Blockchain with Hyperledger Fabric

Second Edition

Build decentralized applications using
Hyperledger Fabric 2

Nitin Gaur

Anthony O'Dowd

Petr Novotny

Luc Desrosiers

Venkatraman Ramakrishna

Salman A. Baset

BIRMINGHAM - MUMBAI

Blockchain with Hyperledger Fabric

Second Edition

Producer: Tushar Gupta
Acquisition Editor – Peer Reviews: Suresh Jain
Content Development Editor: Chris Nelson
Technical Editor: Gaurav Gavas
Project Editors: Carol Lewis, Radhika Atitkar
Copy Editor: Safis Editing
Proofreader: Safis Editing
Indexer: Manju Arasan
Presentation Designer: Sandip Tadge

First published: June 2018
Second Edition: November 2020

Production reference: 3241120

Published by Packt Publishing Ltd.
Livery Place
35 Livery Street
Birmingham B3 2PB, UK.

ISBN 978-1-83921-875-0

www.packt.com

packt.com

Subscribe to our online digital library for full access to over 7,000 books and videos, as well as industry leading tools to help you plan your personal development and advance your career. For more information, please visit our website.

Why subscribe?

- Spend less time learning and more time coding with practical eBooks and Videos from over 4,000 industry professionals
- Learn better with Skill Plans built especially for you
- Get a free eBook or video every month
- Fully searchable for easy access to vital information
- Copy and paste, print, and bookmark content

Did you know that Packt offers eBook versions of every book published, with PDF and ePub files available? You can upgrade to the eBook version at www.Packt.com and as a print book customer, you are entitled to a discount on the eBook copy. Get in touch with us at customercare@packtpub.com for more details.

At www.Packt.com, you can also read a collection of free technical articles, sign up for a range of free newsletters, and receive exclusive discounts and offers on Packt books and eBooks.

Contributors

About the authors

Nitin Gaur currently leads IBM Financial Sciences research practice, as a part of IBM Research. In this role Nitin leads a team that aspires to play a pivotal role in reshaping the future of the financial services industry with faculty, advanced technology, and superior design in the field of financial sciences and financial technology. In his previous role, Nitin served as founder and Director of IBM Digital Asset Labs—serving to device industry standards and use cases, and working towards making blockchain for enterprise a reality. In parallel, Nitin also served as CTO of IBM World Wire—a cross-border payment solution utilizing digital assets. Nitin also founded IBM Blockchain Labs, and led the effort in establishing blockchain practice for enterprises. Prior to this role he worked in capacity of CTO at IBM Mobile Payments and Enterprise Mobile Solutions. Nitin holds an MS in Management Information Systems and MBA in Finance from University of Maryland. He is also an IBM Distinguished Engineer and IBM Master Inventor, with a rich patent portfolio.

Anthony O'Dowd is a Distinguished Engineer at IBM, focusing on Blockchain. He led IBM's contribution to the design and development of the new smart contract and application SDKs found in Hyperledger Fabric v2. Anthony has also made significant contributions to Hyperledger Fabric documentation and samples. He is based in Europe, as part of a worldwide team with a remit to help users build innovative digital solutions which benefit from Blockchain technology. Anthony has a background in messaging, transaction processing, and integration; he has led the development of key IBM middleware, including IBM MQ and the Message Broker/ Integration Bus.

Petr Novotny is a Research Staff Member and Master Inventor at IBM Research with more than 15 years of experience in research and engineering of software systems.

Luc Desrosiers is an IBM Senior Certified IT Architect and the technical leader of the IBM Cloud Pak Acceleration Team. He has worked for many years helping clients and consortiums build blockchain solutions using IBM technologies.

I'd like to thank Mark Cudden for giving me valuable feedback on Governance.

Venkatraman Ramakrishna is an IBM Researcher with 10 years of experience. Following a B. Tech. from IIT Kharagpur and a PhD from UCLA, he worked in Microsoft's Bing Infrastructure team before joining IBM Research—India.

Salman A. Baset currently works at MongoDB, where he is responsible for the strategy and execution of security and compliance for MongoDB's server and cloud.

His last role was CTO Security at IBM Blockchain solutions. In this role, he was responsible for the security and compliance of various blockchain solutions, such as IBM Food Trust and TradeLens. He drove implementation of GDPR for blockchain-based solutions, and co-authored one of the IBM's point of view publications. Moreover, his team built an identity management system for blockchain solutions which is now used by Fortune 500 companies. He has also worked at IBM Research and led teams that contributed to several IBM services and products, such as IBM Container Service, IBM Vulnerability Advisor, and IBM Smart Cloud Enterprise+ patch management system.

He is the recipient of the IEEE INFOCOM Test of Time award (2018), the SPEC Presidential Award (2016), the You Scholars Award by the Marconi Society (2008), and several IBM awards. He has authored over 40 papers and Internet standards, and has over 25 issued patents. He is also an ACM distinguished speaker.

About the reviewer

David Huffman has pretended to be a software engineer at IBM for over 8 years. He graduated from North Carolina State University in 2013 with a Masters in Computer Engineering. David has been a member of the IBM Blockchain team for over one week. He is 5 foot 6 and 1/32 inches short. David enjoys messing with people, including in the creation of this bio.

Varad Ramamoorthy is currently the UI architect for the IBM Blockchain Platform (IBP). Before IBP, he has worked on a number of products as UI architect, including the IBM WebSphere Portal, IBM Business Process Management, and IBM Business Monitor. He is passionate about end-user experience, making product consumption easier.

Mihir Shah is one of the lead architects of the IBM Blockchain Platform. Mihir graduated from North Carolina State University and has been with IBM for over 7 years. He has worked on hardware acceleration using FPGA, IoT, APIs, cloud infrastructure and cloud architecture.

Paul Tippett is currently the Head of Operations for the IBM Blockchain Platform offering in IBM Cloud. Previous assignments include the IBM Container Service and Logging and Metrics Services, also in IBM Cloud. Outside of work Paul spends time mountain biking, working out, and hanging out with his family.

Jason Yellick is an active maintainer of the Hyperledger Fabric project and has contributed to its development since the project was first created. He specializes in consensus and the ordering service, but has spent development time in most aspects of the project, including chaincode lifecycle, channel configuration, and others. In addition to development, Jason works with users who have deployed Fabric in the field to resolve problems, and bring improvements and bug fixes back into the Fabric codebase.

Table of Contents

Preface

We would like to thank our readers for taking time to consume our collective body of work that is representative of the practice, experience, and knowledge gained throughout our careers.

This book was motivated by the desire that we and others have had to contribute to the evolution of blockchain technologies. We were also challenged by a lack of a comprehensive guide that addresses myriad considerations, including but not limited to technology design choices, architecture choices, business considerations, and governance models. We represent a unique and diverse set of skills, and we have strived to cover a lot of ground in this book. We have collectively focused on organization and flow to ensure not only an easy-to-follow and natural flow but also topical modularity.

The contents of this book are aimed at addressing a diverse audience, from business leaders to blockchain developers and anyone who would like to learn from the practitioners' experience expressed in this book. We believe that not only will the audience enjoy and benefit personally and professionally from the book, but also this book will be used as reference material, a handbook of sorts, and aid in making informed design decisions. We encountered various challenges while writing this book, including our own demanding schedules, but ensured that we delivered up-to-date information at the time of publication. The blockchain technology landscape is in flux and keeping up with evolution and innovation is a challenge. We have attempted to distill a model that will enable the reader to create a framework to methodically consume blockchain-related updates and build upon the foundation laid in this book. We have also expended a lot of energy in addressing business design and resulting technology design choices, because unlike other pure technology platforms, **blockchain** (particularly blockchain-powered business networks) is a very business-specific and technology-centric discipline.

We hope the findings and documented considerations from practitioners will arm business leaders and technology managers in making informed decisions and avoiding the failures experienced by the authors.

The technical content covered in this book aims to provide a solid foundation for a diverse set of skills to people such as IT professionals, blockchain novices, and advanced blockchain developers. Modeled after a real-world use case, the application development story weaves in various steps from infrastructure creation to DevOps models and model-driven development, covering various enterprise technology management challenges with a focus on the blockchain network-centric impact of application deployment. We have provided a framework for security and performance design that we hope the technical audience finds particularly helpful in establishing a solid foundation as a technology-design consideration.

We'll conclude the book with a pragmatic overview of various challenges and related opportunities, and call for the community of readers to rise to the challenges and reap the rewards of the resulting opportunities. While this book focuses on **Hyperledger Fabric**, we expect the core topics covered in this book to be universally applicable to the blockchain technology discipline. We sincerely hope that our effort and acumen is well received by our readers and arms them with a strong foundation to make impactful contributions to progressing the blockchain innovation agenda.

Who this book is for

The book benefits business leaders as it provides a comprehensive overview of blockchain business models, governance structure, and business design considerations for blockchain solutions. Technology leaders stand to gain a lot from the detailed discussion around the technology landscape, technology design, and architecture considerations in the book. With its coverage of model-driven application development, this guide will speed up understanding and concept development for blockchain application developers. The simple and well-organized content will put novices at ease with blockchain concepts and constructs.

What this book covers

Chapter 1, Blockchain – An Enterprise and Industry Perspective

You've heard about blockchain and you are wondering, What is all the fuss about? In this chapter, we explore why blockchain is a game changer, what innovation it brings, and what the technology landscape looks like.

Chapter 2, Exploring Hyperledger Fabric

With an understanding of the blockchain landscape, we turn our attention to Hyperledger Fabric. The aim of this chapter is to walk you through the deployment of each component of Hyperledger Fabric while unveiling/building the architecture.

Chapter 3, Business Networks

This chapter introduces the notion of a business network. By understanding how a business network is structured in terms of participants, assets, transactions, and events, we're able to create a framework for analysing how real-world problems and opportunities can be addressed with blockchain technology. This chapter is helpful for technical architects, software developers, and business analysts.

Chapter 4, Setting the Stage with a Business Scenario

This chapter describes a business use case and then focuses on understanding the process of creating a good business network using blockchain, from requirements to design and launch, with instructions to set up prerequisite software and a development environment.

Chapter 5, Designing Smart Contract Transactions and Ledger Data Structure

This chapter talks about how to implement the business logic of the smart contracts of the scenario presented in *Chapter 4, Setting the Stage with a Business Scenario*, and explores the key concepts and libraries necessary for developing a fully functional contract.

Chapter 6, Developing Smart Contracts

This chapter introduces the concept of a multi-part transaction; what it is, why it's important, how it's stored in a blockchain ledger, and how it's generated by a smart contract. Starting with first principles, using fully worked examples, you'll understand how blockchain transactions, ledgers, and smart contracts form the core of a blockchain solution. This chapter is a must-read for technical architects and software developers.

Chapter 7, Developing Applications

This chapter examines and describes how applications can exploit the smart contracts deployed with a Hyperledger Fabric network. Using a broad range of worked examples, we'll see how applications use the three fundamental operations of ledger query, transaction submission, and ledger notification to perform shared transaction processing to improve multi-organization business processing. This chapter is a must-read for technical architects and software developers.

Chapter 8, Advanced Topics for Developing Smart Contracts and Applications

This chapter covers a range of advanced techniques for smart contract and application development. Building on chapters 6 and 7, you'll learn how to customize the SDK, use private and transient data, and make the most of advanced smart contract packaging techniques. This chapter also introduces design patterns that are particularly helpful in asset transfer, asset trading, and other privacy preserving scenarios. The advanced techniques in this chapter are important for technical architects and software developers alike.

Chapter 9, Network Operation and Distributed Application Building

This chapter helps you build and operate a Fabric network and distributed application for the business entities that participate in our trade scenario. This chapter will also help you learn how to build a production-grade ordering service that generates transaction blocks by consensus of a cluster of nodes running the Raft protocol.

Chapter 10, Enterprise Design Patterns and Considerations

This chapter looks at various design patterns and best practices that can be used to build industry-scale blockchain applications.

Chapter 11, Agility in a Blockchain Network

This chapter focuses on the aspects required to maintain agility in a blockchain network. Applying DevOps concepts, the reader is presented with a continuous integration / continuous delivery pipeline.

Chapter 12, Governance – A Necessary Evil of Regulated Industries

Governance is a necessary evil for regulated industries. However, governance is required not only for business networks that deal with use cases for regulated industries, but it also is a good practice to ensure the longevity and scalability of a business network. This chapter explores vital considerations for production readiness for any founder-led blockchain network.

Chapter 13, Life in a Blockchain Network

This chapter aims to raise the reader's awareness on the key activities and challenges that organizations and consortiums may face when adopting a distributed ledger solution, ranging from the management of network and application changes to the maintenance of adequate performance levels. A successful network deployment will hopefully see many organizations join it and the number of transactions increase.

Chapter 14, Hyperledger Fabric Security

This chapter lays the foundation for the security design of blockchain networks. Various security constructs are discussed and Hyperledger Fabric security is explained in detail. An essential chapter to understand security design considerations.

Chapter 15, Blockchain's Future, Protocol, Commercialization, and Challenges Ahead

This chapter looks ahead and discusses the challenges and opportunities that lie ahead. Through the use of open technologies, it invites readers to engage in and promote the blockchain innovation agenda.

Downloading the example code

The code bundle for the book is hosted on GitHub at `https://github.com/HyperledgerHandsOn/trade-network`. Once you follow the instructions carefully, you should be able to import the `trade-contracts` and `trade-apps` repos as submodules.

We also have other code bundles from our rich catalog of books and videos available at `https://github.com/PacktPublishing/`. Check them out!

Conventions used

There are a number of text conventions used throughout this book.

`CodeInText`: Indicates code words in text, database table names, folder names, filenames, file extensions, pathnames, dummy URLs, user input, and Twitter handles. For example; "The code to configure and launch our network using shell scripts can be found in the `bash` folder in our repository."

A block of code is set as follows:

```
PeerOrgs:
  Name: ImporterOrg
  Domain: importerorg.trade.com
  EnableNodeOUs: true
  Template:
    Count: 1
  Users:
    Count: 2
```

Any command-line input or output is written as follows:

```
$ export GOPATH=$HOME/go
```

Bold: Indicates a new term, an important word, or words that you see on the screen, for example, in menus or dialog boxes, also appear in the text like this. For example: "Retain the historical and evolutionary provenance of **Hyperledger Fabric** as a building block."

 Warnings or important notes appear like this.

 Tips and tricks appear like this.

Get in touch

Feedback from our readers is always welcome.

General feedback: Email feedback@packtpub.com, and mention the book's title in the subject of your message. If you have questions about any aspect of this book, please email us at questions@packtpub.com.

Errata: Although we have taken every care to ensure the accuracy of our content, mistakes do happen. If you have found a mistake in this book we would be grateful if you would report this to us. Please visit, http://www.packtpub.com/submit-errata, selecting your book, clicking on the Errata Submission Form link, and entering the details.

Piracy: If you come across any illegal copies of our works in any form on the Internet, we would be grateful if you would provide us with the location address or website name. Please contact us at copyright@packtpub.com with a link to the material.

If you are interested in becoming an author: If there is a topic that you have expertise in and you are interested in either writing or contributing to a book, please visit http://authors.packtpub.com.

Reviews

Please leave a review. Once you have read and used this book, why not leave a review on the site that you purchased it from? Potential readers can then see and use your unbiased opinion to make purchase decisions, we at Packt can understand what you think about our products, and our authors can see your feedback on their book. Thank you!

For more information about Packt, please visit packtpub.com.

1

Blockchain – An Enterprise and Industry Perspective

Blockchain promises to fundamentally solve the issues of time and trust to address inefficiencies and costs in industries such as financial services, supply chains, logistics, and healthcare. Blockchain's key features include immutability and a shared ledger where transactional updates are performed by a consensus-driven trust system, which can facilitate a truly digital interaction between multiple parties.

This digital interaction is not only bound by systemic trust but ensures that the provenance of the transactional record maintains an immutable track record of interaction between parties. This very characteristic lends itself to culpability and non-repudiation and incentivizes fair play. With the blockchain system design, we are attempting to build a system that has implied trust. This trust system leads to reduced risks, and various applied technology constructs – such as cryptography, encryption, smart contracts, and consensus – essentially create gates to not only reduce risk but also infuse added security into the transaction system.

This book endeavors to provide a view into the technology, as well as the skills to bring it into effective use. In addition to being an enhanced version of the original edition of this book, it also focuses on key business-related issues, outlined in the first section of this chapter. The remainder of the chapter will provide an overview of the technology and integrate important business factors and considerations.

We will cover the following topics in this chapter:

- Our approach to this new edition of this book
- Defining a blockchain
- Building blocks of blockchain solutions
- Fundamentals of the secure transaction processing protocol
- Applications of blockchain

Our focus for the new edition

We, this book's original team of authors, have joined forces again to write this new edition. While this book and many of its chapters are dedicated to a technical audience, we wanted to ensure that this book also addresses the linkages to business models and structures. As an industry, blockchain has been in a constant state of flux, resulting in shifting priorities and evolving use cases by businesses attempting to leverage the technology and monetize the resulting constructs. When we released the first edition, blockchain was a technology associated with disruptive decentralized financial technologies, such as cryptocurrency technologies like Bitcoin and Ethereum, and many other competing blockchain-related frameworks. **Hyperledger** is one of the family of frameworks aimed to address the requirements of industry-specific permissioned blockchain business networks.

As blockchain technology matures, the industry itself is shifting, and so is its consumption by businesses, where the conversation has shifted from proofs of concept and experimentation to production-grade deployments and scale. So, in this edition, we will discuss issues such as business models, risk models, consortium structures, and governance to illustrate clearly how the challenges and success criteria go beyond mere technology implementation. Regulated industries are contemplating models of coexistence with current systems as blockchain takes center stage, with a promise to flatten business processes across industries and facilitate huge cost savings for all consortium network members in terms of operations and disintermediation costs.

With this shift in conversation, we have collectively updated our material not only to reflect industry requirements but also technology examples, code samples, and core technical artefacts to ensure you are also up to date with both the blockchain rhetoric and the technology stack needed to implement a viable solution. With blockchain evolving into a mainstream technology, the market for this technology and skilled professionals is growing rapidly. It is our goal to help ensure that our audience is upskilled to meet the challenges of tomorrow, while retaining the historical and evolutionary provenance of **Hyperledger Fabric** as a building block.

We have added content around business considerations, risk models, and overall blockchain protocol commercialization, with a hope that technical and business audiences alike can have a holistic understanding of using the technology and building a technology platform. We have drawn from our collective experience in an effort to relate how business imperatives are closely tied to technology design choices.

These design choices have direct implications for the cost and scalability of the blockchain network design and solution. The design choices include gathering business requirements, risk controls, risk modeling, compliance risk management, and other business-related functions. Business design considerations have a direct impact on network growth and operations, which are embedded in governance tasks such as network management, onboarding, and technical design elements like data obfuscation, data controls, privacy, key management, and so on. As a result, these are very important considerations when launching a blockchain-powered business network. Our attempt will be to address these in detail, arming our audience with the knowledge and skills to apply the right approaches to blockchain projects.

We sincerely hope you benefit from and enjoy these updates.

Defining the terms – what is blockchain?

According to NISTIR 8202 (`https://nvlpubs.nist.gov/nistpubs/ir/2018/NIST.IR.8202.pdf`),

> *Blockchains are tamper evident and tamper resistant digital ledgers implemented in a distributed fashion (i.e., without a central repository) and usually without a central authority (i.e., a bank, company, or government). At their basic level, they enable a community of users to record transactions in a shared ledger within that community, such that under normal operation of the blockchain network no transaction can be changed once published.*
>
> *National Institute of Standards and Technology Interagency or Internal Report (NISTIR) 8202: Blockchain Technology Overview*

A blockchain supporting a cryptocurrency is *permissionless*, in the sense that anyone can participate without a specific identity and the ledger is publicly visible to anyone. Such blockchains typically use a consensus protocol based on **proof of work (PoW)** and economic incentives. In contrast, *permissioned* blockchains have evolved as an alternative way to run a blockchain with a group of known, identified participants.

A permissioned blockchain provides a way to secure the interactions among a group of known entities that share a mutual business goal but don't fully trust each other, such as businesses that exchange funds, goods (supply chain), or information. The entities in permissioned blockchains can choose to make their ledgers public (viewable by anyone) or private (scoped to participants in the permissioned blockchain). For the remainder of this book, we assume that permissioned blockchains also imply that ledgers are not publicly viewable. A permissioned blockchain relies on the identities of the peers, and in so doing can use traditional **Byzantine Fault tolerant (BFT)** consensus (or a flavor of BFT or any leader-based consensus protocol).

Blockchains may execute arbitrary, programmable transaction logic in the form of **smart contracts**, as exemplified by Ethereum (`http://ethereum.org/`). The scripts in Bitcoin were a predecessor of the concept. A smart contract functions as a *trusted distributed application* and gains its security from the blockchain and the underlying consensus among the peers.[7]

Discerning permissioned from permissionless blockchain is vital for enterprises looking to utilize the blockchain platform. The use case dictates the choice of technology, depending on consensus systems, governance models, data structure, and so on. With permissioned blockchains, the idea is to apply traditional technology design (such as three-tier or *n*-tier models) and IT management disciplines (such as ITIL and system management design principles) but in an incrementally better way, which can be significant. In the diagram that follows, you can see how a consortium of banks could use Hyperledger, a type of permissioned blockchain, for clearing and settlement without relying on a central clearing house:

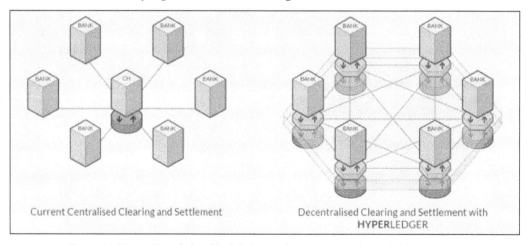

Current Centralised Clearing and Settlement

Decentralised Clearing and Settlement with HYPERLEDGER

Figure 1.1: How a Hyperledger blockchain can change an organization's infrastructure
(Source Hyperledger. Used under Creative Commons Attribution 3.0 Unported. https://creativecommons.org/licenses/by/3.0/)

The core difference between true decentralization versus distributed infrastructure with managed participation is more about governance and rules of engagement on the network. This core difference leads to a new (IT) economic model paving the way to discerning between a utility-based compute model (large, open public networks) or a consortium-based compute infrastructure (consortium-based permissioned networks). This leads to a never-ending debate around permissioned versus permissionless blockchain, and while this chapter will not address the debate, blockchain can present a way to either transform or disrupt current businesses and business models. Most use cases in regulated industries embark on permissioned blockchain models. This is due to regulatory requirements and the economic viability of transaction processing. Whereas permissionless blockchain provides a platform for new business models, such as **peer-to-peer** (**P2P**) transactions and disintermediation-led models, by definition, permissionless blockchain architecture relies on a very compute-intensive compute model to ensure transactional integrity. Regardless of the choice in blockchain models, blockchain provides a lot of possibilities for transformation and disruption.

Blockchain has extraordinary potential as a technology platform. In the enterprise, blockchain can provide:

- A design approach that keeps transaction data, value, and state inherently close to the business logic
- Secure execution of business transactions, validated through a community, in a secure process that facilitates the trust and robust transaction processing that are foundational to blockchain
- An alternative, permissioned technology that conforms to existing regulations

Blockchain promises to solve longstanding industry concerns — and this is where its potential can really be seen, with issues like modernizing financial and trade systems and speeding up securities and trade settlements.

Design considerations for blockchain solutions

In this section, we'll look at the core building blocks for blockchain solutions and then examine some additional capabilities that should be considered.

Four core building blocks

Blockchain solution proposals typically include the following four building blocks:

- **A shared ledger**: The shared ledger appends only the distributed transaction record. Bitcoin blockchain was designed with the intent to democratize visibility; however, with blockchain, consumer data regulations also need to be considered. Using a properly configured SQL or NoSQL distributed database can achieve immutability or append only.

- **Cryptography**: Cryptography in a blockchain ensures authentication and verifiable transactions. Blockchain design includes this imperative because of the computational hardness assumption and a focus on making encryption harder for an adversary to break. This is an interesting challenge with Bitcoin blockchain because of the economic incentive and its system design. When you're working in a less democratic or permissioned business ledger network, considerations around cryptography change.

- **Trust systems or consensus**: "Trust systems" refers to using the power of the network to verify transactions.

  Trust systems are central to blockchain systems; they are at the heart of blockchain applications. We think **trust system** is the preferred term over "consensus system" because not all validation is done through consensus. This foundational element of trust dictates the overall design and investment in a blockchain infrastructure. With every new entrant in the blockchain space, the trust system is modified, forming variations that are specialized for specific blockchain use cases.

  Trust, trade, and ownership are staples of blockchain technology. For intercompany transactions, the trust system governs transactions for trade between participating companies.

  There's still much work needed to define the best trust system for specific use cases, like P2P and sharing economy models with B2B models.

- **Business rules or smart contracts**: Smart contracts are the business terms that are embedded in a blockchain transaction database and executed with transactions. This is the *rules* component of a blockchain solution. It is needed to define the flow of value and state of each transaction.

The following use diagram gives us a good idea of these concepts:

Figure 1.2: Blockchain building blocks

The four building blocks are generally accepted and well understood. They have existed for decades prior to blockchain. Shared ledgers are an evolutionary change, similar to the move to computer-based spreadsheets, but the underlying business rules stay the same.

Additional capabilities to consider

What else should be included in blockchain proposals, especially those within enterprises? The following is a non-exhaustive list of other capabilities to consider:

- **Auditing and logging**: Including auditing and logging in a blockchain solution can help address regulations for the purposes of non-repudiation, technology root cause analysis, fraud analysis, and other enterprise needs.

- **Enterprise integration**: It's also worth considering how the solution will be integrated into the enterprise:

  - **Integration with the incumbent systems of record (SoR)**: The goal here is to ensure that the blockchain solution supports your existing systems, such as CRM, business intelligence, reporting and analytics, and so forth.

  - **Integration as a transaction processing system**: If you want to preserve the SoR as an interim approach to adopting blockchain, integrating it as a transaction processing system makes sense.

- **Design with the intent to include blockchain**: If you intend to share some or part of your data with other enterprises to achieve your business goals, consider designing with your existing system's architecture in mind, as that will accelerate enterprise adoption of blockchain solutions with appropriate data governance. This is because the current data and application architecture will be able to adapt to blockchain-driven transaction processing.

- **Monitoring**: Monitoring is an important capability for addressing regulations and ensuring high availability, capacity planning, pattern recognition, and fault identification.

- **Reporting and regulatory requirements**: Being prepared to address regulatory issues is also very important, even for interim adoption of a blockchain as a transaction processing system. It's recommended that you make connectors to your existing SoR to offload reporting and regulatory requirements until blockchain is enterprise aware, or the enterprise software is blockchain aware.

- **Enterprise authentication, authorization, and accounting requirements**: In a permissioned enterprise world (unlike permissionless Bitcoin blockchain), all blockchain network participants should be identified and tracked. Their roles need to be defined if they are to play a part in the ecosystem.

Let's move on to look at the fundamentals of the secure transaction processing protocol.

Fundamentals of the secure transaction processing protocol

We mentioned previously that cryptography is one of the core building blocks of a blockchain solution. The fundamental security of the Bitcoin blockchain is the elegant cryptographical linkage of all major components of the ledger. Specifically, transactions are linked to each other, mainly through the **Merkle tree**. A Merkle tree is based on the concept of a tree data structure, where every leaf node has a hash calculated of its data and where every non-leaf node has a hash of all its underlying children.

This method provides us with a way to ensure the integrity of the data, but also provides privacy characteristics by allowing us to remove a leaf that is deemed private but leave the hash, thereby preserving the integrity of the tree. The Merkle tree has its roots incorporated into the block header. The block header includes a reference to the block headers that precede it, as shown in the following diagram:

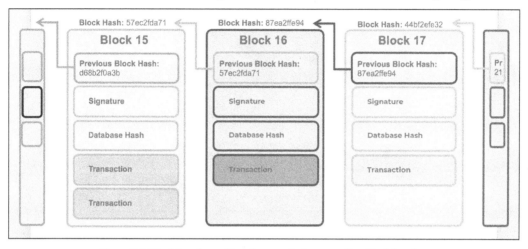

Figure 1.3: Block headers with references to the preceding block headers

That cryptographically enforced interconnectivity fosters the stability and security of distributed ledgers. At any point, if a link between any of the components is broken, it leaves those exposed to malicious attacks.

Transactions are also cryptographically connected to the rest of the blockchain structure mainly through the Merkle tree. Once a transaction is modified within a block, with all other parts remaining stable, the link between all transactions of the block and its header is broken.

The new resulting Merkle tree root does not match the one already in the block header, hence providing no connectivity to the rest of the blockchain. If we proceed to change the Merkle tree root in the block's header, we will, in turn, break the chain of headers and thus the security model of the blockchain itself.

Therefore, if we only change the contents of a block, the rest of the blockchain components remain stable and secure, especially as the block headers provide the connecting links by including a hash of the previous block header in the header of the next block.

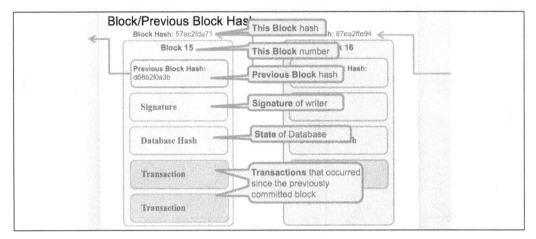

Figure 1.4: Anatomy of a block

Where blockchain technology has been and where it's going

Blockchain has already been a business disruptor, and we expect it to significantly transform industries, government, and our lives in the near future.

The great divide

A significant divide exists between the cryptocurrency and **Initial Coin Offering (ICO)** world, and the world of regulated business. The latter consists of banks and financial institutions working collectively to assess market potential and operational efficiencies.

Both sides of this division have taken advantage of the momentum around blockchain to further their interests. The blockchain ecosystem has challenged the status quo and defied all odds to make a point—often behaving like an adolescent. It is driven by new business models, promises of disintermediation, and interesting technological innovations.

As blockchain has gained momentum, bitcoin value has experienced a comparable rise as an asset class and contributed to the rise of other cryptoassets, such as ether, Bitcoin Cash, and so on. Blockchain momentum also has given rise to alternative finance and fund-raising models, such as **security token offerings (STOs)**, **simple agreements for future tokens (SAFTs)**, and **initial exchange offerings (IEOs)**. These are challenging not only traditional finance structures and business models, but also the regulatory framework that governs the financial infrastructure.

On the enterprise side, there are a growing number of industry initiatives around clearing and settlement to enable faster settlement and interbank transfers, transparency through digitization, symmetric dissemination of information in supply chains, and creating ad hoc trust between **Internet of Things (IoT)** devices.

There's a common theme here—that blockchain is here to stay. As it continues to evolve and generate innovative solutions for industry use cases, it will keep inching toward maturity and deliver on its promises of efficiency and significant cost savings built on the foundation of trust.

An economic model for blockchain delivery

Blockchain networks, underpinned by blockchain technology, may bring transformation or disruption to industries, but in any case, to thrive, blockchain needs an economic model. If disruption is the aim, investments in technology, talent, and market synergy can be combined with the lure of economic incentives. ICOs, for example, typically rely on **tokenomics**, a term that describes the economic system of value generation in those networks. The token is the unit of value created by the system or network—either through making a platform for providers or consumers, or through co-creating a self-governing value network in its business model that various entities can use to their advantage for creating, distributing, and sharing rewards that benefit all stakeholders.

The ICO front, largely funded by cryptocurrencies, has defied current fundraising mechanisms in venture capitalism (led by crowdfunding projects). Importantly, the struggle to discern the difference between a security and utility coin is disruptive in principle.

ICOs look to create an economic system built on the principles of **decentralization**, **open governance** (or *self-governance*), and **transparency**, a system that rewards *innovation* and eradicates disintermediation. ICOs saw some initial failures and some successes, but they nevertheless provide a preview of the future, where cryptoassets will become a basic unit of value—with valuation and fungibility defined by the network they originate from—fueling an economy built for and around innovation.

On the enterprise front, there's been more focus on understanding the technology and reimagining ecosystems, business networks, regulations, confidentiality and privacy, and the business models that impact blockchain networks in various industries. Enterprises looking to explore blockchain want to see quick proof points, use cases that can demonstrate results quickly and help them innovate with blockchain.

Blockchain is helping industries move to a more symmetric dissemination of information by providing built-in control of transactional data, provenance, and historical context. This can lead to more efficient workflows and transform business processes. Many early projects, however, didn't focus on the core tenets of blockchain (which we discuss in some detail later in this chapter), leading to disintermediation, decentralization, and robust self-governance models. There's a good reason for it, though: industries and conventional businesses tend to be focused on their current business agendas, models, growth, and, above all, regulatory compliance and adherence. This emphasis on current business operations means they're not naturally inclined toward disruptive models.

Learning as we go

With any new technology, there is always a learning curve. As blockchain evolved and we began to work with regulated industries, we quickly recognized that, in such industries, there are important design considerations to address — things like identity, confidentiality, privacy, scalability, and performance. These elements can have significant cost implications when it comes to designing blockchain networks, as well as the business models that govern these networks. These challenges have not only been interesting to solve; they've also had a positive effect on conventional, regulated industries and businesses by re-energizing innovation in these organizations and inviting the best talent to join in tackling these challenges. Businesses are recognizing that ecosystems and networks driven by blockchain technology will contribute to progress and success.

Permissioned networks (regulated, conventional, and enterprise business networks) may also need to begin uncovering an incentive model to motivate organizations to join a platform that promotes the idea of creation, distribution, and the sharing of rewards benefitting all stakeholders. The economic incentives behind tokenomics can't be blindly adopted by a lot of conventional businesses and industries, but that doesn't mean those industries shouldn't start the journey to explore possible business models that would enable value creation and elevate some desperately needed modernization efforts.

The promise of trust and accountability

Blockchain technology promises to be the foundation for a secure transaction network that can induce trust and security in many industries that are plagued with the systemic issues around trust and accountability. From a technological point of view, blockchain facilitates a system of processing and recording transactions that are secure, transparent, auditable, efficient, and immutable. These technological characteristics lend themselves to addressing the time and trust issues that plague current-day distributed transaction systems.

Blockchain fundamentally shifts the multitier model to a flat-tier transaction processing model. This carries the promise to disrupt industries fundamentally by disintermediation, inducing efficacy in new system design, or simply creating new business models.

Disintermediation indicates reducing the use of intermediaries between producers and consumers, such as by investing directly in the securities market rather than going through a bank. In the financial industry, every transaction has historically required a counterparty to process the transaction. Disintermediation involves removing the middlemen, which, by definition, disrupts the business models and incentive economies that are based on mediation. There's been a wave of disruption in recent years as a result of digital technologies, which have, in turn, been driven by marketing insights and the desire for organizations to provide a richer user experience.

Blockchain is a technology that aims to catapult this disruption by introducing trade, trust, and ownership into the equation. The technology pattern represented by blockchain databases and records has the potential to radically improve banking, supply chains, and other transaction networks, providing new opportunities for innovation and growth while reducing cost and risk.

Blockchain in the enterprise

The following figure shows a number of blockchain use cases. The variety suggests that there are a lot of application-specific considerations for whether and how to employ blockchain solutions. Let's talk about the principles that should guide the use of blockchain in an enterprise.

Why would an enterprise want to apply blockchain technology to one of its systems or applications?

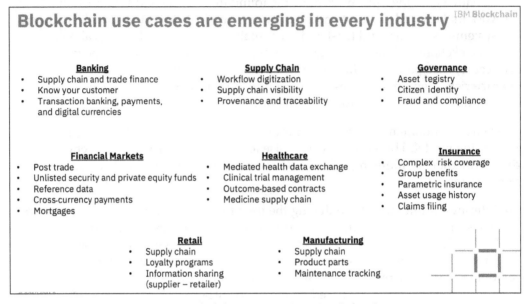

Figure 1.5: Blockchain use cases in various industries

What applications are a good fit?

Organizations will need to establish criteria for use during the application design process to help them assess where they can best apply blockchain technology. The following are some examples of criteria that could help an enterprise determine which applications or systems would benefit from it:

- **Applications that adhere to trade, trust, and ownership**: As described previously, these three tenets—trade, trust, and ownership—are fundamental to any blockchain system. Trade and ownership refer to the flow of assets and transfer of ledger entries, while trust pertains to the otherwise trustless nature of a transaction system.

- **Applications that are fundamentally transactional in nature**: There is often debate about why we can't achieve the benefits of blockchain from a distributed database, that is, a NoSQL or a relational database. But a multi-party transaction is what makes an application suitable for blockchain. There need to be long-running processes with numerous microtransactions that will be verified and validated by the blockchain-powered transaction system. Databases can still be used for persistence or replication to fit enterprise systems, however. Other considerations include a small dataset size that could increase over time, logging overhead, and so on.

- **Business networks that are comprised of non-monopolistic participants**: This third criterion addresses distributed versus decentralized computation models. Blockchain trust systems can work within any model; however, the trust aspect of a blockchain business network comes from multi-party participants with non-monopolistic participation (the consortium permissioned network model). Oligopolistic participation might be acceptable (the private permissioned network model), but it's essential to devise a trust model that assures the prevention of centralized control, even with rational behavior of the participants. Many internal use cases do not adhere to this principle and constitute more distributed application models. (Models are discussed in *Chapter 2, Exploring Hyperledger Fabric*.)

For enterprises trying to understand or determine where to employ blockchain meaningfully, there's a simple approach for thinking through use case selection. An appropriate use case for a sustainable blockchain solution will achieve long-term business objectives and provide a strong return on technology investment.

This starts with an **enterprise problem** — an issue big enough for the enterprise to expend resources/time — and the recognition of cohorts that have the same problem. When companies realize that an enterprise problem is also an **industry problem** (such as securities lending, collateral lending, and so on), they've found a use case where the promise of blockchain has the most potential.

While organizations are determining the benefits of various aspects of blockchain for their enterprise applications, they also need to recognize the fragmentation of the whole blockchain landscape. There are numerous innovative approaches available for solving a specific challenge with blockchain. A lot of vendors offer variants of the trust system specialized to address particular use cases, and they've defined the use cases that will benefit most from blockchain in a given industry, for example. Such specialized vendors often promise a fast solution to meet consumer demands for quick digital interactions.

The tenets of blockchain can be instrumental in delivering rapid consumer-driven outcomes — such as decentralized, distributed, global, permanent, code-based, programmable assets, and records of transaction. We should exercise caution about thinking of blockchain as a hammer to solve every enterprise application challenge, but it can be of use in many transactional applications.

Now, let's discuss how blockchain is perceived in the enterprise and some of the challenges that arise with enterprise adoption of the technology. In the following section, we'll focus on three areas that help set the tone for blockchain in an enterprise context.

Enterprise blockchain business evaluation considerations

In this section, we'll consider important factors in making enterprise-level business decisions about blockchain and its implementation.

A few thoughts on blockchain business models

The following list outlines some important elements related to business models and related design imperatives:

- Business models are an important consideration, as the right business model will dictate the technology design and platform choices not only to seed the network, but also the robust design needed for growth.

- Business model design should provide a platform for business negotiation, contracting vehicles, and other business activities, such as procurement, shared services, legal services, administration, and so on. Business design includes a clear separation of blockchain network functions from business and other technology operations.

- A well-thought-out business model for blockchain networks provides an important avenue for business continuity, funding and sourcing models, and overall growth driven by the economic and financial structure of the business network powered by the tenets of blockchain technology.

- A well-crafted business design restores balance and smooth interactions between various entities that compete with some network participants and need to cooperate and co-create with some other network participants. The co-creation element of a blockchain network is essential for the sustained longevity and growth of the business of the blockchain network.

- Last, a blockchain business network can be a business in itself. A platform that facilitates co-creation and new synergies needs to be managed, operated with defined SLA levels, and have a robust governance structure that not only attracts new participants, but sustains the confidence and business benefit of its founders and existing participants.

Business growth and innovation

We see innovation and micro-innovation everywhere — be it from large companies such as Amazon and Netflix, a smaller start-up ecosystem focused on challenging the status quo, or open source frameworks such as Hyperledger. With access to technology, talent, and digital tools, enterprises small and large are rethinking their business models with a focus on embarking on a journey that has scale built into the business design.

Most businesses go through several stages on this journey:

- Creating the engine of growth: Creating a business model that's well received by the market or target constituents
- Creating a well-oiled network: Establishing iterative processes to optimize operations
- Scaling the business: Growing the business by effectively repeating the repeatable parts

To achieve successful growth and innovation, enterprises employ people, technology, and resources to perfect the business at every stage. When we talk about a business "that has scale built into the business design," we mean to imply a new approach that not only relies on employing people, technology, and resources, but also is inclusive of a co-creative approach, in which users, customers, and ecosystems become co-creators to create more value, growth, and innovation.

How do growth and innovation relate to a blockchain-powered network?

Let's attempt to link the value creation of a blockchain network to co-creation and platform thinking: as blockchain networks evolve and grow, and as new participants are added or removed, the dynamics of the network change and several bilateral and multilateral relationships emerge. Today, these relationships are largely driven by static smart contracts and do *not* capture the essence of blockchain-powered markets.

Now, let's define these two models:

- **A platform thinking approach** to building a business involves figuring out ways in which an external ecosystem of businesses, developers, and users can be leveraged to create value. Common examples include Twitter, Facebook, YouTube, and even Wikipedia.
- **Co-creation** is a concept that brings different parties together (for instance, a company and a group of customers) to jointly produce a mutually valued outcome. Co-creation brings the unique blend of ideas from direct customers or viewers (who are not the direct users of the product), which in turn gives a plethora of new ideas to the organization.

In a true, digitally driven marketplace, the blockchain-powered network ensures that dynamic marketplace relationships and interactions are reflected in a systemic and intelligent way. As we design blockchain networks for industries, we're seeing interesting new business models emerge, leading many organizations to rethink their current business models, the competition, and the overall market landscape.

We're beginning to see network design consist of participants with varied interests focused on a singularity of the assets at the nucleus of the blockchain-driven business network and ecosystem. All of this leads to new partnerships and co-creation. In essence, the blockchain-powered business network has the potential to amalgamate the platform thinking approach and co-creation to exponentially increase value creation in the business transaction network.

Considerations for evaluating the economic value of blockchain entities

How do we value various entities involved in building a blockchain-based business network? There are technology providers, business owners, participants, consortium operators, and many other niche players, ranging from token issuers to blockchain technology players and the business that is using these services to either transform an industry or disrupt it. The following aims to provide an evaluation framework for such an analysis:

- **Business solution**:
    - **Problem domain**: The business problem we are solving, the industry landscape, and evolution through innovation
    - **Addressable market**: The overall cost of the problem domain, that is, the cost of the problem itself and its economic impact on the industry segment
    - **Regulatory and compliance landscape**: The regulatory landscape that can help or impede the adoption of new technology-led business models
    - **Competitive frameworks/alternatives**: The other frameworks and entities trying to solve the issue with or without **distributed ledger technology (DLT)**/blockchain
- **Technology design and architecture**:
    - **Consensus design**: Leads to trust systems and economic viability of blockchain network
    - **Blockchain components**: Shared ledger, crypto elements, smart contracts, and trust system
    - **Blockchain deployment infrastructure**: Cloud, geo-specific deployment, technical talent (or access to it), SLAs, and so forth

- **Monetization strategy**:
    - **Token-based model**: Operation fees — write to the blockchain-powered business network's distributed database
    - **Token as medium of exchange**: Lend or sell the token as a "step-through" currency
    - **Asset-pair trading**: Monetizing margins
    - **Commercialization of the protocol**: Technology services, which include cloud, software lab, and consulting services

- **The power of the network** (also called *network effect*): Extrapolating the power of the network and the exponential power of co-creation models, leading to new business models and resulting economic value

Blockchain investment rubric

It is vital for an enterprise to establish an **investment rubric** as a control and finish risk mitigation technique. An investment rubric is a layered abstraction that represents the investment criteria and landscape. The rubric evaluation criteria have inputs, output, and continual analysis. The inputs are generally assumptions that drive the model, such as technology design, architecture, talent acquisition, compliance costs, cost efficiency versus new business opportunity models, and so on. The output, on the other hand, is the projected performance metric measured against stated input objectives. The investment rubric can also serve as a model, which can be used to evaluate multiple sets of performance metrics based on different assumptions.

This investment rubric is a guide and evaluation tool for blockchain projects. The continual assets of the rubric will enable us to define the merits of a potential investment and objectify the decision and justification of the investment. The rubric is a sort of financial modeling that employs various business valuation techniques such as the following:

- **Net present value (NPV)**: A popular valuation technique used by the financial services industry to compare the delta of present value of cash inflow and cash outflow over a period of time.

- **Benefit-cost ratio (BCR)**: The popular cost-benefit analysis, which defines the overall relationship between the costs employed on the project and the overall benefit to the business.

- **Internal rate of return (IRR)**: In contrast to NPV, this valuation technique relies on calculating the profitability of the investment. This technique is used to determine the rate of return on the investment, as opposed to cash flow.

- **Governance, risk management, and compliance (GRC)**: Analysis that provides a holistic investment and risk profile, which is not considered at the proof of concept phase — a stage with limited experimentation.

Devising the comprehensive investment profile and model is a significant step in communicating to investors, partners, and stakeholders the extent and depth of analysis with a clear defensible plan for project execution, deployment, and subsequent risk mitigation embedded at every layer of the rubric. The investment rubric can be used as an important tool for modeling and analysis with a feedback loop. It serves as a scoring guide of sorts to evaluate the intended investment objective and stated outcome. The idea behind this approach is to have a progressive development model that includes risk mitigation by continual tweaking models to achieve desired objectives. An effective rubric starts with proof points at early stages of technology experimentation and extends to more serious efforts around assessing business models and establishing a minimum viable ecosystem, while testing risks, ROI, and financial and governance models along the way. Used properly, a rubric provides new learning and incremental successes at every stage; it enables us to apply and tweak valuation and risk models, establish autonomic (sense and response) governance policies, and thereby grow and scale the blockchain-powered business ecosystem.

How does the enterprise view blockchain?

Radical openness is an aspect of blockchain as a digital trust web, but in the enterprise, it's vital to consider the impact and implications of radical openness.

A public blockchain can operate with extreme simplicity, supporting a highly distributed master list of all transactions, which is validated through a trust system supported by anonymous consensus. But can enterprises directly apply the model of the trustless system without modifying the fundamental tenets of blockchain?

Do organizations view this disruptive technology as a path to their transformation, or merely a vehicle to help them improvise their existing processes to take advantage of the efficiencies the trust system promises? No matter what, enterprises will want the adoption of blockchain to be as minimally disruptive to the incumbent system as it can be, and that won't be easy to achieve! After all, the design inefficiencies of the incumbent system are what have compelled the enterprise to consider this paradigm shift. A lot of the concepts and use cases for blockchain are still distant from enterprise consumption.

The first industry to experiment with and adopt blockchain was the financial services sector, as it has been facing down the fear of being disrupted by another wave of start-ups. Like many industries, it is also driven by consumer demands for faster, lower-cost transactions.

Financial services have a well-defined set of use cases, including trade financing, trade platforms, payment and remittance, smart contracts, crowd funding, data management and analytics, marketplace lending, and blockchain technology infrastructure. The uses for blockchain we've seen in this industry will likely permeate other areas like healthcare, retail, and government in the future.

Integrating a blockchain infrastructure for the whole enterprise

Any enterprise adoption of blockchain should have the goal of disrupting incumbent systems. Thinking about integration with enterprise systems of record is one way to work toward this. In this manner, an enterprise can implement blockchain-driven transaction processing and use its existing systems of record as an interface to its other applications, such as business intelligence, data analytics, regulatory interactions, and reporting.

It's vital to separate the infrastructure for enterprise blockchain technology from the business domain that uses chain technology to gain a competitive advantage. Blockchain can be seen as an enterprise chain infrastructure that's invisible to business, operating behind the scenes, while promoting **interprise synergy** between various business-driven chains. The idea is to separate the business domain from the technology that supports it. A chain application ought to be provisioned by a business domain that has a suitable trust system. The trust system, as I've stated repeatedly, is central to any blockchain endeavor; therefore, it should be appropriate to the needs of a given business application. The cost of the infrastructure and compute requirements will be dictated by the choice of trust system available to an enterprise.

By separating out the blockchain technology infrastructure, designing an architecture around a pluggable trust system, using trust intermediaries, and a design that promotes flexibility and a modular trust system, the business can focus on the business and regulatory requirements, such as AML, KYC, nonrepudiation, and so forth. The technology infrastructure for blockchain applications should be open, modular, and adaptable for any blockchain variant, thereby making the blockchain endeavor easy to manage.

Interprise synergy suggests driving synergies between numerous enterprise blockchains to enable inter- and intra-enterprise chain (interledger) connections. In this model, the transactions would cross the various trust systems, giving us visibility into the interactions of enterprise governance and control systems. Fractal visibility and the associated protection of enterprise data are important to consider when looking at these interactions between business units and external enterprises.

An invisible enterprise chain infrastructure, as illustrated in the following diagram, can provide a solid foundation to evolve enterprise connectors and expose APIs to make incumbent systems more chain aware. Interprise synergy will flourish due to conditional programmable contracts (smart contracts) between the business chains:

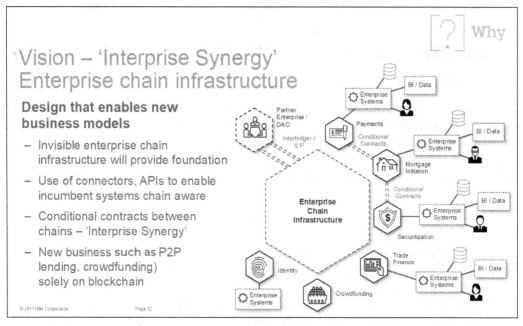

Figure 1.6: An interprise synergy enterprise chain infrastructure

How can an enterprise know if it is ready for blockchain? More importantly, when considering blockchain consumption, should its focus be on integration with incumbent transaction systems, or an enterprise-aware blockchain infrastructure?

To take full advantage of the promise of enterprise blockchain, an integrated enterprise will need more than one use case and will need to drive interprise synergy. The most successful blockchain consumption strategy should focus on technology initially and then consider integration with existing enterprise business systems. This will facilitate collective understanding and accelerate enterprise adoption of blockchain, hopefully on the path of least disruption, leading to seamless adoption of blockchain technology.

Enterprise design principles

As stated previously, blockchain technology promises to be the foundation for a secure transaction network that induces trust and security in industries that are plagued with systemic issues around trust and accountability. It aims to generate market and cost efficiencies.

In the past few years, as blockchain technology has come to maturity, we've focused on how enterprises and businesses can use the technology to relieve pain points and herald new business models. Organizations that have begun to see blockchain's potential are now beginning to reshape business networks that are burdened by the systemic costs of archaic processes, paperwork, and technology.

Business drivers and evolution

In the recent past, organizations would run internal business systems and IT infrastructure out to the internet to harness the collaborative potential of interconnected and accessible systems. Blockchain technology is taking this to the next level, offering true digital interaction facilitated by trusted business networks. In the internet era, successful enterprises adopted and adapted to technological challenges, whereas in the blockchain era, business, rather than technology, is the driver for proliferation.

While blockchain technology is interesting on its own, there are a lot of other mechanics of a business network that ought to be evaluated as well, including:

- **Consensus models**: Which trust system is most fitting for your business network?

- **Control and governance**: What entities are permitted to do what? Who will own the investigative process if there's a system anomaly?

- **Digital asset generation**: Who creates an asset in the system? Who governs it?

- **Authority for issuance**: In a system that's truly decentralized, the notion of authority does not hold together. So, in a blockchain network, who would be responsible for governance, culpability, and eventually regulations?

- **Security considerations**: How will the network address enterprise security, including new security challenges imposed by a shared business network?

We imagine a purpose-built blockchain network that's focused on a plurality of business domains—for example, mortgages, payments, exchanges, clearing, and the settlement of specific asset types. In an enterprise context, we visualize a centralized network in which like-minded business entities share in a consensus consortium. There are several practical reasons to back this idea of a centralized network, including the following:

- The use of **domain-specific business language**, which leads to the construction, management, and governance of smart contracts as proxy business representations

- **A defined asset type**, which leads to governance, management, and valuation (for exchange, fungibility, and so on) of the digital representation of assets

- **Appropriate regulation**, given that every industry and business network is regulated separately, and therefore the burden of adhering to regulations and other related costs can be shared in the business network

- **Other related business functions** such as analysis, analytics, market data, and so forth

We've now covered the business drivers for enterprise blockchain, so next, let's consider what can ensure the sustainability and longevity of a blockchain network.

Ensuring the sustainability of blockchain-based business networks

Blockchain-based business networks are continuing to evolve and grow, and as they do, there will be no turning back on core issues such as trust models, data visibility, and exploiting a network for competitive advantage.

Focusing on sustainability can seem paradoxical because it promotes open collaborative innovation, while at the same time locking down constructs such as consensus or trust systems and the governance systems for managing assets, smart contracts, and overall interaction in a multi-party transaction network. Blockchain system design needs to take all of this into consideration.

A business network with a successful system design needs to align well with the blockchain tenets of trade, trust, and ownership enabling transactionality in a multi-party scenario. Without building on these core tenets, business networks may not realize the promise of blockchain technology in a sustainable way.

There are seven design principles to support and sustain growth in a blockchain business network:

1. The network participants need to have control of their business.
2. The network has to be extensible so that participants have the flexibility to join or leave the network.
3. The network must be permissioned but also protected, to safeguard competitive data while facilitating peer-to-peer transactions.
4. The network should allow open access and global collaboration for shared innovation.

5. The network must be scalable for both transaction processing and encrypted data processing.

6. The network has to be able to accommodate enterprise security and address new security challenges.

7. The network needs to coexist with established systems of record and transaction systems in the enterprise.

In the next section, we'll focus on design principles.

Design principles that drive blockchain adoption

In any enterprise, blockchain adoption is driven by three principles: the *business blueprint*, the *technology blueprint*, and *enterprise integration*. The following are indispensable things to consider when choosing a blockchain framework according to these three principles:

- **Business blueprint**: Blockchain promises to create a business network of value based on trust. To do this, it's vital to understand how various blockchain frameworks handle network interaction patterns, inefficiencies, and vulnerabilities.

- **Technology blueprint**: If technology is to align with business imperatives, organizations need to make appropriate technology and architecture choices for their needs. **Transactions per second** (**TPS**), enterprise integration, external system integration, and regulatory and compliance requirements may all be taken under advisement here. These decisions are part of the technical due diligence necessary to budget properly for blockchain adoption.

- **Enterprise integration**: Integrating blockchain into the enterprise systems, especially an adjacent system, is an important business and technology consideration (because downstream transaction systems affect critical business systems), as well as a cost point. Based on my experience, if organizations don't focus on adjacent system integration early in the planning, it can impede adoption, because it has a significant cost impact on blockchain projects.

In the following sections, we'll cover these design considerations in a bit more detail.

Business considerations for choosing a blockchain framework

Numerous criteria come into play when organizations are evaluating whether to adopt blockchain to address their pain points. Here are some considerations from a business perspective:

- **Open platform and open governance**: The technology standards a business chooses will set the stage for enterprise blockchain adoption, compliance, governance, and the overall cost of the solution.

- **Economic viability of the solution**: Whichever blockchain framework an organization chooses should provide cost alignment to its existing business models, charge backs, compute equity, and account management. This flows into ROI.

- **Longevity of the solution**: As organizations aspire to build a trusted network, they'll want to ensure that they can sustain the cost and operation of the network so it can grow and scale to accommodate additional participants and transactions.

- **Regulatory compliance**: Compliance issues are closely tied to transaction processing and can include events like industry-specific reporting and analysis for business workflow and tasks, both automated and human-centric.

- **Coexistence with adjacent systems**: A blockchain network needs to be able to coexist with the rest of the enterprise, network participants, and adjacent systems, which may have overlapping and complementary functions.

- **Predictable costs of business growth**: Business growth depends upon predictable metrics. Historically, a lot of industries have focused on transactions per second, but that measurement differs from system to system based on system design, compute costs, and business processes.

- **Access to skills and talent**: The availability of talent affects costs, as well as maintenance and the longevity of a blockchain solution as the industry and technology evolve with continued innovation.

- **Financial viability of technology vendors**: When choosing vendors, it's vital to think about their viability when it comes to long-term support and the longevity of your blockchain solution. You should examine the long-term vision and the sustainability of the vendor or business partner's business model.

- **Global footprint and support**: Blockchain solutions tend to involve business networks with a global reach and the related skills to support the network's expansion with minimal disruption.

- **Reliance on technology and industry-specific standards**: Standards are critical not only in helping to standardize a shared technology stack and deployment, but also in establishing an effective communication platform for industry experts to use for problem solving. Standards make low-cost, easy-to-consume technology possible.

Blockchain vendors offer various specializations, including:

- Variant trust systems, such as consensus, mining, PoW, and so on
- Lock-in to a single trust system
- Infrastructure components that are purpose-built for particular use cases
- Field-tested design through proofs of concept

The technological risk of a vendor not adhering to a reference architecture based on a standardized technology set is a fragmented blockchain model for the enterprise.

From a business point of view, an open standards-based approach to blockchain offers flexibility, along with a pluggable and modular trust system, and therefore is the ideal option. This approach keeps an enterprise open to specialized blockchains like Ripple, provides a provisioning layer for the trust system, and offers a separate business domain with the technology to support it.

Technology considerations for choosing a blockchain framework

When organizations consider the technology implications of blockchain, they should start with the premise that it is not just another application. It's a production network that involves risks and costs to ensure correct upkeep and maintenance.

Here are some important things to ponder when evaluating blockchain's technological impact.

Identity management

Identity management is a complicated, involved topic, especially in regulated industries where identities must be managed and have significant business consequences, such as around activities like **know your customer (KYC)**, **anti-money laundering (AML)**, and other reporting and analytics functions. This section describes and discerns between the identity of enterprise participants and the identity of the end users that are the customer base of the participants on the network. By identifying the enterprise or entities that join the network, we are using identity as a permissioning mechanism to identity an enterprise and relying on enterprise to manage end user identity as a client service mandate:

- **Permissioning** is the concept of certification and key management; these enable an entity to be permissioned and identified while transactions are completed. The use case, industry, and business model can define permissioned, that is, the certificate and key management, be it decentralized or distributed or centralized by a consortium network operator.

- **End use identity**, which is maintained by a participating entity in the blockchain network, is the mapping of the LDAP/user registry to the certificates or keys for the sake of tracing (*know your customer*, as well as *know your customer's customer*).

Other identity management considerations include:

- An LDAP or existing user registry won't go away and has to be considered as a design point. This is because there has typically been significant investment and security policies in place for mature authentication and authorization systems.

- Trust systems are at the heart of blockchain technology and must pave the way for trust with identity insertion (for use cases that require transactional traceability).

- Identity is necessary both on the blockchain and for the blockchain. This implies we not only need to identify the direct participants on the network, but also indirect participants who process transactions as the client base of the direct participants.

- Identity acquisition, vetting, and lifecycle need to be accounted for. Identity acquisition is a responsibility of the onboarding entity, which is either a consortium or an operating entity of the network for direct participants and the participants that manage the relationship with indirect participants.

- Identity management should align with trust systems based on use cases. The identity is very much linked to the trust system of blockchain, including consensus voting and also digital signatures for transaction endorsement and processing.

Scalability

Scalability is both a business and a technology consideration, given the way downstream transaction systems can affect critical business systems. Technology choices for scalability—for example, database choices for the shared ledger, adjacent system integration, encryption, and consensus—bring about a system design that can accommodate the predictable costs of growth in network membership or transactions.

Enterprise security

There are four layers of enterprise security to think about:

- The **physical IT infrastructure layer**, which includes use case-specific issues like **Evaluation Assurance Level 5 (EAL5)**, network, and infrastructure isolation requirements.

- The **blockchain middleware layer**, which includes requirements for crypto modules, encryption levels, encryption on data storage, transfer and data at rest, and the visibility of data between participants in the network.

- The **blockchain consensus (trust system layer)**, which is central to blockchain and necessary to guarantee basic **data store** properties. If there are more players in the network, they have to bring capital equity to scale. This is about building a **shared data store** with enterprise data qualities at a lower barrier to entry. Consensus, even minimal consensus, is necessary to ensure this on the architecture in place. There's now a divide between cryptocurrency-based trust systems and non-cryptocurrency-based trust systems. The former model, such as PoW/PoS, isn't sustainable for enterprise use cases aspiring to create permissioned blockchains.

- The **application security** that uses blockchain.

Let's explore development tooling next.

Development tooling

Considerations for development tooling include an integrated development environment, business modeling, and model-driven development.

Crypto-economic models

A crypto-economic model refers to a decentralized system that uses public-key cryptography for authentication and economic incentives to guarantee that it continues without going back in time or incurring other alterations. To fully grasp the idea of blockchain and the benefits of cryptography in computer science, we must first understand the idea of **decentralized consensus** since it is a key tenet of the crypto-based computing revolution.

Decentralization with systemic governance

The old paradigm was centralized consensus, where one central database would rule transaction validity. A decentralized scheme breaks with this, transferring authority and trust to a decentralized network and enabling its nodes to continuously and sequentially record transactions on a public **block**, creating a unique **chain**—thus the term **blockchain**. Cryptography (by way of hash codes) secures the authentication of the transaction source, removing the need for a central intermediary. By combining cryptography and blockchain, the system ensures no duplicate recording of the same transaction.

Blockchain system design should preserve the idea of decentralized digital transaction processing, adapting it into a permissioned network, while centralizing some aspect of regulatory compliance and maintenance activity as needed for an enterprise context.

Enterprise support

Having enterprise support for blockchain is important for the same reasons as the reconsideration of estimation effort. Remember that blockchain should not be thought of as just another application. It's a production network that involves risks and costs for upkeep and maintenance, and it won't be able to simply use existing applications for development, infrastructure, and services.

Use case-driven pluggability choices

To make sure your blockchain solution can allow for use case-driven pluggability choices, consider the following issues.

Shared ledger technology

The use cases, design imperatives, and problem you're trying to address through blockchain will all help determine the choice of shared ledger and database technologies.

Consensus

Consensus guides the trust system and drives technology investment in blockchain application infrastructure—and therefore is at the heart of blockchain. Also, there isn't one consensus type that fits all use cases. Use cases define the interaction between participants and suggest the most appropriate trust system through consensus models.

Consensus is a way to validate the order of network requests or transactions (deploy and invoke) on a blockchain network. Ordering network transactions correctly is critical because many have a dependency on one or more prior transactions (account debits often have a dependency on prior credits, for example).

In a blockchain network, no single authority determines the transaction order; instead, each blockchain node (or peer) has an equal say in establishing the order, by implementing the network consensus protocol. Consensus, consequently, ensures that a quorum of nodes agree on the order in which transactions are appended to the shared ledger. Consensus, by resolving discrepancies in the proposed transaction order, helps guarantee that all network nodes are operating on an identical blockchain. In other words, it guarantees both the integrity and consistency of transactions in a blockchain network.

Consensus algorithms are grouped into three classifications:

- **No-master**: PoW
- **Multi-master**: BFT or Practical Byzantine fault-tolerance (PBFT)
- **Single-master**: HA manager/Raft

Crypto algorithms and encryption technology

Choosing a blockchain system design may be guided by crypto library and encryption technology as well. An organization's use case requirements will dictate this choice and drive technology investments in blockchain application infrastructure. Alternatives to consider include:

- **Asymmetric**: RSA (1024-8192), DSA (1024-3072), Diffie-Hellman, KCDSA, elliptic curve cryptography (ECDSA, ECDH, ECIES) with named, user-defined, and Brainpool curves

- **Symmetric**: AES, RC2, RC4, RC5, CAST, DES, Triple DES, ARIA, SEED

- **Hash/message digest/HMAC**: SHA-1, SHA-2 (224-512), SSL3-MD5-MAC, SSL3-SHA-1-MAC, SM3

- **Random number generation**: FIPS 140-2 approved DRBG (SP 800-90 CTR mode)

As previously stated, use cases will define the interaction between participants and will suggest the most appropriate trust system using consensus models.

Enterprise integration and designing for extensibility

Designing a blockchain network to coexist with the existing systems of record in an organization is important as a cost consideration. Integration should be through both business and technology issues, since downstream transaction systems impact essential business systems. In working with many enterprises, I've found that integrating blockchain with the adjacent systems has a significant cost impact on their blockchain projects. It really needs to be addressed early in the planning stages, so as not to adversely affect enterprise adoption.

It's also important to think about operational issues. By safeguarding the elements of trade, trust, and ownership—and the inherent properties of blockchain such as immutability, provenance, and consensus—a trust system promises to help eliminate redundant and duplicate systems and processes. These duplications cost an organization significant resources, leading to slower transaction processing and associated opportunity costs. One goal with blockchain adoption should be to address the central pain point of the existing process. The aspiration is for a transparent ledger that increases trust, saves time and significant costs, and provides better customer service.

As for network extensibility, designing for extensibility means taking future growth into consideration as you plan the implementation. Extensibility measures a system's ability to extend and the level of effort that will be required to implement extensions. Extensibility is important with blockchain business network design in order to accommodate not only for the dynamic nature of business (with all its regulations, competitive pressures, and market dynamics), but also for network growth (the addition of regulators, market makers, disruptions, service providers, and so on).

The following are some design considerations to help ensure network extensibility:

- **Flexibility with membership**: A blockchain network may start with a finite group of participants and roles, but new participants could later want to join the network, and others may want to leave. So, you have to consider the mechanics of membership changes, including access to (shared) data. The member type is also an important thought when designing for extensibility, as the roles and type of members may change over time.

- **Compute equity**: This is a fairly new concept, and trust systems based on it are different from those based on cryptocurrency. Compute equity is a chargeback model of how much you dedicate compute resources and what you get out of it that mimics cryptocurrency resource models. The types of participants and their business interests in the network are determinants of long-term sustainable infrastructure costs and maintenance. For instance, cost models of regulators may differ greatly from the cost models of the primary beneficiary of a blockchain-powered business network.

- **Shared business interests**: Blockchain networks promise specific advantages for businesses, such as reduced risk, a reliable and predictable transaction network, lower compliance costs, and so on. But these shared interests can lead to other operational issues, like data sharing and ownership as entities join and leave the network. Since regulations around data ownership evolve, as do industry requirements for the durability of data, these should be evaluated carefully when you design a blockchain system.

- **Governance**: Governance includes managing technical artifacts like technology infrastructure and governing data and smart contracts in a blockchain network. Layering governance in the following categories is recommended:

    - Blockchain network/technology governance
    - Blockchain data governance
    - Blockchain smart contract governance
    - Blockchain transaction management governance

When designing for extensibility, the goal should be to ensure that the blockchain network has sustainable operational elements and business growth elements. For example, in a sustainable model, every participant could deploy the chaincode that governs its own business process as it accepts and deals with digital assets, while also putting business participants in control of changing business processes, policies, and regulatory requirements.

Other considerations

There are a few other considerations to keep in mind apart from the previously mentioned aspects. They are briefly explained in the following sections.

Consensus, ACID properties, and CAP

A consensus model will never go to 0 because when NoSQL became the standard, various NoSQL systems solved their problems by understanding the **CAP theorem**, and the RDBMS enterprise community held steadfast to their **ACID** properties. Blockchain technology components and operational models aim to serve primarily as a transaction system. The distributed nature of the infrastructure and transaction processing tends to put the CAP theorem in high gear. It suggests that between the three desired properties of a transaction system—**consistency, availability**, and **partition tolerance**—at any given point, only one or two can be achieved. In the blockchain context, the CAP theorem implies that in the presence of a network partition, you must choose between consistency and availability. On the other hand, ACID properties—**atomicity, consistency, isolation**, and **durability**—constitute a set of properties of database transactions that are intended to guarantee validity even in the event of errors, power failures, and so forth. The technology design needs to consider the CAP and ACID principles when devising a system that can deliver industry and use case requirements.

CAP stands for consistency, availability, network partition tolerance:

- **C – Consistency**: Consensus guarantees only one truth of what happened and in one order.

- **A – Availability**: The fact that all calls to the blockchain are asynchronous allows the *invoking* application to make progress while ensuring consensus and durability. (Chaining also guarantees this.)

- **P – Network partition tolerance**: Consensus again prevents split-brain with conflicts when things get back together after a network partition.

ACID stands for atomicity, consistency, isolation, durability:

- **A – Atomicity**: The chaincode programming model is an all-or-nothing behavior that allows you to group activities together. It either all happens, or it doesn't.

- **C – Consistency**: I think the new world of NoSQL fudges this one. This means the same as the "C" in CAP.

- **I – Isolation**: Isolation indicates that two transactions are serialized, which is exactly what the block construction and chaining do.

- **D – Durability**: The chaining and replication all over the network ensure that if one or more nodes go down, data won't be lost. This is why everyone wants to bring a node and why those nodes should not be co-located.

Attestation – SSCs are signed and encrypted

In **secure service containers (SSCs)**, the software, operating system, hypervisors, and Docker container images cannot be modified. Certificates may be included in the SSC so that they can prove themselves to be genuine to a remote party. For example, including an SSL certificate when building SSCs helps ensure that you're speaking with a genuine instance, since the SSL certificate always stays protected (encrypted) within the SSC.

Use of HSMs

According to Wikipedia (`https://en.wikipedia.org/wiki/Hardware_security_module`), a "**hardware security module (HSM)** is a physical computing device that safeguards and manages digital keys for strong authentication and provides cryptoprocessing." These modules traditionally come in the form of a plug-in card or an external device that attaches directly to a computer or network server.

It can be a real challenge to administer a high-security device like an HSM with sufficient security and controls. In fact, today's standards mandate certain methods and levels of security for HSM administrative (and key management) systems.

Summary

Adopting blockchain in the enterprise requires a balancing act. Organizations not only have to run, manage, and maintain their existing infrastructure, they also need to help pave the way for this new computational model that promises to bring transformation.

In regulated industries, organizations could face a dual impact on the cost of compliance, since even a new technology platform needs to adhere to established regulatory frameworks and proven technology architecture standards and design. Enterprises considering blockchain can look toward a pragmatic approach by adopting a doctrine of layered defense, combining multiple mitigating security controls to help protect their resources and data. With a layered defense approach, digital assets, smart contracts, and ledger data are guarded.

In *Chapter 2, Exploring Hyperledger Fabric*, we will introduce the Hyperledger Fabric project—including the architecture, components, and features of Fabric—and how transactions are processed in Fabric.

References

1. Androulaki, Elli, et al. *Hyperledger Fabric: A Distributed Operating System for Permissioned Blockchains.* (https://arxiv.org/pdf/1801.10228.pdf)

2. Buterin, Vitalik. *Visions, Part 1: The Value of Blockchain Technology.* Ethereum Blog. (https://blog.ethereum.org/2015/04/13/visions-part-1-the-value-of-blockchain-technology/)

3. Cohen, David, and William Mougayar. *After The Social Web, Here Comes The Trust Web.* TechCrunch. (http://techcrunch.com/2015/01/18/after-the-social-web-here-comes-the-trust-web/)

4. Ghalim, Yacine. *Why we should drop the whole "Bitcoin vs blockchain" discussion.* Medium. (https://medium.com/@YacineGhalim/why-we-should-drop-the-whole-bitcoin-vs-blockchain-discussion-e3e38e9a5104#.yi53vmyv5)

5. *Know More: Blockchain – Overview, Tech, Application Areas & Use Cases.* MEDICI. (http://letstalkpayments.com/an-overview-of-blockchain-technology/)

6. Nakamoto, Satoshi. *Bitcoin: A Peer-to-Peer Electronic Cash System.* (https://bitcoin.org/bitcoin.pdf)

7. *National Institute of Standards and Technology Interagency or Internal Report (NISTIR) 8202: Blockchain Technology Overview.* National Institute of Standards and Technology (NIST). (https://csrc.nist.gov/publications/detail/nistir/8202/final)

8. *Unlocking the blockchain: A global legal and regulatory guide – Chapter 1.* Norton Rose Fulbright. (http://www.nortonrosefulbright.com/knowledge/publications/141573/unlocking-the-blockchain-a-global-legal-and-regulatory-guide-chapter-1)

2
Exploring Hyperledger Fabric

The focus of this chapter is the Hyperledger Fabric project—its components, design, reference architecture, and overall enterprise readiness. We will also discuss the broader aim of Linux Foundation-hosted Hyperledger projects and the importance of open source and open standards. The goal is to build an understanding of the diversity of various Hyperledger projects, and what frameworks and tools may be suitable for particular enterprise use cases and software consumption models. While the blockchain technology landscape is constantly in flux, Hyperledger projects represent a structure that supports a mature and peer-reviewed technology geared toward enterprise consumption and fueled by a diverse set of talent and community interests.

This chapter will cover the following topics:

- Building on the foundations of open computing
- Fundamentals of the Hyperledger project
- Hyperledger frameworks, tools, and building blocks
- Hyperledger Fabric component design
- Hyperledger Fabric: the journey of a sample transaction
- Actors and components in a Hyperledger Fabric network

We'll begin by considering Hyperledger's foundations in the open computing movement.

Building on the foundations of open computing

Open source projects, such as Linux and Java, have gained strength in mainstream businesses by serving as low-cost alternatives to commercial software. They provide capabilities that rival those of proprietary software, thanks to support from a large developer community. Popular open source projects can also accelerate **open standards**, the collective building blocks for products, by serving as a common implementation. Businesses and vendors using open standards free up development and services budgets for items that offer higher value and competitive advantage.

Open source is a part of the wider **open computing** movement, along with open standards and **open architecture**, as shown in the following diagram. Together, these initiatives enable integration and flexibility, and benefit customers by helping them avoid vendor lock-in.

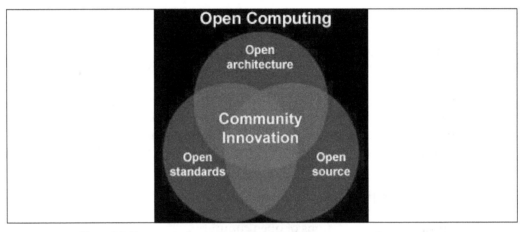

Figure 2.1: Community innovation as a result of the open computing movement

Enterprises are often required to adhere to various industry compliance and technology governance requirements, so it's important to consider the implications of open technology. While it is well understood that blockchain technology powers a business network, it also helps address issues around compliance adherence and technology governance that can have an exponential impact on the cost of technology consumption, governance, and maintenance.

Community-driven open innovation brings order to the chaos by providing a guiding framework for blockchain networks around network-centric software provisioning, deployment, governance, and compliance models.

Because blockchain technology powers the business network, any application defining the network that represents the business application and therefore the impact—technology adoption, costs, and complexity—is also network wide. Therefore, open community-driven technologies and open standards ought to be viewed as a vehicle to risk management and risk mitigation with links to a community-driven governance structure. We aim to discuss this at length with a technological focus in this chapter.

Fundamentals of the Hyperledger project

To start building an understanding of Hyperledger, let's look at some of the key players and fundamental elements of the Hyperledger Fabric space.

The Linux Foundation

The **Linux Foundation** (**LF**) is a world leader in supporting open technology development, and it is highly esteemed in the developer community. The LF fosters partnerships that address some of the world's biggest challenges through open source computing. It has made enormous investments in open source projects since it was founded in 2000 and helped to build an ecosystem that paved the way for the technologies discussed in this book.

Hyperledger

Hyperledger is an open source project that came out of the LF and was created to help advance cross-industry blockchain technologies. It's a global open source collaboration involving leaders from numerous industries.

Open source and open standards

As noted previously, the open computing movement laid the groundwork for blockchain and Hyperledger. Open source is a software licensing model. This means that the user, depending on the specific license details, has the right to use the code freely, enhance it, or even redistribute it, provided this is done on an open source basis.

One of the major advantages of an open source business application is the high level of flexibility provided through open source code, modular components, and standards adherence. This enables an organization to adapt the technology to achieve true usability with minimal effort.

Many applications that are backed by open source technologies can be assembled, like building blocks, to solve business problems. These building blocks come with a core set of functionalities, and each can be enhanced to meet specific business requirements. The different building blocks are easily integrated using open-standard technologies and additional features that can be custom-developed in a modular way.

An open source business application can therefore provide a base set of features at a very low cost, while enabling services engagement to enhance or tailor the application to fully meet business needs.

The open source community also provides a diverse global talent pool, with a wide range of ideas and creativity, which generates more collaborative innovation than any single vendor ever could. It has disrupted markets and created growth opportunities for those who recognize its advantages.

Open source technologies such as Hyperledger and its family of projects provide the following advantages to the industry:

- **Lower cost of software consumption**: Open source technology-driven projects do involve costs associated with deployment, maintenance, management, support, and so forth. The overall costs of development and costs associated with the talent pool, however, are largely reduced. Linking the internal technology governance structure with the community-driven governance structure of a Hyperledger project can greatly reduce the costs of technology governance and compliance. The growing popularity of Hyperledger projects represents the growth of community participation, implying the availability of a diverse talent pool associated with Hyperledger frameworks and tools. This is a huge cost consideration for enterprise business networks as their requirements and business networks grow.

- **Innovation and extensibility**: Enterprise and business networks do not have to have the vendor locked in, but rather can choose from the most innovative and involved communities, taking advantage of fast-paced innovation in the blockchain technology space. Piggybacking on community-based innovation will only amplify the business network's ability to leverage new technology and innovation from projects, and simplify business network operations and governance costs, not to mention the wide array of available competing and complementary technology sets that provide flexibility in enterprise architecture and design.

- **Sustainable development and innovation stream**: The LF provides governance structure to the Hyperledger community. Sustainable development implies peer review and regular software updates by the community that supports it. This enables a vehicle where business networks can enhance their value proposition and create new business models. In many cases, the business network participants may also represent the Hyperledger community, leading to a bidirectional stream of innovation, where the business network feeds business innovation-led improvements and requirements, with the technology community accepting and enhancing innovation.

- **Security and reliability**: The Hyperledger community provides a community of peers that review, debate, and collectively accept the technology's design and innovation. This LF-provided governance structure assumes collective responsibility, as Hyperledger projects are implemented and maintained by a large community of blockchain specialists who can find and address a vulnerability at a much faster pace than a vendor who is provided with proprietary software solutions. Because Hyperledger projects include involvement from their members, who share the costs of development and governance, the Hyperledger framework is reliable, as it is openly governed and peer-reviewed by the community.

- **Speeds up development and market adoption**: Open source projects, such as Hyperledger projects, have diverse communities and member organizations with common interests and a dedicated talent pool to collectively solve emerging problems. Hyperledger projects and the communities behind them provide developers and business networks the opportunity to contribute and consume software at the pace of innovation. The speed of development and market adoption is a critical consideration for many business networks at this stage of rapid technological innovation with respect to consensus, blockchain databases, security frameworks, encryption, and tooling.

So far, we've explored some of the foundational concepts of Hyperledger Fabric, and its position in the wider distributed and open computing industry. In the next section, we'll advance with our discussion by considering the core architecture and building blocks of the Hyperledger project.

Hyperledger frameworks, tools, and building blocks

Now that we've looked at Hyperledger's foundations in the open computing movement, as well as its benefits for industry, let's talk about its frameworks, tools, and building blocks. A summary of the Hyperledger projects is shown in the following diagram:

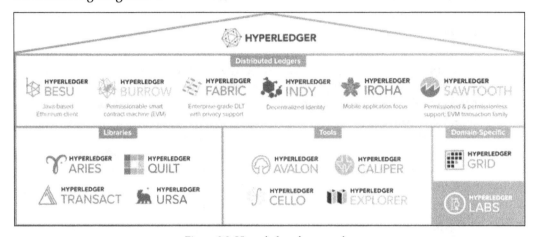

Figure 2.2: Hyperledger frameworks
(Source: Hyperledger.org, used under Creative Commons Attribution 3.0 Unported,
https://creativecommons.org/licenses/by/3.0/)

In this section, we'll discuss each layer of the Hyperledger project, as illustrated in *Figure 2.2*, **Distributed Ledgers**, **Libraries**, and **Tools**, before considering some of the broader building blocks and concepts of Hyperledger Fabric.

Hyperledger distributed ledger frameworks

There are six blockchain frameworks, as follows:

- **Hyperledger Besu**: This is a Java-based **Ethereum Virtual Machine (EVM)** client designed for use in private or public networks and for application in enterprise solutions. It supports several consensus algorithms, including **proof of work (PoW)**, **proof of authority (PoA)**, and **Istanbul Byzantine fault tolerance (IBFT)**, along with permissioning schemes designed for users in a consortium environment.

- **Hyperledger Burrow**: Hyperledger Burrow, which was contributed by Monax and Intel initially, is a modular blockchain that was client-built to the specification of the EVM. It supports advanced event, database, and permissioning features.

- **Hyperledger Fabric**: Hyperledger Fabric, contributed by IBM, is designed to be a foundation for developing applications or solutions with a modular architecture. It allows for plug-and-play components, such as consensus and membership services, and leverages containers to host smart contracts, also called **chaincodes**, that comprise the application logic of the system. The remainder of this chapter will focus on Hyperledger Fabric and its design, components, architecture, and overall enterprise design.

- **Hyperledger Indy**: Contributed by the Sovrin Foundation, Indy is a Hyperledger project made to support decentralized and self-sovereign identity on distributed ledgers. Hyperledger Indy provides tools, libraries, and reusable components for providing digital identities rooted on blockchains or other distributed ledgers.

- **Hyperledger Iroha**: Iroha, designed for mobile and IoT development projects, is based on Hyperledger Fabric and was contributed by Soramitsu, Hitachi, NTT Data, and Colu. It features a modern, domain-driven C++ design, as well as a new chain-based **Byzantine fault tolerant (BFT)** consensus algorithm called **Sumeragi**.

- **Hyperledger Sawtooth**: Sawtooth was contributed by Intel and includes a novel consensus algorithm the company came up with. The algorithm is called **Proof of Elapsed Time (PoET)** and aims to achieve distributed consensus as efficiently as possible. Hyperledger Sawtooth has potential in many areas, with support for both permissioned and permissionless deployments and recognition of diverse requirements. Sawtooth is designed for versatility.

Hyperledger libraries

There are four libraries that serve as building blocks of frameworks and tools, as follows:

- **Hyperledger Aries**: Aries, a library derived from Indy, provides support and mechanisms for creating, transmitting and storing verifiable digital credentials.

- **Hyperledger Quilt**: Quilt, from NTT DATA and Ripple, is a Java implementation of the interledger protocol by Ripple, which is designed to transfer values across distributed and non-distributed ledgers.

- **Hyperledger Transact**: Transact provides a standard interface for design and executing of smart contracts, independent from implementation of distributed ledgers. It serves as a uniform interface for the implementation of various types of smart contract containers.

- **Hyperledger Ursa**: Ursa is a shared cryptographic library that provides implementation of cryptographic functionalities to other Hyperledger projects.

Hyperledger tools

There are five tools currently in the Hyperledger project, all of which are hosted by the LF. These tools are as follows:

- **Hyperledger Avalon**: Avalon is an implementation of Trusted Compute Specifications by the Enterprise Ethereum Alliance that enables the secure movement of blockchain processing off the main chain to dedicated computing resources.

- **Hyperledger Caliper**: Caliper is a blockchain multi-platform benchmark tool that allows users to measure the performance of a specific implementation with predefined use cases. It was contributed by developers from numerous organizations.

- **Hyperledger Cello**: Contributed by IBM, Cello seeks to bring the on-demand "as-a-service" deployment model into the blockchain ecosystem in order to reduce the effort required to create, manage, and terminate blockchains. Cello efficiently and automatically provides a multi-tenant chain service on top of various infrastructures, such as bare metal, virtual machine, and other container platforms. It is currently available for Fabric with the aim to include support for additional platforms.

- **Hyperledger Explorer**: Hyperledger Explorer was originally contributed by IBM, Intel, and DTCC. It can view, invoke, deploy, or query blocks, transactions and associated data, network information (name, status, list of nodes), contracts, and transaction families, as well as other relevant information stored in the ledger of a Fabric network.

- **Hyperledger Grid**: Grid is a library of reference implementations of supply chain-centric data types, data models, and smart contract-based business logic. The implementations are based on existing open standards and industry best practices.

The building blocks of blockchain solutions

As noted in *Chapter 1*, *Blockchain – An Enterprise and Industry Perspective*, blockchain promises to fundamentally solve the issues of *time* and *trust* in industries such as financial services, supply chain, logistics, and healthcare. It seeks to streamline business processes and thereby address inefficiencies.

It's a technology for a new generation of transactional applications built on trust, accountability, and transparency. There are several characteristics shared by all industrial blockchains, including the following:

- A shared single source of truth
- Secure and tamper-proof
- Private unlinkable identity
- Scalable architecture
- Confidential
- Auditable

The following diagram summarizes these characteristics into four tenets:

Figure 2.3: Four tenets of blockchains

Blockchain solutions comprise four building blocks—a shared ledger, privacy, trust, and smart contracts. Allow me to elaborate a bit on each of these building blocks:

- **Shared ledger**: With the Bitcoin blockchain, the intent was to democratize visibility; however, enterprise blockchain requires a different approach due to the regulation of consumer data. Append-only distributed transaction records can be achieved by SQL or NoSQL distributed databases.

- **Privacy through cryptography**: Privacy through cryptography is essential for ensuring that transactions are authenticated and verified. It is imperative to include cryptography in blockchain design for the sake of hardening security and making it more difficult to breach the distributed system. Considerations about cryptography change when you're working with a less democratic or permissioned ledger network.

- **Trust systems or consensus**: Trust means using the power of the network to verify a transaction. Trust is essential in any blockchain system or application, and we prefer the term *trust* system over *consensus* system since trust is the foundational element that dictates a stakeholder's investment in any blockchain infrastructure. The trust system is modified whenever new entrants come into the blockchain space and apply blockchain technology to a new use case or specialization. The trust model is truly the heart of blockchain — it's what delivers the tenets of *trust, trade,* and *ownership.* Trust is what enables blockchain to displace the transaction system, but this can only happen when trade and ownership are addressed by distributed/shared ledgers. There's still much work needed to define an optimized trust system for various use cases. Database solutions are in the works to address scale and mobile use cases, but more work is required around P2P and sharing economy models, as well as B2B models.

- **Smart contracts**: In the context of blockchain, a smart contract is a business agreement embedded into the transaction database and executed with transactions. Rules are needed in business to define the flow of value and state of a transaction, so that's the function of the contract here. The contract is smart because it's a computerized protocol to execute the terms of the contract. Various contractual clauses (such as collateral, bonding, delineation of property rights, and so forth) can be codified to enforce compliance with the terms of the contract and ensure a successful transaction — this is the basic idea behind smart contracts. Smart contracts are designed to reassure one party that the other will fulfill their promise. Part of the objective of such contracts is to reduce the costs of verification and enforcement. Smart contracts must have the following characteristics:

  - **Observable**: Participants can see or prove each other's actions pertaining to the contract

  - **Verifiable**: Participants can prove to other nodes that a contract has been performed or breached

  - **Private**: Knowledge of the contents/performance of the contract should involve only the participants required to execute it

Bitcoin made provisions for smart contracts; however, it lacked some capabilities such as Turing-completeness, lack of state, and so on. Ethereum improved upon Bitcoin's limitations by building a blockchain with a built-in Turing-complete programming language, so that anyone can write smart contracts and decentralized applications by creating their own rules for ownership, transaction formats, and state transition functions.

These advances made it possible for complex contracts to be codified in a blockchain, such as instant transfer of credit to a traveler's bank account when a flight is delayed beyond a certain duration or payment of employee compensation if performance goals are achieved.

How does this work practically? Well, smart contracts are deployed as code on the blockchain nodes, which we might more appropriately call *smart contract code*. This code provides a means for using blockchain technology to complement, or replace, existing legal contracts. This smart contract code is deployed on the blockchain node in a programming language such as Solidity, Golang, or Java. Deploying the code on the blockchain provides three important properties:

- Permanence and censorship resistance inherited from the blockchain

- The ability of the program itself to control blockchain assets, such as by transferring ownership or quantities of an asset among participants

- Execution of the program by the blockchain, ensuring that it will always execute as written and no one can interfere

In the enterprise world, smart contracts would probably involve blockchain's smart contract code, accompanied by a more traditional legal contract. For example, smart contract code may execute on a land registry blockchain network to transfer ownership of a house from one party to another, so that land registry records are updated in real time and all participants, such as the city, realtors, lawyers, and banks, can all update their own records upon completion of the sale. However, the home buyer will insist on a legal contract with indemnity clauses to cover any undiscovered liens.

Hyperledger Fabric component design

Let's discuss various Hyperledger Fabric components that facilitate the key blockchain components of the shared ledger, encryption, the trust system, and smart contracts. The components represent the Hyperledger Fabric infrastructure components and provide isolation from contract's development constructs. Chaincode or smart contract development details will be discussed in detail in a separate chapter.

The following diagram depicts the Hyperledger Fabric infrastructure components:

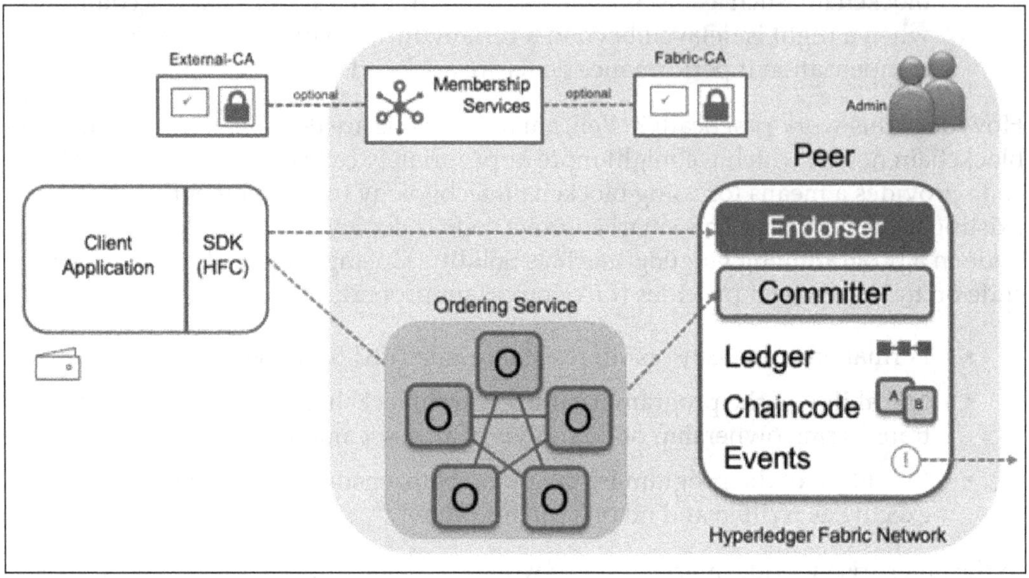

Figure 2.4: Hyperledger Fabric infrastructure components

Let's consider three key components before moving into the design discussion: the membership service, dedicated order nodes, and peers.

The **membership service** provides identity management to network participants:

- Hyperledger Fabric CA is a certificate authority-based implementation of membership services, but you are not required to use it (that is, any X509-based PKI infrastructure that can issue EC certificates can be used)
- Identity Mixer is another implementation available for scenarios requiring a high degree of anonymity and unlinkability of transactions

Dedicated orderer nodes order and batch transactions and sign each batch (block) to create a hash chain (ledger):

- The orderer nodes implement an atomic broadcast API and disseminate newly created blocks into the network
- Hyperledger Fabric provides three implementations—Solo (for development testing), Raft (for production), and Kafka-based implementation for production with high fault tolerance
- The ordering service is pluggable—the implementer needs to provide only an atomic-broadcast API based on the gRPC interface definition

Peers are responsible for existing smart logic (contracts) and maintaining the ledger:

- Endorsement simulates transactions (that is, it executes them, but does not commit them)
- Peers receive batches of endorsed transactions from the orderer nodes and then validate and commit transactions (this eliminates non-determinism)

Now, let's dig a little deeper into the specifics of Hyperledger Fabric's design philosophy, before exploring its reference and runtime architecture models.

Principles of Hyperledger design

Hyperledger Fabric, again, is a blockchain implementation that is designed for deploying a modular and extensible architecture. It has a modular subsystem design so that different implementations can be plugged in and implemented over time. This section covers the design principles of Hyperledger Fabric and describes the details on the various components/modules and their interactions and functions. Understanding the design principles facilitates better solution and technology design decisions, especially around scalability, security, and performance.

While in this book we will discuss the reference architecture of Hyperledger Fabric, please note that all the Hyperledger projects (the frameworks referred to previously) follow a design philosophy that includes the following principles:

- **A modular and extensible approach**: This implies modularity in all components of all frameworks. Components defined by Hyperledger for all projects include (but are not limited to) the following:
    - Consensus layer
    - Contract (chaincode) layer
    - Communication (gossip) layer
    - Data store (persistent, log, shared ledger, and private data)
    - Identity services (root of trust—to identify the participants) APIs
    - Pluggable cryptography
- **Interoperability**: This principle pertains to backward interoperability and *not* the interoperability between the various Hyperledger project-powered blockchain systems or business networks.

- **A focus on secure solutions**: Enterprise and therefore business network security is paramount; hence the focus on security — and not just of the crypto abstraction — on the interaction between components and the structure that governs the permissioning nature of permissioned blockchains. Most industries embarking on the permissioned blockchain are established and regulated industries.

- **A token (or coin or cryptoasset) agnostic approach**: This is discussed in great length in *Chapter 12, Governance – A Necessary Evil of Regulated Industries*, but Hyperledger projects do not use cryptoassets, cryptocurrency, tokens, or coin-like constructs as incentive mechanics to establish trust systems. While there is a notion of asset tokenization that represents a physical, virtual, or dematerialized asset, tokenization of assets is a vastly different concept than a systemic token that is generated in the system as a virtualization of incentive economics.

- **A focus on rich and easy-to-use APIs**: The focus here is to ensure that blockchain systems have not only enterprise middleware access, but also access to business networks, existing participants, and new systems without exposing the details of blockchain-powered business networks.

Hyperledger Fabric reference architecture

Hyperledger Fabric follows a modular design, and in this section, we'll discuss some of the possible components or modules that can be plugged in and implemented. The following diagram shows the overall reference architecture:

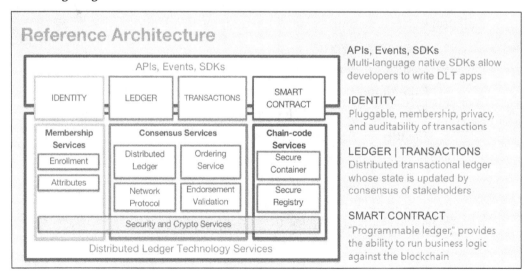

Figure 2.5: Reference architecture

The following list, although not exhaustive, includes some of the important components of the reference architecture:

- **Membership services**: This module acts as a vehicle to establish a root of trust during network creation, but this is also instrumental in ensuring and managing the identity of members. Membership services are essentially a certificate authority as well as utilized elements of the **public key infrastructure** (**PKI**) for things such as key distribution, management, and establishing federated trust as the network grows. The membership services module provides a specialized digital certificate authority for issuing certificates to members of the blockchain network, and it leverages cryptographic functions provided by Hyperledger Fabric.

- **Transactions**: A transaction is a request to the blockchain to execute a function on the ledger. The function is implemented by a contract. Cryptography ensures the integrity of transactions by linking the transaction to previous blocks and ensuring the transactional integrity is protected, by linking the cryptogram or hash from previously linked blocks.

- **Channel**: The Fabric network can be partitioned into several channels, where each channel represents a ledger along with its consensus protocol, contracts, access control policies, peers and other components.

- **State database (DB)**: A state DB, also called a **world state**, represents the current state of the ledger. Unlike the ledger, which contains the whole history of transactions, the world state contains only the latest state resulting from projecting the historical sequence of transactions. It is used by the contract to efficiently query the current state of the ledger. There are two options:

    - LevelDB (default embedded KV DB) supports keyed queries, composite key queries, and key range queries

    - CouchDB (external option) supports keyed queries, composite key queries, key range queries, plus full data-rich queries and indexes

- **Contract services**: A contract is application-level code stored on the ledger as a part of a transaction. Chaincode runs transactions that may modify the world state. Transaction logic is written as a contract (in the Go, Java, or JavaScript language) and executes in secure containers. The transaction transforms data, scoped by the contract on the channel from which it operates. The contract is installed on peers, which require access to the asset states to perform reads and writes. The contract is then instantiated on specific channel and peers. Within a channel the contract can be shared across all peers or with a specific subset.

- **Events**: The process of validating peers and contracts can produce events (predefined channel events and custom events generated by contract) on the network that applications may listen for and take actions on. These events are consumed by event adapters, which may further deliver events using vehicles such as WebHooks or Kafka. The channel provides an event services to publish streams of events to registered listeners. As of v2.0, there are several categories of events, including block events notifying about committed blocks, transactions and transactions' emitted events, block events that include private data specific to organizations, and filtered events limited to confirmations of specific transactions. An event gets published whenever a block is committed to the ledger.

- **Consensus**: Consensus is at the heart of any blockchain system. It also enables a trust system. In general, the consensus service enables digitally signed transactions to be proposed and validated by network members. In Hyperledger Fabric, the consensus is pluggable and tightly linked to the endorse-order-validate model that Hyperledger proposes. The ordering services in Hyperledger Fabric represent the consensus system. The ordering service batches multiple transactions into blocks and outputs a hash-chained sequence of blocks containing transactions.

- **Ledger**: Another component is a distributed encrypted ledger, implemented as an append-only data structure. Each peer maintains a copy of the ledger for each channel of which they are a member.

- **Private data**: Private data allows a subset of organizations participating in one ledger to keep some data private between themselves. This data is stored in a private state database on the peers of authorized organizations, which can be accessed from contracts on authorized peers.

- **Client SDK**: A client **software developer kit** (**SDK**) enables the creation of applications that deploy and invoke transactions atop a shared ledger. The Hyperledger Fabric reference architecture supports both Node.js and Java SDK (while Python and Golang are in development). An SDK is like a programming kit or set of tools that provides developers with the environment of libraries to write and test contract applications. SDKs are critical in blockchain application development and will be discussed in detail in further chapters. Specific capabilities included in the SDK are the application client, contract, users, events, and crypto suite.

Hyperledger Fabric runtime architecture

Now that we've looked at the reference architecture, let's consider the runtime architecture for Hyperledger Fabric, shown in the following diagram:

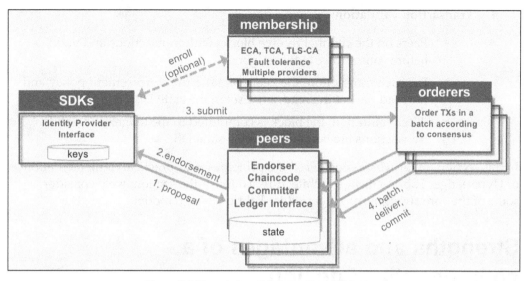

Figure 2.6: Hyperledger Fabric runtime architecture

The following outline demonstrates a Hyperledger Fabric runtime transaction processing flow:

1. **Transaction proposal (client SDK):**
    *   The transaction proposal is submitted by the client SDK
    *   It is sent to multiple endorsing peers (peers designated to participate in consensus) on the channel at the same time

2. **Transaction endorsement:**
    *   Each endorsing peer executes the transaction by calling the specified contract function and signs the result, which becomes the read-write set of the transaction
    *   The endorsed transaction proposal (including the read-write set) is sent back to the client SDK
    *   Each peer may process multiple transactions at the same time, as well as participate in multiple channels, allowing concurrent execution

3. **Transaction submitted to the ordering service:**
    *   The client SDK collects endorsed transaction proposals and submits them to the ordering service
    *   The ordering service accepts endorsed transactions from clients and orders them into blocks and then delivers them to all peers on the channel

4. **Transaction validation**:

- Peers on the channel receive blocks with transactions and validate before committing to the ledger
- For each transaction, the peer validates the endorsement policy and the read part of the read-write set in the state DB
- After validation, the block is committed to the ledger and valid transactions are committed to the state DB

In this section, so far we've considered the principles and practical implementation of Hyperledger Fabric's design architecture. To finish the section, we'll consider some of the core strengths of Hyperledger Fabric's design model.

Strengths and advantages of a componentized design

Hyperledger Fabric's component design offers several advantages. Many of these strengths relate to business network governance, which is an important compliance and costs consideration for Hyperledger Fabric in the enterprise.

These benefits include the following:

- **Delineates development design from runtime design**: Separating development and runtime design is important for development best practices and infrastructure/hybrid cloud variations. It ensures adherence to the current enterprise's and to the business network's application development policies, as well as DevOps practices.
- **Discerns between design imperatives and infrastructure/deployment capabilities**: Componentized design allows us to separate infrastructure design, which includes things such as network connections, security, permissioning, and contractual vehicles, from the overall application design of the business network blueprint that dictates the technology blueprint.

- **Incorporates network design principles**: The modularity of Hyperledger Fabric can address infrastructure scaling issues, such as the number of connections, colocation, security, container deployment practices, and so on. There are various considerations when it comes to network design, such as cloud deployment, hybrid and/or on-premises, and a combination of any of the available options, which are dependent on the requirements of individual members in a business network. Network design also addresses the business challenges of network growth and the resulting performance and security-driven **service level agreements (SLAs)** with its members.

- **Addresses channel design principles**: Modularity, or componentized design, can also address isolation, data privacy, and confidentiality between participants and controlled/permissioned access with robust audit capability. Channel constructs in Hyperledger Fabric enable us to address the business blueprint requirements around implementing business-defined transactions that may be bilateral, trilateral, or event multilateral. Channels also provide an avenue to limit the visibility of transaction data to a few participants or provide full access when required, such as to a regulator. Channel design also addresses critical business requirements around transaction processing, data visibility, business rules enforcement, and so on. It also has technology implications, such as for scalability, security, and the costs of the infrastructure that supports the business network. Finally, channel design addresses the business challenges of network growth and the resulting performance and security-driven SLAs with members.

Each of the advantages of componentized design described has cost implications in terms of the following:

- **Runtime/infrastructure design**: The use of resources and resulting costs
- **Flexible design**: The ability to accommodate when products and relationships morph
- **Longevity of the solution**: The global footprint of the enterprise cloud infrastructure, including robust access to technical and business SMEs in the form of maintenance and support

All of these are essential for the compliance, governance, and longevity of the solution, and resulting business networks powered by blockchain.

Hyperledger Fabric – the journey of a sample transaction

Now, let's look at the journey of a sample transaction with Hyperledger Fabric, as illustrated in the following diagram. This section will facilitate an understanding of the transaction processing protocol of Fabric:

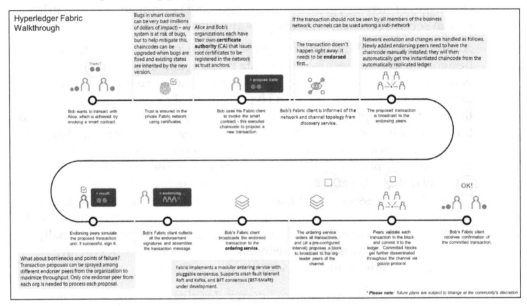

Figure 2.7: Hyperledger Fabric walkthrough

Fabric introduces a newly designed blockchain, preserving the transaction processing architecture and aiming at a secure, scalable, resilient, modular, and confidential design. Hyperledger Fabric 2.0 supports the execution of distributed applications supporting enterprise-friendly programming models. The components in Hyperledger Fabric provide a modular design, optimally suited for a business network made of various enterprises. Hyperledger Fabric introduces a model based on three steps, an *endorse-order-validate* architecture, designed for the distributed execution of untrusted code in an untrusted environment. This separation not only allows for provisioning at scale, but also ensures security by separation at every layer.

The transaction flow is separated into three steps, which may be run on different entities in the system:

1. **Endorsement of a transaction and checking its validity (validation step)**: This step includes members of a channel to inspect and adhere to endorsement policies that define the acceptable agreed-upon approach to validate a transaction proposal. Since peers need to update the ledger (upon transaction finality), the peers (that are subscribed to a channel) review the proposal and provide their ledger's version of the read-write set. This validation step is vital as it provides the first step of transaction validation. This check also acts as a gate and prevents the erroneous downstream processing of a transaction, which can be computationally expensive.

2. **Ordering through an ordering service**: This is a consensus protocol that is meant to be pluggable, irrespective of transaction semantics. The pluggability of the consensus provides enterprise and business networks with tremendous flexibility, as there are consensus mechanism considerations for various types of industries, use cases, and interactions between network participants.

3. **Validation or transaction commitment**: This implies committing a transaction and therefore going through a final set of validations per application-specific trust assumption.

A Hyperledger Fabric transaction involves three types of nodes:

*   **The committing peer** is the node that maintains the ledger and state. The committing peer is the party that *commits* transactions and may hold the smart contract or contract.

*   **The endorsing peer** is a specialized committing peer that can grant or deny the endorsement of a transaction proposal. The endorsing peer has to hold the smart contract.

*   **The ordering nodes** (service) communicate with the committing and endorsing peer nodes; their main function is to approve the inclusion of transaction blocks into the ledger. Unlike the committing peer and endorsing peers, the ordering nodes do not hold the smart contract or the ledger.

Validation can be divided into two roles, endorsement and ordering:

- **Endorsing** a transaction means verifying that it obeys a smart contract; endorsers sign the transaction to complete this aspect of validation
- **Ordering** verifies transactions for inclusion in the ledger; this form of validation helps to control what goes in the ledger and ensures its consistency

What about contract invocation? In a Hyperledger Fabric transaction, simulation (contract execution) and block validation/commit are separate.

There are three phases involved in carrying out a contract operation (in other words, a business transaction) with Hyperledger Fabric:

1. The first phase is contract operation execution through simulation on endorsing peers. It's possible to enable parallel simulation on endorsers to help improve concurrency and scalability since simulation won't update the blockchain state.
2. Next, simulation determines the business transaction proposal, that is, the read-write set, and sends this to the ordering service.
3. A transaction proposal is then ordered with regard to others and broadcasts to committing peers (includes endorsing peers) that validate that its read set has not been modified since simulation and applies its write set automatically.

Channels are also an important aspect of the transaction journey, since peers exchange messages using consensus by way of channels, and they ensure privacy between different ledgers. The following are a few notes regarding channels:

- They don't have to be connected to by all nodes
- Peers connect to channels through an access control policy
- The ordering service orders a transaction broadcast to a channel
- Peers receive transactions in exactly the same order for a channel
- Transactions are delivered in cryptographically linked blocks
- Every peer connected to a channel validates the channel-specific delivered blocks and commits them to the ledger

The next section will cover the roles of various actors and services in Hyperledger Fabric's network.

Actors and components in a Hyperledger Fabric network

In this section we will explore the actors and their roles and responsibilities within a network. In the context of the actors we also look at the list of components of the network. We give a special focus to the role of the developer and the tasks the developer performs in the design of the Fabric-based solution.

Actors in a blockchain network

A blockchain is a network-based infrastructure where network-centric design, development, deployment, management, and support constructs apply. It is therefore vital to understand the various actors and their roles, shown in the following diagram and explained in the following text, that interact with the blockchain network for various purposes such as management, support, business use, regulation, and so on:

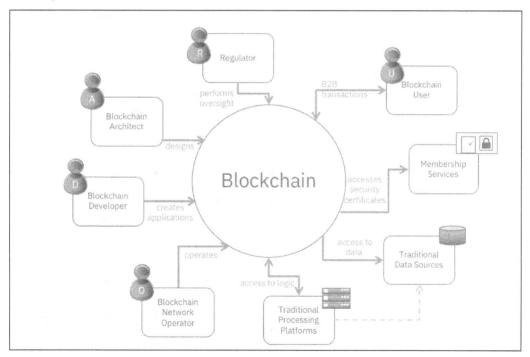

Figure 2.8: Actors in a blockchain network

Each actor has a role and entry point and defines a governance structure that aids in network governance, audit, and compliance requirements. Business network governance (covered in detail in the following points) is an important compliance and cost consideration. Users are the parties who use the blockchain. They create and distribute blockchain applications and perform operations using the blockchain. These actors are consistent, and they are based on cloud computing actors and roles from ISO/IEC 17788:

- **Developers**: Blockchain developers are the actors who create applications for users (client-side) and develop the smart contracts (server-side) that interact with the blockchain, which are then used by blockchain users to initiate transactions. They also write code to enable the blockchain to interact with legacy applications.

- **Administrators**: Blockchain administrators perform administrative activities, such as deployment and configuration of the blockchain network, contracts, or application.

- **Operators**: Blockchain operators are responsible for defining, creating, managing, and monitoring the blockchain network and application.

- **Auditors**: Blockchain auditors have the responsibility of reviewing blockchain transactions and validating their integrity from a business, legal, audit, and compliance perspective.

- **Business users**: This term refers to users operating in a business network. They interact with the blockchain using an application but may not be aware of the blockchain since it will be an invisible transactional system.

Components in a blockchain network

In general, a blockchain system consists of a number of nodes, each of which has a local copy of a ledger. In most systems, the nodes belong to different organizations. The nodes communicate with each other in order to gain agreement on what should be in the ledger.

The process of gaining this agreement is called **consensus**, and there are a number of different algorithms that have been developed for this purpose. Users send transaction requests to the blockchain in order to perform the operations the chain is designed to provide. Once a transaction is completed, a record of the transaction is added to one or more of the ledgers and can never be altered or removed. This property of the blockchain is called **immutability**.

Cryptography is used to secure the blockchain and the communications between the elements of the blockchain system. It ensures that the ledger cannot be altered, except by the addition of new transactions. Cryptography provides integrity on messages from users or between nodes and ensures operations are only performed by authorized entities:

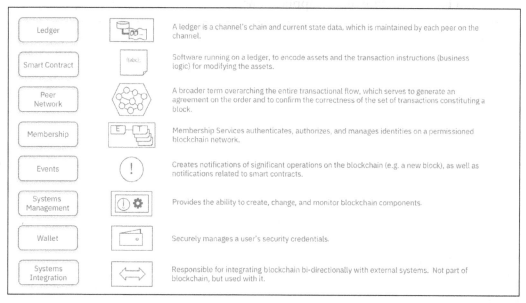

Figure 2.9: Components in a blockchain network

The authority to perform transactions on a blockchain can use one of two models: permissioned or permissionless. In a permissioned blockchain, users must be enrolled in the blockchain before they are allowed to perform transactions. The enrollment process gives the user credentials that are used to identify the user when they perform transactions. In a permissionless blockchain, any person can perform transactions, but they are usually restricted from performing operations on any data but their own. Blockchain owners develop an executable software module called a smart contract implementing a domain-specific business logic, which is installed into the blockchain itself. When a user sends a transaction to the blockchain, it can invoke a smart contract module, which performs functions defined by the creator of the smart contract module.

Developer interaction

As discussed previously in the *Actors in a blockchain network* section, blockchain developers can have many roles, including creating applications for users (client-side) and developing smart contracts. Developers also write code to enable the blockchain to interact with legacy applications.

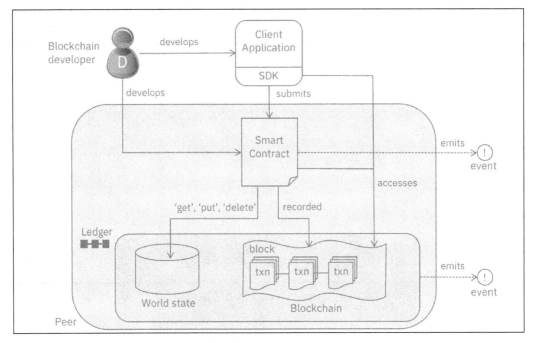

Figure 2.10: Developer interaction with blockchain

A blockchain developer's primary role is to create an application (and integration) and smart contracts, as well as their respective interaction with ledgers and other enterprise systems of the business network and their participants. Due to the separation of the Hyperledger Fabric infrastructure, there is a clear separation between infrastructure constructs—such as peers, consensus, security, channels, and policies—and developer-led activities—such as smart contract development, deployment, enterprise integration, API management, and frontend application development.

From a developer's point of view, the following outline represents an example of developer interaction with Hyperledger Fabric constructs:

- The developer creates an application and a smart contract
- The application can invoke calls within the smart contract through an SDK

- The calls are processed by the business logic built into the smart contract through various commands and protocols:

    - A put or delete command will go through the selected consensus protocol and will be added to the blockchain

    - A get command can only read from the world state but is not recorded on the blockchain

- An application can access block information using REST APIs, such as get block height.

Note the use of delete here, which can delete keys from the world state database, but not transactions from the blockchain, which we've already established are immutable.

The following diagram summarizes all the key roles:

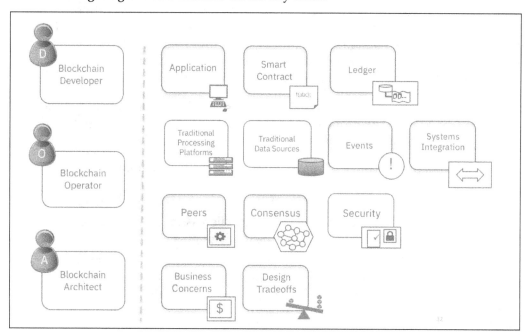

Figure 2.11: Roles in a blockchain network

Now, let's move on to consider the CAP theorem, and how the desired properties of consistency, availability, and partition tolerance are achieved in Hyperledger Fabric.

CAP theorem

In *Chapter 1, Blockchain – An Enterprise and Industry Perspective*, we introduced the CAP theorem in the context of general system properties. Formally, the CAP theorem as postulated by Eric Brewer in 2000 at ACM Symposium on **Principles of Distributed Computing (PODC)** (https://dl.acm.org/citation.cfm?id=343502) states that in a distributed data store it is impossible to guarantee more than any two of the following three properties: **consistency (C)**, **availability (A)**, and **partition tolerance (P)**. A distributed data store thus can be characterized on the two properties it guarantees, namely CA, CP, or AP.

More specifically, the theorem is aimed at distributed systems deployed across unreliable networks (networks with faults and delays, such as the internet), leading to a partitioning of the system components. According to CAP, in these environments, the system design must focus on the balance between availability and consistency. For example, the **ACID (atomicity, consistency, isolation, durability)** approach, typically provided by **relational database management systems (RDBMSes)**, guarantees consistency on a single node at the expense of availability across multiple nodes (CP systems). However, note that different configurations may yield different combinations, namely CA or AP, as well.

In contrast, Fabric is designed, similarly to many other blockchain platforms, as an AP type of system with **eventual consistency**, also referred to as **BASE (basically available, soft state, eventual consistency)**.

In the context of blockchain, CAP properties can be defined as follows:

- **Consistency**: The blockchain network avoids any forks of the ledger
- **Availability**: Transactions submitted by clients are permanently committed to the ledger and available on all the network peers
- **Partition tolerance**: The blockchain network continues to operate despite an arbitrary number of transaction proposals or blocks being dropped (or delayed) by the physical network medium between the peers

Fabric achieves the CAP properties as follows:

- **Consistency**: By a total order of transactions and version control using MVCC
- **Availability**: By hosting a copy of the ledger on each of the peers
- **Partition tolerance**: By maintaining operation despite failed nodes (up to a threshold)

As you can see, availability and partition tolerance (the AP properties of the CAP theorem) are guaranteed by default in most blockchain systems. However, consistency is harder to provide.

Fabric achieves consistency by combining the following elements:

- The transaction processing is split into a sequence of steps across multiple components of the network.

- Clients connect to a communication channel and submit transaction proposals to endorsing peers and then to the ordering service.

- The ordering service orders transactions into blocks with a total order, that is, the order of the transactions is guaranteed to be consistent across the whole network. The blocks once created are broadcasted to each member peer of the channel. The broadcasting protocol guarantees reliable delivery of the blocks to the peers in a correct order, namely total-order broadcast.

- As we will explain when looking at **multiversion concurrency control** (**MVCC**), upon reception of the block on the peer, the peer uses MVCC to validate each transaction based on the key versions stored in the transaction ReadSet. The MVCC validation guarantees consistency of the resulting ledger and of the world state and prevents attacks such as double spending. However, it can also lead to the elimination of otherwise valid transactions that have been submitted in an order violating the ReadSet version validation check. The transactions are then marked either valid or invalid in the ledger.

- The ledger then contains a sequence of totally ordered blocks, where each block contains a sequence of totally ordered transactions (either valid or invalid), yielding a ledger imposing a total order across all transactions.

To round off the chapter, we'll cover a few new features that have been introduced with the most recent version of Hyperledger Fabric.

New features covered in this book

The first edition of this book was published along with Fabric version 1.1. The following is an overview of the new features introduced between version 1.1 and the current version, 2.0:

- **Private data**: Private data allows a subset of organizations participating in one ledger to keep some data private between themselves.

- **Service discovery**: This helps client applications to dynamically discover configuration information about the network peers, cryptographic materials, endorsement policy, and other information needed to submit transactions to the network.

- **State-based endorsement**: This allows the contract-level endorsement policy to be overridden by a policy for a specific key(s).

- **Pluggable system contracts**: Developers can now develop own consensus models by implementing and deploying own system endorsement (ESCC) and validation (VSCC) contracts.

- **Identity Mixer**: This is a new type of membership provider that provides privacy-preserving features including anonymity (the ability to transact without revealing the identity) and unlinkability (the ability of an identity to send multiple transactions without revealing that the transactions were sent by the same identity).

- **New contract languages**: Aside from Golang, Fabric now supports development of contracts in Java and Node.js.

- **Raft ordering service**: This is a new type of ordering service designed as a primary choice for production networks. Implementing the Raft protocol allows the dynamic election of leading ordering nodes, allowing for resilient, crash fault tolerant transaction ordering.

- **New programming model**: This is a new SDK model of objects available for design of client applications allowing for development of resilient and dynamic clients integrating new network features such as service discovery. Aside from the SDK for Node.js, Fabric now offers also an SDK for Java, with SDKs for Golang and Python in development.

- **New governance features**: Version 2.0 offers a host of new features for the management and governance of networks.

Some of these features have been mentioned in this chapter; however, we will encounter them in more detail in the following chapters.

Summary

We have learned about the general concepts that underpin blockchains and reviewed the blockchain frameworks, libraries, and tools currently in development by the LF. Fabric presents a modular and extensible implementation of these general concepts. This design helps us to develop and operate private networks that provide trust to attract new participants, as well as sustaining the confidence of founding and existing participants, all while maintaining business benefits and value. We have also learned about the CAP theorem, which underpins the potential of blockchains, and about the new features included in Fabric since version 1.1.

In the next chapter, we will introduce the notion of a business network and the various concepts of which business networks are composed, including participants, assets, and others.

3
Business Networks

Whenever we encounter a new or complex task, one of the biggest challenges is how to *think* about the problem. That's the point of a **business network**. Once we understand the idea of a business network – its structure and processes – we're able to see how blockchain technology can be successfully applied to our business problem or opportunity.

We're going to explore how the concept of a business network helps us analyze a business. Looking at the set of counterparties with which a business interacts gives us an excellent starting point for understanding that business. By extending our examination to the processes and interactions with those counterparties, we will get a fundamental insight into the value of a business. And that's going to equip us with the necessary intellectual tools to design a viable solution in which a blockchain can often play a key role as a foundational technology building block.

A business network built using Hyperledger Fabric can draw from a rich set of features to simplify the information and processes that knit its constituent businesses together. The resulting benefits include both reduced cost and the creation of new opportunities for participants in the network. Moreover, we'll learn how specific capabilities for transparency and visibility – from fully open ledgers to verifiable privacy – can help us manage risk and comply with a regulatory and compliance framework in a natural way.

It's also worth remembering that although we are often employed to solve an application-specific problem, such as improving energy distribution, most businesses operate in a **network of networks**. For example, an energy company will deal with upstream suppliers, downstream customers, regulators and banks in a variety of information and process sharing tasks.

These partners will do the same because most businesses don't deal exclusively or linearly with one set of counterparties. Thinking in terms of a network of business networks will help us understand the problems and opportunities, but also translate into how we use the technology; there's a direct connection between these ideas and what we'll see in employing Hyperledger Fabric to solve some of the business requirements!

Let's chart our course during this chapter. We'll spend a little time introducing the vocabulary of business networks, including key terms such as **participant**, **asset**, **transaction**, and **event**. We'll then explore examples that show how such elements can be used to analyze a business problem and determine the requirements of a solution. By the end of this chapter, we'll be ready to design software architectures and implementations that use Hyperledger Fabric. And in subsequent chapters, we'll practice this with a real example!

While the idea of a business network is incredibly helpful for implementing a blockchain network, it's also a useful concept for other activities. These include blockchain analytics, integrating with existing systems, and structuring application and enterprise architectures. So, even if you are not going to immediately implement a business network, this chapter can be read standalone.

A final word on Hyperledger Composer before we get started. While the ideas embodied in it remain very helpful for designing a good blockchain solution, as a technology, it has been deprecated. Don't worry about this—its ideas are now found in Hyperledger Fabric, and every example in this edition of this book uses Hyperledger Fabric to achieve the same results and more! This is part of a natural cycle—innovative ideas become standard and then become a commodity. In summary, if you're looking for Composer, you'll find many of its ideas in version 2.0 of Hyperledger Fabric. And if you're used to Hyperledger Fabric, then you're in for a treat—with version 2.0, many once difficult programming tasks just got much easier.

We will be covering the following topics in this chapter:

- A language for business networks
- The business network concept
- Defining a business network
- Introducing participants
- Introducing assets
- Introducing transactions
- Introducing events
- Business network technology

A busy world of purposeful activity

Imagine for a moment that we're flying in a plane over a large city. We can see factories, banks, schools, hospitals, retail stores, car showrooms, ships and boats at the port, and so on. These are the structures that define the city.

If we look carefully, we'll see things happening within and between these structures. Lorries might be delivering iron ore to the factory, customers might be withdrawing money from banks, students might be sitting exams—it's a busy world down there!

And, if we could look a little closer, we would see that all these people and organizations are involved in meaningful activity with each other. Students receiving assessments from their teachers that will subsequently help them get into college. Banks giving loans to clients who can then move home. Factories making components from raw materials, which are assembled into complex objects by their customers. People buying used cars from dealerships that they use to get them to work every day or go on vacation! In a nutshell, things are **connected** through individual **transactions** in which everything has a purpose.

We might marvel at the diversity of all these structures and processes and the transactions that result between them. We might even wonder how it all manages to work together so effortlessly!

We might then reflect upon all these diverse activities and wonder whether they all have something in common? Are there repeatable patterns that allow us to make sense of all this complexity? Is there a resolution at which all this activity looks the same? Are all these people and organizations, in some sense, doing the same thing?

The answer, of course, is **yes**! Let's equip ourselves with a tool—**a language**—which, like a pair of magical glasses, allows us to look at the structures and processes, and see them unified in a simple conceptual framework.

Why a language for business networks?

Thinking about a **business network** allows us to look at a set of activities and describe them using a straightforward vocabulary. And, because we're trying to formulate the world in a language that makes sense to a blockchain, which is a simple technology, we expect that language to be brief and to the point. We'll see that it is!

Why do we want to create a language that a blockchain can understand? Well, if we can, then we can bring all the benefits of the blockchain to a solution that uses that language. Rather than every blockchain solution being different, they all become the same. And the major way in which all blockchain solutions compare is that they all benefit from one thing—**increased trust**.

Increased trust means that the student can show their high school certificates to their college, who can be confident about the veracity of the qualifications. It means that the bank can provide a loan to its customer at the lowest rates because it can be confident about the financial well-being of its client. It means that the component manufacturer can charge a higher price for their output because their customers, in turn, can be sure of the quality of the raw materials, knowing their provenance. And finally, the buyer of the used car can be confident about their purchase because they can prove that it previously only had one, careful, owner!

Defining a business network

Let's summarize the preceding ideas succinctly to introduce the idea of a business network:

> *A business network contains a collection of participants and assets that undergo a life cycle described by a series of transactions. An event can occur when a transaction completes.*

We might be slightly surprised that after all that build-up, we find that a couple of apparently simple sentences describe all this complexity.

Don't be deceived by this simplicity. As we understand in more detail the ideas of a **participant**, **asset**, **transaction**, and **event**, we'll see that we've learned a language vocabulary, which allow us to build sentences, paragraphs, chapters, and even whole books.

Similarly, although a business network is not something we can physically see or touch, like a language, it's the most real of things. It will influence how we see and how we think, how we design and implement our system, and ultimately how it gets used and its success. There is a deeper, more fundamental idea at work here — the language and vocabulary of technology should closely match that of the business domain being analyzed, removing the need for significant translation between business concepts and technology concepts. Thinking of a business network allows us to directly connect blockchain technology to a business. We can reason about a problem or opportunity, design a solution, and translate ideas into a fully operational system with minimal effort.

Practically speaking, it means that while our initial vocabulary for business networks is simple, it is the beginning of a language that can become very rich in structure over time, so long as it describes the details and nuances of what happens in the real world.

We see this in the world; a vernacular form of communication helps systems designers effectively communicate — the particular vocabulary we introduce has terms that are widely used in the businesses to which blockchain technology can be applied.

As if to emphasize this point on common vocabulary, let's start by understanding participants.

Introducing participants

William Shakespeare said that the world is a stage on which men and women are the actors. In a similar way, a business network has a cast — a set of actors who are interacting with each other for some form of mutual benefit. We call these actors the **participants** in a network. For example, the participants in an education network might be students, teachers, schools, colleges, examiners, or government inspectors. The participants in an insurance network might be policyholders, brokers, underwriters, insurers, insurance syndicates, regulators, and banks.

The idea of a participant is crucial to understanding business networks. The key to understanding is in the name — participants *take part* in a business network. It's their actions that we are interested in. Different forms of the word are used to emphasize different aspects of their interactions: participant, party, and counterparty, for example. All these forms have their roots in the idea of action. As usual, we find that the bard knew a thing or two about how the world works!

Learn to love this word, because it's a door-opener! It's shorthand that we understand the founding principle of business — that who one does business with is of paramount importance. It's more important than this, though; identifying the participants in a business network is the first thing that we do when determining whether there's an opportunity to benefit from the use of a blockchain. We must understand the cast before we can really understand what's going on. And, as we learn more about the interactions between the participants, we'll be able to improve our understanding of what it means to be a particular participant. Again, it's just like a play where the more we see of the main characters actions, the more we understand their fundamental nature.

Types of participant

There are different *types* of participants in a business network, and we group them into three broad categories. Surprisingly, the first category we will describe is not the most important one.

Individual participants

Hopefully, this category is a fairly obvious one – the teacher, student, or bank customer are all examples of individual participants. Whether we call them individuals, people, or even humans, this first category is what we would intuitively think of as a participant because we associate them with ourselves.

And we might be forgiven for thinking that individuals are the most important participants in a network. After all, businesses exist to serve the needs of individuals, don't they? Well, yes, they do, but it's a little more subtle than that. While a business network usually exists to serve the needs of individual end consumers, blockchain does this by enabling a business to better coordinate its activities with other businesses, resulting in lower costs and new goods and services for end consumers. That's why we hear people utter sentences like "Blockchain is more important for B2B than B2C, or C2C." They're trying to communicate that the big win for business networks is to use blockchain as a pervasive fabric for efficient and creative business-to-business interactions.

Of course, individual participants are important. Businesses need to know their end consumers, and often, end consumers interact with each other using the services provided by the business network. For example, if I wish to transfer money to you via a banking network, our respective banks need to know who we both are so that the transaction can be properly validated and routed.

Finally, it's a fair rule of thumb that there are more individuals known to a business network than there are businesses in the network. Nothing too surprising here – it's just worth pointing this out so that our understanding of what it means to be an individual participant is complete!

Organizational participants

Organizational participants are the most important actors in a business network. The car dealership, the bank, the school, and the insurance company are all examples of organizational participants. When we first think about a particular business network, we identify these participants, followed by the goods and services they provide to each other and end consumers. These organizational participants provide the infrastructure for the business network – the people, processes, and technology that make it work.

Whereas organizations are made up of individuals, they are conceptually quite separate to them. An organization has its own identity, and its own purpose. It exists in a very real sense, independently of the individuals who belong to it. Organizations provide business networks with a sense of permanence.

While individuals within an organization may change over time, the number of individuals within the organization may grow or shrink, and even different roles within the organization may come and go, the organization remains constant; it is a structure with a longer lifetime than any individual's membership of it.

The final point to note about the nature of the relationship between individuals and their organization is that it is individuals who perform the functions of the organization, as defined by the individual's organizational role. When a bank makes a loan to a customer, it is performed by a bank employee on behalf of the bank. In this way, the individuals are the agents of the organization, and an individual's role determines the set of tasks it can perform. For example, a teacher can set a homework assignment for a student, but it requires a school principal to hire a new teacher. In a nutshell, individuals act on behalf of the organization, and with the authority of that organization.

System or device participants

System or device participants represent the technology components in the business network. They are really a special kind of individual participant, and we can just think of them that way. There are, however, two reasons why we call them out separately.

First, there are a lot of technology components in today's business networks! For example, there are **Enterprise Resource Planning** (**ERP**) systems, payment engines, reservation systems, transaction processors, and much, much more. In fact, most of the heavy lifting inside today's business networks is done by these systems. These systems are associated with organizations that own them, and just like the individuals we discussed earlier, these systems act on behalf of their owning organizations – they too are its agents.

The incorporation of a blockchain into a business network is going to add more system participants with whom the other participants (individual, organizational, and system/device) can interact. It's important to be aware of these blockchain system participants because they are going to provide very useful services to the business network!

Second, devices are becoming a more important part of the business world. And, while many devices today are relatively simple, there's no doubt that devices are becoming more autonomous. We've all heard of self-driving cars, and it's in this spirit that we introduce the concept of **device participants**. It may be increasingly important to think of these devices playing a larger role in business networks. So, while we don't expect cars to become intelligent anytime soon (whatever that might mean!), it's helpful to call out these increasingly autonomous devices as active rather than passive entities in a network.

A participant is an agent

Our examination of participant types shows us that they all have one thing in common — they have a significant degree of agency — they actively do things. Although systems and devices have a level of autonomy that is limited by their programming, it is nonetheless helpful to think of them this way. And, the interactions between these relatively autonomous actors serves as a prompt to the next concept in a business network, namely **assets**. We'll see later that the entities that move between participants — assets — have none of this autonomy. These are subject to the forces exerted upon them by participants. More on this later.

Participant identity

Finally, and very importantly, participants have **identity**. For example, a student has a student ID, a driver has a driving license, and a citizen has a social security number. It's obvious that there is a difference between a participant and what's used to identify a participant. And it's really important to hold these two concepts as closely related but separate from each other.

For example, a participant might have different identities to participate in different business networks — it might be the same bank that participates in an insurance network and a mortgage network. In the insurance network, its identity might correspond to its ability to provide capital to underwriters, whereas in a mortgage network, it might be providing commercial loans to companies. The same bank has to plan for the worst — that its current identity is compromised, allowing them to be impersonated by a rogue participant. In this case, their compromised identity must be revoked, and a replacement identity issued for the bank. The impersonator with the once valid identity is denied, allowing trust to be restored. Different identities, but the same participant — that's the take-away message.

It's because of this concern over impersonation that certain identities are deliberately expired periodically. For example, X.509 digital certificates have an expiry date, after which they are no longer valid. However, just because the certificate has expired, it cannot be assumed that the participant is no longer present.

In fact, it's quite the opposite. The relative permanence of a participant compared to its identity means that it can be used to provide a long-term historical reference of who does what in a business network. The consistency of identity provided by a participant over time helps us reason about the history of interactions in a business network. We could do this without the concept of a participant by just using identities and keeping a clear head about how and when they changed in relation to each other, but it would be less intuitive.

That's just about it on the topic of participants; you're now an expert! Participants are probably the most important thing about a business network, which is why we spent quite a bit of time discussing them. Let's now turn our attention to the objects that move between participants, namely assets.

Introducing assets

We've seen how a business network is defined by the participants who operate within it. These participants are the active agents who perform meaningful interactions within the network, and it's their transactions that are of paramount importance. We now ask ourselves the question, *What flows between participants?* The answer: *an asset*!

Let's look at some asset examples. A student receives coursework from their tutor. The student shows their educational certificate to a university. A car dealer sells a car to a buyer. An insurance company insures that car for a policyholder, issuing a policy. A policyholder makes a claim. These examples all contain assets: coursework, education certificate, car, policy, and claim.

Assets flow between participants

We can see that assets are the objects that flow between participants. Participants have agency over assets, which in turn are passive. This aspect is fundamental to assets—they have meaning to the counterparties who exchange them. That's not to say that other participants aren't interested in these assets, but it does emphasize the passive nature of an asset. So, what makes assets so important? Why are we bothering to talk about these passive objects?

The answer lies in our choice of word—asset. An asset is a thing of *value*. Even though assets are passive, they represent the value that is exchanged between participants. Look at these example assets again with this value-based lens: coursework, education certificate, car, policy, and claim. Coursework is valuable to the teacher and student; an education certificate is valuable to the student and university; a car is valuable to the dealership and buyer; a policy is valuable to the insurance company and policy holder; a claim is valuable to the claimant and insurance company. Hopefully, it is now clear why assets are important, and why they are called assets!

As a minor note, don't think that because we have assets, we must have liabilities—we're not quite using the term this way. It's absolutely true that if we were to measure objects as counting for us, or counting against us, we would term them assets or liabilities, but that's not quite what's happening here—we're using *asset* as a concrete noun, rather than as a quality or abstract noun.

A quick word on vocabulary

The choice of the word *asset* is designed to improve the specificity of an object that moves between participants; specifically, that it has value. We find it helpful to make this distinction because there are many objects in a system under analysis, and getting to the key ones is important. However, if you make this identification naturally, then just use the word object directly. Equally, you might find the term business object a good compromise. What's important is that we identify those key items of value in our analysis.

Tangible and intangible assets

Let's continue our discussion with tangible and intangible assets. Tangible assets are things we can touch and feel — cars, paper money, or coursework. Intangible assets are things such as mortgages, intellectual property rights, insurance policies, and music files. In an increasingly digital world, we're going to see more intangible assets. You'll hear people say that objects are becoming *dematerialized*; for example, files and folders once literally made of paper are now typically known only in their digital forms! The idea of an intangible assets nicely captures these concepts.

Let's consider a couple of points on our usage of the word intangible. First, as we're dealing with a digital ledger, in some trivial sense, everything on a blockchain is intangible — everything is just data in a machine after all! The lesson is that we must be inquisitive. Because we cannot see intangible assets, we must remember to look out for properties and aspects that are not obvious, as they would be in the physical world. It's not as simple as looking at a physical object and asking: *What does that do?*

Second, the use of *intangible* is not intended as a statement of value. Often, in accounting systems, we use this term when we have trouble defining something, such as goodwill. We're not using the word in this sense; our intangible assets have a more concrete, definite, and exchangeable form than this because they are things of value, even if you cannot touch them.

The structure of assets

Let's look a little deeper into the structure of assets. An asset has a set of attributes called **properties** and a set of attributes called **relationships**. Property attributes are easy to understand — they are the characteristics of an object. For example, a car has a date of manufacture, a color, and an engine size, and a mortgage has a value, a lifetime, and a repayment schedule.

A particular asset is identified by a particular set of property **values**. For example, our car might be manufactured in 2015, be white in color, and have a 1.8-liter engine. Another example—our mortgage might be worth 100,000 USD, have a lifetime of 25 years, and be payable monthly. It's important to distinguish this difference between the **structure** of an asset *in general*, its **type**, and the *particular* **instance**.

On the other hand, a relationship is a special kind of attribute—it's a reference to another asset! You can see instantly why this is important. For example, a car has an insurance document. The car is an object of value, and the insurance document is an object of value. Moreover, an insurance document names a policy holder. In our examples, both the subject and the object are assets, and they relate to each other in a way that helps us understand their nature.

We'll see later that understanding assets and their relationships is an extremely important activity because it helps us understand the nature of a system under analysis. And to illustrate this point, in the previous example, we made a deliberate mistake! That's because, in the real world, it's actually a policy document that is central to insurance because it names the car and the policy holder. For example, nowhere in the nature of a car will you find an insurance document—a car is insured by virtue of the fact that it is named in a valid policy document. Moreover, if I want to insure more people to drive the car, I add their names to the policy document, not to the car! Much more on this later—for now, it's enough to remember that assets have properties and references, and particular objects have concrete values for these attributes.

It's also worth mentioning, briefly, the nature of what makes an asset attribute a property, rather than a reference to another asset. A simple answer is when properties get too *big*, we break them out into a separate asset and make a reference. Of course, that's a very unsatisfactory answer. Why? Because we didn't define what makes something big! A better answer is that a reference is required when a property satisfies a separate concern. This principle—**separation of concerns**—is a key design principle in any system. For example, the policy validity date is not a separate concern for an insurance policy, but the car and named drivers are separate concerns. This principle helps us to reason about insurance policies, cars, and drivers independently of each other, which in turn allows us to model the real world more realistically. Finally, on this aspect of assets, property and relationship attributes are **domain-specific**—they relate to the nature of the problem at hand. So, for a car manufacturer, color might be an attribute of a car—but for a paint manufacturer, color is most definitely an asset type!

Ownership

There's one particular kind of relationship that's particularly important in a business network, and that's the concept of **ownership**.

A special kind of relationship

Ownership is an associative relationship such as the insurance policy document we discussed earlier. Let's think about another specific example.

A person owns a car. Is the owner an attribute of the car? Is the car an attribute of the person? After a little thinking, we might realize that neither statement captures what it means to *own* something. Ownership is a mapping between the person and the car. Ownership is a concept that's quite separate to the car and its owner.

It's important to understand this way of thinking about ownership because, in many cases, we model the ownership relationship via the car, or via the owner, and that's sufficient for many purposes.

But the *nature* of an ownership relationship is an associative one, and it's important to realize this. It's important to realize that a blockchain is often used to record ownership and transfer ownership in a business network. For example, governments often hold ownership records — for land or vehicles. In these cases, the primary assets under consideration are the property titles that define the ownership relationships. When a vehicle or land is transferred between participants, it's this ownership record that changes rather than the assets. That's important because we're often interested in the history of a vehicle or piece of land, and while the vehicle or land itself may not change, its ownership most definitely does. It's important, therefore, to be clear about whether we're talking about the history of the asset or the history of ownership. These kinds of history are often called **provenance** — they tell us who has owned an asset and how it has changed over time. Both aspects are important because knowing the provenance of an asset increases our confidence in it.

Ownership and asset tokenization

Increasingly, in blockchain circles, the idea of tokens and tokenization is closely linked to ownership. The token represents the ownership of an asset, and holding the token gives a claim to the bearer on the object.

Moreover, there is a common idea that tokens can be subdivided to represent fractional ownership of an asset. We see this happen a lot in the real world; for example, a set of insurance companies may jointly underwrite a large insurance request. Tokenization is a mechanism that can be used to represent how a single insurance request is shared between multiple counterparties.

Asset life cycles

This idea of provenance leads us very neatly to the concept of an **asset life cycle**. When we consider the history of an asset, in some very meaningful sense, an asset is first created, then changes over time, and ultimately ceases to exist. For example, let's consider a mortgage. It comes into existence when a bank agrees to lend a sum of money to a customer. It remains in existence for the term of the mortgage. As the interest rate changes, it determines the monthly repayment amount according to a fixed or a variable rate of interest. The term of the mortgage may be changed with the agreement of both the bank and the mortgage holder. Finally, at the end of the mortgage, it ceases to exist, although a historic record of it may be kept. The mortgage may be terminated early if the customer wishes to pay it off early (maybe they move), or less fortunately if they default on the loan. In some sense, we see that the mortgage was created, the term was periodically changed, and then the mortgage was completed either normally or unexpectedly. This concept of a life cycle is incredibly important in a business network, and we'll discuss it in detail later when we discuss **transactions**.

Returning to assets, we can see that during their life cycle, assets can also be **transformed**. This is a very important idea, and we consider two aspects of asset transformation—namely whether the transformation involves **division** or **aggregation**, and whether it is a **homogeneous** or **heterogeneous** transformation. These terms may sound a little intimidating, but they are very simple to understand and best described using an example of each.

In the first example, we consider a precious gemstone that has been mined. In general, a mined gemstone is too large for any jeweler to use in a single piece of jewelry. It must be broken into smaller stones, each of which may be used for single item of jewelry. If we were to look at the history of a large, mined gemstone, we would see that it underwent a process of *division*. The initial asset was a gemstone, and it was transformed into a set of smaller gemstones, each of which was related to the original gemstone. We can see that the asset transformation is *homogeneous*, because although the smaller gemstones are most definitely different assets, they are the **same type** as the original asset. A similar process of homogeneous transformation often occurs with intangible assets, for example, when a large commercial loan or insurance request is syndicated among several companies to diversify risk, or when a stock is split.

In our next example, we'll consider the jeweler using a smaller gemstone. We imagine they use the gemstone to create a fine ring for a customer. To make the ring, they use all their skills to set the gemstone in a mounting on a bezel connected to a hoop via a shoulder. A jeweler's craft is to be admired—they transform a small block of silver and a gemstone into a valuable piece of jewelry.

Let's consider for a moment these assets. We can see that the metal block and gemstone have been combined, or *aggregated*, to form the ring. We also note that the ring is a different asset to the gemstone or silver block, which served as inputs. We can see that these inputs have undergone a *heterogeneous transformation* because the output asset is of a different type.

These processes of aggregation and division are seen in many an asset life cycle. As in our example, it's very popular in manufacturing life cycles with tangible assets. But we also see it with intangible assets: in **mergers**, where companies can be combined, or **acquisitions**, where one company ceases to exist by being incorporated into another company. The reverse processes of **de-merger** (**divestiture**) or **spin-off** is neatly described as asset division.

Finally, there is a close relationship between division and aggregation and the idea of tokenization. That's because the divisibility of tokens can often provide a natural mechanism to reflect this process. In homogenous scenarios, there will typically be only one token type, whereas in heterogeneous scenarios, we may see the introduction of new tokens, a process called **minting**.

Describing a life cycle with transactions

Let's consider *how* assets move through their life cycle. We have learned that assets are created and transformed and eventually cease to exist. Although this simple life cycle is a very useful concept, these steps seem somewhat limited in their descriptive power. Surely there are richer descriptions for the set of steps an asset goes through in its life cycle? The answer is yes!

Transactions define a rich, domain-specific vocabulary for describing how assets evolve over time. For example, an insurance policy is requested, refined, signed, delivered, claimed against, paid out against, invalidated, or renewed. Each step of this life cycle is a transaction—and we're going to talk a lot more about transactions in the next section.

Finally, as with assets, participants can go through a life cycle, described by transactions. So, you might be wondering, *what is the difference between assets and participants?* Well, it really comes down to thinking about form versus function. Just because assets and participants both can have life cycles described by transactions, that does not make them the same thing. In the same way that birds, insects, and bats can fly, we classify them differently. Likewise, we think of participants and assets as being in different categories—they are related only in the most general sense.

That ends our discussion on assets! As we saw toward the end of this topic, transactions are of paramount importance in describing the asset and participant life cycles, so let's now turn our attention to them.

Introducing transactions

Our journey so far has involved understanding the fundamental nature of a business network — that it is comprised of participants involved in the meaningful exchange of assets. Now, there's a big concept that underpins a business network, related to the fact that everything, everywhere is constantly changing. The movement of assets between participants involves change. The transfer of value involves change. External forces act on assets and participants forcing them to change or initiate change.

In this section, we formalize the concept of change and discuss in some depth the idea of a **transaction**. A transaction captures how a system and a component within it change. We're going to see how a blockchain introduces a new kind of transaction — a multi-party transaction. Understanding the nature of these transactions will give you a deep insight into what a business network is and why a blockchain like Hyperledger Fabric is so important. But let's start this next section gently.

Change and transactions

In a business network, *change* gives a participant or an asset meaning and purpose.

This may seem like an excessively hyperbolic statement. However, if we think about it for a moment, participants exist meaningfully only in the sense that they exchange goods and services (collectively known as assets) with each other. If a participant does not perform some sort of exchange with another participant, they do not have a meaningful relationship as far as a business network is concerned. It's the same with assets — if they aren't exchanged between participants, then they don't exist in any meaningful way either. There's no point in an asset having a life cycle if it doesn't move between different participants, because the asset is private to a participant and serves no purpose in the business network outside the participant's private context.

Change, therefore, is the fundamental principle in business networks. When we think about exchange, transfers, commerce, buying, selling, agreement, and contracts, all of these motivational ideas are concerned with the business and the effects of change. Change gives the world of business motion and direction.

A transaction is how we describe a change. That's why a transaction is such an important concept in a business network—it defines and records change, change of asset, change of asset ownership, and change of participants. Whenever anything changes in a business network, there's a transaction to account for it.

Transaction definition and instance

The term *transaction* is often used in two closely related, but different ways, and it's important to be conscious of this difference. We sometimes use the term transaction to describe in general terms what happens when something changes.

Most commonly, transaction is used to describe a particular change. For example, we might say that on 16 June 2020, Daisy bought a bicycle from the Winchester bicycle shop for 300 GBP. We're using transaction to describe a particular instance of change—the purchase of goods or services from a bicycle shop.

In the real world, we see examples of transaction instances all the time—whenever we go into a shop to buy some goods, we are offered a receipt! In our previous example, Daisy probably got a receipt for her bicycle. The receipt might be made of paper, though nowadays it is often sent to our phone or email address. This receipt is a copy of the transaction—it's Daisy's personal record of what happened. The bicycle shop also keeps a copy of the transaction record for its own accounting purposes.

But we also use the term transaction as a more general way to describe the process of change. For example, we say that a bicycle transaction involves a buyer purchasing an item from a shop on a certain date in exchange for payment. Or we might define a property transaction where a buyer pays an agreed amount to the owner of the property in exchange for possession of the property and its deeds of title. In this sense, the term transaction is used to describe the general process of exchange in the terms of the participants and assets involved.

It's important to make this distinction; we'll see that a blockchain is going to hold a permanent record of transaction instances, which have been generated by smart contracts that contain transaction definitions. This linkage between transaction definitions and transaction instances is fundamental to understanding how a blockchain system will be relevant to a business network. More on this later!

Finally, although these two senses of "transaction" are quite different, the context almost always makes it clear which one we're talking about. It's the difference between the specific and the general.

Implicit and explicit transactions

In the real world, we don't often see transaction definitions. We just live our lives without worry. Only if something goes wrong, do we get to understand the definition of a transaction. For example, if Daisy's bicycle chain snaps after a couple of days, she might reasonably expect that the chain would be fixed free of charge or the bicycle replaced, or she would get her money back. This is the point at which Daisy determines the true nature of her transaction with the Winchester bicycle shop. For a transaction like this, the definition is encoded in the people, processes, and technology that you interact with. For low-consequence transactions such as Daisy's, the transaction definition is **implicit**.

It looks like this kind of implicit transaction definition only has downsides, but that's not the case. First, every country's laws have explicit notions of a fair transaction that would give Daisy reasonable expectations when she made her purchase at the Winchester bicycle shop. In many countries, this is governed by a Sale of Goods Act (or something similar), and it specifies the rights and responsibilities of all counterparties involved in any commercial transaction. Second, the lack of an explicit contract simplifies the interaction between Daisy and the bicycle shop. Given that, in most cases, bicycles perform well for an extended period after purchase, and a receipt is sufficient for most practical purposes. It would be both costly and timely to re-state what everyone knows to be true every time a simple purchase was made.

For high-consequence transactions, or those with special conditions, the situation is very different—it is vital that the transaction definition is made explicit, in advance. If we look at Daisy's transaction again, we can see that if there was a dispute, there would have been follow-up transactions; for example, the bicycle might have had its chain replaced, or in an extreme circumstance, she might have got her money back. We can see that, in general, we would require several conditional transactions to describe a satisfactory interaction between participants for such a transaction. It means that if Daisy had been getting a mortgage, rather than a bicycle, it would have been necessary to specify several transactions and the conditions under which they could be executed. You have probably heard of a term for such a collection of transactions and conditions—a **contract**.

The importance of contracts

For high value assets, it's vital to have a contract. It defines a related set of transactions and conditions under which they occur. A contract revolves around a particular asset type and involves a well-defined set of participant types. If we look at a real-world contract, it includes a combination of statements about instances and statements about definitions. We see that a contract is an agreement between multiple counterparties that governs transactions relating to assets exchanged between them.

At the top of a contract, all the assets and participants will be laid out with particular values. For example: Daisy (the buyer), Winchester bicycle shop (the seller), 300 GBP (the price), 20 June 2020 (the date of purchase), and so on. It's only after all these type-to-instance mappings have been laid out that the contract is then defined in terms of these types, transactions, and conditions under which they occur, without reference to the particular instance values. This is what makes contracts a little strange to read at first—but once we can see the structure in terms of participants, assets, and transactions, and their respective values, they are actually quite easy to understand, and all the more powerful for this structure.

Signatures

The final thing we see in a contract is a set of signatures. In many ways, signatures are the most important part of a contract because they represent the fact that the named counterparties have agreed to the information contained within it. And of course, we see a lot of signatures in the real world. Daisy's shop receipt normally has her signature on it—either physical or digital. In simple transactions, the store's signature is actually implicit; they put a transaction code on a branded receipt and keep a copy for their purposes—this satisfies the purposes of a signature.

However, for higher-consequence transactions, all counterparties will be required to explicitly sign a contract. Even more pointedly, to ensure that every party is entering the contract with their *eyes open*, an independent third party, such as a solicitor, notary, or regulator, may be required to sign the contract to verify the willing, and free, participation of those counterparties explicitly involved in the transaction.

Smart contract multi-party transactions

These ideas are not particularly complicated, especially when we relate them to things we see and do every day! When we look at a business network, we can see that it is full of **multi-party transactions** governed by contracts. That's why multi-party transactions are such an important concept in a business network; they define and capture the agreed exchanges of valuable assets between different counterparties. And what generates a multi-party transaction? A **smart contract**.

A smart contract is simply a *digital* version of a contract—one that can be easily interpreted and executed by a computer system. In reality, all computer systems that implement transactions implement contracts. The difference is that Hyperledger Fabric has a built-in, formal contract technology with features that make the translation of these real-world transactions into code a 1:1 mapping.

Traditional systems are not just single party — they each implement the intention behind a contract in different ways according to the preferences of the system designer and technology choice. With Hyperledger Fabric, this has become standardized, making it easier and quicker to implement multi-party transaction processing systems.

Digital transaction processing

Smart contracts and transactions are why we like to frame problems using the vocabulary of a business network. It makes the translation from the real world into a computer system as simple as possible. Hyperledger Fabric makes all these ideas quite explicit so that we can easily model and implement a business network. It gives us a technology to implement business networks in a fundamentally **digital** manner — using computer processes, networks, and storage.

As we've seen, transactions are at the center of a business network because they describe a particular change involving a set of participants and assets. However, it's more than this. Even if we add more concepts to the business network, they must always be subject to transactions; they are at the epicenter of a business network. Every object in a business network is subject to transactions.

Initiating transactions

We can see that transactions are usually initiated by one participant in a business network. This participant is usually the consumer of a service available from a particular service provider. For example, Daisy wishes to consume the services provided by the Winchester bicycle shop, that is, buy a bicycle.

Most transactions initiated by participants are concerned with the change in state of an asset, but in some cases, transactions can involve the change in state of a participant. For example, if you change your name by deed poll, then in some sense you — a participant — are the asset being transformed. This reinforces the central nature of transactions — that they capture change no matter what the object.

Transaction history

We know that the history of an asset is important — being able to identify the series of transactions describing the change of an asset over time leads to increased trust. Why? Well, it comes back to those signatures. Because all changes must be agreed by all the participants involved in a transaction, they can be confident that every counterparty consented to the exchange.

A transaction history shows that, at all points in time, every participant in the network has agreed with every change described by every transaction.

A blockchain ledger contains a transaction history held as a **sequenced** order of transactions. For example, if I deposit money into my bank account at 11:00 a.m. and then make a payment at 11:30 a.m., the ledger will contain my 11:00 a.m. transaction, followed by my 11:30 a.m. transaction. And similarly, if *you* deposit money into *your* bank account at 11:00 a.m., and then *you* make a payment at 11:30 a.m., *your* transactions will likewise be recorded in the same blockchain ledger.

Transaction streams

In the preceding example, your transactions and my transactions are **independent transaction streams**; their ordering with respect to each other is not important.

However, let's now ask whether *my* 11:00 a.m. transaction happened before or after *your* 11:00 a.m. transaction? Our 11:30 a.m. transactions? Does it matter whether my 11:00 a.m. transaction is recorded after your 11:30 a.m. transaction, even though it may have occurred, in some sense, before it?

In general, it's not important because you and I are quite independent of each other. But we have to be a little bit careful, because transactions have a nasty habit of becoming entangled with each other. For example, if *my* payment was into *your* account, and you waited on the arrival of my payment into your account before you made your payment, then two otherwise independent transaction streams are dependent on each other. This means that we cannot arbitrarily delay the recording of transactions; my payment occurs before your payment.

In this case, your transaction would be recorded *after* my transaction on the blockchain — because my payment occurred in a very real sense before your payment; my transaction was causal to your transaction. This is an example of **dependent transaction streams**, where transactions are dependent on transactions that are recorded before them.

Notice that we're not talking about the initiation of a transaction at a particular time or in a particular place, but rather the recording of that transaction in the blockchain. That might seem a little overly precise, but it's important. It's a bit like reading an encyclopedic history book from page 1 to page 500. On page 105, we read of Napoleon's excursion to Italy in 1800. On page 110, we read about the founding of the United States Library of Congress in 1800. Finally, on page 120, we read about the completion of the literary work *Kojiki-den* by Motoori Norinaga in Japan, also in 1800.

But did these events occur before or after each other? Were they dependent on each other? It this case, it's unlikely! What's important is that these events are recorded — their order in the book with respect to each other is not necessarily of crucial importance.

That's why we focus on a transaction history as a **sequence** of transactions that have times associated with them. Although an order seems to imply that transactions occur in a time-defined sequence, this is only partially true, as the previous example shows.

A network of networks

Our slightly contrived history book example actually provides us with a deep insight into the design of business networks — that a single record of all interactions in a network of complex interactions is neither necessary nor a good idea. Why? Maybe it would be better to have three different history books? One for French history, one for American history, and one for Japanese history! And for each to have cross-references in the others to show dependent linkages.

This example has important consequences for how we design blockchain networks. It's not just good design, but essential design, to separate different concerns into separate business networks and then link them together. It leads to simpler, more comprehensible, more scalable, more extensible, and more resilient systems. We can start small and grow and be confident that, no matter how things evolve, we can cope with change. We'll see that Hyperledger Fabric explicitly supports this multiplicity using concepts called **networks** and **channels**, and we'll discuss these in more detail later.

So, while it might be tempting to think that there is a single business network, this is true only in a loose, abstract sense. It is good design to actually think of a **network of networks**, where we associate a particular business network with a particular concern, rather than trying to create a single transaction history.

Current value and transaction history

For any given asset or business object, there are typically two aspects that we are interested in. The first is its current value. For example, a bicycle with serial number 12345678 is currently owned by Daisy, cost 300 GBP, and is blue. In general, the current value of a business object is the one that we use when we are accessing it to query or update it, for example.

The second aspect is its transaction history. Think of this as the sequenced set of transactions that have involved this transaction over time. By sequentially applying transactions in order, we can regenerate any particular value of the business object at any point in its history. We think of transaction history as a set of events that occur at different times and places in the business network, and that these determine the changes to the value of all objects in the network.

We will see these two aspects of business networks explicitly expressed in Hyperledger Fabric. We'll see how a Hyperledger Fabric ledger has two components, a **current value** and a **blockchain**. Although it might not sound like it, the current value of a ledger is a set of all the current objects in the ledger, each of which has a set of values as its properties. The blockchain is a sequence of transactions that describes the changes to every object in the ledger, both past and present.

These two elements make Hyperledger Fabric a little more powerful than other blockchain technologies. Like other such technologies, it records all the transactions in a blockchain. Additionally, it also calculates the current value of every asset, making it quite easy to be confident that you're working with the most up-to-date state of a business object. These most recent values tend to be the most important because they represent the current state of the world. And that's what most participants are interested in when it comes to initiating new transactions.

A business network as a history of transactions

In a very real sense, a business network is a result of the history of transactions that formed it. The transaction history of the network describes the totality of changes of every asset initiated by every participant, past and present. For many people, the blockchain element of a ledger is more important than its current value. Because even though we usually deal with the current value of business objects, the nature of those objects is most fully described by its transaction history.

At the same time, a transaction history would be of little consequence unless it described the changes to the assets and participants inside a network. But, although understanding participants and assets and their natures is vital, a sequential history of multi-party transactions describing them is more important. It is the central element that brings everything together into a coherent whole, and in the sense that every transaction is in it, it is the business network.

Regulators

Before we move on from transactions, here is a final word on a special kind of participant that is common to just about every kind of business network—a **regulator**.

In most business networks, there is a participant whose role is to ensure that the transactions obey certain *rules*. For example, in the United States, the **Securities and Exchange Commission (SEC)** ensures that the participants performing transactions involving securities assets do so according to agreed laws and rules, giving investors trust in the stock market. In the United Kingdom, the **Driver and Vehicle Licensing Agency (DVLA)** ensures that vehicles are properly insured, taxed, and exchanged according to UK law. In South Africa, the **Association for Food Science and Technology (SAAFoST)** ensures that transactions involving farming, food distribution, food processing, and food retail comply with appropriate South African law.

A regulator provides proper oversight of a business network; they ensure that everyone plays by the rules. We can see that a business network in which all the transactions are recorded digitally on a blockchain actually allows the regulator to do their job in a more efficient and timely manner.

Of course, you might ask why we need a regulator if all the transactions are available to the appropriately authorized participants who can prove correct or incorrect behavior. The answer is that regulators have the ability to sanction certain participants in the network—for example, to exclude them or confiscate their assets if they are shown to have acted inappropriately. These sanctions are the most powerful transactions in the network as they provide ultimate power and accordingly must be used only in extreme circumstances.

Typically, a regulator would not perform transactions directly in a business network; they are interested in observing and checking what happens, and in the case of bad actors, ensuring transactions occur that create redress.

There's only one more concept to cover in our discussion of business networks: events. Let's move on to this final aspect of business networks.

Introducing events

We've seen so far that the vocabulary of business networks contains a compact set of inextricably linked concepts—participants, assets, and transactions. Though small in number, these concepts are very expressive—they contain big ideas, with many aspects to them, that support and reinforce each other.

It's not that there's something *missing*, but by adding one final concept — **events** — we're going to significantly increase the descriptive and design power of this vocabulary. The good news is that you've heard the term before, and many event-related ideas are quite obvious. But make no mistake, events are a hugely powerful concept. So, let's spend a little time mastering this topic; our investment in this topic will be handsomely rewarded.

A universal concept

We think of an event as denoting the occurrence or happening of a particular fact. For example, the following are all examples of events:

- *The President arrived in Australia*
- *The stock market closed 100 points up today*
- *The truck arrived at the distribution point*

The fundamental idea is simple — an event is a point in time when something significant happens. An event represents some kind of transition; it describes a significant change in the state of a system. This is the nature of events — rather than seeing history as a smooth timeline, we see it as a set of joined dots, each representing a significant event.

In business networks, we can see events *everywhere*. Participants initiating transactions are events. Assets undergoing a series of transformations are events. Assets being exchanged between participants are events. An asset's life cycle is nothing but a series of events. Participants joining and leaving the business network are more events. Think about transaction history — a set of events about participants and assets. Goodness, once we open our eyes, events really are *everywhere*. If we're not careful, we're going to get overwhelmed by these little space invaders!

Event notifications

In the real world, when an event occurs, we are notified by a variety of possible mechanisms — text messages, email, a newsfeed, a Twitter or Facebook feed, and so on. It is helpful to make a distinction between an event and its communication; it illustrates how we are linked to an event via a medium.

Let's now plant the idea — which we will return to later — that although there is a singular event, multiple participants can be notified via separate event notifications. This creates a loose coupling between event-producer and event-consumer. This all means that an event has a slightly intangible quality; it is hard to pin down and perceive only through a notification of its occurrence.

A word of mild caution—we can lose what's important if we obsess about events. The skill is to identity significant events—ones that will result in some kind of significant action. Everything else is just noise; we don't need to consider it. And remember what constitutes significant is going to be domain-specific. A stock market price rise is significant in a financial network but not in an educational network. So, let's use events as a tool for when significant things happen in a business network and we need to understand what prompts participants to act. Let's look at an example.

An event example

Every time a stock goes up or down in price, we can represent this as an event. For example:

At UTC: 2020-11–05T13:15:30:34.123456+09:00

The stock MZK increased in price by 800 from 13000 JPY

We can see that this is a description of an event where the stock MZK increased by 800 Yen at a specific time on 5 Nov 2020.

Just like assets and participants, we can see the term "event" can refer to the type or instance of an event. In our example, we've shown the type and instance information folded into one:

- **event type**: price change
- **time**: 2020-11–05T13:15:30:34.123456+09:00
- **symbol**: MZK
- **currency**: JPY
- **previous**: 13000
- **change**: +800

For each element in the structure, we've shown the particular instance for this event. We can see very clearly from this event what happened in a structured form.

Events and transactions

We can see that events are very closely related to transactions. Indeed, because an event often describes a transaction, it's not uncommon to see the terms used interchangeably. However, events describe a broader class of activity than transactions.

Specifically, while an event often denotes a change, it's a transaction that captures that change. An event is fleeting, a transaction is forever! This means that it's good practice to capture events inside a transaction so that the notification that has communicated the event can be recorded and replayed.

In many cases, a new transaction will generate another event. But think for a moment—events simply describe something happening, and sometimes, those events are *explicitly* created by transactions rather than happening due to a force outside any transaction. In our stock tick example, a transaction might generate an event to signal that the MZK stock has increased by over 5 percent in a single tick:

- **event type**: rapid price change
- **time**: 2020-11–05T13:15:30:34.123456+09:00
- **symbol**: MZK
- **change**: 6.1%

This event is explicitly generated by the transaction, which is part of a business process that needs to identity when a high percentage stock change occurs. The event is, in a very real sense, part of the transaction; without a transaction, it would not have occurred.

Just like in the real world, when an event happens, people and organizations hear about it, process the information in it, and generate actions because of that processing. We see that an event notification often drives a new action, resulting in a subsequent transaction. We'll find it helpful to use the triple concept of **event-condition-action** when designing event-based systems to organize structures and processes within it. Think of an application processing an event notification to perform a new action with some of the event data, probably in combination with other data, to initiate a new transaction, which in turn may result in a new event. And so it goes, on and on!

Let's conclude. While it often makes sense to capture an event as part of a transaction, an event is quite separate from a transaction. Spend a moment reflecting on this—we're really picking apart some subtle, but important, differences.

External and explicit events

It's helpful to think of events as falling into two categories—**external events** and **explicit events**. We don't often think of these two terms as opposites, but they neatly describe the two different types of events in a business network.

Our first event type is an external event — it is generated externally to the business network. This event is processed by participants and will likely result in a transaction. Don't forget, only think about significant events — ones that will result in an action. With an external event, a significant amount of the event content is captured as transaction input, but nothing else about the event is remembered. If we want to record an external event, we must generate an explicit transaction to do so.

Explicit events are different. Because they are generated by a transaction, they are automatically part of the transaction history. When a transaction is committed to the ledger, then these events will be set free into the network — where they will be consumed by any and all participants interested in them. In the case of explicit events, the ledger itself is the event producer.

Loosely coupled design

Let's now return to the seed that we planted a little earlier — **loose coupling**. Event producers and event consumers do not directly know about each other — they are said to be *loosely coupled*. For example, when a participant joins a network, it doesn't need to reach out to everyone and everything it is interested in; it just publishes a *new participant event*. Existing participants simply listen for a *new participant event*. New joiners and existing participants are connected in a loosely coupled manner. Event producers and event consumers find out about each other — indeed everything — using events. This method of communication is very adaptable.

Loose coupling helps us understand another difference between events and transactions. Transactions explicitly bind participants to each other — in a transaction, we name all the counterparties. In an event, we have absolutely no idea of how, or even if, the producers and the consumers of the event are related. From a design perspective, it means that we can create a very flexible system. Participants can be coupled to each other in an almost infinitely flexible way via events, and this really does mirror the richness we see in the real world.

Events are useful!

The sheer utility of events is why we've added them to our definition of a business network. Events allow the business network to be almost infinitely flexible. Revel in this little bit of chaos — it might be, in some sense, a little less easy to predict, but that's okay. Events provide a highly efficient coordination mechanism between participants so that important changes are agreed upon and recorded via multi-party transactions.

Remember that definition of a business network?

> *A business network contains a collection of participants and assets that undergo a life cycle described by a series of transactions. An event can occur when a transaction completes.*

These sentences are maybe a little more powerful than they might first appear — they describe a very rich world indeed. Let's go through an example to see these ideas at work!

Business network technology

On our tour through the concepts of a business network, we've seen the central importance of multi-party transactions, which describe how assets are exchanged between the network's participants. This means that a significant amount of technology is already deployed to implement them.

If you've worked in IT for a while, you've probably heard of the terms **business-to-business (B2B)** and **electronic data interchange (EDI)**. They describe the idea and technology of how businesses exchange information with each other. You might additionally have experience of related protocols such as AS1, AS2, AS3, and AS4. These define standard mechanisms about how to exchange business data between two organizations. Don't worry if you haven't heard of these terms — the key takeaway is that business networks exist today in a very real sense and have a lot of technology applied to them.

What does it mean to *implement* a business network? Well, when it comes to the exchange of tangible assets such as cars or equipment or important documents, a blockchain captures representations of the assets, participants, transactions, and events in a business network. In the case of intangible assets, it's a little different — the increasing dematerialization of assets means that their representation inside a computer system is as real as the asset itself. When we implement a business network using Hyperledger Fabric, we're creating a system that controls and records the activities inside a business network. Hyperledger Fabric is used to create a system that is the *representation* of a business network. But it's a very important representation because it is how most people involved with the network will interact with it.

More dematerialization

One hundred years ago, music was recorded on a revolutionary material called *bakelite*—one of the first plastics. It was a brittle and expensive material, but the benefits of being able to capture and replay sounds were considered magical at the time. Then, through a series of technology innovations, music moved to vinyl, Compact Disc, and digital mini-disc. Each step was cheaper than the previous and of higher quality.

But in 1993, something different happened. The first MP3 format was introduced to support audio capture. Music recording moved from the physical world to the digital world. It became subject to a force that we call *dematerialization*.

This step was quite different from the other steps. Yes, it was cheaper and more convenient. But most importantly, it no longer required a music recording to have a physical representation. This dematerialization pattern is increasingly common— financial products such as bonds, securities, swaps, mortgages, and such are primarily represented digitally. More and more documents and forms are becoming digitized—from airplane and train tickets to more important things like education certificates, employment histories, and health records.

It means that when we implement a business network using Hyperledger Fabric, we are often close to processing the actual assets in a business network. And even when an asset is physical, it's often the case that the information about an asset is as important as the asset itself!

If this seems like hyperbole, let's imagine for a moment that you have an electric car. The car needs to have a charged battery, and it needs to be taxed, serviced, and insured. It needs an annual test to make sure it is roadworthy. It needs a record of ownership that indicates that you own it. Goodness, there's a lot of activity related to this car of yours! This means that the information about the car is very valuable— indeed, over the lifetime of a car, the total running costs will usually be double the cost of the car. So, maybe the information about the car is more valuable than the car itself?

The blockchain benefit

A blockchain can provide a simpler, more comprehensive, approach to B2B information processing across multiple organizations. Whereas EDI protocols such as AS1, AS2, AS3, and AS4 are concerned only with data *exchange*, a blockchain can *share*. The difference between exchanging and sharing is profound.

Specifically, a Hyperledger Fabric blockchain can:

- *Share transaction data* in a replicated **ledger**
- *Share processes* with **smart contracts**
- *Share communications* on a **network channel**

In a blockchain, all the data, processes, and communications that relate to multi-party transactions are integrated into one coherent system.

That's in contrast to a traditional B2B approach where data, processing, and exchange are managed by different systems. This separation directly results in significant amounts of processing to join information across these systems and a lack of overall transparency. The process required to address the different world views between organizations is called **reconciliation**. It ensures that there are not significant differences between the information at different parts of the business network — but it is time-consuming and costly.

We now see the benefits of implementing a business network on a blockchain. Rather than a set of different systems that records the multi-party transactions, there is a shared system — a blockchain. It provides an explicit shared understanding of the asset and its life cycle and of the participants, transactions, and events. This shared nature of blockchain provides increased trust through increased transparency, and that radically simplifies and accelerates processing. Organizations don't have to perform periodic reconciliations because everything tallies all the time in a blockchain.

Let's now have a look at how Hyperledger Fabric is used by the different organizations in a business network.

Interacting with a blockchain

Let's have a look at how participants interact with a Hyperledger Fabric blockchain, starting with the following diagram:

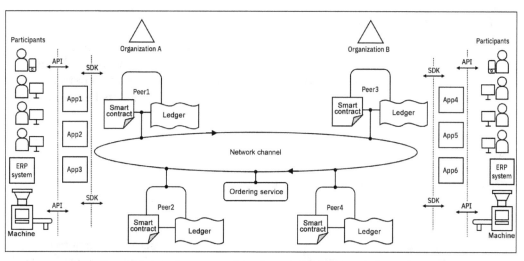

Figure 3.1: A business network implemented using Hyperledger Fabric

Here, we can see a business network built on Hyperledger Fabric. We haven't included every last moving part, but most of the components we've discussed so far in this chapter are on this single diagram. In this section, we'll go through each of the critical elements.

Organizational structure

We can see two distinct organizations in the diagram: A and B. On the left, there are network elements associated with organization A, and on the right, we can see elements associated with organization B. We'll focus on these elements later, but for now, notice how the network is decentralized; organization A and organization B appear (and are) quite equal. There isn't, for example, a "central server" anywhere. We note that it's the *organization* that is central to how the network is structured and how participants interact with it.

 The ordering service, which is discussed in detail elsewhere, is a shared service but not a centralized service. It is typically hosted across multiple organizations in the network but drawn as a single element to emphasize its shared nature.

Technical componentry

At the edges of the diagram, we can see participants, and at the center of the diagram, we can see technology components, such as peers, channels, and so forth. These components provide the technical infrastructure for the business network. The participants in the network use this infrastructure to move assets between each other with transactions and events. We'll see how they do this later.

Participants

Let's look at the different types of participants. In this diagram, we've shown similar sets of participants for organization A and organization B; let's focus on the *types* of participants in organization A.

Notice how the participants with phones and desktops interact with the network. Their proximity is to an application tier located within the technical infrastructure (App1, App2 and App3). It's these applications that act on their behalf to interact with the network. Apps on mobile phones and browsers on desktops will use APIs to connect to the application tier. Although it may seem that the participants are from organization A, notice how this is not actually the case. Participants interacting with the application tier can be from any organization, but every interaction with the network organization will appear to originate from organization A.

We also can see system and device participants — an ERP system and a machine. Just like phones and desktops, these will use APIs to connect to the application tier. If you've heard of *Industrie 4.0*, you'll know that many machines have excellent connectivity to enable exactly this kind of scenario.

In reality, there can be a lot of technical infrastructure between the participants and the application tier, but we can safely ignore this, as all it does is connect the participants to the application tier. If we're designing a whole system, we may not have this luxury, but for the purpose of understanding a business network, we don't need to consider it.

APIs

We can see that each participant communicates with the application tier using an API. Because this application communicates with the end user, we call it **application-centric** because it is described in terms of the business problem being solved. This API is provided and processed by the application tier. We can see that this API is quite removed from the blockchain, as it's the application tier that interacts with the Hyperledger Fabric technical infrastructure shown in the center of the diagram.

At a high level, business network APIs are easy to understand. In a vehicle network, we might have APIs such as buyVehicle(), insureVehicle(), transferVehicle(), registerVehicle(), and so on. These APIs are domain-specific, and the ones just mentioned would be very different from those in a commercial paper network — issuePaper(), movePaper(), and redeemPaper(). It's important that APIs are domain-specific because it makes them meaningful to the participants in the network who are using them — such APIs speak the language of the participants.

In our example, the application tier is only shown using Hyperledger Fabric; in a real system, it might also use databases, messaging engines, and other resource managers to do its work.

Application tier

For both organization A and B, we can see an application tier comprising a set of three applications (App123 and App456). Notice how it's these applications that access the blockchain.

Notice also how App123 and App456 interact with the different technical components of the blockchain using the Hyperledger Fabric SDK. This SDK provides a set of blockchain-centric APIs that allow applications to interact with the blockchain. In practice, this means being able to query the current value of the ledger, submit new multi-party transactions to the ledger, and be notified when the ledger changes. We'll learn much more about this SDK later in this book when we step through a worked example!

Smart contract

The most important solution component in Hyperledger Fabric is the smart contract, and we can see instances of a smart contract installed on every peer in the network.

We're going to spend a lot of time looking at how to program a smart contract. A smart contract contains the program code that generates the transactions that describe the life cycle of *assets* or *business objects*.

Applications use smart contracts to get work done in Hyperledger Fabric. We think of the other components such as *peer* and *ordering service* as parts of the operational infrastructure required to make everything work, but not really that important from a conceptual point of view. Let's not write them off completely, though — nothing will work without them!

We can see that a smart contract is installed in both organization A and B. That's because, ultimately, they will generate the multi-party transactions that are central to a business network and Hyperledger Fabric.

Ledger

On every peer, we also can see an instance of the ledger. For simplicity, we've just shown it as a single symbol, focusing on the blockchain transaction history component rather than the current value component.

A single smart contract instance uses a single ledger instance to generate a transaction that is, ultimately, stored on *every* instance of the ledger in the network via a process called **consensus**. We'll learn a lot more about consensus later in this book; for now, we'll focus on the fact that the ledger is the primary point of reference for a smart contract.

Peer

When we hear people talk about Hyperledger Fabric, we often hear them talk about *peers* very early in the discussion. A peer is the most common *moving part* with Hyperledger Fabric. We can see that it's a peer that holds an instance of the ledger and an instance of a smart contract.

And because there are many peers owned by many different organizations in the network, the network is described as *decentralized*. No single peer is in charge; an application can interact with any peer to get work done. Indeed, we'll see how the SDK makes this very easy to do. We're not going to spend much time on the peer now, however, because although nothing will work without them, they are a relatively low-level detail from a solution perspective.

Ordering service

In the same vein, we notice the *ordering service* in the center of the diagram. If you are used to Bitcoin or Ethereum, then you can think of the ordering service as being like *miners*, but with much less power.

An ordering service creates transaction blocks and distributes them to every organization in the network. It is run by multiple organizations so that no single organization is responsible for blockchain creation and distribution. Unlike miners, however, an ordering service does not access the ledger or validate transactions — it is merely an ordering component. This is *very* important! In Hyperledger Fabric, it's the organizations that own the smart contracts and ledgers that decide how transactions are generated and validated, addressing a major concern with technologies like Bitcoin and Ethereum.

Network channel

We can see that everything is knitted together using a *network channel*, shown in the center of the diagram in *Figure 3.1*. It's the network channel (or simply *channel*) that links the application, smart contract, ledger, peer, and ordering service.

The channel creates a domain-specific network for these components, which the components use depending on the business concern. For example, there would be a different channel for trade finance, food provenance, or international payments.

Hyperledger Fabric is an interesting technology because of its support for multiple channels, giving it the ability to support a *network of networks*. In practice, this means that a peer in Hyperledger Fabric can join different channels with different ledgers and different smart contracts. This allows applications and smart contracts to interact with multiple networks at the same time — the so-called "network of networks." Much more on this later!

Identity

Finally, although it's not shown, just about every component in the diagram — peers, ordering service, application, and organization — has an identity (typically) represented by an X.509 digital certificate. We've not shown identities on the diagram because it would clutter it up, but let's consider them now.

Each component's identity associates it with an organization within in the network, and a network configuration policy (also not shown for simplicity) uses this identity to determine the access rights of that component.

If we spent a little time thinking about it, we'd realize that the participants toward the edge of the diagram do not need such a digital identity as they are connected to the blockchain via the application tier — it's this application's identity that is used to interact with the blockchain. In reality, these participants are authenticated to the application tier using a mechanism that is separate from identity management in Hyperledger Fabric. We'll learn more about this later.

Summary

In this chapter, we've explored the idea of a business network. We've studied participants, assets, transactions, and events and seen that, in some sense, all business networks share the same concerns.

By using a participant—an individual, organization, system, or device—we were able to properly describe what initiates transactions that capture changes in the business network. Using an asset—a thing of value, whether tangible or intangible—we were able to describe and understand the resources that move between participants, and how they express the reason participants interact with each other. In combination, participants and assets allowed us to understand how a change is captured in a transaction. Finally, using events allowed us to understand when significant changes to the network happened and act upon them using loose coupling.

We spent a few moments discussing how these concepts are consumed using APIs, and in the next chapter, we're going focus much more on this aspect—how to demonstrate all these ideas in a real-world example of a business network. We're going to use Hyperledger Fabric so that you can learn how to apply these ideas in practice.

4
Setting the Stage with a Business Scenario

The first three chapters were focused on setting the stage, defining the landscape of a blockchain project, and introducing the concept of business networks. We now understand how the technology works within a business framework, how the various Hyperledger projects aim to solve the problem of time and trust, why different stakeholders would come together to create a business network, and what a business network comprises.

With an understanding of the components that make up Hyperledger Fabric and a generic business network, we will now delve into application design and implementation considerations. The next few chapters will take you through the steps of creating a sample network, building your very own smart contract, and then integrating it into applications.

In order to make these exercises relevant, we will leverage a business use case with roots in older civilizations: trading and letters of credit.

The chapter's objective is to introduce the business concept of a **letter of credit**, walk you through the sample scenario we have selected, and conclude by setting up our development environment and launching a sample network.

In this chapter, we will cover:

- Trading and letters of credit
- Business scenario and use case

- Designing and configuring a Hyperledger Fabric trade network
- Launching a sample trade network
- Configuring our development environment for network operations

Let's begin by exploring the concepts of trading and accounts, which form the theoretical basis of the use case we will be designing and implementing using Hyperledger Fabric.

Trading and letters of credit

Step back in history to a time when merchants traveled across continents to buy cloth in one country to sell in another country. As a Florentine wool merchant, you might make a journey to Amsterdam to buy fine wool in that newly formed city-state, whose port collected resources from the whole of Northern Europe and beyond. You could then transport the wool to Florence, where it could be sold to tailors making fine garments for their wealthy clients. We're talking about 1300 AD—a time when it was not safe to carry gold or other precious metals as a form of currency to buy and sell goods. What was necessary was a form of currency that worked across country boundaries, one that could be used in Amsterdam and Florence, or anywhere!

Marco Polo had been to China and had seen how commerce was conducted in that thriving economy. At the heart of the successful Khan empire were advanced financial techniques that we would recognize today. Fiat currencies, paper money, promissory notes, and letters of credit all arrived in Europe by way of China. Marco Polo brought these ideas back to Europe—they helped form and grow a merchant banking industry for a Europe emerging after the fall of the Roman Empire.

The importance of trust in facilitating trade

Our Florentine merchant could then contact his banker to say that he wanted to buy wool in Amsterdam, and the bank would give him a letter of credit, in exchange for payment on account. This letter could have various stipulations, such as the maximum amount for the trade, how it would be paid (at once or in parts), what goods it could be used for, and so forth. The merchant would then travel to Amsterdam, and after selecting wool from a wool merchant, he would offer the letter of credit as payment. The Amsterdam merchant would happily exchange the wool for the letter because Florentine bankers were famed throughout Europe as being trustworthy when it came to money. The Amsterdam merchant could bring the letter of credit to his banker, who in turn would credit his account. Of course, the Florentine and Amsterdam bankers charged their respective clients— the merchants—for this service! It was good for everyone.

Periodically, Amsterdam bankers and Florentine bankers would meet up to settle their accounts, but this was of no importance to the wool trader and wool merchant. Effectively, what was happening was that the Florentine and Amsterdam merchants were using the trust between their respective bankers to establish a trust relationship with each other—a very sophisticated idea when you think about it. This is why the letter of credit process has remained a fundamental way of conducting business worldwide to this day.

The letter of credit process today

However, over time, due to the massive globalization of trade and the explosion of the financial industry, the number of financial institutions involved in the letter of credit process has exploded! Nowadays, there could be over 20 intermediary financial institutions involved in the process. This requires the coordination of many people and systems, resulting in excessive time, cost, and risk throughout the process for both merchants and banks alike.

> Blockchain technology can enable the creation of a logically singular but physically distributed system that provides a platform for a low-friction letter of credit process. The characteristics of such a system would include greater transparency, timeliness, and automation (resulting in lower costs), and new features such as incremental payment.

In the following sections, we will follow a practical scenario that necessitates various regulatory and transactory processes relevant to our discussion on Hyperledger.

Business scenario and use case

The letter of credit is but one facet of a complex process that parties engaging in international trade must go through. The export of goods across international boundaries involves many entities playing different roles and possessing different, sometimes mutually contradictory, interests. Traditionally, this process has relied on a lot of documentation that has to be physically transferred between entities. This can be quite inefficient, time-consuming, costly, and prone to manipulation by vested interests. But these are exactly the kinds of real-world problems that blockchains were designed to mitigate. Therefore, we have selected an element of an import-export scenario with simplified versions of transactions carried out in the real world as our canonical use case for practical exercises in the next few chapters.

Overview

The scenario we will describe involves a simple transaction: the sale of goods from one party to another. This transaction is complicated by the fact that the buyer and the seller live in different countries, so there is no common trusted intermediary to ensure that the exporter gets the promised money and the importer simultaneously gets the promised goods. Such trade arrangements in today's world rely on the following:

- Intermediaries that facilitate payments and the physical transfer of goods
- Processes that have evolved over time to enable exporters and importers to hedge their bets and reduce the risks involved

Real-world processes

The intermediaries that facilitate payment are the respective banks of the exporter and the importer. The trade arrangement is fulfilled by the existing trust relationships between a bank and its client, and between the two banks. Such banks typically have international connections and reputations to maintain. Therefore, a commitment (or promise) by the importer's bank to make a payment to the exporter's bank is enough to trigger the process. The goods are dispatched by the exporter through a reputed international carrier after obtaining regulatory clearances from the exporting country's government.

Proof of handoff (of the goods) to the carrier is enough to clear payment from the importer's bank to the exporter's bank, and such clearance is not contingent on the goods reaching their intended destination. (It is assumed that the goods are insured against loss or damage in transit.) The promise made by the importer's bank to pay the exporter's bank can be formalized through an instrument like a letter of credit, which specifies a list of documents that are required as proof of dispatch, and the precise method of payment to be made immediately or over a period. Various regulatory requirements must be fulfilled by the exporter before getting documentary clearances that allow it to hand off the goods to the carrier.

Simplified and modified processes

Our use case will follow a simplified version of the preceding process, with certain variations to demonstrate the value of blockchain not just in facilitating this trade but also in opening new possibilities. A promise of payment in two installments is made by the importer's bank to the exporter's bank. The exporter obtains a clearance certificate from the regulatory authority, hands off the goods to the carrier, and then obtains a receipt.

The production of the receipt triggers the first payment installment from the importer's bank to the exporter's bank. When the shipment has reached the destination port, the second and final payment installment is made, and the process concludes.

Terms used in trade finance and logistics

The following terms are used to refer to certain instruments and artifacts that are in play in our trade scenario. The application we will build in this chapter uses very simplified forms of these instruments:

- **Letter of credit**: As we have seen at the beginning of the chapter, this refers to a bank's promise to pay an exporter upon presentation of documentary proof of goods having been shipped. Called **L/C** for short, this document is issued by the importer's bank at the request of its client: the importer. The L/C states the list of documents that constitute proof of shipment, the amount to be paid, and the beneficiary (the exporter in our case) of that amount. A sample L/C is illustrated in the following figure:

Toy Bank, Ltd.

Issue Date: March 1, 2018
L/C Number: 23868

Toy Bank, Ltd. hereby issues this irrevocable documentary Letter of Credit to Lumber Inc. for US$500000 payable immediately upon sight by a draft drawn against Toy Bank, Ltd., in accordance with Letter of Credit number 23868.

The draft is to be accompanied by the following documents:

1. Order Bill of Lading
2. Packing List
3. Invoice

Authorized Signatory
Toy Bank, Ltd.

Figure 4.1: Sample letter of credit issued by Toy Bank, Ltd. in the role of an importer's bank

We will introduce small variations in our use case to make this instrument comprehensible to the reader. First, the L/C will be issued to the exporter's bank rather than directly to the exporter. Second, the L/C states that payment will be made in two identical installments, the first upon production of two documents and the second upon the goods reaching their destination.

- **Export license**: This refers to the approval given by the regulatory authority in the exporter's country for the shipment of the specified goods. In this book, we will refer to it as the **E/L** for short. A sample E/L is illustrated in the following figure:

ABC Government

Department of Forestry: Inspection Services

License to Export Wood

LICENSE NUMBER: 76348

License Holder: Lumber Inc.

FOR THE PURPOSE OF EXPORTING WOOD BY SEA OR AIR

Commencing On: March 1, 2018
Ending on: March 1, 2019

Authorized Signatory,
Department of Forestry

Figure 4.2: Sample export license issued by a regulatory authority to Lumber Inc. for exporting wood

- **Bill of lading**: This is a document issued by the carrier to the exporter once it takes possession of the shipment. Called the **B/L** for short, it simultaneously serves as a receipt, a contract obliging the carrier to transport the goods to a specified destination in return for a fee, and a title of ownership of the goods. This document is also listed in the L/C (as you can see in *Figure 4.1*, the sample letter issued by Toy Bank, Ltd.) and serves as proof of shipment dispatch, which will automatically trigger a payment clearance. A sample B/L is illustrated in the following figure:

Worldwide Shippers	BILL OF LADING FOR OCEAN TRANSPORT
Shipper *Lumber Inc.*	Booking ID *7625901*
Consignee *Toy Company*	Notify Party *Toy Bank, Ltd.*
Place of Receipt *Port ABC*	Place of Delivery *Port LMN*

PARTICULARS FURNISHED BY SHIPPER		
Description of Goods	Weight	Measurement
Wood	*600 tons*	*1000m × 800 m*
Freight Charges *US$40000*		
Authorized Signatory, Worldwide Shippers		

Figure 4.3: Sample bill of lading issued by Worldwide Shippers to Lumber Inc. after taking possession of an export shipment

Shared process workflow

Every instance of the test case scenario presented in this chapter takes a long period of time to complete in real life, involves interactions among different sets of entities at different times, and has many different moving parts that are difficult to keep track of. We hope to simplify this process using our workflow. Implemented as a smart contract on a blockchain, the sequences of transactions described in the following steps (and illustrated in the following diagram) can be carried out in an irrevocable and non-repudiable manner. In this sequence of events, we assume a straight, linear narrative where parties are in agreement with each other and nothing untoward happens; guards are built in the process only to catch errors.

The transactions in our workflow are as follows:

1. The importer requests goods from the exporter in exchange for money
2. The exporter accepts the trade deal

3. The importer asks its bank for an L/C in favor of the exporter

4. The importer's bank supplies an L/C in favor of the exporter, payable to the latter's bank

5. The exporter's bank accepts the L/C on behalf of the exporter

6. The exporter applies for an E/L from the regulatory authority

7. The regulatory authority supplies an E/L to the exporter

8. The exporter prepares a shipment and hands it off to the carrier

9. The carrier accepts the goods (optionally, after validating the E/L) and then supplies a B/L to the exporter

10. The exporter's bank claims half the payment from the importer's bank

11. The importer's bank transfers half the amount to the exporter's bank

12. The carrier ships the goods to the destination

13. The importer's bank pays the remaining amount to the exporter's bank

Here is a diagram to illustrate the transaction workflow:

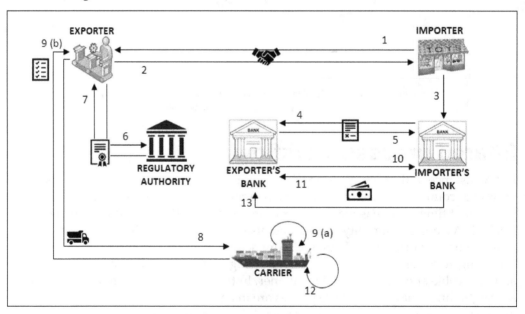

Figure 4.4: Export/import workflow involving traders, banks, carriers, and regulatory authorities

Shared assets and data

The participants in our workflow must have some information in common that gives them a view of the trade arrangement and its progress at any given moment.

The following is a table of the assets owned by the participants, which are shared with each other to drive the process from one stage to the next. (Note that assets need only be shared with selected participants that need to know about them and not with everyone, as we will see later.) This includes documentary and monetary assets. The attributes listed in the table correspond to what is implemented in our project codebase and may not span the entire list of features we discussed earlier in the chapter. For example, an L/C may be issued only by selected participants through a contract (as we will discuss later), and hence we chose not to explicitly add an "issuer" attribute to that asset:

Asset type	Asset attributes
Trade agreement	ID, exporter, importer, amount, and description of goods
Letter of credit	ID, expiration date, beneficiary, amount, and a list of document types
Export license	ID, expiration date, beneficiary (exporter), carrier, approver (regulatory authority), and description of goods
Bill of lading	ID, expiration date, shipper (exporter), consignee/beneficiary (importer), carrier, places of receipt and delivery (source and destination ports), description of goods, and freight amount
Shipment	Shipper (exporter), carrier, beneficiary (importer), description of goods, and freight amount
Payment	Amount in standard currency units

The following are the data elements that circumscribe the options available to participants in each stage:

Data type	Data attributes
Trade agreement	Request and acceptance status: by importer and exporter respectively
Letter of credit	Request, issuance, and acceptance status: by importer, importer's bank, and exporter's bank respectively
Export license	Request and issuance status: by exporter and regulatory authority respectively
Shipment	Preparation and acceptance status: by exporter and carrier respectively Current position or location: by carrier

Participants' roles and capabilities

There are six categories of participants in our scenario: exporter, importer, exporter's bank, importer's bank, carrier, and regulatory authority. The terms in this set refer to the roles an entity can assume in a trade deal; for example, a company exporting goods in one instance may be an importer in another. The capabilities and restrictions of each role are also detailed in the following list:

- Only an importer may apply for an L/C
- Only an importer's bank may supply an L/C
- Only an exporter's bank may accept an L/C
- Only an exporter may request an E/L
- Only a regulatory authority may supply an E/L
- Only an exporter may prepare a shipment
- Only a carrier may supply a B/L
- Only a carrier may update a shipment location
- Only an importer's bank may send money, and only an exporter's bank may receive money

Advantages of blockchain applications over current real-world processes

As discussed at length at the beginning of this chapter, the risks inherent in transferring goods or making payments in the absence of safeguards (such as a trusted mediator) inspired the involvement of banks and led to the creation of the letter of credit and bill of lading. A consequence of these processes was not just additional cost (banks charge commission to issue letters of credit) or additional overhead. Applying and waiting for export licenses to be awarded also increases the turnaround time. In an ideal trade scenario, only the process of preparing and shipping the goods would take a noticeable amount of time.

Recently, the adoption of SWIFT messaging over manual communication has made the document application and collection processes more efficient, but it has not fundamentally changed the game. A blockchain, on the other hand, with its (almost) instantaneous transaction commitments and assurance guarantees, opens possibilities that did not previously exist.

As an example, the one variation we introduced in our use case was payment by installments, which cannot be implemented in the legacy framework because there is no guaranteed way of knowing and sharing information about a shipment's progress. Such a variation would be deemed too risky in this case, which is why payments are linked purely to documentary evidence. By getting all participants in a trade agreement on a single blockchain implementing a common smart contract, we can provide a single shared source of truth that will minimize risk and simultaneously increase accountability.

In subsequent chapters, we will demonstrate in detail how our use case is implemented on the Hyperledger Fabric platform. You will be able to appreciate both the simplicity and elegance of the implementation, which can then be used as a guide for other applications to revamp their archaic processes using this exciting new technology.

However, before diving into the code, we will look at the design of a Hyperledger Fabric network for our trade workflow and set up our development environment to create this network and build applications in it.

Designing and configuring a Hyperledger Fabric trade network

As you already know by now, an instance of a Hyperledger Fabric blockchain is referred to as a channel, which is a log of transactions linked to each other sequentially in a cryptographically secure manner. To design and run a blockchain application, the first step is to determine how many channels are required. For our trade application, we will use two channels, which will maintain the history of trades carried out among the different participants along with associated artifacts like letters of credit, export licenses, bills of lading, bank accounts, and shipment records.

A Fabric peer may belong to multiple channels, which maintain independent and isolated sequences of transactions and resulting datasets. A single peer may thus access ledger data from, and run transactions in, different applications (or contracts) on behalf of its owners (or clients). A channel can run multiple smart contracts, each of which may be an independent application or linked with other contracts (on the same or a different channel) in a multi-contract application. In this book, we will walk the aspiring blockchain developer through the design of a complex multi-channel and multi-contract application in a step-by-step manner. We will show how to create a channel and then develop and deploy a smart contract on it. (Our developer must first learn the crucial art of building smart contracts and decentralized applications without getting lost in the complexity of network management.) The methods will then be replicated to build other channels and contracts. Subsequently, these channels and contracts will be stitched together to build a truly decentralized Fabric blockchain application, one that can be used as a template to build any arbitrary complex production application in the real world.

Before we delve into the mechanics of setting up our system to install an application and run transactions on our smart contract, we will describe how to create and launch a network on which the application will be installed. A sample network structure will be used to illustrate trade operations throughout this chapter. (In *Chapter 13*, *Life in a Blockchain Network*, you will see how this sample network can be modified as the requirements change and evolve.)

Designing a network

The construction of a Hyperledger Fabric network for an application begins by listing the participating organizations. Logically, an organization is a security domain and a unit of identity and credentials. It governs one or more network peers and depends on a **membership service provider** (**MSP**) to issue identities and certificates for the peers as well as clients for smart contract access privileges. (Though an organization can use multiple MSP instances, Fabric recommends a one-to-one mapping between organizations and MSPs.) As described in *Chapter 2*, *Exploring Hyperledger Fabric*, an MSP instance serves as a **certificate authority** (**CA**) and therefore must host a root CA and optionally one or more intermediate CAs within an organization. The ordering service, which is the cornerstone of a Fabric network, is typically assigned its own set of organizations.

The following diagram illustrates a typical peer network structure with clients, MSPs, and logical organization groupings: there are three organizations consisting of a total of six peers to maintain ledger and state replicas and run smart contracts, and two organizations with an ordering service node each to order transactions into a sequence of blocks. A client submits transactions to the network, which validates them using policies framed at the organizational, rather than at the peer's, level (We will describe the anatomy of a transaction in *Chapter 9, Network Operation and Distributed Application Building*):

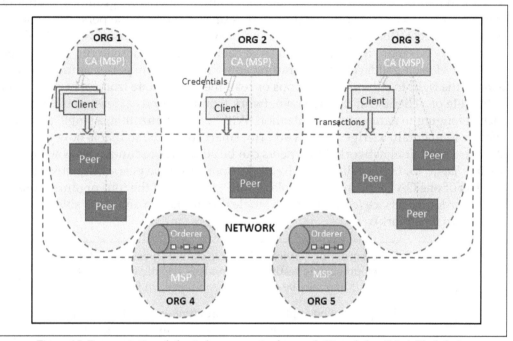

Figure 4.5: Representation of physical components of a sample Hyperledger Fabric blockchain network distributed among organizations. The peer and orderer nodes collectively comprise the transaction-processing network

The set of peers, the organizations they belong to, and the membership service providers serving each organization must be decided before network creation and launch so that the appropriate services can be installed and run on those machines.

A single Fabric network such as the one illustrated in *Figure 4.5* may manage multiple channels, where each channel is exposed to (or shared by) a designated subset of the network. For our demonstration, we will configure two channels, each visible to a portion of the network, though these portions may overlap.

Our sample trade network will consist of four organizations, representing the exporter, importer, carrier, and regulator. The latter two represent the carrier and regulator entities, respectively. The exporter organization, however, represents both the exporting entity and its bank. Similarly, the importer organization represents the importing entity and its bank. As mentioned earlier, an organization represents both a security domain and a business entity; in other words, it provides a trust boundary around a set of entities using an MSP and attests to the veracity of transactions submitted by it. In practice, starting and maintaining an organization with peers and MSPs will require significant investment in resources. Therefore, grouping mutually trusted entities in a single organization makes sense from both the perspective of security and cost. Running a Fabric peer is a heavy and costly business, so a bank, which likely has more resources and a large clientele, may choose to run such a peer on behalf of itself and its clients. A trading entity (that is, an exporter or importer) obtains the right to submit transactions or read the ledger state from its organization in the role of a client. Our blockchain network therefore needs at least four peers, each belonging to a different organization. Within an organization, a single peer is enough to maintain a ledger replica and run smart contracts, so that is how we will structure our initial network. More peers can be added for redundancy, as we will see in *Chapter 13, Life in a Blockchain Network*. Apart from the peers, our network consists of one CA (performing the role of MSP) for each of the four organizations and an ordering service (consisting of a single orderer node running in solo mode in our initial network).

For an ordering service, solo mode should be used only for development and testing. This mode is also deprecated in Fabric 2 onwards and may be eliminated completely in future versions.

In a production application, the ordering service should be set up as a Raft cluster, but for the purpose of demonstrating how to build a blockchain application, the ordering service can be treated as a black box.

The ordering service runs in a single organization with an MSP. The five organizations with their MSPs, peers, and clients of our trading network are illustrated in the following diagram:

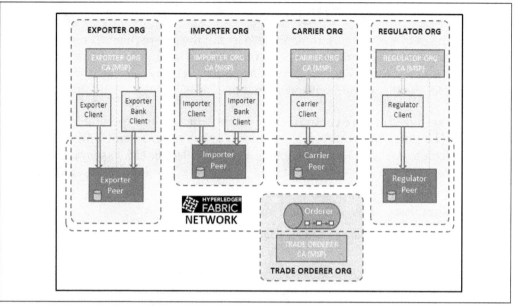

Figure 4.6: A trade network with peers, an orderer, and clients in their respective organizations

You may wonder how, if a trading party and its banker belong to the same organization, the application can distinguish the two (the exporter from the exporter's bank, and the importer from the importer's bank) for the purpose of controlling access to the smart contract and ledger. Two ways of doing this are as follows:

- Embedding access control logic in the service and presentation layers (which we will describe later in this book), whereby users can be distinguished by their IDs (or login names) and an access control list mapping IDs to permitted contract functions is maintained.

- Having an organization's MSP, acting as a CA server, embed distinguishing attributes within the certificates it issues to members of an organization. The access control logic can be implemented in the middleware or even in the contract to parse the attributes and permit or disallow an operation as per business logic requirements.

In our application, we will demonstrate the use of both these mechanisms to distinguish bankers and clients belonging to an organization. You may select either or both mechanisms and implement them in suitable locations to engineer secure client-server applications on Fabric.

Installing prerequisites

With the design of the network in hand, let's install the pre-requisite tools. The instructions below will work on Linux and Mac. On Windows systems, readers should use a solution like Vagrant (with VirtualBox: `https://www.virtualbox.org/`) to run development environments on virtual machines:

1. Make sure you have common application building and code maintenance tools installed on your target machine. For example, on an Ubuntu Linux machine, you should have the following installed: `build-essential`, `git`, `make`, `curl`, `unzip`, `g++`, `libtool`, and `jq`. You may also install the `libltdl-dev` library, which is a package of some of these tools.

2. Ensure that you have the latest version of:

   - Docker, using `https://docs.docker.com/install/`: version 17.06.2-ce or greater

   - Docker Compose, using `https://docs.docker.com/compose/install/`: version 1.14.0 or greater

3. We will be using GitHub to share the source code of our tutorial. To access GitHub, the Git client needs to be installed and configured with authentication to GitHub. For more information, visit GitHub's official website at `https://help.github.com/articles/set-up-git/`.

4. Fabric is implemented in the Go language. To build and run Fabric, we need to download and install Go from `https://golang.org/`.

 The setup of Hyperledger Fabric and the testing of the tutorial application in this book was done using Go 1.14, so the reader is advised to install and use 1.14.x or greater.

5. Next, we need to set up our environmental variables:

   1. `GOPATH` points to a workspace for the Go source code. For example:
   ```
   $ export GOPATH=$HOME/go
   ```

   2. `PATH` needs to include the Go `bin` directory used to store libraries and executables, as we can see in the following snippet:
   ```
   $ export PATH=$PATH:$GOPATH/bin
   ```

Setting up `GOPATH` is a crucial prerequisite to installing Fabric, as we will see later.

6. We will be developing applications in both JavaScript and Java. For JavaScript, we need to install Node.js. The instructions for this vary across platforms, so make sure you install the right version of the software. For Fabric version 2 development, the minimum recommended version of Node.js is 10.15.3. Instructions for Ubuntu Linux are as follows:

   1. If an older version of Node.js is already installed, remove it first:

   ```
   $ sudo apt-get purge nodejs
   ```

   2. To install Node.js version 10, run:

   ```
   $ curl -sL https://deb.nodesource.com/setup_10.x | sudo -E
   bash -
   $ sudo apt-get install -y nodejs
   ```

   This will install the latest minor version of Node.js 10, which is higher than 10.15.3. It will also install the npm package management tool, using which you can reinstall a particular version of Node.js if required.

7. You will need to install Java 11 or above to develop on Fabric version 2, the instructions for which will vary with the platform. Instructions for Ubuntu Linux are as follows:

   1. To install JDK 11 and Maven, run:

   ```
   $ sudo apt-get install -y openjdk-11-jdk maven
   ```

   2. To install Gradle (version 6.3), run:

   ```
   $ wget https://services.gradle.org/distributions/gradle-
   6.3-bin.zip -P /tmp --quiet
   $ sudo unzip -q /tmp/gradle-6.3-bin.zip -d /opt && rm /
   tmp/gradle-6.3-bin.zip
   $ sudo ln -s /opt/gradle-6.3/bin/gradle /usr/bin
   ```

 The Java applications in this book were developed with Gradle 6.3, but you can use newer versions, too.

8. To use the Fabric Node SDK to build applications (we will see how in *Chapter 9*, *Network Operation and Distributed Application Building*), you will need to install Python 2.7 in addition to any other versions of Python you may have installed on your system.

Now we've installed the necessary prerequisites, let's consider how to set up a development environment for testing purposes.

Setting up the development/test environment

Though the reader may use any text editor or IDE for blockchain application development, we recommend the use of Microsoft's **Visual Studio Code** (**VS Code**) as it has support for Hyperledger Fabric development and is also available on most platforms (Linux, Mac, and Windows).

Complete the following steps to set up your environment:

1. To download the VS Code installer and for installation instructions, go to `https://code.visualstudio.com/download`. (Note: For our development, we used version 1.42.1.)

2. To install VS Code, on an Ubuntu Linux machine, for example, let's say you download the installation file as `<code-filename>.deb` in the local folder. You can then install it using the following commands:

    ```
    $ sudo apt update
    $ sudo apt install ./<code-filename>.deb
    ```

3. Start VS Code on your target machine to install the IBM Blockchain Platform extension. For example, on an Ubuntu Linux machine, this would be as follows:

    ```
    $ code
    ```

     If you are developing on a Vagrant virtual machine, you will need to log into that virtual machine with X11 port forwarding enabled.

4. Install the **IBM Blockchain Platform** (**IBP**) extension as follows (instructions are also available at `https://cloud.ibm.com/docs/services/blockchain/howto?topic=blockchain-develop-vscode`):

    1. Select the **Extensions** tab from the left-hand menu (or use *Ctrl + Shift + X*)
    2. Type `IBM Blockchain Platform` in the search box
    3. Click the green **Install** button on the **IBM Blockchain Platform** entry and follow any instructions presented
    4. After a successful installation, you should see an **IBM Blockchain Platform** tab appear in the left-hand menu

5. To complete the setup, you need to install or fix prerequisite software as follows:

    1. Start VS Code

2. Select the **IBM Blockchain Platform** tab from the left-hand menu

3. Fix the missing or mismatched software as indicated in the main window, an example of which is as follows:

   We will be developing applications with the IBP extension in Java and Node.js. Make sure you have (or get) the right version of Node. js (and NPM) installed, as described earlier.

6. Install optional extensions as recommended, including the following:

   - Go

   - Java Extension Pack

   - JavaScript Test Runner

   - Spring Initializr Java Support

7. Ensure that your system meets the system requirements as stated in the panel (for example, 4 GB RAM) and select **I confirm**.

8. Finally, click **Let's Blockchain** to finalize the IBP extension. (This could take some time to complete.)

Next, as an optional step, you can test the IBP extension.

Testing the IBP extension

To ensure that VS Code with the IBP extension is ready to launch networks and build applications, you can run preprogrammed tests as follows:

1. Start VS Code.

2. Select the **IBM Blockchain Platform** icon from the left-hand menu.

3. Under **IBM Blockchain Platform** on the left of the window, you should see four vertical panels labeled **SMART CONTRACTS**, **FABRIC ENVIRONMENTS**, **FABRIC GATEWAYS**, and **FABRIC WALLETS**, respectively.

   In the **FABRIC ENVIRONMENTS** panel, you may see an entry **1 Org Local Fabric (click to start)** under **Simple local networks**. If so, click this entry. Otherwise, create a simple network as follows:

   1. In the **FABRIC ENVIRONMENTS** panel, you should see an entry **Click + to add environments**. Click this entry and select **Create new from template (uses Docker on your local machine)**.

   2. Next, select **1 Org template (1 CA, 1 peer, 1 channel)** to create the most basic Fabric network that can run applications. For the environment name, let's use **1 Org Local Fabric**.

4. Wait for the network configuration to be created. To view output logs, select **View** > **Output** from the top menu. In the **OUTPUT** tab, select **Blockchain** from the drop-down menu. While the network is being created, you should see something like the following:

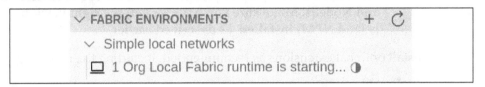

Figure 4.7: The message you see while the default network is being created and launched

5. Eventually, in the **FABRIC ENVIRONMENTS** panel, you should see an entry of **1 Org Local Fabric**. If you move the mouse over it, you should see a message The local development runtime is running. This indicates that a default network consisting of a single peer, a single CA node to run an MSP, and a single ordering service node, has been started, and a single channel has been created.

6. Click the entry **1 Org Local Fabric** to connect to the environment and expand the items in the list. You should see the blockchain network specifications in the **FABRIC ENVIRONMENTS** panel as in the following figure:

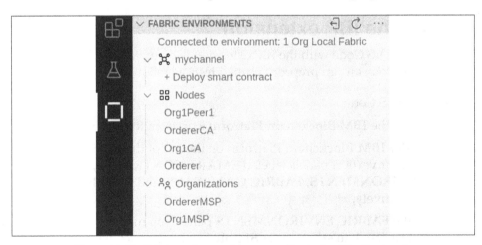

Figure 4.8: The Fabric environment corresponding to the default network
with the channel, nodes, and organizations listed

You can also see that a channel mychannel was created. (Implicitly, the peer Org1Peer1 was joined to this channel too.)

7. Move your mouse over the **FABRIC ENVIRONMENTS** header. You will see a symbol "..." (ellipsis) at the right. Move your mouse over that and you will see a popup labeled **More Actions...**.

8. Click the symbol and select **Teardown Fabric Environment**. Click **Yes** on the popup at the bottom right of the main window. This will perform a reset, deleting the network containers and artifacts. It's important to perform this step so your machine is ready to run the custom trade network from a clean slate.

In the rest of this chapter, we will build and launch a custom network for our trade scenario. (Note that at any given time, you can run and manage only a single Fabric network using the VS Code GUI.)

Forking and cloning the trade-network repository

Now we need to get our own copy of the original source code by forking the repository on GitHub. Then, we can clone the source code into a local machine directory with the following steps:

1. In GitHub, navigate to the following repository: `https://github.com/HyperledgerHandsOn/trade-network`.

2. Fork the repository: Use the **Fork** button at the top-right corner of the page to create a copy of the source code to your account.

3. Get the clone URL: Navigate to your fork of the `trade-network` repository. Click on the **Clone or download** button, and copy the URL.

4. Clone the repository: In the Go workspace, clone the repository as follows:

```
$ cd $GOPATH/src
$ git clone https://github.com/YOUR-USERNAME/trade-network
```

We now have a local copy of all the `trade-network` tutorial materials.

Creating and running a network configuration

The code to configure and launch our network using shell scripts can be found in the `bash` folder in our repository (this is an adaptation of `fabric-samples/first-network`). This folder contains configuration files and scripts that can be run on any Linux or Mac machine.

(These shell scripts were tested on Ubuntu Linux and macOS Catalina and small modifications may be required for other distributions, a task that is left to the users.) This is the most straightforward way to acquaint most developers and network administrators with the process. Once a network is launched using shell scripts (primarily bash/trade.sh), we will switch to using VS Code to connect to this running network and to start developing contracts and applications.

 There is code for an alternative configuration and launch process using Ansible Playbooks in the ansible folder, which we will cover in *Chapter 11, Agility in a Blockchain Network*.

For this exercise, we will run the entire network on a single physical or virtual machine, with the various network elements running in suitably configured Docker containers. It is assumed that the reader has a basic familiarity with containerization using Docker and configurations using Docker Compose. Once the prerequisites listed in the previous section are met, it is enough to run the commands we will demonstrate in this section without any extra knowledge or configuration required of the reader.

Preparing the network

Before running the scripts for network creation and launch, we need to install Hyperledger Fabric tools and create base images for Docker containers. The tools will be used to generate network artifacts and the containers will be used to run network nodes and other functions. There are two ways to obtain base Docker images; (i) build from source, or (ii) download from Docker Hub. The scripts in our project support both mechanisms; if an image corresponding to a given tag (version) cannot be found on the local machine, it will be automatically downloaded from Docker Hub. The default versions used in our project are 2.2.0 for Fabric and 1.4.8 for Fabric CA (values attached to environment variables IMAGE_TAG and CA_IMAGE_TAG respectively in bash/.env and bash/trade.sh in the trade-network repository). But for consistency and to ensure that everything runs smoothly, we recommend that the reader downloads the Fabric source code and build images directly onto the target machine. Instructions for this are as follows:

1. Clone the Fabric (https://github.com/hyperledger/fabric/tree/release-2.2) source code repository. If you are using the git clone command, add the parameter -b release-2.2 as follows:

```
$ git clone https://github.com/hyperledger/fabric.git -b release-2.2
```

Our tutorial was developed for and tested with Fabric release version 2.2, so it is strongly recommended that the reader uses that version. There is no guarantee that our code will work as intended with the `master` branch or with future release versions.

Make sure fabric is downloaded to, or symbolically linked from, the $GOPATH/ src/github.com/hyperledger/ folder. If the Fabric source code is not under GOPATH, subsequent build steps, which rely on Go compilation, will fail as required libraries will not be available in their expected paths.

2. To build Docker images for the peers and orderers, run:

```
$ cd fabric
$ make docker
```

3. To generate the necessary tools to run the network creation commands described in this section, run:

```
$ make configtxgen cryptogen
```

4. Update your system path (for example, the PATH environment variable in Linux) to include .build/bin/ within the Fabric source code folder, which is where these executables are created.

5. Clone the Fabric CA (https://github.com/hyperledger/fabric-ca/tree/ release-1.4) source code repository. (A release-2.2 branch of Fabric-CA was not produced at the time of writing as the release-1.4 version had all the features required by Fabric 2.2.) If you are using the git clone command, add the parameter -b release-1.4 as follows:

```
$ git clone https://github.com/hyperledger/fabric-ca.git -b
release-1.4
```

 Note that the same caveats apply as in *Step 1*.

Make sure `fabric-ca` is downloaded to, or symbolically linked from, the $GOPATH/src/github.com/ hyperledger/ folder. Otherwise, the subsequent build steps, which rely on Go compilation, will fail as required libraries will not be available in their expected paths.

6. To build Docker images for the MSPs, run:

```
$ cd fabric-ca
$ make docker
```

After completion of these steps, your network should be prepared for the next stages of configuration.

Generating network cryptographic material

The first step in the configuration of a network involves the creation of X.509 certificates and signing keys for the MSP (also a certificate authority, or CA) of each peer and orderer organization, and for TLS-based communication. We also need to create X.509 certificates and keys for each peer and orderer node, signed by the MSPs of their respective organizations. Finally, for TLS-based communication among these peers, orderers, and MSPs, we need to create additional certificates and keys, and also corresponding TLS root certificates. (MSPs can play the role of CAs for TLS-based communication, as well.)

The configuration required to generate these cryptographic artifacts is specified in a `crypto-config.yaml` file in the bash folder in our `trade-network` repository. This file contains the organization structure (see more details in the *Generating channel artifacts* section later), the number of peers in each organization, and the default number of users in an organization for whom certificates and keys must be created (note that an `admin` user is created additionally by default). As an example, see the definition of the importer's organization in the file as follows, in the `PeerOrgs` section:

```
PeerOrgs:
  Name: ImporterOrg
  Domain: importerorg.trade.com
  EnableNodeOUs: true
  Template:
    Count: 1
  Users:
    Count: 2
```

This configuration indicates that the organization labeled `ImporterOrg` will contain one peer (`Template` section). Two non-admin users will also be created (`Users` section). The organization domain name to be used by the peer and its organization's CA is also defined.

The `OrdererOrgs` section similarly contains a definition of our single ordering node.

To generate cryptographic material for all the organizations, run the `cryptogen` command (which we built earlier using the Fabric source) as follows:

```
$ cryptogen generate --config=./crypto-config.yaml
```

The output is saved to the `crypto-config` folder. Inside, you will see a subfolder corresponding to the ordering organizations and another corresponding to the peer organizations, the latter containing a subfolder for each user organization, namely the Exporter, Importer, Carrier, and Regulator business domains (refer to *Figure 4.6* in the *Designing a network* section).

In `crypto-config/peerOrganizations/exporterorg.trade.com/users`, you will find crypto artifacts generated for one admin user and two ordinary users, specified in the YAML file. The ordinary users, whose credentials can be found in the subfolders `User1@exporterorg.trade.com` and `User2@exporterorg.trade.com`, represent the Exporter and the Exporter Bank entities. In `crypto-config/peerOrganizations/exporterorg.trade.com/users/User1@exporterorg.trade.com/msp`, you can see a folder named `keystore`, which contains the private signing key for `User1`, and a folder named `signcerts`, which contains its certified public key. In the `crypto-config` folder, you can find similar keys and certificates for other user entities and the peer and orderer nodes of the various organizations. We will revisit these crypto artifacts when creating wallets later in this chapter.

Finally, we would like to emphasize that ordinary and administrative users can be created dynamically by sending requests to organizations' MSPs (which run Fabric-CA servers). Here, we have just demonstrated how to generate user credentials with a static configuration. In *Chapter 9*, *Network Operation and Distributed Application Building*, we will demonstrate the dynamic method, which is the typical way Fabric applications should create user identities in production.

Generating channel artifacts

To create a network according to an organization's structure, and to bootstrap a channel, we will need to generate the following artifacts:

- A genesis block, which contains specifications of organizational groups (called **consortiums** in Fabric parlance) and organization-specific certificates that dictate who is permitted to create and manage network channels. This block is needed to bootstrap the ordering service and will serve as the first block of the **orderer system channel**, which is maintained by the ordering service nodes to track the various application channels created within the network. Creating a system channel using the genesis block is the first step in the creation of our application network.

- A channel configuration transaction.

- Anchor peer configuration transactions for each organization. An anchor peer serves as a fulcrum within an organization, for cross-organization ledger syncing using the Fabric gossip protocol.

Channel profiles

Channel and network properties are specified in a file labeled `configtx.yaml`, which can be found in the `bash` folder in the `trade-network` repository. The organizational structure of our trade network is specified in the `Profiles` section as follows:

```
Profiles:
  FourOrgsTradeOrdererGenesis:
    <<: *ChannelDefaults
    Orderer:
      <<: *OrdererDefaults
      Organizations:
        - *TradeOrdererOrg
      Capabilities:
        <<: *OrdererCapabilities
    Consortiums:
      TradeConsortium:
        Organizations:
          - *ExporterOrg
          - *ImporterOrg
          - *RegulatorOrg
      ShippingConsortium:
        Organizations:
          - *ExporterOrg
          - *ImporterOrg
          - *CarrierOrg
          - *RegulatorOrg
  ThreeOrgsTradeChannel:
    Consortium: TradeConsortium
    <<: *ChannelDefaults
    Application:
      <<: *ApplicationDefaults
      Organizations:
        - *ExporterOrg
        - *ImporterOrg
        - *RegulatorOrg
      Capabilities:
```

```
            <<: *ApplicationCapabilities
    FourOrgsShippingChannel:
      Consortium: ShippingConsortium
      <<: *ChannelDefaults
      Application:
        <<: *ApplicationDefaults
        Organizations:
          - *ExporterOrg
          - *ImporterOrg
          - *CarrierOrg
          - *RegulatorOrg
      Capabilities:
        <<: *ApplicationCapabilities
```

The genesis block's configuration is specified in the `FourOrgsTradeOrdererGenesis` section, which defines two consortiums, namely `TradeConsortium` and `ShippingConsortium`. Each consortium consists of a set of organizations that collectively maintain a channel. `TradeConsortium` consists of `ExporterOrg`, `ImporterOrg`, and `RegulatorOrg`, each of which is defined in a subsection in the `Organizations` section elsewhere in the file. `ShippingConsortium` consists of these three organizations and additionally `CarrierOrg`. The orderer belongs to its own organization called `TradeOrdererOrg`.

The configurations of the two channels our distributed application will consist of (to be described in *Chapter 9, Network Operation and Distributed Application Building*) are given in the `ThreeOrgsTradeChannel` and `FourOrgsShippingChannel` sections; these channels are associated with `TradeConsortium` and `ShippingConsortium`, respectively.

Organization configurations

Each organization section contains information about its MSP (ID as well as the location of the cryptographic material, such as keys and certificates), and the hostname and port information for its anchor peers. As an example, the `ExporterOrg` section contains the following:

```
  - &ExporterOrg
  Name: ExporterOrg
  ID: ExporterOrgMSP
  MSPDir: crypto-config/peerOrganizations/exporterorg.trade.com/msp
  Policies:
    Readers:
      Type: Signature
      Rule: "OR('ExporterOrgMSP.admin', 'ExporterOrgMSP.peer',
'ExporterOrgMSP.client')"
```

```
Writers:
    Type: Signature
    Rule: "OR('ExporterOrgMSP.admin', 'ExporterOrgMSP.client')"
Admins:
    Type: Signature
    Rule: "OR('ExporterOrgMSP.admin')"
Endorsement:
    Type: Signature
    Rule: "OR('ExporterOrgMSP.peer')"
AnchorPeers:
    - Host: peer0.exporterorg.trade.com
    - Port: 7051
```

The names of the organization and its MSP are `ExporterOrg` and `ExporterOrgMSP` respectively, which will be part of the channel's configuration. The `MSPDir` variable (representing a folder) in this specification refers to the location of this organization's cryptographic material we generated earlier using the `cryptogen` command. Policies for reading, writing, and administering the channel are specified in the `Policies` section; for example, write access is given to any entity possessing admin or client privileges in the organization (proved by certificates issued by the exporter organization's MSP). Also specified is the organization's policy for endorsing (that is, signing) a smart contract transaction. Finally, the fully qualified hostname and listening port of the organization's anchor peers is specified in the `AnchorPeers` section; in the previous configuration, `ExporterOrg` possesses just one anchor peer.

Ordering service configuration

A snippet of the `Orderer` section is as follows:

```
Orderer: &OrdererDefaults
    OrdererType: solo
    Addresses:
      - orderer.trade.com:7050
    BatchTimeout: 2s
    BatchSize:
        MaxMessageCount: 10
        AbsoluteMaxBytes: 99 MB
        PreferredMaxBytes: 512 KB
    Policies:
        Readers:
            Type: ImplicitMeta
            Rule: "ANY Readers"
        Writers:
```

```
    Type: ImplicitMeta
    Rule: "ANY Writers"
  Admins:
    Type: ImplicitMeta
    Rule: "MAJORITY Admins"
  BlockValidation:
    Type: ImplicitMeta
    Rule: "ANY Writers"
```

The orderer nodes with their hostnames and listening ports are listed in the `Addresses` section. The `BatchTimeout` and `BatchSize` parameters control block creation; for example, `MaxMessageCount` indicates the maximum number of messages (equivalent to smart contract transactions) contained within a block, and `BatchTimeout` dictates the maximum amount of time to wait for new transactions before creating a block.

The `Policies` section is like the one we saw for the organizations. We specify `ImplicitMeta` policies, which are compositions of simpler (`Signature`) policies, to avoid explicit calling out of the signatories. For example, `"ANY Writers"` indicates that every member of the orderer organizations possesses write access for block creation. `BlockValidation` is an additional policy rule that authorizes ordering nodes to sign blocks.

Finally, the `OrdererType` parameter indicates the configuration of our ordering service. Here it is set to `solo`, the simplest configuration, where an ordering service node creates blocks in isolation without running a consensus protocol with other ordering service nodes. This configuration is meant to be used only in development and test environments. It must not be used in production as it provides no fault-tolerance guarantees whatsoever. The ordering service, once configured, plays no part in application development. Recall `FourOrgsTradeOrdererGenesis` in the `Profiles` section, which includes the previous orderer configuration (using the `OrdererDefaults` alias); a genesis block for a `solo` mode ordering service will be generated on the basis of this section. Fabric does offer more advanced crash fault-tolerance modes of operation, namely Kafka and Raft. The configurations for these are specified in both the `Profiles` and `Orderer` sections. The recommended mode for running an ordering service in Fabric 2 is Raft, and we will discuss how to set up a Raft ordering service in *Chapter 9, Network Operation and Distributed Application Building*.

There are other sections in the `configtx.yaml` file, like `Channel` and `Application`, which are used to set channel- and application-related policies respectively. The `Capabilities` section describes rules for version compatibility. We will not go into detail about these settings here, but we do recommend that the reader uses the default settings for development and refers to the official Fabric documentation for advanced configuration.

Generating channel artifacts using configtxgen

To generate channel artifacts, we will use the `configtxgen` tool we built using the Fabric source. To generate the genesis block for bootstrapping the ordering service, run the following command from the `bash` folder:

```
$ configtxgen -profile FourOrgsTradeOrdererGenesis -channelID trade-
sys-channel -outputBlock ./channel- artifacts/genesis.block
```

The `FourOrgsTradeOrdererGenesis` keyword corresponds to the solo ordering service profile name in the `Profiles` section. The genesis block will be saved in the `genesis.block` file in the `channel-artifacts` folder. The `channelID` parameter is used to specify the name of the orderer system channel.

As mentioned earlier, our application will consist of two channels. Here we will describe how to generate artifacts for one of them, using the profile `ThreeOrgsTradeChannel` defined in `configtx.yaml`. To generate this channel's configuration transaction, run:

```
$ configtxgen -profile ThreeOrgsTradeChannel -outputCreateChannelTx ./
channel- artifacts/tradechannel/channel.tx -channelID tradechannel
```

We use the name `tradechannel` for the channel corresponding to the `ThreeOrgsTradeChannel` profile, maintained by the organizations `ExporterOrg`, `ImporterOrg`, and `RegulatorOrg`, which are members of `TradeConsortium`. This name is specified using the `channelID` parameter, and this channel's initial configuration transaction is stored in `channel-artifacts/tradechannel/channel.tx`. To generate anchor peer configuration for the exporter organization in this channel, run:

```
$ configtxgen -profile ThreeOrgsTradeChannel -outputAnchorPeersUpdate
./channel-artifacts/tradechannel/ExporterOrgMSPanchors.tx -channelID
tradechannel -asOrg ExporterOrg
```

Note that `ExporterOrg` corresponds to the `Name` parameter in the `Organizations` section under the `ExporterOrg` alias in `configtx.yaml`, and we use the `ThreeOrgsTradeChannel` profile for this configuration as well. The anchor peer configuration generation process should be repeated for the other two organizations in `TradeConsortium`, while changing the organization names and output filenames in the preceding command.

The configtxgen command relies on the environment variable FABRIC_CFG_PATH, which must be set to point to the folder that contains the configtx.yaml file. The script file trade.sh (which we will use later) contains the following line to ensure that this YAML file is loaded from the folder in which the command is run:

```
$ export FABRIC_CFG_PATH=${PWD}
```

Generating the configuration in one operation

All trade network operations, including the cryptographic material and channel artifact creation commands described previously, are coded in the trade.sh script in the bash folder. From that folder, you can run the following command instead of running all the cryptogen and configtxgen commands listed in the previous sections:

```
$ ./trade.sh generate -c tradechannel -o 3
```

The -o 3 switch indicates that the ThreeOrgsTradeChannel profile ought to be used to generate artifacts for this channel. Although you can specify any channel name here, keep in mind that applications we will develop later in this book rely on the existence of a channel named tradechannel.

(In *Chapter 9, Network Operation and Distributed Application Building*, we will replicate this process to generate a second channel our distributed application will rely on.)

 This script relies on environment variables in the .env file in the bash folder, notably for the name of the orderer system channel using the variable SYS_CHANNEL.

Composing a sample trade network

Within the bash folder lies a network configuration file, docker-compose-e2e.yaml, which is used to start the network as a set of Docker containers using the docker-compose tool. This file depends on base/peer-base.yaml, which contains the base configurations of peer and orderer nodes, and base/docker-compose-base.yaml, which contains specifications derived from the base configurations for each unique peer and orderer container. Collectively, these files specify peers, orderers, and CAs in the form of services and collections of attributes, allowing us to launch them as interconnected Docker containers in one go, rather than having to manually run instances of these services on one or more machines.

The services we need to correspond to our trade network's nodes are:

- Four instances of a Fabric peer, one for each organization
- One instance of a Fabric orderer running in solo mode
- Five instances of a Fabric CA, corresponding to the MSPs of each organization

As mentioned earlier in this chapter, Docker images for each of the above services can be obtained from the Hyperledger project on Docker Hub (https://hub.docker.com/u/hyperledger/), with the images being hyperledger/fabric-peer, hyperledger/fabric-orderer, hyperledger/fabric-ca for peers, orderers, and MSPs, respectively. But if you followed the earlier instructions to download the Fabric source code and run make docker, these images should already be present on your machine.

Peer node configuration

Our base configuration of a peer is as follows (see base/peer-base.yaml):

```
peer-base:
  image: hyperledger/fabric-peer:$IMAGE_TAG
  environment:
    - CORE_VM_ENDPOINT=unix:///host/var/run/docker.sock
    - CORE_VM_DOCKER_HOSTCONFIG_NETWORKMODE=${COMPOSE_PROJECT_NAME}_trade
    - FABRIC_LOGGING_SPEC=INFO
    - CORE_PEER_TLS_ENABLED=true
    - CORE_PEER_GOSSIP_USELEADERELECTION=true
    - CORE_PEER_GOSSIP_ORGLEADER=false
    - CORE_PEER_PROFILE_ENABLED=true
    - CORE_PEER_TLS_CERT_FILE=/etc/hyperledger/fabric/tls/server.crt
    - CORE_PEER_TLS_KEY_FILE=/etc/hyperledger/fabric/tls/server.key
    - CORE_PEER_TLS_ROOTCERT_FILE=/etc/hyperledger/fabric/tls/ca.crt
    - CORE_CHAINCODE_EXECUTETIMEOUT=300s
  working_dir: /opt/gopath/src/github.com/hyperledger/fabric/peer
  command: peer node start
```

The image property indicates the name and tag of the image this peer will be based on. (IMAGE_TAG is defined in .env as 2.2.0. You can change this to use an image of a different version or even set it to latest for images built locally from source.)

Any Fabric peer configuration parameter (more on that later) can be set here using environment variables, but the default configuration in the `fabric-peer` Docker image is sufficient to get a peer service up and running. In the previous configuration, the `CORE_VM_DOCKER_HOSTCONFIG_NETWORKMODE` variable is set to `net_trade` (the environment variable `COMPOSE_PROJECT_NAME` is defined in the `.env` file), which denotes a common bridge network on which peers and smart contracts will run. `FABRIC_LOGGING_SPEC` defines the logging behavior. Here, it's set to `INFO`, which means that only informational, warning, and error messages will be logged. If you wish to debug a peer and need more extensive logging, you can set this variable to `DEBUG`.

`CORE_PEER_TLS_ENABLED` is set to `true`, indicating that the peer will communicate using TLS connections with other services. Other environment variables down the list indicate where TLS certificates and keys are located; these certificates and keys were created using `cryptogen` and will be synced to the peer container at runtime. Other environment variables affect the behavior of the gossip protocol with which this peer will sync ledger data with other peer services.

The command to run the peer service is specified in the last line of the configuration as `peer node start`. If you wish to run a peer by downloading the Fabric source and building it on your local machine (using `make peer`), this is the command you will have to run (see *Chapter 5, Designing Smart Contract Transactions and Ledger Data Structure*, for examples); here the process will run within a peer's container.

Finally, keep in mind that the `GOPATH` environment variable in a peer's container is set to `/opt/gopath` by default. For advanced users, any additions or modifications to the peer code (written in Go) need to be made in the right locations in the filesystem to achieve the desired effect.

We now need to configure the hostnames and ports for each peer and sync the cryptographic material generated (using `cryptogen`) to the container filesystem. As an example, the peer in the exporter organization is configured in `base/docker-compose-base.yaml` as follows:

```
peer0.exporterorg.trade.com:
  container_name: peer0.exporterorg.trade.com
  extends:
    file: peer-base.yaml
    service: peer-base
  environment:
    - CORE_PEER_ID=peer0.exporterorg.trade.com
    - CORE_PEER_ADDRESS=peer0.exporterorg.trade.com:7051
    - CORE_PEER_LISTENADDRESS=0.0.0.0:7051
    - CORE_PEER_CHAINCODEADDRESS=peer0.exporterorg.trade.com:7052
```

```
    - CORE_PEER_CHAINCODELISTENADDRESS=0.0.0.0:7052
    - CORE_PEER_GOSSIP_EXTERNALENDPOINT=peer0.exporterorg.trade.com:7051
    - CORE_PEER_GOSSIP_BOOTSTRAP=peer0.exporterorg.trade.com:7051
    - CORE_PEER_LOCALMSPID=ExporterOrgMSP
  volumes:
    - /var/run/:/host/var/run/
    - ../crypto-config/peerOrganizations/exporterorg.trade.com/peers/
    peer0.exporterorg.trade.com/msp:/etc/hyperledger/fabric/msp
    - ../crypto-config/peerOrganizations/exporterorg.trade.com/peers/
    peer0.exporterorg.trade.com/tls:/etc/hyperledger/fabric/tls
    - peer0.exporterorg.trade.com:/var/hyperledger/production
  ports:
    - 7051:7051
```

As indicated by the extends parameter, this extends the peer-base service we examined earlier. Note that the ID (CORE_PEER_ID) matches the hostname specified for this peer in configtx.yaml in the exporter organization (ExporterOrg). The ID will be used in the application code later in this book. In the volumes section, you can see that the cryptographic material generated in the crypto-config folder is synced (or copied) to the container. In the same section, a local volume (peer0.exporterorg.trade.com) is maintained to save ledger state across peer restarts. This volume is synced to the folder /var/hyperledger/production in the container, which contains state and history information, including the world state snapshot and chain of blocks.

The peer service itself listens on port 7051 and communicates with installed chaincodes (contracts) on port 7052. Two environment variables specify gossip settings, used to sync the ledger state between peers; the BOOTSTRAP variable is used to advertise a peer's address to other peers within the organization and EXTERNALENDPOINT is used to advertise the address to peers in other organizations. The peers are configured to listen on distinct ports (7051/7052, 8051/8052, 9051/9052, 10051/10052) but it's also possible to make the in-container ports identical (for example, to 7051/7052) and map them to distinct ports on the host machine under the ports section. Lastly, note that the MSP ID specified here matches that in configtx.yaml.

Orderer node configuration

The base configuration of the orderer service is similar to that of a peer, as the following snippet from base/peer-base.yaml indicates:

```
orderer.trade.com:
  container_name: orderer.trade.com
  image: hyperledger/fabric-orderer:$IMAGE_TAG
```

```
    environment:
      - FABRIC_LOGGING_SPEC=INFO
      - ORDERER_GENERAL_BOOTSTRAPMETHOD=file
      - ORDERER_GENERAL_BOOTSTRAPFILE=/var/hyperledger/orderer/
      orderer.genesis.block
      - ORDERER_GENERAL_LOCALMSPID=TradeOrdererOrgMSP
      - ORDERER_GENERAL_LOCALMSPDIR=/var/hyperledger/orderer/msp
      - ORDERER_GENERAL_TLS_ENABLED=true
    ......
command: orderer
volumes:
  - ../channel-artifacts/genesis.block:/var/hyperledger/orderer/
  orderer.genesis.block
  ......
```

The single ordering node in our solo ordering service will run in a container that depends on the preceding base configuration and is defined more specifically in `base/docker-compose-base.yaml` as follows:

```
orderer.trade.com:
  container_name: orderer.trade.com
  extends:
    file: peer-base.yaml
    service: orderer-base
  volumes:
    - ../channel-artifacts/genesis.block:/var/hyperledger/orderer/
    orderer.genesis.block
    - ../crypto-config/ordererOrganizations/trade.com/orderers/
    orderer.trade.com/msp:/var/hyperledger/orderer/msp
    - ../crypto-config/ordererOrganizations/trade.com/orderers/
    orderer.trade.com/tls/:/var/hyperledger/orderer/tls
    - orderer.trade.com:/var/hyperledger/production/orderer
  ports:
    - 7050:7050
```

The orderer runs on the `hyperledger/fabric-orderer` Docker image (which we built earlier with the Fabric source code), and the command to start it is simply `orderer`, as the code indicates. The logging level can be configured using the `FABRIC_LOGGING_SPEC` variable and is set to `INFO` in our configuration.

The value of `ORDERER_GENERAL_LOCALMSPID` matches the MSP ID for the ordering service's organization specified in `configtx.yaml`. `ORDERER_GENERAL_BOOTSTRAPMETHOD` indicates that the genesis block is stored in a file, and `ORDERER_GENERAL_BOOTSTRAPFILE` points to the genesis block file with which this ordering service must be bootstrapped; you will notice in the `volumes` section that this block is a copy of the one we generated earlier using `configtxen`. The `ORDERER_GENERAL_TLS_ENABLED` setting indicates that this ordering node will communicate with other network nodes with TLS enabled. A local volume (`orderer.trade.com`) is maintained to save ordering service state across restarts, just as in the case of the peer; this volume is synced to the `/var/hyperledger/production/orderer` folder in the container.

Combined network configuration with peers, orderers, and CAs

Let's now examine our main launch configuration file `docker-compose-e2e.yaml`, which inherits peers and orderers from `base/docker-compose- base.yaml` (and indirectly `base/peer-base.yaml`). As an example, you can see the carrier's peer's configuration by scrolling down the file, as follows:

```
peer0.carrierorg.trade.com:
  container_name: peer0.carrierorg.trade.com
  extends:
    file:  base/docker-compose-base.yaml
    service: peer0.importerorg.trade.com
  networks:
    - trade
```

This peer's container is built on the `peer0.importerorg.trade.com` specification in the `base/docker-compose-base.yaml` file. Note that every service in the `docker-compose-e2e.yaml` file is instructed to connect to the common trade network that is declared at the top of the file as follows:

```
networks:
  trade
```

In addition, `docker-compose-e2e.yaml` contains service specifications for CA nodes representing organizations' MSPs. The following code shows the exporter organization's MSP service configuration:

```
exporter-ca:
  image: hyperledger/fabric-ca:$CA_IMAGE_TAG
  environment:
    - FABRIC_CA_HOME=/etc/hyperledger/fabric-ca-server
    - FABRIC_CA_SERVER_CA_NAME=ca-exporterorg
```

```
    - FABRIC_CA_SERVER_TLS_ENABLED=true
    - FABRIC_CA_SERVER_TLS_CERTFILE=/etc/hyperledger/fabric-ca-
    server-config/ca.exporterorg.trade.com-cert.pem
    - FABRIC_CA_SERVER_TLS_KEYFILE=/etc/hyperledger/fabric-ca-server-
    config/priv_sk
  ports:
    - "7054:7054"
  command: sh -c 'fabric-ca-server start --ca.certfile /etc/
hyperledger/fabric-ca-server-config/ca.exporterorg.trade.com-cert.
pem --ca.keyfile /etc/hyperledger/fabric-ca-server-config/priv_sk -b
admin:adminpw -d'
  volumes:
    - ./crypto- config/peerOrganizations/exporterorg.trade.com/ca/:/
    etc/hyperledger/fabric-ca-server-config
    - ca.exporterorg.trade.com:/etc/hyperledger/fabric-ca-server
  container_name: ca.exporterorg.trade.com
  networks:
    - trade
```

This MSP instance's root CA (we won't use any intermediate CAs in our basic
network) runs in the `hyperledger/fabric-ca` Docker image (which we built using
the Fabric CA source code) of the version set in `CA_IMAGE_TAG` (specified in `.env`).
The command that we will run in it is `fabric-ca-server`, bootstrapped with the
certificates and signing keys created using `cryptogen`, and using the default login
and password (`admin` and `adminpw`, respectively) configured in the `fabric-ca`
container. The command to start an instance of a Fabric CA server is `fabric-ca-
server start...`, as you can see in the preceding code. The service will listen on port
`7054` within the container by default (we don't override this in our configuration), but
as you can see in the `ports` sections of the different CA services, the listening port is
mapped to different ports on the host machine (`7054`, `8054`, `9054`, and `10054`).

These CAs are configured for TLS-based communication, just as the peers were in
the configurations we viewed earlier. The variables `FABRIC_CA_SERVER_TLS_CERTFILE`
and `FABRIC_CA_SERVER_TLS_KEYFILE` refer to a certificate and private signing key
respectively, created earlier using `cryptogen`. The reader must note that if MSPs
of an organization are TLS-enabled, so should its peers be.

As in the peer and orderer configurations, artifacts created using `cryptogen` are
synced to the CA containers in the `volumes` section. To save and reload CA state
across restarts, the `ca.exporterorg.trade.com` volume maintains information synced
to the `/etc/hyperledger/fabric-ca-server` folder in the container.

As you can observe, `docker-compose-e2e.yaml` does not specify a Fabric CA server (and container) for the orderer's organization. For the exercise we will go through in this book, statically created admin users and credentials for the orderer are enough; we will not be registering new orderer organization users dynamically, so a Fabric CA server for the ordering service is not needed.

Network components' configuration files

We have demonstrated how peers, orderers, and CAs can be configured using `docker-compose` YAML files. To summarize, the services and the containers they run in are:

- **Peer**: `peer: hyperledger/fabric-peer`
- **Orderer**: `orderer: hyperledger/fabric-orderer`
- **MSP**: `fabric-ca-server: hyperledger/fabric-ca`

Each of these containers contains packaged code and configurations, including default settings these services are started with. In our YAML files, the environment variables we have examined are meant to override these default settings. Though a detailed description of these configurations is beyond the scope of this book, we will list the respective files and mention how a user may make changes to them.

For a peer, a `core.yaml` file (`https://github.com/hyperledger/fabric/blob/release-2.2/sampleconfig/core.yaml`) contains all of the important runtime settings, including but not limited to addresses, port numbers, security and privacy, and the gossip protocol. You can create your own custom `core.yaml` file and sync it to the container using Docker volumes or even create a custom `hyperledger/fabric-peer` image; these exercises are left to the reader. You can log in to a running peer container using the following command:

```
$ docker exec -it <container-id> bash
```

You need to replace `<container-id>` with an active ID. For examples, see the next section. You will find the `core.yaml` file in the folder `/etc/hyperledger/fabric/`.

Similarly, an orderer's default configuration lies in an `orderer.yaml` file (`https://github.com/hyperledger/fabric/blob/release-2.2/sampleconfig/orderer.yaml`), which is also synced to `/etc/hyperledger/fabric/` in the container running the `hyperledger/fabric-orderer` image. As in the case of a `core.yaml` file, a custom `orderer.yaml` file must be synced to an orderer container using Docker volumes, or a custom image must be built with this YAML file.

A Fabric CA server also has a configuration file called `fabric-ca-server-config.yaml` (`http://hyperledger-fabric-ca.readthedocs.io/en/latest/serverconfig.html`), which is synced to `/etc/hyperledger/fabric-ca-server/` on the container running the `hyperledger/fabric-ca` image. You can create and sync custom configurations as you would for a peer or an orderer, and also set different administrator names and passwords than the default `admin` and `adminpw`.

Configuring peer databases

By default, a Fabric peer is configured to use an embedded instance of LevelDB as the default ledger state database. LevelDB generally performs faster and is adequate for a variety of query types typically used in Fabric contracts, but it does not support certain kinds of richer query features. For peers running contracts that require such rich query support, Fabric offers the option of using CouchDB instead of LevelDB. As you will see in later chapters, contracts running on peers belonging to the `TradeConsortium` organizations need such support, and hence we need to augment those peers' configurations to use CouchDB. We do this using the Compose file `docker-compose-couchdb.yaml`. The following snippet illustrates how the exporter organization's peer is augmented:

```
couchdb-peer0.exporterorg.trade.com:
  container_name: couchdb-peer0.exporterorg.trade.com
  image: couchdb:2.3
  environment:
    - COUCHDB_USER=
    - COUCHDB_PASSWORD=
  ports:
    - "5984:5984"
  networks:
    - trade
peer0.exporterorg.trade.com:
  environment:
    - CORE_LEDGER_STATE_STATEDATABASE=CouchDB
    - CORE_LEDGER_STATE_COUCHDBCONFIG_COUCHDBADDRESS=
    couchdb-peer0.exporterorg.trade.com:5984
    - CORE_LEDGER_STATE_COUCHDBCONFIG_USERNAME=
    - CORE_LEDGER_STATE_COUCHDBCONFIG_PASSWORD=
  depends_on:
    - couchdb-peer0.exporterorg.trade.com
```

The service `couchdb-peer0.exporterorg.trade.com` represents the CouchDB instance backing the exporter organization's peer running in its own instance. This is based on the `couchdb` image (version 2.3), which is available on Docker Hub. The default username and password are set to blank. By default, the database instance is configured to listen on port 5984, which is mapped to 5984 on the host machine too. CouchDB instances for other peers are mapped to 6984 and 7984 respectively, as you can see by scrolling down the file.

The preceding peer service configuration is only an augmentation of the service in `docker-compose-e2e.yaml`, and hence does not contain `container_name` and `networks` sections. The variable `CORE_LEDGER_STATE_STATEDATABASE` overrides the default database type, and `CORE_LEDGER_STATE_COUCHDBCONFIG_COUCHDBADDRESS` points the peer to the appropriate CouchDB service. The internal port 5984 is specified here rather than the one mapped to the host; this will work because the service name (`couchdb-peer0.exporterorg.trade.com`) specified is unique to the database instance. The username and password values must match those the CouchDB service is configured with; here they are blanks, but readers may use other values on their target machines.

So far, we have created a Docker network configuration and generated channel artifacts and cryptographic material. In the next section, we'll launch our network.

Launching a sample trade network

To launch the sample trade network, all we need to do is start the network using the `docker-compose` command, as follows:

```
$ docker-compose -f docker-compose-e2e.yaml -f docker-compose-couchdb.yaml up
```

You can run this as a background process and redirect the standard output to a log file if you so choose. Otherwise, you will see the various containers starting up and logs from all of them displayed on the console.

To run the basic network using the preceding command and to develop applications in later chapters, ensuring cross-connectivity between services running in various containers is crucial. For this, you may need to map the various container names to the localhost IP address in your host machine's HOSTS file. For example, on a Linux machine, you can add the following entries to /etc/hosts:

```
127.0.0.1        orderer.trade.com
127.0.0.1        peer0.exporterorg.trade.com
127.0.0.1        peer0.importerorg.trade.com
127.0.0.1        peer0.carrierorg.trade.com
127.0.0.1        peer0.regulatororg.trade.com
127.0.0.1        ca.exporterorg.trade.com
127.0.0.1        ca.importerorg.trade.com
127.0.0.1        ca.carrierorg.trade.com
127.0.0.1        ca.regulatororg.trade.com
```

Setting Fabric up can be tricky on some OS configurations. If you run into problems, consult the documentation. A detailed description of how to install a Fabric network and examples is provided at https://hyperledger-fabric.readthedocs.io/en/latest/getting_started.html.

To launch the network with our all-purpose script, simply run:

```
$ ./trade.sh up
```

This starts the Docker network in the background, redirecting container logs into a file logs/network.log by default. You can redirect logs to a different file by adding the optional switch -l <log-file-name> to the preceding command. (This command also starts CouchDB containers for TradeConsortium peers by default; if you wish the peers to use their built-in LevelDB instances, just add the switch -s leveldb to the command.) To view the list of running containers, run the following command from a different terminal window:

```
$ docker ps -a
```

You will see something like the following:

```
CONTAINER ID          IMAGE                             COMMAND            CREATED
  STATUS                PORTS                                            NAMES
56fbc6e92cc2          hyperledger/fabric-peer:2.2.0     "peer node start"      4 minutes ago
  Up 4 minutes          7051/tcp, 0.0.0.0:10051->10051/tcp                peer0.regulatororg.trade.com
1b048d622b4c          hyperledger/fabric-peer:2.2.0     "peer node start"      4 minutes ago
  Up 4 minutes          7051/tcp, 0.0.0.0:8051->8051/tcp                  peer0.importerorg.trade.com
6b8919f83d33          hyperledger/fabric-peer:2.2.0     "peer node start"      4 minutes ago
  Up 4 minutes          0.0.0.0:7051->7051/tcp                            peer0.exporterorg.trade.com
b59a376c5639          couchdb:2.3                       "tini -- /docker-ent…" 4 minutes ago
  Up 4 minutes          4369/tcp, 9100/tcp, 0.0.0.0:7984->5984/tcp  couchdb-peer0.regulatororg.trade.
com
349e1ff13382          couchdb:2.3                       "tini -- /docker-ent…" 4 minutes ago
  Up 4 minutes          4369/tcp, 9100/tcp, 0.0.0.0:5984->5984/tcp  couchdb-peer0.exporterorg.trade.c
om
c6cce0746f7f          hyperledger/fabric-ca:1.4.8       "sh -c 'fabric-ca-se…" 4 minutes ago
  Up 4 minutes          7054/tcp, 0.0.0.0:10054->10054/tcp                ca.regulatororg.trade.com
11b91c51cb85          hyperledger/fabric-ca:1.4.8       "sh -c 'fabric-ca-se…" 4 minutes ago
  Up 4 minutes          7054/tcp, 0.0.0.0:8054->8054/tcp                  ca.importerorg.trade.com
eec812d376ee          hyperledger/fabric-ca:1.4.8       "sh -c 'fabric-ca-se…" 4 minutes ago
  Up 4 minutes          0.0.0.0:7054->7054/tcp                            ca.exporterorg.trade.com
8f29b732f63b          hyperledger/fabric-peer:2.2.0     "peer node start"      4 minutes ago
  Up 4 minutes          7051/tcp, 0.0.0.0:9051->9051/tcp                  peer0.carrierorg.trade.com
1db3793c8121          hyperledger/fabric-orderer:2.2.0  "orderer"              4 minutes ago
  Up 4 minutes          0.0.0.0:7050->7050/tcp                            orderer.trade.com
297b49e50605          hyperledger/fabric-ca:1.4.8       "sh -c 'fabric-ca-se…" 4 minutes ago
  Up 4 minutes          7054/tcp, 0.0.0.0:9054->9054/tcp                  ca.carrierorg.trade.com
8bbc2791a244          couchdb:2.3                       "tini -- /docker-ent…" 4 minutes ago
  Up 4 minutes          4369/tcp, 9100/tcp, 0.0.0.0:6984->5984/tcp  couchdb-peer0.importerorg.trade.c
om
```

Figure 4.9: List of Docker containers for our running network's components

In *Figure 4.9*, we see four peers, three CouchDB instances, four MSPs, and an orderer running in separate containers. You can identify them both by the image names and the launch commands. Our trade network is now up and ready to run our applications!

To view the running logs of a single container, note the container ID (the first column in the preceding list) and simply run:

```
$ docker logs <container-ID>
```

You can use the script for other operations as well. To bring down the network, run:

```
$ ./trade.sh down
```

This, in effect, emulates the following `docker-compose` command (it also includes other Compose files not mentioned, but which we will describe in later chapters):

```
$ docker-compose -f docker-compose-e2e.yaml -f docker-compose-couchdb.
yaml down
```

The network artifacts (genesis block, channel and anchor peer configurations, cryptographic material) remain intact after you run this, as do the container images (those we created earlier and new ones we will create for smart contracts later in this book). To just delete contract images and other temporary images created during the build process, run:

```
$ ./trade.sh reset
```

To delete channel artifacts and smart contract containers and to start from scratch using existing cryptographic credentials, run:

```
$ ./trade.sh clean
```

To start from scratch after deleting cryptographic credentials in addition to channel artifacts and containers, run:

```
$ ./trade.sh cleanall
```

After running `clean` or `cleanall`, you will need to regenerate the artifacts using `./trade.sh generate` and launch another instance of the network.

The `trade.sh` script presents other options, which we will discuss in *Chapter 9, Network Operation and Distributed Application Building*, and *Chapter 12, Governance - A Necessary Evil of Regulated Industries*.

Configuring our development environment for network operations

Our final task in this chapter is to get our application development environment, namely VS Code using the IBP extension, connected to the network we just launched. This is a two-step process:

1. First, we will create and load identity wallets for all our network participants in VS Code.
2. Next, we will create an environment for trade network operations and connect to the running network using identities from these wallets.

Creating Fabric identity wallets

If you do not have VS Code already running, restart it. On an Ubuntu Linux machine, this can be done by running the `code` command. Navigate to the IBP extension by selecting the appropriate tab from the left-hand menu. Now focus on the **FABRIC WALLETS** panel at the bottom left of the main view, which may contain wallets for the organizations of the **1 Org Local Fabric** environment we tested earlier, or be empty as follows (if you tore down the environment):

Figure 4.10: The FABRIC WALLETS panel shows no configured wallets

Now we will create wallets for the nodes in our network and add keys and certificates to them. VS Code will subsequently use these credentials to connect to our running trade network.

You can create wallets at any desired granularity but here we will create one representing each organization. To create a wallet for the orderer, run the following steps:

1. Move your mouse over the **FABRIC WALLETS** header and then over the **+** button. You should see an **Add Wallet** popup. Click the **+** button.

2. Select **Create a new wallet and add an identity** in the menu at the top middle of the window.

3. Enter a name for the wallet and press *Enter*. Let's enter the name `Trade Orderer Wallet`.

4. Provide a name for the identity the orderer node will use in our environment and press *Enter*. This needs to be a signing identity (a certificate and key pair) for an orderer node in the orderer's organization (`TradeOrdererOrg`, as specified in `configtx.yaml`). Let's use the name `trade_orderer`.

5. Enter the MSP ID. This should correspond to the `ID` attribute in the `TradeOrdererOrg` section in `configtx.yaml`: `TradeOrdererOrgMSP`.

6. Select **Provide certificate and private key files**.

7. Select **Browse**.

8. In the file selector dialog box, navigate to the `crypto-config` folder that was created using `cryptogen` earlier in this chapter.

9. Then navigate to the folder `ordererOrganizations/trade.com/users/Admin\@ trade.com/msp/signcerts/` and select the certificate file `Admin@trade.com-cert.pem`.

10. Select **Browse** again and navigate to `crypto-config/ordererOrganizations/ trade.com/users/Admin\@trade.com/msp/keystore/`. You should see a single file named `priv_sk`, which contains the private signing key. Select this file.

11. View logs in the **Output** window after selecting **Blockchain** from the drop-down menu. You should see messages saying `Successfully added identity` and `Successfully added a new wallet`.

In the **FABRIC WALLETS** panel, you should now see the following:

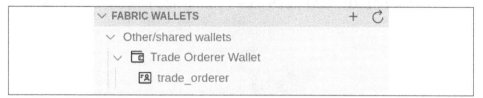

Figure 4.11: A Fabric wallet configured for the trade network's ordering service's organization

Now we will create a wallet for the CA and the peer node in the exporter's organization:

1. Move your mouse over the **FABRIC WALLETS** header and click the **+** button.

2. Select **Create a new wallet and add an identity** in the menu at the top middle of the window.

3. Let's use **Exporter Wallet** for the wallet's name followed by exporter_ca for the name of the identity.

4. Specify the MSP ID as ExporterOrgMSP, as is specified in configtx.yaml.

5. Select **Provide certificate and private key files**, followed by **Browse**.

6. Navigate to crypto-config/peerOrganizations/exporterorg.trade.com/ca/ and select the certificate file ca.exporterorg.trade.com-cert.pem.

7. Select **Browse**, and navigate to the same folder and select the private key file named priv_sk.

8. You should see messages saying Successfully added identity and Successfully added a new wallet in the logs. An exporter wallet has now been created, and an identity for the CA node has been added to it.

9. To add an identity for the peer to this wallet, right-click the **Exporter Wallet** entry in the **FABRIC WALLETS** panel. Select **Add Identity to Wallet**.

10. Let's use exporter_admin as the identity to associate with the peer.

11. Specify ExporterOrgMSP as the MSP ID.

12. Select **Provide certificate and private key files**, followed by **Browse**.

13. Navigate to crypto-config/peerOrganizations/exporterorg.trade.com/ users/Admin\@exporterorg.trade.com/msp/signcerts/ and select the certificate file Admin@exporterorg.trade.com-cert.pem.

14. Select **Browse** and navigate to crypto-config/peerOrganizations/ exporterorg.trade.com/users/Admin\@exporterorg.trade.com/msp/ keystore/. Select the private key file named priv_sk.

15. You should see a message saying `Successfully added identity` in the logs. In the **FABRIC WALLETS** panel, you should now see the following:

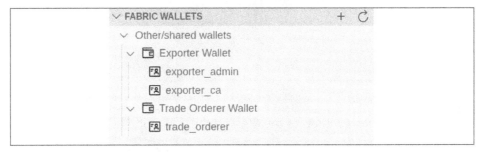

Figure 4.12: Wallets configured for the ordering service's and the exporter's organizations

Now repeat the preceding exercise for the remaining three organizations, selecting the appropriate certificate and key files. After the successful creation of wallets and identities, you should see something like the following in the **FABRIC WALLETS** panel:

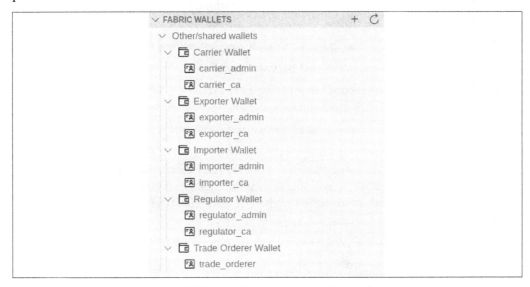

Figure 4.13: Wallets for all the trade network's organizations

As you can see in *Figure 4.13*, you can see the names we have used for the wallets and identities. Next, we'll create a Fabric environment to represent our network.

Creating a Fabric environment

In this section, we will create a Fabric environment to represent our running trade network in the VS Code IDE.

Creating a node file

Before creating the environment, we need to create a node JSON file representing the network's nodes and their connectivity specifications. A description of this file and how it ought to be created is provided in the official documentation at `https://marketplace.visualstudio.com/items?itemName=IBMBlockchain.ibm-blockchain-platform`. Here we will work with a more relevant example. A sample node JSON file for our trade network is given in `bash/samples/node.json` in the repository. You can see that the file contains an array of nine nodes, namely one orderer, four peers, and four CAs. The orderer node is specified as follows:

```
{
    "name": "orderer.trade.com",
    "msp_id": "TradeOrdererOrgMSP",
    "api_url": "grpcs://localhost:7050",
    "type": "fabric-orderer",
    "ssl_target_name_override": "orderer.trade.com",
    "pem": "LS0tLS1CRUdJTiBDRVJUSUZJQ0FURS0tLS0tCk1JSUNPekNDQWVHZ0F3SU-
JBZ0lRQ2duSktBBTHJhUlE4Ym1tMEJHNVlPakFLQmdncWhrak9QUVFEQWpCb01Rc3cKQ1FZ-
RFZRUUdFd0pwWVXpFVE1CRUdBMVVFQ0JNS1EyRnNhV1p2Y201cFlURVdNQlFHQTFFVRUJ4TU-
5VMkZ1SUVaaeQpZVzVqVVVhOamJ6RVNNQkFHQTFVRUNoTUpkSEphWkdUdVkyOXRNUmd3Rm-
dZRFZRUURFdzkwYkhoOalllTNTBjbUZrClpTTNpbWJMjB3SGhjTk1Ua3hNak14TVRRFeE5qQX-
dXaGGNOTWpreE1qSTRNVEV4TmpBZd1dqQm9NUXN3Q1FZRFZRUUcKRXdKVlV6NFVRVNQkVHQT-
FVRUNTUtRMkZzYVdadmNtNXBZVEVVTUJRROExVUVCeE1OVTJGdU1FWlZlVVvQVhOag-
piekVTTUJBROEVUVVUDaE1KZEhKaFpnVXVZMmjl0TVJNdZ0nWURWUVFERXc5MGJITmpZU-
zUwY21Ga1pTTNWpiMjB3Q1dUQVRCZ2NxaGtqT1BRU1JJCZ2dxaGtqT1BRTUJDd05DQUFRRb-
2k1MDhrU3hQY1RNb3J5cGM1Z1V3V3dhWGx6OUEKaEFFJUK1XcjZEKzlYZ1JlNTVjQXIrN-
HhZWjJmWlJYUUJMQlp1b1Yxd3dENE9BajllelM4ZjJjM2lvMjB3YXpBBTwpCZ05WSFE4Qk-
FmOEVCQU1DQWFZd0hRWURWUjBsQkpZd0ZBWUlLd1l1CQlFVSEF3SUdDDQ3NHQVFFVRkJ3TU-
JNQThHHHCkExVWRFd0VCL3dRRk1BTUJBZjh3S1FZRFZSME9CQ01FUUthUHF0NXh0Sk9OcjU-
weEl3L2pvWVI4blVRNk40TTIIKL0tmQnBBENG5TTklLTUFyQ0NDUdTTTQ5QkFGQQ0EwZ0F-
NRVVVDSVFFM0I0dU1uVmN2dGExeGGdoQytYRzR3Q3lsQ0PjWWk5UzRvY1FPVnpaaSDI1L-
1FJZ2JyaUx1OE12bEz2S3ZRcVpGVU40ZjdFQ1RaM3BjjOEhIZmF5bE52akUyUG89Ci0tL-
S0tRU5EIENFUlJRklDQVRFLS0tLS0K"
}
```

The `name`, `msp_id`, and `api_url` values are drawn from `configtx.yaml`. `api_url` and should be modified depending on where you are running your Docker network. The `type` for an orderer node should be set to `fabric-orderer`. The last two attributes need to be used only if TLS is enabled in the orderer. The `ssl_target_name_override` field should be set to the same value as the hostname of the orderer node's container. The `pem` field is a base64-encoding of the contents of the TLS CA's certificate file. In our generated `crypto-config` folder, this is `ordererOrganizations/trade.com/msp/tlscacerts/tlsca.trade.com-cert.pem`. (Note that `crypto-config/ordererOrganizations/trade.com/msp` is the value specified in the `MSPDir` field in the organization's configuration in `configtx.yaml`.)

The peers' JSON configurations should be easy to understand now as they are similar to the orderer's configuration. The certificate file for the exporter's peer, for example, can be found in `crypto-config/peerOrganizations/exporterorg.trade.com/msp/tlscacerts/tlsca.exporterorg.trade.com-cert.pem`.

The CAs' configurations are slightly different. Here is the exporter organization's CA:

```
{
    "name": "ca.exporterorg.trade.com",
    "ca_name": "ca.exporterorg.trade.com",
    "api_url": "https://localhost:7054",
    "type": "fabric-ca",
    "enroll_id": "admin",
    "enroll_secret": "adminpw"
}
```

The `api_url` field requires an `https` rather than a `grpcs` URL. For peers as well as the CA, the ports should be identical to those specified in the Docker Compose files we used to launch the network. The CA enrollment ID and password should be what `fabric-ca-server` was bootstrapped with, as we discussed earlier in this chapter.

To create a JSON node file representing the network (and certificates) we created in this chapter, we can use a simple Node.js program `bash/scripts/gen-node-file.js`. The information needed to generate a node file can be found in the `configtx.yaml` file and the set of Docker Compose files we used to launch the network. But since Docker Compose files can be coded in arbitrary ways and it can be difficult to parse them, we have instead extracted the relevant information into a JSON file `bash/network_defaults.json`. We only need to list the four user organizations here (excluding the orderer organization), indexed by their names as specified in `configtx.yaml`. See the carrier organization's configuration as an example:

```
"CarrierOrg": {
    "peer_ports": [
        {
            "peer0": 9051
        }
    ],
    "cas": [
        {
            "port": 9054,
            "admin_user": "admin",
            "admin_password": "adminpw"
        }
    ]
}
```

As you can see, we have specified a list of ports the different peer services are listening on and also a list of ports the different Fabric CA servers are listening on. For the CA servers, we additionally supply the enrollment username and password they are bootstrapped with. All this information can be extracted from the Docker Compose files we inspected earlier in this chapter. (This JSON structure supports multiple peers and CAs in each organization, but we only have one each in our initial trade network.)

Our script depends on the existence of two files in the bash folder: `configtx.yaml` and `network_defaults.json`. To generate the node JSON file, run the following commands:

```
$ cd scripts
$ npm install
$ node gen-node-file.js > trade_network_node.json
```

A node file `trade_network_node.json` is created in the `scripts` folder that resembles `samples/node.json` in structure.

Creating and connecting to a Fabric environment in VS Code

Now, let's create the environment for our trade network as follows.

 Before you complete the following setup, make sure the nine-node Docker network we launched earlier in this chapter is still running:

1. Move your mouse over the **FABRIC ENVIRONMENTS** header and click the **+** button (you should see an **Add Environment** popup).

2. Select the method **Add any other Fabric network (by providing node JSON files)**.

3. Enter a name for the environment. Let's use the name `Trade Network`.

4. Select **Browse** and navigate to the node file `trade_network_node.json` created earlier. Select that file.

5. Select **Done adding nodes**. (You can also create and import multiple node files with sections of the network in each file, but here we chose to create just one.)

You should see the following in the **FABRIC ENVIRONMENTS** panel:

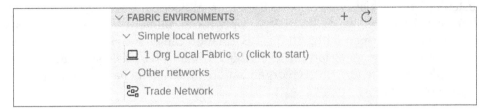

Figure 4.14: An environment created to represent the trade network

You should also see messages in the logs saying `Successfully imported nodes` and `Successfully added a new environment`.

6. Click **Trade Network**. In the output logs, you will see a message: `You must complete setup for this environment to enable install, instantiate and register identity operations on the nodes. Click each node in the list to perform the required setup steps`. In the panel, you will see a list of network nodes displayed as follows:

Figure 4.15: The setup requirements for the Trade Network environment

7. To set up the carrier organization's CA, click `ca.carrierorg.trade.com`.

8. Select **Choose an existing identity** to select one of the identities we have already created in our wallets.

9. Select **Carrier Wallet** followed by `carrier_ca`. Then select **No** as this identity is used only for the carrier organization's CA node. You will see the `ca.carrierorg.trade.com` entry disappear from the list in the panel. In the output logs, you will see the message `Successfully associated identity carrier_ca from wallet Carrier Wallet with node ca.carrierorg.trade.com`.

10. Repeat this process for all the other CAs, selecting the appropriate identities.

11. To set up the orderer node, click `orderer.trade.com`.

12. Select **Trade Orderer Wallet** followed by `trade_orderer`. Then select **No**. You will see the `orderer.trade.com` entry disappear from the list in the panel.

13. To set up the carrier organization's peer, click `peer0.carrierorg.trade.com`.

14. Select **Carrier Wallet** followed by `carrier_admin`. Then select **No**. You will see the `peer0.carrierorg.trade.com` entry disappear from the list in the panel.

15. Repeat this process for all the other peers, selecting the appropriate identities.

You should see the following message in the output logs: `Connected to Trade Network`. The **FABRIC ENVIRONMENTS** panel should now display the following:

Figure 4.16: A successful connection to the running Trade Network

As you can see above, the environment in VS Code now recognizes the various nodes and organizations in our running trade network. There are no channels and smart contracts in the network yet. We will show how to develop and configure those in the next few chapters.

Congratulations, your network setup is now complete, both on your target machine and in the development environment! Now we can move up the stack to application development.

Summary

In this chapter, we introduced the business use case that the following chapters will leverage to create a context around the code we will write. We have also deployed our first Hyperledger Fabric network and have now transitioned from theory to practice. Well done!

The next few chapters will take you through the development of a blockchain application from the bottom up: (1) smart contracts using Java, Node.js, and developer tools, and (2) higher-layer business applications using the Fabric Gateway SDK and VS Code.

Through this exercise, we hope to give you an understanding of the flexibility of the solution and the ability to leverage each tool in the right context. To get ready for the next chapter, you should now stop your network using ./trade.sh down.

5

Designing Smart Contract Transactions and Ledger Data Structures

In Hyperledger Fabric, a **smart contract**, sometimes referred to as *chaincode* or just *contract*, is written by a developer. A contract implements a business logic agreed upon by stakeholders of the blockchain network. The functionality is exposed to client applications for them to invoke, provided they have the correct permissions.

A contract runs as an independent process in its own container, isolated from the other components of the Fabric network. An endorsing peer manages the lifecycle of the contract and of the transaction invocations. In response to client invocations, the contract queries the ledger and generates a transactions proposal.

Fabric provides Contract APIs for the development of contracts in three languages of Go, Java, and Node.js (JavaScript or TypeScript). In the first edition of this book published along with Fabric 1.2, we focused on the development of contracts in Go. The APIs and mechanisms are valid in the current version 2.2 and have been further extended to include new functionality. In this edition we will learn how to develop contracts in Java and Node.js, as these are popular among developers. We will implement the business logic of the smart contracts of the scenario presented in *Chapter 4*, *Setting the Stage with a Business Scenario*, and explore the key concepts and libraries necessary for developing a fully functional contract.

In this chapter, we will be covering the following topics:

- Creating a contract in the VS Code IDE
- Using the VS Code IDE for contract execution and debugging
- Access control
- Implementing contract functions
- Testing contracts in the terminal and with the VS Code IDE
- Contract design topics
- Logging output

Architecture of the trade solution

First, let's look at the architecture of the trade finance solution. In *Figure 5.1*, we can see that the blockchain network consists of two channels, **Trade Channel** and **Shipping Channel**, and that each of the channels hosts two contracts: the trade channel hosts **Trade Contract** and **Letter of Credit Contract** contracts, and the shipping channel hosts **Export License Contract** and **Shipment Contract** contracts. Each contract is designed for a specific business domain, controls the lifecycle of a specific asset type, and can be invoked only by authorized participant roles. For an illustration of the language capabilities and Fabric cross-channel interoperability, each channel hosts one contract implemented in Java and the other in Node.js (specifically in the TypeScript version of JavaScript). The channel configurations and setup procedures will be covered in *Chapter 9, Network Operation and Distributed Application Building*, following on from the procedure outlined in *Chapter 4, Setting the Stage with a Business Scenario*.

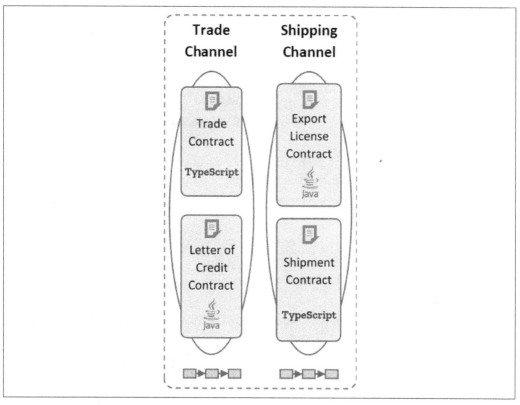

Figure 5.1: Architecture of the Trade Network with channels and contracts

We will talk about the applications, channel operations, and network management in *Chapter 9, Network Operation and Distributed Application Building.*

The following table shows the types of assets managed by each contract:

TradeContract	LetterOfCreditContract	ExportLicenseContract	ShipmentContract
TradeAgreement	LetterOfCredit	ExportLicense	Shipment
TradeAgreementStatus	BankAccount		ShipmentLocation

In the context of the workflow shown in *Figure 4.4* in *Chapter 4, Setting the Stage with a Business Scenario*, the steps map to the contacts as follows:

1. `TradeContract`: The importer requests goods from the exporter in exchange for money.

2. `TradeContract`: The exporter accepts the trade deal.

3. `LetterOfCreditContract`: The importer asks its bank for a letter of credit in favor of the exporter.

4. `LetterOfCreditContract`: The importer's bank supplies a letter of credit in favor of the exporter, payable to the latter's bank.

5. `LetterOfCreditContract`: The exporter's bank accepts the letter of credit on behalf of the exporter.

6. `ExportLicenseContract`: The exporter applies for an export license from the regulatory authority.

7. `ExportLicenseContract`: The regulatory authority supplies an export license to the exporter.

8. `ShipmentContract`: The exporter prepares a shipment and hands it off to the carrier.

9. `ShipmentContract`: The carrier accepts the goods (optionally, after validating the export license) and then supplies a banking license to the exporter.

10. `LetterOfCreditContract`: The exporter's bank claims half the payment from the importer's bank.

11. `LetterOfCreditContract`: The importer's bank transfers half the amount to the exporter's bank.

12. `ShipmentContract`: The carrier ships the goods to the destination.

13. `LetterOfCreditContract`: The importer's bank pays the remaining amount to the exporter's bank.

As a general rule, when a contract requires data from an asset managed by another contract, the requesting contract will invoke the asset-managing contract to obtain the data. However, in our example network of two channels, four contracts, and several peers this approach increases the number of instances of contract containers on each peer (and thus the amount of memory required to run the network). Therefore, in some cases when two dependent contracts run on the same channel, the asset data is retrieved directly from the ledger and not through the contract-to-contract call. This solution allows you to keep the amount of memory needed to run the network reasonable for a typical developer workstation. Note that this is intended only for demonstration purposes and a production solution should follow the design of separation of concerns.

This approach is used to simplify the dependency between `ShipmentContract` and `ExportLicenseContract`. In this case, the `ShipmentContract` does not require the issuance of `ExportLicence` in *Step 7* by `ExportLicenseContract` prior to preparing a `Shipment` in *Step 8*.

In the following sections, we will show code examples in both the Java and Node.js languages and limit to one example contract specific parts of the code.

> While in the next sections we will explore snippets of code related to the concepts, you can get a complete implementation of the contracts at the following address:
>
> `https://github.ibm.com/Hyperledger-Book-2nd-Edition/`
> `trade-contracts/`

Within the repository, artifacts of each contract are placed in a separate folder: `exportLicense`, `letterOfCredit`, `shipment`, and `trade`.

> These can be synchronized as submodules to the `contracts` folder within the `trade-network` repository.
>
> We have two versions of the contracts, one in the `v1` folder and another in the `v2` folder. We need two versions to demonstrate upgrades later in *Chapter 13, Life in a Blockchain Network*. In this chapter, we use the `v1` version to demonstrate how to write contracts.

Starting the contract development

The steps of setting up the VS Code IDE development environment and cloning the source code of the scenario have been explained in *Chapter 4, Setting the Stage with a Business Scenario*. We will now learn how to open, run, and debug the code of the trade contract implemented in TypeScript, and then proceed to detailed contract implementation.

In the following exercises, we will use the IBM Blockchain Platform extension of VS Code. At the time of writing, the extension supporting Fabric v2.x is still in beta version. If at the time of practicing these exercises a release supporting v2.x is not yet available, you can use the latest beta version available at the following page:

`https://github.com/IBM-Blockchain/blockchain-VSCode-extension/releases`

Chapter 9, Network Operation and Distributed Application Building, provides details on setting up the IBM Blockchain Platform extension beta version.

Opening and packaging a contract

In this first exercise, we open the `trade` contract project and package it into a deployable package file:

1. Start VS Code.

2. Choose **File** and **Open...** and select a directory containing the cloned `trade` contract.

3. Disable the access control mechanism.

   The `trade` contract implementation contains an access control mechanism enforcing access control rules prior to the invocation of functions. In order to execute and debug the code in the development environment, we need to disable this part of the code by commenting out the content of the function `beforeTransaction` in the file `trade-contract.ts`. Later in this chapter, we will include and run this code uncommented as part of our tests:

```
public async beforeTransaction(ctx: Context) {
    /*const mspId = ctx.clientIdentity.getMSPID();
    let role = ctx.clientIdentity.getAttributeValue(BUSINESS_ROLE);
    if (!role) {
        role = 'any';
    }
    const tx = ctx.stub.getFunctionAndParameters().fcn;

    const aclSubject = TradeContract.getAclSubject(mspId, role);
    if (!this.aclRules.hasOwnProperty(aclSubject)) {
        throw new Error(`The participant belonging to MSP ${mspId} and role ${role} is not recognized`);
    }

    if (!this.aclRules[aclSubject].includes(tx)) {
        throw new Error(`The participant belonging to MSP ${mspId} and role ${role} cannot invoke transaction ${tx}`)
    }*/
}
```

Figure 5.2: Commented out the access control mechanism of contract

4. Next, on the left menu choose **IBM Blockchain Platform**.

   VS Code will automatically download and start the local Fabric network named **1 Org Local Fabric**. After the initial setup and start, the **OUTPUT** window should contain the following records:

Figure 5.3: Connection to local network

5. In the **SMART CONTRACTS** window, choose **Package Open Project**.

   In this step, VS Code executes npm and packages the contract. After the execution the **OUTPUT** window should contain the following records:

```
OUTPUT   TERMINAL   DEBUG CONSOLE   PROBLEMS                                    Blockchain
[10/6/2020 7:09:04 PM] [INFO] - src/Makefile
[10/6/2020 7:09:04 PM] [INFO] - src/META-INF/statedb/couchdb/indexes/exporterIndex.json
[10/6/2020 7:09:04 PM] [INFO] - src/META-INF/statedb/couchdb/indexes/importerIndex.json
[10/6/2020 7:09:04 PM] [INFO] - src/META-INF/statedb/couchdb/indexes/regulatorIndex.json
[10/6/2020 7:09:04 PM] [INFO] - src/package-lock.json
[10/6/2020 7:09:04 PM] [INFO] - src/package.json
[10/6/2020 7:09:04 PM] [INFO] - src/src/index.ts
[10/6/2020 7:09:04 PM] [INFO] - src/src/trade-contract.spec.ts
[10/6/2020 7:09:04 PM] [INFO] - src/src/trade-contract.ts
[10/6/2020 7:09:04 PM] [INFO] - src/src/tradeagreement.ts
[10/6/2020 7:09:04 PM] [INFO] - src/src/tradeagreementhistory.ts
[10/6/2020 7:09:04 PM] [INFO] - src/src/tradeagreementstatus.ts
[10/6/2020 7:09:04 PM] [INFO] - META-INF/statedb/couchdb/indexes/exporterIndex.json
[10/6/2020 7:09:04 PM] [INFO] - META-INF/statedb/couchdb/indexes/importerIndex.json
[10/6/2020 7:09:04 PM] [INFO] - META-INF/statedb/couchdb/indexes/regulatorIndex.json
```

Figure 5.4: Output of the packaging trade contract

After completion of this sequence, we have a versioned package containing the trade contract and all related artifacts. The **SMART CONTRACTS** window now contains **trade@1.0.0**:

Figure 5.5: Packaged trade contact

Deploying a contract in the testing environment

In the next exercise, we deploy the contract package into the test network and make it available for execution and debug:

1. In the **IBM Blockchain Platform** window **FABRIC ENVIRONMENTS**, under **mychannel**, select **Deploy smart contract**:

Figure 5.6. Deploy smart contract wizard

This will open the **Deploy smart contract** wizard.

2. On the **Step 1** tab, in the **Choose a smart contract to deploy** combo, choose the **trade@1.0.0** option and select **Next**.

3. On the **Step 2** tab, in the **Smart contract definition** combo, choose **trade**. For debugging purposes, we will use the default endorsement policy and thus we do not need to change the **Endorsement policy** text box, so select **Next**.

4. On the **Step 3** tab, we can see the overview of the deployment configuration and proceed by selecting **Deploy**.

    After completion of the deployment process, the trade contract is deployed into the testing network. The **FABRIC ENVIRONMENTS** window, under **mychannel**, now contains an item, **trade@1.0.0**:

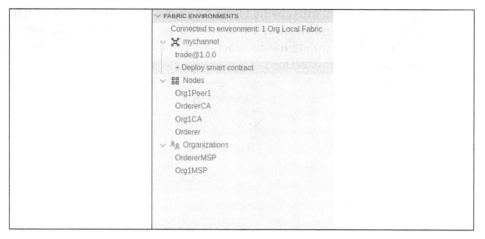

Figure 5.7: Deployed trade contract

5. To invoke functions of the contract, we need to first create a gateway to the local network.

In the **FABRIC GATEWAYS** window, under **1 Org Local Fabric**, click on **Org1**, and select credential **org1Admin** from the **Command Palette**.

Once the gateway is connected, it shows the list of channels, contracts, and functions as follows:

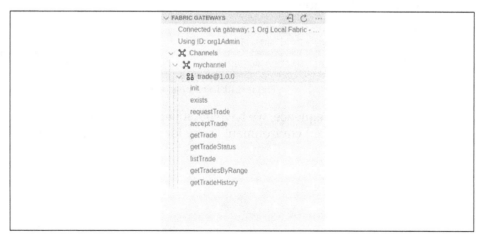

Figure 5.8: Gateway to the local network

6. Next, the contract must be instantiated on the channel. In the **FABRIC GATEWAYS** window, under **trade@1.0.0** are listed all the functions of the contract. To instantiate the contract, open the menu on the **init** function and select **Submit Transaction**:

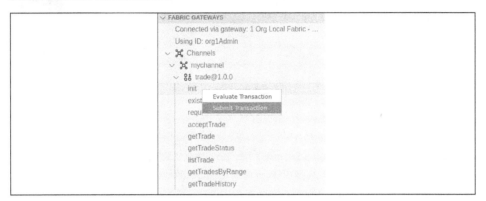

Figure 5.9: Instantiate smart contract

The **Submit Transaction** option opens the **Command Palette** to insert transaction arguments. Since the init function does not have any arguments, we pass through the step by confirming the default value.

After successful transaction execution we should see the following output in the **OUTPUT** window:

```
[10/7/2020 11:36:43 AM] [SUCCESS] Connecting to 1 Org Local Fabric - Org1
[10/7/2020 11:37:29 AM] [INFO] submitTransaction
[10/7/2020 11:37:31 AM] [INFO] submitting transaction init with no args on channel mychannel
[10/7/2020 11:37:33 AM] [SUCCESS] No value returned from init
```

Figure 5.10: Init transaction output

After completion of this sequence, we have deployed and instantiated the trade contract in our development environment ready for testing and debugging.

Invoking and debugging a contract

Now we can proceed with invoking and debugging the contract code:

1. To invoke the requestTrade function, we will select it in the **FABRIC GATEWAYS** window, under **trade@1.0.0** in the list of functions, and select the **Submit Transaction** option:

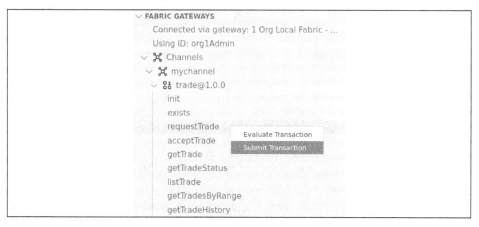

Figure 5.11: Submit requestTrade transaction

2. Next, we fill in the arguments of the function in the **Command Palette**.

   The **requestTrade** function has the following arguments:

   ```
   tradeId: string, exporterMSP: string, descriptionOfGoods:
   string, amount: number
   ```

   We can fill in the following argument values:

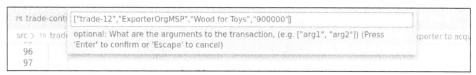

Figure 5.12: Transaction arguments

3. After the execution of the transaction, we should see the following records in the **OUTPUT** window:

```
[10/7/2020 11:45:02 AM] [INFO] submitTransaction
[10/7/2020 11:46:05 AM] [INFO] submitting transaction requestTrade with args trade-12,ExporterOrgMSP,Wood for Toys,900000 on channel
mychannel
[10/7/2020 11:46:07 AM] [SUCCESS] No value returned from requestTrade          ⊙ Successfully submitted transaction
```

Figure 5.13: Transaction execution output

4. Optionally, we can place a breakpoint on any line of the function and after the invocation of the transaction, the code execution will be interrupted at that line and allow for variable state inspection, step-by-step code execution, and so on.

Creating a contract

We are now ready to start implementing our contracts. We will focus on code examples from ExportLicenseContract implemented in Java and TradeContract implemented in Node.js.

 Full documentation of Java and Node.js Contract APIs are available at:

- https://hyperledger.github.io/fabric-chaincode-java/
- https://hyperledger.github.io/fabric-chaincode-node/master/api/index.html

The contract interface

Every contract must implement the ContractInterface, whose methods are called in response to the received transaction proposals.

In Java, the ContractInterface is defined in the org.hyperledger.fabric.contract package and shown in the following code:

```
package org.hyperledger.fabric.contract;

public interface ContractInterface {
  default Context createContext(final ChaincodeStub stub);
  default void unknownTransaction(final Context ctx);
  default void beforeTransaction(final Context ctx);
```

```
    default void afterTransaction(final Context ctx, final Object
result);
    }
```

In Node.js, the contract interface is defined by the `Contract` class in the `fabric-contract-api` package as shown in the following code:

```
class Contract {
    createContext()
    <async> unknownTransaction(ctx)
    <async> beforeTransaction(ctx)
    <async> afterTransaction(ctx, result)
}
```

As you can see, in both `Contract` APIs, the contract interface defines several functions that all have default implementation and thus none of them must be explicitly implemented.

The `beforeTransaction` and `afterTransaction` functions allow you to define code that will be invoked before and after every transaction of the contract. `unknownTransaction` is invoked when the requested transaction is not defined on the contract.

The methods have a single argument ctx of the type `Context`. The `Context` provides access to the `ChaincodeStub` and `ClientIdentity` instances.

The instance of `ChaincodeStub` is the main object that we will use when implementing the contract functionality, as it provides functions for accessing and modifying the ledger, obtaining invocation arguments, and so on.

The instance of `ClientIdentity` provides information about the identity of the transaction submitter.

If needed, we can define a new subtype of the `Context` and return it by implementing the `createContext` function.

Implementing the contract

Let's implement the `contract` file. We will work with the folder structure cloned from GitHub. The contract files we will work with are located in the following folders:

- `ExportLicenseContract` coded in Java: `$GOPATH/src/trade-contracts/v1/ exportLicense/src/main/java/org/trade/`

- `TradeContract` coded in Node.js: `$GOPATH/src/trade-contracts/v1/trade/src/`

You can either follow the steps and inspect the code files in the folders, or you can create a new folder and create the code files as described here.

First, we need to create the contract files:

1. In your favorite editor, create a Java file, `ExportLicenseContract.java`, in the folder `$GOPATH/src/trade-contracts/v1/exportLicense/src/main/java/org/trade/`.

2. Include the following package and import statements:

```
package org.trade;

import static java.nio.charset.StandardCharsets.UTF_8;

import org.hyperledger.fabric.contract.Context;
import org.hyperledger.fabric.contract.ContractInterface;
import org.hyperledger.fabric.contract.annotation.Contract;
import org.hyperledger.fabric.contract.annotation.Default;
import org.hyperledger.fabric.contract.annotation.Transaction;
import org.hyperledger.fabric.shim.ChaincodeException;
import org.hyperledger.fabric.shim.ChaincodeStub;
import org.hyperledger.fabric.shim.Chaincode.Response;
import org.hyperledger.fabric.shim.ledger.CompositeKey;
import org.hyperledger.fabric.contract.annotation.Contact;
import org.hyperledger.fabric.contract.annotation.Info;
import org.hyperledger.fabric.contract.annotation.License;

import com.owlike.genson.Genson;

import java.util.ArrayList;
import java.util.HashMap;
import java.util.Map;
```

In the preceding snippet, we can see following:

- We define a package `org.trade`
- Include `java.nio.charset.StandardCharsets.UTF_8` used for serialization of strings using UTF encoding
- Import standard Fabric interfaces and classes
- Include genson used to serialize complex types
- Include standard Java types

3. Next, we create `trade-contract.js` in folder `$GOPATH/src/trade-contracts/`
   `v1/trade/src/`, and include the following package and `import` statements:

   ```
   import { Context, Contract, Info, Returns, Transaction } from
   'fabric-contract-api';
   import { Iterators } from 'fabric-shim-api';
   import Long = require('long');
   import { TradeAgreement } from './tradeagreement';
   import { TradeAgreementHistory } from './tradeagreementhistory';
   import { TradeAgreementStatus } from './tradeagreementstatus';
   ```

   In the first three lines, we import the standard contract interfaces and classes.
   In the last two lines, we import the definition of assets stored in separate files.

Now we need to define the `contract` classes. Every contract class must have an
annotation providing information about the name, version, license, and other
attributes.

1. Let's add the `ExportLicenseContract` class to the `ExportLicenseContract.`
   `java` file that will implement the contract functions, as shown in the
   following snippet:

   ```
   @Contract(name = "ExportLicenseContract",
       info = @Info(title = "ExportLicense contract",
                    description = "My Smart Contract",
                    version = "1.0.0",
                    license = @License(name = "Apache-2.0",
                             url = ""),
                             contact = @Contact(email =
                             "exportLicense@example.com",
                             name = "exportLicense",
                             url = "http://exportLicense.me")))
   @Default
   public class ExportLicenseContract implements ContractInterface
   {
       public ExportLicenseContract() {
       }
   }
   ```

   The contract class is annotated with the `Contract` attribute with the name
   and additional information about the contract.

2. In the following snippet, we create the `TradeContract` class in trade-contract.ts:

```
@Info({ title: 'TradeContract', description: 'TradeAgreement
SmartContract' })
export class TradeContract extends Contract {

  private static getAclSubject(mspIdVal: string, roleVal:
string) {
  }
}
```

The init method is optional in Fabric 2.2, and it is called once the contract has been installed onto the blockchain network and prior to any transaction. It is executed on endorsement peers that deploy their own instance of the contract and the execution must follow the endorsement policy of the contract. This method can be used for initialization, bootstrapping, and setting up the contract:

3. In our `ExportLicenseContract` implementation, we pass in and store on the ledger configuration arguments, which will allow us to invoke the `TradeContract` hosted on the `tradeChannel`, along with `carrierMSP` and `regulatorMSP` arguments. We will use these later in the implementation of the transactions:

```
@Transaction()
public void init(Context ctx, String tradeChannelName, String
tradeContractId, String carrierMSP, String regulatorMSP) {
    ChaincodeStub stub = ctx.getStub();
    stub.putState(Constants.tradeChannelNameKey,
      tradeChannelName.getBytes(UTF_8));
    stub.putState(Constants.tradeContractIdKey,
      tradeContractId.getBytes(UTF_8));
    stub.putState(Constants.carrierMSPAttr,
      carrierMSP.getBytes(UTF_8));
    stub.putState(Constants.regulatoryAuthorityMSPAttr,
      regulatorMSP.getBytes(UTF_8));
    System.out.println("E/L contract initialized with
Trade channel '" + tradeChannelName + "', contract '" +
tradeContractId + "'");
    System.out.println("Carrier (MSP): " + carrierMSP + ",
Regulatory Authority (MSP) " + regulatorMSP);
}
```

The init function is annotated as a transaction and has one required argument, `Context ctx`. The argument can be followed by an arbitrary number of additional arguments.

In line 3, we obtain a reference to the `ChaincodeStub` by calling `ctx.getStub()`, which provides methods to modify the ledger.

In lines 4 to 7, the string arguments are serialized to bytes and stored into the transaction with the method `stub.putState()`. We will look closer at the method in the following steps.

In lines 8 and 9, the method writes lines into a standard output to report the invocation.

4. In the following snippet, the `init` function of `TradeContract` only reports when it is invoked:

```
@Transaction()
public async init(ctx: Context) {
    console.log('Initializing the trade contract');
}
```

Access control

Before we delve into the implementation of `contract` functions, we need to first define our access control mechanism.

A key feature of a secure and permissioned blockchain is access control. The access control mechanism is typically implemented within the contract and thus enforced during transaction processing on multiple endorsing peers, and the result validated through transaction consensus. Additional access control mechanisms can be inbuilt into application layers interacting with the contract.

In Fabric, the **membership services provider** (**MSP**) plays a pivotal role in enabling access control. Each organization of a Fabric network can have one or more MSP providers. The MSP is implemented as a Fabric **certificate authority** (**CA**). More information on Fabric CA, including its documentation, is available at https://hyperledger-fabric-ca.readthedocs.io/.

Fabric CA issues **enrollment certificates** (**ECerts**) for network users. The ECert represents the identity of the user and is used as a signed transaction when a user submits to Fabric. Prior to invoking a transaction, the user must therefore first register and obtain an ECert from Fabric CA.

Fabric supports an **attribute-based access control (ABAC)** mechanism that can be used by the contract to control access to its functions and data. The ABAC allows the contract to make access control decisions based on attributes associated with the user identity. Users with an ECert can also access a series of additional attributes (that is, name/value pairs).

During invocation, the contract will extract the attributes and make an access control decision. We will take a closer look at the ABAC mechanism in the upcoming chapters.

ABAC

In the following sections, we will show you the steps to register a user and create an ECert with attributes. We will then retrieve the user identity and the attributes in the contract to validate access control. After that, we will integrate this functionality into our tutorial contract.

First, we must register a new user with the Fabric CA. As part of the registration process, we have to define the attributes that will be used once the ECert is generated. A user is registered by running the command `fabric-ca-client register`. The access control attributes are added by using the suffix `:ecert`.

Registering a user

Let's now register a user with a custom attribute named `importer` and the value `true`. Note that the value of the attribute can be of any type and is not limited to Boolean values, as shown in the following snippet:

```
$ fabric-ca-client register --id.name importer --id.secret pwd1 --id.
type user --id.attrs "tradelimit=1000:ecert" -u http://ca:7054
```

The snippet shows us the command line when registering a user with the attribute `tradelimit=1000`. Note that the values of `id.secret` and other arguments depend on the Fabric CA configuration.

The preceding command can also define multiple default attributes at once, such as `-- id.attrs` and `tradelimit=1000:ecert,email=user1@gmail.com`.

The following table contains the default attributes used during user registration:

Attribute name	Command line argument	Attribute value
hf.EnrollmentID	(automatic)	The enrollment ID of the identity
hf.Type	id.type	The type of the identity
hf.Affiliation	id.affiliation	The affiliation of the identity

If any of the attributes are needed in the ECert, they must be first defined in the user registration command. For example, the following command registers user1 with the attribute hf.Affiliation=ImporterOrgMSP, which will be copied into the ECert by default:

```
$ fabric-ca-client register --id.name importer --id.secret
pwd1 --id.type user --id.affiliation ImporterOrgMSP --id.attrs
"tradelimit=1000:ecert,hf.Affiliation=ImporterOrgMSP:ecert"
```

Enrolling a user

Here, we will enroll the user and create the ECert. enrollment.attrs defines which attributes will be copied into the ECert from user registration. The suffix opt defines which attributes of those copied from registration are optional. If one or more non-optional attributes are not defined on the user registration, the enrollment will fail. The following command will enroll a user with the attribute importer:

```
$ fabric-ca-client enroll -u http://importer:pwd1@ca:7054 --enrollment.
attrs "tradelimit,email:opt" --mspdir importer
```

Access control in the contract

In this step, we will retrieve a user's identity and verify attributes during the execution of the contract. Every transaction proposal submitted to the contract carries along with it the ECert of the invoker — the user submitting the transaction. The contract has access to the ECert and to the ABAC functionality through an instance of the ClientIdentity class, which can be obtained in the transaction by calling ctx.getClientIdentity() in Java and ctx.clientIdentity in JavaScript.

The contract can use the certificate to extract information about the invoker, including:

- The ID of the invoker
- The unique ID of the MSP that issued the invoker certificate
- The standard attributes of the certificate, such as its domain name, email, and so on
- The ECert attributes associated with the client identity, stored within the certificate

The functions provided in the Java Contract API by the `ClientIdentity` class are listed in the following snippet:

```java
public final class ClientIdentity {


// returns the ID associated with the invoking identity.
// This ID is guaranteed to be unique within the MSP
public String getId();


// returns the MSP ID of the invoking identity
public String getMSPID();


// returns the value of the client's attribute named attrName.
// If the invoking identity possesses the attribute, returns
// the value of the attribute. If the invoking identity
// does not possess the attribute, returns null
public String getAttributeValue(final String attrName);


// verifies that the invoking identity has the attribute
// named attrName with a value of attrValue
public boolean assertAttributeValue(final String attrName, final String attrValue);


// returns the X509 certificate associated with the invoking identity
public X509Certificate getX509Certificate();


}
```

Similarly, the functions provided in the Node.js Contract API by the `ClientIdentity` class are listed in the following snippet:

```
class ClientIdentity {
    // returns the ID associated with the invoking identity.
    // This ID is guaranteed to be unique within the MSP
    getID()
    // returns the MSP ID of the invoking identity
    getMSPID()
    // returns the X509 certificate associated with the invoking identity
    getIDBytes()
    // returns the value of the client's attribute named attrName.
    // If the invoking identity possesses the attribute,
    // returns the value of the attribute. If the invoking identity
    // does not possess the attribute, returns null
    getAttributeValue(attrName)
    // verifies that the invoking identity has the attribute named
    // attrName with a value of attrValue
    assertAttributeValue(attrName, attrValue)
}
```

Now we can implement our access control policy. We will look at both Java and JavaScript implementations. In Java, the implementation is split between the file `AccessControlUtil.java` and the `beforeTransaction` function within a contract. Note that the code uses string constants defined in a separate file `Constants.java`.

In the following code block, we define an `ACLSubject` class, which represents the MSP and role attributes of an identity. Notice that we override the `hashCode()` and `equals()` functions, which will allow us to store the objects into a map and compare by value:

```
@DataType()
class ACLSubject {
    @Property()
    private String mspId;

    @Property()
    private String role;

    public ACLSubject(String mspId, String role) {
        this.mspId = mspId;
        this.role = role;
    }
```

```java
    public String getMspId() {
        return mspId;
    }

    public void setMspId(String mspId) {
        this.mspId = mspId;
    }

    public String getRole() {
        return role;
    }

    public void setRole(String role) {
        this.role = role;
    }

    @Override
    public boolean equals(Object obj) {
        if (obj.getClass() == ACLSubject.class) {
            ACLSubject aclSubject = (ACLSubject) obj;
            return aclSubject.getMspId().equals(this.getMspId()) &&
            aclSubject.getRole().equals(this.getRole());
        }
        return false;
    }

    @Override
    public int hashCode() {
        return (this.getMspId() + "," + this.getRole()).hashCode();
    }

    @Override
    public String toString() {
        return "MSP ID: " + this.getMspId() + ", Role: " + this.
getRole();
    }
}
```

In the next code block, we define an `AccessControlUtils` class:

```
public class AccessControlUtils {
    public final static String BUSINESS_ROLE_ATTR = "BUSINESS_ROLE";
    private final static Map<ACLSubject,String[]> aclRules = new
HashMap<ACLSubject,String[]>();

    static {
        aclRules.put(new ACLSubject(Constants.regulatorOrgMsp,
        Constants.ANY_ROLE), new String[]{ "init" });
        aclRules.put(new ACLSubject(Constants.exporterOrgMsp,
        Constants.ANY_ROLE), new String[]{ "init" });
        aclRules.put(new ACLSubject(Constants.exporterOrgMsp,
        Constants.EXPORTER_ROLE), new String[]{ "requestEL",
"existsEL", "getEL", "getELStatus" });
        aclRules.put(new ACLSubject(Constants.regulatorOrgMsp,
Constants.REGULATOR_ROLE), new String[]{ "issueEL", "existsEL",
"getEL", "getELStatus" });
    }

    public static String GetClientMspId(Context ctx) {
        return ctx.getClientIdentity().getMSPID();
    }

    public static String GetClientRole(Context ctx) {
        return ctx.getClientIdentity().getAttributeValue(AccessControlU
tils.BUSINESS_ROLE_ATTR);
    }

    public static boolean checkAccess(Context ctx, String mspId, String
role, String function) {
        ACLSubject aclSubject = new ACLSubject(mspId, role);
        if (!aclRules.containsKey(aclSubject)) {
            throw new ChaincodeException("The participant " + mspId + "
role " + role + " is not recognized");
        } else {
            return !Arrays.asList(aclRules.get(aclSubject)).
contains(function);
        }
    }
}
```

On the lines 6 to 10, we define four rules that represent our policy outlining which role issued by which MSP can invoke which type of transaction, for example, transaction init can be invoked by anyone with an identity issued by either regulator or exporter MSPs, while transaction requestEL can be invoked only by role exporter issued by the exporter MSP. These four rules are stored in a map.

We then define function GetClientMspId(), which uses the ctx object to retrieve ClientIdentity and its MSP ID. Next, we define function GetClientRole(), which retrieves the attribute "BUSINESS_ROLE" of the ClientIdentity. This attribute is placed into the ECert by the MSP when registering a user. Finally, we define a function, checkAccess(), that verifies against the map containing our policy whether an identity with a given MSP ID and role is authorized to invoke the requested transaction.

Now we can include the enforcement of our policy in the contract. In the following code block, we define an implementation of the beforeTransaction() function, which uses the AccessControlUtils class to verify the authorization of the transaction invoking identity. On lines 3 and 4 the MSP ID and role of the identity are retrieved, and on line 8 we retrieve the name of the invoked transaction. On line 10 we then use the function checkAccess() to verify the authorization of the identity and throw an exception if the identity is not authorized to invoke the transaction:

```
@Override
public void beforeTransaction(Context ctx) {
    String mspId = AccessControlUtils.GetClientMspId(ctx);
    String role = AccessControlUtils.GetClientRole(ctx);
    if (role == null) {
        role = Constants.ANY_ROLE;
    }
    String function = ctx.getStub().getFunction();

    if (AccessControlUtils.checkAccess(ctx, mspId, role, function)) {
        throw new ChaincodeException("The participant " + mspId + "
cannot invoke transaction " + function);
    }
}
```

By including the verification code in the beforeTransaction() function, the code is guaranteed to be invoked before every transaction request and thus prevents any unauthorized access to or modification of data.

In Node.js, the implementation is considerably shorter and is wholly included within the code of the contract.

Moving to the following code block, within a `TradeContract` contract constructor, in the lines 5 to 10, we define six rules and insert them into an `aclRules` array, which represents our policy outlining which role issued by which MSP can invoke which type of transaction:

```
private aclRules = {};
constructor() {
    super('TradeContract');
    this.aclRules[TradeContract.getAclSubject('ExporterOrgMSP', 'any')]
= [ 'init' ];
    this.aclRules[TradeContract.getAclSubject('ImporterOrgMSP', 'any')]
= [ 'init' ];
    this.aclRules[TradeContract.getAclSubject('RegulatorOrgMSP',
'any')] = [ 'init' ];
    this.aclRules[TradeContract.getAclSubject('ExporterOrgMSP',
'exporter')] = [ 'acceptTrade', 'exists', 'getTrade', 'getTradeStatus',
'listTrade' ];
    this.aclRules[TradeContract.getAclSubject('ImporterOrgMSP',
'importer')] = [ 'requestTrade', 'exists', 'getTrade',
'getTradeStatus', 'listTrade' ];
    this.aclRules[TradeContract.getAclSubject('ExporterOrgMSP',
'exporter_banker')] = [ 'exists', 'getTrade', 'getTradeStatus',
'listTrade' ];
    this.aclRules[TradeContract.getAclSubject('ImporterOrgMSP',
'importer_banker')] = [ 'exists', 'getTrade', 'getTradeStatus',
'listTrade' ];
    this.aclRules[TradeContract.getAclSubject('RegulatorOrgMSP',
'regulator')] = [ 'exists', 'getTrade', 'getTradeStatus', 'listTrade'
];
}

private static getAclSubject(mspIdVal: string, roleVal: string) {
    return JSON.stringify({ mspId: mspIdVal, role: roleVal });
}
```

Next, as in the Java code, we include the enforcement of our policy in the `beforeTransaction()` function, which uses an `aclRules` array to verify authorization of the transaction invoking identity. Lines 2 and 3 retrieve the MSP ID and the role of the identity, and on line 7 we retrieve the name of the invoked transaction. In line 9 we look up a record within our `aclSubjects`, and in line 10 we verify the authorization of the identity and throw an exception if the identity is not authorized to invoke the transaction:

```
public async beforeTransaction(ctx: Context) {
    const mspId = ctx.clientIdentity.getMSPID();
    let role = ctx.clientIdentity.getAttributeValue(BUSINESS_ROLE);
    if (!role) {
        role = 'any';
    }
    const tx = ctx.stub.getFunctionAndParameters().fcn;

    const aclSubject = TradeContract.getAclSubject(mspId, role);
    if (!this.aclRules.hasOwnProperty(aclSubject)) {
        throw new Error('The participant belonging to MSP ${mspId} and
role ${role} is not recognized');
    } else if (!this.aclRules[aclSubject].includes(tx)) {
        throw new Error('The participant belonging to MSP ${mspId} and
role ${role} cannot invoke transaction ${tx}');
    }
}
```

Implementing contract functions

At this point, we now have the basic building blocks of Java and Node.js contracts. We have the init method, which initiates the contract, and the beforeTransaction method, which performs the access control verifications. Now, we need to define the functionality of the contract.

Scenario contracts' functions

Based on our scenario, the following tables summarize the list of functions that record and retrieve data to and from the ledger to provide the business logic of the contracts. The tables also define the access control definitions of organization members, which are needed in order to invoke the respective functions. The access control definitions are listed with the MSP name and role separated by "." (period).

The following tables illustrate the contract modification functions, that is, how to record transactions on the ledger.

The following table illustrated the contract functions of the `ExportLicenseContract`:

Function	Roles permitted to invoke	Description
existsEL	ExporterOrgMSP.exporter RegulatorOrgMSP.regulator	Checks if Export License for the given trade instance exists
requestEL	ExporterOrgMSP.exporter	Creates Export License and records it on the ledger
issueEL	RegulatorOrgMSP.regulator	Issues Export License
getEL	ExporterOrgMSP.exporter RegulatorOrgMSP.regulator	Gets Export License from the given trade ID
getELStatus	ExporterOrgMSP.exporter RegulatorOrgMSP.regulator	Gets current status of the Export License

The following table illustrates the contract functions of the `ShipmentContract`:

Function	Roles permitted to invoke	Description
prepareShipment	ExporterOrgMSP.exporter	Prepares a new shipment
acceptShipmentAndIssueBL	CarrierOrgMSP.carrier	Accepts a shipment and issues a bill of lading
updateShipmentLocation	CarrierOrgMSP.carrier	Updates the shipment location
getShipmentLocation	ExporterOrgMSP.exporter ExporterOrgMSP.exporter_banker ImporterOrgMSP.importer ImporterOrgMSP.importer_banker CarrierOrgMSP.carrier	Gets the current location of a shipment
getBillOfLading	ExporterOrgMSP.exporter ExporterOrgMSP.exporter_banker ImporterOrgMSP.importer ImporterOrgMSP.importer_banker CarrierOrgMSP.carrier	Gets a bill of lading

The following table illustrates the contract functions of the `TradeContract`:

Function	Roles permitted to invoke	Description
exists	ExporterOrgMSP.exporter ExporterOrgMSP.exporter_banker ImporterOrgMSP.importer ImporterOrgMSP.importer_banker	Checks whether a trade exists
requestTrade	ImporterOrgMSP.importer	Requests a trade agreement
acceptTrade	ExporterOrgMSP.exporter	Accepts a trade agreement
getTrade	ExporterOrgMSP.exporter ExporterOrgMSP.exporter_banker ImporterOrgMSP.importer ImporterOrgMSP.importer_banker	Gets trade agreement data
getTradeStatus	ExporterOrgMSP.exporter ExporterOrgMSP.exporter_banker ImporterOrgMSP.importer ImporterOrgMSP.importer_banker	Gets the current status of a trade agreement
listTrade	ExporterOrgMSP.exporter ExporterOrgMSP.exporter_banker ImporterOrgMSP.importer ImporterOrgMSP.importer_banker	Gets the list of trade agreements of the organization the requester is part of

The following table illustrates the contract functions of the LetterOfCreditContract:

Function	Roles permitted to invoke	Description
existsLC	ExporterOrgMSP.exporter ExporterOrgMSP.exporter_banker ImporterOrgMSP.importer ImporterOrgMSP.importer_banker	Checks whether a letter of credit exists
requestLC	ImporterOrgMSP.importer	Requests a letter of credit
issueLC	ImporterOrgMSP.importer_banker	Issues a letter of credit
acceptLC	ExporterOrgMSP.exporter_banker	Accepts a letter of credit
requestPayment	ExporterOrgMSP.exporter_banker	Requests a payment
makePayment	ImporterOrgMSP.importer_banker	Makes a payment
getLC	ExporterOrgMSP.exporter ExporterOrgMSP.exporter_banker ImporterOrgMSP.importer ImporterOrgMSP.importer_banker	Gets letter of credit data
getLCStatus	ExporterOrgMSP.exporter ExporterOrgMSP.exporter_banker ImporterOrgMSP.importer ImporterOrgMSP.importer_banker	Gets the current status of a letter of credit
getAccountBalance	ExporterOrgMSP.exporter ImporterOrgMSP.importer	Gets the current account balance for a given participant

Defining contract assets

We are now going to define the structure of our assets, which will be recorded onto the ledger.

In Java, assets are defined as a class annotated as @DataType(). The class can have multiple member fields annotated as @Property(), which indicates that these fields will be serialized when an object of the class is passed as an argument or returned from a function.

The following snippet shows the definition of the asset ExportLicense in a file ExportLicense.java in the folder $GOPATH/src/trade-contracts/v1/exportLicense/src/main/java/org/trade/. Note that all fields of the class are defined as private and annotated to be serialized:

```java
package org.trade;

import org.hyperledger.fabric.contract.annotation.DataType;
import org.hyperledger.fabric.contract.annotation.Property;

import com.owlike.genson.annotation.JsonProperty;
import com.owlike.genson.Genson;

@DataType()
public class ExportLicense {

    @Property()
    private String id;

    @Property()
    private String expirationDate;

    @Property()
    private String exporter;

    @Property()
    private String carrier;

    @Property()
    private String descriptionOfGoods;

    @Property()
    private String approver;
```

```
    @Property()
    private String status;
}
```

In the next snippet, we define a constructor with the fields as arguments and annotated as @JsonProperty(), which will allow us to load the fields when deserialized from JSON. We also define a set of methods to access and modify the fields. We include only functions for the id and expirationDate fields; however, in the actual code all other fields have respective methods:

```
public ExportLicense(@JsonProperty("id") String id, @
JsonProperty("expirationDate") String expirationDate, @
JsonProperty("exporter") String exporter, @JsonProperty("carrier")
String carrier, @JsonProperty("descriptionOfGoods") String
descriptionOfGoods, @JsonProperty("approver") String approver, @
JsonProperty("status") String status) {
    this.id = id;
    this.expirationDate = expirationDate;
    this.exporter = exporter;
    this.carrier = carrier;
    this.descriptionOfGoods = descriptionOfGoods;
    this.approver = approver;
    this.status = status;
}

public String getId() {
    return id;
}

public void setId(String id) {
    this.id = id;
}

public String getExpirationDate() {
    return expirationDate;
}

public void setExpirationDate(String expirationDate) {
    this.expirationDate = expirationDate;
}
```

Finally, in the following snippet, we define serialization methods, which will allow us to serialize an instance of the `ExportLicense` to and from a JSON string:

```
public String toJSONString() {
    return genson.serialize(this);
}

public static ExportLicense fromJSONString(String json) {
    return genson.deserialize(json, ExportLicense.class);
}
```

In Node.js, assets are defined as a class annotated as `@Object()`. The class can have multiple member fields annotated as `@Property()`, which indicates that these fields will be serialized when an object of the class is passed as an argument or returned from a function.

The following snippet shows the definition of the asset `TradeAgreement` in the file `tradeagreement.java` in the folder `$GOPATH/src/trade-contracts/v1/trade/src/`:

```
import { Object, Property } from 'fabric-contract-api';

@Object()
export class TradeAgreement {

    @Property()
    public tradeID: string;

    @Property()
    public exporterMSP: string;

    @Property()
    public importerMSP: string;

    @Property()
    public amount: number;

    @Property()
    public descriptionOfGoods: string;

    @Property()
    public status: string;
}
```

Coding contract functions

In this section, we will implement the Node.js-based `TradeContract` contract functions we looked at previously. To implement the contract functions, we will use the `ChaincodeStub` with functions that will read assets from the `Worldstate` and record changes. As we have already learned, reads and writes of these functions are recorded into `ReadSet` and `WriteSet` respectively, and the changes do not affect the state of the ledger immediately. Only after the transaction has passed through validation and has been committed into the ledger will the changes take effect.

Creating an asset

Now that we can implement our first contract function, we will move on and implement a `requestTrade` function, which will create a new trade agreement with the status `REQUESTED` and then record that agreement on the ledger.

The following snippet illustrates the `requestTrade` function:

```
@Transaction()
public async requestTrade(ctx: Context, tradeId: string, exporterMSP:
string, descriptionOfGoods: string, amount: number): Promise<void> {
    const exists = await this.exists(ctx, tradeId);
    if (exists) {
        throw new Error('The trade ${tradeId} already exists');
    }
    const trade = new TradeAgreement();
    trade.tradeID = tradeId;
    trade.exporterMSP = exporterMSP;
    trade.importerMSP = ctx.clientIdentity.getMSPID();
    trade.descriptionOfGoods = descriptionOfGoods;
    trade.amount = amount;
    trade.status = 'REQUESTED';

    const buffer = Buffer.from(JSON.stringify(trade));
    await ctx.stub.putState(tradeId, buffer);
}
```

The implementation of the function is shown in the following snippet. It is annotated as `@Transaction()` indicating that a new blockchain transaction will be created as a result of the invocation. Remember that the `beforeTransaction` function is invoked before every transaction and thus when the `requestTrade` function is invoked it is already verified that the submitter identity is authorized to invoke this transaction.

As you can see, in lines 3 to 6 we use the function `exists` to verify that a trade agreement does not exist yet. We will look at the implementation of the `exists` function in the following steps. In line 7 we create a new instance of `TradeAgreement` and in lines 8 to 13 we set the values of the fields to the received arguments.

As we learned earlier, the ledger stores values in the form of arrays of bytes. Thus, in line 14 we serialize `TradeAgreement` with JSON and buffer into an array of bytes. In line 15, we use the `tradeId` argument as an asset key and store the serialized `TradeAgreement` with the function `PutState` into the `WriteSet`.

Reading and modifying an asset

After we have implemented the function to create a trade agreement, we need to implement a function to accept the trade agreement. This function will retrieve the agreement, modify its status to `ACCEPTED`, and put it back on the ledger.

We will first implement functions `exists` and `getTrade`, which tests whether a trade agreement is already stored on the ledger and retrieves the existing trade agreement from the ledger.

The functions are shown in the following snippet:

```
@Transaction(false)
@Returns('boolean')
public async exists(ctx: Context, tradeId: string): Promise<boolean> {
    const buffer = await ctx.stub.getState(tradeId);
    return (!!buffer && buffer.length > 0);
}


@Transaction(false)
@Returns('TradeAgreement')
public async getTrade(ctx: Context, tradeId: string):
Promise<TradeAgreement> {
    const exists = await this.exists(ctx, tradeId);
    if (!exists) {
        throw new Error('The trade ${tradeId} does not exists');
    }
    const buffer = await ctx.stub.getState(tradeId);
    const trade = JSON.parse(buffer.toString()) as TradeAgreement;
    return trade;
}
```

Notice, that the functions are annotated as @Transaction(false) indicating that a function does not result in a new blockchain transaction but serves only as a query that accesses the peer's Worldstate database. Because both functions return a value, in lines 2 and 9 we include annotation @Returns('boolean') and @Returns('TradeAgreement'), which inform us about the resultant data type. The framework will use the annotations of the type to serialize the referenced object when passing it between the server and client.

In line 11, we use the function exists to verify whether the trade agreement exists. In line 15, we use the tradeId as an asset key and retrieve the value with the function GetState. In line 16, we deserialize the array of bytes with JSON and buffer into the instance of the TradeAgreement class, and we then return in line 17.

The following snippet shows the implementation of the acceptTrade function:

```
@Transaction()
public async acceptTrade(ctx: Context, tradeId: string): Promise<void>
{
    const trade = await this.getTrade(ctx, tradeId);

    if (trade.status !== 'REQUESTED') {
        throw new Error('The trade ' + tradeId + ' is in the wrong
status.  Expected REQUESTED got ' + trade.status);
    }
    trade.status = 'ACCEPTED';

    const buffer = Buffer.from(JSON.stringify(trade));
    await ctx.stub.putState(tradeId, buffer);
}
```

In line 3, we use the getTrade function to retrieve the TradeAgreement and in line 4 verify that it has the status REQUESTED.

In line 7, we modify the status so it reads ACCEPTED. In line 9, we serialize the object and finally, in line 10 we store the updated value on the ledger.

Unlike the exists and getTrade query functions, when invoked, the getTrade function generates a new transaction with a ReadSet and WriteSet and will be processed by the transaction processing endorser-orderer-committer protocol.

Testing a contract

Now we can write unit tests for our contract functions. We will focus on testing the Node.js-based `TradeContract` and use the Mocha testing framework (`https://mochajs.org/`) with the Chai assertion library (`https://www.chaijs.com/`), which allows us to write tests as English sentences, and the Sinon mocking library (`https://sinonjs.org/`), which allows us to create stubs of objects.

Note that by convention, the test suite file containing unit tests ends with the suffix `.spec.ts`; therefore, our test suite file will be named `trade-contract.spec.ts` and placed in the same directory as our contract file. The output of the test is written into the standard output, where it can be inspected in the terminal after execution.

 For testing of Java-based contracts, you can use JUnit (`https://junit.org/`).

 The JUnit tests of `ExportLicenseContract` are placed in the file `ExportLicenseContractTest.java` located in folder `$GOPATH/src/trade-contracts/v1/exportLicense/src/test/java/org/trade/`.

Creating a test suite file

In your favorite editor, create a file, `trade-contract.spec.ts`, and include the following package and `import` statements:

```
import { Context } from 'fabric-contract-api';
import { ChaincodeStub, ClientIdentity, Iterators } from 'fabric-shim';
import Long = require('long');
import { TradeContract } from '.';

import * as chai from 'chai';
import * as chaiAsPromised from 'chai-as-promised';
import * as sinon from 'sinon';
import * as sinonChai from 'sinon-chai';
import winston = require('winston');

chai.should();
chai.use(chaiAsPromised);
chai.use(sinonChai);
```

Next, in the following snippet, we define a `TestContext`, which implements the interface of the transaction `Context` and defines mocking stubs for `ChaincodeStub` and `ClientIdentity`. We will use this class instead of the actual `Context` to observe the invocations:

```
class TestContext implements Context {
    public stub: sinon.SinonStubbedInstance<ChaincodeStub> = sinon.crea
teStubInstance(ChaincodeStub);
    public clientIdentity: sinon.SinonStubbedInstance<ClientIdentity> =
sinon.createStubInstance(ClientIdentity);
    public logger = {
        getLogger: sinon.stub().returns(
            sinon.createStubInstance(winston.createLogger().constructor)),
        setLevel: sinon.stub(),
    };
}
```

Defining a test suite

In the following snippet, we define our test suite for `TradeContract` functions. Notice that we define references to the `TradeContract` and `ctx` as our mocking `TestContext`:

```
describe('As an importer, I can enter in a trade agreement with an
exporter to acquire specific goods', () => {
    let contract: TradeContract;
    let ctx: TestContext;
});
```

In the next snippet, we define the function `beforeEach`, which will be invoked before every unit test and sets up the contextual variables of the unit tests. In this function, we create an instance of the `TradeContract` and `TestContext` instances used in the tests and define the state of the stubs. For example, in line 4, we define that when function `ctx.stub.getState` is called with argument `'1000'`, it will return a byte array representation of a JSON-serialized `TradeAgreement` into the following string:

```
'{"tradeID":"1000", "exporterMSP": "ExporterOrg", "importerMSP":
"ImporterOrg", "amount": 1000.0, "descriptionOfGoods": "Apples",
"status": "REQUESTED"}'
```

In this way, we define three `TradeAgreement` assets stored in the ledger prior to invocation of each unit test:

```
beforeEach(() => {
    contract = new TradeContract();
```

```
    ctx = new TestContext();
    ctx.stub.getState.withArgs('1000').resolves(Buffer.
from('{"tradeID":"1000", "exporterMSP": "ExporterOrg", "importerMSP":
"ImporterOrg", "amount": 1000.0, "descriptionOfGoods": "Apples",
"status": "REQUESTED"}'));
    ctx.stub.getState.withArgs('1001').resolves(Buffer.
from('{"tradeID":"1001", "exporterMSP": "ExporterOrg", "importerMSP":
"ImporterOrg", "amount": 1000.0, "descriptionOfGoods": "Apples",
"status": "REQUESTED"}'));
    ctx.stub.getState.withArgs('1002').resolves(Buffer.
from('{"tradeID":"1002", "exporterMSP": "ExporterOrg", "importerMSP":
"ImporterOrg", "amount": 1000.0, "descriptionOfGoods": "Oranges",
"status": "ACCEPTED"}'));
});
```

Unit tests

Now after we have defined our test suite and context functions, we can start to implement the actual unit tests.

In the following snippet, we will define a test of the `init` function. Since the function has no arguments and only writes into the output, the test is as simple as the following code:

```
describe('#init', () => {
    it('should succeed', async () => {
        await contract.init(ctx);
    });
});
```

In the next snippet, we will define two test scenarios of the `requestTrade` function:

```
describe('ImporterOrg creates a trade request to an ExporterOrg Corp',
() => {
    it('should create a trade.', async () => {
        ctx.clientIdentity.getMSPID.returns('ImporterOrg');
        await contract.requestTrade(ctx, '1003', 'ExporterOrg',
'Pears', 1000.0);
        ctx.stub.putState.should.have.been.
calledOnceWithExactly('1003', Buffer.from('{"tradeID":"1003","exporterM
SP":"ExporterOrg","importerMSP":"ImporterOrg","descriptionOfGoods":"Pea
rs","amount":1000,"status":"REQUESTED"}'));
    });
```

```
    it('should throw an error for a trade that already exists.', async
() => {
        await contract.requestTrade(ctx, '1001', 'ExporterOrg',
'Pears', 1000.0).should.be.rejected;
    });
});
```

The first scenario starts at line 2. In line 3, we define 'ImporterOrg' as the MSP ID of the clientIdentity under which we want to test the function. Next, in line 5, a TradeAgreement asset with ID '1003' is created. In line 6, we verify that the putState function of the stub was invoked by the requestTrade function with the respective arguments representing the creation of the TradeAgreement asset.

The second scenario starts at line 10. In line 11, the requestTrade function is called with an ID of a TradeAgreement asset already present on the ledger, and thus we define the function to fail.

The file trade-contract.spec.ts contains an implementation of the full test suite with an exhaustive list of test cases.

Running tests in the terminal

We are now ready to run our tests! Each of the contract folders contains a makefile with configured commands to execute the test suite with all unit tests.

Let's now run the tests in the terminal with the following command:

```
$ cd $GOPATH/src/trade-contracts/v1/trade/:
$ make test
```

The preceding command should generate output similar to the following:

```
echo ">> Running chaincode unit-test"
>> Running chaincode unit-test
docker run  --rm -v /Users/pnovotny/go_workspace/src/trade-network2/
chaincode/trade:/src -v /Users/pnovotny/go_workspace/src/trade-
network2/chaincode/trade/dist:/dist -w /src "node:10.19-slim" sh -c
"npm test"


> trade@1.0.0 pretest /src
> npm run lint


> trade@1.0.0 lint /src
```

```
> tslint -c tslint.json 'src/**/*.ts'


> trade@1.0.0 test /src
> nyc --reporter=lcov --reporter=text-summary mocha -r ts-node/register
src/**/*.spec.ts


2020-07-23T07:07:34.195Z info [c-api:../lib/annotations/object.js]
@Object args: Target -> %s "Function"
2020-07-23T07:07:34.237Z info [c-api:../lib/annotations/object.js]
@Object args: Target -> %s "Function"
2020-07-23T07:07:34.242Z info [c-api:../lib/annotations/transaction.js]
@Transaction args: "Property Key -> init, Commit -> true,","Target
->","TradeContract"
2020-07-23T07:07:34.247Z info [c-api:../lib/annotations/transaction.
js]          @Returns args: ", Property Key -> exists, Return Type ->
boolean,","Target ->","TradeContract"
2020-07-23T07:07:34.248Z info [c-api:../lib/annotations/transaction.js]
@Transaction args: "Property Key -> exists, Commit -> false,","Target
->","TradeContract"
2020-07-23T07:07:34.251Z info [c-api:../lib/annotations/transaction.
js]          @Transaction args: "Property Key -> requestTrade, Commit
-> true,","Target ->","TradeContract"


...


2020-07-23T07:07:37.908Z info [c-api:../lib/contract.js]
Creating new Contract "TradeContract"
Initializing the trade contract
      ✓ should succeed


21 passing (936ms)


=============================== Coverage summary
===============================
Statements   : 100% ( 282/282 )
Branches     : 100% ( 32/32 )
Functions    : 100% ( 59/59 )
Lines        : 100% ( 274/274 )
================================================================================
=========
```

Running tests in VS Code

VS Code provides integrated support for unit testing of Java contracts and allows you to execute individual unit tests or whole test suites.

Let's now run tests of the `ExportLicenseContract`.

Open the **exportLicense** directory in VS Code and then open the `test/java/org/trade/ExportLicenseContractTest.java` file.

Notice that the editor adds **Run Test | Debug Test** links to every unit test as well as to the class containing the tests:

Figure 5.14: Java test suite in VS Code

Next, click on the **Run Test** link above the **ELRequest** function. The test will be started with a debug menu above the code. VS Code supports breakpoints and all other runtime debugging functionalities in tests:

Figure 5.15: Test runtime menu

The output of the test is written to the **DEBUG CONSOLE** window. After completion of the test, the output will be the following:

Figure 5.16: Output of running the ELRequest function unit test

Next, we can run the whole test suite of the contract. Click on the **Run Test** link above the **ExportLicenseContractTest** class. This will invoke in sequence all individual unit tests of the contract.

After completion of the tests, the output will be the following:

Figure 5.17: Output of running the ExportLicenseContract contract test suite

In this section, we have learned about unit testing individual functions and contracts with the use of mocking mechanisms without running the contracts within Fabric. In later sections, we will look at integration testing involving the invocation of multiple components including contracts hosted in Fabric.

Advanced contract design topics

In the following sections, we will explore topics that allow us to develop fully functional contracts including cross-contract and cross-ledger invocations, composite keys, querying techniques, indexing of data, and explain the key transaction mechanisms.

Cross-contract and cross-ledger invocation

In complex business process workflows spanning multiple contracts and channels, a contract may need to invoke other contracts as parts of its logic. In our solution, this happens when transactions of LetterOfCreditContract and ExportLicenseContract require information from TradeContract about TradeAgreements.

Both Contract APIs provide function invokeChaincode, which calls the contract within the same or a different channel. The Java Contract API has the additional invokeChaincodeWithStringArgs, which simplifies the handling of string arguments.

The functions use the transaction context of the calling function to invoke the contract and thus the call does not result in a new transaction. If the called contract is hosted within the same channel, the ReadSet and WriteSet are added to the calling transaction. If the called contract is hosted within a different channel, the call is functioning as a query and the ReadSet and WriteSet will not be added to the calling transaction. As a consequence, if the state of the different channel changes prior to the commitment of the transaction, it will not invalidate the transaction.

The following snippet shows the function available in the Node.js Contract API:

```
<async> invokeChaincode(chaincodeName, args, channel)
```

The following snippet shows the functions available in the Java Contract API:

```
Chaincode.Response invokeChaincode(java.lang.String chaincodeName,
                                   java.util.List<byte[]> args)

Chaincode.Response invokeChaincode(java.lang.String chaincodeName,
                                   java.util.List<byte[]> args,
                                   java.lang.String channel)
Chaincode.Response invokeChaincodeWithSt
ringArgs(java.lang.String chaincodeName,
java.util.List<java.lang.String> args,
java.lang.String channel)

Chaincode.Response invokeChaincodeWithSt
ringArgs(java.lang.String chaincodeName,
java.util.List<java.lang.String> args)

Chaincode.Response invokeChaincodeWithSt
ringArgs(java.lang.String chaincodeName,
java.lang.String... args)
```

In the following example, we will look at the cross-channel invocation of the getTrade function of TradeContract called by the requestEL function of ExportLicenseContract. The requestEL function verifies that the status of a TradeAgreement is not ACCEPTED before a new ExportLincese is recorded.

In the following snippet, the init function of the ExportLicenseContract receives and records on the ledger arguments with the trade channel name and of the trade contract ID, which will be later used by the requestEL function:

```java
@Transaction()
public void init(Context ctx, String tradeChannelName, String
tradeContractId, String carrierMSP, String regulatorMSP) {
    ChaincodeStub stub = ctx.getStub();
    stub.putState(Constants.tradeChannelNameKey,
        tradeChannelName.getBytes(UTF_8));
    stub.putState(Constants.tradeContractIdKey,
        tradeContractId.getBytes(UTF_8));
    stub.putState(Constants.carrierMSPAttr,
        carrierMSP.getBytes(UTF_8));
    stub.putState(Constants.regulatoryAuthorityMSPAttr,
        regulatorMSP.getBytes(UTF_8));
    System.out.println("E/L contract initialized with Trade channel '"
+ tradeChannelName + "', contract '" + tradeContractId + "'");
    System.out.println("Carrier (MSP): " + carrierMSP + ", Regulatory
Authority (MSP) " + regulatorMSP);
}
```

In the following snippet, the requestEL function in lines 5 and 12 retrieves the channel name and trade contract ID and uses these in line 22 to call invokeChaincodeWithStringArgs to invoke the TradeContract:

```java
@Transaction()
public void requestEL(Context ctx, String tradeId) {
    // Lookup trade channel id
    ChaincodeStub stub = ctx.getStub();
    byte[] tchBytes = stub.getState(Constants.tradeChannelNameKey);
    if (tchBytes == null || tchBytes.length == 0) {
        throw new ChaincodeException("No trade channel name recorded on
ledger");
    }
    String tradeChannel = new String(tchBytes);

    // Lookup trade contract ID
    byte[] tcBytes = stub.getState(Constants.tradeContractIdKey);
```

```
   if (tcBytes == null || tcBytes.length == 0) {
      throw new ChaincodeException("No trade contract id recorded on
ledger");
   }
   String tradeContractId = new String(tcBytes);

   // Lookup trade agreemeent by invoking the trade chaincode
   ArrayList<String> tradeArgs = new ArrayList<String>();
   tradeArgs.add(Constants.getTradeFunc);
   tradeArgs.add(tradeId);
   Response tradeResp = stub.invokeChaincodeWithStringArgs(
      tradeContractId, tradeArgs, tradeChannel);
   String trade = tradeResp.getStringPayload();
   if (tradeResp.getStatus() != Response.Status.SUCCESS) {
      throw new ChaincodeException("Error invoking '" + tradeContractId
+ "' chaincode, function '" + Constants.getTradeFunc + "': " + trade);
   }
   if (trade.isEmpty()) {
      throw new ChaincodeException("Unable to locate trade ': " + trade
+ "'");
   }
   @SuppressWarnings("unchecked")
   Map<String, String> tradeObj = genson.deserialize(trade, Map.class);
   String tradeStatus = tradeObj.get(Constants.tradeStatusAttr);
   String tradeExporterMSP = tradeObj.get(Constants.exporterMSPAttr);

   if (!tradeStatus.equals(Constants.ACCEPTED)) {
      throw new ChaincodeException("'" + tradeId + "' is in '" +
tradeStatus + "' state. Expected '" + Constants.ACCEPTED + "'");
   }

   // Exporter, represented by an exporter org MSP
   // (currently, only 'ExporterOrgMSP'), associated with this
   // trade must match the caller's MSP
   if (!tradeExporterMSP.equals(AccessControlUtils.GetClientMspId(ctx)))
   {
      throw new ChaincodeException("'" + tradeId + "' does not belong
to exporter " + AccessControlUtils.GetClientMspId(ctx) + ". Exporter
cannot request EL");
   }
```

```
    // Lookup carrier name from Ledger
    byte[] carrierBytes = stub.getState(Constants.carrierMSPAttr);
    if (carrierBytes == null || carrierBytes.length == 0) {
        throw new ChaincodeException("No Carrier recorded on ledger");
    }

    // Lookup approver name from Ledger
    byte[] approverBytes = stub.getState(Constants.
regulatoryAuthorityMSPAttr);
    if (approverBytes == null || approverBytes.length == 0) {
        throw new ChaincodeException("No Approver recorded on ledger");
    }

    // Create E/L object and record it on the Ledger
    ExportLicense el = new ExportLicense("", "", tradeExporterMSP,
                        new String(carrierBytes),
                        tradeObj.get(Constants.tradeDescOfGoodsAttr),
                        new String(approverBytes), Constants.REQUESTED);
    String elKey = getKey(stub, tradeId);
    String elStr = el.toJSONString();
    stub.putState(elKey, elStr.getBytes(UTF_8));
    System.out.println("E/L issuance recorded with key '" + elKey + "'
and value : " + elStr);
}
```

Composite keys

We often need to store multiple instances of one type on the ledger, such as multiple shipments, letters of credit, export licenses, and so on. In this case, the keys of those instances will be typically constructed from a combination of attributes—for example, "Shipment" plus trade ID, yielding ["Shipment1","Shipment2", ...]. The key of an instance can be composed in the code, or ChaincodeStub provides functions to construct a composite key (in other words, a unique key) of an asset instance based on a combination of several attributes. These functions simplify composite key construction. Composite keys can then be used as a normal string key, which is used to record and retrieve values using the putState() and getState() functions.

The following snippet shows a list of functions that create and work with composite keys:

```
// Creates a composite key by combining the objectType string and the
// given 'attributes' to form a composite key.
createCompositeKey(objectType, attributes)
```

```
// The function splits the compositeKey into attributes from which the
// key was formed.
// This function is useful for extracting attributes from keys returned
// by range queries.
   splitCompositeKey(compositeKey)
```

In the following snippet, we can see a function `getShipmentKey` from the `ShipmentContract`, which constructs a unique composite key of a shipment asset by combining the keyword `Shipment` with an ID of the trade:

```
private getShipmentKey(ctx: Context, tradeId: string): string {
    return ctx.stub.createCompositeKey('Shipment', [tradeId]);
}
```

In more complex scenarios, keys can be constructed from multiple attributes. Composite keys also allow you to search for assets based on components of the key in range queries. We will explore searching in more detail in the next four sections.

Range and composite key queries

As well as retrieving assets with a unique key, `ChaincodeStub` offers functions to retrieve sets of assets based on range criteria. Moreover, composite keys can be modeled to enable queries against multiple components of the key.

The range functions return an iterator (`StateQueryIterator`) over a set of keys matching the query criteria. The returned keys are in lexical order. The iterator must be closed with a call to the function `Close()`. Additionally, when a composite key has multiple attributes, the range query function, `GetStateByPartialCompositeKey()`, can be used to search for keys matching a subset of the attributes.

The following snippet shows a list of range functions:

```
// Returns an iterator over all keys between the startKey (inclusive)
// and endKey (exclusive).
// To query from start or end of the range, the startKey and endKey
// can be an empty.
<async> getStateByRange(startKey, endKey)
// Same functionality as getStateByRange with additional arguments of
// pageSize and bookmark for retrieval if results in pages
<async> getStateByRangeWithPagination(startKey, endKey, pageSize,
bookmark)
// Returns an iterator over all composite keys whose prefix matches the
// given partial composite key.
```

```
// Same rules as for arguments of CreateCompositeKey function apply.
<async> getStateByPartialCompositeKey(objectType, attributes)

// Same functionality as getStateByPartialCompositeKey with additional
// arguments of pageSize and bookmark for retrieval if results in pages

<async> getStateByPartialCompositeKeyWithPagination(objectType,
attributes, pageSize, bookmark)
```

In the following snippet we can see an example of code to search for all trades with an ID within a specific range:

```
@Transaction(false)
@Returns('TradeAgreement[]')
public async getTradesByRange(ctx: Context, fromTradeId: string,
toTradeId: string): Promise<TradeAgreement[]> {
    const resultset = await ctx.stub.getStateByRange(fromTradeId,
toTradeId);
    return await this.processResultset(resultset);
}
```

Note, that during the design time of the range query, it is important to carefully consider the number and type of the resulting keys. This is because, after submission of a transaction that executed a range query, the query will be evaluated again at commitment time and if the state of any of the included keys changed and thus the result of the range query differs from when the transaction was executed at the endorsement peers, the transaction will be marked as invalid.

State queries and CouchDB

By default, Fabric uses LevelDB as the storage for the Worldstate. Fabric also offers the option to configure peers to store Worldstate in CouchDB, which provides multiple operational and performance benefits. When assets are stored in the form of JSON documents, CouchDB allows you to perform complex queries for assets based on the asset state.

In our network example, all peers other than the carrier peer are configured to use CouchDB as the Worldstate database. Since the carrier peer only hosts the Shipment contract that doesn't need advanced query capabilities, LevelDB capabilities are sufficient. However, the Trade contract, which requires advanced query capability, is installed on importer, exporter, and regulator peers, hence they all are configured with the CouchDB Worldstate database.

The queries are formatted in the native CouchDB declarative JSON querying syntax. The current version of this syntax is available at:

`https://docs.couchdb.org/en/stable/api/database/find.html`

Fabric forwards queries to CouchDB and returns an iterator (`StateQueryIterator`), which can be used to iterate over the result set. The declaration of the state-based query function is as follows:

```
<async> getQueryResult(query)
```

Similarly, as with range queries, there is a complementary function that allows us to include pagination in the result:

```
<async> getQueryResultWithPagination(query, pageSize, bookmark)
```

In the following snippet, we can see the `listTrade` function of the `TradeContract` contract, which uses a state-based query to retrieve all `TradeAgreement` assets related to an organization of the submitting identity, that is, where the attribute of `exporterMSP` or `importerMSP` matches the MSP of the submitter. The function submits two queries defined in lines 4 and 10 to find the exporter and importer MSP matches separately and combines the results to return a single array of `TradeAgreements`, shown as follows:

```
@Transaction(false)
@Returns('TradeAgreement[]')
public async listTrade(ctx: Context): Promise<TradeAgreement[]> {
    const queryExporter = {
        selector: {
            exporterMSP: ctx.clientIdentity.getMSPID(),
        },
        use_index: ['_design/exporterIndexDoc', 'exporterIndex'],
    };
    const queryImporter = {
        selector: {
            importerMSP: ctx.clientIdentity.getMSPID(),
        },
        use_index: ['_design/importerIndexDoc', 'importerIndex'],
    };

    const resultsetExporter = await ctx.stub.getQueryResult(JSON.
stringify(queryExporter));
    const resultsetImporter = await ctx.stub.getQueryResult(JSON.
stringify(queryImporter));
```

```
        return this.mergeResults(
                    await this.processResultset(resultsetExporter),
                    await this.processResultset(resultsetImporter));
    }
```

In lines 8 and 14 the queries refer to indexes, which are used by CouchDB during the search. In the next section we will see how to define these indexes.

In the following snippet, we can see implementation of the processResultset function, which combines the returned TradeAgreements into a single array:

```
private async processResultset(resultset: Iterators.
StateQueryIterator): Promise<TradeAgreement[]> {
    try {
        const tradeList = new Array();
        while (true) {
            const obj = await resultset.next();

            if (obj.value) {
                const resultStr = Buffer.from(obj.value.value)
                .toString('utf8');
                const tradeJSON = await JSON.parse(resultStr)
                as TradeAgreement;

                tradeList.push(tradeJSON);
            }

            if (obj.done) {
                return tradeList;
            }
        }
    } finally {
        await resultset.close();
    }
}
```

Note that unlike single key queries or range queries, the queries over state are not recorded into the ReadSet of the transaction. Thus, the validation of the transaction cannot verify whether changes to the Worldstate occurred between the execution and commitment of the transaction. The contract design must therefore take that into consideration; if a query is based on an expected invocation sequence, an invalid transaction may appear.

Indexes

Performing queries on large datasets is a computationally complex task. Fabric provides a mechanism for defining indexes on the CouchDB-hosted Worldstate to increase efficiency. Note that indexes are also required for sorting operations in queries.

An index is defined in JSON in a separate file with the extension *.json. The full definition of the format is available at:

```
https://docs.couchdb.org/en/stable/api/database/find.html#db-index
```

The following two snippets show the two index files defining the indexes for the state-based search queries of the listTrade function shown earlier:

```
File exportIndex.json:
{
    "index": {
        "fields": [ "exporterMSP"]
    },
    "ddoc": "exporterIndexDoc",
    "name": "exporterIndex",
    "type": "json"
}


File importIndex.json:
{
    "index": {
        "fields": [ "importerMSP"]
    },
    "ddoc": "importerIndexDoc",
    "name": "importerIndex",
    "type": "json"
}
```

Here, the index files are placed into the folder /META-INF/statedb/couchdb/ indexes. During compilation, the indexes are packaged along with the contract. Upon installation and instantiation of the contract on the peer, the indexes are automatically deployed onto the Worldstate and used by queries. Notice, that in our TradeContract contract project, the META-INF folder is placed within the contract folder, from where it is picked up during compilation and deployment.

History queries

In some cases, we may need to retrieve the history of a specific asset. The function getHistoryForKey allows us to retrieve from the ledger the information about when the asset was created, updated, and possibly deleted along with the asset states and transaction submitter identity.

The following snippet shows the retrieval of the history of a trade with a specific ID:

```
@Transaction(false)
@Returns('TradeAgreement[]')
public async getTradeHistory(ctx: Context, tradeId: string): Promise<Tr
adeAgreementHistory[]> {

    const resultset = await ctx.stub.getHistoryForKey(tradeId);

    const results = [];
    try {
        while (true) {
            const obj = await resultset.next();
            if (obj.value) {
                const tradeHistory = new TradeAgreementHistory();
                tradeHistory.txId = obj.value.txId;
                tradeHistory.timestamp = Buffer.from(obj.value.timestamp)
                .toString('utf8');
                tradeHistory.isDelete = obj.value.isDelete.toString();
                if (obj.value.value) {
                    const resultStr = Buffer.from(obj.value.value)
                    .toString('utf8');
                    const tradeJSON = await JSON.parse(resultStr)
                    as TradeAgreement;
                    tradeHistory.tradeAgreement = tradeJSON;
                }
                results.push(tradeHistory);
            }

            if (obj.done) {
                return results;
            }
        }
    } finally {
        await resultset.close();
```

```
        }
    }
```

Note that the use of the getHistoryForKey method requires peer configuration core.ledger.history.enableHistoryDatabase to be set to true.

Just like the state-based queries, the history queries are not recorded into the ReadSet, and the contract design must take this into consideration.

Transaction mechanisms

In the following two sections, we will discuss the two key transaction mechanisms related to contract design and implementation, specifically the ReadSet and WriteSet structures used to record information into transactions and the multiversion concurrency control used to ensure consistency between transactions.

The ReadSet and WriteSet

On receipt of a transaction invocation message from a client, the endorsing peer executes a transaction. The execution invokes the contract in the context of the peer's Worldstate and records all reads and writes of its data on the ledger into a ReadSet and WriteSet.

The transaction's WriteSet contains a list of key and value pairs that were modified during the execution by the contract. When the value of a key is modified by a putState function (that is, a new key and value are recorded or an existing key is updated with a new value), the WriteSet will contain the updated key and value pair.

When a key is deleted, the WriteSet will contain the key with an attribute marking the key as deleted. If a single key is modified multiple times during contract execution, the WriteSet will contain the latest modified value.

The transaction's ReadSet contains a list of keys and their versions that were accessed during execution by the contract. The version number of a key is derived from a combination of the block number and the transaction number within the block. This design enables the efficient searching and processing of data. Another section of the transaction contains information about range queries and their outcome. Remember that when a contract reads the value of a key, the latest committed value in the ledger is returned.

If modifications introduced during contract execution are stored in the WriteSet, when a contract is reading a key modified during execution, the committed — not modified — value will be returned. Therefore, if a modified value is needed later during the same execution, the contract must be implemented such that it retains and uses the correct values.

An example of a transaction's ReadSet and WriteSet is as follows:

```
{
    "rwset": {
      "reads": [
        {
          "key": "key1",
          "version": {
            "block_num": {
              "low": 9546,
              "high": 0,
              "unsigned": true
            },
            "tx_num": {
              "low": 0,
              "high": 0,
              "unsigned": true
            }
          }
        }
      ],
      "range_queries_info": [],
      "writes": [
        {
          "key": "key1",
          "is_delete": false,
          "value": "value1"
        },
        {
          "key": "key2",
          "is_delete": true
        }
      ]
    }
}
```

Multiversion concurrency control

Fabric uses a **multiversion concurrency control** (**MVCC**) mechanism to ensure consistency in the ledger and to prevent double spending. Double spending attacks aim to exploit flaws in systems by introducing transactions that use or modify the same resource multiple times, such as spending the same coin multiple times in a cryptocurrency network. A key collision is another type of problem that can occur while processing transactions submitted by parallel clients, and that may attempt to modify the same key/value pairs at the same time.

In addition, due to Fabric's decentralized architecture, the sequence of transaction processing on various components (execution and endorsement, ordering, and commitment) introduces a delay within which key collisions among parallel transactions can occur. Decentralization also leaves the network vulnerable to potential problems and attacks by intentionally or unintentionally modifying the sequence of transactions by clients.

To ensure consistency, computer systems such as databases typically use a locking mechanism. However, locking requires a centralized approach, which is unavailable in Fabric. It's also worth noting that locking can sometimes introduce a performance penalty.

To combat this, Fabric uses a versioning system of keys stored on the ledger. The aim of the versioning system is to ensure that transactions are ordered and committed into the ledger in a sequence that does not introduce inconsistencies. When a block is received on a committing peer, each transaction of the block is validated. The algorithm inspects the ReadSet for keys and their versions; if the version of each key in the ReadSet matches the version of the same key in the Worldstate, or of the preceding transactions in the same block, the transaction is considered valid. In other words, the algorithm verifies that none of the data read from the Worldstate during transaction execution has been changed.

If a transaction contains range queries, these will be validated as well. For each range query, the algorithm checks whether the result of executing the query is exactly the same as it was during contract execution, or if any modification has taken place.

Transactions that do not pass this validation are marked as invalid in the ledger and the changes they introduce are not projected onto the Worldstate. Note that since the ledger is immutable, the transactions stay on the ledger.

If a transaction passes the validation, the WriteSet is projected onto the Worldstate. Each key modified by the transaction is set in the Worldstate to the new value specified in the WriteSet, and the version of the key in the Worldstate is set to a version derived from the transaction. In this way, any inconsistencies such as double spending are prevented. At the same time, in situations when key collisions may occur, the contract design must take the behavior of MVCC into consideration. There are multiple well-known strategies for addressing key collisions and MVCC, such as splitting assets, using multiple keys, transaction queuing, and more.

Logging output

Logging is a vital part of system code, enabling the analysis and detection of runtime problems.

Logging in Fabric is based on the standard Go logging package, https://github.com/uber-go/zaph. The logging mechanism provides severity-based control of logs and pretty-printing decoration of messages. The logging levels are defined in decreasing order of severity, as follows:

```
FATAL | PANIC | ERROR | WARNING | INFO | DEBUG
```

The log messages are combined from all components and written into the standard error file (stderr). Logging can be controlled by the configuration of peers and modules, as well as in the code of the contract.

Configuration

The default configuration of peer logging is set to the level INFO, but this level can be controlled in the following ways:

1. The following command returns the current logging level for a peer:

    ```
    peer logging getlogspec
    ```

2. The following command sets the logging level, and the default logging level, for the peer to warning:

    ```
    peer logging setlogspec warning
    ```

    Note that any module can be configured through the command-line option, as shown in the following snippet. Notice in the example that the command takes the value warning for the gossip and msp components along with a default value info for all other components:

    ```
    peer logging setlogspec gossip=warning:msp=warning:info
    ```

3. The default logging level can also be defined with an `environment` variable
    `FABRIC_LOGGING_SPEC`, as shown in the following snippet:

    ```
    peer0.org1.example.com: environment:
    - FABRIC_LOGGING_SPEC=error
    ```

4. A configuration attribute in the `core.yml` file, defining the configuration of a
    network, can also be used with the following code:

    ```
    logging:
        level: info
    ```

5. The `core.yml` file also allows you to configure logging levels for specific
    modules, such as for the contract or the format of messages, as shown in the
    following snippet:

    ```
    logging:
        level:   error
        shim:    warning
    ```

More details on additional configuration options are provided in the comments of
the `core.yml` file.

Logging API

The Java and Node Contract APIs provide support for `contract` to create and
manage logging objects. The logs generated by these objects are integrated with peer
logs.

The Java Contract API provides a class `Logger`, which extends standard Java `java.`
`util.logging.Logger` and provides additional functions for formatting messages and
writing debug and error messages. The logger functions submit the messages into
peer logs.

The Node Contract API provides the function `newLogger` of class `Shim`, which
returns the logger of the `log4js` library. This logger can be used to format and write
messages into the peer logs.

Standard output and error

Aside from the Contract API logging mechanisms integrated with the peer, during
the development phase, the contract can use the standard output files. The contract
is executed as an independent process and can therefore use the standard output
(`stdout`) and standard error (`stderr`) files to record output using standard functions
such as `System.out.println(…)` in Java or `console.log(…)` in Node.js.

The following snippet shows the logging of a message from the `init` function of `TradeContract` in Node.js:

```
console.log('Initializing the trade contract');
```

Similarly, the following snippet shows the logging of a message from the `init` function of `LetterOfCreditContract` in Java:

```
System.out.println("Initialized exporter account: " + exporterAccount.
toJSONString());
```

During the development phase in VS Code and during testing, the contract logging into the standard output is directed to the console or log files. However, in the production environment when the contract process is managed by the peer, the standard output is disabled for security reasons. When required, it can be enabled by setting the configuration variable `CORE_VM_DOCKER_ATTACHSTDOUT` of the peer. The outputs of the contract are then combined with the outputs of the peer. Keep in mind that these outputs should only be used for debugging purposes and should not be enabled in a production environment.

The following snippet illustrates enabling contract standard output on a peer in a Docker Compose file:

```
peer0.org1.example.com: environment:
- CORE_VM_DOCKER_ATTACHSTDOUT=true
```

In the preceding sections, we have explored the most commonly used functions and mechanisms. To finish the chapter, we'll provide a couple of links where some additional API functions can be explored.

Additional API functions

A complete list of functions is available in the documentation of the respective APIs.

The Java Contract API documentation is available at the following link:

```
https://hyperledger.github.io/fabric-chaincode-java/master/api/overview-
summary.html
```

The Node Contract API documentation is available at the following link:

```
https://hyperledger.github.io/fabric-chaincode-node/master/api/index.html
```

Summary

The design and implementation of a well-functioning contract is a complex software engineering task that requires both knowledge of the Fabric architecture, API functions, and at least one of the contract API languages as well as the correct implementation of the business requirements.

In this chapter, we have learned step-by-step how to use VS Code with the IBM Blockchain Platform extension to open and edit contract projects as well as how to use a VS Code integrated local Fabric network to deploy and debug contracts.

We then learned how to implement the contracts of our scenario. We explored the `Contract`, `Context`, `ClientIdentity`, and `ChaincodeStub` interfaces and classes through which the contract receives requests from clients, explored the access control mechanism, and the various APIs available to the developer to implement contract functionality.

Finally, we learned how to test a contract in the terminal and VS Code, and how to integrate logging functionality into the code. To get ready for the next chapter, you should now stop your network using `./trade.sh down -d true`.

The next chapter covers in detail the programming of contracts addressing diverse business problems and scenarios.

6

Developing Smart Contracts

In this and the following two chapters, we're going to tackle the task of smart
contract and application programming in a business network that uses Hyperledger
Fabric technology. Our first two chapters—this one and *Chapter 7, Developing
Applications*, will explain how to perform the two major tasks a software developer
needs to complete in order to implement a business network:

- Smart contract design and development
- Application design and development

Our third chapter, *Chapter 8, Advanced Topics for Developing Smart Contracts and
Applications*, will introduce more advanced techniques that you'll find helpful as your
requirements expand to support advanced privacy requirements typically found in
real-world networks.

These chapters are not concerned with the management of the technical
infrastructure of Hyperledger. While infrastructure components such as **peers**,
ordering services, and **certificate authorities** are of course important, they are of
little direct interest to the smart contract and application programmer. Their value
comes from the capabilities they make available for smart contracts and applications
to exploit.

By focusing on applications and smart contracts, we're focusing on *what* a network
does rather than *how* it does it. Hyperledger Fabric allows us, correctly, to separate
these two concerns. Moreover, we know that these two distinct aspects of a solution
are performed by a different role within any organization. In a small company, these
two roles might be performed by the same person, but nonetheless they are quite
separate activities.

In larger organizations, you might imagine that the application and smart contract are developed by different roles, but we're not going to make this distinction. That's because Hyperledger Fabric is still a new technology, and in practice it's not a specialist skill to develop a smart contract; indeed, it's quite easy! However, we *will* emphasize the importance of a clear interface between the smart contract and the application.

As we start this chapter, you might be a little intimidated by the prospect of developing a Hyperledger Fabric application and smart contract. You've probably heard about consensus, smart contracts, distributed ledgers, peers, ordering service, certificate authority, cryptography, permissioned and permissionless blockchains, and so on.

Hyperledger Fabric and the ideas behind it are simple. With Fabric 2, these ideas are now also easily accessed by software developers. We'll ruthlessly exploit **separation of concerns** and **abstraction** to assemble smart contract and application designs from small, individually understandable pieces. Each piece will be simple and can be combined with others to build beautiful structures in support of new business processes.

We will be covering the following topics in this chapter:

- Business networks
- Solution application components
- Multi-party transactions
- The ledger
- Consensus
- Smart contracts
- Packaging smart contracts
- Programming languages
- Endorsement policies

Business networks

As we learned in *Chapter 3, Business Networks*, a business network contains a collection of participants and assets that undergo a life cycle described by a series of transactions. We saw at a high level how Hyperledger Fabric provides a technology infrastructure to help implement a business network.

Let's examine the high-level structure of a business network, as shown in *Figure 6.1*:

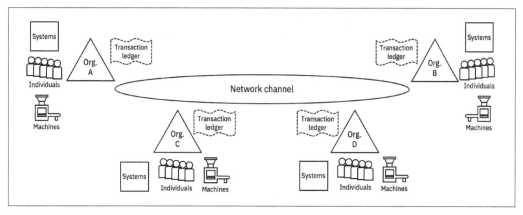

Figure 6.1: Recalling a business network with four organizations and their participants

We see a business network involving four organizations. As we learned in *Chapter 3, Business Networks*, organizations are important because every participant that performs transactions in the network—whether an individual, system, or machine— is associated with an organization.

Figure 6.1 shows that organizations communicate with each other using a **network channel**. This is both simpler and more complex than it seems.

It's *simpler* because the network channel indicates that these organizations are forming a business network for a particular reason. This might be to create a vehicle manufacturing supply chain, or a trade financing network to help the flow of international goods and services. The network channel denotes the **application** purpose that is being addressed, meaning *trade finance* or *vehicle manufacture*. In this context, *application* describes the overall business concern of the network rather than a smaller, technical, system component. In Hyperledger Fabric, we think of organizations coming together on a network channel to transact in particular business applications; trade finance, vehicle distribution, and so on.

It's also *more complex* because organizations typically operate in multiple business applications, rather than just one. For example, a vehicle manufacturer might transact with other manufacturers in a vehicle supply chain network. At the same time, in a financial network, they might perform transactions related to trade financing. Additionally, they might perform transactions in a third network with insurance companies, garages, and government agencies to ensure the proper registration, ownership, and maintenance of private and commercial vehicles. We refer to an organization as participating in a **network of networks**. As we saw in *Chapter 3, Business Networks*:

- It's a better design to think of networks of networks

- Separation of concerns allows us to properly optimize and scale an individual network

- It's easy to link different networks together using transaction and object references

Let's drill a little deeper to see how each organization and its participants transact with each other in a business network.

Solution application components

As we saw in *Chapter 3, Business Networks*, individual participants interact with a Hyperledger Fabric network using one or more applications. These are not the applications that run on a user's desktop or phone, or on the device or machine that wishes to transact in the network. Instead, we're going to look at the application that *provides* the APIs that these desktops, phones, devices, and machines use.

Let's have a look at the main application components in a Hyperledger Fabric network in *Figure 6.2*:

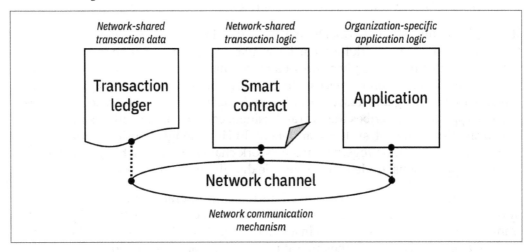

Figure 6.2: The four basic application components of a solution using Hyperledger Fabric

We can see that there are four major application components in a solution that uses Hyperledger Fabric. We're going to discuss these components in some detail during the next three chapters; let's briefly examine them now to give us a high-level map that will help us navigate.

The transaction ledger and multi-party transactions

The ledger is the core of the system; it is where individual transactions are stored. It is a resource that is shared by all organizations in the network. Sharing is achieved via **replication**; multiple copies of the ledger are kept synchronized with each other via a mechanism called **consensus**. This is in contrast to a centrally shared ledger and it's one reason why we call Hyperledger Fabric a *decentralized* network technology.

The individual transactions stored in a ledger record the change of the business objects (assets) that are of interest to the business network. A transaction is described as **multi-party** because it is signed by a set of organizations, rather than a single organization. Multi-party transaction signing is an extremely important idea in Fabric, and we'll examine it in detail throughout this chapter.

All transactions stored on the ledger are validated to determine whether they conform to two basic integrity checks:

- Business object changes described by the transaction are valid
- All necessary organizations agree with the change

This means that although all transactions submitted to the ledger are stored on it, they can be recorded as valid or invalid. While all recorded transactions are important, it is only valid transactions that affect future processing.

Although a ledger is similar to a database, it has significant differences. Specifically, we can only add a transaction to a ledger; an existing transaction cannot be updated or removed. Because of this, we describe transactions on the ledger as *immutable*. Transaction immutability is achieved via cryptographic hashing, as we'll see. What's important is that a transaction cannot be changed once it is written to the ledger.

The cross organizational nature of a ledger allows the network participants to communicate with each other. For example, if one organization submits a transaction to the ledger, then all other organizations that subsequently query the ledger will read a new ledger value. Alternatively, a participant can request notifications whenever the ledger changes. This means the ledger is not tied to a particular organization; the ledger is a vehicle for **shared transaction processing**. We'll elaborate on this idea throughout this chapter.

This shared, decentralized, multi-party, immutable ledger helps the organizations in a business network to trust each other more than they would if they stored transactions in their own, disparate systems. And in turn, this increased trust can be used by these organizations to simplify existing processes and build new ones.

Designing the structure of the business objects that reside on the ledger is a primary task in developing a solution involving Hyperledger Fabric.

Smart contracts

A multi-party transaction is generated by a smart contract. That's what makes a smart contract so important—it's the code that generates a transaction.

Fundamentally, a smart contract is simply a program that generates a set of transactions that describe the life cycle of a business object. For example, a car contract might generate the transactions that describe the manufacture and transfer of cars. The transactions generated by a smart contract will ultimately be stored on the distributed ledger, allowing every organization to have a record of the important transactions affecting a set of business objects.

In a nutshell, whereas a ledger is all about data *structures*, a smart contract is all about *processes*. A smart contract generates the transactions that describe the processes that affect a business object; when it's created, how it changes, and even how it's destroyed or archived.

Like the ledger, a smart contract is a resource shared by the network; it represents the common understanding of the transactions that describe the life cycle of a business object. However, unlike a transaction ledger, which is shared by all organizations in the network, a smart contract is only shared by those organizations responsible for *generating* a transaction. That's important in Fabric—all organizations can record transactions, but only certain organizations can generate a given transaction type. This matches a real-world practicality; my bank and I record a payment involving my account, but it's the bank that generates the payment transaction. In this analogy, we both hold the ledger, but only my bank holds the smart contract.

Designing the smart contracts that describe the life cycle of business objects is also a primary activity when designing a solution that exploits Hyperledger Fabric.

Applications

Applications consume the services provided by a Hyperledger Fabric network. Once the ledger structure and smart contracts have been defined, applications can use them in three distinct ways:

- Query the ledger
- Submit a new transaction to the ledger
- Notification of ledger change

We'll see that these three operations are very easily performed by an application, requiring just a few lines of code.

Unlike a ledger and smart contract, an application is not shared across the organizations in a business network. Indeed, applications are associated with particular organizations; an application describes how an organization has decided to interact with the business network for its own purposes.

An application is primarily concerned with marshalling input from users, systems, or devices, and subsequently deciding how to query the ledger or submit new transactions to it based on those users' requests. Additionally, an application can listen for changes to the ledger and inform users, systems, and devices who can react to these changes.

Of course, an application is usually doing more than just interacting with a blockchain; they might be using a database or performing analytics. Typically, an application combines multiple technologies when providing a business API that is consumed by the users, systems, and devices in their organization; the blockchain or other technology is invisible to these end users.

Designing the applications that query the ledger, submitting new transactions, and processing ledger notifications constitutes a key activity for solution designers.

Network channels

Note that a ledger, smart contract, and application are connected on a Hyperledger Fabric network channel. A network channel allows organizations to satisfy competing operational demands for their technical infrastructure. Specifically, it allows an organization to participate in multiple business networks using the same technical infrastructure, while being confident that these networks can be properly isolated when required — to satisfy privacy, security, and scalability concerns, for example.

Ledgers, smart contracts, and applications operate within the context of a network channel as defined by administrative personnel. Applications, smart contracts, and ledgers on the same channel can thus interact with each other.

Moreover, we'll see how an application and smart contract can also participate in multiple network channels, allowing them to participate in a network of networks. This ability to both reuse and properly isolate technical infrastructure is a key feature of Hyperledger Fabric.

Designing the network channels that connect applications, smart contracts, and ledgers is the fourth major aspect of a solution that uses Hyperledger Fabric.

The multi-party transaction

At the heart of a business network implemented in Hyperledger Fabric is a **multi-party transaction**. This single idea allows us to understand the entire philosophy of Hyperledger Fabric, so it's right to spend a little time making sure we fully grasp this concept.

The good news is that a multi-party transaction is a powerfully simple idea. As we explained in *Chapter 3, Business Networks,* a multi-party transaction describes the change in a set of business objects involving two or more participants.

In the following code, we can see an example of a multi-party transaction that describes the transfer of a car between two participants: Sara Seller and Bob Buyer (we've given them alliterative names to help us recall their roles):

```
car transfer transaction:

  identifier: 1234567890

  proposal:
    input: {CAR1, Sara Seller, Bob Buyer}
    signature: input signed by Sara Seller

  response:
    output:
      {CAR1.currentOwner = Sara Seller,
       CAR1.currentOwner = Bob Buyer}
    signatures:
      output signed by Sara Seller
      output signed by Bob Buyer
```

Code 6.1: A multi-party transaction

Let's examine the structure of this transaction between Sara and Bob.

Transaction type

The first element in *Code 6.1* is the transaction *type*:

```
Car transfer transaction
```

This is a `Car transfer` transaction; the name indicates that this is the *type* of the transaction with which we are dealing. What we're looking at in *Code 6.1* is a *particular instance* of a `Car transfer` transaction between Sara and Bob. It's really important to make this clear distinction between a *type* and an *instance*. In this example, we see an *instance* of a type of transaction.

The word *transaction* is used interchangeably to refer to a transaction type *and* a transaction instance — the context will make it clear what we are referring to.

We note that we cannot see how this transaction was generated — just the *fact* that it was generated. If you recall our discussion in *Chapter 3, Business Networks*, in the real world, a transaction records *what* happened rather than the processes that created it. Of course, the former is very important for us, but that's not what we're looking at here. As we'll see later, this transaction is actually generated by a smart contract.

Transaction identifier

The second element in the transaction reinforces the fact that this is a transaction *instance*:

```
identifier: 1234567890
```

Transaction `identifier` `1234567890` refers to this *particular* transaction between Sara and Bob. An identifier is unique for every transaction; a different identifier would mean a different transaction! And of course, a different identifier may also have a different transaction *type*.

There's not much more to say about this identifier other than it's really important because it's used whenever an application, smart contract, or any other system component refers to a particular transaction.

Proposal

The next element is really interesting — it represents the transaction *proposal*:

```
proposal:
    input: {CAR1, Sara Seller, Bob Buyer}
    signature: input signed by Sara Seller
```

This part of the transaction is describing the `Car transfer` that `Sara Seller` would like to *propose*. We note carefully the choice of words — this is a "proposal"; it's what Sara *would like* to happen. We can see that the proposal has two elements — an input and a `signature`.

The input identifies the inputs to the Car transfer transaction proposal. The transaction does not contain the program logic that acts on this input. But we certainly imagine that this input could be used to start the process of what transfers CAR1 from Sara to Bob.

It is a deliberate design principle of Hyperledger Fabric that we can only see the transaction proposal inputs — and not the program logic that processes them:

- The transaction is a structural record of *what* happened, rather than *how* it happened. The job of the transaction proposal is to capture the *structure* of the input to the contract, rather than the *process* of a smart contract that processes it.

- By keeping the smart contract program logic separate to the transaction instance, we can provide full privacy for the smart contract logic.

  For example, a Car sale smart contract might have a commercially sensitive pricing algorithm that the author of the contract does not want disclosed. Keeping the smart contract logic separate to the transaction is therefore really helpful when the smart contract contains proprietary or sensitive logic. We'll return to this idea later.

The signature field is the most important part of the proposal. We show it as:

```
signature: input signed by Sara Seller
```

What we mean by this is that the input parameters {CAR1, Sara, Bob} are cryptographically hashed using Sara's *private key*, and this hash forms Sara's signature. Along with the cryptographic hash, Sara's signature also contains her *public key*.

The combination of a cryptographic hash and Sara's public key means that anyone with access to this transaction can *verify* the transaction has been generated by Sara. Moreover, Sara's transaction proposal is now *tamper-proof* because changing the input, hash, or signature without access to Sara's private key is, for all practical purposes, impossible!

We've seen the first use of cryptography in Hyperledger Fabric to ensure that individual transactions are verifiable and tamper-proof.

Response

The final element in the multi-party transaction is:

```
response:
  output:
    {CAR1.currentOwner = Sara Seller,
     CAR1.currentOwner = Bob Buyer}
  signatures:
    output signed by Sara Seller
    output signed by Bob Buyer
```

The `response` element describes the response to Sara's transaction proposal. It contains the desired result of the `Car transfer` transaction. Although the smart contract logic is private to the transaction, the transaction response most definitely is not!

Let's examine the `response` element in a little more detail; we can see two fields within it: `output` and `signatures`.

The `output` field describes the output of the `Car transfer` smart contract. Again, even though we cannot see the program logic that generates this output, we definitely can see the result of that logic, the structure of which has two components:

- *before-image*:
    ```
    CAR1.currentOwner = Sara Seller
    ```
- *after-image*:
    ```
    CAR1.currentOwner = Bob Buyer
    ```

The **before-image** represents the state of the ledger before the transaction; that Sara *is* the current owner of CAR1. The **after-image** represents the desired state of the ledger after the transaction — that Bob *will be* the new owner of CAR1. The before-image and after-image therefore represent the current and desired new value of the business objects (assets) involved in the transaction; they have captured the transactional change.

Technically speaking, the states in the before-image and after-image contain the transaction *read-set* and *write-set*, respectively. We think of the read-set and write-set as describing the pre- and post-conditions for the transaction:

- The read-set as a precondition for the transaction expresses the fact that Sara *is* the currentOwner of CAR1. For this transaction change to be valid, the precondition must be true.

- The write-set as the *post condition of the transaction* expresses the desired fact that Bob *will be* the currentOwner of CAR1. If a transaction is valid, then this post-condition will capture the result of the transaction.

We can see that both images are described in terms of the currentOwner attribute of the CAR1 business object. In Hyperledger Fabric, CAR1 together with its properties is called a state. We're going to learn a lot more about states when we program smart contracts.

We think of a ledger as a set of transactions that determine the current value of the ledger. For example, prior to our Car transfer transaction, the ledger's current value might be:

- CAR1:{currentOwner:Sara}
- CAR2:{currentOwner:Aneena}
- CAR3:{currentOwner:Renato}

As a result of our transaction, the current value of the ledger would be:

- CAR1:{currentOwner:Bob}
- CAR2:{currentOwner:Aneena}
- CAR3:{currentOwner:Renato}

Moreover, if we query the current value of the ledger before transaction 1234567890, then CAR1 will be shown as owned by Sara, but if we query the current value after the transaction, the owner will be Bob.

In summary, a transaction response details the nature of the exchange between Sara and Bob in terms of states. It's a full record because it records the state of the world before the transaction, and the state of the world after the transaction. It's vital that we really understand these ideas; so let's make sure we have a solid grasp of the response output before we move on!

The signatures field is the most important element in the response. We show it as:

```
output signed by Sara Seller
output signed by Bob Buyer
```

This is shorthand for the transaction output {CAR1.currentOwner = Sara, CAR1.currentOwner = Bob} being cryptographically hashed once using Sara's *private key* and then using Bob's *private key*.

In a multi-party transaction such as ours, both Sara's hash and Bob's hash, as well as each *public key*, are included. Recall how we did the same thing with the proposal `input signature` field.

The big difference here is that `response` contains *multiple signatures*. Up to this point, the transaction 1234567890 has been like a traditional transaction, but these multiple signatures make it *very different* from a traditional transaction. Unlike a traditional transaction, this transaction has multiple signatories—Bob and Sara. It's not just Sara saying she's happy with the transaction; nor just Bob saying he's happy with it. They are *both* agreeing to this transaction change at the same time! That's what we mean by a multi-party transaction.

As before, the output signature, with its combination of two cryptographic hashes, together with Sara and Bob's public keys, means that *anyone* with access to this transaction can **verify** the transaction response. Moreover, the transaction response is now **tamper-proof** because changing the output, either hash or signature, without access to Sara and Bob's private keys, is to all intents and purposes, impossible. If we thought the transaction input was tamper-proof, then the response is even more so! Again, we see how important cryptography is in Hyperledger Fabric—to ensure that individual transactions are verifiable and tamper-proof.

Again, it's worth us noting that we *cannot* see the program logic that generated this transaction output, and that's deliberate. We simply have a record of the facts of the transaction—who proposed it, who agreed to it, and the business objects that were changed.

Valid and invalid transactions

We might find it surprising to learn that a ledger stores both *valid* and *invalid* transactions. We'll see later, however, that while both types are stored, they do not have the same long-term consequences.

Let's examine the two conditions required for a *valid* transaction:

1. The transaction is properly signed by all the required transaction endorsers.

    In our example, it means that valid car transfer transactions must be signed by Sara and Bob because, as a general principle, the counterparties making the transaction should agree to that transaction. This first validity check ensures that all parties have agreed to take part in the transaction.

    If the transaction is not signed by all required parties, then it will still be added to the ledger as a matter of record, but its post-conditions are not applied. In our example, the car would remain owned by Sara.

2. The second validity check records whether, when a transaction is recorded on the ledger, the before-image preconditions match the current value of the business objects. Recall that the before-image contains the precondition for a valid transaction.

In our example, this means that transaction t1234567890 will only be valid in the state database if CAR1 has the value:

```
CAR1: {Owner: Sara, Make: Volvo, Power: Electric}
```

If CAR1 has any other value, the transaction will still be added to the blockchain but marked as *invalid*. CAR1 will not be updated with Bob as its owner; Sara will remain its owner because the preconditions were not met.

This validity check ensures that business objects transition in a predictable and continuous manner. For example, if one transaction results in Sara as the owner, then any subsequent valid transaction must start with Sara as the owner, not someone else.

Let's move on! We now understand the most important part of Hyperledger Fabric—a multi-party transaction, and are ready to fully grasp the idea of a blockchain!

The ledger

With our solid grasp of a multi-party transaction, we're ready to see how it is stored at the heart of a Hyperledger Fabric blockchain system—in a **ledger**. *Figure 6.3* shows a sample Hyperledger Fabric ledger:

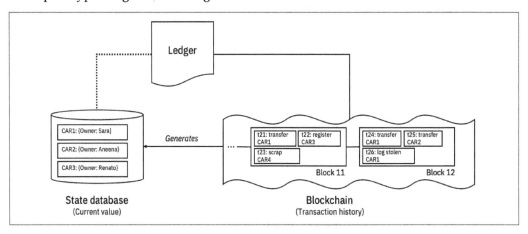

Figure 6.3: A Hyperledger Fabric ledger has two major components: a state database and a blockchain

We can see that there are two parts to a ledger—a state database and a blockchain. The state database holds the current value of all objects in the ledger, while the blockchain holds a history of all transactions affecting these objects. These are the two key data structures with which our smart contracts and application programs will interact.

Make no mistake though, the blockchain is the primary component of the ledger. That's because it *generates* the state database. If the state database was deleted or lost, we could regenerate it from the blockchain by replaying all the transactions contained within it. In contrast, if the blockchain was lost, then while we have the current value of all of the transactions, we no longer have the history of how these current values came to be.

Let's examine these two components in more detail.

State database

The state database is the ledger component that is most frequently accessed because it contains the current value of all business objects. Users are *usually* most interested in the current value of a business object rather than any of its previous historical values. In our example, we are interested in the current owner of CAR1, be it Sara or Bob. We might just as likely be interested in the current balance of a bank account, or our current academic qualifications.

The state database is backed by a real database, either LevelDB or CouchDB, but programs don't need to worry about this. What's important for a program accessing the ledger is the understanding that the state database contains the current value of *all* business objects in the ledger. For this reason, it's often called the **world state**.

The state database is a hugely simplifying data structure. Unlike other blockchains, most notably Bitcoin, the state database means that users of the ledger don't need to individually accumulate the history of changes of every business object—they simply get it from the state database. Of course, the current value of any object is simply the result of all the transactions that have acted upon it, but it's very helpful to have the current value of every object easily accessible.

State

Each state within the state database has a simple structure. It contains a key and a set of name-value pairs.

Let's have a look at an example in *Figure 6.4*:

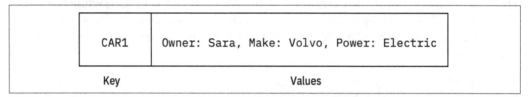

Figure 6.4: A state has a simple structure: a key and a set of properties described as name-value pairs

This state represents the business object CAR1. We can see that the *key* for the state contains the value CAR1. The key is how we refer to it within the state database. We will use the key when we initially create this business object, when we read its value, and when we update it; the key is how we address the business object in all circumstances.

The second part of the state contains a set of attributes expressed as name-value pairs. These attributes represent the properties for this business object. For CAR1, we can see its owner, its make, and its power train. These properties are highly dependent on the real-world problem we're trying to solve. For example, if we were manufacturing a car, we might be more interested in its color, weight, and engine capacity. No matter which properties we decide are important, they are contained right here in the state value.

We see that the ledger state database captures a set of business objects as a corresponding set of states, each accessed via their unique key. The properties of each state represent the current value of a business object. By modifying these values in a transaction, we can effectively move a business object through its life cycle. However, whereas the transactions are recorded in the blockchain, the current value is updated in the state database.

State collections

We think of the world state as being the default *collection* within a ledger—unless otherwise stated, all states are created in this collection. However, we don't always need to use this default world state collection; it is also possible to specify the collection in which a state is created, as we can see in *Figure 6.5*:

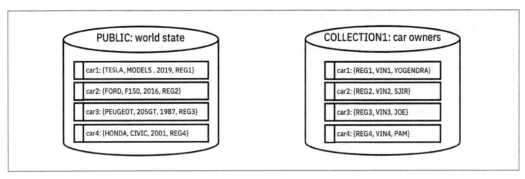

Figure 6.5: States can be contained within a collection. We can consider the world state to be the default collection

The name of a collection also provides a namespace scope for the states within it. In our example, CAR1 in the world state is a different state than CAR1 in COLLECTION1, but it refers to different properties of the same car. The PUBLIC world state CAR1 holds the make, model, year, and registration properties, whereas COLLECTION1 holds more private information — the vehicle identification number (VIN) and owner.

Throughout the chapter, we are going to learn how namespaces and other aspects of collections can prove very helpful when we model privacy structures and processes related to a business network; but for now, we'll think of a collection as a simple grouping mechanism.

Blockchain

Now that we've explored the state database aspect of the ledger, let's now turn our attention to the other side, the blockchain.

As we can recall from *Figure 6.3*, a blockchain contains a historical record of multi-party transactions stored in a sequence of blocks that are linked together — hence the name *blockchain*.

In *Figure 6.6*, we can see a snippet of the entire history of transactions: block 11 and block 12 in a blockchain. For example, when transaction t24 is committed to the ledger, then the owner will be changed for CAR1; and when t26 is committed, CAR1 will be marked as stolen:

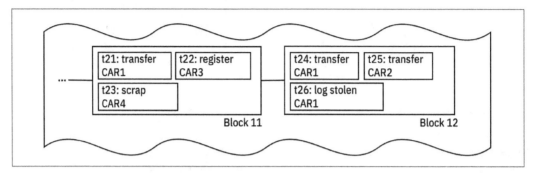

Figure 6.6: A blockchain contains a full transaction history

We can see that every valid transaction recorded on the ledger will result in an update to the state database — the transaction response after-image write-set will replace the corresponding current values in the state database.

Immutable blocks and transactions

As we've seen, a transaction is expressed in terms of a before-image and an after-image of a set of affected states. For example, transaction t1 would detail the before and after states for CAR1 as it is transferred from Sara to Bob. We saw how every transaction is individually cryptographically hashed to ensure it is tamper-proof.

A similar mechanism is also applied to blocks that contain transactions, including the links between subsequent blocks in the chain. Specifically:

- All transactions in a block are hashed together to form a *data hash*, which is stored within that block.
- When a new block is added to the chain, the *previous block hash* is also included in the block, and the block hash above.

This makes the blocks tamper-proof because:

- If we removed or changed a transaction in block 11, its block hash would now be incorrect.
- Likewise, even if we could correctly form block 11, block 12 would also be incorrect, as it implicitly contains the hash of block 11 via its *previous block hash*.

Immutability

This combination of individual transaction signing, block hashing, and block replication across multiple independent organizations is what makes a blockchain *immutable*. Once a transaction is written to the ledger, it cannot be *deleted*; it has been recorded for ever, and inextricably linked with all the other previous transactions in the blockchain.

Moreover, as we'll see later, a Hyperledger Fabric blockchain cannot be *forked* in the traditional sense; in Fabric, every organization can only add to the chain, it cannot replace it. Each Fabric blockchain can never be replaced by a *better* chain. This combination of immutability and predictability makes Hyperledger Fabric suitable as a **system of record** – a term that emphasizes the permanence of the transaction being recorded.

Let us also note that whilst blockchains and their transactions are immutable, the states referred to by those transactions can most definitely be changed. So, for example, the three transactions relating to CAR1 in *Figure 6.6* cannot be removed from the blockchain without breaking it. However, both the existence of CAR1 and its value will change according to these transactions. For example, transaction t21 might have transferred CAR1 from the car dealership to Sara when she bought it new, transaction t24 might transfer CAR1 from Sara to Bob, and t26 might record the unfortunate fact that Bob had his car stolen. These transactions cannot be changed, but the values of the state CAR1 in the state database will most definitely change as a *result* of these transactions.

In summary, we see how *every* copy of the ledger uses transaction signing and block hashing to keep the ledger tamper-proof. Moreover, transaction validity checking additionally ensures that the ledger maintains its *integrity* – it continues to be a true record of the current state of the real world. The widespread distribution of such ledgers means that it would require both immense computational power and systematic collusion across multiple independent organizations to modify an already committed transaction; it's just not feasible. In combination, these features and characteristics provide a high degree of trust in a Hyperledger Fabric ledger.

Primacy of the blockchain

Although most of the time we're interested in the business objects contained within the state database because that represents the current view of the world, we now can see that the fundamental data structure is the *blockchain*.

If you've seen the classic movie *The Wizard of Oz*, it's the blockchain that is behind the curtain! Even though we might think that the state database has all the knowledge, the real power is the blockchain that keeps the current value up to date, and provably correct.

This trust comes from the immutability of the blockchain. Moreover, by replaying its transactions in order, we can regenerate the ledger state database at any point in time, right up to the current value. And if we lose our copy of the blockchain, we can always take a copy from anyone else — being confident that they, or anyone else, has not tampered with it due to transaction signing, block hashing, and chain linking.

Smart contracts

Let's now move on to the primary user of the ledger — a smart contract.

A central role in the network

A ledger is important because it immutably stores multi-party transactions. Our attention now turns to how a smart contract helps generate these transactions in the first place.

As we begin, we issue a gentle caution to the reader! When compared to a program that reads and writes to a database over which it has complete control, a smart contract may not exhibit the behaviors we expect. Specifically, we'll see how a smart contract can sometimes:

- Read and write to the ledger, as we would intuitively expect
- Read from the ledger, but cannot write to it
- Write to the ledger, but cannot read from it

We realize that these statements may seem counterintuitive at the moment, but they stem from the fact that a blockchain is owned by multiple organizations, and every organization must agree to ledger changes in a mechanism called **consensus**.

Fabric 2 often presents the *illusion* that smart contracts have more control over the ledger than they do. This is desirable because it's what we're used to in a single-organization system. But as we'll see, this illusion can be broken in powerful ways for our benefit.

As is often the case, things are not quite as they may appear on the surface!

Smart contracts and consensus

Before we write a smart contract, let's have a look at the framework in which it operates, shown in *Figure 6.7*:

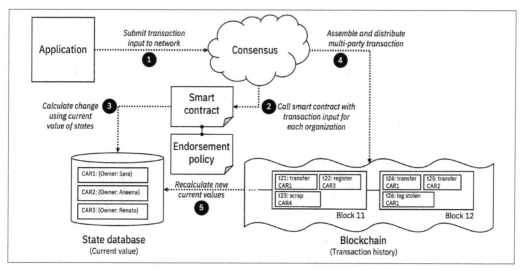

Figure 6.7: Applications and smart contracts operate within a consensus framework

In the figure, we can see how an application submits a multi-party transaction for inclusion in a distributed ledger. Let's examine each of these steps carefully:

- At step **1**, an application submits a transaction input to the network. In our example, our application effectively said, "I wish to submit a transaction to the network that transfers CAR1 from Sara to Bob."

  Note how an application can only submit a transaction input. As we saw in *Code 6.1*, the proposal input is a crucial part of the transaction, but it's not the whole story.

  That's because a fully formed transaction also contains a multi-part response, containing the result of the transfer in a pre-image and after-image, signed by both Sara and Bob.

  At step **1** in our journey, it's enough to know that after an application submits a transaction proposal to the network, Hyperledger Fabric will ensure that all the right things will happen to ensure a signed multi-party transaction is generated for inclusion in every organization's ledger. We're going to focus on what needs to occur, not how it is done. That's what the cloud represents—applications can rest assured that once successfully submitted to Fabric, a transaction proposal will result in a corresponding multi-party transaction being recorded on every copy of the ledger.

- At step **2**, we could imagine Fabric saying, "Hey Sara, hey Bob, there's been a request to transfer CAR1. Can each of you please generate a response representing the change and sign it for me? Once I've got all your responses, I'll get it included in everyone's ledger."

  Therefore, at step **2**, each organization's smart contract is called with the transaction input. And how does Fabric know which organizations need to sign the transaction response?

  Well, every smart contract has an associated **endorsement policy** that details which counterparties need to sign the transaction. Step **2** uses this policy to determine who needs to sign the transaction, and sends a copy of the transaction proposal to each instance of the smart contract in these organizations.

  Note that although it was Sara that submitted the transaction input, our business process requires that both Sara and Bob must sign the resultant transaction before it is considered valid. The term *endorsement policy* neatly captures this idea.

- At step **3**, we can see that a smart contract uses the transaction input to calculate a transaction response.

  The smart contract is accessing the ledger to calculate the before- and after-images for this transaction. Specifically:

  - When a smart contract **gets** a current value of an object, that object is copied into the transaction response before-image.

  - When a smart contract **puts** a new value for an object, that object is copied to the transaction response after-image. It is not written to the ledger.

  We see that the purpose of the smart contract is to generate a transaction response, *not* to update the ledger. Indeed, a smart contract cannot do this unilaterally because the agreement of the whole network is required — via consensus — before this can happen. The smart contract is saying what it would *like* to occur, not what has occurred.

- At step **4**, all responses have been collected from the multiple smart contract invocations, and a fully signed transaction can be assembled. Once assembled, a transaction can be distributed to the network in immutable blocks.

  We may recall from *Code 6.1* that a transaction contains one response output and multiple signatures. However, the signed transaction responses received from each organization each contain an output and signature. We have the right number of signatures, but apparently too many responses!

Of course, each response output *should* be the same. The responses should differ only in the signature hash generated by their respective private keys. The output element should be the same. This means that any response can be used, as they *should* all be the same!

Of course, we have to worry about the case where all response outputs are not the same, whether by accident, or deliberately. In this case, the most popular response is included, and we'll see later how this can still result in a valid transaction!

- We remember that a transaction is signed by a subset of the organizations in the network—only those involved in the contract agreement. However, a transaction must be distributed to the full set of network organizations.

  Step **4** will ensure that all organizations will receive a copy of the transaction for inclusion in their ledger, including the organizations who generated the transaction. In our example, Bob and Sara are sent a copy of the multi-party transaction that they both signed. This makes sense. At step **3**, each signed it for themselves, but as step **4** completes, they each receive a fully signed transaction that includes the other's response signature.

  Transaction distribution is a highly parallel process, so each organization will receive its copy of the block of transactions, and the organizations will append their copies to their ledgers at slightly different times. This is expected in a decentralized network, and each organization maintains their own ledger copies independently of every other organization. They will process the same transactions in the same way to update their ledgers consistently. That's why we sometimes hear a blockchain referred to as "eventually consistent."

- The final stage of consensus occurs at step **5**. Although all transaction blocks are recorded in the ledger, only valid transactions are used to update the current value of the ledger.

  Recall that a valid transaction must have a set of states that match the current value of the ledger. This is easy to check—we merely compare the pre-image in the transaction with the current values in the ledger, and if they match, we have a potentially valid transaction.

  Now we check that this potentially valid transaction is signed by the appropriate number of counterparties. Again, the endorsement policy comes into play. Whereas only a subset of an organization can sign a transaction, *all* organizations have a copy of the endorsement policy, allowing it to be validated by every organization in the network.

If the transaction has been signed by the required number of signatories, then the transaction response after-image is used to update the current value of the ledger.

We remember from step **4** that it might have been the case that not all transaction response outputs matched, and the majority response output was included. In such cases, only a subset of the signature hashes will be valid. If our endorsement policy requires all signatures, then such a transaction will be invalid. However, as we'll see, sometimes an endorsement policy can define a less-than-unanimous set of signatures to be required whereby a transaction is still considered valid. This is fine; every ledger received the same response, and therefore all ledger current values will be updated with the same after-image. Not everyone agreed, but we had *sufficient* agreement as defined by the endorsement policy.

- Consensus has been achieved when step **5** is complete on all nodes in the network. Next, the transaction is successfully incorporated into every organization's ledger in a consistent fashion.

  Subsequent transaction submissions will now use these *new* current values in the ledger to generate their transactions, which will be a reflection of the changes that were agreed.

  At this stage, applications can be informed that consensus is complete for a transaction or block of transactions. Indeed, sometimes applications may be listening for new transactions without having submitted a transaction in the first place.

Writing a smart contract

In *Code 6.1* , we saw a *particular* example of a car transaction: a transfer of ownership between Sara and Bob of an electric Volvo. We saw how an *instance* of a transaction with its signed proposal and multiple signed responses represented the agreement of two parties, Sara and Bob, to undergo the kind of asset exchange we discussed in *Chapter 3, Business Networks*.

Now let's see the mechanics of how a transaction is *generated* using a smart contract. In *Code 6.2*, we can see a very simplified smart contract that generates a set of life cycle transactions for cars:

```
class car fabric-contract {
  createCar(carId, properties) {
    ...
    return true;
  }
  readCar(CarId) {
    ...
    return readCar
  }
  updateCar(CarId, updatedProperties) {
    ...
    return updatedCar;
  }
  deleteCar(CarId) {
    ...
    return true;
  }
  carExists(CarId) {
    ...
    return true;
  }
}
```

Code 6.2: A smart contract describing a basic car life cycle

Smart contract structure

We've initially removed a lot of code from our smart contract to help us focus on the *structure* of a smart contract. We see that a smart contract has a simple structure, because as we saw in *Chapter 3, Business Networks*, a smart contract does a simple thing—it generates transactions that describe the life cycle of an asset or business object.

Contract class and transaction methods

The first thing we can see in *Code 6.2* is a contract for a business object of the car type. In Hyperledger Fabric, we use the built-in fabric-contract class to indicate that we're defining a contract. We'll see later how our smart contract will inherit some helpful behavior from fabric-contract.

The second thing to notice is the five transaction methods that describe the life cycle of a car:

- createCar
- readCar
- updateCar
- deleteCar
- carExists

This is a very obvious structure—cars are created; they are read; they change; they are destroyed. Without getting too philosophical, *everything* comes down to this simple life cycle, and the prevalence of this design pattern has resulted in a handy acronym to remember it by: **CRUD (Create, Read, Update, Delete)**.

Elaborating a smart contract

In reality, CRUD is our *starting point* when we design a smart contract because it helps us focus immediately on the main business objects and the transactions that govern them. We normally prefer a *domain-specific* vocabulary, in which we elaborate these standard verbs to make them relevant to the problem being solved.

We've started this process in *Code 6.3*:

```
class car fabric-contract {

  manufacture(carId, carProperties) {
    ...
    return true;
  }
  assignVIN(carId, vehicleIdentification number) {
    ...
    return true;
  }
  assignRegistration (carId, registration) {
    ...
    return true;
  }
  assignOwner (carId, initialOwner) {
    ...
    return true;
  }
  changeOwner(carId, existingOwner, newOwner) {
```

```
    ...
    return true;
  }
  ...
}
```

Code 6.3: A more realistic set of transaction names in a smart contract

We can see how our smart contract has begun to encode the knowledge of the car manufacture and ownership processes through its choice of vocabulary. We've improved the transaction names to be relevant to someone who knows about the life cycle of cars. Cars are now `manufactured`, rather than `created`. Rather than being generically `updated`, they have `assignVIN`, `assignRegistration`, and `changeOwner` transactions. We might imagine extending this life cycle by defining `scrap`, `searchDetails`, and `registerStolen` transactions.

This process has seen us recast the CRUD verbs as *categories*, inside which we use more descriptive verb-noun method names that describe domain-specific operations for a car life cycle, such as registration or ownership. These new transaction verbs incorporate the domain-specific processes and relationships relevant to the life cycle of a car.

Even though the smart contract has been made more elaborate, we can still see the CRUD structure that underlies it, and it's always worth remembering this basic life cycle when we start the smart contract design process.

Writing smart contract transaction methods

The job of a transaction method is simple — to use a transaction input to generate a signed transaction response. Every organization that agrees to a transaction needs to execute the smart contract to generate the *multiple signatures* required.

In *Code 6.4*, we will see code for the first transaction of a car's life cycle: createCar. (For the moment, ignore the carExists method.) We've used TypeScript in our example, but the contract looks very similar in Java, JavaScript, and Golang, all of which are supported in Fabric 2.

Here's the sample code used to generate a `createCar` transaction response:

```
Import { Context, Contract, Info, Returns, Transaction } from 'fabric-
contract-api';
import { Car } from './car';

@Info({title: 'CarContract', description: 'My Smart Contract' })
export class CarContract extends Contract {

    @Transaction(false)
    @Returns('boolean')
    public async carExists(ctx: Context, carId: string): Promise<boolean>
    {
        const buffer = await ctx.stub.getState(carId);
        return (!!buffer && buffer.length > 0);
    }

    @Transaction()
    public async createCar(ctx: Context, carId: string, owner: string):
Promise<Car> {
        const exists = await this.carExists(ctx, carId);
        if (exists) {
            throw new Error('The car ${carId} already exists');
        }
        const car = new Car();
        car.owner = owner;
        const buffer = Buffer.from(JSON.stringify(car));
        await ctx.stub.putState(carId, buffer);

        return car;
    }
...
```

Code 6.4: A sample car smart contract that generates two different transactions

All transaction methods have the same shape; they marshal their input, access the ledger, and return to their caller. Under the covers, the execution of a smart contract generates a single transaction response from a single transaction proposal. Let's examine each step in a little detail—to see exactly what's happening.

Marshalling the transaction proposal input

We notice that the createCar method has three inputs, each with a specific type:

- ctx: A transaction context. A context is automatically provided by Hyperledger Fabric whenever a smart contract is called. It contains both system and user elements that help the smart contract designer access the ledger or save and recall user-defined information between sequential transaction invocations. We'll see how to exploit a transaction context later.

- carId: A string. This is the first parameter provided by the caller of the smart contract. As we saw in *Figure 6.4*, all ledger states have a key; and carId is provided by the caller as the key for our new car.

- owner: A string. Similarly, we saw that all ledger states have a name-value; owner is provided by the caller and contains the owner of our new car.

The code in createCar checks whether the proposed car ID already exists, and creates a buffer containing the serialized car object.

Accessing the ledger to generate a transaction response

As we discussed earlier in the chapter, the objective of a smart contract is to generate a transaction that describes the change of a set of business objects. Because a transaction is expressed in terms of the existing and desired new values of states in a ledger, a smart contract can simply access the current value of the ledger and generate the desired new values. Under the covers, Fabric will generate the required read-sets and write-sets for inclusion in a transaction.

It is therefore deceptively simple to generate a createCar transaction. When the createCar method checks whether a car exists by calling CarExists, it reads the current value of the ledger using:

```
getState(CarId)
```

getState returns any existing state for the specified key to the smart contract. This value can be used by the smart contract to control its execution, but more importantly, under the covers, the retrieved state will be stored as a state precondition in the transaction response before-image. In the case of creating a new car, the precondition will indicate that the car must not exist for the transaction to be valid.

Given a newly created car does not already exist, the smart contract will continue to generate the post-conditions for the transaction using:

```
putState(carId, value)
```

This generates the transaction post-condition; the new value for a business object. Fabric will capture this value in the transaction response after-image.

For new car creation, it's very important that the smart contract called `getState` before `putState`, because otherwise there would be no precondition. Effectively, there would be no check that `CAR1` does not already exist.

We see how Fabric makes it a very natural process to write a smart contract; a method simply **gets** the current value of the ledger to generate the required preconditions for a transaction, and **puts** the new desired values to generate the post-conditions for the transaction.

Note how a smart contract does not read and write the ledger; it generates transactions that can be written to the ledger!

Specifically, every time a smart contract **gets a state**, it adds a precondition to a transaction before-image. And every time a smart contract **puts a state**, it adds a post-condition to a transaction after-image. A smart contract may *look* like it is changing the ledger, but it's not — it's generating the necessary preconditions for a transaction to be considered valid, and the resultant updates to be applied to the current value of the ledger.

As we saw earlier in *Code 6.1*, while generating transaction response pre- and post-conditions is vitally important, it is not enough to update the ledger. A valid transaction must also contain the signatures of all necessary counterparties involved in the transaction. The general requirement for multiple signatures means that a smart contract can never unilaterally update the ledger; it can merely be used by an organization to generate its piece of the overall agreement to a change.

This is why a smart contract execution is often called *speculative*; it's what one organization would like to happen. The good news is that it means that a smart contract can be written *as-if* a smart contract were accessing the ledger using `putState` and `getState`, but to be clear, that's not what's happening.

If it feels like we're overemphasizing this point — we're not. As we continue our journey, we'll see why understanding the difference between a smart contract generating a transaction and writing to the ledger is fundamental to understand how to get the very most from Fabric.

Accessing the state database

There are, in fact, a large set of APIs that allow smart contract developers to generate transactions. We've just seen two of the most popular APIs used to generate a smart contract transaction response — `getState` and `putState`. These are among the most commonly used APIs:

- `getState(key)` returns a value for the supplied key
- `putState(key, value)` creates or updates a value for the supplied key
- `deleteState(key)` deletes a state for the supplied key

These APIs are quite simple—we can put, get, and delete a state. It may *look* like a smart contract is interacting with the ledger, but that's not the most important thing that's happening; the result returned from a **get**-style operation is of most use to the smart contract to calculate a new transaction response for eventual inclusion in the ledger only after consensus is complete.

There are also a set of more sophisticated query-style APIs—for example, if we need to determine *all blue cars* in the ledger. These APIs typically allow us to query which business objects match a set of relevant criteria:

- `getStateByRange()`
- `getStateByRangeWithPagination()`
- `getStateByPartialCompositeKey()`
- `getStateByPartialCompositeKeyWithPagination()`
- `getQueryResult()`
- `getQueryResultWithPagination()`

The first two `range` APIs allow us to query a set of objects within a key range—for example `CAR1` to `CAR100`. This can be very helpful if we've chosen a particular key style to represent our business objects. The second form is appropriate when we expect to get back thousands of objects—it allows us to process them *N-at-a-time*; hence the term *pagination*.

The next two `PartialCompositeKey` APIs are used when we've built structure into our key! In our previous example, our key was simply the car's identifier. But we could have structured our key more richly. For example, imagine we had a scenario where people owned multiple cars; we might want to structure our keys thus:

- SaraCAR1
- SaraCAR2
- SaraCAR3
- BobCAR1
- BobCAR2
- ...

In these cases, the key is a *composite* of the owner and an identifier. Using these APIs, we could now retrieve all of Sara or Bob's cars with a single API! We can see why key design is important, and a subject in its own right.

The final two `Query` APIs allow us to access states according to their values. As we mentioned earlier, the state database can be configured to store states in LevelDB or CouchDB. However, these APIs are only available if CouchDB has been chosen. Imagine the following two states:

```
CAR1: {Owner: Sara, Make: Volvo, Power: Electric}
CAR2: {Owner: Bob, Make: Honda, Power: Electric}
```

We could use these `Query` APIs to ask the following questions:

- Which cars have:

  ```
  Owner: Sara?
  Result: {CAR1}
  ```

- Which cars have:

  ```
  Power: Electric?
  Result: {CAR1, CAR2}
  ```

These APIs allow us to deep-inspect states to determine which objects match the query criteria. In fact, these APIs simply pass the query through to the underlying CouchDB database, which does all the hard work! That is why these APIs are required. In real-world solutions, we'll want to use these kinds of `Query` APIs all the time, so we recommend that you always configure the state database to use CouchDB, rather than LevelDB.

The APIs above apply to the world state, which we often think of as the public, or default, collection. There are an equivalent set of APIs to access states within a private collection; they vary only in spelling and in the fact that they name the relevant collection. For example:

- getPrivateData(collection, key) is analogous to getState()
- putPrivateData(collection, key, value) is analogous to putState()
- deletePrivateData(collection, key) is analogous to deleteState()

Think of there being a 1:1 correspondence of these APIs to those for the world state.

Returning a signed transaction response

The final part of `createCar` returns control to Fabric, but the story doesn't quite end there!

As we've discussed, under the covers, Fabric has been accumulating a transaction response containing the necessary before- and after- images that describe the transaction. Exiting the smart contract method allows Fabric to sign the transaction with the private key of a participant from the organization executing the smart contract. Again, we don't need to worry about this as the author of the smart contract. We simply write a smart contract, and once deployed, all this happens automatically.

Checking that business objects exist

All smart contracts should have a set of *exist-style* transaction methods. In *Code 6.4*, `carExists` is both a useful method in its own right and is used by other methods, such as `createCar`, to check that a car exists before continuing. `carExists` is a simple operation that merely reads a business object as a state from the ledger world state to verify its presence, returning `true` or `false` accordingly.

For now, such *exist-style* methods seem like a small but practical design point to adopt without question, and we advise you to adopt this pattern. We will return to this topic in *Chapter 8, Advanced Topics for Developing Smart Contracts and Applications*, when we investigate a concept called *private data*, where we'll be lifting this restriction.

We'll also return to this idea of checking whether objects exist in the ledger when we discuss *verify-style* transactions, and the other ways in which we can check whether a business object exists.

Transaction handlers

We've seen how a single smart method generates a particular transaction. Sometimes, however, a contract needs different methods to include the same logic. A smart contract may wish to enforce common security checking or reporting/auditing, for example.

Transaction handlers are designed to allow us to create such common logic:

```
class car fabric-contract {

    ... (user transactions) ...

    beforeTranaction() {
        ...
        return;
    }
    afterTransaction() {
        ...
        return;
    }
    unknownTransaction
        ...
        return;
    }
}
```

Code 6.5: Transaction handlers simplify the programming of common behaviors, such as ACL checking

In *Code 6.5*, we can see the three possible handlers in a smart contract:

- The beforeTransaction handler
- The afterTransaction handler
- The unknownTransaction handler

Respectively, these handlers allow us to add logic at three different points during smart contract processing:

- *Before* every transaction method gets control
- *After* every transaction method relinquishes control — but before it returns to Fabric for transaction response signing
- When an *unknown* transaction is requested by an application

As well as saving us time when we write common logic for different transactions, these handlers also allow us to write better smart contracts because we are forced to *think* about these issues. For example: *What happens if an application invokes a smart contract transaction that has not been defined?*

The good news is that we don't need to worry about transaction handlers at the outset — Fabric provides sensible defaults; if an unknown transaction function is requested, Fabric will return a sensible error message. We can use our own handlers only when we find the default behavior doesn't meet our needs.

Other functionality available in fabric-contract-api

We've already seen how `fabric-contract-api` provides both the contract class, transaction handling, access to the ledger, and transaction handlers.

It also provides many other functions via `ctx.stub.<API>`, which include the APIs we learned about earlier in the chapter — which include the advanced query APIs for the ledger. We're not going to examine them in detail right now — they are important, but we will defer them until later.

Annotations

Finally, you may have noticed a few *annotations* sprinkled around the code in *Code 6.4* — `@Transaction` and `@Info`, for example. You can add these decorations to your code to help describe the smart contract's behavior or structure. For example, if a method is internal to the smart contract, then it is *not* marked with the `@Transaction` annotation.

These annotations can be used by tools to provide an improved user experience. For example, the popular VS Code extension for Hyperledger Fabric uses the @ `Transaction` annotation to test smart contracts by only showing the relevant smart contract transaction functions rather than internal methods. Advanced users can also write tools that exploit these annotations.

Packaging smart contracts

Before a smart contract can be used, it must be packaged for distribution. In Fabric version 2, there is also a new construct associated with a package: a *definition*. Let's have a look at how these two structures are related and used:

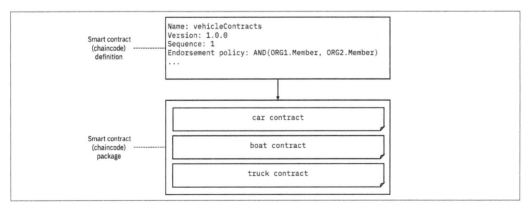

Figure 6.8: An organization packages smart contracts for distribution. An organization also creates an associated package definition.

In *Figure 6.8*, we can see that a smart contract package is simply a collection of smart contracts. The package shown has three smart contracts in it: **car contract**, **boat contract**, and **truck contract**.

A smart contract contains the smart contract code and manifests detailing the contents of the package. Unlike Fabric 1, version 2 has a completely open packaging zip file format, making it both simpler and more accessible to use.

The more significant change in Fabric 2 is the introduction of a package *definition*. As we can see in our example, car contract, boat contract, and truck contract all share the VehicleContracts definition. A definition contains all kinds of interesting information about a package—its name, its version, and most importantly, its *endorsement policy*—something we'll learn about in a moment.

The role of a package definition in Fabric 2 is to formally define a lot of the implicit assumptions that were present in Fabric 1; if you don't know about these assumptions then don't worry—just remember that every organization in a network has a definition that they can use to assert a common understanding of a package.

A word on terminology

This chapter almost exclusively uses the term *smart contract* rather than *chaincode*, and we advise you to do the same. Chaincode is a legacy term, and if you use it outside Fabric circles, you will be met by blank faces. You'll often see it referred to in the Fabric documentation for historic reasons.

Smart contract package definition agreement

For the purposes of analysis, it's helpful to think of a smart contract, its package, and definition as being literally shared across the member organizations in a network—there is one source of code and everyone gets a copy of it. In many cases, organizations will collaborate closely on the development, approval, and deployment of these artifacts to ensure that there is unanimous agreement at all stages.

However, in Fabric, both literal sharing and full agreement is not strictly necessary. What's important is that organizations can agree which transactions are generated and who must sign them before they can be considered valid. This is most easily achieved if the smart contract, package, and definition are the same, but what's important is that smart contract code generates well-formed multi-party transactions with whatever code they use.

A definition is therefore a declaration by an organization of the details of the transactions generated by a particular smart contract package: their name scope, their version, the required signatures, and so on. By each organization declaring which transactions they will generate, the network can determine the conditions under which a given package can be made available on the network, if at all.

If this seems unnecessarily complex, don't worry, it does not affect smart contract or application development. It's a purely operational matter that determines whether or not a smart contract package generating a set of transactions can be made active in the network. In *Chapter 8, Advanced Topics for Developing Smart Contracts and Applications*, we'll exploit this kind of advanced packaging, but until then it can be safely ignored.

Let's now move on from the smart contract to see how it's used by the wider network and applications, in particular. But before we do this, we have a short digression on programming languages.

Programming language

As we discovered earlier in the chapter, at the heart of Hyperledger Fabric is an immutable log of multi-party transactions. This idea transcends any given programming language; indeed, we'd really like as many participants as possible to participate in a network of multi-party transactions.

Moreover, given we have a decentralized system where different organizations develop different smart contracts and applications, it's just not feasible to suggest that only one programming language can be used.

This joint desire and need for language openness is why Hyperledger Fabric allows multiple programming languages to be used for smart contract and application development. At the time of writing, the most popular programming languages are JavaScript, TypeScript, Java, and Golang, and support for these is built into Fabric. Additionally, the Hyperledger Burrow project allows developers to write smart contracts in Solidity, a programming language used by Ethereum.

Developers with different programming language skills, preferences, and experiences can get going immediately in their language of preference. Moreover, because Fabric also allows smart contracts and applications to be written in *different* programming languages to each other, developers can easily modify or add functionality to an existing network using their chosen programming language.

Choice of programming language

Let's keep this simple—all programming languages have trade-offs. Some favor expressivity rather than terseness; some favor static typing rather than more flexible runtime type checking; some favor 100% backward compatibility in preference to a rapidly evolving ecosystem; some favor the declarative power of a functional approach rather than the accessibility of an imperative (*if-then-else*) style of programming.

Much more important than our choice of programming language is good design: good business object design, good design of smart contracts, good design of applications. With good design, we can implement projects in any programming language supported by Fabric. Good programming techniques, in whatever programming language, will mean satisfied end users!

So, look at your team, see what programming skills you have, and use them to the best effect to implement your design.

Using a type system

The only guideline we're going to adopt is that when we build a large system, we're going to advocate the use of a programming language that supports *types*. That's because large systems have structure, and *types embody structure*. Therefore, in this book, we tend to show examples in Java, TypeScript, and Golang.

Because the smart contract is primarily a development artifact rather than the application, it's more important that we use types for a smart contract than for the application. If a smart contract has well-defined inputs and outputs—enabled by the use of a type system—it allows applications flexibility in their choice of a type-based language. That's because the smart contract acts as the arbiter of good behavior when accessing the ledger!

So, while we can use JavaScript for writing applications rather than smart contracts, we're better off sticking to JavaScript when we're designing smaller systems, or prototyping. That's a great trade-off; to be able to use JavaScript when we want to do rapid prototyping to work out our ideas, safe in the knowledge that nothing we do will be programming language dependent.

Modularity – a big idea in Hyperledger Fabric

The ability to choose the programming language for smart contracts and applications is a concrete example of modularity, a key tenet of Hyperledger Fabric.

Hyperledger Fabric is designed as an open system. We know that *open source* is a very important aspect of this philosophy, but so is an *open design*, a principle which allows system components to be interchangeable. In this case, applications and smart contracts can be replaced by those written in a different programming language.

The general idea of modularity allows Hyperledger Fabric to evolve — as new ideas emerge and new technologies are developed, they can be more easily incorporated within a modular framework. You'll see many examples of modularity in Fabric.

Endorsement policy

Now that we understand how a smart contract generates, *for a single organization,* a signed transaction response comprising the before- and after-images of changed states, we're close to understanding how to generate a *multi-party transaction*. We're going to see how an endorsement policy is central to this process.

In *Figure 6.9*, we can see an endorsement policy for the car smart contract we've been discussing:

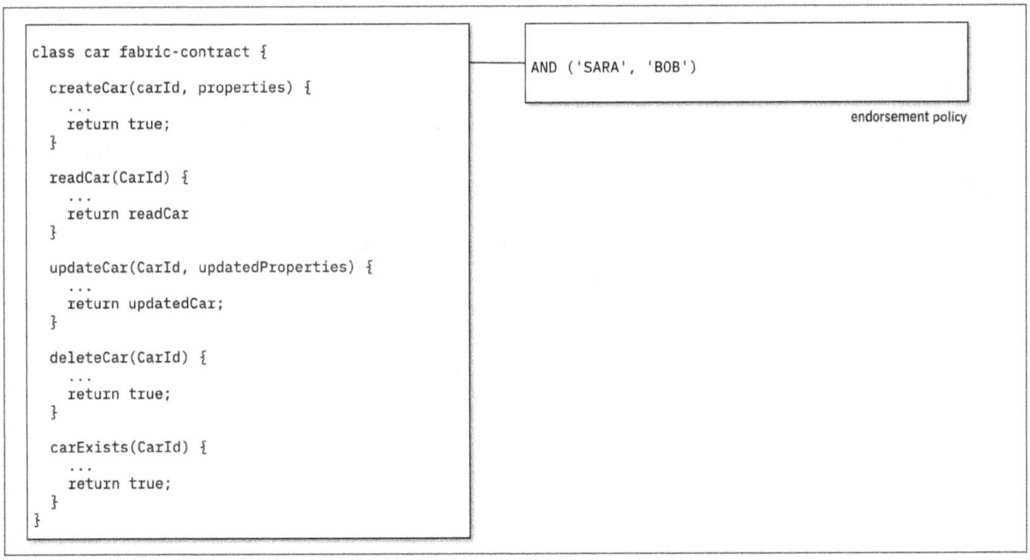

```
class car fabric-contract {

  createCar(carId, properties) {
    ...
    return true;
  }

  readCar(CarId) {
    ...
    return readCar
  }

  updateCar(CarId, updatedProperties) {
    ...
    return updatedCar;
  }

  deleteCar(CarId) {
    ...
    return true;
  }

  carExists(CarId) {
    ...
    return true;
  }
}
```

```
AND ('SARA', 'BOB')
```
endorsement policy

Figure 6.9: A smart contract has an endorsement policy associated with it

The car contract has an associated endorsement policy: AND(SARA, BOB). This says, "any transaction generated by the car smart contract is only valid if it is signed by Sara and Bob."

In Hyperledger Fabric, every smart contract has an associated endorsement policy to describe the set of signatures required for the transaction that generated it to be considered *valid*. Multi-party transactions are the core of Hyperledger Fabric—that's why endorsement policies are so important.

It's the endorsement policy that defines which signatures are required—if a transaction is not signed by Sara and Bob, then it's not valid—it's as simple as that! *Anyone can try* to generate a multi-party transaction, but unless they get it signed by Sara and Bob, the rest of the network will not accept it as a valid transaction.

As we saw in *Figure 6.8*, a smart contract is distributed within a package, and the endorsement policy is actually contained within a definition that points at this package. The essential point is that every smart contract has an endorsement policy associated with it. As we'll continue to see, packages and definitions provide great flexibility in the relationship between a set of smart contracts and a set of endorsement policies—but do not change the fact that every smart contract has an associated endorsement policy.

The structure of an endorsement policy

We can see that an endorsement policy has a simple syntax—it describes the parties that must sign a transaction for it to be valid. In general, an endorsement policy doesn't specify an individual participant like SARA or BOB, but instead any member of an organization, or a particular role within an organization. That's because it is organizations that form the business network and decide which transactions are valid, and we therefore define participants with respect to their owning organization.

So, we might see an endorsement policy like one of these:

```
AND('ORG1.Member', 'ORG2.Member')
OR('ORG1.Member', 'ORG2.Member', 'ORG3.Member')
OUTOF(2, 'ORG1.Member', 'ORG2.Member', 'ORG3.Member')
```

In the first case, both organization 1 and organization 2 must sign a multi-party transaction for it to be valid. In the second case, any of organizations 1, 2, or 3 can sign the transaction. In the final case, any two of the organizations 1, 2, or 3 must sign a transaction before it is considered valid.

As the network gets larger, we'll see that it often makes sense to move an endorsement policy that looks more like an OUTOF type policy to reflect the fact that a large majority is often satisfactory for agreement; it really does depend on what kind of governance we require.

We see that the syntax of an endorsement policy is deceptively simple; it elegantly describes the agreement between the organizations in the network on how the business objects are governed throughout their life cycle. We'll hear the word *governance* a lot in Fabric; this is a good example of it.

Network agreement

It's important that we understand that *every* organization in a network agrees that the same endorsement policy applies to any given transaction generated in a network channel. That's because every organization *independently* validates every transaction as it adds it to its copy of a ledger without reference to other organizations performing the same validation process on identical copies of the transaction being added to their copy of a ledger.

For example, if organization 1 is validating transaction instances according to a policy `AND('ORG1.Member', 'ORG2.Member')`, it makes no sense if organization 2 is using a less restrictive policy `OR('ORG1.Member', 'ORG2.Member')`! Both organizations must use the same policy, or their ledgers will accept different transactions as valid, causing their world states to diverge. In turn, this would adversely impact smart contract execution. Different smart contracts, which use the current value to generate transaction preconditions and post-conditions, would generate different subsequent transactions when using different ledger instances — the system would grind to a halt.

Why endorsement?

If you're familiar with Bitcoin or Ethereum, endorsement policies are the biggest difference between Fabric and these technologies. Although endorsement policies add a little complexity, their use has two distinct benefits:

- Organizations within a network can independently validate transactions rather than external "mining" organizations.

  In the real world, the organizations *involved* in a contractual transaction are the ones who sign it. This normally involves the consumer and provider of a service. Sometimes, for example in the case of property transfer, a legal entity or regulator also signs the contractual transaction. Critically, *all* the parties are formally recognized by each other, and have a stake in the correctness of the transaction. Their identities, as demonstrated by their signature, are the basis of trust.

Bitcoin and Ethereum don't work like this. In these systems, transaction validation is a purely mathematical activity performed by a separate set of organizations unknown to the transaction counterparties. The mathematical nature of transaction validation means that recent transactions can be reversed if a new, longer blockchain is announced by a competing miner. In the real world, when a contract is signed, it cannot be *undone* like this. We call this *finality*, and it's another difference between Fabric and other blockchain technologies.

• Signature-based transaction validation is relatively quick and computationally inexpensive.

Fabric transactions can be validated at low cost and low latency — a significant benefit compared to Bitcoin and Ethereum, where the transaction validation process is computationally very expensive, and wasteful for miners who fail to introduce a successful block. To overcome these concerns, a token lottery is introduced as an incentive to overcome this speculative waste.

Moreover, in Fabric, these lower costs are also *shared* across the network rather than being borne by a particular set of counterparties. Specifically, transactions are signed by endorsing organizations, distributed by ordering organizations, and validated by all organizations. No single set of counterparties suffers a significant computational or latency burden during transaction processing, unlike Bitcoin and Ethereum where miners bear all of the cost of transaction processing.

Endorsement policy – a separate concern

We've seen that while an endorsement policy is very closely related to a smart contract, it is quite separate to it. The principal reason it's separate is because it can change independently of the smart contract.

For example, when organizations are added to or removed from the network, we can simply update the endorsement policy. There is no need to change the smart contract; the network simply agrees a new endorsement policy for a given smart contract, and now transactions generated by this smart contract must conform to these changed requirements.

Secondly, the *nature* of the endorsement policy may change. When networks are small, we will tend to be quite *explicit* about who signs transactions using AND and OR type policies. As the network grows, we will consider using OUTOF type policies to acknowledge the fact that a majority is often enough when validating certain kinds of transactions. In these cases, it really helps that the endorsement policy is separate to the smart contract.

Finally, and probably most importantly, while the endorsement policy is known and agreed by all organizations in the network, the smart contract—in other words, the transaction logic—is not! The smart contract is *private* to the counterparties who sign the *public* transaction response.

This is a key feature in Fabric because it allows *private processing*. For example, a smart contract might have logic containing how a discount rate is calculated for particular consumers, and this must be kept private to the counterparties providing the service. In contrast, the *result* of the transaction—the price paid, for example—can be public. A separate endorsement policy allows us to separate the "how" of processing from the "what" of processing. Again, this is a real-world privacy requirement that Fabric handles through its use of endorsement policies.

State-based endorsement

We've seen how powerful endorsement policies are—they ensure that any change is agreed by the appropriate counterparties, mirroring how things work in the real world. Up to this point, we've seen the endorsement policy associated with every smart contract.

It can also be appropriate for the endorsement policy to be associated with *individual* states to provide more granular transaction approval. *Figure 6.10* shows an example:

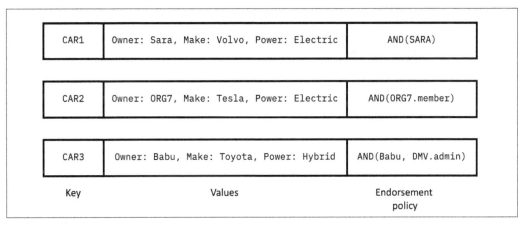

Figure 6.10: Endorsement policies can also be associated with individual policies, which is very appropriate for ownership scenarios

In this case, CAR1 has an endorsement policy of AND(SARA). This means that any transaction that includes a change of this state must also include Sara's signature. This is a powerful idea—it means that change cannot happen without Sara's explicit agreement. If we look at CAR2, we can see a slightly more sophisticated example where any change must be signed by *any member* of ORG7, a less restrictive policy.

Finally, CAR3 has an endorsement policy that is more restrictive — it requires explicit approval from *two* counterparties — both the owner and an administrator from the DMV (the government organization responsible for approving change of ownership requests).

Applying an endorsement policy at an individual state level is a very powerful idea because it closely models the governance of transfer of ownership. But it's not limited to this scenario — we'll find it a helpful tool to have in our blockchain developer kit bag.

A couple of final points on state-based endorsement are worth mentioning. Firstly, as in the ownership examples above, as a state changes, so does the endorsement policy. As CAR1 is transferred to Bob, so the endorsement policy should change to AND(BOB) to reflect the fact that after the transfer, Sara no longer has the ability to create valid transactions that affect CAR1; only Bob does.

Secondly, we usually find that contract-based endorsement and state-based endorsement work closely *together*, as follows: when a state is created, the contract endorsement policy is used to govern this process; at this time an explicit endorsement policy is associated with the state that is subsequently used to govern all changes to it. We'll see an example of this later.

Collection endorsement policy

We've seen that it's possible to define an endorsement policy at the smart contract level or at the state level. These are both helpful:

- A smart contract endorsement policy determines the *general rule* for transaction signing; in the absence of a state-based endorsement policy, this endorsement policy dictates how a transaction must be signed before it can be considered valid.

- A state-based endorsement policy determines the *specific rule* for an individual state.

There is also a third form of endorsement policy, which lies between these two options. It applies to **collections of states**, the so-called *collection endorsement policy*:

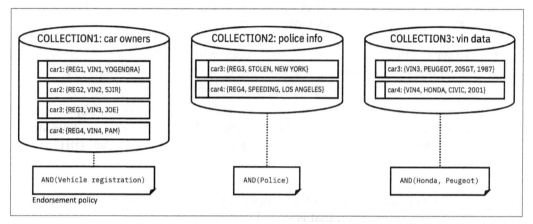

Figure 6.11: Endorsement policies can also apply to collections of states

In *Figure 6.11*, we can see three collections that contain state information corresponding to different aspects of vehicles. COLLECTION1 contains information relating to car owners; COLLECTION2 contains police information on these vehicles; and COLLECTION3 contains vehicle identification data related to the manufacture of Honda and Peugeot cars. We can see how each of these collections have different endorsement policies that determine which organizations need to sign transactions involving states in any given collection.

For example, all transactions involving changes to states in COLLECTION1 must be signed by the vehicle registration organization, and all states in COLLECTION2 must be signed by the police. This makes sense, as these organizations govern the changes to these states. COLLECTION3 also demonstrates how collections can be governed by multiple organizations. Transactions involving states in COLLECTION3 must be signed by both the Honda and Peugeot organizations.

We can see how a collection endorsement policy operates in the space between state-based and contract-based endorsement; it allows us to define rules for transactions involving *particular groups* of states. We'll see later that this can be very helpful for modeling many processes in a business network.

Summary

We've reached the end of our journey on smart contract development in Hyperledger Fabric. Let's spend a few moments recapping the key steps:

- We started by examining the central concept of a *multi-party transaction*, which represents the mutual agreement by a set of organizations in a network consortium to a change to a set of business objects.

- We moved on to see how transactions involving these business objects were stored in a *distributed ledger* replicated across all network organizations, and how it held both the transaction history of these objects and their current value.

- We discussed how smart contracts operate within a consensus framework, and the operations that need to happen for a smart contract to generate a multi-party transaction that is stored in the ledger.

- We examined the important interplay between a smart contract and the ledger's current value in generating a transaction response expressed as before- and after-images. We saw how multiple signed transaction responses were assembled into a multi-party transaction that was distributed to every ledger for inclusion. We saw how only a valid transaction resulted in current value changes to the ledger.

- Moreover, we saw how a *smart contract* could be used to capture the business logic used to generate the set of transactions that govern the *life cycle* of these business objects using `fabric-contract-api`.

- We then explored how an *endorsement policy* dictated which counterparties need to sign a transaction before it can be considered valid.

- We broadened the scope of an endorsement policy from just applying it at the smart contract level to applying it at the state and collection levels.

- Finally, we discussed how smart contracts are packaged and distributed, and how a package definition is used to agree to a consistent endorsement policy for smart contracts across a network.

In the next chapter, we're going to see how an application uses everything we've learned about smart contracts to submit multi-party transactions to the ledger.

7
Developing Applications

Let's build on what we learned about ledgers and smart contracts in the preceding chapter as we consider application design and development. In *Chapter 6, Developing Smart Contracts*, we saw that smart contracts were responsible for generating the multi-party transactions that describe a business object's life cycle. These transactions were captured on a distributed ledger, replicated across a set of organizations connected via a network channel, as shown in the following illustration.

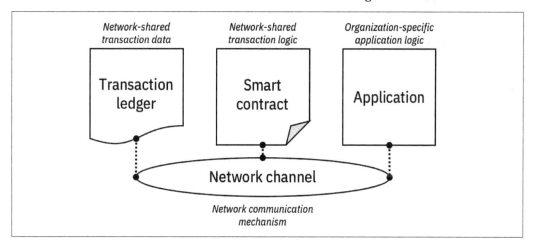

Figure 7.1: Recalling the components of a solution that uses Hyperledger Fabric

We saw that a ledger has two major components. The most important was the blockchain because it held an immutable history of multi-party transactions. The valid transactions in a ledger contributed to the ledger's current value; and it was this current value that was most frequently used. This is because users are normally most interested in the current value of a business object.

The focus of this chapter is how applications interact with smart contracts and the ledger. We'll see that there are three basic operations that an application can perform:

- Query the ledger
- Submit a new transaction
- Listen for ledger notifications

This chapter will explore these ideas in more detail. We will be covering the following topics:

- Applications
- Wallets and identity
- Gateway
- Accessing networks and smart contracts
- How to query the ledger
- How to submit a new transaction
- Events and notifications

Applications

Chapter 6, Developing Smart Contracts, gave us a solid understanding of the main structures that a Hyperledger Fabric smart contract developer needs to understand:

- Multi-party transaction
- Ledger
- Smart contract
- Endorsement policy

Let's look at an example set of applications interacting with these components within a Hyperledger Fabric infrastructure:

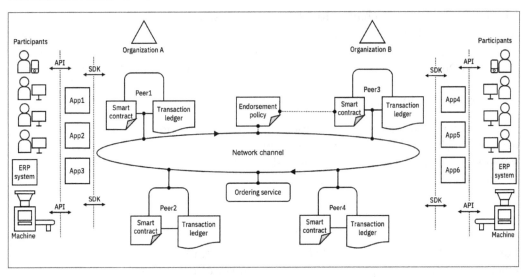

Figure 7.2: An example of a two-organization Hyperledger Fabric network where applications interact on behalf of participants

While *Figure 7.2* might seem a little complex, its structure will become more familiar and simpler as we examine it throughout the chapter.

In this example, we can see a set of six applications (App1-App6) in two organizations, acting on behalf of their organization's participants. These applications interact with a set of network Hyperledger Fabric infrastructure components that provide the ledgers, smart contracts, and network channels that allow participants to create and exchange transactional information with each other.

We're going to explore what applications like these can do and how they do it.

The three basic application operations

Applications can interact with a Hyperledger Fabric network in three distinct ways:

- Query a ledger
- Submit a new transaction
- Receive notification of a change to a ledger

Figure 7.2 might seem to have a lot of moving parts, but it shows a relatively simple network in which our applications wish to interact. With just two organizations, we can see four peers, an ordering service, ledgers, deployed smart contracts, and their respective endorsement policies. Imagine how a network with more organizations could present an almost overwhelming arrangement of peers, ledgers, smart contracts, and endorsement policies for an application to navigate.

If this wasn't enough, many applications will be participating in *multiple* networks, each of which could be as complex as *Figure 7.2*, in the so-called **network of networks**. There's clearly potential for all this infrastructure complexity to completely overwhelm an application programmer.

The application SDK

Fortunately, the Hyperledger Fabric application SDK makes interacting with *any* Fabric topology simple. No matter the number of networks with which an application needs to interact, no matter how their organizations, ledgers, smart contracts, endorsement policies' peers, and ordering services are structured, the SDK shields the application from the complex topology, while at the same time allowing an application to exploit this richness.

Moreover, as the network topology changes, the SDK has logic inside it to exploit potential application benefits, like high availability or resiliency. For example, if an application's organization has two peers, the SDK will automatically use one that is available if the other isn't running; or if one peer fails, the SDK will automatically switch to the available peer to continue processing. Applications get all the richness provided by the network without worrying about any of its implementation details.

Declarative APIs and the fabric-network package

In a nutshell, applications request *what* they want to do, and the SDK manages *how* that request is achieved. We describe the Fabric SDK API as declarative, rather than imperative.

This philosophy makes a Hyperledger Fabric programmer's life easy. We'll see concrete examples of the declarative nature of the SDK APIs later in this chapter.

If you've used a previous version of Hyperledger Fabric with the old SDK, you're in for a treat; the version 2 SDK fabric-network package makes applications simpler and allows them to exploit the network in ways that simply weren't possible with the old fabric-client SDK.

To be explicit, we strongly recommend that applications use the `fabric-network` packages for JavaScript, TypeScript, Java, and Golang. These packages contain the declarative APIs that will make application programs easier and quicker to write, more reliable, more resilient, and higher performing. The Hyperledger Fabric application `fabric-network` package represents an enormous investment that you can exploit in your application programs.

Indeed, my opinion is you should never use `fabric-client`! Moreover, convert your existing Fabric applications as soon as possible to use the idioms and capabilities in `fabric-network`; you'll be making your programs better in every way, and exploiting features of Fabric that you could not practicably do before.

Separating the physical from the logical

The other thing you'll notice about the SDK is that its APIs make no reference to the physical infrastructure component types in Fabric, namely peers, certificate authorities, and ordering services. This is deliberate.

Although it's true to say that a Hyperledger Fabric network would not, indeed *could not*, work without these components, it is also true to say that they are not part of the application architecture. Network administrators may create or reconfigure peers, ordering services, and certificate authorities in any number of ways, but this is of little concern to the application that simply wishes to query the ledger, submit new transactions, or receive notification of ledger change.

It's also worth noting that the client application doesn't usually need to be aware of the smart contract endorsement policy either. That's because the SDK will use the Fabric process of *discovery* to find all the smart contract endorsement policies, and then calculate what needs to be done to generate a valid transaction.

The situation is slightly different for state-based and collection-based endorsement policies where the endorsement policy is part of an *integrated* application/smart contract design. We'll see that the new SDK has made this process easier too, and we'll explore these cases as a part of advanced usage in *Chapter 8, Advanced Topics for Developing Smart Contracts and Applications*.

Querying the ledger

Let's start our exploration with the simplest and most common operation an application can perform — querying the ledger.

In *Figure 7.3*, we can see the three steps required to complete a query:

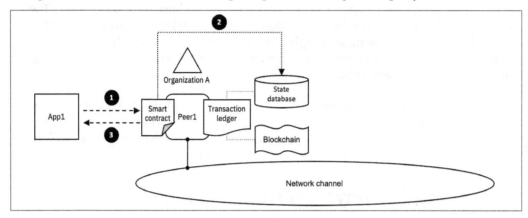

Figure 7.3: An application queries the ledger using a smart contract to access the current value of the ledger

Consider application App1. We can see that querying the ledger is a simple operation that begins with an application sending a query input to a smart contract on Peer1 (step **1**). The smart contract uses the input to determine the query result using the state database (step **2**) and returns this result in a response to the application (step **3**).

We note that at step **2**, the smart contract reads the current state of the ledger using the state database rather than the blockchain. That's because applications are typically interested in the current value of business objects. Smart contracts are able to read the blockchain if they require, but at this stage of our learning, it's enough to know that a smart contract uses the get-style ledger APIs we explored in *Chapter 6, Developing Smart Contracts*, to generate a query response.

Let's place this individual application query in the context of a wider network:

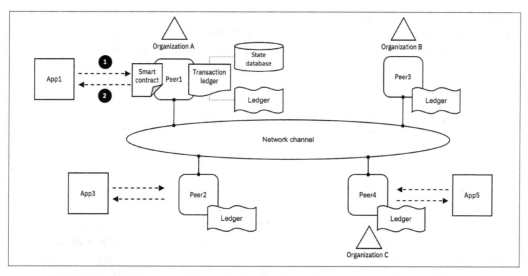

Figure 7.4: Applications typically use their local organization's peers to satisfy query responses

In *Figure 7.4*, we can see that App1 uses a ledger instance hosted on Peer1 for its query; a peer that is owned by organization A. On the other hand, App3, also from organization A, is querying the ledger instance hosted on Peer2. We've only shown the smart contract and ledger components for Peer1; the other peers in the network have a similar structure of a smart contract and two-part ledger. In summary, organization A has two peers that host the ledger in support of queries from applications within organization A.

By contrast, App5 is querying the instance of the ledger hosted on Peer4 owned by organization C. Because the ledger is fully replicated across both organizations and their peers, we see that an application can query *any* ledger in the network channel.

Now, while an application can, in principle, query any instance of the ledger in the network and receive the same answer, in practice, applications query *their own* organization's ledger instances. That's why, in *Figure 7.4*, App1 and App2 query the ledger instance on Peer1 and Peer2, whereas App5 queries the ledger instance on Peer4.

This ability to query any peer highlights how a Hyperledger Fabric network is *decentralized*. Each organization has full control of its own infrastructure, independent from every other organization.

Moreover, for the purposes of ledger query, an organization can use this independence to improve security, latency, throughput, resource consumption, resilience, and manageability when querying its own peers, safe in the knowledge that every other organization is behaving the same way. Indeed, in a network comprising many organizations, any given organization's applications will not be aware of other organizations' infrastructure when it comes to querying the ledger. (The situation is a little different when it comes to submitting new transactions to the ledger, as we'll soon see.)

Finally, as we mentioned earlier, the application doesn't need to worry about any of this physical peer topology! It simply tells the SDK that it wishes to query the ledger, and the SDK will choose an appropriate peer from its organization, send it the request, and wait for a response, which it returns back to the application as it receives it. If the application so wishes, it can ask the SDK to do this *asynchronously*, so that it can get on with other work while the query is in progress!

Submitting a new transaction

The second most common, but most important, operation an application can perform is to submit a new transaction to the ledger. As we know, a transaction records the changes to a set of business objects in the ledger as a set of before-images and after-images using the current value of the ledger, which must be signed by the necessary organizations before it can be considered valid.

The process

In the following diagram, we show the steps that need to occur for an application to submit a new transaction to the ledger:

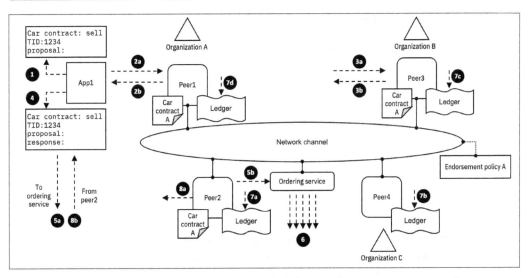

Figure 7.5: Submitting a new transaction to the ledger in a three-organization network

A quick inspection of *Figure 7.5* shows that the process to submit a new transaction to the ledger is much more complex than querying the ledger. As we saw in *Chapter 6, Developing Smart Contracts*, we give this entire process a name — **consensus**. It is the mechanism by which new transactions are consistently agreed on by every organization in the network. Consensus is the most important process in Hyperledger Fabric, and its consensus mechanism is quite different from that of Bitcoin and Ethereum. We're going to examine it in the following sections.

At the end of this examination, we'll see that an application doesn't need to worry about the mechanics of consensus; it simply *submits* a new transaction, and the SDK makes sure that everything shown in *Figure 7.5* happens behind the scenes. Even so, it's really helpful for us to appreciate at a high level what the SDK does on behalf of an application. We'll use this knowledge later to understand why we program applications in a particular way and when we use more advanced features of Hyperledger Fabric.

How the SDK makes consensus easy

In *Figure 7.5*, we can see the discrete steps, marked with circles, that happen when an application submits a new transaction using the submitTransaction API. These steps occur in three distinct phases: **transaction signing**, **distribution**, and **validation**:

Transaction signing

In our example, App1 wishes to submit transaction 1234 to the ledger recording the sale of a car. As we saw in *Chapter 6, Developing Smart Contracts,* a multi-party transaction starts with a transaction proposal containing a transaction identifier and a signed transaction input generated by the transaction submitter.

At step **1**, the application generates a signed transaction proposal comprising a transaction identifier and private key-signed transaction input. In the subsequent steps, this proposal will be sent into the network, and the signed response outputs used to build a multi-party transaction. Let's see how that happens.

Transaction responses are generated by car contract A, and the SDK can inspect endorsement policy A to determine that both organization A and organization B need to sign the transaction. Recall that an endorsement policy has to be agreed on by the network channel and is available for every organization to refer to. Therefore, at steps **2a** and **3a**, the SDK knows to send the proposal to a peer in organization A and a peer in organization B. Each of these organizations has an installed instance of car contract A, which can generate signed transaction responses for these organizations using their respective private keys.

We note that the smart contract is installed on Peers 1, 2, and 3 owned by organization A and B, but not on Peer4 owned by organization C. That's OK because organization C does *not* need to sign car transactions, but it does need to validate them, so while it doesn't have the car contract installed, it does have access to endorsement policy A, and will use it later, as we'll see.

We see the importance of **Fabric discovery** in this phase of consensus. Discovery helps the SDK identify that the car contract is installed on Peers 1, 2, and 3 and that transactions must be signed by organizations A *and* B as defined by endorsement policy A for them to be accepted by the whole network as valid.

Steps **2b** and **3b** show the return flow of the signed transaction responses, which the SDK can now assemble into a fully formed multi-party transaction. We see the multi-party transaction assembled at step **4**, where the responses **2b** and **3b** are packaged together with the initial proposal. At step **4**, the SDK has formed a valid multi-party transaction, but the ledger remains unchanged. For the ledger to change, this transaction must be distributed to the network for inclusion in each organization's ledger.

It's worth mentioning that the SDK sends out transaction proposals and collects transaction responses in parallel, reducing latency. Moreover, it will *automatically* avoid peers that are not running or ones that fail. The application doesn't need to worry about this—the SDK takes care of everything!

Transaction distribution

Steps **5** and **6** show transaction distribution into the network. Now that transaction 1234 has been signed, it needs to be distributed to every peer in every organization in the network, and this is the role of the orderer. Specifically, the SDK forwards the signed multi-party transaction to the ordering service for distribution to the entire network. We see this process represented by steps **5a**, **5b**, and step **6**.

In step **5a**, we can see that App1 forwards transaction 1234 to the ordering service. Although the ordering service may acknowledge receipt of the transaction, the consensus process has only just begun, and the SDK must wait to be informed that the ledger has been updated before it can return control to the application. This is represented by step **8b** in the diagram, which will happen much later.

The ordering service receives the multi-party transaction from App1, represented by step **5b**. In a busy network, the ordering service will simultaneously receive transactions from many applications. Its job is to package these transactions into blocks, ready for distribution to every peer in the network. Step **6** shows the ordering service distributing copies of every transaction block it forms to all the peers in the network.

The exact mechanism by which an ordering service distributes blocks to Peers 1, 2, 3, and 4 is not important to discuss here; suffice to say that it's both efficient and comprehensive. Every peer in the network receives these blocks and processes them independently of every other peer. It is a highly parallel, asynchronous process.

Transaction validation

In this final phase of consensus, the blocks that have been distributed to the network are processed by every peer joined to the network channel. Steps **7a**, **7b**, **7c**, and **7d** indicate how Peers 1, 2, 3, and 4 independently process copies of the block containing transaction 1234.

Again, each peer independently processes its own block. The block is first added to a peer's blockchain instance. Then each transaction in the block is validated to determine whether it is valid. As we saw in *Chapter 6, Developing Smart Contracts*, valid transactions update the ledger's current value, whereas invalid transactions do not. In this way, each peer has a blockchain containing both valid and invalid transactions, and a state database containing an accumulation of all valid transactions over time.

Recall that transaction 1234 must pass two tests. First, it must be signed by organization A and organization B, per the contract's endorsement policy. Second, it must also represent a continuous change of state. For example, if the transaction before-image says the car owner is Sara, then the current owner must be Sara; any other current owner representation is invalid. If the before-image is indeed Sara, then the after-image is applied to the state database, making Bob the current car owner.

Once a peer has fully processed a block of transactions, it will notify all applications that have requested notification. In *Figure 7.5*, step **8a** shows an event notification being generated by Peer2.

Applications don't need to worry which peers to use for notification because, by default, the SDK registers with all peers in the application's organization. We'll see in *Chapter 8, Advanced Topics for Developing Smart Contracts and Applications* how an application can customize this default behavior using a **notification strategy**.

Once the SDK has received all necessary notifications, it will return control to App1, along with an indication of whether the transaction was valid or invalid. In our example, the SDK has registered for notifications from Peer2 only; and step **8b** shows this notification arriving at the SDK.

Moreover, we can see that Peer1 and Peer3, which signed the transaction, also validate it, *even though they generated the transaction in the first place*. We remember that when these two peers generated their respective transaction responses, the ledger was not updated; the ledger update occurs in the validation phase, not the signing phase.

It's important that we fully grasp these three phases of consensus — the transaction has gone on a very long journey to be committed! It was started in the application, was signed by Peer1 and Peer3, packaged and distributed by the ordering service, and validated by every peer. The application was informed the submission was complete only after the SDK was confident that consensus was complete.

Requesting ledger notification

The third and final ledger operation available to an application is similar to a ledger query, both conceptually and in its simplicity. As we saw earlier, an application often wishes to query the ledger; for example, to query the current owner of a car. In the case of a ledger query, we say that an application makes an *active* choice to interact with the ledger. This might be because the request is being issued to satisfy an online user request.

However, there are scenarios where a complementary approach is helpful, whereby the application is notified whenever the ledger changes. This might be because a user has requested to be informed if and when car ownership changes. In contrast to queries, **ledger notification** is a fundamentally asynchronous process, and in the following diagram, we see how it works:

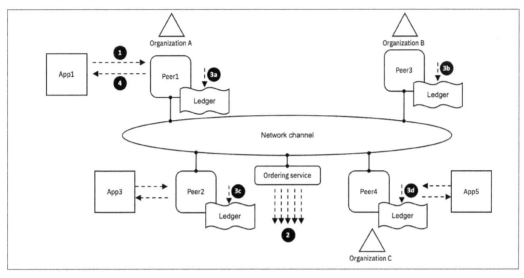

Figure 7.6: Applications can also be notified when the ledger changes without having to actively query it

Let's examine *Figure 7.6*. App1 is requesting notification from the ledger instance hosted on Peer1, and App3 from the ledger on Peer2. Both peers are owned by organization A. In contrast, App5 is requesting ledger notification from Peer4 owned by organization C. As with a query, because the ledger is fully replicated, an application can request ledger notification from any peer in the network channel. As with a query, an application should request notification from its own organization's peers.

Notification is a simple process. The application initially sends a notification request to a peer (step **1**), at which time control is immediately returned. This peer remembers the application's notification request. At the same time, other applications submit new transactions. In step **2**, we see new transaction blocks thus being distributed by the ordering service as a result of these new transactions, and at steps **3a**, **3b**, **3c**, and **3d**, we see Peers 1, 2, 3, and 4 add these transactions to their respective ledgers.

As each peer updates its ledger, it can inform all connected applications who have requested notification. We see this indicated in step **4**. Here, App1 is informed of change **3a** to the ledger on Peer1. We can see that step **4** happens asynchronously to step **1**; compare this to the process of querying, in which a peer returns a result to the application immediately.

Although not shown explicitly in *Figure 7.6*, applications can request two different kinds of notification; event notification and block notification. We'll see later how a transaction can generate custom event information for use by a notified application.

Upon receipt of a notification, an application will typically query the current value of the ledger. Recall our car ownership example; an application made aware of a car ownership change may wish to subsequently query the new owner details.

We see again how notification reflects **decentralization**; each organization uses its own peers to improve security, latency, throughput, resource consumption, resilience, and manageability, independent of every other organization in the network. Organizations and their applications *are not aware* of other organizations' infrastructure when they are registering for, or receiving, ledger notifications.

As with query and new transaction submission, an application doesn't need to worry about any of this physical topology! It simply tells the SDK that it wishes to be notified when the ledger changes, and the SDK chooses the appropriate peer from its organization, sends it the request, and waits for notification, informing the application when required.

We've seen that an application can perform three distinct operations when connected to a Hyperledger Fabric network:

- Query a ledger
- Submit a new transaction to a ledger
- Receive notification of a change to a ledger

We've also seen how the SDK simplifies these operations, especially when the underlying network infrastructure is complex. Let's now use this understanding to program an application to achieve these tasks.

Wallets and identity

We've already seen how **identity** is central to multi-party transactions; the transaction input is signed by the transaction proposer, and the transaction responses are signed by the endorsing organizations. Moreover, we're going to see how a user's identity associates them with a role in their organization, which in turn determines how they can access resources in the network.

Using an identity

Because of the central role that identity plays in a Hyperledger Fabric network, it makes sense that the first thing an application must do is select an identity to use. Let's look at an example:

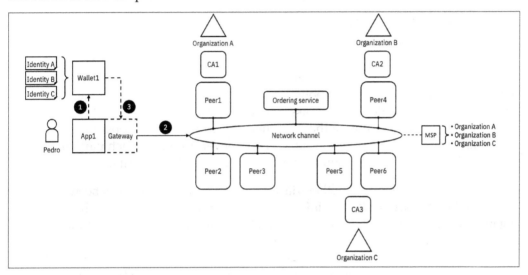

Figure 7.7: A wallet stores a user's identity for interaction with the network

In *Figure 7.7*, we can see how organizations A, B, and C use a channel to form a blockchain network. Organization A owns a set of infrastructure components for use in this network channel, namely Peers 1, 2, and 3 and a certificate authority CA1. Similarly, organization B uses Peer4 and CA2, and organization C has Peer5 and Peer6, and CA3. Finally, there is an ordering service that distributes transactions to the network channel, though in this example we're not concerned with which organizations own the ordering service.

Application App1 is being used by a participant, Pedro, and is connected to the network. Pedro has a wallet with three identities in it (A, B, and C), which can be used when his application accesses the network. These identities associate Pedro with organization A; they have been issued by CA1, a certificate authority associated with this organization.

By using different identities, Pedro can access the network with different roles, each of which provides him with different levels of authority. For example, using identity A, he might only be able to query the ledger, whereas with identity B, Pedro might be able to submit new transactions to the ledger. Finally, identity C might give Pedro full administrative rights over the network.

Indeed, it's not just Pedro that has an identity in the network. Every component in this diagram has a unique identity that associates it with its owning organization:

- Application (via Pedro's identities)
- Peer
- Ordering service node
- Certificate authority
- Organization

In Hyperledger Fabric, each component's individual identity is represented by a unique X.509 certificate and their associated private keys, which must be kept securely by each component. In theory, other certificate types are possible, but are so rare as to not be worth mentioning; you will never use them. Each participant's X.509 certificate is issued by their organization's certificate authority.

All components are bound together via a network channel, which has been configured with a set of **MSP definitions**. These definitions describe each organization and the key roles within them. For example, the MSP for organization A contains the X.509 certificate of CA1 so that anyone in the network can easily identify participants from organization A. So, when an application using Pedro's identity connects to any component in the network, he can immediately be identified as coming from organization A.

Moreover, an MSP also defines the key roles within an organization. In our example, Pedro's identity C identifies him as an administrator for organization A.

Consequently, whenever Pedro connects *any* node in the network via the application SDK, his identity can be used to identify his role within a specific organization, which will determine which actions Pedro can perform. It means that the identity selected by Pedro to access the network is fundamental in determining which actions he can perform.

Using a wallet

Identities are held within a **wallet**, and step **1** in *Figure 7.7* shows how App1 uses Wallet1 to access the different held identities within it. An application is able to associate multiple wallets with it if required, though this is not typical. An application can access a wallet with a single line of code:

```
const wallet = new FileSystemWallet('../identity/user/pedro/wallet');
```

This snippet also nicely illustrates how there are different storage locations for a wallet. Most commonly, a wallet is stored on the filesystem, as you can see in the above example.

However, a wallet can also be stored in:

- **Local memory**: This is useful when an application is running in a browser.
- **A CouchDB database**: Use this when an application is already making significant use of CouchDB as an application store.
- **Hardware Security Module (HSM)**: An HSM is ideal when an application wants to store its X.509 certificates and private keys very securely. HSMs optionally provide improved compute performance for cryptographic signing.

No matter which of these mechanisms our application uses, it selects the appropriate wallet with a single line of code!

It is Pedro's responsibility to manage the identities in the wallet; he must ensure, in advance, that any wallet used by his application has the required identities. As we've seen, because Pedro is associated with `organization` A, his identities are provisioned by `CA1` ahead of time in a process called **enrollment**, discussed in *Chapter 4, Setting the Stage with a Business Scenario*.

We see that step **1** is relatively passive; an application is merely bringing a wallet into the current program context. The first active operation happens at step **2** where Pedro's application interacts with the network.

Recall the three different interaction styles that are possible. It's at step **2** where `App1` will interact with the network to query the ledger, submit a new transaction, or request ledger notification. It's at this point where a particular identity must be retrieved from `Wallet1`.

We can see how identity retrieval works at step **3**. When an application interacts with a Hyperledger Fabric network channel, it uses an SDK abstraction called a **gateway**. We're going to learn more about gateways in a moment, but for now, it's enough to know that an application uses one to interact with the network.

A gateway has a set of *connection options* that are used to configure how it interacts with the network:

```
const userName = pedroId1@orgA.example.com';
const wallet = new FileSystemWallet('../identity/user/pedro/wallet');

const connectionOptions = {
  identity: userName,
```

```
    wallet: wallet,
    eventHandlerOptions: {
      commitTimeout: 100,
      strategy: EventStrategies.MSPID_SCOPE_ANYFORTX
      }
    };

  await gateway.connect(connectionProfile, connectionOptions);
```

Code 7.1: Using a wallet

The code snippet in *Code 7.1* shows how a gateway's `connectionOptions` specify the wallet and identity that should be used. When a `gateway` is used to interact with the network, the identity `pedroId1@orgA.example.com` from the wallet stored on the file system will be used.

This identity will be automatically used to sign new transactions that are submitted to the network, using the private key safely stored in Pedro's wallet. Likewise, when the SDK needs to interact with different nodes in the network using this gateway, it will pass Pedro's public certificate into the network so that it can be used by other network components for access control.

Let's examine in a little more detail how a gateway is used by an application.

Gateways

The concept of a gateway radically simplifies Hyperledger Fabric 2 application programming. Let's understand why.

It has not escaped our notice that there are a *lot* of moving parts in Hyperledger Fabric: smart contracts, transactions, ledgers, peers, ordering services, certificate authorities, channels, MSPs, policies, and identities. Individually they may be easy to understand, but in combination, they present a significant mental hurdle.

Why gateways are useful

A gateway elegantly brings together all the components of Hyperledger Fabric in a single, easy-to-understand and easy-to-use concept, allowing an application to focus on three simple operations: query, submit, and notification.

Let's look more closely at the idea of a gateway in the following example:

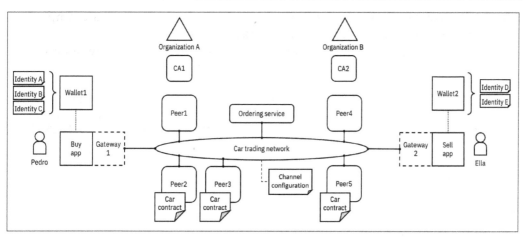

Figure 7.8: A gateway in the network access point for an application interacting with a network channel

In *Figure 7.8*, we see a relatively small Hyperledger Fabric topology sufficient for us to understand what a gateway is, and how to use it. In the real world, we would see more participating organizations, each of which had many peers, hosting different smart contracts with multiple channels, ordering services, and so on. A gateway will allow us to scale our application to work with arbitrarily complex networks without any difficulty! Let's examine this simple configuration to see how.

The network channel has two organizations within it, A and B. We can see that CA1 is associated with organization A, as are Peers 1, 2, and 3. A contract, car contract, governing the life cycle of cars is installed on Peer2 and Peer3. We can see that CA2 is associated with organization B, as are Peer4 and Peer5. The smart contract is also installed on Peer5.

This network is being accessed by two applications. Pedro from organization A is using the buyApp, and Ella from organization B is using the sellApp. These applications access the network using their respective gateways.

We can easily imagine a much larger network than this; more organizations, more channels, more peers, more smart contracts, and more applications. Moreover, as we've discussed, networks can change; network channels are joined for new and different business purposes, organizations come and go within these networks, peers are added for scale and resiliency, new smart contracts are added to provide new functionality within a channel, and new function consumers result in new applications accessing ledgers and smart contracts. It's a dynamic system!

Think of a gateway as a **network access point** for an application. In our example, buyApp accesses the car trading network via gateway1, whereas sellApp accesses it via gateway2. Let's see how Pedro's application uses a gateway as a network access point in *Code 7.2*:

```
connectionProfilePath = path.resolve(__dirname, 'connection-orgA.
json');
connectionProfile = JSON.parse(fs.readFileSync(connectionProfilePath,
'utf8'));

connectionOptions = {
  identity: userName,
  wallet: wallet,
  eventHandlerOptions: {
    commitTimeout: 100,
    strategy: EventStrategies.MSPID_SCOPE_ANYFORTX
  }
};

await gateway.connect(connectionProfile, connectionOptions);
network = await gateway.getNetwork('CarTrading');
```

Code 7.2: Using a gateway to connect to a network

We can see that using a gateway is very straightforward:

- connectionProfile defines the network infrastructure for organization A. We'll examine connection-orgA.json in a moment to see how it does this.

- connectionOptions defines how an application wants a gateway to interact with a network — for example, the wallet and identity to use.

- The gateway.connect API brings these two concepts together. The SDK knows *which* set of infrastructure components it can interact with and *how* it has been instructed to interact with them!

Let's examine connectionProfile in a little detail:

```
name: vehicle-networks
version: 1.0.0

organizations:
  OrgA:
    mspid: OrgA.MSP
    peers:
    - peer1.orgA.example.com
    certificateAuthorities:
    - ca1.example.com

peers:
  peer1.orgA.example.com:
    url: grpc://peer1.orgA.example.com:7051

certificateAuthorities:
  ca1.example.com:
    url: http://ca1.example.com:7054
    caName: ca1.orgA.example.com
```

Code 7.3: A typical connection profile is very simple

The first thing to notice in *Code 7.3* is that a connection profile is quite simple. It only needs to specify a minimal set of information, because once the SDK has connected to *part* of the network, discovery will find the rest of the topology. A connection profile is mostly a *network* bootstrap — it gets an application connected, but subsequently, Fabric discovery will augment and supersede the connection profile. Let's examine the main elements in the profile:

- organizations: This object identifies the organizations the connection profile is aware of, and which peers and certificate authorities belong to them. Again, the names of the peer and certificate authority refer to objects later in the file: peer1.orgA.example.com and ca1.orgA.example.com, respectively.

- peers: This is where the peers referred to earlier in the connection profile have their connection information defined. We can see that peer1 can be contacted at grpc://peer1.orgA.example.com:7051.

- certificateAuthorities: This is where the certificate authorities referred to earlier in the connection profile have their connection information defined. We can see that ca1 can be contacted at http://ca1.orgA.example.com:7054.

Discovery

A `connectionProfile` is simple because of a process in Hyperledger Fabric called **discovery** in which network components find each other using a communications protocol called **gossip**. It means that a connection profile just needs to identify one peer in the network and this can be used to discover everything relevant for channels to which the peer is connected.

In our example, we only have a connection to `peer1`. That's okay—`peer2` and `peer3` will be discovered, including the fact that they have smart contracts installed on them. By default, the SDK will assume all the peers that have a smart contract installed on them can be used for endorsement, and we'll see in *Chapter 8, Advanced Topics for Developing Smart Contracts and Applications*, how we can modify this behavior using a `connectionOption` strategy or handler.

Discovery works on more than peers; it also works on organizations. Our connection profile only has `organization` A defined because peers in one organization are able to discover other organizations using an **anchor peer** defined within a channel configuration. In our example, `peer1` might be the anchor peer for `organization` A, whereas `peer4` might be the anchor peer for `organization` B.

These anchor peers mean that peers in `organization` A can discover all the peers in `organization` B, and that `peer5` has `car` contract installed and can therefore be used for endorsement.

Gateways, connection profiles, and the process of discovery mean that it's very easy for an application to interact with one or more Hyperledger Fabric networks with just a few lines of code.

A network view for an application

To complete our understanding of gateways, let's now consider `gateway2` for the `sellApp` application in organization B. Its connection profile would be quite different from the `buyApp` application in organization A. That's because its connection profile only needs to identify `peer4` for bootstrapping. Moreover, initially it only needs to know about `organization` B, its peers, and any certificate authorities; the rest can be discovered!

It's very likely that once the discovery process is complete for `gateway1` or `gateway2`, they will have likely discovered the same information. We often can think of different gateways as having different *initial* starting points but the same resulting endpoint—a full understanding of the topology.

We can also consider a connection profile as representing a particular initial view to a set of Hyperledger Fabric networks. Because topologies are arbitrarily large and can change over time, it's neither necessary nor desirable for a connection profile to define all the components of a topology. And as we mentioned earlier, an application can subtly modify how the SDK interacts with a particular network topology using **strategies**.

It means that although two gateways may have discovered the same set of network components as each other, their resultant behavior, via the SDK, can be different according to the different strategies defined in the gateway connectionOptions. We'll learn more about how to customize gateway behavior in *Chapter 8, Advanced Topics for Developing Smart Contracts and Applications*.

Accessing networks and smart contracts

Now that our application has connected to a gateway, it's time to start interacting with smart contracts in the available networks. Let's look at an expanded scenario for Pedro, whose organization has access to multiple networks:

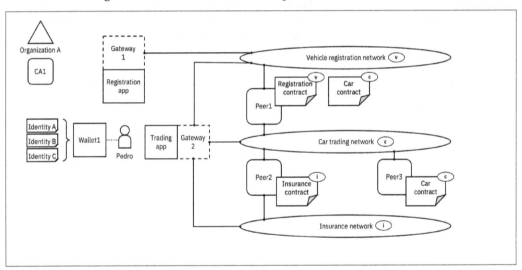

Figure 7.9: A gateway provides access to multiple network channels and smart contracts

In *Figure 7.9*, we can see that Pedro has two applications that he's using — a registration application, and a trading application. We can see three network channels to which these applications are connected, the **Vehicle registration network**, the **Car trading network**, and the **Insurance network**.

Figure 7.9 also shows how only certain peers are connected to certain networks, and that only certain smart contracts are available on certain peers. As we saw in earlier chapters, this helps management and scalability. For example, Peer1 must be used for vehicle-registration access, but it can also be used for car-trading access. In contrast, Peer3 can only be used for access to the car trading network. In the following sections, we'll see how these applications interact with this network topology.

This diagram shows the network from the perspective of organization A, but there are other organizations in the network. A network administrator only has control over their own organization's infrastructure within the network. It means that Peer1, Peer2, and Peer3 are the only peers with which organization A needs be concerned, and as we'll see, service discovery keeps this to a minimum for applications both within organization A, as well as applications in other organizations connected to the network channel.

Single network gateway

In *Figure 7.9*, we can see that the registration application is connected to the vehicle-registration network using gateway1. We can also see that only Peer1 is joined to the vehicle-registration network and has a copy of the registration smart contract installed.

Let's have a look at how the registration application accesses this network in *Code 7.4*:

```
const userName = pedroId1@orgA.example.com';
const wallet = new FileSystemWallet('../identity/user/pedro/wallet');

connectionProfilePath = path.resolve(__dirname, 'vehicle-registration.
json');
connectionProfile = JSON.parse(fs.readFileSync(connectionProfilePath,
'utf8'));

connectionOptions = {
  identity: userName,
  wallet: wallet,
  eventHandlerOptions: {
    commitTimeout: 100,
    strategy: EventStrategies.MSPID_SCOPE_ANYFORTX
    }
};

await gateway1.connect(connectionProfile, connectionOptions);
```

```
network = await gateway1.getNetwork('vehicle-registration');

contract = await network.getContract('RegistrationContract');
contractResponse = await contract.submitTransaction('updateRegistrati
on', ...);
```

Code 7.4: Accessing a smart contract on a network channel

As with our previous examples, Pedro's wallet location is specified together with one of his available identities in the gateway `connectionOptions`. We can also see how `connectionProfile` identifies the `vehicle-registration` network via the `vehicle-registration.json` file. We will examine its details in a moment.

But first, look at how the call to `gateway1.getNetwork('vehicle-registration')` connects Pedro's app to a named network channel. Because a gateway provides access to channels, this call associates the `network` variable with the particular `Vehicle-registration` network. Pedro's application now has access to all the smart contracts in this network.

See how `network.getContract('RegistrationContract')` is then used to access the relevant smart contract. Of course, a network will often contain more than one smart contract.

And although we're not going to examine it now, the final line of code shows how easy it is to submit a new `updateRegistration` transaction to the ledger using the `contract.submitTransaction()` method.

Let's now return to examine the details of the `vehicle-registration.json` connection profile used to connect to `gateway1` in *Code 7.5*:

```
name: vehicle-networks
version: 1.0.0

organizations:
  OrgA:
    mspid: OrgA.MSP
    peers:
    - peer1.orgA.example.com

peers:
  peer1.orgA.example.com:
    url: grpc://peer1.orgA.example.com:7051
```

Code 7.5: Connection profile for a single network gateway

The key points to note in this connection profile are:

- The initial interaction with the network will be via peer1. Recall from *Figure 7.9* that while peer1 may discover other organizations in this network channel and their peers, it will not discover peer2 and peer3 because they are not connected to this channel.

  Indeed, no matter which channel the application tries to connect to, peer1 will be used to determine whether it exists; it means that the application will only be able to connect to networks to which peer1 is joined. For this reason, we sometimes call peer1 a **gateway peer**.

- This connection profile only has information for organization A and peer1; other information will have to be found using service discovery.

This gateway example exemplifies the concept of a gateway as an access point to a wider network topology. In this case, using this connection profile will allow an application to interact fully with organizations and their relevant peers in the vehicle-registration network.

Indeed, this connection profile could also allow gateway1 to access the car-trading network, as Peer1 is also connected to it.

Multi-network gateway

We can also see in *Figure 7.9* how an application can use different gateways simultaneously. Moreover, a gateway can provide access to more than one network. Whereas gateway1 is only used to access the vehicle-registration network, gateway2 provides the trading application access to the vehicle-registration, car-trading, and insurance networks.

Unlike the registration application that only needs to register and query car registrations, the trading application needs to trade cars, check their registration status, and insure them. To do this, it requires access to multiple networks.

Let's have a look at some sample code to see how it does this:

```
const userName = pedroId1@orgA.example'.com;
const wallet = new FileSystemWallet('../identity/user/pedro/wallet');

connectionProfilePath = path.resolve(__dirname, 'multi-network.json');
connectionProfile = JSON.parse(fs.readFileSync(connectionProfilePath,
'utf8'));

connectionOptions = {
  identity: userName,
  wallet: wallet,
  eventHandlerOptions: {
    commitTimeout: 100,
    strategy: EventStrategies.MSPID_SCOPE_ANYFORTX
  }
};

await gateway2.connect(connectionProfile, connectionOptions);

network1 = await gateway2.getNetwork('vehicle-registration');

network2 = await gateway2.getNetwork('car-trading');

network3 = await gateway2.getNetwork('insurance');

...
```

Code 7.6: Applications can access multiple networks from the same gateway

Using gateway2, the trading application can easily access all networks with a single line of code. Because it's the same gateway, the SDK will use the same connection options across all three networks—for example, the same identity from the same wallet.

In *Chapter 8, Advanced Topics for Developing Smart Contracts and Applications*, we'll examine the many different connectionOptions that can be set when an application connects to a gateway, such as time-out and notification strategies.

The trading application in *Code 7.6* uses a slightly different multi-network.json connection profile to the registration application:

```
name: vehicle-networks
version: 1.0.0

organizations:
  OrgA:
    mspid: OrgA.MSP
    peers:
      - peer1.orgA.example.com
      - peer2.orgA.example.com
      - peer3.orgA.example.com

peers:
  peer1.orgA.example.com:
    url: grpc://peer1.orgA.example.com:7051
  peer2.orgA.example.com:
    url: grpc://peer2.orgA.example.com:7052
  peer3.orgA.example.com:
    url: grpc://peer3.orgA.example.com:7053
```

Code 7.7: A connection profile can provide access to all the networks the identified peers are joined to

We note some key points about the connection profile in *Code 7.7*:

- Three network channels are accessible to a gateway that uses this profile, namely the vehicle-registration, car-trading, and insurance networks.

- peer1 can be used for the initial interaction with the vehicle-registration and car-trading network channel. peer1 can discover both peer2 and peer3 from the car-trading network. peer1 cannot interact with the insurance network.

- peer2 can be used for the initial interaction with the car-trading and insurance network channels. peer2 can discover peer1 and peer3 from the car trading network channel. peer2 cannot interact with the vehicle-registration network channel.

- peer3 can only be used for the initial interaction with the car-trading network channel. peer3 can discover peer2 from the car-trading network channel. peer3 cannot interact with the vehicle-registration or insurance network.

Of course, an application might wish to use multiple gateways to allow it to use different connection options with the same or different networks. Using multiple gateways can be very helpful when an application is acting as a proxy for many different users or user types.

A common example of this is when an application uses OAuth to authenticate mobile or web applications connected to it, and subsequently maps these identities to different Fabric identities, which interact with different network channels. Using multiple gateways is a very natural way to achieve this.

These examples show us how a gateway provides access to a network of networks. By providing minimal bootstrap information, a gateway makes it easy for an administrator to provide applications with comprehensive network connectivity.

The Fabric application SDK uses the bootstrap information in a connection profile in combination with service discovery to find all the topology information required to interact with the different network components. This allows applications to focus on the application logic of querying the ledger, submitting new transactions, or listening for receiving ledger notifications.

Let's now see how an application connected to a gateway can query the ledger!

Querying the ledger

The simplest operation an application can perform is to query a ledger. Let's examine how the registration and trading applications query a ledger in different networks:

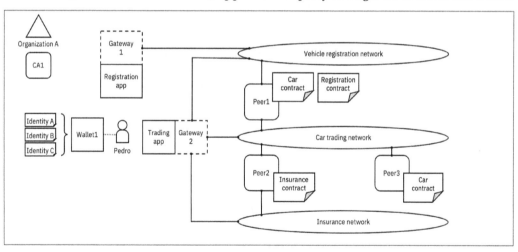

Figure 7.10: The simplest operation an application can perform is to query a ledger

In *Figure 7.10*, we can see that peer1 has the registration contract installed, making it available to all applications connected to the vehicle-registration network. Similarly, Peer1 also has car contract installed for participants in the car-trading network. The registration application uses the registration contract to query the registration ledger, and the car contract to query the trading ledger.

But where are the `registration` and `car` ledgers in *Figure 7.10*? Let's take a closer look at the smart contracts to find out.

Smart contract packaging and namespaces

Smart contracts are placed in a package for both logical grouping and distribution. Consider an example:

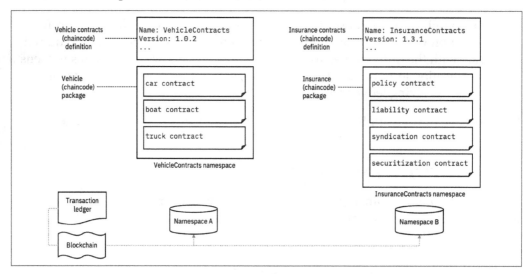

Figure 7.11: A smart contract package name partitions the current value of the ledger into different namespaces

In *Figure 7.11*, we can see two smart contract packages and their associated definitions. When an application accesses a smart contract in the network, it needs to be clear about both the smart contract and package name. See how the `car`, `boat`, and `truck` contracts all have an associated package name of `vehicleContracts`. The four contracts in the insurance package all have an associated package name of `insuranceContracts`.

The package name also provides a namespace for a set of current values accessed by all smart contracts in the same package. In this example, the `car`, `boat`, and `truck` contracts can only see states in `Namespace A`, whereas the insurance package contracts can only see states in `Namespace B`.

We can consider these namespaces to be distinct ledgers from the perspective of a smart contract. Of course, the transactions for these different ledgers are held in the same blockchain, but critically, a transaction generated by a smart contract can only refer to states in that smart contract's namespace.

Therefore, a single blockchain can populate multiple current value state database namespaces. These namespaces allow the current value of the ledger to be partitioned such that different smart contracts do not interfere with each other. It means that when we see a smart contract shown on a network diagram, we can consider it as accessing a particular ledger namespace within the state database.

It's often convenient to package a single smart contract in chaincode and give the package the same name as the smart contract, but this is not required. Indeed, as we develop more sophisticated smart contracts, and use inheritance and polymorphism to encapsulate different behaviors, our packaging strategy and naming will become more important. We'll investigate this in more detail in *Chapter 8, Advanced Topics for Developing Smart Contracts and Applications*.

Using EvaluateTransaction to query the ledger

Let's use this information to see how the `registration` application queries the `vehicleContracts` ledger:

```
network = await gateway1.getNetwork('vehicle-registration');

contract = await network.getContract('RegistrationsPackage',
'registration');
response1 = await contract.evaluateTransaction('queryRegistration',
'CAR0001');
console.log('result is: ${response1.toString()}');

response2 = await contract.evaluateTransaction('queryRegistration',
'CAR0002');
console.log('result is: ${response2.toString()}');
```

Code 7.8: Query the ledger with evaluate transaction

As we can see in *Code 7.8*, querying the ledger only requires a few lines of code. Note the following important points:

- `gateway1.getNetwork` provides access to all channels that are accessible through the connection profile used by this gateway. In this example, the `vehicle-registration` network is being accessed.

- `network.getContract` provides access to all packages within a network channel. We've used the long form of the API to make it clear that we're accessing the particular `registration` contract in `RegistrationPackage`.

- `contract.evaluateTranasaction` allows us to query a particular registration using the `queryRegistration` method in the `registration` contract.

- The first `evaluateTransaction` call queries the registration for the car with identifier `CAR001`; the response is subsequently written to the console.

- The second `evaluateTransaction` call queries the registration for the car with identifier `CAR002`; the response is subsequently written to the console.

We can see how easy it is to query the ledger; we simply access the smart contract on the required network channel and *evaluate* the appropriate method in the smart contract, which returns the query result defined by the smart contract.

Separating the logical from the physical

See how there is no reference to any physical network component? Even though a peer must be used to run the smart contract to return a response, this is not of any concern to the application program. It simply issues `EvaluateTransaction`, and under the covers the SDK will interact with the appropriate network components.

The reason the `fabric-network` package is so easy to use is that there is an excellent separation between the business logic and the network topology. All network topology is encapsulated in the gateway and used by the SDK to execute the query efficiently in support of the application developer who wishes to simply query a ledger using a smart contract.

In *Figure 7.10*, `peer1` is used by the SDK to generate the response because it is the only peer that is joined to the `vehicle-registration` network. We'll look at the `car trading` application in a moment, which has a more complex topology, and we'll see that the application logic is no more complex. Indeed, no matter how large or small a network becomes, the application programmer is unaware—the SDK manages all the complexity.

Synchronous and asynchronous queries

We note that the default form of the `evaluateTransaction` API is to wait for a reply before returning control to the application. In JavaScript, the `await` expression waits for `evaluateTransaction` to complete, at which point the query result from the smart contract is available. Other SDK languages such as Java and Go use appropriate language idioms for the synchronous form of this API.

Simple queries typically involve retrieving a single object from the ledger and are therefore usually executed synchronously. Moreover, an application often needs to know a query result before continuing.

However, as we discussed in *Chapter 6, Developing Smart Contracts*, it is also possible to perform large or complex queries, for example with the getStateByRange or getQueryResult ledger APIs. These types of queries take significantly longer to execute, and it can therefore be appropriate for an application to perform other logic during this time. This style of smart contract query lends itself nicely to asynchronous notification, rather than synchronous execution.

Applications that generate reports often use this processing idiom to execute lots of work in parallel. For now, it's easiest to learn using the synchronous forms; we'll examine how applications can perform ledger operations asynchronously in *Chapter 8, Advanced Topics for Developing Smart Contracts and Applications*. The good news is that the syntax change is minimal.

Query in a more complex topology

Let's now look at the car trading application. It is used by Pedro who wishes to buy a new car. To do so, Pedro's application will need to interact with each of the three networks in *Figure 7.10*:

- The vehicle-registration network to check the car registration details
- The car-trading network to check the purchase details of the car for sale
- The insurance network to find out how much it costs to insure the car

This might seem like it's going to require lots of application code, but in fact the program is quite simple:

```
const userName = pedroId1@orgA.example'.com;
const wallet = new FileSystemWallet('../identity/user/pedro/wallet');

connectionProfilePath = path.resolve(__dirname, 'multi-network.json');
connectionProfile = JSON.parse(fs.readFileSync(connectionProfilePath,
'utf8'));

connectionOptions = {
  identity: userName,
  wallet: wallet,
  eventHandlerOptions: {
    commitTimeout: 100,
    strategy: EventStrategies.MSPID_SCOPE_ANYFORTX
    }
};
```

```
await gateway2.connect(connectionProfile, connectionOptions);

// Check car is registered and retrieve its registration information.
// Lookup uses car registration plate - CAR0001

regNetwork = await gateway2.getNetwork('vehicle-registration');
contract = await network.getContract('RegistrationPackage',
'Registration');
regInfo = await contract.evaluateTransaction('getRegInfo', 'CAR0001');

//Check car registration info is OK
...

// Check car is for sale and retrieve its sales information.
// Lookup uses car registration plate - CAR0001

tradeNetwork = await gateway2.getNetwork('car-trading');
contract = await network.getContract('CarPackage', 'Car');
saleInfo = await contract.evaluateTransaction('getSaleInfo',
'CAR0001');

// Check car sale info is OK
...

// Find out how much it would cost to insure this car
// Lookup uses car registration plate - CAR0001

tradeNetwork = await gateway2.getNetwork('insurance');
contract = await network.getContract('InsurePackage', 'Insure');
insureInfo = await contract.evaluateTransaction('getFullPolicyInfo',
'CAR0001');

// Check car insurance policy info is OK
...
```

Code 7.9: Querying multiple networks

Note the following important points about the application in *Code 7.9*:

- The multi-network.json connection profile is used to create a gateway that provides access to all three networks.

- The same identity — pedroId1@orgA.example.com — is used in all three networks.

- The SDK will interact with the different network peers using the same strategies—as specified in `connectionOptions`. For example, the same timeout of 100 ms will be used.

- Access to each network is achieved using the `gateway2.getNetwork` API.

- Lookup in each of the three networks uses the car registration `CAR0001`.

See how simple the application logic is to query these three networks; the SDK is using the gateway information to interact with the different peers as follows:

- `peer1` is the only peer joined to the `vehicle-registration` network, so it is always used to perform registration ledger queries using the `registration` contract.

- `peer1` is also joined to the `car-trading` network, and has the car contract installed, so it can be used to perform car sale ledger queries.

- `peer2` is joined to the `car-trading` network, but does not have the car contract installed, so it *cannot* be used for car sale ledger queries.

- `peer2` is joined to the `insurance` network, and has the `insurance` contract installed, so it can be used for insurance ledger queries.

- `peer3` is joined to the `car-trading` network, and has the `car contract` installed, so it can be used for car sale ledger queries.

Submitting a new transaction

Now that Pedro has performed sufficient query checks about `CAR0001`, he wishes to use the car trading application as follows:

- To submit a new transaction to the `car-trading` network to purchase the car

- To submit a new transaction to the `vehicle-registration` network to update the purchased car registration details

- To submit a new transaction to the `insurance` network to insure the car

Let's return to our network topology to see the network context in which the car trading application is operating:

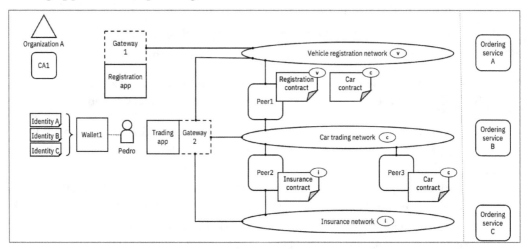

Figure 7.12: Submitting a transaction to three different networks using a gateway

In *Figure 7.12*, we've updated our diagram to show the ordering services for the different networks. These ordering services are used to package and distribute transactions to the different networks. Specifically, `ordering-service` A handles transactions for the `vehicle-registration` network, `ordering-service` B for the `car-trading` network, and `ordering-service` C for the `insurance` network.

While these ordering services are vital to ensure that transactions are packaged and distributed, they are of no concern to the `car trading` application submitting its transactions in *Code 7.10*:

```
saleInfo = await contract.submitTransaction('buyCar', 'CAR0001');

//Check sale info
...

regInfo = await contract.submitTransaction('updateRegistration',
                                           'CAR0001',
                                           'New owner');

//Check updated registration
...

policyInfo = await contract.submitTransaction('insureCar',
                                              'CAR0001',
                                              'ComprehensivePolicy');
```

```
//Check policy info
...
```

Code 7.10: Submitting new transactions to multiple networks

This code is a continuation of the code in the *Query in a more complex topology* section. We can see that each transaction submission requires just a single line of code.

From an application perspective, submitting a new transaction is as simple as querying the ledger. We simply use the existing smart contract with the `contract.submitTransaction()` API, and the SDK makes it happen. There is no reference to ordering services; these are discovered as required and used by the SDK to ensure that multi-party transactions are distributed.

When the `submitTransaction` API returns control, consensus is complete for the submitted transaction. Again, we see no reference to the underlying topology of peers, ordering services, or certificate authority—the SDK perfectly separates the logical act of submitting a transaction from the underlying Hyperledger Fabric network components. Of course, *behind the scenes*, the SDK is performing a lot of work, but the application doesn't need to worry about this.

The other organizations in the network

The final thing to notice about the `car trading` application is that we see no reference to the other organizations in the network. Let's widen our view for a moment to the overall topology:

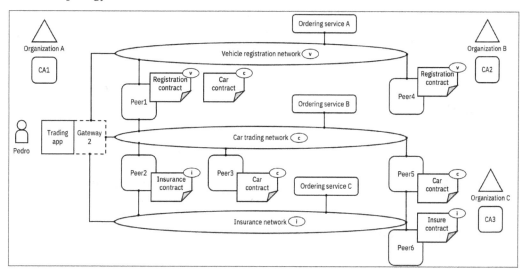

Figure 7.13: A wider view of the network

In *Figure 7.13*, we've elaborated on *Figure 7.12* to show organization B and organization C, and their infrastructure components in each network:

- Organization B owns Peer4, and it is joined to the vehicle-registration network.

- Organization C owns Peer5, which is joined to both the car-trading and insurance networks. It also owns Peer6, which is only joined to the insurance network.

We can also see that these peers host smart contracts, which allows them to run smart contracts in support of applications that wish to query the ledger or submit new transactions. Let's examine the different peers and their installed smart contracts:

- Peer4 has the registration contract installed, and because it's joined to the vehicle-registration network it can support both evaluateTransaction and submitTransaction requests for this contract.

- Peer5 has the car contract installed, and because it's joined to the car-trading network it can support both evaluateTransaction and submitTransaction requests for this contract. Peer5 is also joined to the insurance network but does not have the insure contract installed. It means that although Peer5 has a full copy of the ledger (both transaction history and current value), it cannot support evaluateTransaction and submitTransaction requests for this contract, or indeed any other. We'll see later that Peer5 can still play a very important role in the insurance network.

- Peer6 has the insure contract installed, and because it's joined to the insurance network it can support both evaluateTransaction and submitTransaction requests for this contract.

The final piece of the network jigsaw is the endorsement policies for these smart contracts. We're going to assume very simple policies are applied:

- RegistrationPackage policy: AND('ORGA.Peer', 'ORGB.Peer')
- CarPackage policy: AND('ORGA.Peer', 'ORGC.Peer')
- InnsurancePackage policy: AND('ORGA.Peer', 'ORGC.Peer')

We can see that for new transactions to be accepted onto the ledger, they need to be signed by all organizations in the consortium for that network channel. This might be a very typical policy approach for a set of organizations with equal status — they all have to endorse transactions before they are considered valid.

It's important for us to remember that this network has been set up by administrators in the different organizations; peers have been added to network channels and smart contract packages installed on them. All this is out of the control of the application! Moreover, the topology can change — new peers can be added, new smart contracts installed, and endorsement policies modified. Again, none of this needs to affect the application.

However, for applications to issue `evaluateTransaction` and `submitTransaction`, it's the intelligence in the SDK that implements the necessary interactions, getting a predictable answer no matter what the topology. While we don't need to understand how the SDK does this, it's really helpful to understand what it needs to do.

What it means to evaluate and submit a transaction

We might find it a little strange why we query the ledger with an API called `evaluateTransaction`, but rest assured there's a good reason.

Let's recall that the fundamental difference between querying the ledger and submitting a new transaction is twofold:

- A query transaction only requires a smart contract to be executed on a single peer to generate a query response. In *Figure 7.13*, peer1 and peer3 host the car smart contract, and each has an equivalent copy of the ledger, so the SDK can simply direct an `evaluateTransaction` request to one of these peers, get the response, and pass it back to the application.

  No further action is required — the SDK doesn't need to send anything to the orderer and no other peer in the network will be aware of this request. For example, let's imagine that the SDK selected peer1 to handle a queryCar request — peers 2, 3, 4, 5, and 6 would *all* be unaware of the operation.

  That's one of the reasons why it's called `evaluateTransaction` — because even though a smart contract is executed to generate a transaction response, the response is not distributed to the network for inclusion in peers' ledgers; it is merely *evaluated on the target peer with no further consequence* — even on the target peer. This verb emphasizes the lack of consequence of the smart contract execution.

- To emphasize the point, we could use `evaluateTransaction` with a transaction method like buyCar — which is typically used to update the ledger. But because the SDK would not build a multi-party transaction to be ordered, no peer ledgers in the network (including peer1) would receive a signed transaction, and all ledgers therefore remain unchanged. The transaction has been *evaluated*, but it was not *submitted*.

- In contrast, submitting a new transaction requires the smart contract to be executed on *multiple peers* — one in every organization that is required to sign the transaction response before a multi-party transaction can be constructed; a single peer execution is not enough. For example, in *Figure 7.13*, an updateRegistration transaction must be signed by peer1 and peer4; a buyCar transaction must be signed by peer1 (or peer3) and peer5; and an insureCar transaction must be signed by peer2 and peer6.

  These smart contract executions have not changed the ledgers on which they were executed. For this to happen, their responses must be aggregated into a multi-party transaction for distribution to every peer in the network, for inclusion on every peer's ledger.

  For example, in *Figure 7.13*, a buyCar transaction will be executed on peer3 and peer5, and the resulting multi-party transaction distributed to peer1, peer2, peer3, and peer5 for inclusion in their ledgers. The initial execution of the smart contract on peer3 and peer5 was conceptually the same as evaluateTransaction because it had no effect until the multi-party transaction was distributed to the wider network. The buyCar transaction only has an impact on any peer's ledger (including peer3 and peer5) when that peer receives a block with the buyCar transaction in it.

  That's why we change the ledger with submitTransaction; smart contracts are not merely evaluated on peers to generate responses; those responses are used to generate a multi-party transaction that is distributed via a block for inclusion in every organization's ledger.

These two reasons are at the heart of why the SDK APIs are named evaluateTransaction and submitTransaction. When an application calls evaluateTransaction, a single contract on a single peer generates a transaction response, but it is not forwarded in the network, but instead simply returned to the application. It means that an *evaluated* transaction does not result in a new transaction being submitted to the network for inclusion in every peer's copy of the ledger.

In contrast, when an application calls submitTransaction, multiple peers in different organizations must be called, and they must each generate a signed transaction response, so that a multi-party transaction can be formed from all the responses, for inclusion on every peer's ledger.

This is why we use evaluateTransaction to query the ledger, but submitTransaction to change it. Indeed, we could evaluate a transaction that changed the ledger, but the SDK would not submit it to the network for inclusion in the ledger; we'd merely be *evaluating* what the result would be, *if* we were to submit it. Moreover, we could *submit* a transaction that merely queried the ledger. This could be helpful if we wished to record queries.

If you understand why we use `evaluateTransaction` to query the ledger and `submitTransaction` to update the ledger, then you have a really solid understanding of the multi-party, transaction, and distributed nature of a Hyperledger Fabric DLT. Don't worry if these ideas initially seem a little unintuitive—the key point is to use `evaluateTransaction` to query the ledger, and `submitTransaction` to update it.

The network topology doesn't matter!

The punchline remains that the network topology doesn't matter to the application designer. It's not that the topology isn't important—it is! It's just that it's important for the SDK rather than the application programmer.

There is, however, an opportunity for the application to influence *aspects* of SDK behavior, and we'll investigate how this is done in *Chapter 8, Advanced Topics for Developing Smart Contracts and Applications*, when we consider SDK strategies.

Atomic transactions within and across networks

We saw in *Figure 7.13* how easy it was for the `car trading` application to submit three different transactions to three different networks. It's important to realize that these three transactions are committed to the ledger independently of each other; they are atomic.

That's because when the `car trading` application gets control back from a `submitTransaction` operation of buyCar, that transaction has been finalized on the ledger. Likewise, the subsequent `updateRegistration` and `insureCar` transactions are independently committed. Even if we processed these transactions asynchronously, without waiting for completion, they would be separate, atomic operations.

This is an important design consideration; a single `submitTransaction` operation on one channel is completely independent of every other `submitTransaction` operation on any other network channel, including the same channel.

It is currently not possible in Hyperledger Fabric to include such transactions in a *single unit of work*. Every `submitTransaction` operation is committed independently and cannot be coordinated with other `submitTransaction` requests.

Combining transactions in a single unit of work

It is, however, possible to combine transactions *within* a network channel into a single unit of work with a little extra work. Let's consider a simple transaction where Sara wishes to sell two cars to Bob in a single transaction.

If an application issues two submitTransaction requests to transfer each car, it will result in two separate multi-party transactions. What we require is a single composite transaction containing both car transfers. Let's examine these options in the following diagram:

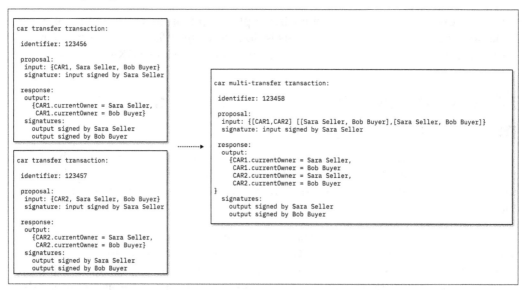

```
car transfer transaction:

  identifier: 123456

  proposal:
    input: {CAR1, Sara Seller, Bob Buyer}
    signature: input signed by Sara Seller

  response:
    output:
      {CAR1.currentOwner = Sara Seller,
       CAR1.currentOwner = Bob Buyer}
    signatures:
      output signed by Sara Seller
      output signed by Bob Buyer


car transfer transaction:

  identifier: 123457

  proposal:
    input: {CAR2, Sara Seller, Bob Buyer}
    signature: input signed by Sara Seller

  response:
    output:
      {CAR2.currentOwner = Sara Seller,
       CAR2.currentOwner = Bob Buyer}
    signatures:
      output signed by Sara Seller
      output signed by Bob Buyer
```

```
car multi-transfer transaction:

  identifier: 123458

  proposal:
    input: {[CAR1,CAR2] [[Sara Seller, Bob Buyer],[Sara Seller, Bob Buyer]]}
    signature: input signed by Sara Seller

  response:
    output:
      {CAR1.currentOwner = Sara Seller,
       CAR1.currentOwner = Bob Buyer
       CAR2.currentOwner = Sara Seller,
       CAR2.currentOwner = Bob Buyer
    }
    signatures:
      output signed by Sara Seller
      output signed by Bob Buyer
```

Figure 7.14: Composing multiple transactions into a single transaction

On the left-hand side of *Figure 7.14*, we can see *two* independent car transfer transactions involving the transfer of CAR1 and CAR2 from Sara to Bob. On the right-hand side, we can see *one* multi-transfer transaction that transfers both CAR1 and CAR2 from Sara to Bob. We can see that we've adjusted the transaction inputs and responses to include all the relevant inputs and responses from the two independent transactions. What we've done is made up for Fabric's current lack of transaction coordination with a single composite transaction.

We can achieve this with the following smart contract design:

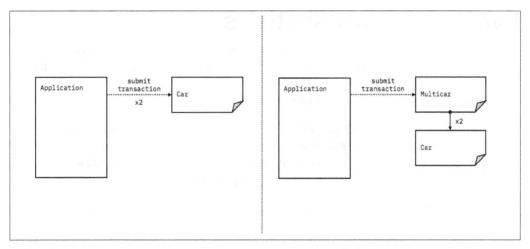

Figure 7.15: Using a smart contract to compose multiple transactions

In *Figure 7.15*, we see how to achieve this objective. On the left-hand side of the diagram, we can see how an application can generate two independent transactions by invoking the Car contract twice, once for CAR1 and a second time for CAR2. On the right-hand side, we've introduced a new Multicar contract that simply de-marshals the input parameters and invokes the existing Car contract to generate the appropriate transaction responses for CAR1 and CAR2. It's relatively simple to do, but it does require the introduction of a new smart contract. That makes it less responsive from an application perspective, but it is a relatively simple way to address the issue of coordinated transactions in a single channel.

Indeed, we can use this mechanism to compose arbitrary transactions — they do not all have to be of the same kind. Beware — as we compose transactions of different types, we may find that our transaction inputs become somewhat arbitrary, leading to a decrease in smart contract simplicity and comprehension.

Moreover, as we start to compose multiple transactions, we may need transactions to be signed by multiple different counterparties, and the composite smart contract endorsement policy may become unwieldy.

Therefore, although smart contract transaction composition is a pragmatic approach to the problem today, this author hopes that the SDK will, in time, allow an application to request that multiple transaction responses are grouped into a single coordinated transaction, to avoid the need to create a new smart contract, something that is outside of the control of many application developers, as service consumers, rather than service providers.

Events and notifications

The two primary interactions we've examined in detail so far in this chapter have been to query the ledger and submit new transactions. The final class of interaction is to listen for ledger notifications. These notifications complement query and submit operations; let's explore when and how to use them.

Unlike querying and submiting, which are fundamentally *synchronous* in nature, listening for an event is an *asynchronous* activity. That's because an application can register for a notification at any time, but when and whether a notification is received is outside the control of the listening application.

Let's see how applications in our network can exploit event notification:

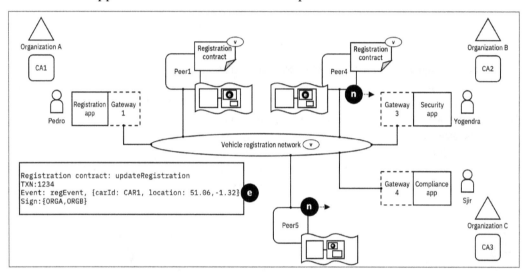

Figure 7.16: Applications can receive notifications as the ledger changes

In *Figure 7.16*, we have expanded the `vehicle-registration` network to include notification applications as follows:

- Yogendra, from `organization B`, is running a security application that will check registrations to see if they are suspicious.

- Sjir, from `organization C`, is running a compliance application that will check that all registered cars are insured.

Yogendra and Sjir are from different organizations and are unaware of each other. Moreover, both are unaware of Pedro, from `organization A`, who registers vehicles. Ledger notifications are a great way to establish loose coupling between these types of network participants.

Transactions, events, and smart contracts

We're already aware that a transaction records the changes to a set of business objects and is signed by a set of endorsing organizations. Additionally, a transaction can record one or more transaction events.

Transactions and events

In *Figure 7.16*, we notice that the updateRegistration transaction also contains an event labeled regEvent. This event represents the fact that a car has been registered and has an associated event payload. In our example, it's the GPS location where the car is registered.

It means that whenever a car registration is updated, there will be a corresponding event recorded in the corresponding ledger transaction.

In *Code 7.11*, we notice that an event is not like a state. Specifically, an event doesn't have a before-image or an after-image, it just *is*. As we discussed in *Chapter 3, Business Networks*, that's the nature of an event—it represents a fact. A situation may have occurred, or not occurred—the event merely establishes this fact. A transaction ledger therefore contains a record of events as well as a record of business object changes. Our ledger has become even more useful:

```
Registration updateRegistration transaction:
  identifier: 1234567890
  proposal:
    input: {CAR1, Bob, {51.06,-1.32}}
    signature: input signed by Pedro
  response:
    output:
      {CAR1.currentOwner = Sara Seller,
       CAR1.currentOwner = Bob Buyer,
       event:{"regEvent",{car: CAR1, location: 51.06,-1.32}}}
    signatures:
      output signed by Sara Seller
      output signed by Bob Buyer
```

Code 7.11: A transaction can also contain one or more events

Smart contracts and events

It's very easy for a smart contract to generate an event:

```
import { Context, Contract, Info, Returns, Transaction } from 'fabric-
contract-api';
import { Car } from './car';
import { Registration } from './registration';
import { Location } from './location';

@Info({title: 'RegistrationContract', description: 'The registration
smart contract' })
export class RegistrationContract extends Contract {

...

    @Transaction()
    public async updateRegistration(ctx: Context, CarId: string,
                                    newReg: Registration,
                                    coord: GpsLocation)
                                 : Promise<Registration> {
        const exists = await this.registrationExists(ctx, carId);
        if (!exists) {
            throw new Error(`Cannot find registration for car ${carId}.`);
        }
        const updatedReg = new Registration();
        updatedReg.value = newReg;
        const buffer = Buffer.from(JSON.stringify(updatedReg));
        await ctx.stub.putState(CarId, buffer);

        const eventPayload: Buffer = Buffer.from(
          {'CarId': CarId, 'location': coord});
        await ctx.stub.setEvent('regEvent', eventPayload);
        return updatedReg;
    }
...
```

Code 7.12: A smart contract generates an event with the setEvent API

In *Code 7.12*, we can see how the `updateRegistration` method has been modified to generate a transaction that contains an event named `RegEvent`. Moreover, we can see the event payload contains the GPS location as provided as input to the smart contract.

We notice that event payloads (`carId` and `coord`) are passed to the smart contract, so they are also recorded as input parameters to the transaction. Although it is common for smart contract inputs to be used in event payloads, the payload is completely independent of the smart contract. However, we must remember that if our smart contract generates event information, then it must do so predictably, as the smart contract will be executed in each organization to generate a signed transaction response—and the event is included in the signature hash.

So far, so good; we now have an event recorded in our transaction. But as we saw in *Figure 7.16*, Yogendra and Sjir wish to receive notifications of this event; let's see how they accomplish this.

Event listening and notification

We've seen how a smart contract generates a transaction containing an event. Let's see how Yogendra can be notified of this event:

```
const userName = yogendraId@orgB.example'.com;
const wallet = new FileSystemWallet('../identity/user/yogendra/
wallet');

connectionProfilePath = path.resolve(__dirname, 'registration-network.
json');
connectionProfile = JSON.parse(fs.readFileSync(connectionProfilePath,
'utf8'));

connectionOptions = {
  identity: userName,
  wallet: wallet,
  eventHandlerOptions: {
    commitTimeout: 100,
    strategy: EventStrategies.MSPID_SCOPE_ANYFORTX
    }
};
```

```
await gateway.connect(connectionProfile, connectionOptions);
regNetwork = await gateway.getNetwork('vehicle-registration');
contract = await network.getContract('RegistrationPackage',
'Registration');

// Listen for regEvent notifications
console.log(`Listening for registration event.`);
const listener =
      await contract.addContractListener('reg-listener',
                                          'regEvent',
(error: Error, event: any) => {
   if (error) {
      console.log('Error from event: ${error.toString()}');
      return;
   }

   const eventString: string = 'chaincode_id: ${event.chaincode_id},
         tx_id: ${event.tx_id}, event_name: "${event.event_name}",
         payload: ${event.payload.toString()}';

   console.log('Event caught: ${eventString}');
});
...
```

Code 7.13: Applications can register for an event notification

In *Code 7.13*, we can see the code for Yogendra's security application that is listening for car registration events. The structure is similar to previous applications:

- It uses an identity, yogendraId@orgB.example.com
- This is stored in a file system wallet located at ../identity/user/yogendra/ wallet
- This is used to connect to a gateway using a connection profile registration-network.json
- This provides access to the vehicle-registration network channel and the Registration smart contract within it

However, this application's intent is not to subsequently query the ledger or submit a new transaction to it, but to listen for notification, which it does with the contract.addContractListener() API.

We can see that the addContractListener API takes three parameters:

- The name of the listener, reg-listener, is simply a name used by the SDK to identify this listener.

- The name of the event, regEvent, is the event name for which the reg-listener listener is waiting.

- The event handler function, (error: Error, event: any) => {...}, that will be called when a notification for this event is generated.

  In our example, we've declared the function in-line using the JavaScript arrow notation => {...}, so that we can easily see the handler code. Larger programs typically pass a named, rather than anonymous, function to the API, and define that function elsewhere in their program to aid readability.

After the addContractListener API completes, the notification request has been remembered by a peer, and processing continues as normal in the application.

Subsequently, every time a valid transaction is committed to the ledger with a regEvent in it, the application event handler will be called by the SDK and will be passed two parameters by the SDK:

- error: As you'd expect, a variable to indicate if there's been an error

- event: Details of the event that has generated the notification

The event notification we receive has a structure containing the following elements:

- chaincodeId is the name of the smart contract package that generated the event. Recall that the event was contained within a transaction, generated by a smart contract in a package.

- tx_id is the identifier of the transaction containing the event.

- event_name is the event name that generated the notification.

- event_payload is the payload that was put in the event when the smart contract generated the event.

In our example, we can see how these elements are accessed; it's very straightforward. Of course, our example doesn't *do* anything with the event other than write its details to the console—in reality, the event payload would be used to initiate other processing.

We see that listening for event notifications is straightforward; as with query and submit, it's a single addContractListener API call. But because it's an asynchronous process, registering for notifications is just the first half of the process—the real action happens when the event notification is generated and passed to the event handler function. And this happens irrespective of what the application is doing when the notification is generated; the event handler can be called at any time.

We should mention of course that event handlers are subject to the same scoping rules as other functions. If Yogendra's application ends for any reason, normally or abnormally, then the event handler will be deleted automatically, and notifications will not be received. Of course, the events will still be generated, emphasizing why we think of events as *loosely coupling* applications together; applications can come and go, but the number of events remains constant, only the number of notifications changes.

Listening – how it works

As with query and submit, the SDK makes it very easy for applications to listen for, and receive, event notifications. While it's not necessary to understand what's happening under the covers, it is helpful if we appreciate what the SDK does during event processing. As we'll see in *Chapter 8, Advanced Topics for Developing Smart Contracts and Applications,* an application can define strategies that affect how the SDK interacts with Hyperledger components, and to use these effectively, *some knowledge* of the underlying processes is helpful. Let's gain that now.

In *Figure 7.16*, the update registration transaction contains a regEvent event with a payload that identifies the car that was registered and its location. This transaction will be distributed to every peer in the vehicle-registration network where it will be validated and stored on every ledger instance. Indeed, we can see that peers 1, 4, and 5 each have a copy of the event.

At the point where a transaction is considered valid by a peer and committed to the ledger, an event notification is generated—by the peer—for every application that has registered for an event notification for this event. When the notification is received by the SDK, it calls the application's registered event handler with the details.

Any and all peers have the ability to generate event notifications. However, because network administrators may wish to balance which peers are used for event notification, only peers that are configured as an **event hub** will generate event notifications. In *Figure 7.16*, peer4 and peer5 are event hubs that can generate notifications. In contrast, peer1 is not an event hub, so while it has a copy of the event, it will not generate notifications.

Moreover, we can see that peer5 does not have a copy of the smart contract—it can *only* be used as an event hub; it cannot service evaluateTransaction or submitTransaction API requests.

Again, we see how the SDK in general, and the concept gateway in particular, helps separate the business logic of an application from the network topology, making it easy for applications to operate in a loosely coupled interaction style.

Asynchronous responses

As we've seen, the process of consensus is simple in principle, but complicated in practice. The simple request to submit a transaction to the ledger necessarily involves many parties agreeing that a transaction is valid—indeed, this is what consensus means.

We've seen how the SDK makes the task of submitting a new transaction to the ledger simple; the application constructs the request, submits it to the network, and *waits* for a reply. There are multiple options on how an application waits for a reply to a transaction submission, as shown in the following diagram:

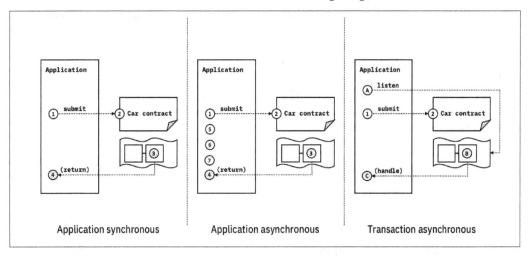

Figure 7.17: An application can wait for transaction submission to complete synchronously or asynchronously

In *Figure 7.17*, we can see the three ways in which applications can process transaction submission responses.

Application synchronous

This is the simplest and most common mechanism—an application makes a request and simply waits synchronously for the Fabric SDK to return control when the transaction has been successfully validated on the ledger. In this mode, transaction submission looks completely synchronous, as shown by the linear sequence 1, 2, 3, 4; although many other things are going on in parallel—the application perceives the whole process as synchronous.

The advantage of using this mechanism is that it is simple. Moreover, sometimes an application implements a process as a series of sequential steps that cannot proceed until the previous step completes. This is a simple and effective way to achieve this.

Application asynchronous

We can see a second option in *Figure 7.17*, where the application submits a transaction but does not synchronously wait for a reply. Instead it uses the appropriate programming language idiom to be notified when the `submitTransaction` SDK method completes. It means that the application can perform steps **5**, **6**, and **7** while steps **1**, **2**, **3**, and **4** proceed as before. The `fabric-network` SDK has been designed to work with different programming language asynchronous processing idioms to allow this programming style.

In JavaScript and TypeScript, the SDK returns a `promise` that completes when the SDK has received a notification that consensus has been reached. In Java, we can use `completableFuture` to dispatch submit transaction onto a separate thread and be notified when it completes, and in Go, the `go`, `defer`, and `waitgroup` language constructions achieve the same goal.

Using these features is relatively straightforward; just be aware that your application logic must allow different tasks to proceed independently. In our example, steps **5**, **6**, and **7** must not depend on step **4**.

Transaction asynchronous

In this processing model, the application considers the process of transaction submission at steps **1** and **2** as quite independent to transaction notification at steps **A**, **B**, and **C**. The application can both submit transactions and listen for events at the same time; it is almost as though these are separate applications. Indeed, our application in *Figure 7.17* includes steps **A**, **B**, and **C** but not steps **1** and **2**—these were performed in another application.

This option acknowledges the fundamentally asynchronous nature of consensus; the act of transaction submission and ledger updating are clearly related, but highly independent. In this model, an application will use listen to register a handler for ledger commit events at step **A,** before it issues submitTransaction for steps **1** and **2**. Subsequently, a quite separate part of the application will handle the event notification at step **C** as a result of a new block added to the ledger at **B**.

In summary, you can use these three different forms of synchronous and asynchronous processing with Fabric to meet your application needs for simplicity, parallelism, and processing style.

Summary

Here, we conclude our tour on application development in Hyperledger Fabric. Let's recap a few of our key learning points:

- We started the chapter by examining the three fundamental operations an application can perform:

    - Query a ledger

    - Submit a new transaction

    - Listen for ledger notifications

- We discussed how the primary rationale of the fabric-network SDK package was to make these three operations simple for application programmers by abstracting the often-complex network topology found in a Hyperledger Fabric network.

- We explored in closer detail the process of querying, transaction submission, and ledger notification. We examined the interactions required between Hyperledger Fabric components to make these capabilities available to application programmers.

- We examined how applications embody these operations in code, looking at the main SDK abstractions that are used to simplify network interactions. Specifically,

    - We saw how wallets hold the identities that are used by an application when interacting with a network and how to use wallets and identities in our applications.

- We explored how a gateway is used to separate the network topology from the application logic. We saw how a connection profile bootstraps an application to a network and works with Fabric discovery to enable the SDK to interact with the necessary network components on behalf of the application.

- We saw how a gateway could be used in practice to access a single network or multiple networks without increasing the complexity of an application. We examined examples of how smart contracts were accessed within these networks.

- We looked at a detailed example of how an application queried the ledger using a smart contract.

- We examined several detailed examples of how an application submitted a transaction to the ledger using a smart contract.

- We discussed the concept of transaction events, how to generate them, and how they are used by applications performing the ledger notification operation.

- We examined synchronous and asynchronous application programming.

In the next chapter, we're going to look at some advanced topics that you'll want to be familiar with as your processing requirements become more sophisticated. Rest assured that they too are easy to understand and use—building upon all we've learned so far.

8

Advanced Topics for Developing Smart Contracts and Applications

In this, the last of three chapters on application and smart contract development, we cover a series of more advanced topics related to Hyperledger Fabric smart contract and application development.

Chapter 6, Developing Smart Contracts, and *Chapter 7, Developing Applications*, introduced the central topic of a multi-party transaction. Such a transaction captures a specific change to a set of business objects. It is also signed by multiple organizations to indicate their agreement with this change. Hyperledger Fabric provides a decentralized technical infrastructure, owned by multiple organizations, for the processing of multi-party transactions:

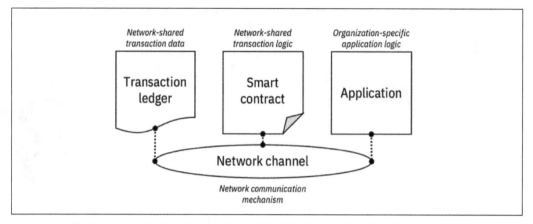

Figure 8.1: Recalling the main Hyperledger Fabric programming abstractions

Figure 8.1 recalls the key programming abstractions within a Hyperledger Fabric network. An application can generate a multi-party transaction using a smart contract. The transaction is stored immutably in a distributed ledger backed by a blockchain. A valid transaction results in updates to the current values in a set of business objects in the ledger. Applications can also query the current value of business objects in the ledger using a smart contract. Finally, applications can request notifications when the ledger changes to allow them to dynamically respond to new transactions and events.

As we design more complex solutions involving Hyperledger Fabric, there is a set of techniques and capabilities that build upon and expand these concepts. Understanding and mastering these techniques will help us design better solutions with Hyperledger Fabric. We'll also deepen our understanding of how to get the most from this technology.

To achieve this, we'll cover the following topics:

- Customizing SDK behavior
- Transient data
- Private data
- Collection and state endorsements
- Smart contract transaction patterns
- Advanced smart contract packaging

Customizing SDK behavior

As we've seen, an application can perform three fundamental tasks: query the ledger, submit new transactions, and listen for notifications. The SDK provides applications a simple API that hides the detailed network interactions required to achieve these goals by separating *what* the application wants to achieve from *how* it is achieved.

This principle of **separation of concerns** means that an application can focus on business logic, and let the SDK handle all the detailed interactions with the underlying Hyperledger network components.

To provide this simplicity, the SDK makes a lot of network interaction decisions on behalf of the application. That's because a Hyperledger Fabric network can be arbitrarily complex, and complexity introduces choices.

Like a good friend, the `fabric-network` package will always make a sensible default choice on behalf of the application. An obvious example might be not to use a peer that isn't running. Often it doesn't matter which choice is made—for example, a query can go to any available peer in the application's organization. Other choices might seem a little more arbitrary—the SDK will wait up to 300 seconds for a response to a transaction submission.

Sometimes the choice made by the SDK is not suitable because the application has a different preference. It's not that the choice is wrong, it's just that an application would prefer the SDK to adopt a different strategy when interacting with the network.

Let's look at an example in the following diagram:

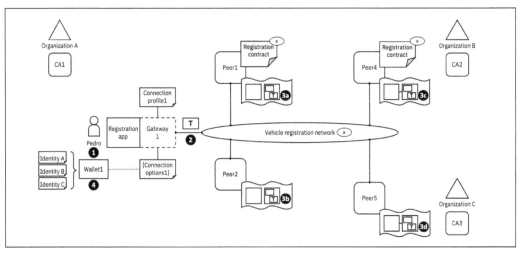

Figure 8.2: Connection options allow an application to customize how a gateway interacts with the network

In *Figure 8.2*, we can see a `Registration` app that wishes to use Pedro's `identityA` from his wallet to submit a new transaction, `T`, to the `vehicle registration` network.

As we can see, the network comprises three organizations and four peers, each hosting a ledger that will contain a copy of `T` after consensus is complete. By default, the SDK will confirm that the transaction has been successfully committed after all available peers from `organization A` have notified it that `T` has been added to their ledger. This is sensible; it's a reasonable assumption that if all peers in Pedro's organization have committed the transaction, then so have other ledgers. Moreover, any peer in `organization A` can now be used to query the ledger as they all have a copy of `T`.

But what if the `registration` application wants to be more optimistic than this? What if it is confident that once *any* of the organization's peers (1 and 2) confirm the transaction, then it can assume every other peer will do so? Can the application ask the SDK to adopt the application's consensus preference instead of the SDK's default strategy? The answer is, of course, "Yes"!

Connection options to the rescue

We recall that an application's interaction with a network is determined by a gateway. In *Figure 8.2*, we can see that the `registration` application uses `gateway1` to interact with the `vehicle registration` network. The information in `connection profile1` allows the SDK to bootstrap the network discovery process and identify the available set of organizations, peers, smart contracts, and endorsement policies for the `vehicle registration` network. Moreover, this network may be just one of many networks available to the gateway.

While `connection profile1` is essential to configure the gateway, it also requires a second object, `{connectionOptions1}`. Let's see an example of this in the following code:

```
const userName = pedroIdentityA@orgA.example.com';
const TlsName = pedroIdentityC@orgA.example.com';
const wallet = new FileSystemWallet('../identity/user/pedro/wallet');

connectionProfilePath = path.resolve(__dirname, 'registration-network.
json');
connectionProfile1 = JSON.parse(fs.readFileSync(connectionProfilePath,
'utf8'));

connectionOptions1 = {
  identity: userName,
  wallet: wallet,
```

```
  clientTlsIdentity: TlsName,
  eventHandlerOptions: {
    commitTimeout: 100,
    strategy: EventStrategies.MSPID_SCOPE_ANYFORTX
    }
};

await gateway1.connect(connectionProfile1, connectionOptions1);

regNetwork = await gateway1.getNetwork('vehicle-registration');

...
```

Code 8.1: Connection options allow the application to express its preferences for network interaction

As we saw in *Chapter 7, Developing Applications*, interaction point **1** in *Figure 8.2* demonstrates how two connection options are *required* by all gateways. Specifically, a wallet and identity must be provided to associate an identity with all interactions.

In *Code 8.1*, identity pedroIdentityA@orgA.example.com from wallet ../identity/ user/pedro/wallet is used to configure gateway1. The code also highlights other application preferences for how the gateway interacts with the network at points **2**, **3**, and **4** in *Code 8.1*:

- Point **2** shows a gateway being used to submit a transaction T to the network. By default, the gateway would wait for up to 300 seconds for all required peers to confirm that the transaction has been committed to their ledger. *Code 8.1* shows how gateway1 has been configured to wait only 100 seconds using the commitTimeout connection option.

- Points **3a**, **3b**, **3c**, and **3d** show transaction T being committed to the ledgers on peers 1, 2, 4, and 5 respectively. The behavior for gateway1 is to wait up to 100 seconds for *both* peer1 and peer2 to confirm that T has been committed. However, in our example code in *Code 8.1*, the application uses the MSPID_ SCOPE_ANYFORTX connection option value to indicate that it only wishes to wait for *either* peer1 *or* peer2 to confirm transaction T.

  EventStrategies.MSPID_SCOPE_ANYFORTX is effectively saying "it is sufficient for any peer in my organization to confirm T for me to consider consensus complete." This is an optimistic strategy—an application reasonably assumes that as all peers are fundamentally the same when it comes to committing T, as soon as one peer confirms, then all peers will eventually do the same. Contrast this with a much more pessimistic strategy, EventStrategies. NETWORK_SCOPE_ALLFORTX, which requires *all* peers in the available network to confirm T before consensus is considered complete.

An application might wish to use a pessimistic strategy if it has a very important transaction that it needs to confirm with all organizations before continuing—maybe the transfer of a high-value asset. In contrast, an optimistic strategy may be more appropriate if we know that other organizations can process the transaction asynchronously to the submitter without any disadvantage.

- Point **4** is another example of a wallet interaction. When a gateway interacts with a network, the *primary* identity it uses is the one that signs transaction **T**. However, it is also possible for network components (such as peers) to be configured to require applications to use secure communications. In this case, an application can also specify a secondary identity for communications using the `clientTlsIdentity` connection option.

  In *Code 8.1*, we can see that identity `C` is used quite distinctly from identity `A`. Indeed, it should be kept completely separate; identity `A` is used to sign transaction `T`, recorded in every peer in the network, whereas `clientTlsIdentity` does not extend beyond communications between the gateway's network interactions.

Notice how any particular connection option allows an application to influence *how* the SDK interacts with the available network, allowing an application to focus on *what* it wants it to do. See how `commitTimeout` specifies the time to wait for each peer, but it doesn't say how to implement the timers, or whether the requests can be in parallel (they are, in fact). See how `MSPID_SCOPE_ANYFORTX` does not say which peer to wait for, but rather that any peer within the application's organization will do.

These examples are just a few of the many connection options available to applications. And remember that the SDK's default choice is always a sensible choice, so don't feel it necessary to explicitly configure connection options until you need to do so.

Event handler functions

In principle, it should be enough for a single peer in the application's organization to confirm a transaction has been committed because all peers will, in time, have the *same* set of transactions committed to their ledger.

The default strategy, `MSPID_SCOPE_ALLFORTX`, requires that all available peers within the application's organization confirm the transaction. This is helpful because it allows both subsequent queries to be sent to any peer within the application's organization knowing that all ledgers are up to date.

While the four available strategies—MSPID_SCOPE_ANYFORTX, MSPID_SCOPE_ALLFORTX, NETYWORK_SCOPE_ANYFORTX, and NETWORK_SCOPE_ALLFORTX—cover most common application requirements for application query, transaction submission, and ledger notification, it can be helpful to sometimes have more control over the actual peers used by the SDK.

For example, an application may wish to direct all large queries to a particular peer or limit the number of available peers an application can use in order to reduce the aggregate number of network sessions.

This is where a custom event handler can be helpful. It allows an application to participate in the consensus process, deciding which peers are used for network interactions. But wait a moment, doesn't this break the principle of separation of concerns?

No! We note that even though the application is involved in network interactions when it specifies an event handler, this doesn't break the principle of separation of concerns because the event handler code is quite separate from the application logic and the query, submit, or listen logic. Let's see an example in *Code 8.2*:

```
...

const connectOptions: GatewayOptions = {
    transaction: {
        strategy: MyEventhandler
    }
}

const gateway = new Gateway();
await gateway.connect(connectionProfile, connectOptions);

...
}

import { TxEventHandler } from 'fabric-network';

class MyEventHandler implements TxEventHandler {

    ...

}
```

Code 8.2: A custom event handler is completely separate from the application contract and the ledger logic

Custom event handlers are aware of the network topology, but as with the design point of the SDK, they separate the *how* from the *what*. The main part of the application is unaffected by the custom handler. It focuses on the *what* — submit, query, and listen — whereas the handler focuses on the *how* — which peers to use and when. The handler is aware of the network topology, the rest of the application is not.

In general, custom event handlers are only required in larger networks. Most importantly, you do not need to worry about custom event handlers when you design your application or smart contract. They can be added after the fact. This is very good news indeed, and we advise you to not worry about custom event handlers until and unless you need to do so!

Checkpoint handler

As we've seen, transaction events are permanently stored in the blockchain within transaction blocks. We saw how an application can listen for notifications of both transaction events and block events committed to the ledger. Under the covers, the SDK registers with a peer to ensure that an application receives all notifications to fulfill its listen request.

By default, an event hub peer will generate events for all the blocks it receives to satisfy its current listeners. For example, if application A starts listening at 0700 hours, it will receive notifications for every transaction added to the ledger after 0700, whereas application B, which started listening at 0800 hours, would only receive notifications from 0800 hours onward.

Until it ends gracefully, an application will continue to receive event notifications. Upon graceful termination, an application is effectively unsubscribed from the peer and no longer receives notifications.

Behind the scenes, the SDK has a *default checkpoint handler* that records, in a file, the most recent notifications received by the application. In the event of an application failure, the SDK uses this FILE_SYSTEM_CHECKPOINTER to identify the last notification received by the application so that it can request from an event hub any events the application may have missed during the period it was not started.

It is rarely necessary to replace the default checkpoint handler with a custom checkpoint handler. However, it can be done quite easily. For example, an application may wish to store the checkpoint file in a particular location or store the information in a local database.

We won't discuss the detailed mechanics of custom checkpoint handlers. It's enough to know that they exist and can be used when the default mechanism isn't sufficient.

This first section shows how an application can easily customize and extend SDK behavior without violating the principle of the separation of concerns. The SDK benefits from progressive disclosure. It is easy to get started, and as our needs grow, we can build on previous knowledge to achieve increased capabilities.

We now move on to a new capability called **transient data**, the first of two important privacy functions in Hyperledger Fabric, along with **private data**, which we'll learn about later.

Transient data

As we've seen, Hyperledger Fabric allows an application to submit a transaction generated by a smart contract to a distributed ledger. Any instance of the ledger can be subsequently queried to determine the result of a submitted transaction. Finally, an application can listen for ledger notifications indicating that new transactions have been committed.

Explicitly recording transaction input

Hyperledger Fabric records the submitter's digitally signed input, as well as the digitally signed transaction responses from each of the endorsing organizations. Remember, these were the organizations required to sign a transaction in order for it to be considered valid.

These ideas are illustrated in *Figure 8.3*:

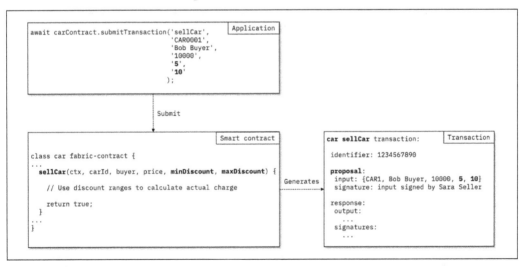

Figure 8.3: Applications use smart contracts to generate multi-party transactions that capture the inputs and responses

In *Figure 8.3*, an application invokes the `car contract` smart contract method to generate a `sellCar` transaction to be recorded on the ledger.

We've slightly modified the `car contract` smart contract from *Chapter 7, Developing Applications*, to incorporate a discount the seller would be prepared to accept. The submitting application has to provide the minimum and maximum discount that they are prepared to give the seller. In our example, we can see that the minimum and maximum discounts for this particular sale are **5**% and **10**%, respectively.

The smart contract takes these input parameters and uses an algorithm to calculate the actual charge to the buyer of the car. The details of this algorithm are not important to us since it's arbitrary business logic. What is important is that these **5**% and **10**% discounts are recorded in the transaction and are therefore available for all organizations to see.

All transaction inputs are recorded and distributed throughout the network, which makes it "public" information to the network channel. So, while the car contract is only available to those organizations who host the smart contract, and that's great for the privacy of the algorithm, the *discounts* are available for all to see, as they are recorded in the transaction distributed to the network.

Hiding the transaction input

There are situations where recording particular transaction inputs is not ideal, and a mechanism in Hyperledger Fabric called **transient data** allows an application and smart contract to avoid this issue. Let's see how it works in *Figure 8.4*:

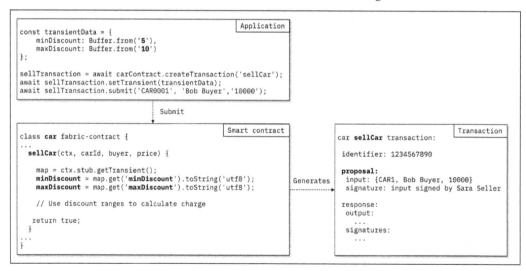

Figure 8.4: Transient data allows smart contracts to receive application input without it being recorded in a transaction

We can see the same basic structure as *Figure 8.3*; an application submits a sellCar transaction to the ledger using an appropriate smart contract. But we notice that the inputs are slightly different from *Figure 8.3*.

Let's start by looking at the transaction. The transaction input now shows {CAR1, Bob Buyer, 10000} representing the car, buyer, and price, respectively. There is no reference to the 5% and 10% discount figures in our previous example.

Likewise, if we look at the smart contract, we can see that its formal input parameters no longer contain these discounts:

```
class car fabric-contract {
...
  sellCar(ctx, carId, buyer, price) {
```

Code 8.3: Not all inputs used by a smart contract are specified in the method definition

Instead, we can see that the smart contract retrieves the discounts via the getTransient API:

```
map = ctx.stub.getTransient();
minDiscount = map.get('minDiscount').toString('utf8');
maxDiscount = map.get('maxDiscount').toString('utf8');
```

Code 8.4: A smart contract uses the getTransient API to access transient data from a map passed by the application

Notice how the application creates this transient data and passes it to the smart contract:

```
const transientData = {
    minDiscount: Buffer.from('5'),
    maxDiscount: Buffer.from('10')
};
sellTransaction = await carContract.createTransaction('sellCar');
await sellTransaction.setTransient(transientData);
await sellTransaction.submit('CAR0001', 'Bob Buyer','10000');
```

Code 8.5: The transaction object provides fine-grained control over transaction submission

The request to submit this type of transaction looks a little different from our first example in *Code 8.2*.

First, that example only used the contract.submitTransaction API; this example creates an *explicit* sellTransaction from carContract, which uses the sellTransaction.submit API to submit the transaction.

The second and most important difference is the use of the `setTransient` API. It stores the previously constructed `transientData` map, which contains the `minDiscount` and `maxDiscount` values of 5% and 10% respectively. We previously saw in *Code 8.4* how these values are retrieved using the `getTransient` method.

Note that you can always use the `contract.createTransaction` and `transaction. submit` combination in preference to a single `contract.submitTransaction` API. The latter is simply shorthand for the former. The advantage of using an explicit `transaction.submit` is that it's slightly more explicit, quicker to type, and required if you're using transient data.

That's it; the SDK and smart contract API make transient data simple to understand and simple to use. It's a powerful technique to have in your back pocket when you need to keep critical information off the ledger, while allowing effective communication between an application and smart contract.

Private data

Although often confused with transient data, private data is a completely different mechanism provided by Hyperledger Fabric. While transient data keeps transaction inputs off the ledger, private data keeps transaction outputs off the ledger.

To see why private data is useful, it helps to look at a concrete example:

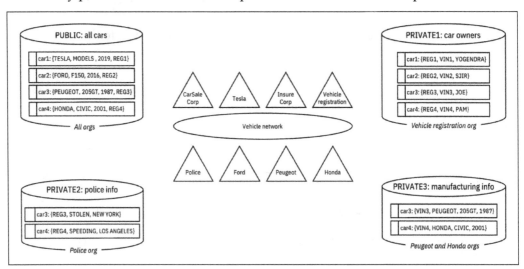

Figure 8.5: In a network consortium, ledgers can be shared by all organizations or restricted to subsets of organizations

In *Figure 8.5*, the **Vehicle network** contains a consortium comprising eight organizations sharing transactional information about vehicles. These organizations include motor manufacturers, a car retailer, an insurance company, the police, and a national vehicle registration agency.

Up to this point, we've mostly concerned ourselves with ledger data like that shown in PUBLIC: all cars, where current values are shared by all organizations in the network. For example, everyone can see that car3 is a 1987 PEUGEOT 205GT with registration REG3, or that car1 is a 2019 TESLA MODELS with registration REG1.

As we know, the all cars set of states is called the ledger *world state*. We'll find it really helpful to think of the world state as a special kind of *collection*. Cars in the world state collection are seen by all organizations in the network, and we denote this at the bottom of the PUBLIC collection with All orgs (note that we don't need to show the peers for these organizations.)

We recall the world state is subject to name-spacing — *Figure 8.5* doesn't show any smart contract packages, but if it did, different smart contract packages would provide their own namespace for the world states created by that package. We still think of the world state as globally shared, it's just that it's namespaced at the same time.

Let's now turn our attention to the PRIVATE1 collection of states. These states are uniquely accessible to the Vehicle registration organization which holds information on the owners of each car in the PUBLIC collection. For example, the Vehicle registration organization can see that YOGENDRA is the owner of car1, SJIR is the owner of car2, and so on. Unlike the world state, which all organization peers host, only Vehicle registration peers host a copy of PRIVATE1 data. Thus we call PRIVATE1 a private data collection.

There are important things to recognize about the PRIVATE1 private data collection:

- Only the Vehicle registration organization has a copy of the PRIVATE1 collection; the other members of the consortium *do not have a copy* of PRIVATE1. We'll see later how transactions are recorded in the blockchain to make this possible, but for now, recognize that PRIVATE1 is only available on Vehicle registration peers.

- The states in PRIVATE1 are scoped to PRIVATE1; even though the states in PRIVATE1 have the same keys as those in the PUBLIC collection, they are different states. PRIVATE1 effectively provides a namespace for the state keys within it, keeping them separate from the world state and other private data collections. A little like a smart contract namespace, a private collection provides a natural scope for its states, keeping them quite separate.

- In our example, because the states in PUBLIC and PRIVATE1 refer to the same business object, it's appropriate to use the same state keys in these collections. But this isn't required; a private data collection can have any number of different states and keys that may or may not correspond to other states in the ledger. Because private collections provide a natural scope, it is a smart contract design choice whether collection state keys have any correspondence with those in other collections.

- The PRIVATE1 states hold less information than those in the PUBLIC collection—the owner of the car, its registration, and the vehicle identification number (VIN). But again, this isn't a requirement. A state in a private data collection has no special limits on the information it can hold.

Now that we've understood the structure and rationale of PRIVATE1, it's worth comparing and contrasting with PRIVATE2. This collection is held only by the Police organization and holds information on a subset of cars. We can see that car3 is recorded as being stolen, and that car4 has recently been speeding! Notice that PRIVATE2 is more sparsely populated than PUBLIC or PRIVATE1, as we'd expect—the police only hold information about relevant cars, not every car.

Finally, with PRIVATE3, we can see that a private data collection is not limited to a single organization. The PRIVATE3 collection holds information for two of the manufacturers: Honda and Peugeot. We can see how they are sharing VINs for each of the cars that they manufacture. (It's just a coincidence that these are the same cars that are in PRIVATE2.) Again, the other organizations in the network do not have a copy of PRIVATE3. Only Honda and Peugeot have a copy of PRIVATE3.

When we look at *Figure 8.5*, we see that collections give us the ability to partition information between different organizations. This can create a situation where no single organization has the full picture. For example, every organization can see the public information about cars. However, the Vehicle registration, Police, Honda, and Peugeot organizations can also augment the public information with information from their respective private collections.

Let's reflect on this for a moment. Our primary rationale for a blockchain was to make sure that every organization had a shared copy of the ledger; that is, they all saw the *same transactions* about the *same business objects*. Now we seem to be stepping away from that idea, or at least modifying it a little. We'll return to this topic in a short while when we look at smart contract design patterns for transaction sharing.

Using private data collections

As we've seen, private data collections provide a simple way for a subset of organizations in a network channel to limit the distribution of a specific scope of states to other organizations. Let's now see how to use private data collections in a smart contract, and then some useful design patterns for private data collections.

Smart contract exploitation

Now that we've seen what collections are, let's see how they are used by applications and smart contracts. As we saw in *Figure 8.5*, the first thing to note about a collection is it has a name—we can see PRIVATE1, PRIVATE2, and PRIVATE3. In practice, we'll use more meaningful names for collections, to represent their function—OwnerInfo, PoliceInfo, or ManufacturingData, for example.

Let's see how a private data collection is accessed using a smart contract:

```
import { Context, Contract, Info, Returns, Transaction } from 'fabric-
contract-api';
import { CarOwner } from './car-owner';
const collectionName: string = 'OwnerInfo';

@Info({title: 'CarOwner', description: 'Smart Contract for Vehicle
owner data' })
export class CarOwnerContract extends Contract {

...

public async readCarOwner(ctx: Context, carOwnerId: string):
Promise<string> {
    const exists: boolean = await this.carOwnerExists(ctx, carOwnerId);
    if (!exists) {
        throw new Error('The owner info for car ${carOwnerId} does not
exist');
    }

    let privateDataString: string;
    const info: Buffer = await ctx.stub.getPrivateData(collectionName,
carOwnerId);

    infoString = JSON.parse(info.toString());
    return infoString;
    }

...
```

Code 8.6: Accessing a private data collection in a smart contract using the getPrivateData API

The first thing to notice about *Code 8.6* is that it's the smart contract that accesses the private data collection; an application is not involved. In fact, an application cannot and should not be able to tell that a smart contract is using a private data collection. It merely uses `transaction.submit` or `transaction.evaluate` and everything else is handled by the smart contract.

This is a good thing for the application developer. It means that private data collections are an implementation detail from the application's perspective. This makes sense — collections relate to how organizations keep their data private from each other, and while applications should be subject to this constraint, it should be bound within a smart contract design.

The second thing to notice is that accessing a private data collection is almost exactly the same as accessing the world state with which we're familiar. The `getPrivateData` API is almost exactly the same as the `getState` API. The only difference is that it requires a collection name. Once a smart contract knows a collection name, the instruction to read a state from it is very simple.

Likewise, writing a private data state is straightforward, as we can see in *Code 8.7*:

```
import { Context, Contract, Info, Returns, Transaction } from 'fabric-
contract-api';
import { CarOwner } from './car-owner';
const collectionName: string = 'OwnerInfo';


@Info({title: 'CarOwner', description: 'Smart Contract for Vehicle
owner data' })
export class CarOwnerContract extends Contract {

public async updateCarOwner(ctx: Context, carOwnerId: string):
Promise<void> {
        const exists: boolean = await this.carOwnerExists(ctx, carOwnerId);
        if (!exists) {
            throw new Error('The owner info for car ${carOwnerId} does
not exist');
        }

        const newOwner: CarOwner = new CarOwner();

        const transientData: Map<string, Buffer> = ctx.stub.getTransient();
        if (transientData.size === 0 || !transientData.has('newOwner'))
        {
```

```
        throw new Error('New owner not in transient data.');
    }
    newOwner.owner = transientData.get('newOwner').toString('utf8');

    const newOwnerBuffer = Buffer.from(JSON.stringify(newOwner));
    await ctx.stub.putPrivateData(collectionName, carOwnerId,
newOwnerBuffer);
    }
```

Code 8.7: Updating a private data collection in a smart contract using the putPrivateData API

In this example, we've added a new method to the `CarOwnerContract` contract that will update the car owner in the `OwnerInfo` private data collection.

The key API to update the car owner is `putPrivateData`. It takes the collection name, the state key, and the new value of the state. As with `getPrivateData`, this API is analogous to the `putState` API a smart contract would use for world states. Again, it's a simple process for a smart contract to write data to a private data collection.

Of course, as with regular states, this API does not update the data when the smart contract executes; it is generating the new current value of the state in `OwnerInfo` for this transaction, which will only be applied if the transaction is valid. The observant reader will have lots of questions on how this works, and we'll return to the mechanism by which this happens a little later in this chapter; for now, we can *think* of a private state write as analogous to a world state write.

Private data with transient data

In *Code 8.7*, it's also worth noticing the use of transient data to keep the new car owner off the ledger. See how `newOwner` is *not* specified in the `updateCarOwner` method signature. If it was, the `newOwner` would have appeared in the transaction input, in a similar manner to *Code 8.6*. Instead, our smart contract retrieves the new owner from the transient data passed by the calling application, in a similar manner to *Code 8.7*.

As we mentioned earlier, this is why it is easy to get confused between transient data and private data. They are often used together, but they are quite different. In our previous example, we used transient data to keep data private between an application and a smart contract so that discount processing could be kept fully private. In this example, transient data is used to keep data fully private, which also requires the use of private data collections.

We can see again that the mechanics of using a private data collection is straightforward.

Understanding private data collections

Our initial examination of private data suggests that there are many cases in which we can use private data as we would use world state. Private collections have a name and a similar API. That's it, right?

Not quite. As we moved from a public collection to private data collections, something fundamental *changed*. When we use the public collection, every organization can see every state, and this makes the system highly symmetrical. But with private collections, only certain organizations can see certain data. We've created an asymmetry between organizations. As we're about to see, this will introduce both new processing restrictions and new opportunities.

Let's stand back for a moment to take a closer look at what's going on when we use private data:

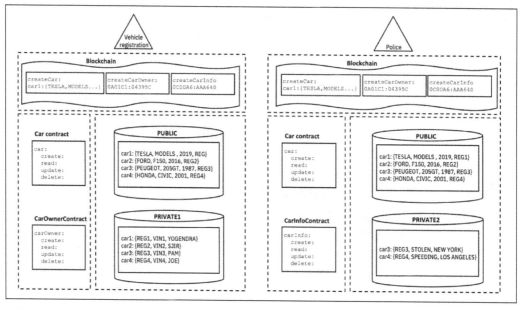

Figure 8.6: The blockchain holds private data key hashes for verification; state values are limited to owning organizations

In *Figure 8.6*, we've elaborated on how the information in *Figure 8.5* is stored for the Vehicle registration and Police organizations.

For Vehicle registration, we can see a copy of the blockchain containing three transactions (to simplify, we've not shown the blocks). We can also see that they host a copy of the PUBLIC collection containing general information on all cars, and PRIVATE1, which contains registration information about these cars. Specifically, it contains their registrations, owners, and VINs.

Let's examine the blockchain, public world state, and private data collections for the Vehicle registration organization:

- As we expect, the blockchain contains a createCar transaction for car1 with the full information for this business object, namely {TESLA, MODEL5, 2019...}.

- However, the createCarOwner transaction does not contain the business object data relating to the creation of the owner information for car1. Instead, it contains two SHA256 hashes of this data—a hash of the object key car1, and a corresponding hash of the values of car1. (We've only shown the first 6 bytes of the SHA hash.)

  These two hashes are generated from the PRIVATE1 collection state car1:{REG1, VIN1, YOGENDRA}:

  - The key hash 0A01C1 is calculated as the SHA256 hash of PRIVATE1car1 (note how we combine the collection name with the key).

  - The value hash 04395C is generated from the SHA256 hash of REG1, VIN1, YOGENDRA.

  Notice how the blockchain in the Police organization has exactly the same transaction, including hashes, but it does not have a copy of the PRIVATE1 collection containing car1.

- Similarly, the createCarInfo transaction does not contain business object data relating to the creation of the police information for car3. Again, it only contains two SHA256 hashes of this data—one hash of the object key for car3, and a corresponding hash of the values of car3.

  These hashes have been generated from the PRIVATE2 collection holding the state car3:{REG3, STOLEN, NEW YORK}:

  - The key hash 0C0DA6 is calculated as the SHA256 hash of PRIVATE2car3 (again, we combine the collection name with the key).

  - The value hash AAA640 is generated from the SHA256 hash of REG3, STOLEN, NEW YORK.

  Again, notice how although Vehicle registration has a blockchain with the hashes for the createCarInfo transaction, it does not have a copy of the PRIVATE2 collection, which contains car3; only the Police organization has this data.

We can similarly inspect the blockchain, public world state, and private data collections for the `Police` organization, and we will see the same blockchain information with the corresponding `PUBLIC` world state. However, the `Police` organization hosts the `PRIVATE2` data collection, which holds the police information.

Private data consensus and off-chain data

While the mechanics of consensus for private data are intricate, we can summarize a few key points:

- The blockchain contains private data hashes rather than private data.
- Private data is distributed via gossip between the organizations defined in the collection policy.
- A private data collection is updated if the transaction signatures satisfy the relevant endorsement policies.

Because of these facts, you'll sometimes hear private data referred to as off-chain data or off-chain transactions. This terminology can be helpful; it comes from the Bitcoin and Ethereum communities, who use a similar pattern to overcome potential performance challenges in these systems. However, in these systems, private data is held outside the platform; it is under the control of application-specific processes. This is unlike Fabric, where the private data is held in databases managed according to an agreed private data policy.

But in the main, these approaches are the same. The blockchain provides a cryptographic anchor for a transaction that proceeds by other means. In Fabric, this is the gossip protocol private data exchange. In Bitcoin and Ethereum there are myriad such layer 2 protocols, such as the Lightning Network, which ultimately anchor into the main blockchain.

Layer 2 protocols also attempt to achieve other things in Bitcoin and Ethereum networks, but their key similarity to private data is that they ultimately refer back to the blockchain as the root of trust.

Such off-chain solutions are a common pattern in blockchain. Indeed, some application architects and developers will use only a Fabric public state to save hashes of data in external systems. This can be a highly effective pattern when there is existing data that needs to be verifiably referred to in a transaction. You will find private data techniques helpful for such design approaches even if you don't use private data.

Private data collections and verifiability

As we can see, when an organization uses private data in solution design, it is deliberately limiting who can see certain data. In our example, the Vehicle registration organization can see ownership information, but it cannot see police information. Similarly, the Police organization cannot see registration information but has full access to its private data on speeding and stolen cars.

Even though the data collections that each organization hosts are different, their blockchains are the same. The hashes contained within them allow these organizations to verify private data objects, even though they cannot read them. This concept of verifiability is at the heart of understanding how private data collections work and how to design smart contracts that use them.

The fact that an organization that does not have a copy of a private data collection may be able to verify business objects within it makes a private data collection different to a local database. The hashes mean that although an organization may exclusively host a private data collection, it is not free to tamper with it (by whatever means) as this would be detectable by any other organization on the network channel by referring to its blockchain.

Verifiability means that an organization can independently verify a fact represented as a current value in the ledger. For example, any organization in the network could determine whether Car1: {REG1, VIN1, YOGENDRA} is currently true or not simply by calculating whether hashes for the key and value match those in its blockchain.

Of course, the verifying organization has to know to ask this question. That's why verifiability goes hand-in-hand with *assertions*; one organization asserts that something is true, and all other organizations with access to the blockchain can *verify* that assertion.

Recapping on styles

As we discussed earlier, the idea of a transaction style or pattern is helpful—it allows us to name a conceptual idea and thereby add a code pattern to our kit bag of problem-solving tools. We now encounter a powerful idiom, the verify-style transaction pattern.

The verify-style transaction

Because this idea of *verifiability* is so important, this author recommends that all smart contracts that manipulate private data have so-called *verify-style* transaction methods associated with them.

Let's have a look at a smart contract structured this way:

```typescript
import { Context, Contract, Info, Returns, Transaction } from 'fabric-contract-api';
import { CarOwner } from './car-owner';
const collectionName: string = 'OwnerInfo';

@Info({title: 'CarOwner', description: 'Smart Contract for Vehicle owner data' })
export class CarOwnerContract extends Contract {

public async verifyCarOwner(ctx: Context,
                            carOwnerId: string,
                            verifyProperties: CarOwner):
Promise<boolean> {

  const hash: Buffer = await ctx.stub.getPrivateDataHash(collectionName, carOwnerId);

  if (hash.length === 0) {
    throw new Error('No private data hash with the Key: ${carOwnerId}');
  }

  const actualHash: string = pdHashBytes.toString('hex');

  // Convert user provided object into a hash
  const propertiesHash: string = crypto.createHash('sha256')
                            .update(JSON.stringify(verifyProperties))
                            .digest('hex');

  // Compare the hash of object provided with the hash stored on
  // public ledger
  if (propertiesHash === actualHash) {
    return true;
  } else {
    return false;
  }
}
}
```

Code 8.8: Smart contracts that use private data should have verification methods

In *Code 8.8*, we can see that the carOwnerContract contract has a verifyCarOwner method. It takes a set of properties corresponding to an assertion for a particular car. It returns a boolean indicating whether or not the assertion is true.

The code is straightforward; it retrieves the hash for CarId in the OwnerInfo collection using the getPrivateDataHash API. Conceptually, this API retrieves the hash from the blockchain. The contract then computes the hash for the properties that have been provided and returns the appropriate true or false response.

Writing smart contracts this way makes it very easy for applications to follow the assert-verify pattern:

```
verifyOwner = await carContract.createTransaction('verifyCarOwner');

let isTrue: boolean = await verifyOwner.evaluate ('CAR1',
                                                  'REG1, VIN1, YOGENDRA');
```

Code 8.9: An application can assert a business object easily if smart contracts are structured with a verify method

In *Code 8.9*, we can see that it takes a couple of lines of application code to determine whether Yogendra is indeed the owner of a particular car!

We might ask how the application issuing this request got the data to make this assertion, and this comes back to the underlying business process. Imagine, for example, Yogendra asking his insurer to provide a policy for his car. Yogendra is asserting to the insurance company that he owns car1. The insurance company has been provided with all the data from Yogendra so that they can verify his assertion. The insurer can use the smart contract to verify whether or not this is true. Private data collections are an excellent implementation choice whenever we see this kind of assert-verify pattern in a business process.

Applications, organizations, and private data

The code in *Code 8.9* shows how easy it is for an application to verify a business object that lives in a private data collection. However, an application always runs with an identity, and this associates it with a particular organization. Moreover, a smart contract needs to be deployed within an organization before it can access the blockchain.

These organizational facts mean that it's important to understand the extent to which smart contracts can access private databases in their organizational location. Let's see how this works in a simple example:

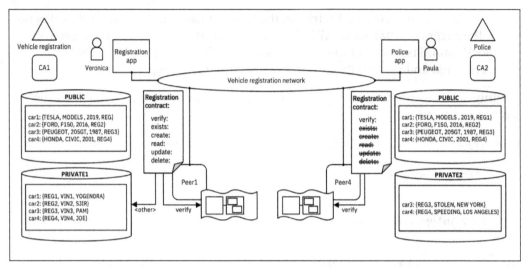

Figure 8.7: An application uses a contract to read its organization's private data but verify any organization's private data

In *Figure 8.7*, we can see Veronica from the Vehicle registration organization using a registration application connected to the Vehicle registration network. In the Police organization, Paula is using a police app, also connected to this network. We can see that the registration contract has been deployed on peers owned by each organization. This topology means that although the contract is available to both applications, they will each use it in quite different ways.

Let's imagine that Joe is driving in Los Angeles, and in a moment of thoughtlessness exceeds the speed limit and is stopped by the police. The police officer asks Joe if he's the owner of the car that he's driving—a Honda Civic. The police officer is connected to the police app in the same way as Paula in the diagram, and therefore can access the vehicle registration network and the registration contract, which provides access to registration information.

Let's look at the registration contract deployed on Peer1. The full range of contract methods is available because this contract has access to both PRIVATE1 *and* the blockchain. The verify method uses the blockchain to perform its logic. The other contract methods need access to PRIVATE1 because their logic requires them to read business objects using the getPrivateData API. In total, it means that the contract on Peer1 can generate any of the transactions listed in the smart contract.

The situation is somewhat different for the same smart contract installed in the police organization's Peer4 because it does not host a copy of PRIVATE1. This means only the verify method can execute correctly on Peer4. While Peer4 has access to its copy of the blockchain, it cannot read any of the data in PRIVATE1. Any method that requires data to be read from PRIVATE1 using **get**-style APIs on Peer4 will fail. To indicate this, we've struck through the other contract functions — they cannot be executed successfully on Peer4.

This means that if the police application wishes to access the full functionality of the contract, it must use Peer1 or any other peer in the Police organization. Applications that want access to read a private collection must come through the collection-owning organization to do so. Of course, this is not typical for read-type smart contract operations. The whole point of a decentralized network was to permit pervasive queries, making the network scalable and independent. With private data, this is only true for verification (not for ledger querying).

In our example, this means the police app can call the verify method in the registration contract on its local peer. This will verify that Joe is indeed the registered owner of the car he's driving. Keep in mind, the police are not able to see every car's registered owner. Also notice that the police subsequently make a record of Joe's misdemeanor in PRIVATE2!

This *assert-verify* style of interaction is very powerful. Private data collections make it simple to distribute a smart contract widely among other organizations in the network. This allows them to verify business objects *without* disclosing those business objects through the world state.

In the following sections, we'll review some other important design patterns related to smart contracts to allow us to maximize their benefits.

Private data consensus

To fully understand these patterns, it is important to understand the consensus mechanism for transactions that involve private data. This understanding will be the basis for structuring our smart contracts for the advanced design patterns typically required by Hyperledger Fabric-based solutions.

Our previous example illustrated this. By understanding that *only certain* organizations hold private data keys and values but *all* organizations hold the key/value hashes, we can create smart contracts with verify-style transaction methods.

Let's build on the example in *Figure 8.7* and update the owner of `car1` from Yogendra to Rebecca:

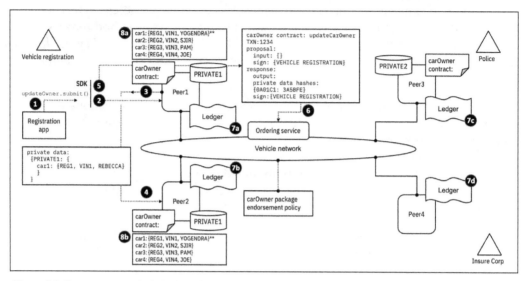

Figure 8.8: Transactions include hashes of private data key/values, but the key/value data is shared privately via gossip

Figure 8.8 shows the process steps required to update the owner of `car1` to Rebecca:

At step **1**, the `registration` app submits an `updateOwner` transaction. The transaction input is to change the owner of `car1` from `Yogendra` to `Rebecca`. The application uses transient data to keep these inputs from being recorded in the transaction.

At step **2**, the SDK chooses `Peer1` to endorse the transaction according to the endorsement policy. This policy could be satisfied equally well by `Peer2` if required. Let's not worry about the specifics of the endorsement policy right now. What's important is that it's `Peer1` that will run the `updateOwner` transaction method and sign the transaction response on behalf of the `Vehicle registration` organization.

At step **3**, the smart contract executes and accesses the `PRIVATE1` collection to create a state that reflects the car owner to be Rebecca; `car1: {REG1, VIN1, REBECCA}`. The smart contract uses the `putPrivateData` API to do this. As was the case with world state transactions, no change to `car1` in `PRIVATE1` occurs at this time. Updates to `PRIVATE1` will happen much later at steps **8a** and **8b**, when the overall transaction is committed.

Since the transaction involves private data, there is an additional communication from `Peer1`. It distributes the proposed `car1` state update to `Peer2`, which also holds a copy of `PRIVATE1`. In our example, `PRIVATE1` is held exclusively by the `Vehicle registration` organization, so the distribution is quite straightforward. In *Figure 8.5*, we saw that multiple organizations may host a private data collection, in which case distribution will be made to multiple organizations.

At step **4**, `Peer2` receives the updates to `car1`. Again, all updates are not applied to `PRIVATE1` until later (when the transaction is committed).

At this point in the consensus process, both peers in the `Vehicle registration` organization have the new values of `car1` but have not applied them to their copy of `PRIVATE1`.

At step **5**, the `updateOwner` contract method has returned a transaction response containing the private data hashes to the SDK. The SDK then created transaction 1234 and submitted it to the ordering service.

The most important thing to note is that transaction 1234 does not contain any explicit or calculable record of `PRIVATE1` or the new `car1` state, other than the hashes:

- Key `0A01C1`: A SHA256 hash of `PRIVATE1car1`
- Value `355BFE`: A SHA256 hash {`REG1`, `VIN1`, `REBECCA`}

In our example, we note that because the application used transient data, there are also no inputs captured in the transaction. Moreover, the transaction response does not contain any updates to the public world state collections. That is because our smart contract only updates private data collections. It is perfectly reasonable to write smart contracts that generate transactions that contain public world state and private data updates, it's just that our example does not require it.

At step **6**, transaction 1234 is ordered. It will be included in a transaction block along with other transactions. As usual, the ordering service performs a largely technical role in collecting transactions into blocks and distributing those blocks to the leading peers of the organizations participating in the network channel.

In our diagram, we can see that the orderer will distribute this transaction to peers 1, 2, 3, and 4. These peers will perform transaction validation as normal.

At step **7a** and step **7b**, the peers in the `Vehicle registration` organization validate transaction 1234. Specifically, the presence of the private data hashes for `car1` allow both `Peer1` and `Peer2` to update `car1` from {`REG1`, `VIN1`, `YOGENDRA`} to {`REG1`, `VIN1`, `REBECCA`}.

Note that this validation uses the same endorsement policy checks as a normal transaction. For private data, this policy could be in an individual private data state, a collection policy, or a smart contract definition. The validation process merely checks that all required signatures are present in the transaction output. We'll return to this later in this chapter, but for now, validation proceeds as we expect.

At step **7c** and step **7d**, we can see validation occurring for the Police and Insure Corp organizations. As they do not host PRIVATE1, they simply record the transactions in their blockchain, no other processing is required. As with steps **7a** and **7b**, any public world state data would be processed as normal.

At steps **8a** and **8b**, PRIVATE1 is updated with the new state for car1. We've marked car1 with ****** to indicate this fact.

The insert-style transaction

The same principles enable and encourage another really useful design pattern for smart contracts; the **insert-style** transaction method. This transaction style is most similar, but still significantly different, to the standard or *create-style* methods that we have seen up to this point. They can be very helpful for initiating and transferring work between organizations in a network channel while maintaining data privacy.

Let's have a look at a bank securities network to see an example at work:

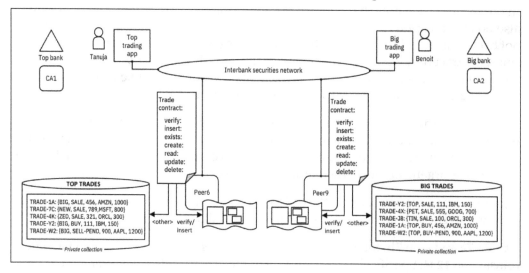

Figure 8.9: Smart contracts can verify and insert private data information even though they cannot read it

In *Figure 8.9*, we can see how Top bank and Big bank are using the Interbank securities network to record stock trades that they perform with other counterparty banks in the network.

We've simplified things a little, focusing on how each bank uses a single organization's private data collection. This collection is dedicated to recording all the organization's trades (sales and purchases of securities) with other banks in the organization.

For example, if we look at the TOP TRADES collection, we can see that Top bank has used the Trade contract to create TRADE-1A to represent its sale of 456 units of AMZN stock at a price of 1000 USD to Big bank. Top bank has also created two other trades to record sales to NEW bank (TRADE-7C) and ZED bank (TRADE-4K). We can also see that Top bank has also created TRADE-Y2 to record the purchase of 111 units of IBM stock from Big bank at 150 USD. Finally, we can see a pending transaction TRADE-W2 to buy 900 units of AAPL stock from Big bank at 1200 USD.

None of Top bank's trade information is available to any other bank in the network because the TOP TRADES private data policy only distributes these private trade states to peers within the Top bank organization. As with the example shown in *Code 8.6*, every organization in the network has the ability to *verify* any particular Top bank trade, if that counterparty can *assert* its details.

If we look at Big bank's BIG TRADES collection, we can see a similar pattern of transactions. BIG TRADES are private in the same way as TOP TRADES. Inside BIG TRADES, we can see the other halves of the transactions with Top bank as well as trades with PET bank and TIN bank. Neither of these transactions is visible to any other bank in the network other than Big bank. However, because Top bank and Big bank have half of TRADE-Y2 they can easily verify that the other has correctly recorded the corresponding part of the trade. For example, Big bank can use TRADE-Y2: {TOP, SALE, 111, IBM, 150} to *verify* that TOP TRADES contains TRADE-Y2: {BIG, BUY, 111, IBM, 150}. This pattern is worth understanding fully. It's a slightly more advanced form of a verify-style transaction involving police and vehicle registration data. It can be used for a large number of scenarios, as we'll discuss in a later section.

The most important trade

However, the most important entry in TOP TRADES is TRADE-W2. That's because unlike the other trades in TOP TRADES, it was not originated by Top bank! This statement seems to fly in the face of everything we've learned about private data collections, but it's a very important and helpful fact to understand. Let's see how it happened.

In our scenario, Big bank wants to buy 900 units of AAPL stock at a unit price of 1200 USD from Top bank. Of course, Top bank must want to sell this stock; it has to be a mutually agreeable exchange. The process starts with the Big bank buyer first indicating that they would like to purchase this stock, and to do this they create a *pending* transaction with the Top bank seller.

TRADE-W2 in TOP TRADES represents the pending sale to Top bank, and it was originated by the trade contract insert method on Peer9, owned by Top bank. That's right, it is Big bank, not Top bank, that originates the *pending* transaction TRADE-W2 into TOP TRADES! Big bank is effectively saying to Top bank "I'd like you to sell me that APPL stock. The details are in TRADE-W2. Can you agree to it?" It will be Top bank's responsibility to accept or reject this trade of course, but the proposal has been put there by Big bank; the ledger is capturing this stage in the process.

It's also worth noting that, as part of the same process, Big bank also used the trade contract's create method on Peer9 to create the TRADE-W2 pending purchase trade in BIG TRADES. This means that Top bank can now verify that Big bank has made a transaction using the verify method on Peer6, which it may wish to do as part of validating TRADE-W2.

This is an example of the *insert-style* transaction, and it captures some very important ideas:

- This behavior has been agreed by the smart contract. Top bank, Big bank, and probably other banks in the network have had to install and approve this smart contract before it was made available for use. Big bank is not able to insert random information wherever it likes — this behavior has been agreed by the business developers who created the smart contract and the operations personnel who deployed it; it is controlled behavior.

- Big bank is *writing* information to TOP TRADES, it is not *reading* data from it. We often think about writing data as more powerful than reading data because we associate writing with creation and change; writing indicates that things are happening. However, with private data, *reading* is the more valuable operation, because our primary concern is privacy. In the case of privacy, *reading* is more powerful than *writing*.

  This is why we make a conceptual distinction between *create-* and *insert-style* transactions. A create-style transaction has to determine whether a business object exists before it is written, whereas an insert-style transaction writes without reading beforehand. This difference is crucial because an insert-style transaction does not require the originating organization to host the target private data collection. Because the write operation is performed at validation time, insert-style transactions can be performed by organizations that do not host the collection. However, they still satisfy the endorsement policy.

We might think of `Top bank` as saying to the network:

- No organization can read from my private mailbox.

- I will accept requests to sell stock via my private mailbox. Insert your request, and I'll look at it.

- The following organizations are allowed to write to my private mailbox.

In this analogy, the mailbox is the private data collection, the insertion of a request is the `putPrivateData()` API, and the allowed organizations are the collection-level endorsement policy.

- As part of this operation, `Big bank` does not read TOP TRADES, it only writes to it. Indeed, because `Big bank` cannot read TOP TRADES, it can only write a pending transaction to this collection.

  This operation starts the life cycle of a pending trade, and as defined by the `trade` contract. This is how `Big bank` posts a pending request to `Top bank's` mailbox; the `insert` transaction allows authorized members of the network channel to write to `Top bank's` mailbox, but ultimately, it's up to `Top bank` to accept the pending transaction.

  We've shown a simplified data structure where sales, purchases, and pending transactions are all in the same collection. Usually these would be held in different collections. That's another reason why using the term *insert* to describe this transaction style is a good fit.

- As with all transactions, an endorsement policy will apply. It effectively allows a private data hosting organization to define who can write insert-style transactions because as long as the endorsement policy is satisfied, any organization can insert data into a private collection. Again, this is in stark contrast to organizations that wish to read data, as this requires the data to be hosted on its peers.

How smart contracts are packaged can also be important. In our example, we've shown how the same functionality can be made available everywhere in the network. That's because `Top bank` and `Big bank` are, in many senses, peers of each other.

We'll see later how we can package different parts of a smart contract to provide different organizations with different levels of functionality.

Insert-style smart contract

As is often the case, the code required for a smart contract to implement an insert-type pattern is quite small. Still, the design of the smart contract is important.

Let's have a look at the outline of the trade contract `insertTrade()` transaction method:

```
import { Context, Contract, Info, Returns, Transaction } from 'fabric-contract-api';
import { Trade } from './trade';

@Info({title: 'Trade', description: 'Smart Contract for trades'})
export class TradeContract extends Contract {

public async insertTrade (ctx: Context): Promise<void> {

// Get trade details from transient data

tradeId = transientData.get('tradeId').toString('utf8');
buyer = transientData.get('buyerCode').toString('utf8');
newTrade.seller = transientData.get('sellerCode').toString('utf8');
newTrade.price = transientData.get('price').toString('utf8');
...

// Check trade details
...

// Insert the transaction

  const tradeBuffer = Buffer.from(newTrade);
  collectionName = newTrade.sellerCode;

  await ctx.stub.putPrivateData(collectionName, tradeId, tradeBuffer);
}
```

Code 8.10: Insert-style transactions show how external organizations can write to a collection, without needing to read from it

The small number of lines of code in *Code 8.10* is in contrast with the important points to note:

- The transaction signature for `insertTrade()` does not contain any input parameters. Any such input would be recorded in the generated transaction divulging information about the proposed trade. In this case, we have minimized the *explicit* transaction inputs to a minimum to ensure that the blockchain transaction does not leak potentially sensitive information relating to a trade.

  If required, we can define an insert-style transaction with explicit inputs, but be aware that they will be visible to all organizations in the network channel.

- The trade details are passed in transient data; these include the `tradeId` and other trade details. We've shown the `buyer` and `seller` banks and `price` for illustrative purposes. Again, to reinforce the point, this data will not appear in the blockchain; it is private to the calling application and the `trade` contract.

- The collection name is calculated, rather than fixed. Indeed, notice that there are few constants in this transaction method. That is typical of real-world smart contracts.

  Note how in our example, we only have one collection per bank that keeps *all trades* with any other bank in the network. This means that every time a new bank joins the Interbank network, it only needs to add a single collection to participate.

  Indeed, it wouldn't matter if we had separate collections for purchases, sales, and pending transactions as long as each contained all such trades with other banks. This pattern avoids data structures per counter-party, where a bank would use a different collection for trades with different counterparties. Such an approach would require each bank to have different numbers and types of collections that increase as a bank traded with more counterparties, which is clearly not a desirable pattern.

  Of course, a few tactical multi-lateral collections in a network is OK, but such multi-lateral collections should not be systematized.

  If we recall the network design in *Code 8.2*, Honda and Peugeot had a shared collection between them. We could make this more scalable by assigning a single collection for all motor manufacturers with an open-sharing policy. Alternatively, information could be kept private but verifiable, assigning a single collection per manufacturer in which they store their information. Bilateral sharing would be possible using the insert-style transaction between counterparty organizations.

- The smart contract uses the putPrivateData() API to generate the pending proposal in the appropriate buyer's TRADE collection. As we've seen, this API merely places a set of hashes in the transaction response and distributes the collection data via gossip to the organizations that host the collection. In our example, Trade-W2 can be inserted into TOP TRADES by Big bank, even though Big bank does not host the collection. That's because the interbank network TRADE collections have been defined to allow non-member organizations to write to it by setting the memberOnlyWrite: false property for these collections. This is not something a developer needs to worry about; they merely write to the collection.

We note carefully that the smart contract doesn't *read* from the seller's collection, it only *writes* to it. This is very important—any read would typically fail because a smart contract will only have access to the collections hosted in the organization where it executes.

Insert-style application transaction submission

Once we've designed a contract method such as insertTrade(), it's very easy for an application to consume this functionality:

```
const tradeDetails = {
    tradeId: Buffer.from('TRADE-W2'),
    counterparty: Buffer.from('BIG'),
    units: Buffer.from('900'),
    symbol: Buffer.from('AAPL'),
    price: Buffer.from('1200')
};

insertTrade = await tradeContract.createTransaction('insertTrade');
await insertTrade.setTransient(transientData);
await insertTrade.submit();
```

Code 8.11: Applications can transparently consume insert-style transactions

In *Code 8.11*, we can see that an application is largely unaware of the implementation of the insert-style smart contract. The application simply puts the trade details in the transient data and submits an insertTrade transaction to the network. This separation of concerns is important as it allows applications to participate in the proper maintenance of secure information with minimum burden; the smart contract has encapsulated all the data privacy concerns.

Read your own writes

As we've seen, the insert-style transaction is an important design pattern to master, as it allows us to design systems that maintain verifiability and privacy to a high degree. Insert-style transactions exploit asymmetric behavior in Fabric: reads are immediate, writes are deferred. That is to say when a smart contract reads data using get-style APIs, access to the underlying data store returns the results immediately to the smart contract. However, when a smart contract writes data using put-style APIs, the update does not complete until the transaction is committed.

As we've seen this can have beneficial consequences for insert-style transactions. They can maintain the privacy of collections, while allowing specific forms of controlled access that can be beneficial in particular use cases, such as our trading network in *Figure 8.9*.

However, this pattern applies to all smart contracts in Hyperledger Fabric. It is often summarized as Hyperledger Fabric smart contracts cannot read their own writes. It comes down to the fact that as implemented in Fabric today, get-style APIs simply pass through to the underlying database (LevelDB or CouchDB, for example), whereas put-style APIs simply store create a write-set that is put in the database at validation time. The result is that a smart contract's own writes are not available to it.

This is an important detail to notice as we write smart contracts: any data we read in a smart contract will not be affected by data we write in the same invocation.

We note that this behavior is not fixed for all time; it is possible for Fabric to keep a buffer of uncommitted writes that it could use in combination with the current data in the database to calculate a result set that reflects uncommitted writes, effectively allowing a smart contract to read their own writes. However, the current behavior has been established over two releases and we need to be aware of this effective restriction.

In summary, this is an important but relatively minor restriction for Hyperledger Fabric. The important thing is to be aware of it and design our smart contracts appropriately.

Collection and state endorsements policy

As we've seen, private data collections provide a powerful framework for organizations within a network to share verifiable information at scale while maintaining privacy. We've seen how private data APIs mirror those for the public world state collection and have an extra API that allows smart contracts to verify the hash of a state in a private data collection.

Our next topic expands our understanding of an endorsement policy. In *Chapter 6, Developing Smart Contracts*, we focused on smart contract endorsement policies and mentioned that collection and state endorsement policies were also possible. Let's now see how these two policy types are used in practice. We'll see how along with the *verify*-style and *insert*-style transactions, endorsement policies form the basis of a new, *transfer*-style transaction.

Levels of endorsement policy

The first thing to note is that endorsement policies can exist at three levels. We've already seen two of them, and we'll now introduce a third:

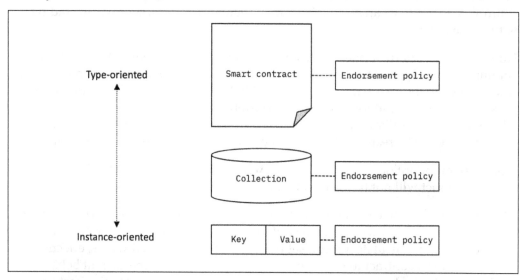

Figure 8.10: An endorsement policy can be defined at the smart contract, collection, or state level

In *Figure 8.10*, we can see that endorsement policies can be defined at the smart contract, collection, and state level. There is an explicit precedence order — endorsement policies must be satisfied first at the state and then at the collection level, and finally at the smart contract level. All appropriate endorsement policies must be satisfied before a transaction is considered valid.

This is all very sensible behavior — endorsements on specific objects have precedence over endorsements over collections of objects, which in turn have precedence over the most general smart contract behavior. It mirrors what we see in the real world: general rules are overridden in more specific situations when appropriate.

Let's consider an example. We've enhanced the Vehicle network (introduced in *Figure 8.5*) to use private data collections for each manufacturer. Each manufacturer will store car vehicle identification numbers:

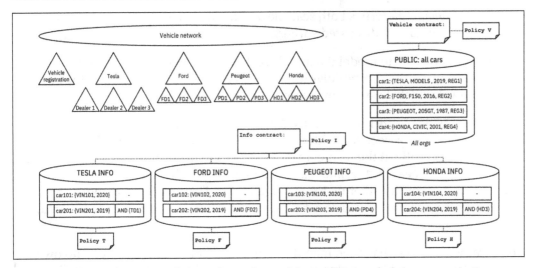

Figure 8.11: Endorsement policies can be used to model ownership transfer between organizations

In *Figure 8.11*, we can see how each manufacturer hosts its own private collection of vehicle information to keep car information private, but verifiable. The public collection, or world state, exists as usual. We'll consider the various endorsement policies as we examine the vehicles in these collections.

Consider the Tesla organization. When car101 is manufactured, only Tesla knows about it—exactly as we'd expect. It has not entered the supply chain yet and is not ready to be registered, so it exists only in the TESLA INFO collection. We can see similar cars for other manufacturers: car102, car103, and car104 have been similarly manufactured, have a VIN, and are verifiable, but they're not visible to the whole network as registered vehicles.

All these pre-registered vehicles have their VIN info stored in their respective organization's private collections as dictated by the Info contract. Notice that both the Info contract and every INFO collection has an endorsement policy associated with it. Let's consider the two important implications of this:

- When car101 is created, it will be Policy T that dictates the organizations that must sign the transaction that created car101, not Policy I. That's because a collection endorsement policy takes precedence over a smart contract endorsement policy.

- Each organization has a different endorsement policy for its INFO collection. Tesla has Policy T, whereas Honda has Policy H, and so on. It means that each organization can use the same smart contract but tailor the endorsement policy to define how valid transactions must be signed. It allows Tesla, Ford, Peugeot, and Honda to endorse using its own peers, yet still using the same smart contract.

- This design pattern is both scalable and flexible; these are key network design goals we discussed earlier.

This design allows us to model the initial creation of vehicles that have not yet entered the supply chain, a popular idiom when assets have started their life cycle but are not yet widely known throughout the network.

Let's now consider `car201` in the `TESLA INFO` collection. We can see that it has an endorsement policy associated with it. To understand the reason for this policy, we need to look carefully at the members of the network consortium in *Figure 8.11*. We notice that `Tesla Dealer 1, 2,` and `3` are also members of the network consortium. The same is true for the other motor manufacturers. This structure supports the business process that occurs once a car has been manufactured and is distributed, as we'll now explore.

Specifically, once a car has been manufactured, it is sent to a dealership, who owns the car before it is sold to a customer. We can enforce this control using state-based endorsement.

Consider `car201`, which has been moved to `Tesla Dealer 1` (`TD1`) and has an endorsement policy that requires the `TD1` organization to sign any transactions that change `car201`. We can see similar endorsement policies for `car202`, `car203`, and `car204` — their owning dealerships have been made the endorsing organizations for any change to them. It means that once `car201` has been updated in `TESLA INFO` by the `Info` contract as part of its transfer, `TD1` will subsequently be required to sign any transaction that updates it. Again, we notice two important implications of this:

- The state-based endorsement policy was added to `car201` when its ownership was transferred to `TD1`. This transactional change was made by the `Info` smart contract and was signed by the Tesla organization in accordance with `Policy T` at the collection level. Once this transaction is committed, `car201` will contain a state-based endorsement.

- The state-based endorsement for `car201` takes precedence over `Policy T`, the collection endorsement. For `car201`, it is the policy `AND(TD1)` that now dictates that any change must be signed by `TD1`. For `car201`, state-based endorsement allows finer-grained instance-based control.

- Different cars, whether in the same or different collections, can have different endorsement policies. For example, the `Info` contract inserted `car201` into `TESLA INFO` with an owner `TD1`, and `car204` into in `HONDA INFO` with an owner `HD4`.

  We see that `INFO` states are manipulated by the `Info` contract, but it is the policy within a state that determines which organizations must sign any transactional change, rather than an endorsement policy at a collection or smart contract level.

These design points allow us to model the transfer of ownership of specific assets between counterparties in the supply chain. Our example has demonstrated a change of custody, but the flexibility of state-based endorsements supports sophisticated ownership patterns to be supported. For example, assets can be owned by multiple organizations with the application of the appropriate endorsement policy.

The final stage in the business process is cars being sold by dealers and being formally registered in the PUBLIC all cars world state. This is controlled by the Vehicle contract, and transactions must be signed as dictated by Policy V, which applies to this smart contract. This is a standard process that we learned about extensively in *Chapter 6*, *Developing Smart Contracts*, and *Chapter 7*, *Developing Applications*, so we won't elaborate further, other than to say that public world states can also have state-based endorsement. This can be useful to allow all network participants to view an asset but restrict the set of organizations that can change it; a powerful pattern.

A note on collection policies

Collection policies contain more than just the endorsement policies that are used to validate transactions, but these tend to be of little interest to the application programmer.

For example, a collection policy defines maxPeerCount and requiredPeerCount, which control how many peers must receive a private state update before control is returned to the application calling a smart contract. Of course, this is purely for an administrator to configure and has no bearing on how an application works. It can, of course, affect performance, but this is not something the application or smart contract developer can or should be concerned with in isolation.

In summary, it's only the endorsement policy aspects of a collection policy that are of interest to an application or smart contract developer.

The transfer-style transaction

We conceptualized the functionality of private data collections and the processing paradigms they support by thinking about verify-style and insert-style design patterns for smart contracts. In the same way, we can use the transfer-style pattern for contract methods that use state-based and collection-based endorsement.

Let's have a look at the structure of a transfer-style smart contract:

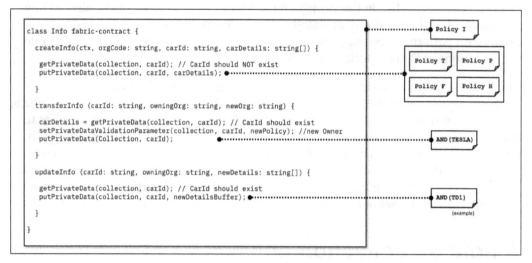

Figure 8.12: A transfer-style contract contains the privacy and endorsement aspects of private data collections for applications

In *Figure 8.12*, we can see the major transactions in a transfer-style contract. We've significantly simplified the code to allow us to see the concepts at work, and how the relevant APIs are used. We've not shown transient data in this example as we want to illustrate the transfer semantic rather than privacy. It would be a simple matter to transpose this smart contract to use transient data. We'll show you how to do that when we demonstrate how an application consumes this smart contract. Let's walk through this contract.

The createInfo transaction

Let's examine the transaction:

- createInfo starts the info life cycle. It is responsible for creating the VIN information for cars in a given organization.

- Because each organization hosts its own INFO collection, createInfo can read it to check that a new asset does not already exist within its organization. This basic check is analogous to the Exists method we saw earlier in *Chapter 6, Developing Smart Contracts*. We contrast this method with an insert-style transaction, which creates a new state in a target organization without checking whether it exists within its own organization as it does not have access to the target private data collection.

- `putPrivateData` writes a new object into the ledger. As we've learned, this operation is deferred. The current value of the ledger will not be updated until consensus is complete.

- A transaction created by `createInfo` must be signed according to the appropriate collection-level endorsement policy. For example, when Tesla creates a new car in the `TESLA INFO` collection, it will be `Policy T` that governs how transactions must be signed before they are included in the ledger. Likewise, for `HONDA INFO`, it will be `Policy H`, and so on.

  We note that `Policy I`, which applies at the contract level, does not come into play. That's because new objects are created within a collection, and it's therefore that collection's endorsement policy that determines how transactions must be signed.

  As we saw in *Code 8.9*, such policies need their smart contracts to be well-defined in terms of their behavior, while still being flexible to each organization's requirements. Specifically, Tesla, Honda, Peugeot, and Ford all have the same smart contract, which ensures that each of their `INFO` collections behaves in the same way. However, they each have a different endorsement policy to give them per-organization customizing for transaction validation.

- We cannot see by inspecting the `createInfo` code which specific endorsement policy applies for a given object. It is necessary to understand the full transaction life cycle as defined by the smart contract and its endorsement policies, and the relevant collection and their endorsement policies.

  This is not ideal; it would be better if smart contracts had some kind of metadata that could be used to help in this regard. As we'll see a little later, this does have an impact on the application.

The transferInfo transaction

Let's examine the details of this transaction:

- This method is responsible for changing the ownership of the `carInfo` object from a manufacturer to a dealership; for example, Tesla transferring ownership to `TD1`.

- This method signature identifies the car to be transferred, the current organizations, and the new organizations. Even though the owning organization is not necessary from an endorsement perspective, smart contracts often encapsulate the business rules that govern the transfer of business objects. For example, a transfer of `car201` from Tesla to `TD1` will check that the car is currently owned by Tesla.

- As we can see in *Figure 8.11*, cars are created according to a collection-level endorsement policy. The `transferInfo` transaction will add an endorsement policy identifying the new organization as the owner. It does this using the `setPrivateDataValidationParameter()` API, which sets a new policy for the state in a collection. In our example, `car201` will have an endorsement policy of `AND(TD1)` assigned to it.

- Although a transaction generated by `transferInfo` sets a dealership such as `TD1` as the owner, this transaction must be signed by Tesla. Because when the transaction is validated it is this endorsement policy that must be fulfilled. This makes sense since it's analogous to a transfer of an object from me to you — it requires my approval for it to be considered valid.

- Once a `transferInfo` transaction has been validated, a car will have a state-based endorsement policy associated with it, and this will now govern subsequent changes to that object.

- Unlike `createInfo`, the `transferInfo` code does give us some insight as to which endorsement policy applies for a given object.

    The `setPrivateDataValidationParameter()` indicates that state-based endorsement is in use, and may therefore apply to other transactions in the life cycle.

    However, it is still necessary to examine the rest of the smart contract to understand the transaction life cycle and relevant endorsement policies that will apply.

The updateInfo transaction

Let's examine this transaction's details:

- An `updateInfo` transaction is used by a dealership to modify the details of a particular car.

- It is a simple operation; it checks that a car object exists and updates it using the appropriate `get` and `put` ledger APIs.

- The transaction generated by `updateInfo` must be signed by an individual dealership such as `TD1` because `transferInfo` added a state-based endorsement policy. It's this policy that any collection-level policy applied when it was initially created.

- updateInfo does not make use of the setPrivateDataValidationParameters() API as it is not changing ownership. However, any changes to objects are subject to the policy that was set by this API in the transferInfo transaction method.

- As with createInfo, we cannot see by looking at updateInfo which endorsement policy rules for a given object. Again, it is necessary to understand the transaction life cycle and relevant endorsement policies.

We can see that the skeleton code for this transfer-style smart contract is deceptively simple. That's because the collections and their endorsement policies work in concert with the smart contract code to provide sophisticated behavior. Once we have a clear understanding of what we want to do we can implement sophisticated logic in a relatively small amount of code.

It means that when we examine the createInfo and updateInfo transactions, we only see a part of the picture. We must examine the full transaction life cycle as defined by the smart contract, its endorsement policies, the relevant collections, and their endorsement policies if we want to understand the semantics of the contract.

The transferInfo transaction is a little easier to understand. The use of the setPrivateDataValidationParameter() API hints at the fact that interesting things are being done to a state! However, without reference to the other transaction methods in the contract, collections, and endorsement policies that apply to them, we will struggle to glean the full meaning of this method.

Therefore, this author encourages you to make full and proper use of the smart contract interface to implement clear business object life cycles that encapsulate all operations on a business object of a given type. In other words, adopting an object-oriented approach will help the design and comprehensibility of your smart contracts.

The transfer-style application transaction submission

Once we've designed a contract such as Info, it's very easy for an application to consume its functionality. Let's see how the different organizations in the network can use this smart contract life cycle.

Firstly, let's see how Tesla or a similar manufacturer brings the car201 info into existence:

```
const createDetails = {
    owningOrg: Buffer.from('TESLA'),
    carId: Buffer.from('Car101'),
    carVin: Buffer.from('VIN101'),
    carYear: Buffer.from('2020')
};

createInfo = await infoContract.createTransaction('createInfo');
await createInfo.setTransient(createDetails);

endorsingOrgs = ['TESLA'];
await createInfo.setEndorsingOrganizations(...endorsingOrgs);

await createInfo.submit();
```

Code 8.12: An application can use setEndorsingOrganizations to meet a transaction endorsement policy

In *Code 8.12*, we can see how a Tesla application creates the Vin and Year info for car201. It uses transient data to keep the transaction input details off the ledger and submits a createInfo transaction. It's a very simple invocation that results in car201 residing in the TESLA INFO collection, as we've seen.

However, this createInfo transaction must be endorsed by TESLA according to the TESLA INFO collection endorsement policy. Therefore, the Tesla application uses the setEndorsingOrganizations to identify the endorsing organization (Tesla), which must sign the createInfo transaction.

It must make this call because it is not currently possible for discovery to help in this scenario. The SDK has no way to link this transaction to the TESLA INFO collection. This is an implementation detail, encapsulated in the program logic of createInfo, and therefore must be set by the application.

Ideally, Fabric would have a mechanism to allow the SDK to determine the correct endorsers. In the meantime, it can make sense for applications to encapsulate this logic inside a slightly higher-level API that mirrors submitTransaction and relieves the caller from calling the setEndorsingOrganizations API. However, it is helpful to retain a sense of perspective. This is a relatively simple task no matter how it's implemented!

Similarly, we can see how `Tesla` transfers the car to the `TD1` dealer:

```
const transferDetails = {
    owningOrg: Buffer.from('TESLA'),
    newOwner: Buffer.from('TD1'),
    carId: Buffer.from('Car201'),
};

transferInfo = await infoContract.createTransaction('transferInfo');
await transferInfo.setTransient(transferDetails);

endorsingOrgs = ['TESLA'];
await transferInfo.setEndorsingOrganizations(...endorsingOrgs);

await transferInfo.submit();
```

Code 8.13: Transfer-style contracts use contracts that rely on setEndorsingOrganizations to transfer ownership

In *Code 8.13*, we can see an identical pattern to *Figure 8.12*. However, in this case, although the `transferInfo` transaction will set the endorsement policy to `TD1` according to the `newOwner` transient data, it requires a signature from Tesla to make this a valid transaction. We see again how the Tesla application uses the `setEndorsingOrganizations` API to ensure the correct signing occurs.

Once this transaction has been successfully added to the ledger, it can now be updated by the `TD1` organization, as we can see in *Code 8.14*:

```
const updateDetails = {
    owningOrg: Buffer.from('TD1'),
    carId: Buffer.from('Car201'),
    carModification: Buffer.from('FILTER4'),
};

updateInfo = await infoContract.createTransaction('updateInfo');
await updateInfo.setTransient(updateDetails);

endorsingOrgs = ['TD1'];
await updateInfo.setEndorsingOrganizations(...endorsingOrgs);

await updateInfo.submit();
```

Code 8.14: A transfer-style contract uses setEndorsingOrganizations to match a state-based endorsement policy

The only difference here is that the TD1 dealer application must ensure that the transaction is signed by the TD1 organization.

Note that we have not spent a lot of time on the business rules inside a smart contract as these are highly dependent on the business problem being solved. There are many options available that we've not shown explicitly:

- createInfo could ensure that a supplied VIN complied with the standard format and had not already been issued.

- transferInfo could ensure that the transaction was submitted by the organization that owned the car, and that transaction submitters had sufficient authority as defined by their organizational role.

- updateInfo could ensure that the transaction was submitted by the organization that owned the car and that the changes were valid.

In reality, it's these business rules — where we implement the business logic that governs the life cycle of the assets in our business network — that we will spend the most time on now that we have a clear understanding of how Hyperledger Fabric works.

Summarizing smart contracts, transactions, and applications

We're at the end of our journey on advanced use of smart contracts and the transactions they generate that update the ledger. We've also seen how the careful design of smart contracts makes it easy for applications using the SDK to achieve powerful results with a small amount of code.

We should also note how we've seen a range of options for transaction sharing; from a relatively simple model where all organizations in a network perform similar operations to each other with relatively open sharing of information, to one where organizations have more specialized roles and use Hyperledger Fabric to verify transactions and transactional data within a more restricted sharing regime.

In reality, most solutions will use a combination of features, so it's important that we are comfortable with the myriad of options available.

Advanced smart contract packaging

The final section in this chapter is a short but important one — how to best exploit smart contract packaging. In *Chapter 7, Developing Applications*, we learned that packaging was a fairly straightforward activity, and in many cases it will be so.

However, when using private data, verify-style, insert-style, and transfer-style contracts, there are opportunities and traps of which we should be aware.

In summary, proper packaging of smart contracts can:

- Allow different endorsement policies to be applied to the same smart contract
- Ensure organizations only see the smart contract code they need to see
- Minimize distribution of unnecessary code

As we saw in *Chapter 6, Developing Smart Contracts*, Fabric 2 has significantly improved smart contract packaging. The most important change is the introduction of a smart contract package (chaincode) *definition*. In most cases, there will be a one-to-one mapping between the smart contracts in a package and their associated endorsement policy, but let's now examine the opportunities we can exploit using the separation of the package from the definition.

Multi-definition packages

In Fabric 2, it is now possible for the same package to have different definitions. We see this illustrated in the following diagram:

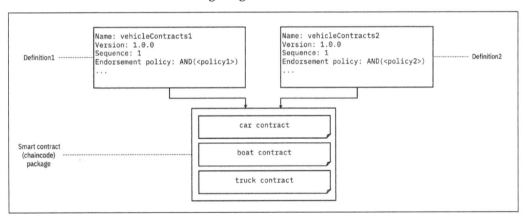

Figure 8.13: Two definitions can point to the same smart contract package

In *Figure 8.13*, we see that a package can be addressed using the vehicleContracts1 or vehicleContracts2 definition. While the smart contract package is the same for both definitions, each is a completely *different set of transactions*.

Specifically, applications that use the car contract via vehicleContracts1 generate completely different transactions to applications using the car contract via vehicleContracts2. So, while the code is the same and the transaction shapes are the same, they will be stored in different namespaces, and the endorsement policy rules will be different.

Multiple definitions are helpful because they allow the same smart contract code to be packaged and used in different ways without renaming. Essentially, they are a powerful reuse mechanism for smart contracts.

Functional packaging

Figure 8.13 showed how the *same* package can be used by *different* definitions. It's also possible for *different* definitions to use the *same* package. We see this illustrated in the following diagram:

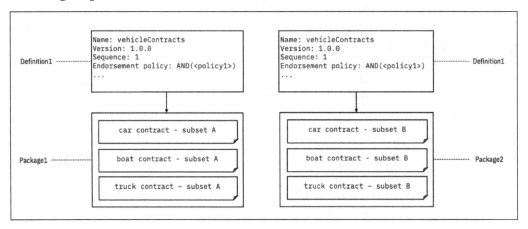

Figure 8.14: The same definition can be used to refer to different packages

In *Figure 8.14*, we can see how vehicleContracts can refer to package1 or package2. We note that even though it looks like there are two different definitions, their contents are the same — they refer to version 1.0.0 of the vehicleContracts definition with endorsement policy <policy1>. In this example, it is the package contents that are different.

Examining these packages more carefully, we can see that package1 has a particular set of transactions within it, namely subset A of the car contract, subset A of boat contract, and so on. Likewise, package2 has subset B of these contracts. We call this **functional packaging** because different packages can generate different transactions from the total pool of possible transactions; different packages therefore contain different *business functions*.

Let's look at an example of why this can be very powerful by returning to our trade contract:

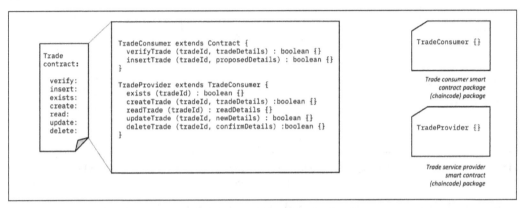

Figure 8.15: A contract arranges its transactions in a hierarchy for distribution to service consumers and providers

In Figure 8.15, we can see an elaboration of the trade contract from the Interbank securities network in Figure 8.7. We can see that the trade contract is not structured as a simple class, but as a class hierarchy.

We have placed verifyTrade and insertTrade in a TradeConsumer subclass of the built-in Fabric Contract base class. We have placed all other transactions such as createTrade and readTrade in a derived class, TradeProvider.

The relationship between the participants in the network is captured and reflected in this structure, a hierarchy. We have designed a hierarchy where TradeProviders can perform every function that TradeConsumers can and more. We've then placed different transactions into appropriate TradeConsumer and TradeProvider packages for distribution.

However, as the following diagram illustrates, we can choose different inheritance relationships to target the functionality of certain classes of participants:

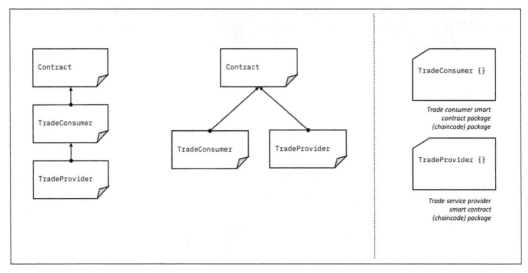

Figure 8.16: Contract hierarchies are designed to reflect and capture the relationships between business network participants

In *Figure 8.16*, the left-hand structure allows TradeProvider to do everything that TradeConsumer can do and more. In the second case, TradeProvider and TradeConsumer have no overlapping functionality.

Returning to *Figure 8.15*, we see a hierarchy of transactions—those in TradeConsumer are in some sense the most generic and least powerful, while those in TradeProvider are the most specific and most powerful. The intention is to make TradeConsumer transactions widely available to the network and keep TradeProvider transactions available to the organizations that provide the service.

However, *Figure 8.16* shows that we have choices when we design transaction inheritance structures and packages. They can reflect and capture the different roles in a network.

In networks where all participants perform the same role, the class inheritance will be flatter. In networks where different participants perform very different roles, the inheritance structure will be deeper. And we recall that in most simple cases we place all contracts in a single package and distribute it to all organizations.

But in the Interbank network, this is not desirable; careful packaging has significant benefits, both functional and operational:

- Contracts can have commercially sensitive information in them. For example, while `insertTrade` merely requests a trade to be made, `createTrade` will have access to the rules governing whether or not to make a trade. We may well want to limit the distribution of the latter transaction's logic.

- Allied to this, if we distribute smart contract logic to many different actors then we give them access to code that they could potentially maliciously exploit. Of course, our system should be safe even if rogue actors have access to the code, but limiting its distribution in the first place reduces the attack surface.

- Organizations that need to perform simple operations should have simple contracts. It makes a system easier to understand and easier to debug if things go wrong if we separate concerns between different participant types.

The inheritance and packaging designs in *Figure 8.15* are used to target functionality to certain types of participants according to their relationships.

Of course, at the end of the day, everything must work. Applications in one organization using smart contracts in the `TradeConsumer` package must be able to work with applications using the `TradeProvider` package in a different organization. We cannot place functionality in arbitrary packages without regard to the ways in which they will be used but, as we've seen, careful design has significant benefits.

Finally, let's put all these ideas together in the `Vehicle network`:

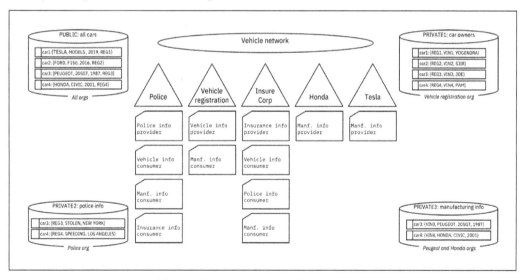

Figure 8.17: Smart contract (chaincode) packages are distributed to the service consumer and provider organizations

In *Figure 8.17*, we can see how different organizations provide and consume different services according to the smart contracts available to them. For example, it is only the police that can generate a `police info` transaction or `Vehicle registration` that can generate a `car owner` transaction. Each of the five organizations is a service provider for transactional information over which they are sovereign.

In contrast, note who can consume transactional information. In our network, both `Police` and `Insure Corp` can verify `vehicle info`, `police info`, and `manufacturing info`. In contrast, manufacturers do not have access to these transactions. They do not have the smart contract transactions that form the hashes or other transactions that would allow them to otherwise transact with these organizations.

We can see how careful smart contract packaging makes the Vehicle network more intelligible, private, and secure. We've also seen how a smart contract package (chaincode) and its definition allows a network to agree on which transactions are generated and their respective endorsement policy. Careful design of smart contract inheritance allows a network of organizations to deliver precise functionality to the different network participants according to their needs.

We saw that if a network uses multi-definition packaging, then it's the *same* code being used to generate different transactions, which was helpful for code reuse. If a network uses functional packaging, then the same *definition* generates *different* transactions. This can be helpful to restrict unnecessary and sometimes unwanted code distribution, effectively limiting the transactions particular organizations can generate.

Summary

We conclude our chapter on advanced smart contract and application development topics for Hyperledger Fabric. Let's recap a few of our key learning points:

- We started the chapter by continuing our examination of the fundamental operations an application can perform:
  - Query a ledger
  - Submit a new transaction
  - Listen for ledger notifications

- We then took a deeper dive into advanced topics, including how to customize how the application interacts with the network using *strategies* and *handlers*. We saw how they allow applications to incrementally increase their influence over how the SDK interacts with the network without ever worrying about the network details.

- Our extensive tour of *private data collections* allowed us to design networks that support *privacy* and *verifiability*.

- We looked at both *state-based* and *collection-based endorsement* and saw how they complement contract-based endorsement.

- We learned how smart contract *patterns* allow us to encapsulate the advanced functionality provided by private data and advanced endorsement.

- We showed how patterns such as *verify-style, insert-style*, and *transfer-style* help smart designers implement common network idioms and create easy-to-use application interfaces.

- Finally, we examined contract *hierarchies, inheritance*, and *packaging* to keep contracts simple, understandable, and secure.

This chapter also concludes the last of three chapters dedicated to smart contract and application design. You'll find the ideas in it both helpful to your understanding of how Fabric works and how to architect, design, and develop useful solutions that involve Hyperledger Fabric.

Let's continue our exploration of Hyperledger Fabric 2 beyond application and smart contract development.

9

Network Operation and Distributed Application Building

In previous chapters, we established the foundations of a business network and application spanning multiple organizations and stakeholders:

- In *Chapter 4, Setting the Stage with a Business Scenario*, we configured and ran a barebones trade network from a set of specifications
- In *Chapter 5, Designing Smart Contract Transactions and Ledger Data Structure*, we built the core of a blockchain application in the form of a set of smart contracts that directly read and manipulate the ledgers that are the systems-of-record for your network

The bulk of the configuration and application logic development is done, but our task is far from finished.

As you can imagine, the contracts, which act on data used by multiple organizations, are sensitive pieces of code that ought to be accessible only via safe channels with built-in protections against misuse. Therefore, it is standard practice among blockchain developers to layer one or more applications above the contracts, exposing the contracts' capabilities in ways that provide adequate security and privacy safeguards. These applications, unlike smart contracts, can be engineered as typical enterprise applications using well-known technology stacks. They can also be integrated with existing enterprise applications used by organizations that participate in blockchain networks.

Unlike a smart contract, which acts on a shared backing store (ledger) whose state is held in consensus by network participants, the higher-layer enterprise applications don't necessarily have to act on behalf of the entire network. In fact, the various organizations and stakeholders within them may have unique and specific business logic requirements, requiring the development of different applications serving selected clientele. Therefore, a single blockchain network may end up exposing different ledger views and contract capabilities to different stakeholders. Further, these applications may run in enterprise security domains maintained independently by the different organizations. Collectively, though, the set of smart contracts and higher-layer applications can be viewed as a distributed application acting on a common data storage layer.

In this chapter:

- We will learn how to build and operate a distributed Fabric application for the business entities that participate in our trade scenario:
    - We will recap the Hyperledger Fabric ledger setup and transaction pipelines
    - We will show how each step is performed using code and configuration samples

- At the end of this process, you will understand how to:
    - Bootstrap network ledgers
    - Install contracts
    - Engineer applications as web services that can be exercised by users through commands on a terminal or from a web browser

- We will learn how to build a production-grade ordering service that generates transaction blocks by consensus of a cluster of nodes running the Raft protocol

We will begin this chapter by discussing the nature of a multi-layered distributed Fabric application: first in generic terms, and subsequently using our trade scenario as an example. Later, we will demonstrate how to develop and bootstrap such an application to enable our trade scenario.

Stages in a Fabric network's life cycle

Before we dive into the details of application-building, it is important to first gain a broader perspective on how a Fabric network is created and bootstrapped in readiness for deploying and running applications, and what streams of developmental activities must be undertaken. *Figure 9.1* illustrates these stages and activities from the perspectives of three groups of subjects: operators and maintainers, developers, and users:

- Network setup and bootstrapping activities are classified into operations, which is the responsibility of network operators designated by their respective organizations or by the consortium. Operators will also typically oversee DevOps.

- Development, which involves designing, writing, and testing application code, can occur before or concurrently with operations. The developers responsible for this are typically distinct from operators and do not need to know operational details, though they need to know the organizational and channel structure to write proper code.

- Finally, the exercising of the applications' business logic is classified into runtime activities, and this is done by members and clients of the enterprises that belong to the network consortium.

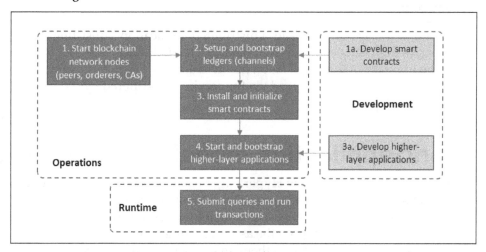

Figure 9.1: A Fabric network's life cycle categorized into operational, developmental, and runtime stages

The operations stage (steps **1** to **4** in *Figure 9.1*) begins with the process of starting up individual components of a network (step **1**), namely the peers belonging to designated organizations that share channel ledgers, ordering nodes (typically) belonging to their separate organizations, and nodes running Fabric CA servers and acting as CAs for their respective organizations. We demonstrated this process in *Chapter 4, Setting the Stage with a Business Scenario*.

Next, we set up channels and associate each network peer with one or more channels (step **2**). We walked through an example of defining a channel's configuration and creating the artifacts necessary to start up those channels in *Chapter 4, Setting the Stage with a Business Scenario*. In this chapter, we will see how to create channels and bootstrap their ledgers (or chains). Smart contract development (step **1a**) can occur together with the channel definition and setup; since contracts running on different channels may need to communicate at runtime, the contract developers must know channel names and organizational affiliations beforehand.

Having completed *Chapter 5, Designing Smart Contract Transactions and Ledger Data Structure*, you should already know how to implement a contract. Once the channels are set up, each contract must be installed and initialized on a given channel (step **3**), which we will see how to do later in this chapter. Finally, the higher-layer applications can be started (step **4**); these can be developed (step **3a**) at any point in time using knowledge of the API offered by each contract, but must be started for users to complete this exercise.

At the end of the operations stage, a distributed application, consisting of multiple service apps exercising contracts that manage channel states, is ready. In the runtime stage, the life cycle of this application involves arbitrary sequences of transaction submissions and queries triggered via the service APIs offered by the higher-layer applications (step **5**).

Fabric application model and architecture

In earlier chapters, we saw how Hyperledger Fabric can be viewed as a transaction processing system over a distributed database (corresponding to channel ledgers) maintained by the network peers, exposing information through a set of views. It is the developer's job to expose the assets and data items in the ledgers, as well as the transactions and queries on them, in a way that hides the complexity of the underlying network and channel architecture. In addition, the developer must provide differentiated capabilities to various enterprise users affiliated with the network's organizations, with appropriate security and privacy safeguards built in. *Figure 9.2* illustrates what such a distributed Fabric application looks like:

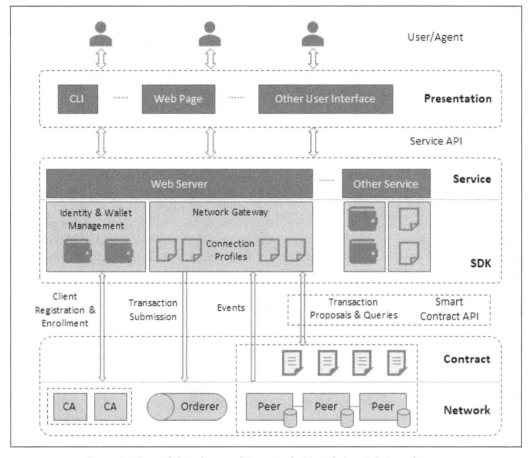

Figure 9.2: Typical three-layer architecture of a Hyperledger Fabric application

As we can see, the **Network** layer at the bottom, consisting of network peers, ordering nodes, and CAs, is the infrastructure on which applications are deployed. Channels created and maintained in peers' databases are also parts of this infrastructure. Above the infrastructure and interfacing with users or software agents is the distributed application built as a three-layer stack. The lowest layer consists of smart contracts, like those we developed in *Chapter 5, Designing Smart Contract Transactions and Ledger Data Structure,* that read and write directly to channel ledgers (maintained in the peers' databases). The middle layer consists of a set of services, typically built as web servers offering REST APIs, each of which manages the Fabric network's identities and triggers transactions and queries on the smart contracts using the Fabric SDK libraries. At the top is the presentation layer, which offers interfaces to users, typically through a command-line terminal or a web browser, to invoke the APIs offered by the servers in the layer.

Fabric application development overview

In this chapter, we will see how to develop the service and presentation layers of a distributed trade application and run them on our trade network. Most developers will be familiar with building command-line interfaces or web pages that a presentation layer will comprise. Our discussion of the service layer will be more instructive to a blockchain developer, as this is where the orchestration of application life cycle tasks that involve submitting transactions to, or reading state from, smart contracts takes place.

The applications in this layer translate user requests to transactions and queries supported by the smart contract APIs, and extract results to provide information that's comprehensible to the user. Such applications can also be viewed as wrappers around the smart contract, though they may often contain much more business logic than typical wrappers would. (Depending on requirements, a service-layer application, like a typical enterprise web application, may maintain private off-chain databases that can be used to cache states from channel ledgers to avoid the latency of a contract query.) In almost all cases, such applications must have suitable access control logic programmed into them. The access control rules will be determined based on what smart contract assets and operations a given end user is entitled to access, and this is a design decision that should be made a priori by the organization that will build and run such an application.

The developer must keep in mind (and this is where blockchain applications differ from traditional enterprise backend applications) that every Hyperledger Fabric transaction is asynchronous; that is, the result of the transaction will not be available in the same communication session in which it was submitted. This is because, as we have seen in previous chapters, a transaction is processed through a pipeline composed of independent stages:

1. The client submits transaction proposals for endorsements to multiple peers

2. Valid transaction proposals with endorsements are submitted in an envelope to the ordering service, which batches transactions into blocks

3. Network peers commit transactions to their ledger databases after verifying their validity

In short, this is the consensus protocol through which a transaction is collectively approved by network peers, and each instance may potentially take an unbounded amount of time. Hence, submitting a transaction request to a smart contract is akin to submitting a job request, and the requester gets a response through events using a publish-subscribe mechanism.

Fortunately, the transaction pipeline's complexity can be hidden (or wrapped) in an SDK that Fabric provides in three different languages: Node.js, Java, and Go. This SDK allows applications to connect to Fabric networks using **gateways** with **connection profiles**, submit transactions, and get back responses synchronously using the gateway API. The SDK also offers features for identity management and storage of credentials in **wallets**. It offers API functions to dynamically register new network clients with desired roles and attributes (by connecting to **Membership Service Providers** (**MSPs**) and automatically store the credentials into local wallets. Gateway operations require possession of valid credentials that can be looked up from these wallets. We will discuss gateways, connection profiles, and wallets in more detail through code samples later in this chapter. You can see how a typical service layer application is built in *Figure 9.2*, with a web server offering a REST API above and exercising the SDK API below.

Finally, the applications in the service and presentation layers should not be considered part of a single application stack. Each service could be built on an independent technology stack that's tailor-made for a given organization or user with its own presentation layer. They will likely run in production in different domains guarded by their enterprises' firewalls. But every application here will use Fabric SDK API functions to connect to the common network and the common set of smart contracts linking the different organizations. Shortly, we will demonstrate how our trade scenario consists of distinct web applications serving different organizations, namely exporter, importer, carrier, and regulator; some applications are built using Java and others using JavaScript.

 The thinking behind this architecture and the principles driving it are independent of the underlying blockchain technology. To implement an identical application on a different blockchain platform than Hyperledger Fabric, only the smart contract and SDK layer must be reimplemented. The rest of the application can remain untouched with the end user not noticing any difference.

Architecture of a Fabric application for trade

In *Chapter 4, Setting the Stage with a Business Scenario,* we created a network specification for our trade scenario consisting of four organizations:

- An exporter organization (ExporterOrg) that is managed by the exporter's bank and serves both the bank and exporters who had accounts with it

- An importer organization (ImporterOrg) that is managed by an importer's bank and serves the bank and importers

- A carrier organization (CarrierOrg) that serves the carrier that ships goods from exporters to importers

- A regulator organization (`RegulatorOrg`) that serves a governmental authority that issues export licenses to exporters

It makes sense, therefore, to build distinct service-and-presentation applications to serve each of these four organizations. The architecture of our distributed trade application is illustrated in *Figure 9.3*:

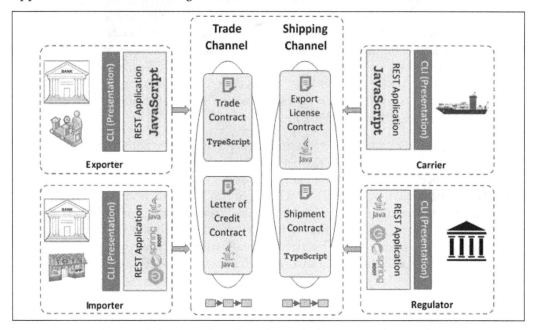

Figure 9.3: Architecture of a trade application built using Hyperledger Fabric

Our application has two channels consisting of different assets and data items. The **Trade Channel** tracks the details and progression of trades arranged between an exporter and an importer as well as the life cycles of letters of credit facilitating those trades. The **Shipping Channel** tracks the shipment of goods involved in these trades as well as the export licenses needed to clear those shipments.

As you can see in *Figure 9.3*, the contracts we built in *Chapter 5, Designing Smart Contract Transactions and Ledger Data Structure* are distributed across these two channels. The **Trade Contract**, written in TypeScript, and the **Letter of Credit Contract**, written in Java, are installed on the **Trade Channel**. Installed on the **Shipping Channel** are the **Export License Contract**, written in Java, and the **Shipment Contract**, written in TypeScript. These four contracts collectively manage states held in the two channels through business logic that links them; for example, the Letter of Credit and Export License contracts look up the existence and properties of a trade by querying the **Trade Contract**, and the **Letter of Credit Contract** processes payments by looking up shipment status from the **Shipment Contract**.

The interests of different entities involved in a trade are not restricted to single contracts but rather span the state managed collectively by the four contracts on the two channels. None of these entities needs a full view of the ledger, and as we saw when we were developing the contracts, there are access control rules restricting the operations a given entity can perform through a contract. The set of applications in *Figure 9.3* therefore reflects a real-world division of interests among organizations.

For the carrier and the regulator, we will show how to build separate applications serving those entities, exposing a certain set of operations and information queries that are relevant only to those roles. In the case of the exporter and the importer, we will build separate applications, each managing users possessing bankers' and clients' roles and with access control logic to distinguish the two.

To show that these applications in the service layer are truly independent from both a development and a deployment perspective, we will use different languages and frameworks. The exporter and carrier applications will be written as JavaScript web applications exposing REST APIs. The importer and regulator applications will be written in Java using the Spring Boot framework.

For each application, we will build a common **command-line interface (CLI)** presentation layer application that will be replicated across the four service-layer applications. This CLI application will make REST calls to the respective services using the services' APIs.

Operations – network setup and bootstrap

Now we can get to work, equipped with the:

- Knowledge of what steps are involved in the creation and running of a Fabric application
- Architecture of the trade application we would like to build

We have already completed two of the steps illustrated in *Figure 9.1*:

- Created a network that we can launch using a single command
- Developed code for the four smart contracts illustrated in *Figure 9.3*

In this section, we will demonstrate steps 2 and 3, namely **channel setup** and **contract installations**.

Operations overview – channel and contract setup

Figure 9.4 expands the Operations stage illustrated in *Figure 9.1*. Once the number of channels required for our distributed application has been determined and each channel has been assigned a unique name, each channel is *created* by submitting a request to the network's ordering service. This channel creation is appended as a block to the system channel maintained by the ordering nodes.

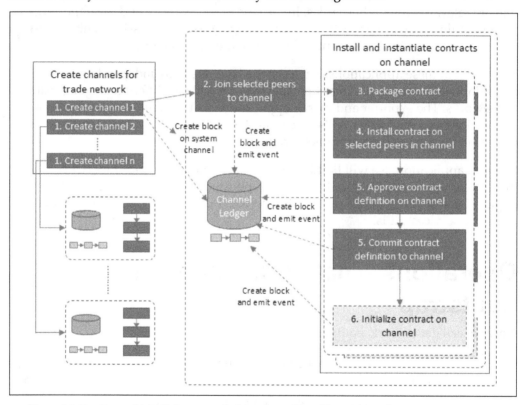

Figure 9.4: Creating and initializing network channels, and installing and initializing contracts on them

For every channel that is successfully created, selected network peers belonging to organizations that are part of the channel's consortium (see *Chapter 4, Setting the Stage with a Business Scenario*) can be *joined* to that channel, a procedure that results in those peers being initialized with the channel's ledger (that is, a chain of blocks as well as the current world state). At this stage, every peer joined to a channel is only a committing peer because no contracts have been installed yet. The act of joining is triggered by a request to the ordering service and appends a block to the channel's ledger.

Next, one or more contracts are installed in each channel. This is a 4-5 step process. First, the contract source code is packaged in a certain format. A subset of peers joined to the channel is designated to have endorsement privileges for this contract, and the package is installed on each such endorsing peer. Then, an administrator from each organization maintaining the channel must independently *approve* a definition of the contract by submitting a request to the ordering service, resulting in a new block on the channel's ledger. Finally, an administrator from any of the channel's organizations must *commit* a contract's chaincode definition to the channel, again by sending a request to the ordering service and appending a new block to the ledger.

Finally, each contract can optionally be *initialized* by submitting a transaction that bootstraps the contract's state on the ledger. (This step was mandatory in Fabric 1.) Depending on how this contract's business logic has been implemented, this step may not be necessary, and the contract may be ready for regular operation right after a successful commit.

Now that we have understood the design and the process of setting up channels and contracts, we can move from theory to practice. In the next few sections, we will perform the steps in the Operations stage using code and commands from our `trade-network` project repository.

Prerequisites – creating all channel artifacts

Before we can perform the operations in *Figure 9.4*, we must generate the necessary channel artifacts and start the network (if it is not already running).

Creating all channel artifacts

Let's revisit the code in our `trade-network` repository and navigate to the `bash` folder. In *Chapter 4, Setting the Stage with a Business Scenario*, we saw how the channel configuration file, `configtx.yaml`, defines two profiles:

- `ThreeOrgsTradeChannel` for the consortium named `TradeConsortium` consisting of three organizations: `ExporterOrg, ImporterOrg, RegulatorOrg`

- `FourOrgsShippingChannel` for the consortium named `ShippingConsortium` consisting of four organizations: `ExporterOrg, ImporterOrg, RegulatorOrg, CarrierOrg`

We created a channel named `tradechannel` based on the `ThreeOrgsTradeChannel` profile as follows:

```
$ ./trade.sh generate -c tradechannel -o 3
```

This produced a genesis block named `genesis.block` in the `channel-artifacts` folder and a channel configuration transaction and anchor peer configurations in the `channel-artifacts/tradechannel` folder. (Note that if you deleted the crypto artifacts for the network or the channel artifacts associated with `tradechannel` using the `clean` or `cleanall` options with `trade.sh`, you should run the preceding generate command again.)

Now, to generate equivalent channel artifacts for another channel named `shippingchannel` based on the `FourOrgsShippingChannel` profile, run:

```
$ ./trade.sh generate -c shippingchannel -o 4
```

The `-o 4` switch results in the `FourOrgsShippingChannel` profile being used. You will see that `genesis.block` in the `channel-artifacts` folder is not replaced, but a new folder named `channel-artifacts/shippingchannel` is created and contains the `channel.tx`, `ExporterOrgMSPanchors.tx`, `ImporterOrgMSPanchors.tx`, `RegulatorOrgMSPanchors.tx`, and `CarrierOrgMSPanchors.tx` files.

Launching the network

If you still have the network launched in *Chapter 4, Setting the Stage with a Business Scenario*, running, you can skip to the next step. Otherwise, if you brought down the network at the end of that chapter, launch it again as follows:

```
$ ./trade.sh up
```

This will start the Docker network in the background, redirecting container logs into `logs/network.log` by default. If you run `docker ps -a`, you should see four peer containers, four CA containers, three CouchDB containers, and one orderer container.

Overview of Fabric tools and commands

Fabric peers, orderers, and CAs (or MSPs) communicate using gRPC (https://grpc.io/). Each endorsing peer that launches a contract in a container (we will see how this is done later) also communicates with the contract process using gRPC. The contract (also called **chaincode** in Fabric parlance) itself exports a service endpoint implementing the JSON RPC 2.0 specification (http://www.jsonrpc.org/specification) for transactions and queries. Fortunately, Hyperledger Fabric provides developer- and administrator-friendly interfaces and APIs that abstract away the low-level specifications and enable applications (or scripts) above them to directly run the channel and contract operations in *Figure 9.4*.

These interfaces come in two varieties: CLI and **software development kit (SDK)**. For all operations illustrated in *Figure 9.4*, we will use CLI commands, which in Fabric 2 and above is the default recommended way. The Fabric SDK has discontinued support for these operations in recent versions and is today meant exclusively for exercising contracts in the runtime stage, and we will see examples later in this chapter.

For ease of development, Fabric offers a packaged collection of all necessary and available CLI commands in a Docker container named hyperledger/fabric-tools. If you built Docker containers from a cloned copy of the Fabric source in *Chapter 4, Setting the Stage with a Business Scenario,* using make docker, this image should already be present on your system. Otherwise, when you run the channel commands in the next section using the trade.sh script, it will automatically be downloaded from Docker Hub.

Creating channels

First, we must start the tools container, which is configured in bash/docker-compose-cli.yaml. Some portions of the file are as follows:

```
cli:
  container_name: trade_cli
  image: hyperledger/fabric-tools:$IMAGE_TAG
  stdin_open: true
  ......
  command: /bin/bash
  volumes:
    - /var/run/:/host/var/run/
    - ./crypto-config:/opt/gopath/src/github.com/hyperledger/fabric/
    peer/crypto/
    - ./channel-artifacts:/opt/gopath/src/github.com/hyperledger/
    fabric/peer/channel-artifacts/
    - ./cli_scripts:/opt/gopath/src/github.com/hyperledger/fabric/peer/
    scripts
    - ./../contracts/:/opt/gopath/src/github.com/hyperledger/fabric/
    peer/contracts/
  networks:
    - trade
```

The base image of this container is `hyperledger/fabric-tools`, as we discussed earlier. The `stdin_open` attribute instructs the container to start an interactive shell, waiting for users to run commands using the Bash shell (as set by the `command` attribute) instead of terminating after launch. In the `volumes` section, we are syncing the crypto artifacts, the channel artifacts, the contract source code, and scripts (in `bash/cli_scripts/`) to the container.

Launch the tools container (again, from the `bash` folder):

```
$ docker-compose -f docker-compose-cli.yaml up >logs/network-cli.log
2>&1 &
```

The container is now running in the background and its console logs are streamed to `logs/network-cli.log`. Log into this container:

```
$ docker-compose -f docker-compose-cli.yaml up >logs/network-cli.log
2>&1 &
```

The container is now running in the background and its console logs are streamed to `logs/network-cli.log`. When you run `docker ps -a`, you should see a container named `trade_cli`.

We can now create our first channel by running:

```
$ docker exec -e CHANNEL_NAME=tradechannel trade_cli scripts/channel.sh
create
```

This runs a `scripts/channel.sh create` command from within the `trade_cli` container. The output you see on the console should end as follows, indicating that `tradechannel` has been created:

```
2020-09-01 17:05:50.190 UTC [channelCmd] InitCmdFactory -> INFO 001 Endorser and orderer connection
s initialized
2020-09-01 17:05:50.195 UTC [cli.common] readBlock -> INFO 002 Expect block, but got status: &{NOT_
FOUND}
Error: can't read the block: &{NOT_FOUND}
+ peer channel create -o orderer.trade.com:7050 -c tradechannel -f ./channel-artifacts/tradechannel
/channel.tx --tls true --cafile /opt/gopath/src/github.com/hyperledger/fabric/peer/crypto/ordererOr
ganizations/trade.com/orderers/orderer.trade.com/msp/tlscacerts/tlsca.trade.com-cert.pem --connTime
out 120s
+ res=0
+ set +x
2020-09-01 17:05:50.303 UTC [channelCmd] InitCmdFactory -> INFO 001 Endorser and orderer connection
s initialized
2020-09-01 17:05:50.370 UTC [cli.common] readBlock -> INFO 002 Received block: 0
===================== Channel 'tradechannel' created =====================

========= Channel creation completed ===========
```

Figure 9.5: Successful creation of tradechannel

The command that triggers the channel creation can be seen in the preceding screenshot:

```
peer channel create -o orderer.trade.com:7050 -c tradechannel
-f ./channel-artifacts/tradechannel/channel.tx -tls true -
cafile /opt/gopath/src/github.com/hyperledger/fabric/peer/crypto/
ordererOrganizations/trade.com/orderers/orderer.trade.com/msp/
tlscacerts/tlsca.trade.com-cert.pem -connTimeout 120s
```

The `peer` command can be used to run a range of channel and contract operations, and we will use it extensively in this section. Here, the `channel create` option indicates that a channel ought to be created. The `-c tradechannel` switch indicates the name of the intended channel, and the `-o orderer.trade.com:7050` switch indicates the address of the orderer node to send this request to. The `-f` switch points to the channel configuration transaction file we created earlier for `tradechannel`. The other parameters specify key and certificate files for TLS communication, and a connection timeout.

Returning to the command we ran earlier, you can see that we ran a script named `channel.sh`, which lies in the `cli_scripts` folder on your host machine. If you open this script file, you will see channel creation instructions in the function `createChannel`:

```
createChannel() {
    setEnvironment exporterorg
    set -x
    fetchChannelConfig
    set +x
    if [ -f $CHANNEL_NAME.block ]
    then
        echo "Channel already created"
        return
    fi

    ......

        peer channel create -o orderer.trade.com:7050 -c $CHANNEL_NAME
-f ./channel-artifacts/${CHANNEL_NAME}/channel.tx --tls $CORE_PEER_TLS_
ENABLED --cafile $ORDERER_CA --connTimeout 120s >&log.txt

    ......

    echo "===================== Channel '$CHANNEL_NAME'
    created ===================== " echo
}
```

The `setEnvironment` function sets the signing identity to that of an admin member of `ExporterOrg`. Note that a channel can be created by any admin member of a consortium in that channel's profile, so we could have used `importerorg` or `regulatororg` with `setEnvironment` (for `ImporterOrg` or `RegulatorOrg` respectively) instead of `exporterorg`. If you examine the `setEnvironment` function, you will see that it sets a collection of environment variables, including the organization's MSP ID, the peer address, the MSP configuration folder in the crypto artifacts, and TLS connection information, including the root certificate. The `peer channel create` command, under the hood, uses the key associated with the signing identity to sign the channel configuration transaction (`channel.tx`) before submitting to the orderer.

The `fetchChannelConfig` function attempts to fetch the latest channel configuration block (in this instance, for `tradechannel`). Here, since the channel has not yet been created, this operation will fail, and the block will not be recorded to the filesystem (you can see this in the console output too).

Finally, you can see the `peer channel create` command in the preceding snippet, which we observed earlier in the console output. After this command succeeds, a file named `tradechannel.block` containing the created channel's new configuration block will be recorded on the container's filesystem.

Using the trade.sh script as a shortcut

Now that we have examined the details of what it takes to trigger a channel creation procedure, we can take a step back and look at our all-purpose `trade.sh` script, which provides a shortcut to create a channel. Instead of running the `docker exec` command, we could instead have simply run:

```
$ ./trade.sh createchannel -c tradechannel
```

If you examine the `trade.sh` code, you will see that the preceding command executes a `peer channel create` command for `tradechannel` with appropriate parameters.

Verifying block creation

We saw in *Figure 9.4* that the creation of a channel results in a block being appended to the orderer system channel. We can verify this by querying blocks on the system channel (named `trade-sys-channel` in `bash/.env`, as we noted in *Chapter 4, Setting the Stage with a Business Scenario*). Log into the `trade_cli` container and set your signing identity as an orderer organization (`TradeOrdererOrg`) administrator:

```
$ docker exec -it trade_cli bash
$ export CORE_PEER_ADDRESS="orderer.trade.com:7050"
$ export CORE_PEER_LOCALMSPID="TradeOrdererOrgMSP"
```

```
$ export CORE_PEER_MSPCONFIGPATH="/opt/gopath/src/github.com/
hyperledger/fabric/peer/crypto/ordererOrganizations/trade.com/users/
Admin@trade.com/msp"
$ export CORE_PEER_TLS_CERT_FILE="/opt/gopath/src/github.com/
hyperledger/fabric/peer/crypto/ordererOrganizations/trade.com/orderers/
orderer.trade.com/tls/server.crt"
$ export CORE_PEER_TLS_KEY_FILE="/opt/gopath/src/github.com/
hyperledger/fabric/peer/crypto/ordererOrganizations/trade.com/orderers/
orderer.trade.com/tls/server.key"
$ export CORE_PEER_TLS_ROOTCERT_FILE="/opt/gopath/src/github.com/
hyperledger/fabric/peer/crypto/ordererOrganizations/trade.com/orderers/
orderer.trade.com/tls/ca.crt"
```

Now fetch the newest block in the orderer system channel as follows:

```
$ peer channel fetch newest sys_newest.block -o orderer.trade.com:7050
-c trade-sys-channel --tls --cafile /opt/gopath/src/github.com/
hyperledger/fabric/peer/crypto/ordererOrganizations/trade.com/orderers/
orderer.trade.com/msp/tlscacerts/tlsca.trade.com-cert.pem
```

You should see an output like the following:

```
bash-5.0# peer channel fetch newest sys_newest.block -o orderer.trade.com:7050 -c trade-sys-channel
 --tls --cafile /opt/gopath/src/github.com/hyperledger/fabric/peer/crypto/ordererOrganizations/trad
e.com/orderers/orderer.trade.com/msp/tlscacerts/tlsca.trade.com-cert.pem
2020-09-01 17:14:04.175 UTC [channelCmd] InitCmdFactory -> INFO 001 Endorser and orderer connection
s initialized
2020-09-01 17:14:04.179 UTC [cli.common] readBlock -> INFO 002 Received block: 1
```

Figure 9.6: Fetching a block from the orderer system channel corresponding to the creation of tradechannel

The latest block is numbered 1. This is actually the second block in the channel, as the first block (which is the genesis.block we created earlier) is numbered 0. If you look into the block file (sys_newest.block), you will see specifications of tradechannel and the TradeConsortium that is attached to that channel. (You don't need to understand the details of the contents, though we will discuss block structure in the context of channel configuration updates in *Chapter 13, Life in a Blockchain Network*.)

Now that we have created and verified tradechannel, we can create our other channel, which we named shippingchannel, as follows:

```
$ ./trade.sh createchannel -c shippingchannel
```

In the logs, you should see very similar output to what you saw when tradechannel was created. You should see a shippingchannel.block containing this channel's initial configuration written to the container's filesystem. To verify the creation, you can log into the trade_cli container as we did earlier and fetch the newest block from the system channel using the orderer administrator's signing identity. This time, you will see the latest block numbered 2.

Joining organization peers to channels

Consider `tradechannel` first. Three organizations, each containing one peer, are associated with it. To instantiate the channel's ledger (chain of blocks), we must initialize that ledger on each peer and start the gossip protocol that enables the peers and the ordering service to communicate with each other to sync blocks and world states. This process is called the joining of peers to the channel and must be done separately for each peer in the channel's organizations. For `tradechannel`, these peers run in the containers named `peer0.exporterorg.trade.com`, `peer0.importerorg. trade.com`, and `peer0.regulatororg.trade.com`. To join them to the channel, run:

```
$ ./trade.sh joinchannel -c tradechannel -o 3
```

The `-o 3` switch tells the command to join the three peers listed previously to `tradechannel`. If you monitor the output in `logs/network-cli.log`, you will see something like the following after a successful operation:

```
+ peer channel join -b tradechannel.block
join
Having all peers join the channel...
+ res=0
+ set +x
2020-09-01 17:17:42.043 UTC [channelCmd] InitCmdFactory -> INFO 001 Endorser and orderer connection
s initialized
2020-09-01 17:17:42.433 UTC [channelCmd] executeJoin -> INFO 002 Successfully submitted proposal to
 join channel
==================== peer0.exporterorg.trade.com joined channel 'tradechannel' ====================
==

+ peer channel join -b tradechannel.block
+ res=0
+ set +x
2020-09-01 17:17:45.568 UTC [channelCmd] InitCmdFactory -> INFO 001 Endorser and orderer connection
s initialized
2020-09-01 17:17:45.908 UTC [channelCmd] executeJoin -> INFO 002 Successfully submitted proposal to
 join channel
==================== peer0.importerorg.trade.com joined channel 'tradechannel' ====================
==

+ peer channel join -b tradechannel.block
+ res=0
+ set +x
2020-09-01 17:17:49.027 UTC [channelCmd] InitCmdFactory -> INFO 001 Endorser and orderer connection
s initialized
2020-09-01 17:17:49.355 UTC [channelCmd] executeJoin -> INFO 002 Successfully submitted proposal to
 join channel
==================== peer0.regulatororg.trade.com joined channel 'tradechannel' ====================
===

========= Channel join completed ===========
```

Figure 9.7: Joining three organizations' peers to tradechannel

As you can see, each of our three peers in separate organizations is joined successfully to the channel. Behind the scenes, the `trade.sh` script runs the `channel. sh` script within the `trade_cli` container, which in turn runs the following command to trigger each join request:

```
peer channel join -b tradechannel.block
```

If you examine `cli_scripts/channel.sh`, the `joinChannelWithRetry` function runs this command for each organization and peer (which defaults to peer0) combination using the `setEnvironment` function. This updates the environment variables, determining the current signing identity as in the channel creation step. The `join` command also uses the latest channel configuration block, `tradechannel.block`, which was written to the filesystem after channel creation. Finally, you will see retry logic in the function, which exists simply for fault tolerance as join requests may occasionally fail.

To verify the join, we can check for the presence of a new block on the `tradechannel` chain using the following command (from the host machine):

```
$ ./trade.sh fetchconfig -c tradechannel -b tradechannel_newest.block
```

You will see the channel's newest block in a newly created file, `tradechannel_newest.block`. If you check the container logs, you will see something like the following:

```
fetch
Fetch the channel configuration block...
Fetching the most recent configuration block for the channel
+ peer channel fetch config tradechannel.block -c tradechannel --connTimeout 120s
+ res=0
+ set +x
2020-09-01 18:40:08.410 UTC [channelCmd] InitCmdFactory -> INFO 001 Endorser and orderer connections initialized
2020-09-01 18:40:08.412 UTC [cli.common] readBlock -> INFO 002 Received block: 0
2020-09-01 18:40:08.413 UTC [channelCmd] fetch -> INFO 003 Retrieving last config block: 0
2020-09-01 18:40:08.414 UTC [cli.common] readBlock -> INFO 004 Received block: 0
========== Channel configuration fetched ===========
```

Figure 9.8: Fetching first (configuration) block from tradechannel

The channel's configuration is the first block, numbered 0, indicating that the ledger (or chain of blocks) has been initialized.

Let's repeat the join process for our other channel, `shippingchannel`. We have four organizations associated with this channel and one extra peer to join, namely peer0. carrierorg.trade.com. Run the following command:

```
$ ./trade.sh joinchannel -c shippingchannel -o 4
```

The `-o 4` switch tells the command to join four peers listed previously to `shippingchannel`. If you monitor the output in `logs/network-cli.log`, you will see successful join attempts for four peers. To verify the join, you can fetch the newest block of `shippingchannel` using the `trade.sh fetchconfig` command, which should fetch a block numbered 0, just as in the case of `tradechannel`.

If you are familiar with the first edition of this book, you will recall that channel create and join operations were demonstrated in a Node.js app using the Fabric-SDK-Node library. Both create and join operations could be performed using an instance of a `fabric-client` object that was exported by this SDK. But `fabric-client`, which offers lower-level functions and is a little complex to use, is a legacy (deprecated) API in 2.x (currently 2.2).

The `fabric-network` module, which co-existed with `fabric-client` in 1.4, is the only application-level SDK library in 2.2. It offers features to exercise contracts in the runtime stage but does not support administrative features to be exercised in the operations stage. This includes channel create and join operations as well as contract installation and initialization. Those features are now only supported using the CLI, as we have demonstrated partially in the preceding sections.

That said, `fabric-client` will still work with a Fabric 2.x peer network, and for the benefit of the curious reader, we have created a simple application that was adapted from the `middleware` code in the first edition of this book into the `legacy_sdk_1.4` folder (at the same level as `bash`). This supports channel creation and joining using credentials that are either loaded from our previously generated crypto-artifacts, or using dynamic registration and enrollment with organizations' MSPs. (We will discuss registration and enrollment later in this chapter when we develop our service apps.) An example of creating `tradechannel` using the signing identity of an `ImporterOrg` administrator (created using `cryptogen`) and joining peers to it is (after re-launching the network):

```
$ node prepareChannel.js tradechannel load
importerorg
```

Repeat the preceding command (you'll have to re-launch the network again):

```
$ node prepareChannel.js tradechannel enroll
importerorg
```

You should refer to the `README.md` file in the folder for more instructions. Note that you should delete the `bash/client-certs/` folder and re-launch the network before resuming this chapter.

Setting organization anchor peers on channels

Another administrative operation that must be performed is the setting of an anchor peer for each organization on a channel. An organization's anchor peer acts as a point of contact for peers in other organizations. For example: an anchor peer in ExporterOrg can respond to queries from a peer in ImporterOrg and share connectivity information for all other peers in ExporterOrg. This kind of reachability information is necessary for the gossip protocol among peers to work and sync ledger data.

Recall that our configtx.yaml file contains a definition for an anchor peer for each organization other than the orderer's. (In our initial configuration, we only have one peer in each organization, so the selection is moot.) For example, the anchor peer for ExporterOrg is peer0.exporterorg.trade.com listening on port 7051, and the configuration file we created for this peer on tradechannel using configtxgen (see *Chapter 4, Setting the Stage with a Business Scenario*) is channel-artifacts/ tradechannel/ExporterOrgMSPanchors.tx. Three organizations participate in tradechannel, hence we need to run three channel configuration updates to set anchor peers for ExporterOrg, ImporterOrg, and RegulatorOrg. We can do this simply by running:

```
$ ./trade.sh updateanchorpeers -c tradechannel -o 3
```

The -o 3 switch tells the command to join peer0 in each of the three organizations mentioned to tradechannel. If you monitor the output in logs/network-cli.log, you will see something like the following after a successful operation:

```
anchor
Set anchor peers...
+ peer channel update -o orderer.trade.com:7050 -c tradechannel -f ./channel-artifacts/tradechannel
/ExporterOrgMSPanchors.tx --tls true --cafile /opt/gopath/src/github.com/hyperledger/fabric/peer/cr
ypto/ordererOrganizations/trade.com/orderers/orderer.trade.com/msp/tlscacerts/tlsca.trade.com-cert.
pem --connTimeout 120s
+ res=0
+ set +x
2020-09-01 18:45:18.435 UTC [channelCmd] InitCmdFactory -> INFO 001 Endorser and orderer connection
s initialized
2020-09-01 18:45:18.476 UTC [channelCmd] update -> INFO 002 Successfully submitted channel update
===================== peer0.exporterorg.trade.com set as anchor in exporterorg in channel 'tradecha
nnel' =====================

+ peer channel update -o orderer.trade.com:7050 -c tradechannel -f ./channel-artifacts/tradechannel
/ImporterOrgMSPanchors.tx --tls true --cafile /opt/gopath/src/github.com/hyperledger/fabric/peer/cr
ypto/ordererOrganizations/trade.com/orderers/orderer.trade.com/msp/tlscacerts/tlsca.trade.com-cert.
pem --connTimeout 120s
+ res=0
+ set +x
2020-09-01 18:45:21.597 UTC [channelCmd] InitCmdFactory -> INFO 001 Endorser and orderer connection
s initialized
2020-09-01 18:45:21.628 UTC [channelCmd] update -> INFO 002 Successfully submitted channel update
===================== peer0.importerorg.trade.com set as anchor in importerorg in channel 'tradecha
nnel' =====================

+ peer channel update -o orderer.trade.com:7050 -c tradechannel -f ./channel-artifacts/tradechannel
/RegulatorOrgMSPanchors.tx --tls true --cafile /opt/gopath/src/github.com/hyperledger/fabric/peer/c
rypto/ordererOrganizations/trade.com/orderers/orderer.trade.com/msp/tlscacerts/tlsca.trade.com-cert
.pem --connTimeout 120s
+ res=0
+ set +x
2020-09-01 18:45:24.756 UTC [channelCmd] InitCmdFactory -> INFO 001 Endorser and orderer connection
s initialized
2020-09-01 18:45:24.785 UTC [channelCmd] update -> INFO 002 Successfully submitted channel update
===================== peer0.regulatororg.trade.com set as anchor in regulatororg in channel 'tradec
hannel' =====================

========= Channel configuration updated with anchor peers ===========
```

Figure 9.9: Updating anchor peer configurations for organizations in tradechannel

The `update` command for the `ExporterOrg` peer is:

```
peer channel update -o orderer.trade.com:7050 -c tradechannel -f ./
channel-artifacts/tradechannel/ExporterOrgMSPanchors.tx --tls true
--cafile /opt/gopath/src/github.com/hyperledger/fabric/peer/crypto/
ordererOrganizations/trade.com/orderers/orderer.trade.com/msp/
tlscacerts/tlsca.trade.com-cert.pem --connTimeout 120s
```

As with channel create and join, the transaction is submitted to the orderer using appropriate TLS credentials, and the configuration file `ExporterOrgMSPanchors.tx` is supplied. A similar peer `channel update` command is run for the other two organizations.

Each such update appends another block to the `tradechannel` chain, so we can verify the success of these operations by fetching the latest block (as we did after the peer join):

```
$ ./trade.sh fetchconfig -c tradechannel -b tradechannel_newest.block
```

The output should be something like the following:

```
fetch
Fetch the channel configuration block...
Fetching the most recent configuration block for the channel
+ peer channel fetch config tradechannel.block -c tradechannel --connTimeout 120s
+ res=0
+ set +x
2020-09-01 18:59:15.790 UTC [channelCmd] InitCmdFactory -> INFO 001 Endorser and orderer connection
s initialized
2020-09-01 18:59:15.793 UTC [cli.common] readBlock -> INFO 002 Received block: 3
2020-09-01 18:59:15.793 UTC [channelCmd] fetch -> INFO 003 Retrieving last config block: 3
2020-09-01 18:59:15.795 UTC [cli.common] readBlock -> INFO 004 Received block: 3
========= Channel configuration fetched ===========
```

Figure 9.10: Fetching the latest block from tradechannel, containing an anchor peer update transaction

As we can see, three blocks have been appended to the chain since the join, as we would expect after three anchor peer updates.

Now we can update the anchor peers for the four organizations of shippingchannel as follows:

```
$ ./trade.sh updateanchorpeers -c shippingchannel -o 4
```

If you fetch the newest block in the shippingchannel chain, you will see that it is numbered 4.

Running all channel operations in one go

As a shortcut for the user, we have a script called startAndJoinChannels.sh in the bash folder that creates, joins, and updates anchor peers for both our channels in one shot. Instead of running the various commands we have demonstrated and analyzed in the preceding sections, we could have instead run:

```
$ ./startAndJoinChannels.sh
```

(If you choose to run this command, you should first bring down the network using ./trade.sh down and then bring it up again using ./trade.sh up.)

Installing and initializing contracts

Now we can install our contracts on the two channels we have created and bootstrapped. Referring to *Figure 9.3*, we intend to install two different contracts on each channel. As we discussed earlier in this book, contracts only need to be installed on peers that serve as endorsers; that is, peers that run procedures and affix their signatures to the results. Also, typically, the endorsement of one peer belonging to an organization is enough to deem a given transaction as meeting the approval of that organization.

We can conceive of more complex organizational dynamics where different peers represent different spheres of authority, but for our application, we will keep it simple.

Therefore, the selection of peers to install a given contract on is driven by **endorsement policy** (more on that later), which in turn is determined by the business scope of that contract; only organizations that are concerned with that portion of the business logic encoded in the contract need to have it installed in their peers.

The other criteria we must use for endorsement peer selection are dependencies between contracts. Our contracts are programmed to invoke each other for different purposes, as we saw with the examples in *Chapter 5, Designing Smart Contract Transactions and Ledger Data Structure*. In the Fabric model, it is only possible for a contract to invoke another if the latter is also installed on the local peer. Further, if the invocation involves writing a value to a key, the endorsement policy of the caller contract must be stricter than the endorsement policy of the called contract. In our application, cross-contract invocation happens only for reading key values, so this concern doesn't arise.

With these guidelines in mind, let's see where our four contracts will be installed:

- trade: This governs trade deals between exporters and importers; hence, it must be installed on ExporterOrg and ImporterOrg peers. In addition, the regulatory authority export licenses must have visibility into these deals, so it must be installed on RegulatorOrg peers too.

- exportLicense: This governs the issuance of an export license to an exporter by a regulator; hence, it is enough to install it on ExporterOrg and RegulatorOrg peers. This contract invokes the trade contract, which is installed on peers belonging to both these organizations.

- shipment: This governs the shipment life cycle, and hence must be installed on ExporterOrg, ImporterOrg, and CarrierOrg peers.

- letterOfCredit: Trade financing concerns exporters, importers, and their respective banks; hence, this must be installed on ExporterOrg and ImporterOrg peers. Regulators have no interest in this process, so it need not be installed on RegulatorOrg peers. This contract invokes both the trade and shipment contracts, both of which are installed on ExporterOrg and ImporterOrg peers as well.

In the scenario described in *Chapter 4, Setting the Stage with a Business Scenario*, it was suggested that the dispatch of a shipment would be dependent on the existence of a valid export license. For our implementation, we chose not to add this dependency primarily for resource reasons. It would involve running both exportLicense and shipment on the peers of all four organizations, which may prove to be difficult on users' machines with limited CPU and memory, as each contract instance runs in a separate container. But users with more powerful machines are encouraged to augment the contract code and the installation process for experimentation and learning purposes.

Jumping from theory to practice, we will now follow the five-step process illustrated in *Figure 9.4* (see steps **3-6**) and demonstrate them in two different modes: (i) using CLI tools like the ones we use for channel operations, and (ii) using the VS Code IBP extension.

Using CLI tools to install and initialize contracts

We will demonstrate CLI mode first, using the trade_cli container, which should already be running from the channel create, join, and anchor peer update exercise.

Prerequisites for contract installation

First, if you have not already done so, make sure that the contract source code is present by running the following from the root folder of your clone of trade-network:

```
$ git submodule update --init
```

You should see the source code in the contracts folder under two different versions; for the current exercise, we will use the code in the v1 folder.

First, we must prepare the contracts for packaging. To build the trade contract, run (from the root folder):

```
$ cd contracts/v1/trade/
$ make build
```

A dist folder and a node_modules folder should be created if they are not already present. Repeat this exercise for the other three contracts. In shipment, the other contract written in TypeScript, you should see similar folders getting created. In the Java-based contracts, letterOfCredit and exportLicense, you should see folders named dist and build.

We will now demonstrate the five-step process using the trade contract as an example.

Packaging a contract

Package the trade contract in the trade_cli container as follows:

```
$ docker exec -e CHANNEL_NAME=tradechannel -e CC_LANGUAGE=node -e CC_
LABEL=trade -e CC_VERSION=v1 trade_cli scripts/chaincode.sh package
```

This runs scripts/chaincode.sh package from within the trade_cli container, which in turn runs the following command:

```
peer lifecycle chaincode package trade_v1.tar.gz --path ./contracts/v1/
trade/ --lang node --label trade
```

If you log into the container using docker exec -it trade_cli bash, you will see a zipped archive named trade_v1.tar.gz in the current folder, which represents this contract's package.

Installing a contract on peers

Install this package on peers peer0.exporterorg.trade.com, peer0.importerorg.trade.com, and peer0.regulatororg.trade.com as follows:

```
$ docker exec -e CHANNEL_NAME=tradechannel -e PEERORGLIST="exporterorg
importerorg regulatororg" -e CC_LABEL=trade -e CC_VERSION=v1 trade_cli
scripts/chaincode.sh install
```

This runs scripts/chaincode.sh install from within the trade_cli container. This command calls the installChaincode() function, which in turn calls installChaincodeInOrg() three times, once for each peer in our list, specified using the PEERORGLIST environment variable. If this is not the case, you should see something like the following in the console:

```
install
Installing chaincode on org peers...
+ peer lifecycle chaincode install --connTimeout 300s trade_v1.tar.gz
+ res=0
+ set +x
2020-09-02 08:19:23.201 UTC [cli.lifecycle.chaincode] submitInstallProposal -> INFO 001 Installed r
emotely: response:<status:200 payload:"\nFtrade:5a86ee79965ac1385c84b1ac212c844c2860851f5437971cf04
76240d2b116a2\022\005trade" >
2020-09-02 08:19:23.201 UTC [cli.lifecycle.chaincode] submitInstallProposal -> INFO 002 Chaincode c
ode package identifier: trade:5a86ee79965ac1385c84b1ac212c844c2860851f5437971cf0476240d2b116a2
===================== Installed chaincode on peer0.exporterorg.trade.com for channel 'tradechannel'
 =====================

+ peer lifecycle chaincode install --connTimeout 300s trade_v1.tar.gz
+ res=0
+ set +x
2020-09-02 08:19:23.435 UTC [cli.lifecycle.chaincode] submitInstallProposal -> INFO 001 Installed r
emotely: response:<status:200 payload:"\nFtrade:5a86ee79965ac1385c84b1ac212c844c2860851f5437971cf04
76240d2b116a2\022\005trade" >
2020-09-02 08:19:23.435 UTC [cli.lifecycle.chaincode] submitInstallProposal -> INFO 002 Chaincode c
ode package identifier: trade:5a86ee79965ac1385c84b1ac212c844c2860851f5437971cf0476240d2b116a2
===================== Installed chaincode on peer0.importerorg.trade.com for channel 'tradechannel'
 =====================

+ peer lifecycle chaincode install --connTimeout 300s trade_v1.tar.gz
+ res=0
+ set +x
2020-09-02 08:19:23.658 UTC [cli.lifecycle.chaincode] submitInstallProposal -> INFO 001 Installed r
emotely: response:<status:200 payload:"\nFtrade:5a86ee79965ac1385c84b1ac212c844c2860851f5437971cf04
76240d2b116a2\022\005trade" >
2020-09-02 08:19:23.658 UTC [cli.lifecycle.chaincode] submitInstallProposal -> INFO 002 Chaincode c
ode package identifier: trade:5a86ee79965ac1385c84b1ac212c844c2860851f5437971cf0476240d2b116a2
===================== Installed chaincode on peer0.regulatororg.trade.com for channel 'tradechannel
' =====================

========= Chaincode installations completed ===========
```

Figure 9.11: Installing the trade contract on three organizations' peers in tradechannel

Ultimately, the installation command for a given organization's peer is run using the following command:

```
peer lifecycle chaincode install --connTimeout 300s trade_v1.tar.gz
```

Only an organization administrator may run this command, so the signing identity is first set using appropriate environment variables in the setEnvironment function. Chaincode package installation involves building code and generating an executable, which can take a significant amount of time, especially for contracts written in Java (as you may observe when you run the preceding command). Therefore, we set a timeout of 5 minutes (300 seconds) using the --connTimeout 300s switch.

Approving a chaincode definition on the channel

Next, organizations on a channel must agree on a **chaincode definition** (*chaincode* being synonymous with *contract* in Fabric) for a given contract, a process involving the submission of an approval request to the ordering service by an administrator of each organization that wishes to run the contract on its peers. The definitions proposed by different organizations must match each other, effectively expressing an agreement among the organizations. The policy used to agree on a chaincode definition is set in the `Application:Policies:LifecycleEndorsement` attribute in `bash/configtx.yaml` as follows:

```
Application: &ApplicationDefaults
  ......
  Policies:
  ......
  LifecycleEndorsement:
    Type: ImplicitMeta
    Rule: "MAJORITY Endorsement"
  ......
```

Even without this specification, the default policy requires a majority of channel members (organization administrators) to agree on a definition. This policy applies to definition commitment, which we will discuss in the next section, rather than approval: every organization must independently approve, while only a majority of organizations' approvals are needed to commit. Since `tradechannel` has three organization members, at least two are required to agree on an identical definition for the contract's deployment to proceed. (This is a channel-level policy and is independent of which organization's peers have the contract code installed.)

A chaincode definition is composed of a set of attributes. (See the full list at `https://hyperledger-fabric.readthedocs.io/en/latest/chaincode_lifecycle.html#step-three-approve-a-chaincode-definition-for-your-organization`). For our `trade` contract, we are interested in setting the following values:

- **Name**: This should be a unique name on the channel, and we will set this to `trade`.
- **Version**: This represents a new version of the contract code and should be unique for the contract; we will set this to `v1` for our initial installation.
- **Sequence**: This is a number indicating how many times the chaincode has been defined; hence, we will set this to 1.

- **Endorsement policy**: This is a policy specifying different sets of channel members whose signatures are required on any transaction on this contract before it can be committed to the ledger. In the CLI command, we use a Boolean syntax involving ANDs and ORs to define such a policy (a different JSON syntax can be used in the VS Code installation process that is functionally similar to this Boolean syntax). For our `trade` contract, we will specify a policy that requires a member of each of the three organizations to endorse a transaction, as follows: `AND('ExporterOrgMSP.member', 'ImporterOrgMSP.member', 'RegulatorOrgMSP.member')`. For more discussion of endorsement policies, see `https://hyperledger-fabric.readthedocs.io/en/latest/endorsement-policies.html`.

- **Initialization**: This is an optional flag (`--init-required`) indicating that you have defined an initialization function (typically, though not mandatorily, called `Init`) in your contract, which needs to be called before any other transaction can be invoked. Strictly speaking, an initialization function is not required for the contracts we have developed using the Fabric contract API (it is required for contracts developed using the Fabric chaincode shim API). Still, it is a good development practice, and we use it to initialize the ledger with certain key-value pairs that subsequent invocations will depend on.

For our scenario, we don't care about the other chaincode definition attributes, such as collection configuration and ESCC/VSCC Plugins.

Let's now run the definition approval for our three channel organizations:

```
$ docker exec -e CHANNEL_NAME=tradechannel -e NUM_ORGS_IN_CHANNEL=3 -e
PEERORGLIST="exporterorg importerorg regulatororg" -e CC_LABEL=trade -e
CC_VERSION=v1 trade_cli scripts/chaincode.sh approve
```

You should see three distinct approvals in the console, like the following:

```
approve
Approving chaincode definition for orgs...
+ peer lifecycle chaincode approveformyorg --connTimeout 120s -o orderer.trade.com:7050 --ordererTL
SHostnameOverride orderer.trade.com --channelID tradechannel --name trade --version v1 --signature-
policy 'AND('\''ExporterOrgMSP.member'\'','\''ImporterOrgMSP.member'\'','\''RegulatorOrgMSP.member'
\'')' --init-required --package-id trade:5a86ee79965ac1385c84b1ac212c844c2860851f5437971cf0476240d2
b116a2 --sequence 1 --tls true --cafile /opt/gopath/src/github.com/hyperledger/fabric/peer/crypto/o
rdererOrganizations/trade.com/orderers/orderer.trade.com/msp/tlscacerts/tlsca.trade.com-cert.pem
+ res=0
+ set +x
2020-09-02 08:25:46.116 UTC [chaincodeCmd] ClientWait -> INFO 001 txid [d39a422b319809045cc19b5cb73
2e621fc42d3840a753386b672d8b39783f360] committed with status (VALID) at
===================== Approved chaincode definitions for exporterorg for channel 'tradechannel' ===
==================

+ peer lifecycle chaincode approveformyorg --connTimeout 120s -o orderer.trade.com:7050 --ordererTL
SHostnameOverride orderer.trade.com --channelID tradechannel --name trade --version v1 --signature-
policy 'AND('\''ExporterOrgMSP.member'\'','\''ImporterOrgMSP.member'\'','\''RegulatorOrgMSP.member'
\'')' --init-required --package-id trade:5a86ee79965ac1385c84b1ac212c844c2860851f5437971cf0476240d2
b116a2 --sequence 1 --tls true --cafile /opt/gopath/src/github.com/hyperledger/fabric/peer/crypto/o
rdererOrganizations/trade.com/orderers/orderer.trade.com/msp/tlscacerts/tlsca.trade.com-cert.pem
+ res=0
+ set +x
2020-09-02 08:25:49.279 UTC [chaincodeCmd] ClientWait -> INFO 001 txid [b848d4fe783344c6c57c4354e51
0c1e7d6e1ac3c660696ba8fbc1cfe54a0123c] committed with status (VALID) at
===================== Approved chaincode definitions for importerorg for channel 'tradechannel' ===
==================

+ peer lifecycle chaincode approveformyorg --connTimeout 120s -o orderer.trade.com:7050 --ordererTL
SHostnameOverride orderer.trade.com --channelID tradechannel --name trade --version v1 --signature-
policy 'AND('\''ExporterOrgMSP.member'\'','\''ImporterOrgMSP.member'\'','\''RegulatorOrgMSP.member'
\'')' --init-required --package-id trade:5a86ee79965ac1385c84b1ac212c844c2860851f5437971cf0476240d2
b116a2 --sequence 1 --tls true --cafile /opt/gopath/src/github.com/hyperledger/fabric/peer/crypto/o
rdererOrganizations/trade.com/orderers/orderer.trade.com/msp/tlscacerts/tlsca.trade.com-cert.pem
+ res=0
+ set +x
2020-09-02 08:25:51.936 UTC [chaincodeCmd] ClientWait -> INFO 001 txid [97f0228d8229def299d65ee787a
8e182900f2aac68b2bcf3d4fcab8890632b94] committed with status (VALID) at
===================== Approved chaincode definitions for regulatororg for channel 'tradechannel' ==
==================

========== Chaincode definitions approved ==========
```

Figure 9.12: Approving trade chaincode definition for three organizations in tradechannel

Each peer lifecycle chaincode approveformyorg command is run with a different organization administrator's signing identity, set using the setEnvironment function in cli_scripts/chaincode.sh. This command takes the various chaincode definition attributes we defined as parameters, as you can see in the preceding screenshot. In addition, it specified TLS parameters and a connection timeout of 120 seconds. The –package-id parameter specifies the ID of the trade contract created after the previous installation step. This ID is obtained by running the following command after logging into the container (using docker exec -it trade_cli bash):

```
peer lifecycle chaincode queryinstalled
```

You should see an output like the following (each of our three peers will generate the same ID):

```
vagrant@bash$ docker exec -it trade_cli bash
bash-5.0# peer lifecycle chaincode queryinstalled
Installed chaincodes on peer:
Package ID: trade:5a86ee79965ac1385c84b1ac212c844c2860851f5437971cf0476240d2b116a2, Label: trade
bash-5.0#
```

Figure 9.13: List of installed chaincodes on a peer in tradechannel

The package ID query and the subsequent approval submissions are scripted in the approveChaincodeDefinitions() and approveChaincodeDefinitionForOrg() functions in cli_scripts/chaincode.sh.

Just to track the evolution of our blockchain, we can try to fetch the latest block follows by running the following command in the container (using docker exec -it trade_cli bash):

```
$ peer channel fetch newest -c tradechannel tradechannel_newest.block
```

You should see something like the following:

```
bash-5.0#
bash-5.0# peer channel fetch newest -c tradechannel tradechannel_newest.block
2020-09-02 10:43:20.626 UTC [channelCmd] InitCmdFactory -> INFO 001 Endorser and orderer connection
s initialized
2020-09-02 10:43:20.630 UTC [cli.common] readBlock -> INFO 002 Received block: 6
bash-5.0#
```

Figure 9.14: Fetching the latest block from tradechannel, containing a trade chaincode approval transaction

Remember that the newest block number we found after updating anchor peer configurations was 3. And now, after three chaincode definition approvals recorded by admins of our three tradechannel organizations, three more blocks were added and the latest block number is 6, as you can see in the preceding screenshot.

 You can also use the peer channel getinfo command to find out the current block height of a channel. See https://hyperledger-fabric.readthedocs.io/en/latest/commands/peerchannel.html#peer-channel-getinfo for more instructions.

Committing a chaincode definition to the channel

The final step in the contract installation process involves committing an already approved chaincode definition to the channel. This can be done by the administrator of any of the organizations (it just needs one) using their signing identity to send a commitment request to the ordering service. We can run the following command from the host machine to commit the definition:

```
$ docker exec -e CHANNEL_NAME=tradechannel -e NUM_ORGS_IN_CHANNEL=3 -e
PEERORGLIST="exporterorg importerorg regulatororg" -e CC_LABEL=trade -e
CC_VERSION=v1 trade_cli scripts/chaincode.sh commit
```

If it succeeds, you should see something like the following in your console:

```
commit
Committing chaincode definition...
Chaincode definition approved by exporterorg
Chaincode definition approved by importerorg
Chaincode definition approved by regulatororg

+ peer lifecycle chaincode commit --connTimeout 120s -o orderer.trade.com:7050 --ordererTLSHostname
Override orderer.trade.com --channelID tradechannel --name trade --version v1 --sequence 1 --signat
ure-policy 'AND('\'\''ExporterOrgMSP.member'\'','\''ImporterOrgMSP.member'\'','\''RegulatorOrgMSP.mem
ber'\'')' --init-required --tls true --cafile /opt/gopath/src/github.com/hyperledger/fabric/peer/cr
ypto/ordererOrganizations/trade.com/orderers/orderer.trade.com/msp/tlscacerts/tlsca.trade.com-cert.
pem --peerAddresses peer0.exporterorg.trade.com:7051 --tlsRootCertFiles /opt/gopath/src/github.com/
hyperledger/fabric/peer/crypto/peerOrganizations/exporterorg.trade.com/peers/peer0.exporterorg.trad
e.com/tls/ca.crt --peerAddresses peer0.importerorg.trade.com:8051 --tlsRootCertFiles /opt/gopath/sr
c/github.com/hyperledger/fabric/peer/crypto/peerOrganizations/importerorg.trade.com/peers/peer0.imp
orterorg.trade.com/tls/ca.crt --peerAddresses peer0.regulatororg.trade.com:10051 --tlsRootCertFiles
 /opt/gopath/src/github.com/hyperledger/fabric/peer/crypto/peerOrganizations/regulatororg.trade.com
/peers/peer0.regulatororg.trade.com/tls/ca.crt
+ res=0
+ set +x
2020-09-02 10:53:06.578 UTC [chaincodeCmd] ClientWait -> INFO 001 txid [5ed9d4947136f61c6be60e2ecf9
b97aa1ed9b212422fe900c19e1932b0fc90a4] committed with status (VALID) at peer0.importerorg.trade.com
:8051
2020-09-02 10:53:06.639 UTC [chaincodeCmd] ClientWait -> INFO 002 txid [5ed9d4947136f61c6be60e2ecf9
b97aa1ed9b212422fe900c19e1932b0fc90a4] committed with status (VALID) at peer0.regulatororg.trade.co
m:10051
2020-09-02 10:53:06.701 UTC [chaincodeCmd] ClientWait -> INFO 003 txid [5ed9d4947136f61c6be60e2ecf9
b97aa1ed9b212422fe900c19e1932b0fc90a4] committed with status (VALID) at peer0.exporterorg.trade.com
:7051
===================== Committed chaincode definition on channel 'tradechannel' ===================
=
========= Chaincode definition committed ==========
```

Figure 9.15: Committing the trade chaincode definition to tradechannel

The command calls the commitChaincodeDefinition() function in cli_scripts/
chaincode.sh. The first action in the function is a check for readiness of the channel
to commit the trade contract's chaincode definition, and this involves running the
following function:

```
peer lifecycle chaincode checkcommitreadiness --connTimeout 120s
--channelID tradechannel --name trade --version v1 --init-required
--sequence 1 --tls true --cafile /opt/gopath/src/github.com/
hyperledger/fabric/peer/crypto/ordererOrganizations/trade.com/orderers/
orderer.trade.com/msp/tlscacerts/tlsca.trade.com-cert.pem --output json
```

This returns a JSON structure like the following, indicating that all three
organizations have approved the definition:

```
{
  "approvals": {
    "ExporterOrgMSP": true,
    "ImporterOrgMSP": true,
```

```
      "RegulatorOrgMSP": true
  }
}
```

In the preceding screenshot, you can see that parsing this JSON results in three assertions in the form `Chaincode definition approved by <org-name>`. (According to the majority policy we discussed in the previous section, we only needed two out of three organizations to have approved the definition for a commitment to succeed.)

The `peer lifecycle chaincode commit…` commitment command is run next, with the same chaincode definition attributes that were used in the approval command, and additionally connectivity (address, port, and TLS certificate) information specified for the peers of the three organizations. An event indicating successful commitment is emitted to each of the peers, as can be seen in the preceding screenshot below the command. In the `commitChaincodeDefinition()` function, you can see that we also run a `peer lifecycle chaincode querycommitted` command to verify the commitment on `tradechannel`.

As we did after the approval step, we can check the status of the blockchain by fetching the latest block in `tradechannel` within the `trade_cli` container as follows:

```
bash-5.0#
bash-5.0# peer channel fetch newest -c tradechannel tradechannel_newest.block
2020-09-02 10:57:39.642 UTC [channelCmd] InitCmdFactory -> INFO 001 Endorser and orderer connection
s initialized
2020-09-02 10:57:39.645 UTC [cli.common] readBlock -> INFO 002 Received block: 7
bash-5.0#
```

Figure 9.16: Fetching the latest block from tradechannel, containing a trade chaincode commitment

You can see that the latest block number is 7, which indicates that a block containing a commitment transaction was added.

If you now run `docker ps` to view the list of running containers, you will see that three new containers have been created, each running a contract and communicating with a different peer using gRPC, as follows:

```
vagrant@bash$ docker ps
CONTAINER ID        IMAGE
                                                                        COMMAND
                     CREATED          STATUS          PORTS
    NAMES
07044574874f           dev-peer0.importerorg.trade.com-trade-5a86ee79965ac1385c84b1ac212c844c2860851f5
437971cf0476240d2b116a2-f7d027c25e70884e7932b716ae1549989e27569678e5fc7fea0740aa3eada6ce     "docker
-entrypoint.s…"    7 minutes ago      Up 7 minutes
    dev-peer0.importerorg.trade.com-trade-5a86ee79965ac1385c84b1ac212c844c2860851f5437971cf0476240d
2b116a2
cf699c38a9ce           dev-peer0.regulatororg.trade.com-trade-5a86ee79965ac1385c84b1ac212c844c2860851f
5437971cf0476240d2b116a2-3360bf216937e6402df5075d3715f3fa74add3994e9c6a8f2e8f484a02c818ce     "docker
-entrypoint.s…"    7 minutes ago      Up 7 minutes
    dev-peer0.regulatororg.trade.com-trade-5a86ee79965ac1385c84b1ac212c844c2860851f5437971cf0476240
d2b116a2
742f95458e67           dev-peer0.exporterorg.trade.com-trade-5a86ee79965ac1385c84b1ac212c844c2860851f5
437971cf0476240d2b116a2-6743396e2a7bd7701daef01fd477298acf626c66fa481618ff260ceb092d2811     "docker
-entrypoint.s…"    7 minutes ago      Up 7 minutes
    dev-peer0.exporterorg.trade.com-trade-5a86ee79965ac1385c84b1ac212c844c2860851f5437971cf0476240d
2b116a2
```

Figure 9.17: List of running trade chaincode containers in tradechannel

The name of each contract, or chaincode, container is prefixed by dev-, and contains the peer service name (such as peer0.regulatororg.trade.com), the contract name (trade), and the package ID that was computed after the install step.

Deploying a contract in one step

We can run the four steps—packaging, installation, approval, and commitment—in one go using our trade.sh script. For the trade contract, we could simply have run:

```
$ ./trade.sh installcontract -c tradechannel -p trade -o 3
```

The -o 3 switch tells the command that there are three organizations on tradechannel. You will see something like the following in your console after a successful operation:

```
Installing contract on channel for contract 'trade' on channel 'tradechannel'
LOCAL_VERSION=2.2.0
DOCKER_IMAGE_VERSION=2.2.0
CLI container running
Packaged contract trade in channel tradechannel
Installed contract trade in channel tradechannel
Approved contract trade definitions in channel tradechannel
Committed contract trade definition in channel tradechannel
```

Figure 9.18: Installing the trade contract and committing the chaincode definition on tradechannel

Deploying the remaining contracts

We can now install our three remaining contracts using single commands. First, we install the letterOfCredit contract on tradechannel:

```
$ ./trade.sh installcontract -c tradechannel -p letterOfCredit -o 3
```

You should see messages indicating that the four steps involved in deployment were successful. The following lines in the installContract function in trade.sh show that this is a Java contract, and that it is installed on two peers (in ExporterOrg and ImporterOrg):

```
function installContract () {
  ......
  elif [ "$CONTRACT_NAME" == "letterOfCredit" ]
  then
    CC_LANGUAGE=java
    PEERORGLIST="exporterorg importerorg"
  ......
```

Similarly, to install the exportLicense contract on shippingchannel (two peers, in ExporterOrg and RegulatorOrg), run:

```
$ ./trade.sh installcontract -c shippingchannel -p exportLicense -o 4
```

And finally, run the following to install the shipment contract on shippingchannel (three peers, in ExporterOrg, ImporterOrg, and CarrierOrg):

```
$ ./trade.sh installcontract -c shippingchannel -p shipment -o 4
```

If you now run docker ps, you will see new chaincode containers: two for letterOfCredit, two for exportLicense, and three for shipment.

Initializing the contracts

Initializing a contract (strictly an optional step in Fabric 2) involves invoking an initialization function before submitting any other transactions to it. Though not mandatory (it is called out as an optional step in *Figure 9.4*), it is good practice to exercise such a function and initialize a contract's state on the ledger with values that all subsequent transactions can use. As we observed in the approval and commitment steps, our trade chaincode definition included the --init-required parameter, indicating that this contract requires initialization. We can initialize the trade contract from the host machine as follows:

```
$ docker exec -e CHANNEL_NAME=tradechannel -e PEERORGLIST="exporterorg
importerorg regulatororg" -e CC_LABEL=trade -e CC_FUNC=init -e CC_
ARGS="" trade_cli scripts/chaincode.sh init
```

You should see something like the following upon success:

```
init
Initializing chaincode...
+ peer chaincode invoke --connTimeout 120s -o orderer.trade.com:7050 --ordererTLSHostnameOverride o
rderer.trade.com -C tradechannel -n trade --isInit --tls true --waitForEvent --cafile /opt/gopath/s
rc/github.com/hyperledger/fabric/peer/crypto/ordererOrganizations/trade.com/orderers/orderer.trade.
com/msp/tlscacerts/tlsca.trade.com-cert.pem --peerAddresses peer0.exporterorg.trade.com:7051 --tlsR
ootCertFiles /opt/gopath/src/github.com/hyperledger/fabric/peer/crypto/peerOrganizations/exporteror
g.trade.com/peers/peer0.exporterorg.trade.com/tls/ca.crt --peerAddresses peer0.importerorg.trade.co
m:8051 --tlsRootCertFiles /opt/gopath/src/github.com/hyperledger/fabric/peer/crypto/peerOrganizatio
ns/importerorg.trade.com/peers/peer0.importerorg.trade.com/tls/ca.crt --peerAddresses peer0.regulat
ororg.trade.com:10051 --tlsRootCertFiles /opt/gopath/src/github.com/hyperledger/fabric/peer/crypto/
peerOrganizations/regulatororg.trade.com/peers/peer0.regulatororg.trade.com/tls/ca.crt -c '{"functi
on":"init","Args":[]}'
+ res=0
+ set +x
2020-09-02 11:31:37.490 UTC [chaincodeCmd] ClientWait -> INFO 001 txid [cb6058dd8e4749c75fd4e2374a6
719f980ad9f48041f9fa339a5926a94d11c22] committed with status (VALID) at peer0.regulatororg.trade.co
m:10051
2020-09-02 11:31:37.559 UTC [chaincodeCmd] ClientWait -> INFO 002 txid [cb6058dd8e4749c75fd4e2374a6
719f980ad9f48041f9fa339a5926a94d11c22] committed with status (VALID) at peer0.exporterorg.trade.com
:7051
2020-09-02 11:31:37.594 UTC [chaincodeCmd] ClientWait -> INFO 003 txid [cb6058dd8e4749c75fd4e2374a6
719f980ad9f48041f9fa339a5926a94d11c22] committed with status (VALID) at peer0.importerorg.trade.com
:8051
2020-09-02 11:31:37.595 UTC [chaincodeCmd] chaincodeInvokeOrQuery -> INFO 004 Chaincode invoke succ
essful. result: status:200
===================== Initialized chaincode on channel 'tradechannel' =====================
========= Chaincode initialized ===========
```

Figure 9.19: Initializing the trade contract on tradechannel

The initialization, like any transactions or queries that follow, only requires the contract name and not its version, because Fabric keeps track of, and invokes, the latest version (in our case, it is v1).

The command we ran executed the initializeChaincode() function in cli_scripts/chaincode.sh, which in turn triggered the peer chaincode invoke command you see in the screenshot. (Note that contract invocation does not require administrator permissions, and so the setOrganization exporterorg User1 command sets the signing identity of the transaction submitter to that of an ordinary user.)

Contract invocation requires a function name and list of arguments, which we supply in the CC_FUNC and CC_ARGS variables respectively. In the peer chaincode invoke command (see preceding screenshot), this is translated into a JSON spec, '{"function":"init","Args":[]}', indicating that a function named init in our trade contract is called with no arguments. The invocation command also contains a --isInit parameter, indicating that the function being invoked is an initialization function. A list of peer addresses and other connectivity information is provided so endorsements can be collected for this transaction. Finally, the --waitForEvent parameter tells the command to wait for a ledger commitment event to be emitted before returning. The output following the command in the screenshot indicates that three endorsements (as per the endorsement policy we framed) for this initialization transaction were obtained, resulting in a successful operation.

To verify that the init() function in the trade contract was indeed executed, you can view the logs of any of the containers running it (prefixed by dev-). You should see something like the following at the bottom:

```
2020-09-02T11:28:36.521Z info [c-api:lib/handler.js]                    Successfully regi
stered with peer node. State transferred to "established"
2020-09-02T11:28:36.522Z info [c-api:lib/handler.js]                    Successfully esta
blished communication with peer node. State transferred to "ready"
Initializing the trade contract
2020-09-02T11:31:35.227Z info [c-api:lib/handler.js]                    [tradechannel-cb6
058dd] Calling chaincode Init() succeeded. Sending COMPLETED message back to peer
vagrant@bash$
```

Figure 9.20: Last portion of the trade chaincode container logs after initialization

Also, as we did after the definition commitment step, we can check the status of the blockchain by fetching the latest block in tradechannel within the trade_cli container. You will see that the latest block number is 8, which indicates that a block containing a contract transaction (executing the init() function) was added.

Our trade.sh script offers an alternative, and shorter, command to carry out the preceding operation:

```
$ ./trade.sh initcontract -c tradechannel -p trade -t init
```

We can use this command to similarly initialize the other three installed contracts. For letterOfCredit, run:

```
$ ./trade.sh initcontract -c tradechannel -p letterOfCredit -t init -a
'"trade","shippingchannel","shipment","ExporterOrgMSP","LumberBank","10
0000","ImporterOrgMSP","ToyBank","200000"'
```

Among the list of arguments provided to this contract, we can see three that depended on our setup configuration: "trade" and "shipment" represent the names of two of our other contracts on which letterOfCredit depends, and "shippingchannel" represents the name of the channel on which the shipment contract is installed.

The exporter's and importer's identities in this contract are represented by their organizations' MSP names (ExporterOrgMSP and ImporterOrgMSP respectively). Sample values are provided here for the other arguments, and you can select different bank names and amount values if you wish.

The exportLicense contract, which depends on the trade contract installed on tradechannel, is initialized as follows:

```
$ ./trade.sh initcontract -c shippingchannel -p exportLicense -t init
-a '"tradechannel","trade","CarrierOrgMSP","RegulatorOrgMSP"'
```

And the `shipment` contract is initialized as follows:

```
$ ./trade.sh initcontract -c shippingchannel -p shipment -t init
```

You can view the respective container logs to view any information recorded during the execution of the contracts' `init` functions.

As a shortcut, the `bash` folder contains a `sampleChaincodeOperations.sh` script that installs and initializes all four contracts using a single command.

Note that in a typical production network, each organization will independently maintain its signing credentials. It will use those credentials (signing identities) to join its peers to a given channel, package and install contracts on its peers, and submit chaincode definition approvals to an ordering service. The scripts we have used to orchestrate these operations from a single machine are strictly meant for ease-of-use and testing.

Installing contracts using the VS Code IBP extension

We now outline an alternative mechanism to installing contracts via the VS Code IBP extension instead of the CLI tools we demonstrated in the previous section. The process of installation remains the same; the only difference is that you get a GUI to select a contract and specify common chaincode definition parameters and click a few buttons to trigger the process.

This section is meant purely for reference and to utilize in any other projects our readers may wish to develop on Fabric. At the time of publication, the Fabric 2 contract installation feature in the IBP Extension is still in beta (see the release list here: `https://github.com/IBM-Blockchain/blockchain-vscode-extension/releases`), so it was not possible for us to do a full-fledged demonstration with a production-ready version. Until such a version is available, our readers are encouraged to use the CLI tools in `trade-network` for contract operations.

For demonstration, we will deploy the shipment contract on `shippingchannel`. Readers can replicate the same procedure to install the other three contracts. Here are the instructions:

1. Make sure the `trade` network is running and that all operational steps described earlier in this chapter have been completed.

2. If you do not have VS Code already running, start it and select the **EXPLORER** tab from the left-hand menu.

3. Select **File** | **Add Folder to Workspace...** from the top menu.

4. Navigate to your local copy of the `trade-contracts` repository. (You can also find this in the `contracts` folder within `trade-networks`.) Select the `v1/shipment` folder. You will see something like the following in the **EXPLORER** pane (Make sure you have built the contract already using `make build` within this folder using a command-line terminal, which should create the `dist` and `node_modules` folders):

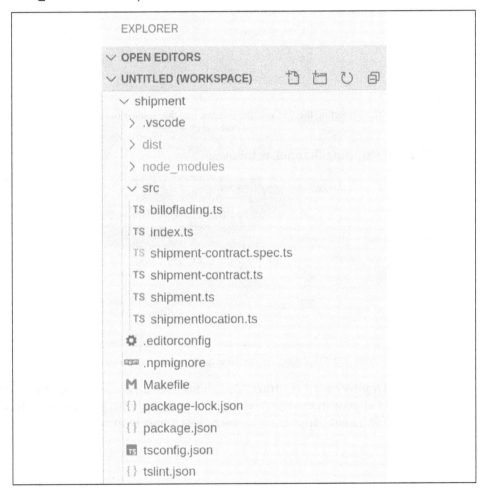

Figure 9.21: The shipment contract project loaded in the VS Code workspace

5. Select the **IBM Blockchain Platform** tab from the left-hand menu.

6. Repeating steps from *Chapter 4, Setting the Stage with a Business Scenario*, if your trade environment is not already connected to the running network, click **Trade Network** in the **FABRIC ENVIRONMENTS** panel. You should see the message Connected to Trade Network in the logs in the **Output** window (after selecting **Blockchain** from the drop-down menu). You should see the instantiated channels in the **FABRIC ENVIRONMENTS** panel:

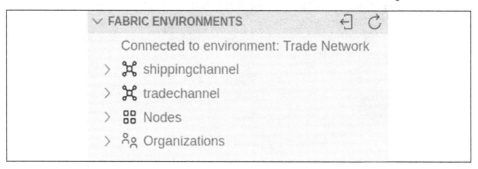

Figure 9.22: Connecting the VS Code IBP extension to the running trade network and displaying its nodes and ledgers

7. Expand **shippingchannel** as follows:

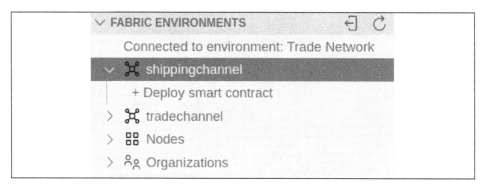

Figure 9.23: Displaying the option to deploy a smart contract on shippingchannel

8. Click **+Deploy smart contract**. You should see a panel titled **Deploy Smart Contract** appear in the main window as follows, with the currently loaded project (shipment) appearing in the **Select smart contract** drop-down menu:

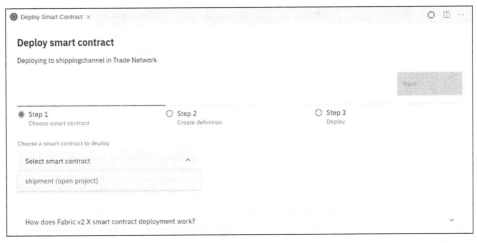

Figure 9.24: Displaying the option to select a smart contract to deploy on shippingchannel

9. Select **shipment (open project)** and click the **Package open project** link that appears as follows (an alternative way of packaging an open project is using the **SMART CONTRACTS** panel on the left, just above the **FABRIC ENVIRONMENTS** panel):

Figure 9.25: Displaying the option to package a smart contract (shipment) selected for deployment

In the output logs, you will see messages indicating a successful packaging of the project into a zipped archive. The chaincode will be installed with the name shipment_1.0.0:

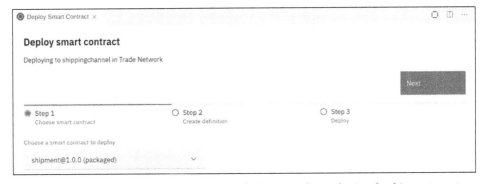

Figure 9.26: Displaying the option to continue deployment after packaging the shipment smart contract

10. Click the blue **Next** button in the top right to proceed with the installation. You will get a GUI to specify the chaincode definition as follows. Let's set the version to **v1** and the endorsement policy to `AND("ExporterOrgMSP.member"`, `"ImporterOrgMSP.member"`, `"CarrierOrgMSP.member")` as we did when we installed the contract using the CLI tools (we will ignore the collections configuration):

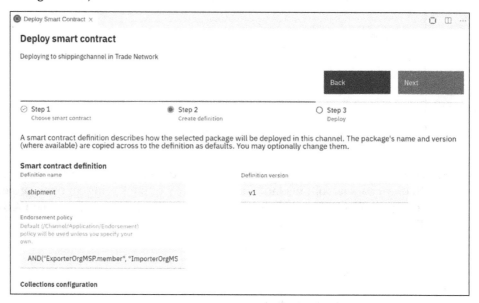

Figure 9.27: Displaying the chaincode definition options for the shipment contract deployment

11. After clicking the blue **Next** button in the top right, you should see a view describing the approval and commitment process. (The peer selection process has not been implemented yet in the beta version, though it may be available in production by the time our readers get to this part of the book.) Click the blue **Deploy** button in the top right:

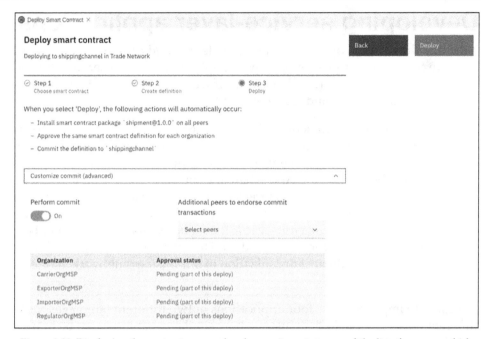

Figure 9.28: Displaying the contract approval and commitment steps, and the list of peers on which the shipment contract will be installed

In the output logs, you should see messages such as Successful installed on peer <peer-name> (corresponding to each of the four peers on this channel), Successfully approved smart contract definition, Successfully committed smart contract definition, and Successfully deployed smart contract.

12. If you run docker ps in a terminal window, you should see four new chaincode containers with the dev- and shipment_1.0.0 keywords in the container names; each corresponds to a different peer on shippingchannel.

This tool does not provide the ability to initialize the contract. For that, you can use either the CLI tool demonstrated in the previous section or a gateway created through the IBP extension (we will see how to do this later in this chapter).

You can try to install the other three contracts using similar methods. We are now ready to move up one layer in the application stack.

Developing service-layer applications

Now that the network operations, including ledger and contract setup, are out of the way, we can focus on the development of applications that a user or software agent in the real world will use. (In other words, if we examine *Figure 9.2*, everything in the bottom layer is complete and ready for use.)

Figure 9.3 showed the architecture of our application from a component-based view. The middle portion contains the contracts representing the lowest layer of our technical stack. The components in the outer portion represent the applications we still need to build and run. And where the contracts were designed in a *ledger-centric* manner (because they act on the ledgers as if they are common databases, even though those ledgers are shared among multiple peers), our higher-layer applications are designed in a *user-centric* (or *organization-centric*) manner because they act on behalf of different stakeholders. Therefore, we have four applications, one representing each distinct organization in our business network, in the periphery of *Figure 9.3*.

We chose to implement the four applications in two different languages for two different reasons. First, to demonstrate how similar capabilities can be implemented in either Java or JavaScript, allowing users to pick their language of choice while they develop other applications, using ours as guides. And second, to show that these applications can be engineered independently by different enterprises using different technology stacks, with only the network structure, channel configuration, and contract API being common knowledge.

Application runtime life cycle

Each service-layer application we build must implement the operations supposed to be performed in the runtime stage illustrated in *Figure 9.1*, namely submitting transactions to, and querying, smart contracts. A more descriptive view of this stage is provided in *Figure 9.29*, which illustrates the life cycle of such an application and the blockchains (ledgers) it acts on via the smart contracts. Such a life cycle consists of an arbitrary sequence of transactions and queries submitted to any of the installed smart contracts on any of the active channels; a transaction's success or failure is reported back through an event. This life cycle is typically initiated, and can sometimes be punctuated, by the registration and enrollment of a user with an organization's MSP (an instance of a Fabric CA server); this results in the possession of credentials that can be stored in wallets maintained on the filesystem or in a database. A user can submit service requests along with appropriate wallet credentials to a gateway, which translates the requests into contract transactions or queries and synchronously returns responses, as shown in the following figure:

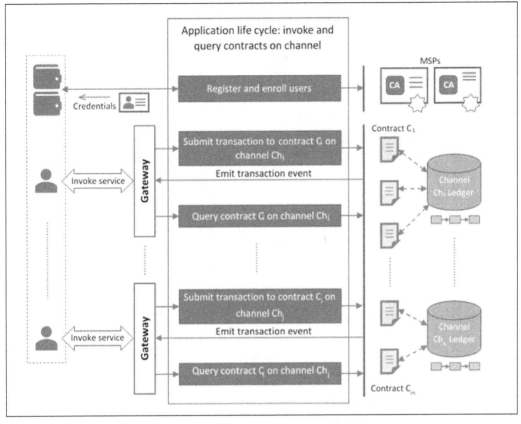

Figure 9.29: An application's runtime life cycle

In the next few sections, we will demonstrate application development using primarily one application as a guide, though there will be occasional references to applications developed in a different language for the benefit of our readers.

An application for the importer's organization

In our design, this application is hosted and run by a well-known bank that assumes the role of an importer's bank and serves both bankers and clients (who assume the role of importer), as illustrated in *Figure 9.30*. Depending on the relative power and reputation differential between importers and banks, this application could have been designed the other way around: hosted by a well-known trader in an importer's role, serving both the trader and various banks it associates with:

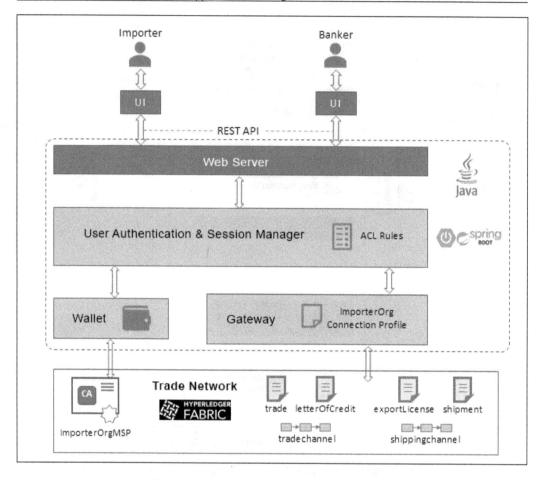

Figure 9.30: Architecture of the importer application

 We select the application developed for `ImporterOrg` because, in addition to implementing the enrollment and contract invocation capabilities, it also differentiates users by their roles *within the organization*. The ACL rules enforced by our contracts expect these different roles to be specified in certificate attributes, as we saw earlier.

This importer application is written in Java and is developed using the Spring Boot framework (`https://spring.io/projects/spring-boot`), which allows developers to easily create web services and run them automatically using Apache Tomcat (`http://tomcat.apache.org/`). The VS Code IDE, which we installed and used in *Chapter 4, Setting the Stage with a Business Scenario*, can be used to program and launch this application.

Figure 9.30 shows a specific instance of the generic application architecture presented in *Figure 9.2*. It maintains a wallet for the identities of bankers and importers, obtained through communication with the importer organization's MSP. It uses a connection profile for the importer organization's portion of the network (more on this later) to invoke the four contracts we have installed and initialized on the two channels. The web server offers a common REST API to all users, with functions for registration, login, and smart contract operations. The **User Authentication and Session Manager** module manages the creation of user identity and role and controls access to different REST API functions; after a successful access control check, it passes the user's request down the stack. This module also manages sessions using JSON web tokens, enabling an authentic logged-in user to execute multiple operations using a dynamically generated token.

 We implemented an application from scratch for demonstration purposes. But most enterprises (such as banks or traders) may already be running a suite of tried-and-trusted enterprise applications. That leaves our readers who are production enterprise developers with a choice: build an application from scratch or augment their existing applications to run transactions and queries on a newly created Fabric network. If they make the latter choice, the code we will discuss in the next few sections (and which is provided in full in our GitHub repository) should be used as inspiration, and adapted to create libraries that can be imported into existing enterprise applications.

Importer application structure

If you followed the instructions in the contract installation section, your copy of `trade-network` should already have the applications submodule (in the `apps` folder) synced. The importer application project code can be found in the `apps/importer` folder. This is a VS Code project built on Spring Boot and Gradle.

To create a new empty Spring Boot project, you can do the following:

1. Launch VS Code. In Linux, this involves running `code` from the command line

2. Press *Ctrl + Shift + P* and enter `Java Overview` in the textbox

3. Select the **Create a Spring Boot project...** link, as shown in the following figure, and follow the instructions:

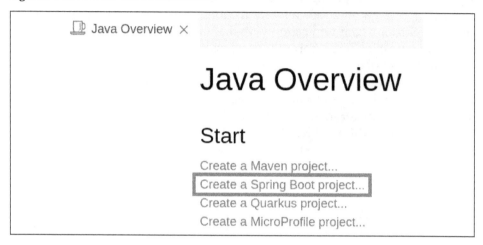

Figure 9.31: Displaying the Java project creation options

Here, though, we will load our existing project from the `apps` submodule within the `trade-network` repository, which we have cloned to our machine. Readers can adapt this code for their purposes rather than create projects from scratch:

1. In VS Code, select **File | Add Folder to Workspace...** from the top menu.

2. Navigate to the `apps/importer` folder and select it.

3. In the **EXPLORER** pane on the left side of the window, as shown in the following figure, you can see the file and folder structure of this project, consisting of the source code and configuration files required for building. The files of interest to us lie in the `src` folder, expanded in the following figure. The source code lies in `src/main/java/org/trade/importer`, within the `org.trade.importer` package. Various properties for runtime use are specified in `src/main/resources/application.properties`, and a placeholder unit test file, `ImporterApplicationTests.java`, created in `src/test/java/org/trade/importer`. We leave writing the unit tests as exercises for our readers:

Figure 9.32: Displaying the importer application file and folder structure in EXPLORER

The source code file structure is highly simplified because we wanted to focus on the essential features that distinguish a Fabric application from any generic enterprise application. For production development, the reader is encouraged to follow best practices, such as the creation of specific folders for data models, API endpoints, common interfaces, common utilities, security functions, and so forth. (The companion application for the exporter organization in apps/exporter, programmed in JavaScript, does differentiate source code files into controllers, models, and routes, as a suggestive guide to our readers.)

Project dependencies

In this section, we outline the project dependencies:

- This project is meant to be built and run using Gradle 6.3, and this setting is made in `gradle/wrapper/gradle-wrapper.properties` as follows:

  ```
  distributionBase=GRADLE_USER_HOME
  distributionPath=wrapper/dists
  distributionUrl=https\://services.gradle.org/distributions/
  gradle-6.3-bin.zip
  zipStoreBase=GRADLE_USER_HOME
  zipStorePath=wrapper/dists
  ```

- All other important dependency settings are configured in `build.gradle`. The version of Spring Boot this project is built on is specified in the `plugins` section as follows:

  ```
  plugins {
      id 'org.springframework.boot' version '2.2.6.RELEASE'
  ```

- The project is built on the **Java Development Kit (JDK)** 11, which is configured as follows:

  ```
  sourceCompatibility = '1.11'
  ```

- The relevant Maven repositories from which external libraries must be fetched are configured in the `repositories` section, and the library names and versions are configured in the `dependencies` section. Notably, our project depends on the Fabric Java SDK (Gateway API) 2.2.0 (*the latest version at the time of publication*), which is configured as follows:

  ```
  dependencies{
      implementation 'org.hyperledger.fabric:fabric-gateway-
  java:2.2.0'
  ```

As a reference for the reader, source code for the Fabric Gateway SDK in Java lies in `https://github.com/hyperledger/fabric-gateway-java/`. There are several other settings that are automatically configured by Spring and Gradle, and can be used without change in any project you wish to build.

We will now turn our attention to the code that is specific to our application and to Hyperledger Fabric development.

Setting application properties and generating a connection profile

The aforementioned `application.properties` file contains the following by default:

```
jwt.secret=fabrichacker
connectionProfilesBaseDir=/config/gateways/importerorg
connectionProfileJson=connection.json
walletsBaseDir=/config/wallets/importerorg
```

This configuration was created to run the application within a Docker container, but in our current exercise, we will run it in the host machine from VS Code. This requires the following changes in the configuration:

1. Create subfolders named `wallets` and `gateways` in the root folder of `trade-network`

2. Create a subfolder under `gateways` named `importerorg`

3. Create a subfolder under `wallets` named `importerorg`

4. Set `connectionProfilesBaseDir` to the absolute path of the `gateways/importerorg` folder on your machine

5. Set `walletsBaseDir` to the absolute path of the `wallets/importerorg` folder on your machine

6. Save `application.properties`

The connection profile we will use is named `connection.json` and the importer application will expect to find it in the `connectionProfilesBaseDir` folder. We can generate this profile in two different ways. The first way is through the IBP extension in VS Code as follows:

1. Make sure the trade network is running and that all operational steps described earlier in this chapter have been completed.

2. With VS Code running, select the **IBM Blockchain Platform** tab of the menu on the left.

3. If your trade environment is not already connected to the running network, click **Trade Network** in the **FABRIC ENVIRONMENTS** panel. You should see the message `Connected to Trade Network` in the logs in the output window (after selecting **Blockchain** from the drop-down menu). You should see the instantiated channels in the **FABRIC ENVIRONMENTS** panel:

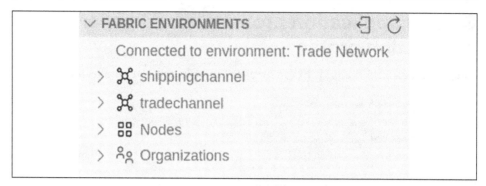

Figure 9.33: Connecting the VS Code IBP extension to the running trade network and displaying its nodes and ledgers

4. Now, move your mouse over the **FABRIC GATEWAYS** header and then over the **+** button. You should see an **Add Gateway** popup. Click the **+** button.

5. Select **Create a gateway from a Fabric environment** in the menu at the top of the window.

6. Enter a name for the gateway and press *Enter*. Let's use the name **Importer Gateway**.

7. Select **ImporterOrgMSP**.

8. Select **ca.importerorg.trade.com**.

9. You should see the message Successfully added a new gateway in the output log and the following in the **FABRIC GATEWAYS** panel:

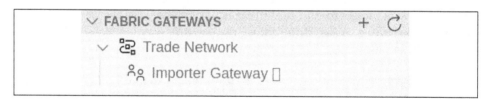

Figure 9.34: Displaying the newly created gateway to the importer organization

10. Right-click **Importer Gateway** and select **Export Connection Profile**. Navigate to the gateways/importerorg folder we created earlier and save (export) the file as Importer Gateway_connection.json. (This is a temporary file that we must adjust before it is ready for use in our application.)

Let's examine the contents of the connection profile. This file will be used by our application to connect to ImporterOrg peers and CAs. The client section contains organization and timeout settings:

```
"client": {
  "organization": "ImporterOrgMSP",
  "connection": {
    "timeout": {
      "peer": {
        "endorser": "300"
      },
      "orderer": "300"
    }
  }
},
```

The `organization` value (`ImporterOrgMSP`) is simply a key into the organizations structure:

```
"organizations": {
  "ImporterOrgMSP": {
    "mspid": "ImporterOrgMSP",
    "peers": [
      "peer0.importerorg.trade.com"
    ],
    "certificateAuthorities": [
      "ca.importerorg.trade.com"
    ]
  }
},
```

The `mspid` field contains the actual MSP ID of `ImporterOrg`. The `peers` and `certificateAuthorities` fields are arrays of keys into the `peers` and `certificateAuthorities` sections further down in the file.

The `peers` section contains the configuration of the sole peer in `ImporterOrg`:

```
"peers": {
  "peer0.importerorg.trade.com": {
    "url": "grpcs://localhost:8051",
    "tlsCACerts": {
      "pem": "-----BEGIN CERTIFICATE-----\
nMIICbjCCAhSgAwIBAgIRAM3/1/pOGmHZOI/3ecz3KeUwCgYIKoZIzj0EAwIwgYAx\
nCzAJBgNVBAYTAlVTMRMwEQYDVQQIEwpDYWxpZm9ybmlhMRYwFAYDVQQHEw1TYW4g\
nRnJhbmNpc2NvMR4wHAYDVQQKExVpbXBvcnRlcm9yZy50cmFkZS5jb20xJDAiBgNV\
nBAMTG3Rsc2NhLmltcG9ydGVyb3JnLnRyYWRlLmNvbTAeFw0yMDA1MjExNDMxMDBa\
nFw0zMDA1MTkxNDMxMDBaMIGAMQswCQYDVQQGEwJVUzETMBEGA1UECBMKQ2FsaWZv\
ncm5pYTEWMBQGA1UEBxMNU2FuIEZyYW5jaXNjbzEeMBwGA1UEChMVaW1wb3J0ZXJv\
```

```
ncmcudHJhZGUuY29tMSQwIgYDVQQDExt0bHNjYS5pbXBvcnRlcm9yZy50cmFkZS5j\
nb20wWTATBgcqhkjOPQIBBggqhkjOPQMBBwNCAATZzKnkzKwwTDAVTd6/aOT8PtI5\
nJWUS1KPIA6BlDGEtoYM3NsVcAGDwDQhKSFI2C/KbhiyEp2ZV7BJxiis3WAYgo20w\
nazAOBgNVHQ8BAf8EBAMCAaYwHQYDVR0lBBYwFAYIKwYBBQUHAwIGCCsGAQUFBwMB\
nMA8GA1UdEwEB/wQFMAMBAf8wKQYDVR0OBCIEIMbBSbrr4MJc+QmE9rWWOkXp2qud\
nDm99cNOTr9Gc1g00MAoGCCqGSM49BAMCA0gAMEUCIBrvrQI3rRM91CArVjnnNzEZ\nur2w
OzaQWQRF17IMl7XJAiEAosRz3Pv2MuVt6dT60MNihfNXKPfM+Gx2YlGWEeiK\ntTA=\n---
--END CERTIFICATE-----\n"
    },
    "grpcOptions": {
      "ssl-target-name-override": "peer0.importerorg.trade.com"
    }
  }
},
```

The url field specifies the peer's endpoint URL for clients to connect to and the tlsCACerts field specifies the TLS certificate that we created using cryptogen. (The contents in the pem field are meant only for representative purposes.) The ssl-target-name-override attribute contains the peer service's name as embedded in its TLS certificate (in the Common Name, or CN, attribute), and this corresponds to the identity of the importer organization's peer we created earlier.

The certificateAuthorities field similarly contains connectivity information for the sole CA belonging to the importer organization.

This connection profile misses the following key features our importer application needs:

- The Fabric SDK built for Java requires the name override value in grpcOptions to be specified in the hostnameOverride attribute.
- The caName field in the CA configuration must match the identity of the CA as configured using the FABRIC_CA_SERVER_CA_NAME environment variable in our network compose file, bash/docker-compose-e2e.yaml. For the importer organization's CA, this is ca-importerorg.
- The CA's TLS certificate must be specified for client connectivity.

These fixes can be made using the Node.js bash/utils/manage-connection-profile.js utility file. The reader is encouraged to examine the code, which involves parsing our configtxgen.yaml file and reading the certificate contents from the generated crypto-config folder. To generate the desired connection profile, navigate to the bash/utils folder and run the following command:

```
$ node manage-connection-profile.js --update ../../gateways/
importerorg/Importer\ Gateway_connection.json ../../gateways/
importerorg/connection.json ca-importerorg
```

The desired `connection.json` profile has been created in the `gateways` folder, as expected by our importer application. If you view the contents of this file, you will see that the `peers` and `certificateAuthorities` sections have been updated as follows:

```
"peers": {
  "peer0.importerorg.trade.com": {
    "url": "grpcs://peer0.importerorg.trade.com:8051",
    ......
    "grpcOptions": {
      "ssl-target-name-override": "peer0.importerorg.trade.com",
      "hostnameOverride": "peer0.importerorg.trade.com"
    }
  }
},
"peers": {
  "certificateAuthorities": {
    "url": "https://ca.importerorg.trade.com:8054",
    "caName": "ca-importerorg",
    " tlsCACerts ": {
      "pem": "..............."
    }
  }
},
```

We mentioned earlier that there were two different ways to create such a connection profile, and we just demonstrated the first one. The second way involves simply running our Node.js utility script with different parameters to generate the profile using the network configuration files and generated crypto artifacts already present in the `bash` folder. After backing up the existing `connection.json` file, simply run:

```
$ node manage-connection-profile.js --generate importerorg
ImporterOrgMSP 8051 8054
```

You will see that the new `connection.json` file possesses an identical set of attributes to the old file, except for a difference in profile name. (The `manage-connection-profile.js` program was created for our `trade-network` project and the configurations specified within it. If you change settings in the network YAML and compose files, you will need to modify this utility program accordingly.)

The preceding steps can be used to create connection profiles for each of our other three applications: exporter, regulator, and carrier. To generate all four connection profiles using one command, run:

```
$ node generateAllProfiles.sh
```

 A connection profile need not be limited to one organization, like the ones we have created and examined in this section. For an example of a multi-organization profile, see `legacy_sdk_1.4/ connection_profile.json`. This describes all peers and CAs in our trade network. Before attempting connection with a gateway to a given organization, you must set the value of the `client. organization` field appropriately. Keep in mind that connection profiles in real-world Fabric networks are not meant to be shared among organizations, so a multi-organization profile ought to be used strictly for testing purposes.

For more information about connection profiles, you can read the documentation at `https://hyperledger-fabric.readthedocs.io/en/latest/developapps/ connectionprofile.html`. The connection profile we have created will be used by a dynamic gateway, to use the terminology from this web page. Dynamic gateways need minimal connectivity information from profiles, with further information obtained using service discovery, as we will see later in this chapter.

Designing a service API for the importer application

The design of any enterprise application must begin with a specification of the interface it wishes to expose to users and other software agents. As is common practice in the enterprise world, our importer application exposes its services through a REST API that can be invoked by any HTTP client. In a Spring Boot application, this API is defined and partly implemented in a type that carries the `org.springframework.web.bind.annotation.RestController` annotation. If you open the `ImporterController.java` file, you can see that we define an `ImporterController` type to encapsulate the REST API as follows:

```
@RestController
public class ImporterController {

        @RequestMapping("/")
        public String index() {
                return "<h1>You have reached the Importer Organization Portal!</h1>";
        }
```

Figure 9.35: Displaying the ImporterController class with an action defined for the default importer application server URL

You can see that the index() function handling the default URL (that is, with a server and port name ending in a /) returns sample HTML. This function is annotated by the org.springframework.web.bind.annotation.RequestMapping class, which is used to map a URL suffix to a given function. The controller will ensure that the return values of such functions are wrapped in HTTP responses. Knowing this, we can identify (by their annotations) functions within the ImporterController class that comprise our REST API:

- register (POST /register): This function is invoked by an administrator to create an identity and a password for a user, be it banker or client
- login (POST /login): This function is invoked by a user with an existing identity to obtain session tokens (more on that later) that allow it to be "logged in" for a fixed duration
- requestTrade (POST /requestTrade): This function is used by an importer (client) to request the creation of a trade with a given exporter
- requestLC (POST /requestLC): This function is used by an importer (client) to submit a **letter of credit (L/C)** application to the importer's bank
- issueLC (POST /issueLC): This function is used by an importer's banker to issue an L/C
- makePayment (POST /makePayment): This function is used by an importer's banker to process a payment installment from an importer's account to an exporter's account
- getTrade (GET /getTrade): This function is used by any user to obtain details of a trade
- getTradestatus (GET /getTradeStatus): This function is used by any user to obtain the status of a trade
- getLC (GET /getLC): This function is used by any user to obtain details of an L/C
- getLCStatus (GET /getLCStatus): This function is used by any user to obtain the status of an L/C
- getShipmentLocation (GET /getShipmentLocation): This function is used by any user to obtain the present location of a shipment
- getBillOfLading (GET /getBillOfLading): This function is used by any user to obtain the details of a **bill of lading (B/L)**
- getAccountBalance (GET /getAccountBalance): This function is used by an importer (client) to obtain its present account balance
- listTrades (GET /listTrades): This function is used by any user to obtain a list of all trades involving that user, with details

Apart from /register and /login, all functions in this list map directly to smart contract API functions. Among these, functions that trigger contract transactions are exposed as POST methods, whereas functions that query contracts are exposed as GET methods. In subsequent sections, we will see how user access to these REST endpoints is controlled.

User registration, login, and session management

Our application uses **JSON Web Tokens (JWTs)** (https://jwt.io/introduction/), a popular and secure way to manage user authentication and client-server sessions. The basic idea is that when a user attempts to log in using their credentials (typically a known username-password combination), the server generates a signed token with an embedded expiration time and other optional attributes. The user subsequently invokes services using this token (which is a long and hard-to-guess string of characters); the server maps the token to a username and runs access control and expiration checks before deciding whether to allow or deny service.

Functions for the creation, validation, and parsing of JWTs in our project lie in SecurityUtils.java, and the code to exercise these functions for user authentication and access control lies in ImporterWebSecurityConfig.java. We will not delve into the details of JWT operations in these files, which is largely standard code readers are encouraged to experiment with. Our focus here will be on code specific to user management and authentication.

 The applications written in JavaScript also rely on JWTs for login and session management. In the exporter application (the apps/exporter folder), the code for this lies in app.js and routes/routes.js and depends on the npm libraries express-jwt and jsonwebtoken.

User records, that is, username and password, are managed in our project using the **Data Access Object (DAO)** pattern, which enables the isolation of business logic from storage logic. We use an object of type org.springframework.security.provisioning.InMemoryUserDetailsManager for this purpose, as specified in the ImporterController class in ImporterController.java as follows:

```
@RestController
public class ImporterController {

  ......

  @Autowired
  private InMemoryUserDetailsManager userDetailsService;

  ......
```

We use another org.springframework.security.provisioning.
InMemoryUserDetailsManager object in the JwtRequestFilter class in
ImporterWebSecurityConfig.java as follows:

```
@Component
class JwtRequestFilter extends OncePerRequestFilter {
  @Autowired
  private InMemoryUserDetailsManager userDetailsService;

  ......
```

This object maintains user records in memory, and is enough for demonstration and
testing, but in production one would use a class that persists records on disk, such as
JdbcUserDetailsManager.

The @Autowired annotation tells Spring to ensure the availability of a dependency
and inject it in the right fields. Here, a common instance of userDetailsService is
available to both the classes defined previously at runtime.

Let's see how to register a new user in the register function in ImporterController.
java:

```
@Autowired
private AuthenticationManager authenticationManager;

......

@RequestMapping(value = "/register", method = RequestMethod.POST)
public ResponseEntity<String> register(String registrarUser, String
registrarPassword, String username, String password, String role)
throws Exception {
  role = role.toUpperCase();
  try {
    Authentication authResult = authenticationManager.authenticate(new
UsernamePasswordAuthenticationToken(registrarUser, registrarPassword));

    ......

    if (!userDetailsService.userExists(username)) {

      ......

      userDetailsService.createUser(User.withUsername(username).
password(new BCryptPasswordEncoder().encode(password)).roles(role).
build());
    }
```

Registration of a user requires the /register endpoint to be called by an administrator (termed a *registrar* to be consistent with Fabric terminology) with existing credentials that are passed in the registrarUser and registrarPassword parameters. First, the registrar is authenticated using built-in authentication logic. We create such a registrar user after instantiation in the createDefaultAdminUser function as follows:

```
@PostConstruct
public void createDefaultAdminUser() {
    userDetailsService.createUser(User.withUsername("admin").password(new
BCryptPasswordEncoder().encode("adminpw")).roles(SecurityUtils.
registrarRole).build());
```

We use the same username and password here that we used to set up our Fabric CA instances just for convenience; there is no connection between the credentials possessed by an administrator of a service application and the credentials possessed by an administrator of the corresponding organization's MSP.

If our in-memory user database doesn't already contain username, a record will be created with username, password (encrypted), and role, as you can see in the register function.

The created username and password are communicated to the user out-of-band, who can then log in by calling the /login endpoint, implemented in the login function as follows:

```
@RequestMapping(value = "/login", method = RequestMethod.POST)
public ResponseEntity<String> login(String username, String password)
throws Exception {
    try {
        authenticationManager.authenticate(new UsernamePasswordAuthenticati
onToken(username, password));
    ......
    final UserDetails userDetails = userDetailsService.
loadUserByUsername(username);
    final String token = securityUtils.generateToken(userDetails);
    JSONObject tokenObj = new JSONObject();
    tokenObj.put("token", token);
    return ResponseEntity.ok(tokenObj.toString());
}
```

The user's credentials are first authenticated using the built-in authentication function by matching the passed parameters with the stored values. The user record is then looked up and a JWT is generated by calling the generateToken method on the securityUtils object, which is an instance of the SecurityUtils class defined in SecurityUtils.java. This token is then wrapped in a JSON object and returned to the user.

Finally, we note that the expiration time for the returned token is set to 15 minutes in SecurityUtils as follows:

```
public static final long JWT_TOKEN_VALIDITY = 15 * 60 * 60;
```

Anyone possessing such a token may call one or more REST API functions within a 15-minute period (apart from /register and /login endpoints, which have no restrictions). After 15 minutes, the user must re-login and get a fresh token.

User roles and access control

As we discussed earlier, an importer application user can assume the role of a banker or client (importer in a trade instance). In the previous section, we encountered a third kind of user, a registrar. Registrars can be designated by the bank maintaining this application, and they play no role in the business logic apart from creating credentials for bankers and clients. Specification and validation of roles is done in SecurityUtils.java as follows:

```
protected static final String registrarRole = "REGISTRAR";
protected static final String adminRole = "ADMIN";
protected static final String bankerRole = "BANKER";
protected static final String clientRole = "CLIENT";

protected static boolean recognizedRole(String role) {
  role = role.toUpperCase();
  return (role.equals(adminRole) || role.equals(bankerRole) || role.
equals(clientRole));
}
```

We define a fourth role called ADMIN as a placeholder for a user who is not a registrar but can perform channel and contract management operations on the network; this role is not exercised in our application at present.

The register function in ImporterController takes a role parameter, as we saw earlier, thereby allowing the registrar to associate a given username with a given role. This function also checks to see if the passed role is recognized (which means it must be one of the defined roles other than the registrar):

```
@RequestMapping(value = "/register", method = RequestMethod.POST)
public ResponseEntity<String> register(String registrarUser, String
registrarPassword, String username, String password, String role)
throws Exception {
    ......

    if (!SecurityUtils.recognizedRole(role)) {
        return new ResponseEntity<String>(role + " is not a recognized
role", HttpStatus.BAD_REQUEST);
    }
    ......
```

In `SecurityUtils.java`, we define functions to determine roles from tokens after those tokens have been authenticated: `isRegistrar`, `isBanker`, `isImporter`. Though these functions are presently not used in the application, they can be used if more advanced authentication logic is desired.

Roles are used to control access to the REST API functions offered by the server, and access control rules are specified in the `configure` function in the `ImporterWebSecurityConfig` class, as we can see in the following code snippet from `ImporterWebSecurityConfig.java`:

```
@Override
protected void configure(HttpSecurity httpSecurity) throws Exception {
    ......

    .authorizeRequests().antMatchers("/register", "/login").permitAll()
    .antMatchers("/issueLC", "/makePayment").hasRole(SecurityUtils.
bankerRole)
    .antMatchers("/requestTrade", "/requestLC", "/getAccountBalance").
hasRole(SecurityUtils.clientRole)
    .antMatchers("/getTrade", "/getTradeStatus", "/getLC", "/
getLCStatus", "/getShipmentLocation", "/getBillOfLading", "/
listTrades").hasAnyRole(SecurityUtils.clientRole, SecurityUtils.
bankerRole)
    ......
```

Anyone is permitted to call the /register and /login endpoints. But only a user passing valid registrar credentials will be able to perform a registration, as we saw earlier. Similarly, only a user possessing a valid username and password (created through registration) will be able to log in and obtain a session token (JWT).

Most endpoints triggering contract queries, which involve only reading data off the channel ledgers, such as getTrade, can be called by a user in either a client or banker role. Only a banker is permitted to perform the issueLC and makePayment functions, which trigger contract transactions. Only an importer, in a client role, is permitted to perform the requestTrade and requestLC functions, which similarly trigger contract transactions. getAccountBalance triggers only a contract query, but since only importers maintain accounts, it makes sense for this operation to be restricted to users possessing client roles.

Fabric registration, enrolment, and identity wallets

The code we have examined thus far, for user and session management and for access control, is representative of what we would find in any web application. Now our importer application's backend must, in turn, obtain access credentials and permissions that will be recognized by the Fabric network we have launched. We have already generated access credentials for administrator and ordinary users using cryptogen earlier in this book and used those credentials to perform various channel and contract setup operations. But cryptogen is a convenience tool meant purely for static configurations. A platform like Fabric must offer the ability to dynamically create identities and credentials, and it does so through the Fabric CA server. There is another reason to create credentials dynamically for our importer application: our deployed contracts rely on special attributes to be present in callers' certificates to enforce access control rules, and the statically created certificates don't possess such attributes.

We can implement the Fabric identity creation logic in our application in different ways. A fixed set of identities can be created during application launch and used for multiple banker and client users. Alternatively, a different Fabric identity can be created and mapped to every unique banker and client. Which option one should pick is largely a maintenance question for application developers, so we chose to demonstrate the latter through our project code.

The code for Fabric identity creation and maintenance lies in the FabricIdentityUtils class defined in FabricIdentityUtils.java. The creation of a new identity is a three-step process:

1. Enrollment of registrar
2. Registration of user
3. Enrollment of user

Enrollment of registrar

When we started a Fabric CA server (for each organization), we created an administrator user by providing a username (admin) and password (adminpw) as command-line arguments. This administrator user acts as registrar for the CA, but to do so, it must first enroll with the CA, a process that involves generating a public-private key pair and obtaining an X.509 certificate from the CA by sending the public key with a **certificate signing request**. The certificate with other metadata is stored in the local wallet. In FabricIdentityUtils.java, this logic lies in the enrollRegistrar function. First, we try to load the identity if it already exists in the wallet:

```
private static String adminUser = "admin";
private static String adminPassword = "adminpw";
......
public static boolean enrollRegistrar(String orgMspId) {
protected void configure(HttpSecurity httpSecurity) throws Exception {
    ......
    Wallet orgWallet;
    try {
        orgWallet = Wallets.newFileSystemWallet(Paths.
get(walletsBaseDir, orgMspId));
        Identity adminIdentity = orgWallet.get(adminUser);
        if (adminIdentity != null) {
            System.out.println("Successfully loaded admin user 'admin'
of org   " + orgMspId + " from wallet");
            return true;
        }
    } catch (IOException ioe) {
        ioe.printStackTrace();
        return false;
    }
}
```

The SDK defines classes for Wallet and Identity in the org.hyperledger. fabric.gateway package. A filesystem-based wallet is instantiated using the newFileSystemWallet function and identity files loaded from the path (walletsBaseDir) we set in application.properties. If the admin user, identified by the registrar's pre-configured name (admin), already exists in the wallet, nothing else need be done. Otherwise, an enrollment is initiated as follows:

```
HFCAClient caClient = getCAClientForOrg(orgMspId);
if (caClient == null) {
    return false;
}
Enrollment enrollment;
```

```
try {
    enrollment = caClient.enroll(adminUser, adminPassword);
    // This is always hardcoded
    if (enrollment == null) {
        return false;
    }
}
......
try {
        orgWallet.put(adminUser, Identities.newX509Identity(orgMspId,
enrollment));
}
......
```

To enroll, we need a client handle of type `HFCAClient` (offered by the SDK), which is obtained by using the `getCAClientForOrg` function and passing the MSP ID of the CA's organization (in our application's case, this will be `ImporterOrgMSP`). This function parses the connection profile we created earlier, obtains connectivity information for the sole CA defined there (`ca.importerorg.trade.com`), and creates an `HFCAClient` using that info. Subsequently, an enrollment is attempted using the registrar's username and password, which if successful returns an `Enrollment` object. A new identity is created in the wallet under the name `admin` and stored in a file. Later, when we run the application, we will see what an identity file looks like.

Registration of user

The enrolled registrar uses its certificate to submit a registration request for a user by providing a username to the CA. The CA internally creates an identity for the user and returns a secret to the registrar. The code for this (and the user enrollment following this) lies in the `registerAndEnrollUser` function in `FabricIdentityUtils`:

```
public static boolean registerAndEnrollUser(String orgMspId, String
userId, String role) {
    Identity adminIdentity;
    ......
    HFCAClient caClient = getCAClientForOrg(orgMspId);
    ......
    Enrollment enrollment;
    try {
        User admin = new User() {
            @Override
            public String getName() {
                return adminUser;
            }
        }
        ......
```

```
            @Override
            public String getAffiliation() {
                return "org1.department1";
            }

            ......

            @Override
            public String getMspId() {
                return orgMspId;
            }
        };
```

To register a user, an object that implements the `org.hyperledger.fabric.sdk.User` interface must be created. The notable functions that should be implemented are indicated in the previous snippet. The identity of the registrar should be returned by the `getName` function and the organization's MSP ID by the `getMspId` function. The affiliation returned by the `getAffiliation` function should be one of those specified in the CA server's configuration file, which we briefly discussed in *Chapter 4, Setting the Stage with a Business Scenario.* (Refer to `fabric-ca-server-config.yaml`, an example of which can be found at `http://hyperledger-fabric-ca.readthedocs.io/en/latest/serverconfig.html`.) By default, the `org1.department1` affiliation is one of those specified in the configuration that accompanies the default `fabric-ca` image, so using that will work for our application. Now a registration is attempted by submitting a `RegistrationRequest` to the CA:

```
RegistrationRequest regReq = new RegistrationRequest(userId);
if (role.toUpperCase().equals(SecurityUtils.adminRole)) {
    regReq.setType("admin");
} else {
    regReq.setType(HFCAClient.HFCA_TYPE_CLIENT);
    String appRole = role.toUpperCase();
    if (!contractRoles.containsKey(appRole)) {
        throw new NullPointerException("Role " + appRole + " does not
map to any Fabric contract role");
    }
    regReq.addAttribute(new Attribute(BUSINESS_ROLE_ATTR,
contractRoles.get(appRole), true));
}
String enrollmentSecret = caClient.register(regReq, admin);
if (enrollment == null) {
    throw new NullPointerException("Enrollment failed");
}
```

The role parameter represents the role assigned to the user by our web server when the /register endpoint is invoked. As we mentioned earlier, our application supports a user with an admin role (for channel and contract operations), and such a user can be registered with a Fabric CA if we pass the hardcoded "admin" value in the RegistrationRequest.setType method. Otherwise, we pass the value HFCAClient.HFCA_TYPE_CLIENT, indicating the user should be an ordinary client that should be granted privileges only for contract invocations. But we do need to distinguish ordinary client users into bankers and clients (importers) as our contracts expect. This is done by the addAttribute method, to which we pass the appropriate role, stored in the contractRoles map:

```
public final static String BUSINESS_ROLE_ATTR = "BUSINESS_ROLE";
public final static String IMPORTER_BANKER_ROLE = "importer_banker";
public final static String IMPORTER_ROLE = "importer";
public static HashMap<String, String> contractRoles = new
HashMap<String, String>();
static {
    contractRoles.put(SecurityUtils.bankerRole, IMPORTER_BANKER_ROLE);
    contractRoles.put(SecurityUtils.clientRole, IMPORTER_ROLE);
}
```

Therefore, in a registration request, a user with the CLIENT role is assigned the importer attribute and a user with the BANKER role is assigned the importer_banker role. The effect of this is that whenever the registered user tries to enroll, the CA will issue a certificate with this attribute value embedded in it.

Finally, as we can see from the earlier code snippet, the registration request is submitted to the CA listed in our connection profile, and a secret obtained by calling the caClient.register function. (There is logic in the beginning of the registerAndEnrollUser function that checks for the presence of an identity file for the user. If such a file exists, the function returns successfully without attempting a registration.)

Enrollment of user

The user can now enroll with the CA just like the registrar did earlier, providing its username and the secret obtained in the previous step as a password. An identity is created under the name passed to registerAndEnrollUser in the userId parameter and stored in a file in the wallet directory. The code for this resembles what lies in the enrollRegistrar function, which we discussed earlier.

The three-step process described in the preceding sections is triggered whenever the /register endpoint is called by a user (see ImporterController.register in ImporterController.java). If identities for the registrar and/or user already exist in the wallet, they are read from the filesystem and no further communication with the Fabric CA server is required, as you can see in the beginning of the registerAndEnrollUser function.

 For the equivalent of wallets and registration functions in JavaScript, let's examine the exporter application. The /register and /login endpoints are configured in src/routes/routes. js. Through src/controllers/identityController.js, these endpoints ultimately call the registerUser and enrollUser functions, which are defined in src/models/identityModel. js. These functions in turn use the Fabric CA SDK (the npm library fabric-ca-client) for registration, enrollment, and wallet identity creation.

Contract invocations through gateways

Now that we have seen how identities can be created, let's see how these identities can be used by our application to run appropriate contract operations based on user requests.

Example – requesting a trade

We will use the /requestTrade endpoint as an example. Here is what this function looks like in ImporterController.java:

```
@RequestMapping(value = "/requestTrade", method = RequestMethod.POST)
public String requestTrade(@RequestHeader Map<String, String> headers,
String tradeId, String exporterMSP, String descriptionOfGoods, double
amount) {
    String username = securityUtils.getUserNameFromTokenHeaders(heade
rs);
    if (username == null) {
        return errorObj("Unable to get username from headers");
    }
    return FabricNetworkUtils.invokeContract(username,
FabricNetworkUtils.tradeChannel, FabricNetworkUtils.tradeContractId,
false, "requestTrade", tradeId, exporterMSP, descriptionOfGoods,
Double.toString(amount));
}
```

The SecurityUtils.getUserNameFromTokenHeaders library function uncovers the caller's username, which is then used to submit a contract transaction using the catch-all FabricNetworkUtils.invokeContract function. This invokeContract function takes the username (for wallet identity purposes), channel name (tradechannel), and contract ID (trade) as arguments. The fourth parameter (false) tells the function to submit a transaction rather than a query to this contract. Then follows the contract function name (requestTrade) and list of arguments this function expects ([<trade-id>, <exporter-MSP>, <description-of-goods>, <amount>]). As you can see in the function definition, the user is expected to supply these four contract arguments; the headers parameter value is supplied by Spring whenever this function is called.

Fabric network utility functions

Functions to exercise gateways and contracts are defined in the FabricNetworkUtils class in FabricNetworkUtils.java, with the invokeContract function as the entry point for the controller functions. After some sanity checking of arguments, this function instantiates an object of type org.hyperledger.fabric.gateway.Network:

```
public static String invokeContract(String userId, String channelName,
String contractId, boolean isQuery, String func, String ...args) {
    ......

    Network network = getNetworkForOrgAndChannel(connectionProfileJson,
importerOrgMsp, userId, channelName);
    ......
```

The network object is created by the getNetworkForOrgAndChannel function, which takes as parameters the importer organization's MSP (ImporterOrgMSP), the caller's username, and the channel name (in this scenario, tradechannel). In addition, it takes the filename of our connection profile, which is set after application launch by the ImporterController.createDefaultAdminUser function (see ImporterController.java):

```
@Value("${connectionProfilesBaseDir}")
private String connectionProfilesBaseDir;

@Value("${connectionProfileJson}")
private String connectionProfileJson;

@Value("${walletsBaseDir}")
private String walletsBaseDir;

@PostConstruct
```

```
public void createDefaultAdminUser() {
    ......
    FabricNetworkUtils.connectionProfilesBaseDir =
connectionProfilesBaseDir;
    FabricNetworkUtils.connectionProfileJson = connectionProfileJson;
    FabricIdentityUtils.walletsBaseDir = walletsBaseDir;
}
```

The @Value annotations tell Spring to look up the values of the variables declared previously from application.properties. This includes the base directories of the gateways and wallets folders we set earlier in this chapter and the connection profile filename (connection.json).

This is how the getNetworkForOrgAndChannel function creates a Network object:

```
public static Network getNetworkForOrgAndChannel(String
connectionProfile, String walletDir, String userId, String channelName)
{
    try {
        // Initialize connection profile
        Gateway.Builder builder = Gateway.createBuilder();
        Path connectionProfilePath = Paths.
get(connectionProfilesBaseDir, connectionProfile);

        // Initialize wallet
        Path walletPath = Paths.get(FabricIdentityUtils.walletsBaseDir,
walletDir);
        Wallet wallet = Wallets.newFileSystemWallet(walletPath);
        builder = builder.identity(wallet, userId).networkConfig(connec
tionProfilePath).discovery(true);

        // Connect to gateway
        Gateway gateway = builder.connect();
        Network network = gateway.getNetwork(channelName);

        return network;
    } catch (IOException e) {
        e.printStackTrace();
        return null;
    }
}
```

The builder object, created using `Gateway.createBuilder()`, is used to configure gateway options before connecting to a running Fabric network. The next few lines of code result in the creation of a `wallet` object that can be used to load identities (of the kinds we created through registration and enrollment) from the filesystem, in the location set in `application.properties`. The identity of the user, passed in the `userId` parameter and that ought to have been created in the wallet, is then associated with the `builder` object using `builder.identity(wallet, userId)`. Subsequently, the connection profile we created earlier (`connection.json`) is associated with the `builder` object using `networkConfig(connectionProfilePath)`.

Finally, service discovery is enabled in this gateway builder using `discovery(true)`. Service discovery is a feature that enables the SDK to find out current network information dynamically from a discovery service exposed by each peer rather than reading it from a static configuration. This network information includes, among other things, the addresses of active peers as well as the contracts' endorsement policies.

For service discovery to work, each peer must be known to the **discovery service** of a network. This involves setting an environment variable, `CORE_PEER_GOSSIP_EXTERNALENDPOINT`, for that peer. If you recall the network creation steps, we did this for each peer container in the compose file, `bash/base/docker-compose-base.yaml`, in the `trade-network` repository. (In the importer organization's peer, this value was set to `peer0.importerorg.trade.com:8051`.)

Now, having enabled service discovery on our gateway builder, all our gateway will have to do is connect to the discovery service using the importer peer's address specified in the connection profile. Information needed for contract transaction submissions will then be made available to it. (For more information about service discovery, check out `https://hyperledger-fabric.readthedocs.io/en/latest/discovery-overview.html`.)

Having configured all the gateway options, a gateway can be created by calling `builder.connect()`, and a handle to the network channel (`tradechannel` in this case) created using `gateway.getNetwork(channelName)`. This handle is returned to the calling function.

Creating and running operations on a contract object

Returning to the `invokeContract` function, a `contract` object is instantiated for contract operations from the network channel handle:

```
Contract contract = network.getContract(contractId);
```

Depending on the isQuery value passed to invokeContract, the passed function name and arguments are sent to the contract either for a query (evaluateTransaction) or transaction (submitTransaction):

```
if (isQuery) {
    response = contract.evaluateTransaction(func, args);
} else {
    response = contract.submitTransaction(func, args);
}
```

A call to evaluateTransaction involves just a peer executing a contract function and returning the output. A call to submitTransaction results in contract function execution followed by ordering service block creation. Then, transactions in blocks are validated and committed independently by peers, and finally a success or failure event is bubbled up to the application, which then returns a value to the waiting caller. Thereby an asynchronous multi-operation pipeline is abstracted into a synchronous submitTransaction call.

 For the equivalent of gateways and contract invocation functions in JavaScript, let's examine the exporter application. As an example, the endpoint to accept a trade, /trade/:tradeId/accept_trade, is exposed in src/routes/routes.js. Through src/controllers/tradeController.js, this endpoint ultimately calls acceptTrade in src/models/tradeModel.js. This function in turn uses the Fabric SDK (the npm library fabric-network) to call submitTransaction, just as in its Java equivalent. In src/models/tradeModel.js, you can also see examples of evaluateTransaction, used for contract queries.

Launching and testing the application

We have seen what the essential portions of the code look like, so now we are ready to run a simple test involving a user running a transaction all the way down into the blockchain. To do this, we first need to launch the application, which will start a web server that listens for requests on port 5000, which is configured in application.properties through the server.port setting. The Spring Boot framework takes care of adding missing dependencies (such as beans) by looking at the classpath and various annotations we have made in the code (such as @Autowired). It also automatically configures the embedded Tomcat instance on which the web server runs.

Our `trade.sh` script offers `invokecontract` and `querycontract` functions to emulate `submitTransaction` and `evaluateTransaction` respectively but using the peer CLI commands in a `fabric-tools` container (`trade_cli`). But these commands won't work with certificates generated statically using `cryptogen`, as they don't contain the right attributes. To use `trade.sh` to submit transactions and queries, you will need to replace certificates in the `trade_cli` container with ones created dynamically and bearing attributes (such as those in the `wallets` folder).

Yet another way to exercise the smart contract API outside of our service-layer applications is using VS Code. In the FABRIC GATEWAYS panel, if you select any gateway and sync it with a running network, the contract API will be listed in the view. You can right-click on any API function and submit a transaction or a query, as the case may be.

The convenience class for launching an application, created automatically by Spring Boot, is `ImporterApplication` in `ImporterApplication.java`. This is a very simple piece of code:

```
@SpringBootApplication
public class ImporterApplication {
    public static void main(String[] args) {
        SpringApplication.run(ImporterApplication.class, args);
    }
}
```

Much of the heavy lifting is done by the `@SpringBootApplication` annotation, which tells Spring to add various dependencies. (We will not go into details of how this works; interested readers can use this reference as a starting point: `https://spring.io/guides/gs/spring-boot/#initial`.)

Before you launch the application, make sure the network is running, channels are set up, and contracts are installed according to the procedures we have demonstrated in this chapter and in *Chapter 4, Setting the Stage with a Business Scenario.*

To launch the application, click the **Run** link over the function declaration as indicated in the following VS Code screenshot. Make sure a terminal window is on by selecting **View** from the top menu followed by **Terminal** (alternatively, use *Ctrl +* ` as a shortcut):

```
@SpringBootApplication
public class ImporterApplication {

    Run| Debug
    public static void main(String[] args) {
        SpringApplication.run(ImporterApplication.class, args);
    }

}
```

Figure 9.36: Displaying the option to launch the importer application built on Java and Spring Boot

In the terminal window, you should see console output beginning with a Spring Boot logo that looks something like the following:

Figure 9.37: Displaying the Spring Boot logo and initial logs in a terminal indicating that ImporterApplication has started

If you scroll down the terminal window, you should see messages like the following, indicating that the server was started on Tomcat, listening on port **5000**:

```
2020-09-02 21:03:34.154  INFO 11878 --- [  restartedMain] org.trade.importer.ImporterApplication    :
No active profile set, falling back to default profiles: default
2020-09-02 21:03:34.451  INFO 11878 --- [  restartedMain] .e.DevToolsPropertyDefaultsPostProcessor  :
Devtools property defaults active! Set 'spring.devtools.add-properties' to 'false' to disable
2020-09-02 21:03:34.462  INFO 11878 --- [  restartedMain] .e.DevToolsPropertyDefaultsPostProcessor  :
For additional web related logging consider setting the 'logging.level.web' property to 'DEBUG'
2020-09-02 21:03:40.618  INFO 11878 --- [  restartedMain] o.s.b.w.embedded.tomcat.TomcatWebServer   :
Tomcat initialized with port(s): 5000 (http)
2020-09-02 21:03:40.706  INFO 11878 --- [  restartedMain] o.apache.catalina.core.StandardService    :
Starting service [Tomcat]
2020-09-02 21:03:40.714  INFO 11878 --- [  restartedMain] org.apache.catalina.core.StandardEngine   :
Starting Servlet engine: [Apache Tomcat/9.0.33]
2020-09-02 21:03:41.215  INFO 11878 --- [  restartedMain] o.a.c.c.C.[Tomcat].[localhost].[/]        :
Initializing Spring embedded WebApplicationContext
2020-09-02 21:03:41.216  INFO 11878 --- [  restartedMain] o.s.web.context.ContextLoader             :
Root WebApplicationContext: initialization completed in 6750 ms
2020-09-02 21:03:43.477  INFO 11878 --- [  restartedMain] o.s.s.web.DefaultSecurityFilterChain      :
Creating filter chain: any request, [org.springframework.security.web.context.request.async.WebAsyncM
anagerIntegrationFilter@5741889b, org.springframework.security.web.context.SecurityContextPersistence
Filter@60bac377, org.springframework.security.web.header.HeaderWriterFilter@2dd3f339, org.springframe
work.security.web.authentication.logout.LogoutFilter@518fa715, org.trade.importer.JwtRequestFilter@78
8d31a6, org.springframework.security.web.savedrequest.RequestCacheAwareFilter@71857ee0, org.springfra
mework.security.web.servletapi.SecurityContextHolderAwareRequestFilter@337c9c09, org.springframework.
security.web.authentication.AnonymousAuthenticationFilter@38814f95, org.springframework.security.web.
session.SessionManagementFilter@44641936, org.springframework.security.web.access.ExceptionTranslatio
nFilter@7d71949, org.springframework.security.web.access.intercept.FilterSecurityInterceptor@2fbc7c5f
]
2020-09-02 21:03:44.695  INFO 11878 --- [  restartedMain] o.s.s.concurrent.ThreadPoolTaskExecutor   :
Initializing ExecutorService 'applicationTaskExecutor'
2020-09-02 21:03:46.567  INFO 11878 --- [  restartedMain] o.s.b.d.a.OptionalLiveReloadServer        :
LiveReload server is running on port 35729
2020-09-02 21:03:46.662  INFO 11878 --- [  restartedMain] o.s.b.w.embedded.tomcat.TomcatWebServer   :
Tomcat started on port(s): 5000 (http) with context path ''
2020-09-02 21:03:46.673  INFO 11878 --- [  restartedMain] org.trade.importer.ImporterApplication    :
Started ImporterApplication in 14.602 seconds (JVM running for 16.787)
```

Figure 9.38: Displaying the log output during ImporterApplication launch, with port 5000 indicated

The importer application's server is ready to receive and handle requests now. To submit HTTP requests, we will use the `curl` tool. Our first action will be to register a user in a client role (or as an importer). From a command-line terminal on your host machine, run the following:

```
$ curl -X POST http://localhost:5000/register -H "content-type:
application/x-www-form-urlencoded" -d 'registrarUser=admin&registrarPas
sword=adminpw&username=importer&password=password&role=client'
```

We can pick any username and password for the importer, and for the purpose of this exercise, we picked `importer` and `password` respectively. The registrar username and password (`admin` and `adminpw`) must match those we hardcoded in `ImporterController.java`.

In production, we clearly would not want to send passwords in the open, so our web server ought to be secured with TLS for confidential client-server communication and expose an `https` URL. But the server we are running is enough to demonstrate Fabric's capabilities, which is our primary goal.

If the registration is successful, you should see the following output:

```
{"roles":["CLIENT"],"username":"importer"}
```

This indicates that a user named `importer` has been registered with the role of `CLIENT` in the application. But that's not all. If you look into your wallet folder (the path to which was set in the `walletsBaseDir` property in `application.properties`), you should see a newly created folder named `ImporterOrgMSP` (corresponding to the importer organization's MSP ID). This folder in turn should contain two files named `admin.id` and `importer.id`, the former created after enrollment of the registrar with the importer organization's MSP and the latter created after registration and enrollment of the `importer` user. The contents of `importer.id` should look something like the following:

```
{"version":1,"mspId":"ImporterOrgMSP","type":"X.509","crede
ntials":{"certificate":"-----BEGIN CERTIFICATE-----\nMIICiD
CCAi+gAwIBAgIUDdNA9FQaIMyZNVnGWxqm89iOJkgwCgYIKoZIzj0EAwIw\
nfTELMAkGA1UEBhMCVVMxEzARBgNVBAgTCkNhbGlmb3JuaWExFjAUBgNVBAcTDVNh\
nbiBGcmFuY2lzY28xHjAcBgNVBAoTFWltcG9ydGVyb3JnLnRyYWRlLmNvbTEhMB8G\
nA1UEAxMYY2EuaW1wb3J0ZXJvcmcudHJhZGUuY29tMB4XDTIwMDYyNDIwNTAwMFoX\
nDTIxMDYyNDIwNTUwMFowJDEPMA0GA1UECxMGY2xpZW50MREwDwYDVQQDEwhpbXBv\
ncnRlcjBZMBMGByqGSM49AgEGCCqGSM49AwEHA0IABFcaQNHrV4cnFuR4q46UzJq4\
nvyRyPIE3uyrk5HYXBG04X5L+ulwm72/lgM2J4QXVB114o04YMdCEU9IQYjcXyPej\
ngeUwgeIwDgYDVR0PAQH/BAQDAgeAMAwGA1UdEwEB/wQCMAAwHQYDVR0OBBYEFH56\
nKfJ8X6huaHEuIpRTnXgKu8ybMCsGA1UdIwQkMCKAIB68GDb3i6+V5NodqNwD9n+O\
neUkL2qHcd6x28uhbjiU2MHYGCCoDBAUGBwgBBGp7ImF0dHJzIjp7IkJVU0lORVNT\
nX1JPTEUiOiJpbXBvcnRlciIsImhmLkFmZmlsaWF0aW9uIjoiIiwiaGYuRW5yb2xs\
nbWVudElEIjoiaW1wb3J0ZXIiLCJoZi5UeXBlIjoiY2xpZW50In19MAoGCCqGSM49\
nBAMCA0cAMEQCIAuJNBpAiH3HvZ8X0QANLSzcpjejXTWMih2qQHgbF0VRAiBNgak0\
nRkpuOd9GI6kbu2jMNJxUhb7moeLQBCtCTZHIPg==\n-----END
CERTIFICATE-----\n","privateKey":"-----BEGIN PRIVATE KEY-----\
nMIGTAgEAMBMGByqGSM49AgEGCCqGSM49AwEHBHkwdwIBAQQgjdTS9ZZA71SD6iJY\
na2z0/Dl8hkQVjcoptozlo8TaLyygCgYIKoZIzj0DAQehRANCAARXGkDR61eHJxbk\neKuO
lMyauL8kcjyBN7sq5OR2FwRtOF+S/rpcJu9v5YDNieEF1QddeKNOGDHQhFPS\nEGI3F8j3\
n-----END PRIVATE KEY-----\n"}}
```

This is a JSON structure, with notable fields including the MSP ID (`mspId`), the `importer` user's private key (`privateKey`), and its certificate issued by the MSP (`certificate`). This represents the signing identity of `importer` and will allow it to submit contract operations.

If you look at the terminal window in VS Code, you should see messages indicating that the `importer` user was enrolled and its identity was imported into the wallet corresponding to `ImporterOrgMSP`, as in the following screenshot:

Figure 9.39: Displaying logs indicating the enrollment of the importer user identity and the addition of that identity to the wallet

Now the `importer` user can log in to obtain an access token by running:

```
$ curl -X POST http://localhost:5000/login -H "content-type:
application/x-www-form-urlencoded" -d 'username=importer&password=passw
ord'
```

Upon success, you should see something like the following in the output:

```
{"token":"eyJhbGciOiJIUzUxMiJ9.
eyJzdWIiOiJpbXBvcnRlciIsImV4cCI6MTU5MzA4Nzk5NSwiaWF0IjoxNTkzMDMzOTk1fQ.
WFr-iV0ECo5NTMHyDVNm1WQSNjcGuaVYfwi4xeOPtKXAT4MZ7ivEPQyijv-VK4Pm3ufW7j-
tsGH3nRLApAjf3g"}
```

The value of `token` in this JSON structure is the JWT we can use to invoke other endpoints. Let's now try to request a trade, which is the first step in our business workflow. Remember that only a user in an importer's role is permitted to make this request as per the `trade` contract logic, so this ought to be a safe operation. Run the following command:

```
$ curl -X POST http://localhost:5000/requestTrade -H
"content-type: application/x-www-form-urlencoded"
-H "authorization: Bearer eyJhbGciOiJIUzUxMiJ9.
eyJzdWIiOiJpbXBvcnRlciIsImV4cCI6MTU5MzA4Nzk5NSwiaWF0IjoxNTkzMDMzOTk1fQ.
WFr-iV0ECo5NTMHyDVNm1WQSNjcGuaVYfwi4xeOPtKXAT4MZ7ivEPQyijv-VK4Pm3ufW7j-
tsGH3nRLApAjf3g" -d 'tradeId=trade-12&amount=90000&descriptionOfGoods=W
ood&exporterMSP=ExporterOrgMSP'
```

You can see how we supplied the token value in the `authorization` header, prefixed by `Bearer`. We also provided values for trade ID, amount, description of goods, and the exporter's MSP ID, all of which were ultimately used as arguments to the contract's `requestTrade` function. Upon success, you should see the following:

```
{"result":true,"payload":""}
```

This indicates that the operation succeeded in committing a trade request to the `tradechannel` ledger. The `payload` field is empty because the `requestTrade` function in our `trade` contract does not return a value on success. If this operation had failed, you would have seen an error message in the console.

Just to confirm that our trade request indeed succeeded, and to try out a query for variety, let's run the `getTrade` operation to obtain details of the recorded trade request:

```
$ curl -X GET http://localhost:5000/getTrade?tradeId=trade-12
-H "content-type: application/x-www-form-urlencoded"
-H "authorization: Bearer eyJhbGciOiJIUzUxMiJ9.
eyJzdWIiOiJpbXBvcnRlciIsImV4cCI6MTU5MzA4Nzk5NSwiaWF0IjoxNTkzMDMzOTk1fQ.
WFr-iV0ECo5NTMHyDVNm1WQSNjcGuaVYfwi4xeOPtKXAT4MZ7ivEPQyijv-VK4Pm3ufW7j-
tsGH3nRLApAjf3g"
```

If successful, the output should be something like the following:

```
{"result":true,"payload":"{\"amount\":90000,\"descriptionOfGoods\":\"Wo
od\",\"exporterMSP\":\"ExporterOrgMSP\",\"importerMSP\":\"ImporterOrgMS
P\",\"status\":\"REQUESTED\",\"tradeID\":\"trade-12\"}"}
```

The `result` value indicates that the query succeeded, and the `payload` value contains the attributes of the trade. These attributes should match those supplied by us in the `requestTrade` operation.

We have now successfully completed all the stages of our Fabric network-building and distributed application development.

Event management

As we discussed earlier, a Fabric transaction is inherently asynchronous, and its success or failure is revealed only as events to which one must subscribe. But the Fabric SDK masks this behavior and presents a synchronous API to the application developer, handling event subscriptions under the hood. But the API also offers features for event subscription that will be useful in complex enterprise applications. But if we are developing a complex enterprise application, it may be necessary for a process to know and track whether a transaction submitted by a different process or service succeeded. To enable this, the SDK exposes features for the subscription of different classes of events (contract operations and network changes) through the API. Our readers are encouraged to examine the API documentation and experiment with this feature. Java developers should check out the following:

- `https://github.com/hyperledger/fabric-gateway-java/`
- `https://github.com/hyperledger/fabric-sdk-java`

And JavaScript developers should check out the following:

- `https://github.com/hyperledger/fabric-sdk-node/`

Exercising the application through a presentation layer

The service-layer applications we have designed, such as the importer application, expose REST APIs for invocation by users. The most direct way for a user to exercise these applications is by sending an HTTP query. But an HTTP query, though simple to frame for a technically skilled person, may look cryptic to the laypeople who are our applications' target users. Therefore, it is common practice to mask the complexity of framing such HTTP queries through applications that provide more intuitive interfaces, which present easy-to-understand information and options to users. For example, consider the trade request we demonstrated earlier using `curl`. All an importer really needs to specify is the ID of the proposed trade, the description of goods, the amount, and the exporter to whom the proposal is being made. An ideal presentation application would prompt the user to enter these pieces of information, and possibly offer a list of exporters to select from. Underneath, this application would implement an HTTP client to send requests to the application server and present responses to the importer in an easy-to-read format (unlike the JSON we saw earlier).

As indicated in *Figure 9.2* earlier in this chapter, presentation application interfaces come in two modalities: CLIs and **graphical user interfaces (GUIs)**. CLI applications present prompts, menus, and selections to users on command-line terminals using text. They can also present basic forms of images through text (such as ASCII art). These applications can be implemented using popular languages such as Node.js; for example, using tools like Commander (`https://www.npmjs.com/package/commander`) and Inquirer (`https://www.npmjs.com/package/inquirer`).

GUI applications are typically implemented as web pages (using HTML and JavaScript) that allow users to exercise services through web browsers, though other tools, such as Java applets, can also be used. GUIs offer more capabilities than CLIs, as they can present forms and visuals (images, videos, animations) in addition to textual information, menus, and selections. Event notifications can also be posted to web pages using **web sockets** (`https://developer.mozilla.org/en-US/docs/Web/API/WebSockets_API`).

Regardless of language or modality, presentation applications for our Fabric applications are essentially wrappers around web clients. Most developers can write such applications with ease by following online documentation and tutorials, so demonstrating an implementation is beyond the scope of this book. Instead, we will use `curl` commands, which are simple and convenient HTTP clients, to exercise the complete smart contract API using the four service-layer applications illustrated in *Figure 9.3*.

Launching applications

First, we must prepare and start all four applications: importer, exporter, regulator, and carrier. We continue where we left off in the previous section and assume that the importer application is still running. (If that application was stopped, run it again using the given instructions.)

 Note that the applications' servers must listen on unique ports on your host machine.

In the `wallets` folder, create subfolders corresponding to the other three organizations: exporter, carrier, and regulator.

If you have not created connection profiles in the `gateways` folder corresponding to each of the four organizations, do so now using the instructions supplied earlier in this chapter.

The next application we will run is the regulator application, which, like the importer application, was developed using Java:

1.   In VS Code, select **File | Add Folder to Workspace...** from the top menu.

2.   Navigate to the `apps/regulator` folder and select it.

3.   Open `src/main/resources/application.properties`. Since our importer application server is already listening on port 5000, we choose a different port here (6000), as you can see in the following line:

```
server.port=6000
```

4.   Now open `src/main/java/org/trade/regulator/RegulatorApplication.java` in VS Code, and click the **Run** link over the main function definition as follows:

```
@SpringBootApplication
public class RegulatorApplication {

    Run | Debug
    public static void main(String[] args) {
        SpringApplication.run(RegulatorApplication.class, args);
    }

}
```

Figure 9.40: Displaying the option to launch the regulator application built on Java and Spring Boot

You will see server logs in a new console at the bottom of the screen in the **TERMINAL** panel.

Next, we will run the exporter application, which was developed using JavaScript. Though we can run this from VS Code as well, it is simpler to launch it from the command line.

Open a new terminal window and navigate to the `apps/exporter` folder. You can start the app by simply running `npm start`, but we must tell the server where our `gateways` and `wallets` folders are located (the root folder of your `trade-networks` project clone). This is because the default path in the application is configured for integration tests running in Docker containers (see *Chapter 11, Agility in a Blockchain Network*). As an example, if your copy of `trade-networks` lies in `/home/blah`, the path you must supply to the app during launch using the `CONFIG_PATH` environment variable is `/home/blah/trade-networks`. Then, the command you should run is the following:

```
$ CONFIG_PATH=/home/blah/trade-network npm start
```

You will see something like the following in the console. Note that this server is configured by default to listen on port 4000, which is fine as the two other running apps are listening on ports 5000 and 6000 respectively:

```
> node ./src/app.js

[2020-09-02 11:38:11.488] [INFO] TradeExporterApp - ****************** SERVER STARTED *************
*********
[2020-09-02 11:38:11.495] [INFO] TradeExporterApp - ***************  http://0.0.0.0:4000  *********
*********
```

Figure 9.41: Launching the exporter application, with the server listening on port 4000

Finally, we will run the carrier application, which, like the exporter application, was developed using JavaScript. Open a new terminal window and navigate to the apps/carrier folder. We must specify a CONFIG_PATH at launch, and optionally a PORT for this application's server to listen on (which must be different from the other three applications' server ports). By default, the port is set to 7000 for the carrier application. Run the following command to launch the carrier app (with or without the PORT specification):

```
$ CONFIG_PATH=/home/blah/trade-network PORT=7000 npm start
```

You will see something like the following in the console:

```
> node ./src/app.js

[2020-09-02 11:40:14.015] [INFO] TradeCarrierApp - ****************** SERVER STARTED *************
*********
[2020-09-02 11:40:14.022] [INFO] TradeCarrierApp - ***************  http://0.0.0.0:7000  *********
*********
```

Figure 9.42: Launching the carrier application, with the server listening on port 7000

An end-to-end scenario – trade request to final payment

Now we will run the complete 13-step workflow illustrated in *Chapter 4*, *Setting the Stage with a Business Scenario*, switching among different users to drive the workflow. Services are invoked using curl commands with different parameters. These commands are also present in shortcut shell scripts in the apps/sample-cli-curl/ folder for convenience.

Users and their credentials

Usernames and roles are as follows:

- In the exporter application, we will create a user named exporter in the
  CLIENT role, and a user named eb in the BANKER role

- In the importer application, we will create a user named importer in the
  CLIENT role (we already did this in the previous section), and a user named ib
  in the BANKER role

- In the carrier application, we will create a user named carrier in the CLIENT
  role

- In the regulator application, we will create a user named regulator in the
  CLIENT role

Passwords for all six usernames will simply be set to password.

Registering users

To register exporter and eb with the exporter application, run:

```
$ curl -X POST http://localhost:4000/register -H "content-type:
application/x-www-form-urlencoded" -d 'registrarUser=admin&registrarPas
sword=adminpw&username=exporter&password=password&role=client'
$ curl -X POST http://localhost:4000/register -H "content-type:
application/x-www-form-urlencoded" -d 'registrarUser=admin&registrarPas
sword=adminpw&username=eb&password=password&role=banker'
```

The output you should see for each is:

```
true
```

We have already registered importer, so we just need to register ib with the importer
app:

```
$ curl -X POST http://localhost:5000/register -H "content-type:
application/x-www-form-urlencoded" -d 'registrarUser=admin&registrarPas
sword=adminpw&username=ib&password=password&role=banker'
```

You should see the following output:

```
{"roles":["BANKER"],"username":"ib"}
```

To register `carrier` with the carrier application, run:

```
$ curl -X POST http://localhost:7000/register -H "content-type:
application/x-www-form-urlencoded" -d 'registrarUser=admin&registrarPas
sword=adminpw&username=carrier&password=password&role=client'
```

You should see the following output:

```
true
```

To register `regulator` with the regulator application, run:

```
$ curl -X POST http://localhost:6000/register -H "content-type:
application/x-www-form-urlencoded" -d 'registrarUser=admin&registrarPas
sword=adminpw&username=regulator&password=password&role=client'
```

You should see the following output:

```
{"roles":["CLIENT"],"username":"regulator"}
```

To run all six registrations in one command, you can run the script `registerAll.sh`. But keep in mind that this is meant to be run on a newly created network that doesn't have any users registered already (such as `importer`, which we registered earlier).

The `wallets` folder on your machine now contains identities created by the four applications using different Fabric SDKs. Examples are:

- `wallets/importerorg/ImporterOrgMSP/importer.id` for the `importer` user
- `wallets/exporterorg/ExporterOrgMSP/eb.id` for the exporter bank user
- `wallets/carrierorg/CarrierOrgMSP/carrier.id` for the `carrier` user

As we discussed in an earlier section, these identities are specified as JSON objects containing (among other attributes) the organization's MSP ID, the client's private signing key, and the certificate issued for the client by the MSP.

If you are familiar with the code written for the first edition of this book, you will notice that the identity format created and maintained by the SDK has changed. Fabric SDK version 1.4 and earlier maintained a client's identity in a folder named after the username. This folder contained three files:

- A private key with a name like c89176ffd0c328218f0307 a914571f96c3bfcbe55785681dc6c3af5fc52ca0c3-priv

- A public key in a similarly named file like c89176ffd0c3 28218f0307a914571f96c3bfcbe55785681dc6c3af5fc52 ca0c3-pub

- A file named after the username (like exporter or ib) that contains a JSON with certificate and organization MSP ID among other attributes

Just for experimentation, if you run the legacy code in the legacy_ sdk_1.4 folder, you will see such identities created in bash/ client-certs. For our readers' benefit, we have created a utility script, upgrade-wallet-id-1_4-to-2_0.js, to convert a Fabric SDK 1.4 identity to a Fabric SDK 2.x identity. This script lies in the bash/utils folder in the trade-network repository. You can run this script by navigating to the bash/utils folder and running:

```
$ node upgrade-wallet-id-1_4-to-2_0.js exporter
<identity-folder-path>
```

Here, <identity-folder-path> refers to a folder named after a username (such as exporter or ib).

Logging in users

After registering users, we need to log them in to their respective applications and obtain tokens for each of them. We did this for importer earlier in this chapter, and we need to repeat the procedure for all the other users. As an example, run the following to log in the exporter:

```
$ curl -X POST http://localhost:4000/login -H "content-type:
application/x-www-form-urlencoded" -d 'username=exporter&password=passw
ord'
```

You should see a JSON output of the form { "token": <token> }. Because we will need to reuse these tokens for multiple operations, it is better to save it in an environment variable. Using the script loginExporter.sh, you can save the exporter's token in JWT_EXP and export it in your shell's environment:

```
JWT_EXP=$(curl -X POST http://localhost:4000/login -H "content-type:
application/x-www-form-urlencoded" -d 'username=exporter&password=passw
ord' 2>/dev/null | jq .token)
JWT_EXP=${JWT_EXP:1:${#JWT_EXP}-2}
export JWT_EXP
```

Before running this script, make sure you have the jq tool installed. To save the exporter's token in JWT_EXP, run:

```
$ . loginExporter.sh
```

If you ran this on a Linux machine with a bash shell, run the following to verify the login:

```
$ export | grep JWT
```

You should see something like:

```
declare -x
JWT_EXP="eyJhbGciOiJIUzI1NiIsInR5cCI6IkpXVCJ9.eyJleHAiOjE1OTMxMTgwMDc
sInVzZXJuYW1lIjoiZXhwb3J0ZXIiLCJpYXQiOjE1OTMxMTM4Njd9.I4W_cFqrq87BPMR
bwsmXWoG9o2iOK5_n_wEY4hyIeVk"
```

To log in all six users with one command, simply run:

```
$ . loginAll.sh
```

The tokens for the different users are saved in variables as follows:

- importer: JWT_IMP
- ib: JWT_IMPBANK
- exporter: JWT_EXP
- eb: JWT_EXPBANK
- carrier: JWT_CAR
- regulator: JWT_REG

Requesting a trade as an importer

Now we can resume the workflow we began in a previous section where an importer user requested a trade and verified that a request was recorded on the ledger. Note that if you've recreated the network since then, you must run the `requestTrade` operation again. You can do this using the shortcut script:

```
$ ./requestTrade.sh
```

And you can verify the existence of a trade request by running:

```
$ ./getTrade.sh
```

The trade we are going to be driving has the ID `trade-12` and obliges the importer to pay an amount of `90000` units to the exporter.

Accepting a trade as an exporter

Now that the importer (`importer`) has requested this trade, you can switch your persona to the exporter (`exporter`) and accept it by running:

```
$ ./acceptTrade.sh
```

You should see this output:

```
true
```

As the importer, you can get details of the trade and verify acceptance with:

```
$ ./getTrade.sh
```

The output should look like this:

```
{"result":true,"payload":"{\"amount\":90000,\"descriptionOfGoods\":\"Wo
od\",\"exporterMSP\":\"ExporterOrgMSP\",\"importerMSP\":\"ImporterOrgMS
P\",\"status\":\"ACCEPTED\",\"tradeID\":\"trade-12\"}"}
```

You can just check the status of the trade as the exporter by running:

```
$ ./getTradeStatus.sh
```

The output should look like this:

```
{"Status":"ACCEPTED"}
```

Requesting a letter of credit as an importer

We now move to the letter of credit stage. Switching back to assuming the role of importer, you can request a letter of credit:

```
$ ./requestLC.sh
```

The output should look like this:

```
{"result":true,"payload":""}
```

Issuing a letter of credit as an importer's bank

Assuming the role of the importer's bank (ib), you can issue a letter of credit against trade-12 by running:

```
$ ./issueLC.sh
```

The bank supplies an L/C ID, expiration date, and required documents as parameters; these are hardcoded in the script, but you can edit them to whatever values you desire. The output should look like this:

```
{"result":true,"payload":""}
```

To check the contents of the L/C, you can run the following (we do this using the persona of the exporter's bank, but either of the trading parties or their banks can run this query):

```
$ ./getLC.sh
```

The output should look like the following, indicating that the L/C was issued:

```
{"amount":90000,"beneficiary":"ExporterOrgMSP","expirationDate":"11/3
0/2020","id":"lc-12","requiredDocs":[{"docType":"B/L"},{"docType":"E/
L"}],"status":"ISSUED"}
```

Accepting a letter of credit as an exporter's bank

Assuming the persona of the exporter's bank (eb) now, you can accept the L/C against trade-12 by running:

```
$ ./acceptLC.sh
```

You should see this output:

```
true
```

To check the status of the L/C as the importer's bank, run:

```
$ ./getLCStatus.sh
```

The output should look like the following, indicating that the L/C was accepted:

```
{"result":true,"payload":"{\"Status\":\"ACCEPTED\"}"}
```

Requesting an export license as an exporter

We now move to the export license stage. Assuming the persona of the exporter, you can request an export license:

```
$ ./requestEL.sh
```

You should see this output:

```
true
```

Assuming the persona of the regulator (regulator) now, you can view the contents of the license request by running:

```
$ ./getEL.sh
```

The output should look like the following, indicating that an **export license (E/L)** has been requested:

```
{"result":true,"payload":"{\"approver\":\"RegulatorOrgMSP\",\"carrier\
":\"CarrierOrgMSP\",\"descriptionOfGoods\":\"Wood\",\"expirationDate\"
:\"\",\"exporter\":\"ExporterOrgMSP\",\"id\":\"\",\"status\":\"REQUEST
ED\"}"}
```

Issuing an export license as a regulator

Remaining in the persona of the regulator, you can issue the export license by running:

```
$ ./issueEL.sh
```

The regulator supplies an E/L ID and expiration date as parameters; these are hardcoded in the script, but you can edit them to whatever values you desire. The output should look like this:

```
{"result":true,"payload":""}
```

To check the status of the E/L as the exporter, run:

```
$ ./getELStatus.sh
```

The output should look like the following, indicating that the E/L was accepted:

```
{"Status":"ISSUED"}
```

Preparing a shipment as an exporter

We now move to the shipment and payments stage. Assuming the persona of the exporter, you can prepare a shipment:

```
$ ./prepareShipment.sh
```

The exporter supplies shipment details like amount, description of goods, carrier, and beneficiary identities as parameters; these are hardcoded in the script, but you can edit them to whatever values you desire. You should see this output:

```
true
```

Accepting a shipment and issuing a bill of lading as a carrier

Assuming the persona of the carrier (carrier) now, you can accept the shipment and issue a B/L:

```
$ ./acceptShipmentAndIssueBL.sh
```

The carrier supplies a B/L ID, expiration date, source, and destination posts as parameters; these are hardcoded in the script, but you can edit them to whatever values you desire. You should see this output:

```
true
```

At this point, the shipment's location should be set to SOURCE. Assuming the persona of the importer (though you can do this in the persona of either of the trading entities, their banks, or the carrier), you can verify this by running:

```
$ ./getShipmentLocation.sh
```

The output should look like the following:

```
{"result":true,"payload":"{\"Location\":\"SOURCE\"}"}
```

To view the B/L contents in the persona of the exporter's bank, run:

```
$ ./getBillOfLading.sh
```

The output should look like the following:

```
{"amount":90000,"beneficiary":"ImporterOrgMSP","carrierMSP":"CarrierO
rgMSP","descriptionOfGoods":"Wood","destinationPort":"LosAngeles","e
xpirationDate":"03/05/2021","exporterMSP":"ExporterOrgMSP","id":"bl-
12","sourcePort":"Mumbai"}
```

Requesting a partial payment as an exporter's bank

Now that the shipment has been dispatched, the request for the first payment installment can be made. Assuming the persona of the exporter's bank, run:

```
$ ./requestPayment.sh
```

You should see this output:

```
true
```

Before processing payments, let's check the account balances of the importer and exporter that were set during the initialization of the letterOfCredit contract. Assume the persona of the exporter and view its balance by running:

```
$ ./getExporterBalance.sh
```

The output should look like the following:

```
{"Balance":100000}
```

Assume the persona of the importer and view its balance by running:

```
$ ./getImporterBalance.sh
```

The output should look like the following:

```
{"result":true,"payload":"{\"Balance\":200000.0}"}
```

Making a partial payment as an importer's bank

Now assume the persona of the importer's bank and make a payment by running:

```
$ ./makePayment.sh
```

The output should look like the following:

```
{"result":true,"payload":""}
```

Assume the persona of the exporter and view its balance by running:

```
$ ./getExporterBalance.sh
```

The output should look like the following:

```
{"Balance":145000}
```

45000 units were credited to this account, which is half the total amount of 90000, as per the terms encoded in the letterOfCredit contract. Now assume the persona of the importer and view its balance by running:

```
$ ./getImporterBalance.sh
```

The output should look like the following:

```
{"result":true,"payload":"{\"Balance\":155000.0}"}
```

45000 units were debited from this account, as expected.

Delivering a shipment as a carrier

Now assume the persona of the carrier and mark the shipment as delivered by updating its location to DESTINATION:

```
$ ./updateShipmentLocationDestination.sh
```

You should see this output:

```
true
```

To check the shipment's location in the persona of the importer, run:

```
$ ./getShipmentLocation.sh
```

The output should look like the following:

```
{"result":true,"payload":"{\"Location\":\"DESTINATION\"}"}
```

Requesting the balance payment as an exporter's bank

Now that the shipment has been delivered, the balance payment can be requested. Assuming the persona of the exporter's bank, run:

```
$ ./requestPayment.sh
```

You should see this output:

```
true
```

Making the balance payment as an importer's bank

Now assume the persona of the importer's bank and make the balance payment by running:

```
$ ./makePayment.sh
```

The output should look like the following:

```
{"result":true,"payload":""}
```

Verify that the remainder of the payment (45000) was credited to the importer's account. Assume the persona of the importer and view its balance by running:

```
$ ./getImporterBalance.sh
```

The output should look like the following:

```
{"result":true,"payload":"{\"Balance\":110000.0}"}
```

Verify that the remainder of the payment (45000) was debited from the exporter's account. Assume the persona of the exporter and view its balance by running:

```
$ ./getExporterBalance.sh
```

The output should look like the following:

```
{"Balance":190000}
```

Viewing the list of active or processed trades as an importer

Let's now see the list of unique trades that have been processed or are being processed by our combination of contracts. Assuming the persona of the importer, run:

```
$ ./listTrades.sh
```

The output should look like the following:

```
{"result":true,"payload":"[{\"amount\":90000,\"descriptionOfGoods\":\"W
ood\",\"exporterMSP\":\"ExporterOrgMSP\",\"importerMSP\":\"ImporterOrgM
SP\",\"status\":\"ACCEPTED\",\"tradeID\":\"trade-12\"}]"}
```

The `payload` field contains an array of trades. Since we have processed just one trade thus far, this array has only one element (the attributes of the trade identified by `trade-12`).

We have successfully concluded a trade using our combination of smart contracts running on multiple channels, with four independent service applications intermediating the different personas with the blockchain.

The scenario we walked through can be tested end-to-end in an automated manner by launching applications within Docker containers and running integration tests. See *Chapter 11, Agility in a Blockchain Network*, for instructions.

Using a production-grade ordering service

The network we have built and run contracts and service applications on uses an ordering service that runs in `solo` mode, as we saw in *Chapter 4, Setting the Stage with a Business Scenario*. This is a trivial ordering service consisting of a single node that is completely in charge of ordering transactions into blocks. Needless to say, centralizing block creation violates core blockchain principles and therefore cannot be the basis for any production-grade enterprise network that requires a multi-node consensus-based ordering service. And Hyperledger Fabric 2 does support and recommend ordering services built on Raft clusters. (Fabric 1 supported Kafka- and ZooKeeper-based ordering services, though support for Raft was added in 1.4.)

So why did we run our network construction and development exercise on a solo orderer that will never be used in production? There are two reasons. One, we wanted to demonstrate to our readers that all aspects of channel setup, contract development, and higher-layer application development are completely independent of the nature of the ordering service, which can be treated as a black box after its configuration is specified in a configtx.yaml file and artifacts are created. Second, the creation of a more complex ordering service will require more nodes in more containers to be created. Since we already have a somewhat elaborate application that spawns multiple containers for four different contracts, the overhead of a multi-node orderer may prevent users from running our applications on resource-poor machines.

But the setting up of a Raft ordering service is a necessary skill for a Fabric developer, and we will demonstrate how to do that by augmenting our trade network in this section. This is not meant to be a primer on Raft, for which readers are encouraged to seek online resources such as https://raft.github.io/. It is also not meant to be a broad discussion of the various ordering service modes supported by Fabric, for which the starting point is https://hyperledger-fabric.readthedocs.io/en/latest/orderer/ordering_service.html.

We will be rebuilding our network from the bottom up, as a new ordering service requires the recreation of channel artifacts. So, before embarking on this exercise, you should bring down the network we were ran earlier (using ./trade.sh down). You also have a choice: whether to augment the existing set of cryptographic artifacts or recreate the entire set using cryptogen. If you wish to do the latter, you should run this exercise from a fresh copy of the trade-network code.

The configuration we will use to build our new network lies in the bash/multiple_orderers folder. This contains a configtx.yaml to replace the one in the bash folder and a crypto-config.yaml to augment the one in the bash folder.

This configtx.yaml file is different from the one in the bash folder in two respects: it contains a profile of a five-node Raft ordering service (the latter defines a single-node Raft orderer under the unused TradeMultiNodeEtcdRaft profile) and these five nodes are included in the TradeOrdererOrg organization. A snippet from the TradeMultiNodeEtcdRaft profile in multiple_orderers/configtx.yaml illustrates this as follows:

```
TradeMultiNodeEtcdRaft:
    ......
    Orderer:
        ......
        <<: *OrdererDefaults
        OrdererType: etcdraft
```

```
EtcdRaft:
  Consenters:
  - Host: orderer.trade.com
      Port: 7050
      ClientTLSCert: ../crypto-config/ordererOrganizations/
          trade.com/orderers/orderer.trade.com/tls/server.crt
      ServerTLSCert: ../crypto-config/ordererOrganizations/
          trade.com/orderers/orderer.trade.com/tls/server.crt
  - Host: orderer2.trade.com
      Port: 7050
      ClientTLSCert: ../crypto-config/ordererOrganizations/
          trade.com/orderers/orderer2.trade.com/tls/server.crt
      ServerTLSCert: ../crypto-config/ordererOrganizations/
          trade.com/orderers/orderer2.trade.com/tls/server.crt
  - Host: orderer3.trade.com
      Port: 7050
      ClientTLSCert: ../crypto-config/ordererOrganizations/
          trade.com/orderers/orderer3.trade.com/tls/server.crt
      ServerTLSCert: ../crypto-config/ordererOrganizations/
          trade.com/orderers/orderer3.trade.com/tls/server.crt
  - Host: orderer4.trade.com
      Port: 7050
      ClientTLSCert: ../crypto-config/ordererOrganizations/
          trade.com/orderers/orderer4.trade.com/tls/server.crt
      ServerTLSCert: ../crypto-config/ordererOrganizations/
          trade.com/orderers/orderer4.trade.com/tls/server.crt
  - Host: orderer5.trade.com
      Port: 7050
      ClientTLSCert: ../crypto-config/ordererOrganizations/
          trade.com/orderers/orderer5.trade.com/tls/server.crt
      ServerTLSCert: ../crypto-config/ordererOrganizations/
          trade.com/orderers/orderer5.trade.com/tls/server.crt
  Addresses:
    - orderer.trade.com:7050
    - orderer2.trade.com:7050
    - orderer3.trade.com:7050
    - orderer4.trade.com:7050
    - orderer5.trade.com:7050
  Organizations:
    - *TradeOrdererOrg
  ......
```

The orderer type (OrdererType) is specified as etcdraft, indicating that this profile defines a Raft orderer (as opposed to the FourOrgsTradeOrdererGenesis profile, which we have been using thus far). The orderer type to be used for the network is specified in the Orderer section as follows:

```
Orderer: &OrdererDefaults

  ......

  OrdererType: etcdraft
```

Lastly, the Organizations section has an augmented TradeOrdererOrg as follows:

```
Organizations:
  ......
  - &TradeOrdererOrg
    ......
    Name: TradeOrdererOrg
    ......
    ID: TradeOrdererOrgMSP
    ......
    OrdererEndpoints:
      - orderer.trade.com:7050
      - orderer2.trade.com:7050
      - orderer3.trade.com:7050
      - orderer4.trade.com:7050
      - orderer5.trade.com:7050
    ......
```

The endpoints of the orderer nodes in this organization correspond to those defined in the TradeMultiNodeEtcdRaft profile.

Turning to cryptographic configuration, our crypto-config.yaml in the bash/multiple_orderers folder defines four more ordering nodes than crypto-config.yaml in the bash folder. Each node in the orderer configuration corresponds to a node in our Raft cluster:

```
OrdererOrgs:
  ......
  - Name: TradeOrderer
    Domain: trade.com
    ......
    Specs:
      - Hostname: orderer
      - Hostname: orderer2
      - Hostname: orderer3
```

```
    - Hostname: orderer4
    - Hostname: orderer5
```

To employ our `trade.sh` script for Raft-based network building and launching, we must use an extra switch in the command: `-m prod`. This is the mode parameter, which by default (that is, if omitted) is set to `test`, indicating that a solo ordering service must be created and run. To generate crypto artifacts for our network and channel artifacts for `tradechannel`, run the following from the `bash` folder:

```
$ ./trade.sh generate -c tradechannel -o 3 -m prod
```

If you are running this on an existing configuration, the `crypto-config` folder will simply be augmented with credentials for the four new ordering nodes, leaving existing credentials intact. If you look into the `crypto-config/ ordererOrganizations/trade.com/orderers/` folder, you will see folders named `orderer2.trade.com`, `orderer3.trade.com`, `orderer4.trade.com`, and `orderer5. trade.com`, to accompany `orderer.trade.com`.

The contents of the `channel-artifacts` folder will be replaced though, and you will see a `genesis.block` (the orderer system channel genesis block) of a bigger size. `channel-artifacts/tradechannel` will be similar to what we created earlier in this book. To generate (or regenerate) artifacts for `shippingchannel`, run:

```
$ ./trade.sh generate -c shippingchannel -o 4 -m prod
```

We are ready to launch our new network now. For our network configuration, we will use the `bash/docker-compose-raft-orderer.yaml` compose file, which inherits the peers, CAs, and solo orderer configurations in `bash/docker-compose-e2e.yaml` (which is the file we have been using thus far). In addition, it specifies configurations for four more orderer nodes: `orderer2.trade.com`, `orderer3.trade.com`, `orderer4. trade.com`, and `orderer5.trade.com`. Each configuration is identical to that of our earlier solo orderer node, `orderer.trade.com`, except for the container names and service ports exposed. For example, the configuration of `orderer2.trade.com` is as follows:

```
orderer2.trade.com:
  container_name: orderer2.trade.com
  extends:
    file: base/peer-base.yaml
    service: orderer-base
  volumes:
  - ./channel-artifacts/genesis.block:/var/hyperledger/orderer/
  orderer.genesis.block
  - ./crypto-config/ordererOrganizations/trade.com/orderers/orderer2.
```

```
trade.com/msp:/var/hyperledger/orderer/ms
- ./crypto-config/ordererOrganizations/trade.com/orderers/
orderer2.trade.com/tls/:/var/hyperledger/orderer/tls
- orderer2.trade.com:/var/hyperledger/production/orderer
ports:
  - 8050:7050
networks:
  - trade
```

The orderer service within this container runs a service that listens on port 7050, which is mapped to 8050 on the host machine. Other orderers' ports are mapped to 9050, 10050, and 11050.

Run the following command to launch the network with a five-node Raft ordering service:

```
$ ./trade.sh up -m prod
```

If you run docker ps now, you will see something like the following:

CONTAINER ID	IMAGE	COMMAND	CREATED
STATUS	PORTS		NAMES
aefc5df276c7	hyperledger/fabric-peer:2.2.0	"peer node start"	10 seconds ago
Up 6 seconds	7051/tcp, 0.0.0.0:10051->10051/tcp		peer0.regulatororg.trade.com
8c8fa8eeed83	hyperledger/fabric-peer:2.2.0	"peer node start"	10 seconds ago
Up 7 seconds	7051/tcp, 0.0.0.0:8051->8051/tcp		peer0.importerorg.trade.com
79bc5415e610	hyperledger/fabric-peer:2.2.0	"peer node start"	12 seconds ago
Up 7 seconds	0.0.0.0:7051->7051/tcp		peer0.exporterorg.trade.com
1c74a63cb932	hyperledger/fabric-orderer:2.2.0	"orderer"	19 seconds ago
Up 10 seconds	0.0.0.0:10050->7050/tcp		orderer4.trade.com
2cac53944747	couchdb:2.3	"tini -- /docker-ent…"	19 seconds ago
Up 10 seconds	4369/tcp, 9100/tcp, 0.0.0.0:7984->5984/tcp		couchdb-peer0.regulatororg.trade.com
a920fe53f82c	couchdb:2.3	"tini -- /docker-ent…"	19 seconds ago
Up 10 seconds	4369/tcp, 9100/tcp, 0.0.0.0:6984->5984/tcp		couchdb-peer0.importerorg.trade.com
1738f3b1f01a	hyperledger/fabric-ca:1.4.8	"sh -c 'fabric-ca-se…"	19 seconds ago
Up 10 seconds	7054/tcp, 0.0.0.0:9054->9054/tcp		ca.carrierorg.trade.com
cb1937458e03	hyperledger/fabric-ca:1.4.8	"sh -c 'fabric-ca-se…"	19 seconds ago
Up 11 seconds	0.0.0.0:7054->7054/tcp		ca.exporterorg.trade.com
558b5dfcb9da	hyperledger/fabric-orderer:2.2.0	"orderer"	19 seconds ago
Up 11 seconds	0.0.0.0:11050->7050/tcp		orderer5.trade.com
e2cd619027d5	couchdb:2.3	"tini -- /docker-ent…"	19 seconds ago
Up 11 seconds	4369/tcp, 9100/tcp, 0.0.0.0:5984->5984/tcp		couchdb-peer0.exporterorg.trade.com
7f583450914e	hyperledger/fabric-orderer:2.2.0	"orderer"	19 seconds ago
Up 13 seconds	0.0.0.0:8050->7050/tcp		orderer2.trade.com
786932e1560d	hyperledger/fabric-orderer:2.2.0	"orderer"	19 seconds ago
Up 13 seconds	0.0.0.0:7050->7050/tcp		orderer.trade.com
c2cc365dba89	hyperledger/fabric-ca:1.4.8	"sh -c 'fabric-ca-se…"	20 seconds ago
Up 14 seconds	7054/tcp, 0.0.0.0:8054->8054/tcp		ca.importerorg.trade.com
8b809fa5a6c2	hyperledger/fabric-orderer:2.2.0	"orderer"	20 seconds ago
Up 15 seconds	0.0.0.0:9050->7050/tcp		orderer3.trade.com
97238ba1cfdc	hyperledger/fabric-peer:2.2.0	"peer node start"	20 seconds ago
Up 11 seconds	7051/tcp, 0.0.0.0:9051->9051/tcp		peer0.carrierorg.trade.com
8b9fcccbe777	hyperledger/fabric-ca:1.4.8	"sh -c 'fabric-ca-se…"	20 seconds ago
Up 12 seconds	7054/tcp, 0.0.0.0:10054->10054/tcp		ca.regulatororg.trade.com

Figure 9.43: List of running trade network containers with five nodes in a Raft ordering service cluster

A total of 16 containers will be running: four peer nodes, four CA nodes, three CouchDB instances, and five ordering nodes.

You can now repeat the steps described earlier in this chapter to set up channels, install contracts, run service applications, and exercise the applications using our `curl`-based scripts. None of those steps require any changes to work with the Raft ordering service, which lies underneath the application and produces blocks using a different mechanism than the solo ordering service did.

Summary of key steps

As a reference to our readers, we list the sequence of operations that must be performed to bring up a network and distributed application from scratch and run transactions on it. We supply shortcut commands using the Bash scripts in `trade-network` wherever applicable. You should choose the ordering service type in the beginning and run all commands in the appropriate mode:

1. Create cryptographic and channel artifacts (the -m switch is optional):

```
$ ./trade.sh generate -c tradechannel -o 3 [-m prod]
$ ./trade.sh generate -c shippingchannel -o 4 [-m prod]
```

2. Launch the network:

```
$ ./trade.sh up [-m prod]
```

3. Create channels, join peers to channels, and set anchor peers for organizations:

```
$ ./startAndJoinChannels.sh
```

4. Install and initialize contracts. You can do this manually using VS Code or by running the following shortcut command:

```
$ ./sampleChaincodeOperations.sh
```

5. Create a `wallets` folder in the `trade-network` root. Create `exporterorg`, `importerorg`, `carrierorg`, and `regulatororg` subfolders within `wallets`.

6. Create a `gateways` folder in the `trade-network` root. Create `exporterorg`, `importerorg`, `carrierorg`, and `regulatororg` subfolders within `gateways`.

7. Create a connection profile named `connection.json` in each subfolder under `gateways`. You can do this by exporting a connection profile from the trade network environment in the IBP extension in VS Code and fixing its attributes using:

```
$ cd bash/utils
```

```
$ node manage-connection-profile.js --update <vscode-exported-
connection-profile> ../../gateways/<org-name>/connection.json
<org-ca-name>
```

Or you can generate all four profiles using a single command:

```
$ cd bash/utils
$ ./generateAllProfiles.sh
```

8. Launch the four service applications in the apps folder (exporter, importer, carrier, and regulator) according to instructions given earlier. To automate these launches, refer to the integration testing steps described in *Chapter 11, Agility in a Blockchain Network*.

9. Run scripts in the apps/sample-cli-curl/ folder to register new identities and run trade operations.

This completes the sequence of operations to bring up a network and application and populate the ledger with data.

You can perform the following cleanup operations as well, should you choose to:

- To bring down a running network and delete all ledger data, run:

```
$ ./trade.sh down [-m prod]
```

If you wish to retain ledger data (channel and contract states), add the -r switch to the preceding command.

- To delete dynamically created identities and credentials (you must do this if you run trade.sh down without retaining ledger data) and delete Docker images created for the contracts, run:

```
$ ./trade.sh reset
```

- To delete identities, contract images, and channel artifacts, run:

```
$ ./trade.sh clean
```

- To delete identities, contract images, channel artifacts, and cryptographic artifacts, run:

```
$ ./trade.sh cleanall
```

The preceding command will ensure that you can start from scratch if you wish to rebuild a network.

Summary

Building a complete blockchain application is an ambitious and challenging project, not just because of the range of skills it requires — systems, networking, security, and web application development, to name a few — but because it requires concerted development, testing, and deployment by multiple organizations spanning multiple security domains.

In this chapter, we built a distributed application over a Fabric network using our trade scenario as a practical development guide. We began with a barebones four-organization network and four smart contracts and ended with a distributed application and the ability to orchestrate an entire trade workflow by six independent personas spanning four organizations. The attributes of trade- and finance-related artifacts and the history of these workflows were recorded in a pair of tamper-resistant, shared, replicated ledgers. In the process, we learned how to build and operate multiple channels, and selectively join certain organizations' peers to each channel. Further, we learned how to install and initialize smart contracts on subsets of the peer network with custom endorsement policies. Once the smart contracts were ready to be exercised using well-defined APIs, we learned how to expose their capabilities in differentiated ways to different organizations' members using REST APIs.

We learned how an end user application typically follows a three-layer pattern, with the bottom layer acting on common network databases, whereas service and presentation layers above serve subgroups of the network and also act as integration points with traditional enterprise systems. And we saw how the new Fabric Gateway API provides wallet capabilities and makes application development simple by abstracting away the complexity of the transaction pipeline.

We ended the chapter by demonstrating how to build a production-grade ordering service consisting of a cluster of nodes running the Raft protocol in a decentralized manner.

The Hyperledger platforms and tools will, no doubt, evolve over time to serve industry and developer needs, but the architecture and methodology we described in our application-building exercise should continue to serve as an educational guide in the long term. Our journey so far has taken us to the foundation of the Hyperledger Fabric framework. We have worked with channels and contracts and integrated applications using the Fabric Gateway SDK API. These are essential skills.

In the next chapter, we will learn about various design patterns and best practices that can be used to build industry-scale blockchain applications.

10
Enterprise Design Patterns and Considerations

By now, you know how to build a distributed application over a Fabric business network. But building and deploying a production-quality enterprise system requires a developer to be cognizant of other practical considerations. We delved into one such consideration in *Chapter 9, Network Operation and Distributed Application Building,* by demonstrating how our network could use a Raft-based ordering service for better fault tolerance. In this chapter, we will discuss topics such as service design patterns, reliability, and other common engineering concerns. Although these concerns apply to every distributed application, we will discuss the special needs and issues that arise in blockchain-based (and particularly Fabric-based) applications. Our target is an experienced enterprise developer who can apply this knowledge to design distributed blockchain applications and integrate them with existing systems and processes.

When discussing end-to-end solutions with customers, we often explain that blockchain-related components represent a very small percentage of the overall footprint. This is still a very important set of components, but nonetheless they represent a small footprint. As we discussed in *Chapter 9, Network Operation and Distributed Application Building,* service-layer applications represent the integration points between enterprise systems (legacy or otherwise) and blockchain. In **trade-network** service apps, we have implemented a minimal set of integration capabilities. A production application could be an extension of our project with more business logic wrapped around these capabilities, or it could be a separate system that relies on the REST APIs exposed by the service apps. Either way, there is more to building and deploying a full enterprise system than what we demonstrated in the previous chapter.

This chapter will focus on the touch points between our traditional systems and the Hyperledger Fabric API. The service-layer applications we demonstrated earlier represent integration points between enterprise systems (legacy or otherwise) and blockchain. A production application could be built using standard software design patterns with business logic wrapped around the blockchain components, or it could be a separate system that relies on the REST APIs exposed by the service apps. We will explore various patterns of integration that can be leveraged and see how some non-functional requirements can influence the integration deployment. Finally, we will explore some additional considerations that integrators will need to keep in mind when designing their integration layer.

In this chapter, you will:

- Understand the design considerations of the integration layer
- Review the integration design patterns
- Explore the impact of application-independent requirements on system building and integration

Design considerations

By now, you have experience with the Fabric SDK which service applications can use to connect to a Fabric peer network and invoke contracts. While this is certainly the main tool of the trade when it comes to integration, it is part of an ecosystem, and there needs to be an alignment of the business processes of the enterprise to make sure the integration makes sense.

There are various considerations for integration design, and we will look at the following:

- The impact of decentralization
- Process alignment
- Message affinity
- Service discovery
- Identity mapping

Managing heterogeneity

Many attempts have been made to standardize IT functions and capabilities, but the reality is that no two organizations have the same IT landscape. Even for those who have selected the same ERP vendor, the systems will have been customized for the organization's processes and to meet its needs.

This means that, when planning your integration design, you should keep in mind that each organization in a blockchain network consortium may have its own way of invoking smart contracts and may have different IT capabilities and policies from other organizations.

As an example, exposing events through WebSockets (`https://tools.ietf.org/html/rfc6455`) may make sense for an organization that is familiar with cloud-based technologies, but other organizations may not have the skills, or their IT security policies may not allow them to use the protocol.

While it may seem surprising to some, keep in mind that a network can be a mix of Fortune 500 organizations and start-ups. Consider the supply-chain industry for a moment; you will find some trucking companies with little to no IT infrastructure, all the way to industry behemoths. Clearly, one size may not fit all.

Having said that, from a network perspective, you should consider the degree of support the network wants to provide to joining organizations. There are two possible approaches:

- **The network provides an integration asset**: This can take the form of a gateway that each participant deploys in their own infrastructure. The gateway is standard for everyone and manages the invocation of the smart contracts in a consistent manner. (The simplification of contract invocations using the gateway pattern in Fabric 2 was meant to boost standardization.) This can provide the benefit of accelerating the on-boarding process, but requires consideration about who owns, manages, and supports this IT component. Furthermore, some organizations may not want to deploy this piece of infrastructure due to trust issues.

- **Each participant builds their own integration layer**: The obvious downside of this approach is the reinvention of the wheel by all participants, but it reduces the potential support issues created by deploying a common component in every organization. This may also be the preferred approach for use cases requiring deep system integration to achieve the benefit of process optimizations.

Process alignment

The integration layer will have to deal with two different viewpoints:

- **Organization IT system and business process viewpoint**: An organization's business process may be hosted in an ERP such as SAP. In such a situation, when a specific business event warrants the invocation of a smart contract, this may be issued through a **Business API (BAPI)** call from the SAP system. The API call from the ERP may contain a variety of data structures, some of which will be completely irrelevant to the blockchain network.

- **Smart contract viewpoint**: This viewpoint has the particularity of having a data representation that is application- and organization-agnostic. This means that all participants of the network will understand the nature of the data being processed.

Thus, there is both organization-specific process and data and common network process (that is, contracts) and data. It is up to the integration layer to reconcile the two viewpoints (and process and datasets) and ensure that proper semantics of a transaction is maintained in both systems. This may imply:

- **Mapping**: Moving data from one field name to another
- **Transformation**: Aggregating, splitting, or computing a new value based on input
- **Cross-referencing**: Leveraging a reference table to map application-specific codes to values recognized by the network

In addition, the integration layer must orchestrate transactions that act on both in-organization and common network data in a way that ensures the integrity of business process and data.

The point here is that even if your network agrees to use the Hyperledger Fabric gateway demonstrated in *Chapter 9, Network Operation and Distributed Application Building*, there is still work that needs to be done by each participant to ensure that the integration fits into the overall business processes of the organization.

Message affinity

This is an issue that impacts any application that must handle multiple concurrent requests from independent clients. While this is not strictly a blockchain integration concern, ignoring it can lead to serious issues that will typically surface during integration or performance testing.

We refer to message affinity as a situation that occurs when a system issues a series of inter-dependent transactions, which are issued in a short period of time. Because each transaction is issued separately, they are subject to being processed in a different order than when they are issued by the client. The result may be unpredictable, as the following example shows. To make it concrete, let's look at an **Order** process that would issue three separate transactions, as shown in the following diagram:

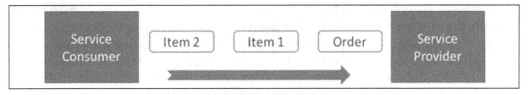

Figure 10.1: Processing service requests in order

Because the **service provider** is multi-threaded, the order of processing can vary depending on the load at the time. A potential result is illustrated in the following diagram:

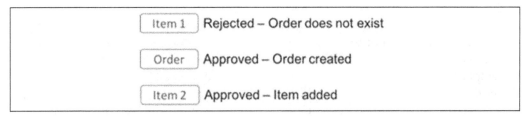

Figure 10.2: Potential service processing result

The first item being processed out of order would be rejected because the order object hasn't been created yet. However, the two subsequent objects would succeed and leave the system in a state where the order is recorded as having a single item instead of two.

The challenge with this situation is that it is hard to troubleshoot. An unaware developer may not be able to reproduce this behavior on their development platform.

Now, you may be wondering, how does this relate to blockchain and Hyperledger Fabric? Considering that Fabric transactions are asynchronously processed by multiple components in a pipeline (endorsing peers followed by ordering nodes followed by committing peers) and that they are validated against every world state, this situation can arise quite frequently. In one scenario, the client will issue the transaction and may asynchronously receive a message saying that the transaction was invalid because it did not correspond to the world state. In another scenario, two clients belonging to separate organizations may be contending for a common data element. Only one will succeed because the ordering service imposes a sequence among transactions and committing nodes process transaction sequences in deterministic ways. Finally, the "losing" client will asynchronously receive a transaction failure message.

There are two lessons one can learn from this. One is that an API should be designed at business event-level granularity. Too many fine-grained transactions only lead to high message affinity, increased latency, and the potential for integrity issues, as described here. The second is more relevant to the integration layer, which is responsible for transaction orchestration. Logic can be written in this layer to monitor ledger state, track transaction failures, and perform remedial actions to ensure business process integrity.

Service discovery

In the first edition of this book, we described service discovery for a Fabric network's peers, CAs, and orderers as a pressing need for any developer, and that providing this capability was part of the Hyperledger Fabric roadmap. Since then, this feature has been added to the Fabric SDK in a way that makes it extremely simple for any developer to use. As we demonstrated in *Chapter 9, Network Operation and Distributed Application Building,* the gateway API in Fabric 2 supports the enabling or disabling of service discovery using a Boolean flag. Enabling it avoids all the complexity around collecting endorsements for a transaction from multiple peers, validating and matching the responses, and creating a transaction envelope to send to the ordering service. The developer need not even know the endorsement policy, whereas in the earlier versions of Fabric 1, they would have to know the policy and the complete network topology. Just having a minimal **dynamic** connection profile is enough in Fabric 2, and the application code and runtime can remain unchanged in the face of network topology changes.

To conclude, service discovery was an integration layer concern in earlier versions of Fabric but is not anymore unless the developer chooses to make it so. Fabric does still offer the ability to perform lower-level orchestration of transaction stages. But given that it offers a robust transaction processing subsystem and an API that masks that subsystem's complexity, integration developers are strongly encouraged to use the gateway API.

Identity mapping

Identity mapping is the process of converting the identity of an individual or an organization to an identity that is recognized on the network. We demonstrated how to do this in our trade network's service applications in *Chapter 9, Network Operation and Distributed Application Building*, and here we will discuss why it is important, even crucial, for businesses participating in a network.

When looking at the solution from a business network perspective, what is the granularity of the identity that needs to be recognized? Will other organizations care whether Bob or Ann from ACME issued a transaction? In most cases, the answer will be no. Knowing that the transaction was issued by ACME will be sufficient.

Why is that, you may wonder? It is directly related to the concept of trust. Remember the concepts presented in *Chapter 1, Blockchain – An Enterprise and Industry Perspective*; blockchain solves the problem of time and trust. Understanding where the trust issues come from helps us rationalize what identities should be used to transact on the network. In most cases, our experience has been that trust issues occur between organizations.

If you think about a use case where a bank customer transacts through their bank portal, the customer will not care about the backend systems; they trust their bank's security system.

Having said that, there are situations where an identity will need to be mapped:

- Business partners transacting through the integration layer of the organization
- Different departments with varying levels of privilege
- Users with different roles that drive different access privileges

In this case, the integration layer will need to convert the inbound credentials (API key, user ID and password, JWT token, and so on) into a Hyperledger Fabric identity.

As we demonstrated with the Fabric Gateway and Wallet APIs, you can configure the service (or integration) layer to support multiple users. The server leverages the wallet framework to manage this authentication. This provides the flexibility of supporting different models (for example, user ID/password, JWT, and OAUTH).

Once the client is authenticated to the server, there is an additional step that consists of loading the Fabric wallet identity into the server's user repository. There needs to be implicit trust between the client and the server, as the wallet identity contains the private key and the server itself acts as a client (on behalf of Ann or Bob) with respect to the Fabric network.

The takeaway for you is that an organization's clients are trusted by the network (that is, by other organizations) only by virtue of getting credentialled by that organization. In effect, they **borrow** trust from the organization. The network may mandate different access rules for different users, like we have demonstrated in our smart contracts. But determining which end user gets what privileges (implemented through certificate attributes in Fabric) is left to the organization. On the flipside, an organization's clients completely trust it to act as a proxy between them and the blockchain.

Integration design patterns

We will now look at some of the viable integration patterns we have seen in the industry. The list is by no means exhaustive, and even though we have deployed and validated many Hyperledger Fabric solutions, we expect that new patterns will emerge as people and organizations become more comfortable with the technology.

In this section, we consider organizations' preexisting enterprise systems that predate their joining of the network. These systems have their own concepts and paradigms, and we will require a form of abstraction to reconcile the two worlds.

Integrating with an existing system of record

Following is a diagram to illustrate the integration of a blockchain network with an existing system of record:

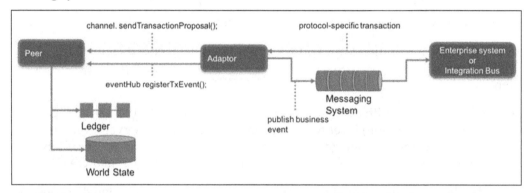

Figure 10.3: Integrating the blockchain network with an existing system of record

Most large enterprises looking at joining a business network will eventually aim at integrating their system of record to make sure that they benefit from the real-time transparent distribution of transactions. In these circumstances, the process alignment we previously mentioned will be tremendously important.

As depicted in the preceding diagram, the approach will consist of leveraging an adaptor pattern to act as a data mapper between the two worlds. The adaptor will adopt the enterprise system application protocol and data structure to receive transaction requests. Optionally, it can also leverage existing foundations such as messaging services to propagate responses from gateways, including ledger events.

The important thing to note here is that this type of integration will be specific to an organization, and very little reuse will be possible.

As a variant of this pattern, some organizations will break the adaptor into two parts:

- **REST gateway**: Exposing a REST interface that exposes Fabric smart contract capabilities. This interface may be aligned with the smart contract API, or it could offer functions at larger granularities.
- **Integration bus**: Mapping the fields and connecting the enterprise systems.

While in this variant reuse is higher, the same considerations only get moved one layer down.

Integrating with an operational data store for blockchain analytics

Here is a diagram that illustrates the integration of the blockchain network with an operational data store:

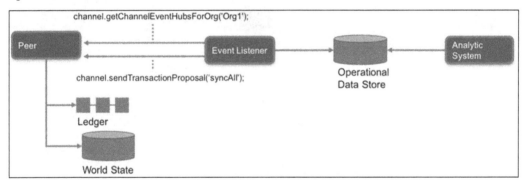

Figure 10.4: Integrating the blockchain network with an operational data store

Often, organizations are looking at ways of running analytics on the information from their ledgers. However, issuing multiple/large queries against the organization's peers will only impact the online performance of the system. Generally, the recognized approach in enterprise system design is to move the data to an operational data store. The data can then be easily queried. Additional views on the data can be created by enriching the data using different data sources.

In this pattern, the event listener subscribes to the Fabric organization events. As such, it can receive transactions from all channels the organization is entitled to. If the preservation of the data's integrity is important, the event listener can calculate a hash of every record and store them alongside the records. (The preceding diagram presents a general blockchain transaction pattern that is asynchronous and communicates results through events. In Hyperledger Fabric 2, as we have seen, the asynchronicity can be masked by the gateway, which can be substituted for the Event Listener in the diagram.)

You will notice that the pattern also accounts for a syncAll function that would allow the event listener (or gateway) to re-synchronize the data store with the latest view of the world state. Keep in mind that the implementation of this syncAll function will need to be done carefully and will most likely require that the function supports the pagination of the result sets.

Microservice and event-driven architecture

The following diagram illustrates microservice and event-driven architecture for a blockchain application. You may recognize its similarity to the architecture of our distributed trade application that was presented in *Chapter 9, Network Operation and Distributed Application Building*:

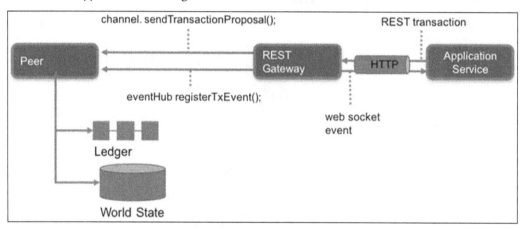

Figure 10.5: Microservice and event-driven architecture for a blockchain application

We've labeled this as microservice and event-driven because these are the patterns most often seen in those types of architectures. Microservices are small services performing minimal functions that typically cannot be decomposed any further. An event-driven architecture is one where system components notify each other about state changes; coupled with a microservice architecture, this avoids the need for a hard-to-maintain common store or a wasteful polling mechanism.

However, the particularity of these patterns in a blockchain application comes from the gateway. Such a system will not perform any data mapping; it will leverage a common communication protocol (HTTP) and data format (typically JSON, but it could be XML). There is also an expectation that the services will already be designed to understand the semantics of the data being transacted. Events are also propagated through the same protocol and data format.

Again, microservice applications tend to be newer applications, and they benefit from a more fine-grained interface. As such, they tend to evolve more quickly and be in positions to adapt and adhere to the transactions from the network. Similarly, event-driven applications will benefit from their low coupling to the other components of the system, and so are good candidates for this pattern.

Resiliency and fault tolerance

In the concluding part of this chapter, we will move our focus from application design to network operation.

The failure of software or hardware components is a fact of life for any industrial application, so you must design your application network to tolerate failures and minimize downtime. We will discuss three key guidelines that are widely used in the industry to build and maintain systems, and briefly examine how they apply to an application built using Hyperledger Fabric tools. Though these guidelines ought to be kept in mind when designing any software system, our focus will primarily be on Fabric network design and operation. Integration-layer applications also ought to be robust and scalable, but the process to build and maintain these is well-known in the IT industry. Operational concerns involved in setting up ledgers and deploying contracts, on the other hand, are peculiar to blockchain solutions and deserve more attention.

Reliability and availability

A **reliable** system is one that runs for as long as possible without failing. Further, it ensures correct operation in the face of failure, thereby making the system **fault tolerant**. This entails the following things:

- Comprehensive unit and integration testing prior to deployment
- Continuous self-monitoring of the system
- Detection of failure or corruption in a component
- Fixing the problem and/or failing over to a working component

The **availability** criterion is closely related to reliability, but it is more about ensuring system uptime with high probability, or as a corollary, minimizing the probability of system downtime. This entails the following things:

- Determination of a desired availability level (typically a percentage)
- Allocating an adequate number of redundant or self-correcting resources
- Testing, monitoring, and resource reallocations in production environments

Reliability and availability require similar preparations and remedial actions. Although various practices have evolved in industry, common (or even universal) techniques are:

- Ensuring adequate redundancy for components
- The detection of failed components
- Timely failover

These are the keys to ensuring that your application will remain operational, even when one or more components fails.

Let's apply these guidelines and mechanisms to a Fabric network of the kind we have built for trade. Recall that Fabric has many different components that must work in concert (though in a loosely coupled manner) to ensure successful operation. The ordering service is one such key component that would completely stall the transaction pipeline were it to fail. Therefore, when building a production version of, say, our trade application, you must ensure that the orderer has enough redundancy built in. In practice, this means ensuring that there are enough nodes in the Raft cluster to take up the slack should one or more fail.

Similarly, the reliability of peers for endorsement and commitment is key to ensuring transaction integrity. Although blockchains, being shared replicated ledgers, are designed to be somewhat robust to peer failures, their vulnerabilities may vary depending on the application and configured policy. If an endorsing peer fails, and if its signature is necessary to satisfy the transaction endorsement policy, transaction requests cannot proceed beyond the endorsement stage. If an endorsing peer misbehaves and produces incorrect execution results, the transaction may reach the end of the pipeline but will then fail validation at the commitment stage. Either kind of failure will reduce system throughput or make the system fail altogether. To prevent this from happening, you should ensure that there are enough redundant peers within each organization, especially the ones that are key to satisfying an endorsement policy. The following diagram illustrates a possible mechanism whereby transaction proposals are made to multiple peers, and absent or incorrect responses are discarded using a majority rule:

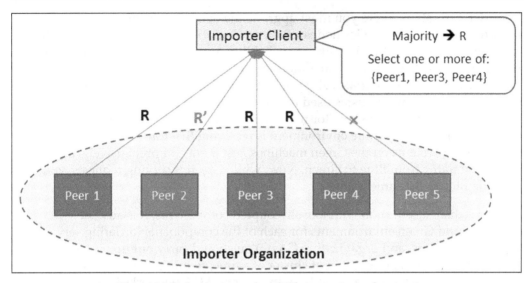

Figure 10.6: Redundant peers for reliable transaction endorsement

The level of reliability one gets from a system depends on the amount of resources devoted to monitoring and failover. For example, five peers in the preceding diagram are enough to counter two peer failures, but this now requires four more peers in the organization than what we used in our example network. To determine and ensure that your network provides the expected level of reliability and availability, you will need to run periodic integration tests on your complete system and adjust redundancy levels dynamically.

The application developer does not need to know or worry about peer or orderer network reliability and availability, other than to program safeguards in the application against catastrophic failure (for example, all network peers crashing simultaneously, which is a low-probability event). Ensuring redundancy and failover is the network operator's concern, and thanks to Hyperledger Fabric features such as service discovery, network structure can arbitrarily change with no impact on higher-layer application behavior.

Serviceability

Serviceability or **maintainability** is the ease with which you can replace or upgrade parts of your system without impacting the system as a whole.

Consider a situation where you must upgrade the operating system on one or more of your ordering service nodes, or if you need to replace a faulty peer within an organization. As with reliability or availability, having redundant (or parallel) resources to which application operations can be switched seamlessly is the way to handle this in an industrial-scale system. So-called Blue-Green deployment is one of the popular mechanisms used for this purpose. In a nutshell, you have two parallel environments (let's say, for the ordering service), one called Blue and one called Green, where the Blue environment is receiving live traffic. You can upgrade the operating systems on the Green machines, test them comprehensively, and then switch the traffic from Blue to Green. Now, while Green is serving requests, you can upgrade Blue in the same manner.

In a blockchain application with loosely coupled components, it is advisable to have Blue and Green environments for each of the components (ordering service, organization peers, and organization CAs). You should carry out upgrades and testing in stages, or one component cluster at a time, to minimize the chances of a mishap. For example, you can keep the peer and CA networks intact while upgrading an ordering service, which has some nodes belonging to a Blue Raft cluster and others to a Green Raft cluster. Once the upgrade is complete and verified, you can upgrade the peers and the CAs if required.

Summary

In this chapter, following on from the application-building exercise in the previous chapter, we learned about various design patterns and best practices that can be used to build industry-scale blockchain applications. We also learned about the considerations to keep in mind while building robust Hyperledger Fabric networks and integrating applications built on this technology with existing systems and processes. The Hyperledger platform offers basic capabilities to build fault-tolerant networks and applications using configuration files. We have provided an understanding of what kinds of configurations will be useful in an enterprise scenario, and it is up the developer to create suitable configurations for any given enterprise solution using Fabric tools. The design and integration patterns we have described in this chapter should serve as an educational guide in the long term regardless of how Fabric and equivalent blockchain technologies evolve.

In the next chapter, we will learn how to maintain a network and its code base in an agile manner. This topic also ties to *Chapter 13*, *Life in a Blockchain Network*, which addresses the evolution of a network during its life cycle.

11
Agility in a Blockchain Network

At this point, if all went well, you should have a fully functional decentralized application, with the associated smart contracts running on Hyperledger Fabric. With this knowledge in hand, life is going to be good, right? Well, like anything, solutions evolve. It could be a change in regulations, the introduction of a new member in the consortium, or a simple bug in your smart contract—whatever the cause, the solution will grow. Without robust development and operational practices, changes will be slow, and your life will be painful.

Considering that maintaining agility in the development processes of an IT organization is already very challenging, how can it be done in a consortium? How can companies of various cultures with different velocities come together, to deliver and maintain the solution in a time frame that allows them to keep the competitive edge that the network provides?

While a lot has been written on IT agility and DevOps, this chapter will focus on applying these concepts to a blockchain solution. Our attention will be on those DevOps concepts that are specific to blockchains. Through automation and the deployment of a **continuous integration** (CI) and **continuous delivery** (CD) pipeline, we will discuss the impact that a blockchain network has on the people, the process, and the technology.

In this chapter, we will cover the following topics:

- Defining the promotion process
- Configuring the CI pipeline
- Protecting the source control
- Extending the pipeline to include CD
- Keeping the network up to date
- The implication of the consortium on team structures

Defining the promotion process

As you may already be aware, the promotion process represents the essential set of activities and gates that any system modification will need to go through. It typically encompasses the development, packaging, testing (for example, unit testing, functional verification, and integration testing), versioning, and deployment. Usually, an organization will have a standardized approach that will document what is expected from the project and its support teams.

In the case of a Hyperledger Fabric network, two different types of components may have different life cycles (evolve at different rates) and thus follow different promotion processes:

- **Smart contracts**: As these components set the rules of the network and guide the business interactions, they require additional scrutiny and validation. Governance of the network will typically dictate how often new versions will be published.

- **Integration layer**: The integration layer translates requests from systems of records or user interfaces to smart contract invocation. Frequently, consortiums will provide this layer and the associated user interfaces as a way to accelerate the onboarding of new organizations to the network. However, an organization may prefer to integrate the blockchain network directly to their system of records, in which case they will own the integration. Understanding these two models will allow us to define a promotion process aligned with the business reality of the network and its members.

Also, consider that the change control process could expand to cover the policies of the network. For example, the endorsement and private data collections are closely aligned to the smart contract, so modifying the endorsement policy to add a new member will require updating the smart contract's deployment.

Before jumping straight into the configuration of the pipeline, let's spend a bit of time understanding the particularities of each application layer in relation to the major phase of the deployment process.

Aligning the promotion process to components

As we already highlighted, the nature of a component and its role in the solution defines its life cycle in the solution. It directly impacts how we define the promotion process. These impacts can range from additional validation requirements during testing to different packaging and distribution approaches. However, to get to more specific aspects, we will break down the process into two major sets of activities:

- **Continuous integration** (CI): The activities aimed at ensuring our components meet a level of quality and reliability, and that they can function together to support the goal of the system/network.
- **Continuous delivery** (CD): A set of activities specific to the deployment of our solution in the various organization environments.

For each of these phases of the promotion process, let's have a look at the considerations for the smart contracts and the integration layer.

Smart contract considerations

As we've already mentioned, smart contracts are vital to business interaction between the participants of any blockchain network. Since they contain the rules and conditions under which a transaction is deemed valid, we need to ensure that every participant and organization agrees to its validity. Otherwise, this trust will be compromised.

From a CI perspective, considerations for the smart contract would include the following:

- **Traceability of an issue**: Is this a bug fix or a new feature? Along with this element, there might be a need for organizations to approve the issue before it moves to implementation.
- **Successful execution of all tests**: This may be self-evident for some, but most tests should be automated, and the results captured.
- **Code review from key parties**: Would you sign a contract without reviewing its terms and conditions? Well, the code review serves a similar purpose.

- **Impact assessment**: Is the new version of the smart contract backward compatible? Changes that are not backward compatible will require additional planning.

- **Sign-off from key parties**: Preceding all the other points, do you have the blessing of all relevant parties? Where will you record this?

The definition of *key parties* will be something that will be left for the consortium to define. Key parties could be all organizations that currently use that smart contract, or perhaps the term could refer to a subset of technical leads or members of the founder organization.

From a CI perspective, the considerations would include things like:

- **Chaincode distribution**: It is important to realize that smart contracts may be scoped by various subsets of participants of the network. When defining a channel with participants, the smart contract will not be visible to the rest of the network members who are not members of the channel. Before it can be committed to the ledger, the chaincode needs to be distributed, installed, and approved. How will this be done safely?

- **Deployment frequencies**: Promotion frequency can be contentious. Some organizations are used to quarterly cycles, while others are comfortable with weekly deployments. The rate of promotion can have a direct impact on the operational expense of an organization since it can require the mobilization of many specialists. Thus, friction is bound to occur if such factors are not discussed initially.

- **Version management**: The scoping of these smart contracts and various permutations and combinations represent a challenging problem: how do we track what is deployed where?

- **Fallback process**: The deployment of chaincode is pretty much an all or nothing activity, meaning that each organization can only run a single version of the contract. Techniques like blue/green or canary deployment are not possible with smart contracts. This removes the ability to gradually deploy a new version and increase the need to carefully consider the fallback process in case of issues.

The point is that the conditions and process of modifying a smart contract should be defined upfront by the consortium, to avoid any misunderstandings and frustration. In a sense, this is no different than a traditional contract being modified; the terms for the conditions of a contract modification need to be agreed on upfront to avoid conflicts.

Integration layer considerations

As we have seen in *Chapter 9*, *Network Operation and Distributed Application-Building*, there are a few patterns that an organization and a consortium can use to invoke transactions on the network. The selected pattern will help drive the management of the promotion process. If the service layer of an application directly invokes the Fabric SDK, then the owner of the system will have to manage its promotion process. If, instead, the consortium imposes the use of a REST gateway, then you can expect that its deployment will follow a process like the one for a smart contract.

No matter the owner of the integration component, the abstraction provided by the integration layer should isolate the application from the smart contract, and as such, it would be expected that they evolve independently. Updating the smart contract should not automatically mean that we need to redeploy the integration layer. Vice versa, it should be possible to modify an integration layer without worrying about the smart contract. It is possible to achieve such an approach if proper tests and controls are in place to detect compatibility issues.

That is not to say that impact assessments are not always required. Keep in mind that the integration layer represents the boundary between the organization and the network. Any change should be assessed to understand its extent and the risk it creates for the organization and the network.

From a CI perspective, the integration layer shares a lot of the considerations presented in the *Smart contract considerations* section. However, it also adds:

- **The need for contract testing**: Contract testing focuses on the interactions between a service consumer and a service provider. It ensures that changes to the contract (that is, the interface) are identified early. As such, it does not require the full solution to be deployed and instead relies on mocked components. By identifying breakage of contracts early on, we avoid runtime issues after deployment.

- **End-to-end process validation**: Business networks rely on blockchain to support and gain visibility of key business processes. As such, it is important to not only run through unit testing but also consider the end-to-end process. There should be provisioning to automate the full process.

From a CI perspective, there are additional capabilities that can be leveraged to ensure the effective deployment of integration layers:

- **Identity management**: How and when are Hyperledger Fabric identities provisioned for your integration layer? Understanding what responsibility is placed on the deployment of your integration layer is important. Should every upgrade of your services also automate the renewal of certificates, or should a separate process manage it?

- **Semantic versioning**: With a proper deployment strategy, you could rely on semantic versioning (https://semver.org/) to adopt a different deployment strategy, depending on whether it is a patch or a minor or a major update.

- **Deployment strategy**: In line with the semantic versioning consideration, the integration layer tends to be stateless, and that characteristic provides us with the flexibility to deploy those services in various fashions, supporting concepts like blue/green deployments, A/B testing, and canary releases.

Continuous integration

This section focuses purely on the definition and configuration of the CI pipeline. We will start by defining a process that aligns with our trade network and take you through the steps to configure your Git client and repository, as well as the Travis pipeline.

Promotion process overview

With these concepts defined, let's turn our attention to the promotion process of our application. As we are using Git as our software configuration management tool, we will leverage its social coding features to support our promotion process:

1. We can use Git issues to record new features or bug fixes
2. We can use Git branches to isolate proposed modifications
3. Git GPG is used to sign every commit and tag
4. Pull requests are used to enforce governance

The following diagram summarizes the process we will use to configure our application:

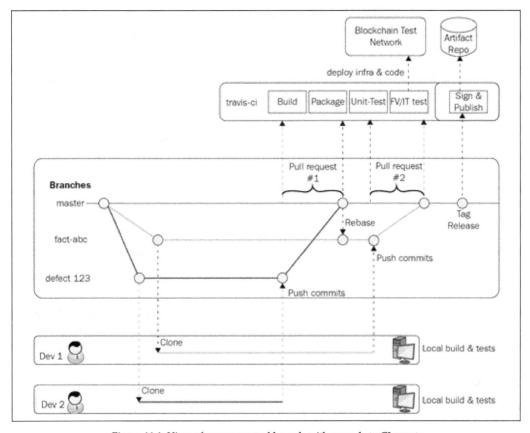

Figure 11.1: View of source control branch with regards to CI events

Wondering what a pull request is?

This chapter assumes that you are already familiar with many Git concepts. If this is not the case, it might be a good idea to pause and explore what Git has to offer.

As a quick summary, a pull request is a process by which people can submit code changes between forks (that is, different repositories) or branches (within a repository). It provides a controlled way to review, comment on, and ultimately approve all code changes.

Let's look at the process in detail and focus on the issue of trust and the provenance of the code. Since smart contracts are at the heart of blockchain networks, we need to ensure that we carefully track their evolution to avoid unfortunate events. From that perspective, we will want to have traceability from the requirements (Git issues) all the way to the deployment.

As such, every code modification should start with the creation of a Git issue. It should adequately identify what its scope is — feature request or bug fix — and then describe what work is expected.

We will cover the governance aspect in a few chapters, but for now, we can assume that the issue will have been prioritized so that we can assign work according to the consortium's priority.

Once the developer is assigned to work on the issue, their first step will be to create a temporary Git branch (feature branch) to track all code changes related to this Git issue. Code modification should never be done on the master branch as it represents the stable version of the code, and new features and bug fixes should be reviewed before their integration into the stable stream.

We expect that developers will run all the appropriate tests within their local environments and only commit back to the branch when the code is ready, and all the unit tests complete successfully.

When the time comes to commit the changes, Git provides a feature that allows you to sign all your work using **GPG**. What is GPG, you ask? It stands for **GNU Privacy Guard**, and it is an open implementation of the OpenPGP standard. It provides a tool that helps you sign and encrypt data using your private key. Git has implemented GPG to allow developers to sign their work. Each commit or tag can be signed using the GPG key of the author, thereby providing nonrepudiation of commits.

Why sign code modifications using GPG? It can be perceived as overhead and more complex since you need to have additional components and need to make a private key. However, consider that the code being modified represents a legal contract and is at the root of the trust of the network. From this point of view, it might be desirable to ensure that the identities of the authors of the code are proven beyond a doubt.

Using single-factor authentication for commits may not be sufficient to prove their authorship; consider all the reports on the internet of people spoofing the identities of others.

Without signed commits, we can imagine a situation where a rogue developer modifies a smart contract for their benefit, and gets away with it by claiming they were not the real author of the code change. Such an event would jeopardize the viability of the network and far outweigh the inconvenience of signing commits.

Now that the developer has signed the commits, they are ready to submit a pull request.

The pull request has been configured to check the following criteria:

- The temporary branch is up to date with the content from the master
- Every commit is signed
- The code owners have reviewed and accepted the code changes
- The CI pipeline has completed

The pipeline will be automatically triggered when the pull request is created. Once all the conditions are met, then one of the code owners may merge the code with the master branch and commit those changes (while signing the commit, of course).

In a real-life scenario, the consortium would have other environments (user acceptance environment, staging environment, and so on) where the complete solution stack would be tested.

The final step described in the diagram focuses on tagging the release. The idea here is that a single release may be built from a series of multiple pull requests. When the consortium is ready to release a new version, it should tag it to represent the official version.

It is on this event that the pipeline will be triggered again, but with a different objective; that is, to build, test, sign, and publish the smart contract to an artifact repository. This artifact repository could be one of many popular solutions out there, but in our case, for simplicity's sake, we will attach the smart contract to a Git release.

You may be wondering why we are not deploying directly on the network nodes. The intent is to maintain a clear delineation between the centralized build process and the decentralized nature of the network. Each organization can be notified of the new smart contract to deploy, pull the archive, validate it against the signature, and finally deploy it using their continuous deployment pipeline.

In summary, here are a few points on the promotion process:

- Every code change is tied to a change request
- Developers sign their modification using GPG
- The pull request process preserves master branch integrity
- The pipeline builds and tests the code for pull requests
- The pipeline publishes the smart contract to the artifact repository when changes are tagged
- Each organization receives a notification when a new version is available

In the next section, we will start configuring the CI pipeline we have just defined.

Configuring a CI pipeline

Not all languages are created equal, and while we could debate the benefits of strongly typed languages such as Java and Go versus untyped ones such as JavaScript, the fact is that we need to rely on unit tests to ensure that the code is working as intended. It is not a bad thing in itself—every code artifact should be supported by a set of tests with adequate coverage.

What does that have to do with a CI pipeline, you may be wondering? Well, it's all about the tests and, in the case of JavaScript code, this is very important. The pipeline will need to ensure the following:

- The code meets all quality rules
- All unit tests are successful
- All integration tests are successful

Once these criteria are met, then the process will be able to package and publish the result.

So, in the next few sections, we will experiment with the deployment and configuration of our pipeline using one of the most popular cloud-based CI services: Travis CI.

We will cover the following elements:

- Customizing the pipeline process
- Publishing our smart contract against a repository

Once this is all done, we will move on to configuring our Git repository to control how changes are validated and integrated. So, without further ado, let's get started.

Customizing the pipeline process

You may recall that, in our promotion process, we identified two events within the life cycle meant to trigger the pipeline:

- Pull requests
- Tag releases

You may wonder why we specifically chose only those events. If you recall the process, the developers are expected to run tests on their local environment manually, so there is not an absolute need to trigger the pipeline every time someone delivers code to their branch. However, when initiating the process of moving the code to the master branch, it is crucial to validate that the code can be built, deployed, and tested before accepting changes. The same goes with tagging a release — this is an indication that a new version has been created, so it makes sense to rerun the pipeline one last time to publish the deployment unit (the smart contract package, in our case).

In any case, this is the approach we have set for our pipeline, but other teams may choose differently. You should consider this as a guideline and not a final design for CI.

Local build

Before we dive into the configuration of the pipeline, let's quickly look at how the build process is organized. The first thing to note is that our solution is now technology-rich: Fabric, Java, and TypeScript, as well as Node.js.

These technologies have quite a few dependencies that need to be in place for the build to work. Think about the prerequisites for Fabric, the JavaScript SDK, and chaincode libraries, as well as components like nvm, npm, Node, and all the packages deployed via `package.json`.

To get a consistent build output between the local and remote environments, we need to have a way to reduce and contain the dependencies. This is where the approach of using **Docker** and **Make** comes in:

- Docker provides us with an environment that helps contain the dependencies and makes the execution consistent between environments

- Make helps us manage the dependencies, and because it is built into most operating systems (except Windows, unfortunately), it reduces the need for additional tool deployment and configuration

This combo allows developers to run the build on their systems with minimum effort. There is no need to deploy additional packages; if the system has Docker and Make, then it is good to go.

 Windows users: While Windows does come with Make, we would recommend that you look at GNU Make. You can follow the installation instructions from this site: `http://gnuwin32.sourceforge.net/packages/make.htm`.

As we've already mentioned, Docker provides a pre-built environment that exists within the container, thus avoiding the need to deploy the plethora of tools on the local workstation.

The **Makefile** is the file that contains the set of tasks that can be triggered via the Make tool. For example, invoking this command:

```
make build
```

will invoke this task from the Makefile:

```
.PHONY: build
build: $(DIST_DIR)
    echo ">> Building chaincode"
    docker run --rm -v $(ROOT_DIR):/src -v $(DIST_DIR):/dist -w /src
${DOCKER_IMAGE} sh -c "$(BUILD_CMD)"
```

Let's break down the `docker run` command:

- `--rm`: Removes the container at the end of the build
- `-v`: Mounts the `src` and `dist` directories from the Git clone folders
- `-w`: Makes the container's `src` directory the working directory
- `DOCKER_IMAGE`: Container image with node 10.19 deployed and configured
- `sh -c "$( BUILD_CMD)"`: The build command to run

As you can see, with minimal configuration, the build is now taking place within the container but using the local Git clone files and folders. The nice thing about this is that the container will behave the same, whether running locally or in our build pipeline.

 Why `.PHONY`, you ask? A Makefile is an excellent but ancient tool. As such, it initially focused on file dependencies. If someone ever defined a file called `build` or `test`, Make would consider that the task was up to date and do nothing. `.PHONY` tells Make not to consider those tags as a file.

From a Makefile task's perspective, we can define dependencies between tasks. For our project, this ensures that we only package the chaincode if the build and tests are up to date and complete successfully. This diagram illustrates the dependencies:

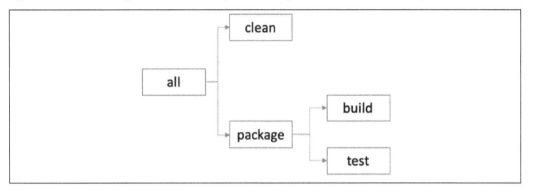

Figure 11.2: Makefile task dependencies

In the next section, we will make use of the make build and make test commands to execute our pipeline.

Configuring Travis CI

Travis CI is one of the numerous tools out there providing the ability to orchestrate a CI pipeline. Once configured, Travis CI will listen for events from your GitHub repository and trigger the pipeline when appropriate.

Getting started with Travis CI is pretty straightforward. You need to point your browser to the www.travis-ci.org website, authenticate using your GitHub identity, and authorize Travis to access your GitHub account. Travis CI will then create a profile for you and sync it with your GitHub account. Once this is done, you will be presented with a list of projects from your GitHub organization. You only need to flick the switch next to our project, and Travis CI will start tracking the events in your GitHub repository.

The following screenshot shows the activation of the Travis CI pipeline for the trade project, which resides in the GitHub `HyperledgerHandsOn` organization:

Figure 11.3: Activating the Travis CI pipeline for the GitHub trade project

Customizing the pipeline using .travis.yml

While Travis CI is now tracking our Git repository, it is not yet smart enough to know what to do with it when an event occurs. To tell Travis CI what to do, we need to create a special file within the root of the repository. Whenever a Git event happens (for example, a Git pull request), the `.travis.yml` file will be processed and used to orchestrate the pipeline's execution.

In the case of our smart contract, we have the following `.travis.yml` file in the root of our Git repository:

```
sudo: required
language: minimal
services:
- docker
dist: xenial
cache:
  directories:
  - v1/trade/node_modules
script:
- cd v1/trade && make build
- make test
- cd ../exportLicense && make build
- make test
```

```
- cd ../letterOfCredit && make build
- make test
```

Since our Makefile is making use of Docker containers to make the build independent, we need to let Travis know about this. Hence, the first three lines of the file indicate that the build process will make use of Docker, and minimal language support is required.

The `dist: xenial` key fixes the Linux distribution to ensure there's consistency in the system's behavior.

The important lines represent the two significant steps of the process:

1. `cache`: This is an optimization of the build to ensure `node_modules` is not always reloaded.
2. `script`: This is where the build commands are provided. In this case, this step includes the following:

    - **`make build`**: Builds the chaincode
    - **`make test`**: Executes the unit test

Note that the script includes all four smart contracts. From a book perspective, we made the conscious decision to keep all contracts within the same repository. In reality, project teams may decide to keep these separate to allow them to be released independently. In any case, as we are building the whole repository's content, the `script` section invokes Make for each smart contract.

The details of the code for trade chaincode was covered in *Chapter 10, Enterprise Design Patterns and Considerations*, so we won't cover those details again. However, we will focus on the build and explore the stanza of the `package.json` file:

```
[...]
    "scripts": {
        "lint": "tslint -c tslint.json 'src/**/*.ts'",
        "pretest": "npm run lint",
        "test": "nyc mocha -r ts-node/register src/**/*.spec.ts",
        "start": "fabric-chaincode-node start",
        "build": "tsc",
        "build:watch": "tsc -w"
    },
[...]
```

You will find the `package.json` file under the `trade-apps` repository.

Let's quickly review each of the default commands:

- lint: Runs the **tslint** tool, which is a tool we use to analyze the code while searching for patterns. The rules applied by this tool can be adjusted through the .tslint.json file.

- pretest: Ensures that **lint** always executes before the **test**.

- test: The Mocha unit test framework will run the tests that are located in the project test directory and will be invoked by the **nyc** tool. The nyc tool is used to measure the coverage of the Mocha tests.

- start: Invoked when the Peer nodes start the chaincode.

- build: Compiles the TypeScript files.

- build:watch: Watches for file changes and automatically starts the compiler.

To control code coverage, nyc provides the following controls:

```
"nyc": {
    "extension": [
        ".ts",
        ".tsx"
    ],
    "exclude": [
        "coverage/**",
        "dist/**"
    ],
    "reporter": [
        "text-summary",
        "html"
    ],
    "all": true,
    "check-coverage": true,
    "statements": 100,
    "branches": 100,
    "functions": 100,
    "lines": 100
}
```

By adjusting the package.json file, we can now control the "gates" that run the verification process for test coverage and code quality. It fails if the minimum is not met.

Publishing our smart contract package

At this point, in traditional deployments, we could consider automating the deployment of our application to push it to production automatically. However, in the case of a blockchain network, allowing a single process to install, approve, and commit the various chaincode packages for all organizations could become the Achilles heel of the network. Such an approach would, in effect, pass control to a central authority and make it possible to introduce change unbeknownst to the participants.

Instead, we will publish the package file to a trusted store (in this case, the GitHub release) and let every organization pull the right archive to deploy for their peer nodes.

Fortunately for us, Travis CI has a function that's used within the deploy step that allows us to attach the smart contract package to a tagged release automatically. The service requires an OAUTH_TOKEN to be configured on our GitHub account, and it needs to be added to the Travis configuration to allow Travis to attach the smart contract to the release.

While that configuration could be done manually, there is a simple command-line interface for Travis that will automatically push the token to GitHub and add the deploy section to the .travis.yml file.

We can install the Travis CLI using the following command:

```
gem install travis
```

Additional installation details can be found in the Travis documentation.

Once the CLI is installed, we first authenticate using the following:

```
$ travis login
We need your GitHub login to identify you.
This information will not be sent to Travis CI, only to github.com.
The password will not be displayed.

Try running with --github-token or --auto if you don't want to enter
your password anyway.

Username: githubid@somedomain.com
Password for githubid@somedomain.com: ***********************
```

We can then run the following command:

```
$ travis setup releases
Username: githubid
Password for githubid: ********
File to Upload: ./dist/trade.tgz
Deploy only from HyperledgerHandsOn/trade-contracts? |yes|
Encrypt API key? |yes| no
```

The tool will ask for a few pieces of information: our GitHub user ID, password, the location of the file we want to upload, whether we want to only deploy from our repository, and if we want to encrypt our API key. On this last question, it is important to say no. We will soon explain why.

The tool will add a section like the following at the end of the .travis.yml file:

```
deploy:
  provider: releases
  api_key: 3ce1ab5452e39af3ebb74582e9c57f101df46d60
  file_glob: true
  file: ./**/dist/*.tgz
  on:
    repo: HyperledgerHandsOn/trade
```

The first thing we will do is copy the API key to our workstation clipboard and go back to the Travis CI site. On the main dashboard, you should see your repository, and on the right-hand side, you will see a button called **More Options**. By clicking it and selecting **Settings**, you will be presented with a panel, split into a few sections.

Scroll down a bit, and you will find the **Environment Variables** section. Go through the following steps:

1. In the **Name** field, type OAUTH_TOKEN

2. In the **Value** field, paste the API key you copied in the .travis.yml file

3. Click **Save**

The results should be as follows:

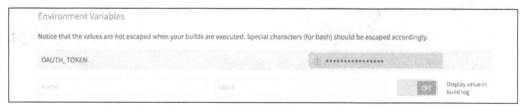

Figure 11.4: Adding the OAUTH_TOKEN as a variable to the pipeline

You see, while we could have kept the OAUTH_TOKEN encrypted in our .travis.yml file, it would have been stored in our GitHub repository to be viewed by everyone. By moving the key to the environment, we avoid this. We can now modify the configuration file so that it refers to the environment variable we just defined:

```
deploy:
  provider: releases
  api_key: ${OAUTH_TOKEN}
  file_glob: true
  file: ./**/dist/*.tgz
  on:
    branch: master
    repo: HyperledgerHandsOn/trade
    tags: true
```

The on: section provides you with the ability to restrict the publication process to the tag event on your repository.

With package.json and the .travis.yml file modified, we just need to update our repository by committing and pushing our changes to the master branch. Our pipeline is now fully configured! In a few sections, we will see how network participants can be notified of the new release and retrieve the archive, but for now, let's look at what we need to configure in Git.

Configuring your GitHub repository

In this section, we will see how to protect our GitHub repository by doing the following:

- Setting the code owners of our smart contract
- Protecting the master branch
- Configuring Git for commit signing and validation
- Testing the process by submitting a pull request

Setting the code owners of our smart contract

We will start by defining the code owners for our smart contract. Ideally, in a large consortium, the code owners should not be the same group as the one that modifies the code. Remember, these steps are meant to reinforce the trust in the network, so a segregation between who writes the rules and who validates them is in order.

Code owners are defined in a file called CODEOWNERS, which can reside either in the root directory or the .Github directory. GitHub allows us to define different code owners depending on file patterns, so while we could get very creative, the design has already partitioned the business logic into different smart contracts. We can leverage that structure to assign different owners to different contracts.

Depending on the scope, the content could also be further broken down by functional areas separated using folders.

The following represents a basic set of rules concerning the CODEOWNERS, based on the authors of this book. Feel free to adjust it to your team. The important point to note here is that the last pattern to match will be the one used to identify the owners who need to perform the review. As such, we must be careful regarding the order of the rules:

```
# In this example, README.md and build files are part
# of the default match. Default owners if nothing else matches.
# Any changes to the build process should be reviewed by everyone
* @ldesrosi @rama @P-Novotny
Makefile @ldesrosi @rama @P-Novotny

# Code related to trade should be validated by Rama.
/trade/ @rama

# Code related to Letter of Credit should be validated by @ldesrosi.
/letterOfCredit/ @ldesrosi

# Code related to Export License should be validated by @P-Novotny.
/exportLicense/ @P-Novotny

# Code related to Shipment should be validated by @rama.
/exportLicense/ @rama
```

Instead of listing each member of the team in the rules, we could have used the concept of GitHub teams to assign code ownership.

With the CODEOWNERS file defined, we can now focus on submitting it to the master branch.

Using a command-line prompt, go through the following steps:

1. Navigate to the location of the clone of your repository.

2. Create the CODEOWNERS file according to the content defined in the previous section.

3. Commit the new file and directory:

```
git add -A
git commit -m "Setting initial code ownership."
```

4. Push the commits to the master branch:

```
git push
```

Protecting the master branch

As we previously discussed, since the master branch represents the stable version of our smart contract, we need to control how code changes are introduced to this branch. We will now configure our repository to ensure that only pull requests can alter the content of the master branch. The first step is to open a browser and point it to your GitHub repository.

Once the web page has loaded, go through the following steps:

1. Looking at the top tabs of the GitHub pages, you should be able to locate the **Settings** tab. Click the tab, and a side menu should appear on the left-hand side of the page.

2. Select the **Branches** menu item. You should be able to see the **Protected branches** section.

3. Click the **Add Rule** button.

This will open the page that contains all the options we need to set to protect the master branch properly.

The content should be set to the following:

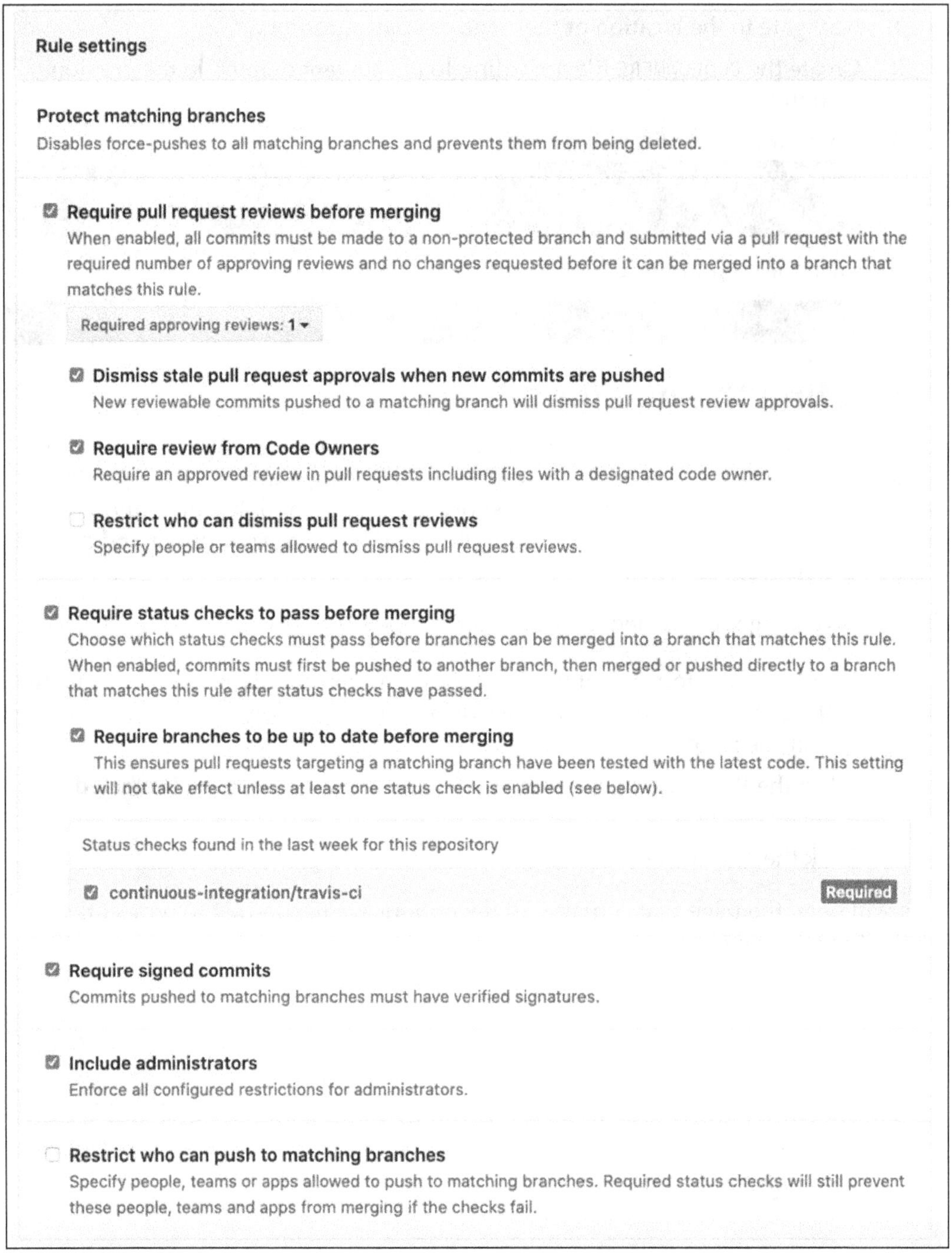

Rule settings

Protect matching branches
Disables force-pushes to all matching branches and prevents them from being deleted.

☑ **Require pull request reviews before merging**
When enabled, all commits must be made to a non-protected branch and submitted via a pull request with the required number of approving reviews and no changes requested before it can be merged into a branch that matches this rule.

Required approving reviews: 1 ▾

   ☑ **Dismiss stale pull request approvals when new commits are pushed**
   New reviewable commits pushed to a matching branch will dismiss pull request review approvals.

   ☑ **Require review from Code Owners**
   Require an approved review in pull requests including files with a designated code owner.

   ☐ **Restrict who can dismiss pull request reviews**
   Specify people or teams allowed to dismiss pull request reviews.

☑ **Require status checks to pass before merging**
Choose which status checks must pass before branches can be merged into a branch that matches this rule. When enabled, commits must first be pushed to another branch, then merged or pushed directly to a branch that matches this rule after status checks have passed.

   ☑ **Require branches to be up to date before merging**
   This ensures pull requests targeting a matching branch have been tested with the latest code. This setting will not take effect unless at least one status check is enabled (see below).

Status checks found in the last week for this repository

   ☑ continuous-integration/travis-ci   `Required`

☑ **Require signed commits**
Commits pushed to matching branches must have verified signatures.

☑ **Include administrators**
Enforce all configured restrictions for administrators.

☐ **Restrict who can push to matching branches**
Specify people, teams or apps allowed to push to matching branches. Required status checks will still prevent these people, teams and apps from merging if the checks fail.

Figure 11.5: GitHub branch protection option

This first set of options ensures that every change to the master branch is done through pull requests and that the approval process can only be done on up-to-date code, and by the code owners only.

We have highlighted this section because, while these are very important when working in teams, it should be **disabled** for our exercise. GitHub will not let you review your own pull requests and will prevent you from completing the steps later.

The second set of options provides us with the ability to define checks to be performed before allowing the code to be merged. We will add one of these checks in the next section.

The final option also ensures that even administrators of the repository need to follow the process of pull requests when modifying the code.

 Travis CI needs to have run at least once to appear in the status check list. If it does not appear, you can trigger a build and come back to this configuration page later.

Configuring Git for commit signing and validation

At this point, we have protected our Git branch and identified who should be reviewing code changes. We also know that signing commits is a good way for a developer to prove that they were the author of a code change. However, unless everyone signs their commits, how can you be sure that unsigned commits are valid?

Fortunately, there is now an option to require signed commits as part of the master branch's protection. Going back to the settings page for branch protection, make sure this option is selected:

☑ **Require signed commits**
Commits pushed to matching branches must have verified signatures.

Figure 11.6: GitHub branch protection—signed commits option

Configuring GPG on your local workstation

To make sure everything is working nicely, we will now set up GPG on our local workstation and test our repository by submitting a pull request. In this section, we will do the following:

1. Install GPG and generate our set of GPG public and private keys
2. Import our GPG public key in our GitHub profile
3. Submit a pull request to the master branch with a signed commit

The client application for GPG can be found on the www.gnupg.org website. From the website, you may download either the source code or the precompiled binaries. Depending on your operating system and the option chosen (**Source code** or **Binaries**), follow the instructions provided on the website and install the client.

To configure the system to use GPG keys to sign our Git commits, we will need to do the following:

1. Generate a GPG key
2. Export the public key
3. Import the public key in our GitHub account
4. Configure our Git client to make use of our GPG key

To get started, open a terminal and type the following command:

```
gpg --full-generate-key
```

The GPG tool will now ask a few questions about the characteristics of the key:

- **Kind of key**: Select the default (RSA and RSA)
- **Key size**: Select the maximum size (4,096)
- **Key validity period**: Make sure that the key does not expire

With the characteristics of the key provided, the GPG tool will ask about the identity associated with the key:

- Real name
- Email
- Comment: You may want to use the comment box to indicate the purpose of this identity (signing GitHub commits)

Make sure that the email matches the entries of your GitHub profile, or else the system will not be able to reconcile the identity to the commit.

Remember that case matters for GitHub: `yourID@email.com` is not the same email as `YOURID@email.com`.

Finally, the tool will ask for a passphrase to protect the private key and ask you to generate entropy by moving the mouse around. After a few seconds, you should see an output such as the following:

```
gpg: key 3C2784EA997D marked as ultimately trusted
gpg: directory '/Users/yourID/.gnupg/openpgp-revocs.d' created
gpg: revocation certificate stored as '/Users/yourID/.gnupgprevo
cs.d/962F917E83EA997D.rev'
public and secret key created and signed.
pub rsa4096 2018-02-03 [SC]
962F9129F7E83EA997D
uid Your Name (GitHub Signing Identity) <yourID@email.com>
sub rsa4096 2018-02-03 [E]
```

With the GPG key created, we now need to export the key in a format that GitHub will be able to understand. To achieve this, run the following command:

```
gpg --armor --export <<email-you-use-to-generate-the-key>>
```

The tool will output the public key directly in the console and should look as follows:

```
-----BEGIN PGP PUBLIC KEY BLOCK-----
mQINBFp1oSYBEACtkVI1fGR5ifhVuYUCruZ03NglnCmrlVp9Nc417qUxgigYcwYZ
[…]
vPF4Gvj20/l+95LfI3QAH6pYOtU8ghe9a4E=
-----END PGP PUBLIC KEY BLOCK-----
```

Copy the whole key to the clipboard, including the header, and using your browser, go to your GitHub profile and select the SSH and GPG keys tab from the left-hand side menu. You should see two sections—SSH and GPG. Click the **New GPG Key** button and paste the contents of your clipboard into the entry field that shows up. Finally, click the **Add GPG Key** button, and, if everything goes well, GitHub should show you an entry similar to the following:

| GPG | Email address: ███████████████
 Key ID: ████████████████
 Subkeys: ████████████████
 Added on 3 Feb 2018 | Delete |

Figure 11.7: Adding the GPG key to your GitHub profile

Take note of this and copy the Key ID to your clipboard. We will reuse that key to configure our Git client.

Back in the console, type the following command:

```
git config --global user.signingkey 3C27847E83EA997D
```

At this point, you should have a fully configured pipeline and protected Git repository. We're now ready to start testing our configuration. To facilitate the testing steps in the next section, we have not activated the GPG signing configuration in our Git client. We will enable it in the next section.

> **An important consideration for enabling the Require signed commits option**
>
> To work properly, this option needs to be enabled from the first commit of the repository. Adding this configuration later will cause all pull requests to fail since some commits on the master branch will not have the verified signature!

Testing considerations for the trade network

So far in this chapter, we have focused on setting up the various artifacts to protect our code base. However, we have not covered one key element of a pipeline: providing a proper set of tests to ensure the resiliency of our solution. In this section, we will look into some of the key aspects of the testing that went into the trade network.

We will limit our focus to the **trade smart contract** and the **exporter rest gateway**, which are written in TypeScript/JavaScript. However, these concepts extend to the Java components of the solution.

Unit testing

If the smart contracts define the rules of the network, then surely the unit tests are the guardians of those rules. Well-written unit tests effectively coerce source code into delivering the business intent. The challenge is in developing quality tests that properly validate the behavior of the system while being easy to maintain and resilient to change.

We say resilient to changes because not every source code modification should require an adjustment to the unit test. For example, should your test track error message content? If you establish that the error message for attempts to accept a trade in the wrong status should always say The trade is in the wrong status, then the moment someone modifies the message, you will need to update any unit tests that contain it. So, we need to define a set of tests that focuses primarily on the business rules and avoids getting caught in the details of lesser importance.

The good news is that there is plenty of literature describing good testing practices. **Behavior-driven development (BDD)** and **test-driven development (TDD)** are widely known methods for ensuring that code delivers the intended capability. The main differences between the two is the viewpoint from which test cases are created:

- BDD focuses on ensuring the behavior is correct
- TDD focuses on ensuring that a function/component is working as designed

It is important to note that they are not mutually exclusive, meaning that nothing prevents you from combining the two approaches. The important part is adhering to the approach advocated by these methodologies:

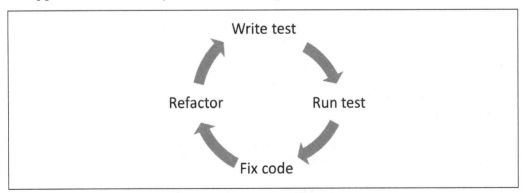

Figure 11.8: TDD cycle

The process is iterative in nature, but more importantly, it always starts with the creation of the test. In the case of BDD, the definition of a set of business scenarios describing the behavior of the system is the first step that comes before the creation of the test.

Since the source code in our GitHub repository already contains the final state of the unit tests, it is not easy to understand the thought process that went into it. In the next few sections, we will assume that we are starting from scratch and rebuild our tests and smart contracts, applying BDD and TDD concepts throughout.

Defining our user story and business scenarios

Since our focus is on the trading process happening between the importer and the exporter, let's start describing the user story that covers the trading aspect of our solution:

> *"As an importer, I can enter into a trade agreement with an exporter to acquire specific goods."*

With this user story, we understand that there are two key actors: the importer and the exporter. We also understand that there will be a trade agreement that will describe goods that the importer wants to acquire and that the exporter will sell.

From there, we can define a series of scenarios:

- ImporterOrg creates a trade request to ExporterOrg
- ImporterOrg reviews its trade requests
- ExporterOrg reviews the pending trade requests
- ExporterOrg accepts a trade request

These broadly describe what the importer and exporter can do with the system. However, as you will notice, none of these scenarios is technology focused. We are just describing that actual actions that each actor can take, but nothing is said of the underlying technology.

For each scenario, we can refine our description to include three elements that contribute to the definition of the behavior of the system:

- **GIVEN**: Provides a context for the scenario, in essence, establishing the preconditions
- **WHEN**: Describes the action or the event taking place
- **THEN**: Describes the outcome expected

If there are multiple conditions, actions, or outcomes, you can use an AND condition to complete the description.

The following shows our five scenarios fully fleshed out:

- **ImporterOrg creates a trade request to ExporterOrg**

  GIVEN ImporterOrg is a member of the trade network

  AND ImporterOrg is recognized as an importer

  WHEN they request a trade

  THEN a trade request is created on the ledger with a status of REQUESTED

- **ImporterOrg reviews their trade requests**

  GIVEN ImporterOrg is a member of the trade network

  AND ImporterOrg is recognized as an importer

  WHEN they retrieve their existing trade requests

  THEN a list of trade requests is returned

- **ExporterOrg reviews the pending trade requests**

  GIVEN ExporterOrg is a member of the trade network

  AND they are recognized as an exporter

  WHEN they request to retrieve trade requests where they are the exporter

  THEN a list of trade requests is returned

- **ExporterOrg accepts a trade request**

  GIVEN ExporterOrg is a member of the trade network

  AND they are recognized as an exporter

  AND ImporterOrg has submitted a trade request

  AND the trade is in status REQUESTED

  WHEN they accept the trade

  THEN the trade request is updated with the status ACCEPTED

So, we now have a series of scenarios that describe the expected behavior of the system. As you may have noticed, there could be many more scenarios (like rejecting a trade); however, the intent here is to show the concepts. The benefit is that any non-technical folks can easily validate these scenarios, and they provide important input to the definition of our tests.

We will now look at how these scenarios can be mapped to specific unit tests, but before that, we will look at the "plumbing" required to support the tests, which is what we generally call the **test fixture**.

Test fixture

Earlier in this chapter, we briefly covered the configuration of the `package.json` file and the associated test task. For our unit tests, we are using the following frameworks:

- **Mocha**: A unit test framework that supports BDD and TDD constructs
- **Sinon.JS**: A framework to stub and mock JavaScript and TypeScript objects
- **Chai**: An assertion library that provides a rich language to assert conditions

As we go through our existing unit tests, you will get to see how these three components come together to support our testing approach.

Since the unit tests are running in an isolated runtime outside the boundary of the blockchain network, we will need to mock some of the key elements of a transaction. In order to assert the outcome of a transaction, we first need to be able to control the input.

Consider a typical transaction like this one:

```
@Transaction(false)
@Returns('TradeAgreement')
public async getTrade(ctx: Context, tradeId: string):
Promise<TradeAgreement> {
```

And focus on the two inputs:

- `tradeId`, a primitive of the type `string`
- `ctx`, a `Context` object from Hyperledger Fabric

We can easily control the value of the type `string`; however, we need to create a mocked version of the `Context` to be able to manage its behavior. As such, we define a class as follows:

```
class TestContext implements Context {
  public stub: sinon.SinonStubbedInstance<ChaincodeStub> =
            sinon.createStubInstance(ChaincodeStub);

  public clientIdentity: sinon.SinonStubbedInstance<ClientIdentity> =
                    sinon.createStubInstance(ClientIdentity);
```

```
    public logger = {
        getLogger: sinon.stub().returns(
        sinon.createStubInstance(winston.createLogger().constructor)),
        setLevel: sinon.stub(),
    };
}
```

We are using a framework called Sinon.JS (https://sinonjs.org/) to create stubs of the objects that are expected within the context. This test context class will need to exist and be properly configured before we can invoke any transaction.

The next thing we need to worry about is the state of the ledger. After all, we need to reproduce the behavior of the trade network, and as such, we would expect to find some entries in the world state. However, we need an easy way to "reset" the world state between tests to ensure that they can be run independently. To achieve this, we will use the beforeEach construct from the Mocha framework (https://mochajs.org/). As its name implies, this function will be called before each test:

```
beforeEach(() => {
  contract = new TradeContract();
  ctx = new TestContext();

  ctx.stub.getState.withArgs('1001').resolves(
    Buffer.from('{"tradeID":"1001", "exporterMSP": "ExporterOrg",
                "importerMSP": "ImporterOrg", "amount": 1000.0,
                "descriptionOfGoods": "Apples",
                "status": "REQUESTED"}'));

  ctx.stub.getState.withArgs('1002').resolves(
    Buffer.from('{"tradeID":"1002", "exporterMSP": "ExporterOrg",
                "importerMSP": "ImporterOrg", "amount": 1000.0,
                "descriptionOfGoods": "Oranges",
                "status": "ACCEPTED"}'));
});
```

You can notice that the function does three things:

1. Creates a TradeContract instance, which will be the object under tests
2. Creates a TestContext, which will be passed to the transaction being invoked
3. Declares how the stub should reply to the method's invocation

Since the stub is an instance of `sinon.SinonStubbedInstance`, we can invoke the following functions:

- `withArgs`: Indicates which parameter value to respond to. If the method is called with a value that was not defined, then an undefined value is returned.

- `resolves`: Defines what value to return when an invocation is made with arguments matching the ones from `withArgs`.

So, from there, you can see that before any test, there will always be two trades in the world state:

- Trade ID 1001 with the state `REQUESTED`
- Trade ID 1002 with the state `ACCEPTED`

This is all we need for now in terms of the test fixture. We will now map our scenarios to Mocha constructs.

Mapping scenarios to Mocha

The following code extract shows how the user story and business scenarios can be mapped to Mocha:

```
describe('As an importer, I can enter in a trade agreement with an
exporter to acquire specific goods', () => {
    describe('ImporterOrg creates a trade request to an ExporterOrg',
() => {
        it('should create a trade.', async () => {});
        it('should throw an error for a trade that already exists.',
async () => {});
    });

    describe('ImporterOrg reviews his trade requests', () => {
        it('should retrieve their existing trade requests', async () =>
        {});
        it('should return an empty list if they have no trade
requests.', async () => {});
    });

    describe('ExporterOrg reviews the pending trade requests', () => {
```

```
        it('should retrieve existing trade requests where they are the
exporter', async () => {});
        it('should return an empty list if they have no requests.',
async () => {});
    });

    describe('ExporterOrg accepts a trade request', () => {
        it('should be able to accept a trade', async () => {});
        it('should not be able to accept a trade that is in the wrong
state', async () => {});
    });
});
```

The describe function can be used to aggregate our tests. They can be nested to allow us to organize our tests to represent our **user story** and our **scenarios**.

The it will be aligned to our WHEN criteria. The GIVEN will eventually become part of the setup of the test and the THEN will become part of the assertion tests.

In real-life projects, you would not have all of those scenarios created upfront. Instead, you would start by defining your user story and then iteratively add scenarios as you implement them.

Implementing unit tests

With the structure in place, we can start implementing our tests. The following example shows the test that covers the scenario of requesting a new trade.

Note that the test starts by configuring the condition (WHEN) with regards to the identity of the requester. It then ensures that the new trade object has been put against the correct trade ID:

```
describe('ImporterOrg creates a trade request to an ExporterOrg', () =>
{

  it('should create a trade', async () => {
    ctx.clientIdentity.getMSPID.returns('ImporterOrg');

    await contract.requestTrade(ctx, '1003', 'ACME', 'Pears', 1000.0);
```

```
    ctx.stub.putState.should.have.been.calledOnceWithExactly(
      '1003',
      Buffer.from(
        '{"tradeID":"1003","exporterMSP":"ACME",
          "importerMSP":"ImporterOrg","descriptionOfGoods":"Pears",
          "amount":1000,"status":"REQUESTED"}'));
  });
```

In a pure BDD/TDD process, the unit tests are created first, and then we implement the transaction. As scenarios are added, the business logic is enriched.

While most rules can be implemented as behavior, you will notice that some functions, like `beforeTransaction`, are tested separately. The rationale is that, depending on the context, it is easier and better to centralize some test cases. In particular, centralizing the access control test makes more sense than distributing them across multiple behavior scenarios.

Furthermore, as you may remember, earlier in this chapter, we set some code coverage expectations to 100%. This means complete code coverage by the unit tests! This might be seen as a daunting task, but, thankfully, using tools like Istanbul code coverage, we can quickly assess the existing gap.

The following screenshot was taken after running `npm run test` and accessing the report from `trade-contracts/v1/trade/coverage/lcov-report/index.html`:

```
64        @Transaction()
65   1x   public async requestTrade(ctx: Context, tradeId: string, exporterMSP: string, descriptionOfGoods: string, amount: number): Promise<void> {
66   1x     const exists = await this.exists(ctx, tradeId);
67   1x     [I] if (exists) {
68           throw new Error(`The trade ${tradeId} already exists`);
69         }
70   1x     const trade = new TradeAgreement() statement not covered
```

Figure 11.9: Example from a unit test report

Again, while the BDD approach will cover a large part of these scenarios, there are situations where just a good unit test will allow us to complete our code coverage.

We've focused our effort on the smart contract as it represents the more novel part of the development process. Note that the user stories and scenarios could equally be applied to the REST gateway and its associated classes and components. We will not cover the unit tests for those components as the approach is essentially the same. Instead, we will look at how we can run integration tests that include both the REST gateway and the blockchain network.

Integration testing

Unit tests are great for ensuring that each component delivers the functions and behavior we need. However, it does not ensure that the system as a whole is working. Between the various runtime components, their configuration, and the execution of the business process, there can still be gaps that create defects.

Integration tests are often relegated to a set of manual activities. Test specialists will write a series of test plans and then go through the test scenarios and test steps, validating business processes and outcomes. While the unit tests allowed us to find issues early on, this subsequent phase becomes a tedious and costly phase due to the fact that it is manual and labor-intensive.

However, it does not have to be. Integration tests can be automated like unit tests.

For our trade network, we have written a series of integration tests that exercise the complete process, from the request of a trade to the final payment. As shown in the following diagram, our integration tests focus on the interactions between the four REST gateways and the blockchain network:

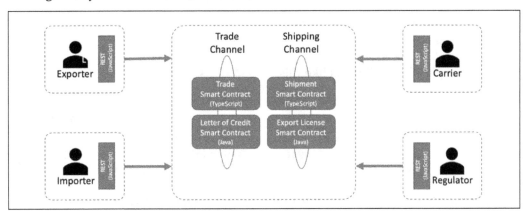

Figure 11.10: Overview of the network and its participants

 The integration tests can be found under `trade-apps/_ integration/src/trade-exchange.spec.js`.

Setting up the integration tests

For the integration test to be effective, we need to be able to authenticate against each gateway and orchestrate the execution of each test to validate that the system correctly supports the business process. The main difference here is that the tests are modifying the actual state of the system, so there is a dependency between each test and the one that follows it. The failure of one test pretty much means that the remaining ones are also bound to fail. It also means that we need to ensure the uniqueness of the records we create. If our input values are too static, we will need to tear down and recreate our network between test cycles. In the case of our business network, this is easy since most of the transactions are based on the trade identifier. Hence, this instruction provides us with a guaranteed uniqueness across each invocation: `const tradeId=new Date().valueOf();`.

For the integration tests, we are using a JavaScript test framework called `supertest`, which has the advantage of being able to integrate with a framework like Chai to perform assertions.

Initializing an instance of `supertest` against a REST gateway is done like this:

```
const IMPORTER_URL='localhost:5000';
const importerRequest = supertest(IMPORTER_URL);
```

While making a REST call looks like this:

```
const res =
    await request
        .post('/login')
        .send('username='+user+'&password='+userpw)
        .expect(200);
```

The first function (`post`) indicates the path and HTTP method to use, the second (`send`) provides the parameter to pass to the `post` function, and the last one asserts the expected HTTP status code.

You will find two convenience functions within the integration test file:

- `register`: Invokes the `register` function against a specific gateway. The function will register a new identity against the corresponding Fabric CA server and enroll it.

- `login`: Authenticates against a specific gateway. The function will return the JWT token to be used during subsequent calls.

These two functions are using in the `before` method to make sure that the identities and required tokens are properly generated:

```
before(async () => {

    await register(importerRequest, 'admin', 'adminpw', 'importer',
'importerpw', 'client');
    await register(importerRequest, 'admin', 'adminpw',
'importerBanker', 'bankerpw', 'banker');
    await register(exporterRequest, 'admin', 'adminpw', 'exporter',
'exporterpw', 'client');
    await register(exporterRequest, 'admin', 'adminpw',
'exporterBanker', 'bankerpw', 'banker');
    await register(regulatorRequest, 'admin', 'adminpw', 'regulator',
'regulatorpw', 'client');

    tokenImporter = await login(importerRequest, 'importer',
'importerpw');
    tokenImporterBanker = await login(importerRequest,
'importerBanker', 'bankerpw');
    tokenExporter = await login(exporterRequest, 'exporter',
'exporterpw');
    tokenExporterBanker = await login(exporterRequest,
'exporterBanker', 'bankerpw');
    tokenRegulator = await login(regulatorRequest, 'regulator',
'regulatorpw');

});
```

 Notice that we are using `before` and not `beforeEach`. This means that the registration and authentication calls will be done only once per test cycle.

Testing the trade business process

With the prerequisites set up, we can start adding test cases for each significant portion of the trade business process. Each test case aims to exercise a transaction that alters the state of the network, followed by a query from a different organization, which helps confirm that the transaction was properly replicated across peer nodes.

For example, in the following test case, the importer identity initiates a new trade request, which is then followed by the retrieval of the trade by the exporter:

```
it('importer can create a trade and exporter can see it.', async
function () {
    const newTradeRes = await importerRequest
        .post('/requestTrade')
        .set('authorization', 'Bearer ' + tokenImporter)
        .send('tradeId=${tradeId}&exporterMSP=${exporterMSP}&
amount=${amount}&descriptionOfGoods=${descriptionOfGoods}')
        .expect(200);

    const tradeLookupRes = await exporterRequest
        .get('/trade/${tradeId}')
            .set('authorization', 'Bearer ' + tokenExporter)
            .expect(200);
});
```

Notice a couple of things:

- `tokenImporter` and `tokenExporter` are used against their relative REST gateway to ensure that the authentication session is preserved.

- The trade lookup is done via the `exporterRequest`. This implies that the first invocation against the blockchain network has been successful and that the data has been propagated to the exporter peers.

Running the integration tests

To run the integration tests, we will need to start the network and ensure that the REST servers are started as Docker containers. To do so, we can run the following:

```
cd trade-network/bash
./startAll.sh
```

The script will deploy the network, create the channel, deploy the chaincode, and start the REST servers. Once this is done, we can run the tests, as follows:

```
cd ../../trade-apps/_integration
npm install
npm run e2e
```

Exercising the end-to-end process

With all of the configuration done and the unit tests ready, we will run through a simple scenario that will allow us to test our setup and ensure that everything is working smoothly.

The scenario will consist of addressing the need to add a new transaction. To deliver this new feature, we will perform the following steps/tests:

1. Create a new transaction for our business network.

    Once we are done coding, we will then try to do the following:

    1. Push a commit to the master branch directly

    2. Submit a pull request with an unsigned commit

2. Add test cases to cover our new transaction:

    1. Amend our commit to be signed

    2. Add our test case and submit an additional signed commit

3. Release the new version of the business network:

    1. Merge the pull request on the master branch

    2. Create a new release and check that the chaincode package is published

Creating a new transaction

For the purpose of our tests, we will keep the new transaction relatively simple: the transaction will merge two trades into one and add their values in the process.

Let's define the new transaction in the `trade-contracts/trade/src/trade-contract.ts` file:

```
@Transaction()
public async mergeTrade(ctx: Context, tradeIdFrom: string, tradeIdTo:
string): Promise<void> {
    const tradeFrom = await this.getTrade(ctx, tradeIdFrom);
    const tradeTo = await this.getTrade(ctx, tradeIdTo);

    // To merge, trades must be in status REQUESTED and
    // from same exporter and importer.
    if (tradeFrom.status !== 'REQUESTED' || tradeTo.status !==
'REQUESTED') {
        throw new Error('One of the trades is in the wrong status.');
```

```
    }

    if (tradeTo.exporterMSP !== tradeFrom.exporterMSP) {
        throw new Error('The exporterMSP don\'t match.');
    }

    if (tradeTo.importerMSP !== tradeFrom.importerMSP) {
        throw new Error('The importerMSP don\'t match.');
    }

    if (tradeTo.descriptionOfGoods !== tradeFrom.descriptionOfGoods) {
        throw new Error('The description of goods don\'t match.');
    }

    tradeTo.amount += tradeFrom.amount;

    const buffer = Buffer.from(JSON.stringify(tradeTo));
    await ctx.stub.putState(tradeIdTo, buffer);
    await ctx.stub.deleteState(tradeIdFrom);
}
```

That's all there is to it! Of course, some may remark that we are not following a good methodology — where are our unit tests for this code? Let's proceed. Don't worry; it's all part of the plan!

Pushing a commit to the master branch directly

With the code modification done, let's try to add the source code to our Git repository. To do so, we will go through the following steps:

1. Navigate to the location of the clone of your repository.

2. Commit the new file and directory:

```
git add -A
git commit -m "Testing master branch protection."
```

3. Push the commits to the master branch:

```
git push
```

The push command should fail with an error message, such as the following:

```
$ git push
Counting objects: 3, done.
Delta compression using up to 8 threads.
Compressing objects: 100% (2/2), done.
Writing objects: 100% (3/3), 367 bytes | 367.00 KiB/s, done.
Total 3 (delta 0), reused 0 (delta 0)
remote: error: GH006: Protected branch update failed for refs/heads/
master.
remote: error: Required status check "continuous-integration/travis-ci"
is expected.
To https://github.com/HyperledgerHandsOn/trade-contracts.git
 ! [remote rejected] master -> master (protected branch hook declined)
error: failed to push some refs to
'https://Github.com/yourID/trading-contracts.Git'
```

If you get a similar message, you know you're on the right path. If the push command succeeds, it means that the code was directly applied to your master branch, thus the branch protection was not enforced. You should probably go back to the *Protecting the master branch* section.

Submitting a pull request with an unsigned commit

Continuing from our previous attempt, we know that we need a separate branch to store our work before we can submit a pull request to the master branch. Now that we've committed a change, we need to be careful not to lose our work. The first thing we will do is undo our commit by running the following command:

```
git reset HEAD^
```

To save our work, we will use a nice function from Git that will temporarily store our work:

```
git stash
```

With our modification saved, we can then create the new branch locally by running the `git checkout` command. For those who are less familiar with Git, the `-b` option specifies the name of the new branch, and the last parameter indicates that the new branch is based on the master branch:

```
git checkout -b MergeTrade
```

With the new branch created locally, we can restore our modification using the following:

```
git stash pop
```

Finally, we can commit our code and push it to the `MergeTrade` branch:

```
git add -A
git commit -m "Adding mergeTrade transaction."
git push --set-upstream origin MergeTrade
```

With these commands executed, our `MergeTrade` branch should now contain the additional transaction code. Let's switch to our browser and create the pull request on GitHub:

1. Select the `MergeTrade` branch and click the **New pull request** button
2. Make sure the branches can merge and click the **Create pull request** button

The result on the next screen will show that the pull request is failing the Travis build. The details for the build should show that the test coverage is not sufficient to meet the threshold we established previously:

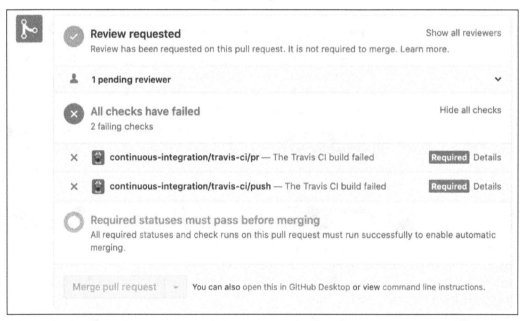

Figure 11.11: Failed pull request

We will now correct our build and add the necessary tests!

Adding the mergeTrade unit test

Let's add the content of this additional test case to the `test/logic.js` file:

```
describe('#mergeTrade', () => {
    it('should merge two trades', async () => {
        ctx.clientIdentity.getMSPID.returns('ImporterOrg');
        await contract.mergeTrade(ctx, '1000', '1001');
        ctx.stub.putState.should.have.been.calledOnceWithExactly('1001'
,Buffer.from(
'{"tradeID":"1001","exporterMSP":"ACME","importerMSP":"ImporterOrg",
"amount":2000,"descriptionOfGoods":"Apples","status":"REQUESTED"}'));
        ctx.stub.deleteState.should.have.been.
calledOnceWithExactly('1000');
    });

    it('should fail merge in wrong state', async () => {
        ctx.clientIdentity.getMSPID.returns('ImporterOrg');
        await contract.mergeTrade(ctx, '1000', '1002').should.be
            .rejectedWith(/One of the trades is in the wrong status./);
    });

    it('should fail merge with exporter MSP not matching', async () =>
    {
        ctx.clientIdentity.getMSPID.returns('ImporterOrg');
        ctx.stub.getState.withArgs('1003').resolves(
            Buffer.from('{"tradeID":"1003", "exporterMSP":
"SOMEOTHERORG",  "importerMSP": "ImporterOrg", "amount": 1000.0,
"descriptionOfGoods": "Oranges", "status": "REQUESTED"}'));

        await contract.mergeTrade(ctx, '1000', '1003').should.be
            .rejectedWith(/The exporterMSP don't match./);
    });

    it('should fail merge two trades with importer MSP not matching',
async () => {
        ctx.clientIdentity.getMSPID.returns('ImporterOrg');
        ctx.stub.getState.withArgs('1003').resolves(
            Buffer.from('{"tradeID":"1003", "exporterMSP": "ACME",
"importerMSP": "SOMEOTHERORG", "amount": 1000.0, "descriptionOfGoods":
"Oranges", "status": "REQUESTED"}'));

        await contract.mergeTrade(ctx, '1000', '1003').should.be
```

```
                .rejectedWith(/The importerMSP don't match./);
    });

    it('should fail merge two trades with goods not matching', async ()
=> {
        ctx.clientIdentity.getMSPID.returns('ImporterOrg');
        ctx.stub.getState.withArgs('1003').resolves(
            Buffer.from(
            '{"tradeID":"1003", "exporterMSP": "ACME", "importerMSP":
"ImporterOrg", "amount": 1000.0, "descriptionOfGoods": "Oranges",
"status": "REQUESTED"}'));
        await contract.mergeTrade(ctx, '1000', '1003').should.be
            .rejectedWith(/The description of goods don't match./);
    });
});
```

We won't cover the details of this test case, as it has been covered in previous sections.

It is always a good idea to locally run the test, and we can do so, using this command:

```
npm test
```

Be aware that when copying text from this book, whitespaces can get in the way and cause the npm test run to fail. Fix those before submitting the next commit.

With all tests passing, we can now type the following commands:

```
git add -A
git commit --amend -m "Adding mergeTrade transaction."
git push -f
```

We need to force push the changes as we are amending our commits. Typically, amending commits should only be done on a branch where you are sure you are alone working on.

If you go back to the browser and look at the pull request, after a moment, you should now have something like the following:

Figure 11.12: Pull request blocked due to missing signed commits

This is great. The build and unit tests have completed successfully; however, the pull request has been blocked because you did not sign the commit. Let's remediate that now.

Submitting a pull request with a signed commit

We can now finalize and activate our GPG signing. In the console, type in the following command:

```
git config --global commit.gpgsign true
```

Now, instead of having to create a separate branch and go through the same steps all over again, we will simply amend our commit once more and add our signature to it:

```
git commit --amend -S -m "Adding mergeTrade transaction."
```

> You may get the following error when trying to amend your commit:
>
> error: gpg failed to sign the data
> fatal: failed to write commit object
>
> If you do, you may need to set the following environment variable:
>
> export GPG_TTY=$(tty)

This command will delegate the signing to GPG, and you should be asked for your GPG passphrase. Once this is completed, we can push our changes to our branch using the following command:

```
git push --force
```

We should now have solved the last problem—the signing of commits. From the browser's perspective, you should be able to see this:

Figure 11.13: Commit status with the Verified tag

This should automatically trigger our build pipeline, which should complete successfully and leave our pull request in the following state:

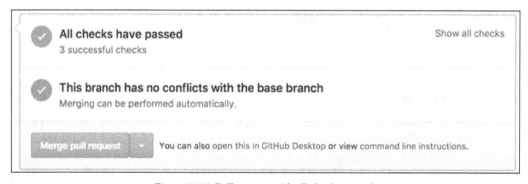

Figure 11.14: Pull request with all checks passed

This should allow you to merge the pull request. Click the **Merge pull request** button, confirm the merge, and get ready to create your first release!

If your pull request is not green and asks for a code review, you may have forgotten to uncheck the **Require pull request reviews before merging** option, as mentioned in the *Protecting the master branch* section.

Releasing the new version

We are now ready to release our new business network archive. Go to your web browser and navigate to the **Code** tab of your GitHub repository. You should see a **releases** option in the top navigation bar, as shown in the following screenshot:

Figure 11.15: GitHub repository header showing the releases

Click on the **releases** button and then click on the **Create a new release** button. Fill in the form in a similar way to the following example:

Figure 11.16: GitHub release form

Click on the **Publish release** button at the bottom of the form. It should trigger your build pipeline one final time, and, after a few minutes, you should have the chaincode package file attached to the list of assets associated with your release:

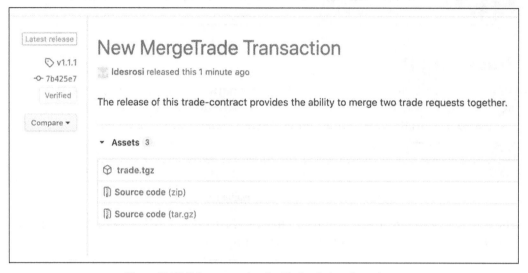

Figure 11.17: Release populated with the chaincode package

Well done! We've configured a complete pipeline using Travis CI and GitHub and are able to sign and protect our smart contracts.

Our last step will now be to see how the various network participants can automate the continuous deployment of the network artifacts, chaincode archive, and REST gateway.

Continuous delivery

The terms CI and CD are too often conflated into CI/CD, causing the nuance between the two processes to be lost. Hopefully, by the end of this chapter, we will have clarified the two.

Up until this point, our attention has been primarily on CI, the process of building and testing the software components of the solution. If CI is there to ensure the quality of our software, CD ensures the consistency of the configuration of our infrastructure.

In the traditional data center world, workloads tended to be long-lived, and the management of the configuration was an eternal battle as manual intervention created an opportunity for configuration drift and made systems hard to maintain and troubleshoot.

Now, with the advent of software-defined infrastructure, the cloud, Docker, and Kubernetes, there is a big push toward automation. Through automation, we can now define infrastructure through declarative languages, and we can manage those configurations as assets in our source control.

In this section, we will discuss a few key deployment considerations and explore how they fit into a CI process. While we will cover most of the components of the solution, we will target the blockchain-specific elements.

Specifically, we will look at:

- The underlying technologies involved in the deployment of a blockchain network
- An overview of the deployment process
- Deployment strategies

Kubernetes as a platform for Hyperledger Fabric

As we have seen, Hyperledger Fabric is delivered as a set of Docker images that you are free to download from Docker Hub or build yourself. So far, we have been using our `trade.sh` script to deploy our network. Under the cover, our script relies on Docker Compose files that describe the list of containers and their associated configuration. This is all good for a local test environment, but a production-grade network will want to ensure that the nodes are genuinely decentralized, and from that standpoint, a local Docker Compose file will not cut it.

Each organization may want to host and own their nodes. For high-availability reasons, they may also want to distribute their peers across multiple data centers or geographic regions. As it progresses, the number of containers will grow, and the network topology will become more complex. This is where a pure Docker-based solution does not cut it.

When comparing **virtual machines** (**VMs**) to containers, the analogy is often made of pets versus cattle. A VM tends to be long-lived and, as such, it requires a lot of attention (similar to a pet), while a Docker container is just one of many more. Containers come and go. We treat containers as cattle because when one fails, we simply replace it with another instance.

The challenge comes when the number of containers grows, and the topology becomes more complex. How do you know which container has failed and where it has been deployed, as well as which system it should be communicating with? To solve such a problem, we need a way to orchestrate and track the deployment of those containers.

This is where a solution like Kubernetes comes in. There are multiple technologies in the field of container orchestration, but Kubernetes has a definite edge compared to the other options. Many Hyperledger Fabric service providers like IBM Blockchain Platform heavily depend on its capabilities, which is why we will provide a very short overview here.

The following diagram shows the high-level architecture of a Kubernetes cluster. The main runtime components are the Master nodes and the Worker nodes. Roughly speaking, the Master nodes are responsible for coordinating and keeping track of the workloads deployed on the Worker nodes. When we request deployment of an application on the cluster, the Master nodes will evaluate the deployment characteristics, look at the state of the cluster, determine which Worker node has the resources, and deploy the container in a component called a pod. Once the pod is up and running, it will have a network address, and it will be able to access storage to persist data:

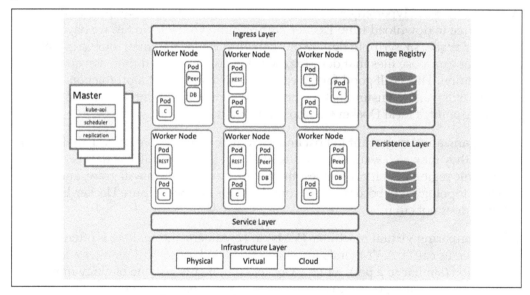

Figure 11.18: Kubernetes component overview

Here are a few of the key components of a Kubernetes cluster:

Component	Definition
Pods	The smallest deployable unit of compute that can be made up of one or more containers.
Containers	Running instantiation of a Docker image. Containers tend to be immutable to minimize configuration drift.
Docker Image	A set of layered binaries that represent a "snapshot" of the application and configuration of a specific service/process.
Image Registry	Stores Docker images so that anyone with access can retrieve the image and pull it to its local system. A registry can be public, like Docker Hub, or private.
Namespace	Entity used to group and isolate objects. It allows a community of users to organize and manage their content in isolation from other communities.
Deployments	Application templates that bring together different components/pods of an application, best suited for stateless applications. They ensure the prescribed number of replicas are active at all times.
Services	Internal abstraction layer, providing a hostname that makes the pod accessible to other pods or external applications.
Ingress	Mechanism to expose services to the outside world.

With the right networking conditions, a Kubernetes cluster can manage Worker nodes across multiple data centers (often referred to as multi-availability zone clusters). Because of the ability to manage compute, network, and storage using a declarative language, Kubernetes allows us to get a consistent deployment across multiple environments. It is that specific capability that makes it so compelling to Hyperledger Fabric networks: each organization can have its cluster and still maintain a consistent deployment of its peer nodes.

However, while Kubernetes is great for deploying and managing containers, we know that there is additional configuration and policies that need to be managed. For example, how would you handle the addition of a new member of a channel? Adding a member to a channel involves modifying the configuration block, and that requires a coordinated effort between the member of the network to sign the transaction payload and ultimately update the configuration. If Kubernetes cannot help with this, is there another way to do this, or do we need to start writing more Bash scripts?

Infrastructure as Code and Ansible

In *Chapter 13, Life in a Blockchain Network*, we will explore the various tasks administrators need to perform to support and maintain a network. From creating peer nodes to managing channels and deploying chaincode, there are command-line interfaces that enable you to achieve those things. However, you need to contend with large numbers of parameters, and you need to apply the right identity to sign every action you take.

As the administrator, you could choose to write Bash scripts to automate a large part of those tasks and then just invoke them when needed.

The problem with this approach is that Bash scripts are procedural and do not take into account the current state of the system; they just execute each command. What if the system is not in the right state? Will the script succeed or break some components? You can add more condition checking in the script, but that tends to increase its complexity further and make it harder to maintain.

In our experience, using Bash scripts to manage a large-scale network tends to be a brittle approach. The script may not react to a new error condition and fail. The last thing any organization wants is a failed deployment due to faulty scripts.

Let's be clear: Bash scripts are not all bad. In fact, the network in this book was started using a Bash script (`trade.sh`). However, as complexity increases, we need a better way to handle the various conditions that can occur. Now, what will happen if you run the script a second time? Will it work, or will it delete some valuable information?

```
if [ $? -ne 0 ]; then
    echo "ERROR !!!! Unable to start network"
    exit 1
fi
```

 From `trade.sh`: How many status codes should we monitor?

This is where Infrastructure as Code technologies like Ansible can help. By focusing our efforts on describing the system state as opposed to the tasks to perform, we provide a way to deliver a solution that is easy to extend.

The following extract from the Ansible script shows how we can represent an organization:

```
-organizations:
  - &ExporterOrg
    msp:
      id: "ExporterOrgMSP"
      admin:
        identity: "exporterOrgAdmin"
        secret: "exporterOrgAdminpw"
      ibp:
        display_name: "ExporterOrg MSP"
    ca: &ExporterOrgCA
      id: "exporterorgca"
      admin_identity: "admin"
      admin_secret: "adminpw"
      tls:
        enabled: true
      ibp:
        display_name: "ExporterOrg CA"
    peers:
      - &ExporterOrgPeer1
        id: "exporterorgpeer1"
        identity: "exporterOrgpeer1"
        secret: "exporterOrgpeer1pw"
        database_type: couchdb
        tls:
          enabled: true
          identity: "exporterOrgpeer1tls"
          secret: "exporterOrgpeer1tlspw"
```

Notice how it only includes a description of the organization? It declares that the organization is called ExporterOrg, that it's MSP ID is ExporterOrgMSP, and that it has a CA and one peer. It doesn't mention how the peer node should be deployed or where the identities should be stored. It focuses purely on the outcome.

Furthermore, Ansible aims to be idempotent, which means that it can be applied multiple times without changing the outcome. Only a change to the organization details will change the system.

This section is not a full tutorial on Ansible. We will only cover the basics and focus on its usage in a blockchain network.

If you are interested in learning more, you can go to `https://docs.ansible.com/ansible/latest/user_guide`.

How is this achieved, you may be wondering? Let's look at a few concepts:

- Playbooks
- Roles
- Modules
- Tasks

A **playbook** is the top-level script that we use to describe our system. It can contain variables, roles, and tasks. An example of a playbook can be found under the project trade-network/ansible/playbook.yaml.

A **role** is a logical construct meant to represent the role that a specific node plays in a deployment. Originally, Ansible was used with VMs or bare-metal servers. Each system was assigned a role. For example, a web application could be deployed on two servers: an app server and a database server. Each server would be tagged to a role so that the first one would get the app server code deployed and configured to point to the database server. In turn, the database server system would have the software deployed along with the required data model. Ultimately, a role represents a grouping of tasks.

Modules provide us with a way to encapsulate roles and tasks in a reusable fashion. There are plenty of modules that have been published on Ansible Galaxy (https://galaxy.ansible.com/) that can help you accelerate your deployment. In fact, IBM has published an official collection of Ansible tasks: https://ibm-blockchain.github.io/ansible-collection/index.html. In part of our exercise later in this section, we will also rely on an Ansible module stored in our GitHub organization.

Tasks are the atomic entities in Ansible. Tasks can be as simple as creating a directory or a file or as complex as deploying a Fabric CA server.

In the following example, taken from the Ansible blockchain module, the task ensures that the generated root CA, persisted in the variable result.json.result. CAChain, is first Base64 decoded and then copied to the tls-root.pem of the organization wallet:

```
- name: Copy the TLS CA root certificate (for all components)
  copy:
    content: "{{ result.json.result.CAChain | b64decode }}"
    dest: "{{ organization.wallet }}/tls-root.pem"
  when: ca.tls.enabled
```

Importantly, Ansible provides us with a way to define conditions under which the task should take place. In this specific case, a copy of the certificate should only be made if the CA has TLS enabled.

Later in this chapter, we will exercise Ansible to see how it deploys our trade network. Now that we have looked at some of the infrastructure technologies like Kubernetes and Ansible, we will look at how we can define a deployment process.

Deployment process overview

From a continuous deployment perspective, we need to consider the complete stack and not just the smart contract or application layer. With the automation capabilities available today, ensuring that all components' deployments are scripted means fewer issues related to human errors.

Looking at the network stack, the following diagram shows the deployment sequence of events:

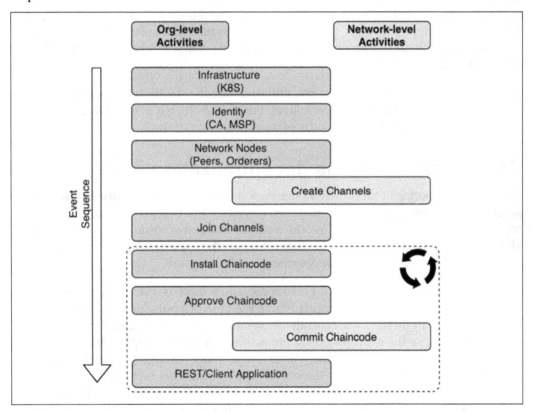

Figure 11.19: Org-level versus network-level deployment activities

The preceding diagram illustrates the activities that happen at the organization level versus the ones that impact the whole network.

Organization-level activities have little to no dependency on the other members of the network. This means that, for example, at any point, an organization could decide to add a peer to a channel without requiring intervention from other members. However, activities at the network level will require coordination between members. For example, while the approval of chaincode can be done independently and at any point in time, the commit requires coordination across the members of the channel.

Also, notice the dotted box around the chaincode deployment activities and the REST client application. This simply represents the fact that those activities will tend to happen regularly while other actions like channel creation will be much less frequent.

Taking these facts into account means that CI should be designed so that the organizations can be provisioned independently from the rest of the network. It also means that the deployment of chaincode is something that can benefit from being separate, to enable the CI pipeline to only act on the components being changed: the chaincode and the REST server.

Chapter 13, *Life in a Blockchain Network*, will dive into the details of the various activities that happen at the network level. For now, suffice it to say that the continuous deployment should address the automation of the full stack.

Centralization versus decentralization

You may have noticed that our trade network deployment is all controlled from a single script (trade.sh). All organizations' identities and components are deployed together on a single system. This works for local and test environments, but what about production-grade networks? Depending on the operational structure of the network or the consortium, the deployment model can vary.

Centralizing the CI pipeline could make sense when there is a single entity managing the solution. Think of it in the context where the network outsources the operation to a third party. In those cases, centralization may make sense. It can simplify the scripts and remove the need to coordinate activities across multiple organizations. However, in instances in which there is no single entity managing the network, decentralizing the deployment is the only viable option. This means that the organization needs to be able to provision their clusters, generate their identities, and deploy the required peers and smart contracts independently. Once identities are created, these organizations will need to share their MSP details (the public certificates of their CAs and administrators) so that they can be added to channels. The delineation of organization-specific and network-specific activities becomes crucial in these cases.

As we get ready to test our deployment strategy for our trade network, we will be taking on a centralized approach as we have the constraint of running on a single system: your local workstation.

Notifying the consortium

In the context of a decentralized deployment, there are a few approaches that can be applied to ensure that every organization is notified that a business network is ready to be updated.

The one thing that is for sure is that manual notification is not an option; as the number of smart contracts and participants grows, you need a reliable notification process.

The following diagram depicts a process for deploying a business network, following the delivery of a new release:

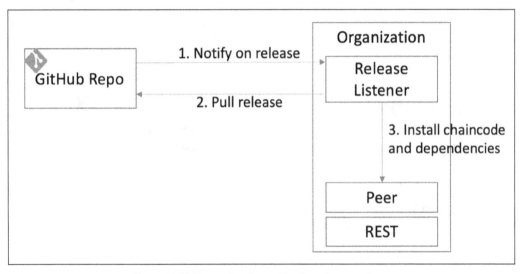

Figure 11.20: Processing the notification of a new release

By not distributing the chaincode package, we ensure that the network has a single source of truth (GitHub) when it comes to retrieving and deploying packages. It also enables our system to be automated to react to an event (new release). Finally, it reduces the risk of distributing a package that has not been properly vetted. Instead, the notification only informs every organization of the existence of a new release and lets the consortium retrieve and deploy the archive.

This is effectively what the concept of the release listener is doing: listening for notifications and then issuing a request to GitHub to retrieve the archive of the new release.

The release listener is a concept that would need to be implemented by a consortium, should they decide to adhere to this approach.

The release listener could be implemented to listen for events coming from one of two sources:

- **GitHub webhooks**: By providing the URL of the release listener, GitHub webhooks can be configured to send a JSON message based on specific events. In our case, it would be the release event.

- **Travis CI notification**: There is also a concept similar to the webhook in Travis CI. There are also other mechanisms, such as Atom feed and Slack integration, that may be more suitable to your team.

The choice of mechanism depends on your business requirements but, generally, the use of GitHub webhooks should be preferable as they are triggered by the actual event we are interested in — the release of a new version of the smart contract.

Even if someone were to send a false notification to the release listener, because it only retrieves released binaries from GitHub, it would not be possible for a third party to inject a bad archive.

Applying these concepts to our network

Normally, we would set up a webhook, and we would have a process triggering our Ansible script to update our organization with the latest version of the smart contract and the application. This could be driven by a pipeline like the one we created in Travis CI or with similar tools.

However, given the constraint of a single system, we will be manually triggering the update of the network. At this point, we will assume that we have received a notification and that we are in charge of deploying the new version.

Our deployment will consist of the following steps:

1. Setting up Ansible on your system
2. Starting the network using Ansible
3. Downloading the new version
4. Updating the business network

Setting up Ansible

The playbook we will use to deploy our network is based on the IBM Blockchain Platform Manager, which is available here: `https://github.com/IBM-Blockchain/ansible-role-blockchain-platform-manager`.

For convenience and to ensure that we work with a fixed version, we have included the role directly under `trade-network/ansible/roles/ibm.blockchain_platform_manager`.

The setup for Ansible is fully described at the preceding URL. As a quick summary, we have included the important steps here:

1. Set up Python 3.7:

    Each operating system will have different requirements. Look up your operating system here: `https://www.python.org/downloads/release/python-370/`.

2. Install Ansible 2.8:

    Higher versions might work, but the script was tested with version 2.8. You can download Ansible from this site: `https://docs.ansible.com/ansible/2.8/installation_guide/intro_installation.html`.

3. Install the Hyperledger Fabric and Fabric CA command-line interfaces:

    These should already be present on your system since we built these in earlier chapters. You will need to make sure that they are part of the `PATH` environment variable so that the script can find them.

4. Install the Docker SDK for Python:

    With Python 3.7 installed, you can run this command to deploy the Docker SDK:

    ```
    pip install docker
    ```

    Note that, depending on your system, you may need to use `pip3` as the command.

5. Install additional utilities:

    There are two mandatory utilities required to perform modifications to the config block:

    *   `jq`: `https://stedolan.github.io/jq/download/`
    *   `sponge`: From the `moreutils` library (limited to macOS and Linux)

With those steps completed, you should now be ready to start the network with Ansible.

Starting the network using Ansible

With Ansible set up, we can now start the script. If you still have your network running with Bash, we recommend that you stop and tear it down using the `trade-network/bash/stopAll.sh` convenience script.

Once this is done, we are ready to start the network using Ansible. Run the following commands:

```
cd trade-networks/ansible
ansible-playbook playbook.yaml
```

The convenience script, `trade.sh`, is also included in this folder. Running `./trade.sh up` will start the network, while `./trade.sh down` will clean up resources.

 `./trade.sh down` will properly clean up your system, removing old images and all volumes. If you encounter any issues, it's always a good idea to run this script first.

Once the script has completed, you should see this message on the console:

```
PLAY RECAP ***********************************************************************************************************************
localhost                  : ok=695  changed=248  unreachable=0    failed=0    skipped=29   rescued=0    ignored=0
```

Figure 11.21: Expected results from the Ansible script

Make sure that the `failed` count is set to zero and proceed to the next section.

Your trade network is now up and running with version 1.0.0 of the trade contract.

Pulling a new chaincode release

Given that we have just released the new version and that the pipeline has added the binary to the release, we can simply download the archive using the `curl` command, as follows:

```
curl https://github.com/HyperledgerHandsOn/trade-contracts/releases/
download/v1.1.0/trade.tgz \ -L -o trade.tgz
```

The -L option is used to tell curl to follow any redirect command. Following the execution of this command, the chaincode package file should be on your local filesystem.

We now need to move the archive trade.tgz into position for the update. To do so, copy the file to trade-networks/contracts/v1/trade/dist.

Upgrading the network

With the archive in place, we now need to update our playbook with the latest version of our contract. Locate the playbook.yaml in the trade-networks/ansible folder and change the version field from 1.0.0 to 1.1.0:

```
- package: "{{ source.contracts.trade }}"
  channels:
    - <<: *TradeChannel
      definitions:
        - name: trade
          version: 1.1.0
```

 Extract from playbook.yaml.

With the file modified, we can now start the upgrade using:

```
cd trade-networks/ansible
ansible-playbook playbook.yaml
```

Notice that we only need to specify the version we are deploying. No additional changes are required. Ansible will detect that the system is already up and running and only update the smart contract.

If all goes well, the script should complete with the following message:

```
PLAY RECAP **************************************************************************************************
localhost                  : ok=560  changed=10   unreachable=0    failed=0    skipped=143  rescued=0    ignored=0
```

Figure 11.22: Ansible output showing skipped tasks

Again, ensure that the failed count is at zero. Also, observe that since the network was already running, only 10 tasks modified the state of the system.

With that, we've completed the delivery of a new transaction. From the initial GitHub configuration to the pipeline being set up, then to the unit and integration tests to the deployment, we have exercised the full CI/CD pipeline.

Summary

Hopefully, this chapter has given you a good overview of the challenges and considerations required to align a consortium around the promotion process. CI and CD pipelines are an essential part of providing velocity to a consortium, removing manual processes, and ensuring that every organization can review and approve code changes before they go live. We've looked at some of the key events, such as pull requests and tag releases.

Over the course of this chapter, you have configured a complete CI pipeline, including testing and publishing the chaincode archive. Furthermore, you have seen how we can secure the production-ready code by protecting the master branch, as well as ensuring that every change is subject to a code review by key participants from organizations. We have also looked at how we can ensure we maintain the provenance of each Git commit using a GPG signature. Finally, we have reviewed a process used to deploy updates in a trusted manner.

One thing is for sure: automation is the key to agility — by eliminating repetitive manual tasks and providing a structure to how we modify the code, we enable organizations to be more agile and respond quickly, whether this is to defects or new requirements. This chapter was, of course, only a small introduction to this approach and its associated concepts; some of these topics could warrant their own books.

Managing the deployment of a smart contract is one key activity that needs to be coordinated by the various members of a network. However, how do you get all parties to agree to the upgrade? How do you ensure the rules of engagements are clear? To be successful a network needs to agree on a set of common rules and a decision process. This will be the topic of the next chapter.

12

Governance – A Necessary Evil of Regulated Industries

For those of you who have experienced projects without transparent decision-making, you'll have probably felt disengaged. Politics gets in the way, and the objectives of the project end up getting challenged, budgets get cut, and the long-term vision is either missing or confusing. As decisions get revisited and directions change, you are left wondering when it will all come to an end. While this is something that can happen in a traditional IT project, a blockchain project has the characteristic of having a great deal more stakeholders. A typical business network is composed of organizations that are sometimes competing and sometimes cooperating. In this context, it is not hard to see that there are high risks of finding conflicting perspectives, points of view, and interests.

Whether you are a developer or a **Chief Information Officer** (**CIO**), understanding how a governance model can help alleviate some of the issues may help to prepare you for what is to come.

This chapter presents a few of the patterns across various industries. It explores how businesses form blockchain business networks and how the underlying governance model operates.

This chapter provides an overview of the following topics:

- What is governance?
- Various business models
- The role of governance in a business network

- Typical governance structure and phases
- Roles and processes to consider
- Impact on IT solutions

Decentralization and governance

You may be wondering why we are covering such a topic in a blockchain book. After all, aren't blockchain networks supposed to be decentralized and, therefore, guarded against the control of a single entity? The reality is that, behind the technology, there are humans who shape the direction of the solution. For an enterprise-grade blockchain network to succeed, it requires many decisions throughout its life cycle.

Even Bitcoin, the decentralized, anonymous, permissionless network, must deal with hard decisions. A case in point is the controversy around Bitcoin's block size. In the early days of Bitcoin, the developers set a block size limit of 1 MB. As the network scaled up, this limit became problematic. Numerous proposals were issued, but the need for a consensus across the entirety of Bitcoin nodes made the change a challenge to agree upon. The debate started in 2015, but the community had to wait until February 2018 for a partial solution, **SegWit**, to be partially adopted. We say "partially" because SegWit, which stands for "segregated witness," only alleviates the problem by separating the signatures from the transaction payload, thereby allowing the inclusion of more transactions within a block—a lot of discussion and exchanges to reach a partial answer. Furthermore, consider that blockchain business networks are meant to create trust in an environment where not all participants fully trust each other. How will they reach a consensus on how to manage a network?

Knowing there are conflicts and disparate views, how can we address this? Well, we need a process that involves the decision-makers of each key organization. There needs to be a basic agreement regarding a process that participants agree to follow and respect the outcome. We need a way to govern the network—we need **governance**.

So, is governance about decision-making? Not really. Governance is about providing a framework that guides the decision-making process. It does so by providing a clear delineation of roles and responsibilities. It ensures that there are agreed processes to reach and communicate decisions.

We've been generically talking about decisions, but what are the types of decisions that the governance process should manage? The *Business domains and processes* section should answer this question; however, for now, suffice it to say that everything that deals with funding, the functionality roadmap, system upgrades, and network expansion are crucial topics that should be covered by a governance process.

There is plenty of existing literature covering business and IT governance topics at length. As such, standards have emerged, and there are a few IT governance standards that aim to define a proven structure to guide practices within the IT industry. Two examples of such standards are:

- **Information Technology Infrastructure Library (ITIL)**: ITIL's primary focus is on how IT renders services to the business and aims to define a process model that supports IT service management, essentially expressing an IT service as a function of the business benefits they bring instead of the underlying technical details.

- **Control Objectives for Information and Related Technologies (COBIT)**: This standard is broken down into two parts: *governance* and *management*. The governance portion of COBIT focuses on ensuring that the enterprise can meet its objectives through a series of controls around the evaluation, direction, and monitoring processes.

To be clear, these are IT governance frameworks, and they have been designed to focus on a single organizational structure. They are not immediately suited to a decentralized business network. So, while some ideas, concepts, and artifacts from these standards can be reused, they will need to be adjusted and tailored to the business model and context of the network.

Exploring business models

A business model focuses on creating a structure that describes the flow of how an organization creates and captures value in a market.

In the context of a business network, it is interesting to look at the value chain and understand where that value originates. What makes a blockchain network so appealing from a financial perspective? Well, as we have seen in *Chapter 1, Blockchain – An Enterprise and Industry Perspective*, blockchain technologies offer an opportunity to solve the issues of time and trust, thereby reducing inefficiencies and operational costs.

Blockchain benefits

What types of benefits can come from addressing the issues of time and trust?

The benefit of time means reduced delays to settle a transaction. It means that by providing a shared replicated ledger made up of entries reached through a consensus, we can eliminate delays caused by each organization performing its validation.

The benefit of trust is that organizations can eliminate the costly verification process and rethink the way they do business by:

- Providing an immutable ledger that records the provenance and consensus of transactions

- Ensuring that ledger content will not be modified (immutable) and will always be on the ledger (final)

Let's look at a few examples of how different industries can apply blockchain to their use cases.

Supply chain management

The supply chain is made up of many actors, from the exporter to the logistic service providers, port authority, freight carrier, importer, and, ultimately, the consumer. The industry must deal with a variety of regulations, and while there are many data exchanges in place between different organizations, getting a single version of the truth is not possible. The lack of trust in a supply chain stems from the fact that many organizations fear that data might be leaked to competitors. It translates to the following issues:

- **Visibility**: Where is my order? Where is my container? Without transparency, the manufacturer's forecasting is impacted and can lead to production delays.

- **Administrative overhead**: Data needs to be keyed in multiple times, requiring human effort and the need for a reconciliation process to detect errors.

- **Disputes**: The lack of access to a common source of information leads to discrepancies in the perception of the different actors, turning these discrepancies into conflicts.

- **Investigation**: As a consequence of the dispute, efforts have to be made by multiple parties to gather facts and resolve the issue. In this context, a decentralized, permissioned ledger means that every order and every shipment could be tracked in real time, all while preventing competitors from accessing sensitive information. This model would contribute to eliminating duplicate data entries, reducing human error, and expediting the investigation, as the provenance of each transaction could easily be demonstrated.

Given the worldwide economy, it is not hard to imagine the potential savings. Imagining a world where there is a single source of truth that is managed through a permissioned ledger, and where all relevant actors can get access to the information, we can see the immediate benefits that this would bring throughout the supply chain.

Healthcare

The healthcare industry has a wide range of use cases that can be explored, including the pharmaceutical supply chain, clinical trials, and electronic health records. This last use case is the focus of this example, as it is closer to our heart (literally).

The promise of electronic health records has always been appealing, and the benefits, at first glance, seem to be numerous:

- **A complete view of a patient's history**: By eliminating the inherent duplication of paper-based records, a patient should get more accurate diagnostics and receive more coherent long-term care, all in a timely fashion.

- **Reduction in duplication**: Whether from different doctors requesting the same tests or the fact that every clinic and hospital has to maintain its records, there is a potential waste of resources in the healthcare system.

- **Prevention of fraudulent actions**: From double accounting by rogue clinics to claims for false prescriptions, there are many scenarios where the duplication of records creates the opportunity for abuse.

While the benefits may seem obvious, the lessons from existing electronic health record projects would seem to hint that they are expensive and may not immediately deliver the expected benefits. Some researchers found that:

- Digitally documenting patient/doctor sessions created additional work for the doctor

- Electronic health record systems were creating an increase in IT spending
- Change management and training were generating additional cost and effort

Since then, recent studies have shown that such solutions tend to have a positive return on investment in the long run (taking around five years to achieve a benefit). Given that the value and benefits come from a wide, standardized adoption of the technology, and given the extent of the medical networks of many countries, it is not hard to see how this type of endeavor is fraught with political complexities.

Can blockchain networks improve an area that has been long touted as a prime area of innovation for centralized technologies? While, technically, we can envision an elegant blockchain solution where clinics and hospitals join the network to get access to a patient's records, could the real challenge lie in governance?

Letters of credit

At this point in the book, you should be familiar with the concept of the **letter of credit**. However, let's quickly recap the concept behind it, as illustrated in the following diagram:

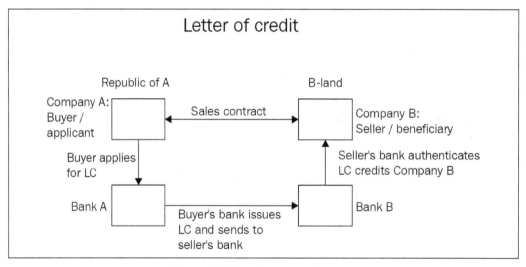

Figure 12.1: How a letter of credit works

The letter of credit is a payment vehicle whereby, on request from a buyer, a bank issues a letter of credit to a seller, stating that when the trade terms and conditions are met, the payment can be issued.

As we covered in previous chapters, the letter of credit process is not new. However, today's letter of credit process is a complex one. While examples typically involve two banks, the reality is that there can be many more participants involved in such a network. It translates into a process that is costly and constrained by the time it takes to execute it. A blockchain network can create an opportunity to optimize the process; with a blockchain network, we can store the letter of credit on the ledger and, by the nature of the **multiversion concurrency control** (**MVCC**) process, prevent a double-spending scenario, whereby the owner of the letter could attempt to cash it again. We can measure the benefit by the reduction in time delays, and costs, but it also provides the significant benefit of reducing the underlying risks associated with such a transaction. Finally, banks can also now consider introducing new services, such as the ability to make incremental payments to the seller. The fact that transactions on the ledger are final is what makes this scenario appealing to banks. It also gives us the ability to start with a smaller network, get an initial value, and expand as the solution becomes proven, substantially reducing the amount of early coordination required to establish the network.

From benefits to profits

Whatever the market or the business model, there must be a return on the investment in such a way that the following formula holds:

Value created by blockchain - Network operation cost > 0

With a positive return, and out of shared business interests, a network-level business model can emerge. The objective is to maximize the value and minimize the costs, thereby delivering higher margins. It is not hard to understand that when the network can deliver a positive return, an organization's motivation to join can be strong. That is unless the business model favors a few at the expense of many. The selection of a business model that is fair and equitable for its members is a deciding factor in the success or failure of the network.

B2B and B2C considerations

If blockchain for the enterprise focuses on bringing together various businesses and organizations, it represents what we call a **business-to-business** (**B2B**) relationship.

An example of B2B could be the use of blockchain in the manufacturing industry to track the delivery of raw materials to the manufacturing plant, the purpose being dispute resolution and service-level adherence.

In such a scenario, the benefits and the members of the network are purely limited to the businesses of that supply chain. Furthermore, there is no inherent competition between the key participants. The network exists to reduce the operational costs associated with tracking service levels and resolving disputes.

Even in the case of an enterprise blockchain network, there are times where the customer can directly feel the benefits; think, for example, of insurance claim systems. Due to the complexity of the process and the amount of information that needs to be shared, the time required to settle a claim directly impacts the customer experience. Using blockchain to address the time aspect, the network could provide the various insurance company stakeholders with a verified and consistent view of the claim, reducing the processing time. In this case, the network brings the benefit directly to the customer, and we talk about a **business-to-customer (B2C)** relationship.

Finally, there is the scenario where organizations can come together to form a marketplace. This provides a means for them to advertise their goods and services. Through a portal, the customer can get access to these businesses and buy from them. This is akin to what Amazon is providing. Businesses have the incentive to expose their services because they get exposed to a very large set of potential customers. In this situation, we see the need for two types of interactions:

- **Marketplace**: A public place to foster competition
- **Peer-to-peer transactions**: Enable organizations to transact in complete privacy

This type of model is called **B2B2C**. Here, businesses enter into an agreement with other businesses in order to gain access to new markets or new customers. In this model, the customer is essentially the prize; the organizations will agree to pay for the right to compete and gain access to customers that they otherwise would never have reached.

By identifying the types of relationships enabled by the business network, we can get an appreciation for the type of incentive the solution will create. It also provides a good perspective on the level of competition that takes place in the network.

Without some form of collaboration, a business network could not exist. From the governance to the development of a smart contract, the members need to agree to collaborate, while recognizing that, in many cases, their objectives will be to win the business. That means competition.

Looking back at the previous examples, there are many models where competition might not be an issue. In the preceding B2B and B2C scenarios, there are no concerns around competition since the objective is to optimize existing processes.

However, the B2B2C model is not so clear. In this case, the balance between collaboration and competition needs to be clearly planned to avoid a breakdown of the network.

Understanding the level of collaboration versus competition will be essential to understand the objections and incentives each member may have. By recognizing these facts, we can ensure that there are some benefits for every participant and that the business network is fair.

Network business models

So now that we understand the importance of the fair business model, let's look at some of the business models we have observed in the industry so far:

- Founder-led network
- Consortium-based network
- Community-based network
- Hybrid models

The following sections cover each of these models.

Founder-led networks

There are many valid situations in which a founder-led network can be valuable. A normal founder-led network has the following architecture:

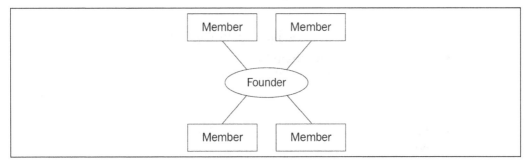

Figure 12.2: Founder-led network architecture

However, we start with a warning: a founder-led network should not be a way to avoid hard business discussions with potential network participants. From our experience, many organizations feel overwhelmed at the idea of decentralizing the control of the network. While they believe in the value of blockchain networks, they end up creating a roadmap focused on technology.

They postpone the business discussion until subsequent phases. The result is typically a fabric network hosted within the founder's infrastructure, exposing the network through an API gateway. In some cases, it goes as far as not providing a different identity (that is, a private key and certificate) to the participants. The risk here is that while the solution is technically viable, it fails to deliver value according to the tenets of blockchain networks.

This is not to say that organizations should not adopt a founder-led approach with a phased roadmap, but it is essential to get buy-in from potential participants early during the establishment of the network to avoid either a lack of adoption or significant rework efforts.

The following types of organizations typically leverage the founder-led network:

- **Start-ups**: These organizations tend to have a unique perspective on their industry and bring innovation and fresh ideas. They orient their business model toward providing an added value service to the industry. While innovation may propel them to industry recognition, their success hinges on credibility and funding.

- **Industry leaders**: From their industry perspective, they have enough influence to establish their network. They get the support of their suppliers and other organizations to define the agenda and use cases they should support.

- **Interdepartmental blockchain projects**: This model may not initially qualify as a business model, given that it is meant to serve the purpose of internal coordination in an organization. However, they are good projects to enable an organization to:

    - Learn and master blockchain technology in a safe environment.

    - Introduce a shadow chain to the central system of records of the enterprise. The shadow chain can replicate a slice of the system of record's functionality and then contribute to the elimination of satellite systems focused on reconciliation tasks.

    - Position the organization to evolve the solution beyond the boundaries of the organization.

As a founding member, they get the opportunity to define the policies and the focus of the network. Organizations that succeed with their networks get a leadership position and maintain significant influence in shaping the network optimally for their benefits. These benefits could be financial (membership fee), functional (driving feature roadmaps for their use), or competitive (creating an advantage others can't leverage).

However, these advantages do come at the risk of the need to convince other organizations to join. They also bear the complete burden of investing capital in getting the project started and getting the required expertise to deliver the solution. Finally, they are exposed to the risk of significant rework if other industry leaders request changes before joining.

Consortium-based networks

A consortium is a grouping of two or more organizations leveraging their business network to achieve their common objectives. The architecture of this network is as follows:

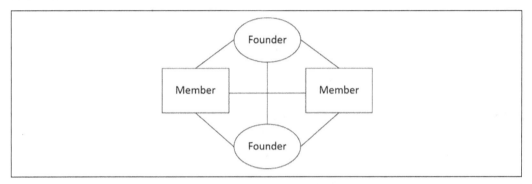

Figure 12.3: Consortium network architecture

These organizations can be in the same industry or from closely related industries. This association exists because of the level of synergy in the processes and a common, shared benefit. A vital feature of a consortium is that each member retains their legal entity and status. Through the creation of the consortium, they typically enter contractual and legal agreements that guide the governance, activities, and investments required to turn their vision into a reality.

We make a distinction between a consortium founder and member since the former faces a similar situation as a single organization adopting a founder-led network model. Although they have to deal with similar issues as a founder-led network, they are able to offset the risks through expanded industry participation. Consortium founders may also choose to monetize the network as other organizations join.

Additionally, members of a consortium may have taxation benefits, contribute to improving the regulatory posture of the industry, or create a voice that has increased influence. However, they need to deal with the potential liability and nonperformance of a founder who is not able to contribute as equally as the other.

Community-based networks

The community-based network is, in essence, a more informal consortium of like-minded organizations. Together, they form a business ecosystem that aims to foster collaboration across different industries to create new business opportunities. The architecture of this network is as follows:

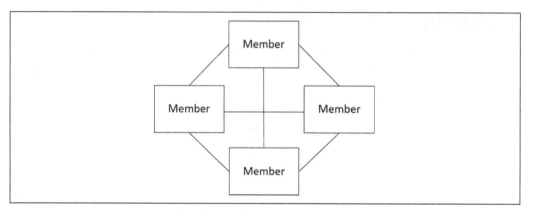

Figure 12.4: Community-based network architecture

In this model, the solution may evolve into a marketplace where each member may work to offer added-value services. The power of this model comes from the implicit free structure and the freedom for the best idea to surface. It is the best model to support the concept of a decentralized network and governance. It can, however, suffer from the same issues as the consortium if the contributions of its members are not well aligned.

Hybrid models

Business models are not static and can evolve. So, while a network may start as a community, it is conceivable that it could evolve into a consortium. Furthermore, any of these models can benefit from the two models that we discuss here.

Joint venture

In the joint venture model, a few organizations agree to own and form a new legal entity jointly. Each organization can contribute funding to gain equity in the venture. They share revenue and operational expenses. The control of the joint venture lies in the parties that form it, not with the joint venture itself.

New corporation

The **new corporation** (**NewCo**) model is similar to the joint venture model but is a complete spin-off from an enterprise or a consortium. This NewCo may provide a service to the parties that contributed to its creation; however, the NewCo wholly owns the profits and losses.

Funding models

In discussing business models, there is an implicit understanding that to be viable, these organizations need to get access to resources:

- **Human resources**: These include designers, system architects, and developers to create and deploy the required solution
- **Physical resources**: From offices to physical servers and cloud resources, these are the infrastructure a team will need
- **Financial resources**: These are required to gain access to the human and physical resources

So how can the required capital be raised to support not only the initial phases of the network but cover the operation and subsequent phases required to evolve? This is an important point: the funding needs to sustain the evolution of the network. There needs to be a way, either through revenue or a constant flow of investment, to keep the initiative afloat, or it will either fail or slowly lose members to another shiny new network. Let's take a look at some of the various approaches to raise those much-needed funds.

Token-based models

Since the blockchain revolution started with cryptocurrencies, it is almost natural that new initiatives would leverage this mechanism to generate the required funds to kickstart their projects. While there are subtleties and variations in the model, it basically consists of exchanging fiat or cryptocurrency for a quantity of tokens. The start-up can then use and convert the cryptocurrency back into fiat to pay for the required resources.

Surely, the event that sparked the interest in this new model was the **Ethereum initial coin offering** (**ICO**) that took place in 2014 and raised over $18 million in 42 days. It enabled Ethereum to grow to become a mainstream blockchain network and it's now the de facto choice when it comes to selecting a platform to run an ICO.

What exactly does one get by acquiring these tokens? Generally, the tokens can be categorized as:

- **Utility tokens**: These tokens are meant to be used as a means to access the services or goods of a platform. This means they only hold value in the context of the business network in which they are issued.

- **Cryptocurrency:** The main difference here is that the token can be used between any parties that recognize the token as holding a value.

- **Asset-backed tokens**: The value of these tokens is directly tied to the value of associated assets. It is worth mentioning that, in that context, assets can be fungible (that is, interchangeable), like a stock share, or non-fungible, like a property or an art piece.

Organizations going down the ICO route rely on a document called the **white paper** to describe the problem they aim to solve, their approach to solving it, how the funds will be used, and the team behind the initiative. This enables potential investors to assess the merits and make decisions based on it.

It is worth mentioning that the frenzy for ICOs has attracted not only investors but also scammers. Considering the high risk for fraud, along with the potential return on investments, ICOs have been the focus of many countries' financial regulators.

Traditional models

While the hype has been around the new funding model presented by ICOs, enterprise-grade networks will tend to rely on existing funding models like venture capital and corporate funding.

Venture capital focuses primarily on investment in the early stages of start-ups with high growth potential. While this is great for founder-led networks that have a market differentiator, it is not applicable to all business models. For example, the community-based network may not be focused on growth and short-term returns.

Corporate funding, on the other hand, will be something frequently seen in consortium-based networks. Many examples of such networks exist today: B3i, TradeLens, and We.Trade are all examples of consortiums where members have jointly decided to invest in the endeavor.

Having said that, this does not mean that these sources of funding are infinite. As we mentioned in the *From benefits to profits* section, there needs to be sufficient revenues and profits to sustain the operation and evolution of the network.

Membership considerations

As we will see in the next few sections, not every participant of a network has the same incentive or capability to play an active role in the network. So how do you distribute the cost of operation? Who will pay for the smart contract upkeep? Who will cover the cost of the governance board?

In addition to these costs, it is important to understand who is generating the value of the network. There might be some organizations you do not charge simply because their data feeds are mandatory for the network to exist.

One approach is to evenly distribute the cost across all members, but then, for some, the entry barrier will be too high. Modeling the membership fee structure to reflect the reality of the various types of members while taking into account the cost is not a trivial task.

Some of the models that have been explored are:

- **Membership tiering**: From bronze to gold membership, the idea, here, is that each tier ensures that the cost is aligned to the required support, infrastructure, and capabilities. In defining each tier, it is important to understand what the incentives for a participant are to upgrade their membership. If the lower tier is too generous, then the network could become unbalanced and make it unviable.

- **Transaction fees**: Membership tiers alone create a risk of having an imbalance in the load that is generated on the network. By allocating a fee per transaction, a network can avoid a situation where a bronze member is consuming a disproportionate amount of resources.

Just to reiterate, in our experience, the modeling of fee structures to ensure the network is viable is a complex process that will require multiple iterations. It will also evolve as the network grows and the types of participants evolve.

At this point, you should have a good appreciation for the various organizational structures that can frame a business network. With this basic understanding, we will now turn our attention to the real objective of this chapter: the governance of a blockchain business network.

Governance of a business network

Having reviewed the various business models, we can see that the control that each participant has varies based on the model. By understanding the model and the interests of each party, we can create a decision process that makes sense to everyone.

So, while we understand that governance is about the process to reach a decision, should the governance process manage all business decisions, operational decisions, and technical decisions? Some would argue that the governance process should cover only essential topics, but then what are these topics? It is the role of a governance model to define each decision domain and make sure everyone understands the level of **ceremony** required for each category of decision. By "ceremony," we mean the level of formalisms to apply to each process and decision. A bug fix in a smart contract may not require much attention, but an upgrade to the blockchain technology may require a heightened degree of focus. Agreeing upfront on how to handle each of these categories can help both current and future participants understand what the network expects from them. Another consideration that needs to be addressed by the governance model is the level of decentralization of decision-making.

Distributing the power of decision-making may make the process seem fair, reduce the risk of undue control, and encourage freethinking. Still, in doing so, it may create delays in the achievement of a consensus. While this makes sense in the context of a community-driven network, would it work with a founder-led network?

Probably not. If the founder is investing capital and resources, they may not want to share control over the network. Keep in mind that this is not an absolute rule. How critical the decision is plays a significant role in the amount of control that is applied.

In the case of a bug fix in a smart contract, we can expect that the decision as to when to deploy the fix should be decentralized, but that the decision as to the next feature to implement should be centralized.

The following table shows the relationship between governance and business models, and (generally speaking) how the business model can drive the governance structure. We can see that, on both sides of the scale, we have the community-based network, which tends to be a completely decentralized business model, and thus can only survive with equally decentralized governance:

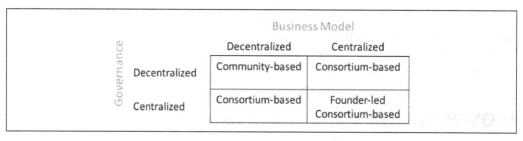

		Business Model	
		Decentralized	Centralized
Governance	Decentralized	Community-based	Consortium-based
	Centralized	Consortium-based	Founder-led Consortium-based

Figure 12.5: Relationships between business models and governance

An attempt at centralizing governance would probably compromise its very existence as the community members would either reject the control or push for the creation of a consortium. On the other end of the spectrum, we have the founder-led network, which, by its very nature, tends to retain control as the founding organization. Consortium business models tend to be variable and depend very much on their nature. A highly regulated industry may require an equivalent degree of centralization to ensure that all parties adhere to the established standards. Then again, a consortium could achieve decentralized governance by adopting a consensus mechanism for decision-making.

Mapping business roles to blockchain roles

In the context of a business network, hosting a node comes with a set of responsibilities—both business and technical. Organizations need to ensure that they adequately secure their infrastructure, provide a satisfactory level of system availability, upgrade their software, deploy smart contracts, and, ultimately, support the business process implemented by the network.

Now, every organization of a business network is bound to be different. From a bank to a trucking company, they are all of varying shapes and sizes. As such, the technological solution should aim to reflect this reality. Can we expect a small or medium-sized organization to have the same IT capability as a large corporation?

Understanding the roles and relationships of each type of organization that is involved in a business network is important because it allows us to start defining a model that accounts for those differences. It ensures that they are not going to place undue responsibilities on an organization that either cannot meet those responsibilities or that only derives marginal benefits.

Having introduced the notion that not all members need to play the same role and that there are various approaches to interact with a network, we can start seeing that there might be a way to *layer* the design of a blockchain network in such a way that:

- Organizations and people that do not have an identity interact with the network through a portal or API gateway of one of the members
- Smaller members of the network have an identity and sign their transaction but may not require or want to manage a peer
- Key influencers of the network will not only have an identity but also host and manage peers

From our experience of real-life projects, we have come to realize that these layers can be mapped to a predefined set of participant types. This list identifies some of the recurring roles and the name we have given to each of them:

- **Indirect participants**: This type of participant has not signed up to the governance charter. They also do *not* have an identity in the network. They are represented here because they interact with others through a direct participant. They will generally agree to the terms and conditions of the direct participant they chose.

- **Direct participants**: These participants' interactions are covered by and subject to the governance charter. Every direct participant holds an identity in the network. However, they may have different levels of involvement in governance. Trustees, stewards, and custodians are all direct participants.

- **Trustees**: These are direct participants of the network that have agreed to abide by the governance charter. This category of direct participant owns an identity and is responsible for submitting transactions. However, they do not operate a node.

- **Stewards**: Stewards are trustees who are also responsible for the governance of the network and for operating the nodes (peers) that maintain the distributed ledger.

- **Guardians**: These are stewards who also agree to hold and manage one or more of the trustees' identities on their behalf. They are often considered to be hosting nodes that are called **multi-tenant** nodes. All dependent identities managed by a guardian could eventually become stewards.

- **Custodians**: These are stewards who are responsible for supporting the existence of the business network. They are responsible for establishing and managing the trust framework. They can run the ordering nodes, although it is not strictly necessary that each custodian does so.

The following diagram shows the relationships between each type of participant:

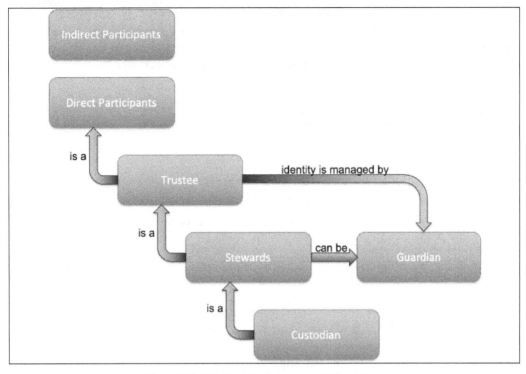

Figure 12.6: Relationships between participant types

This layering approach enables a governance organization to structure itself along those lines but also drives some of the technological decisions. By moving the business roles into the various layers, we create a funnel or a way to segregate access control going from both:

- Large crowds of participants (tens of thousands) to a very select few (tens)
- A user population that may have little IT infrastructure to organizations that are operating mature IT landscapes

Through this approach, we create not only a network that can scale but also the foundation for the governance structure. Through the assignment of an organization to a role, we start understanding the involvement that it will have in the governance of the network. We will now look at the structure of the governance board.

Governance structure

So far, in this chapter, we have:

- Looked at the various business models
- Assessed the impact of centralization versus decentralization
- Identified the roles and responsibilities of each type of member

We can now see how organizations have been structuring themselves to provide a coherent approach that deals with the different levels of focus that decision-makers have, depending on their roles.

While the centralized and decentralized governance models can appear to be very different from each other, in reality, there are shades of grey. Some functions may be central while others are decentralized. Again, much of this has to do with the business model and imperatives driving the network.

Centralized governance

While a network may adopt centralized or decentralized governance, each organization also has a mechanism to control who makes decisions. Typically, organizations rely internally on centralized governance. The implication of this is that we need to consider not only network governance but also each organization's structure, as shown in the following diagram:

Figure 12.7: Organizational structure

In a centralized model, decisions tend to flow from the top to the bottom, and only unresolved issues at the lower tiers of the organization percolate to the top. This creates a framework where there is a clear-cut process to deal with the problems and the vision, but which leaves little room for changes to the structure.

In this model, we typically see three significant layers of governance:

- Strategic
- Tactical
- Operational

The next section defines each one and explores the types of decision-makers for each layer.

Exploring the levels of governance

We are now going to dive in and explore how each of these layers influences the evolution of the organization.

Strategic governance

Strategic governance represents the top of the decision pyramid. This governance tier requires executive sponsorship from various organizations and business units and is responsible for ensuring that the vision and strategy align with the network objectives. It should focus on ensuring the realization of business benefits.

Strategic governance focuses on the following:

- Creating a common business vision
- Defining a clear mandate and governance structure (stakeholder-driven)
- Setting the agenda regarding the priorities of the network
- Ensuring that the organization meets its business objectives
- Developing and evolving network competencies

Tactical governance

Tactical governance focuses on converting the vision into a program with milestones that meet the requirements of the network. It generally involves business stakeholders, directors, IT architects, and legal counselors.

As a result of these concerns, the focus is on the following:

- Defining ownership
- Developing and maintaining standards, privacy requirements, and regulations
- Creating a common approach for services and smart contracts
- Managing a common approach to defining business and technical requirements
- Common technology infrastructure

Operational governance

Operational governance focuses on the day-to-day activities that are centered around the running and operation of the network. At this level, the focus is on aspects like the design, build, and operation of the network. It includes various stakeholders from the business, legal, and technical teams. Tasks can include elements such as the following:

- Enforcing standards
- Smart contract code reviews
- Deployment planning
- Organization onboarding
- Security audits
- Reporting

Mapping governance to organizational structure

Understanding the levels of governance is all good, but how it gets reflected in real life is a different matter. How should those levels of governance be implemented? Is there a single organization making decisions or many? Can decisions be reached through simple communication channels like email, or do representatives of each organization need to meet?

A simple network or founder-led network might be able to address the strategic, operational, and tactical governance levels in a relatively informal manner; however, for consortiums, the story is different.

In a large consortium, having a clear communication plan, which describes the various communication channels (email, web conferences, and face-to-face meetings) and the rules of engagement, will ensure that everyone is clear on the expectations.

Generally, these large consortiums are made up of two different bodies:

- The board of directors
- Advisory boards

The board of directors will consist primarily of the executive-level representation from each organization, focus on strategic-level decisions, and also act as an arbitration body when conflicts arise between members.

Advisory boards, by contrast, will be separated into different topic areas like:

- Marketing
- Legal
- Security
- Technology

The advisory boards take the form of council meetings, where members represent their organization and, together, are empowered to make decisions. Membership of a board can be permanent or based on a rotation.

For large consortiums, it makes sense to limit the participation to a smaller set of people to ensure a consensus can be reached. In such cases, relying on a rotation of members ensures that the process remains fair and every organization has the opportunity to have its voice heard.

Decentralized governance

The decentralization of governance is a way to bring transparency and fairness to the decision process. Keep in mind that every organization has its governance structure (the three tiers), and those governance bodies need to agree on the decision. It is not a trivial task considering that the strategic governance of each organization may have a different imperative. It means that the network needs to reach decisions through the form of a consensus — a voting process — that is fair and transparent and brings together the governance bodies of all the network's organizations. It also retains the same levels of governance (strategic, tactical, and operational) as a centralized network. Still, this model fosters an open model where community calls and events allow participants to discuss issues and topics. In such a model, the documentation of the decisions is even more essential to ensure a proper level of transparency. Without a public audit trail, how can one know that the decision process is equitable?

It should be noted that while the model is decentralized and can be more lightweight and agile, it is no less important to document the model and get the participant's buy-in. Note that decentralized does not mean easier.

While decentralized network governance aligns closely with the nature of blockchain technologies, it introduces some challenges. For instance, since there is no central body that controls the strategic decisions, how can a network move toward a common goal? How can you avoid a hard takeover or network fragmentation?

Such a model can work while the business objectives are aligned. However, when a corporation's agenda is delayed because the majority of the community is voting for different priorities, this is bound to generate tension, disputes, and delays. As we have seen with the Bitcoin block size debate, getting a consensus takes time and creates the opportunity for fragmentation. This is not to say that the solution lies in a centralized model—in fact, similar risks exist in that model, too—but the decentralized nature of the model may mean that participants' business objectives are not always closely aligned.

To conclude our examination of the role of governance in a business network, let's quickly look at the kinds of decisions that a business network needs to address:

- **Membership life cycle**: Decisions associated with the process of onboarding and offboarding participants to the network.

- **Funding and fees**: Decisions focused on how to fund the network. Funding may cover areas such as centralized infrastructure, shared services, and staffing.

- **Regulation**: Decisions pertaining to regulatory issues. Most industries need to meet specific regulations that are often geographically bound. This category focuses on ensuring that these regulations are met and enforced.

- **Education**: Decisions on the level of training and support to provide to members. It can focus on the use of the network and integration into it.

- **Service life cycle**: Decisions related to IT components and covering aspects such as the deployment of new smart contracts, bug fixes, and system updates.

- **Disputes**: Decisions dealing with the resolution process. This is important because at least some disputes are almost always unavoidable.

In the next section, we will dive into each of these areas and explore some of their intricacies. However, it is worth noting that, in every decision category, there is a balancing act between the following:

- Cost versus risk
- Competition versus cooperation
- Formalism versus agility

Business domains and processes

In this section, we will look at the scope of operations that a governance model should aim to address. To avoid bad surprises, each of these decision areas should be considered by any network. Not every decision needs to be bound by a formal process, but considering these elements can avoid problems down the road.

Membership life cycle

As we know, a blockchain network is meant to be fully decentralized. Thus, the expansion of participants is a normal thing that we would expect to see in a healthy network. However, since this is an enterprise-grade network that is subject to rules and regulations, some things need to be established upfront during network formation and the onboarding of new participants:

- *Who owns the privilege to invite organizations to the network?*

  It should include considerations as to who can submit a proposal to create a new organization and also considerations for channel-level invitations. Are there privacy and confidentiality constraints that we need to account for during the onboarding?

- *What are the minimum-security requirements that an organization needs to meet?*

  An organization that cannot correctly secure its peers would risk exposing its ledger data and compromising its private keys. Dealing with fraudulent transactions would lead to chaos and painful investigations. Clearly articulating the security requirements helps a new participant to understand the level of investment it needs to make.

- *What are the standard contractual agreements that participants should accept?*

  As we mentioned in previous chapters, the network members need to accept the smart contract as the enforcer of the rules of the network. However, it also needs to be bound by contractual agreements that not only recognize this fact but also state the expectations of the participant and the dispute processes.

- *What are the IT service-level agreements that the participant needs to adhere to?*

  As we have seen in *Chapter 11*, *Agility in a Blockchain Network*, getting an agreement on the frequency of promotion to smart contracts and the implicit evolution of the integration layer is crucial. It is only an example, but from a service-level agreement, there are other aspects, such as availability, performance, and throughput, that can impact the network.

Through the onboarding process, an organization needs to deploy its infrastructure, integrate transactions into its enterprise system, and complete a round of testing before it can start transacting. During its life on the network, the governing body may dictate that some audits should be performed on the participant's infrastructure to demonstrate adherence to the terms and conditions.

The event of offboarding is a situation that is sometimes overlooked. There are two events that could cause this to occur:

- The participant's interest in the network changes, and it no longer wants to transact
- A breach of contract or a dispute causes the participant to be removed

No matter what the reason is, if there are no provisions for this event, there can be issues related to the ownership of the organization's data and the resolution of pending trades or disputes. Within the context of the legal agreement of the network, the parties may agree to have the distributed ledger stored in everyone's peers; however, once that agreement comes to an end, what happens?

Funding and fees

As you saw earlier, the network cannot operate itself. There are smart contracts to develop, common infrastructure to deploy (ordering nodes, for example), and legal agreements to be written. The model that can be adopted here varies widely depending on the chosen business model. A founder-led network may incur all the funding costs; though, in turn, it might charge a fee that will not only cover the cost but also generate a profit.

On the other hand, a community-driven network may choose to have participants cover the cost of those common elements. In any case, the governance board should not only define the funding and fee structure but also consider monitoring and billing aligned to system usage.

Regulation

This area depends mainly on the industry and geography in which the network is operating. Still, at that level, there should be an identification of the compliance requirements and regulations to which participants are meant to adhere.

A good example is the **General Data Protection Regulation (GDPR)**, which has recently come into effect. GDPR is a regulation proposed by the European Commission to strengthen and reinforce data privacy rules. Under the new law, users can request to have their data permanently erased from any organization. Ignoring such regulations could result in a smart contract that persists personal information, creating a significant problem for all participants of the network when a request for erasure is received.

In this area, the focus should be on the following:

- Identifying the relevant regulations
- Auditing smart contracts and participants to ensure they are compliant

Finally, it is worth mentioning that different versions of some business networks have been deployed in different countries or regions to ensure regulations are met.

Education

This may not apply to all types of business models. For example, a community-driven model may choose not to provide education services, letting their participants manage it on their own. In contrast, a founder-led network may decide to invest in education to expedite the onboarding process and recoup the investment faster.

Service life cycle

The service life cycle deals, specifically, with the technology side of the network. Much consideration should be given upfront, from the initial design and implementation to the operation of the network.

In the initial stages of the network, key decisions include areas such as the following:

- Design authority and standards
- Requirement management (including non-functional aspects like performance and scalability)
- Data governance
- Configuration management
- Key management
- Testing processes

Once the network is ready for prime time, the operational aspect will then quickly surface:

- Infrastructure operations (network, server, and storage)
- Changes, upgrades, release management, and maintenance
- Business continuity plan, archiving, and backups
- Security, controls, and policy enforcement
- Service-level objectives around availability, capacity, scalability, and performance
- Incident and problem management

Disputes

Nobody likes to think about disputes any more than they like to think about the offboarding process; however, it is crucial to define a process to address these disputes. In that context, the governance model should cover areas such as the following:

- **Raising grievances**: Where should those issues be raised? We will cover the governance structure in the next section, but what if you are working in a truly decentralized model? Do you have a forum in which to raise this?

- **Investigation**: How will facts be gathered? How will the issue be documented? If someone questions the output of a smart contract, will it be extracted from the ledger?

- **Resolution**: Disputes will not always have happy conclusions, but what is the process to resolve them? Is there a subset of participants that should decide on the issue? Should this become a legal prosecution?

Blockchain as a governance tool

So far, in this chapter, we have focused primarily on the human side of governance. We have looked at the impact of the business model on governance, the business processes to consider, and the various potential structures, but what about the technology? What is the effect of the governance model on technology, and how does technology impact governance?

While the primary focus of blockchain projects is on solving business and enterprise issues, the foundation still relies on technology. In this section, we will look at the significant policy capabilities of Hyperledger Fabric and how it can support governance.

Managing network policies

As you now know, the system ledger is used to store the organizations, policies, and channels that make up the network. Storing configurations on the ledger means that any modifications need to be signed and approved.

Hyperledger Fabric is, therefore, excellent from an audit perspective, as it provides the configuration with the characteristics of the blockchain approach itself:

- **Consensus**: Configuration changes are endorsed and validated by members of the network according to the defined policies.
- **Provenance**: Configuration changes are signed by the initiator of the change and all other endorsers, thus preserving the provenance of the change.
- **Immutable**: Once added to the blockchain, the configuration block cannot be modified. A subsequent transaction is required to alter the configuration.
- **Finality**: As the transaction is recorded on the system ledger and distributed to all peers of the network, it provides a unique and final place to assert the configuration of the system. There is no need to look at configuration files to understand which peer your anchor should communicate with.

Now, while this is a highly valuable feature, it comes with a level of complexity. The high-level process to modify the configuration is as follows:

1. Retrieve the latest configuration block
2. Decode the configuration block and alter the configuration accordingly
3. Encode the block and calculate the delta/difference compared to the previous block to establish the RW set

4. Sign the transaction and share it with other participants so that they can sign it according to the network policy

5. Submit the signed transaction back to the network

These steps require a good understanding of the foundation of Hyperledger Fabric and a way to track and manage the signings by other parties. Given its decentralized nature, there might be a lot of different parties that need to be involved.

Types of policies

In this section, we will briefly explore the various types of policies that can be enforced by Hyperledger Fabric and understand how they support the governance of the network.

Keep in mind that the policies presented here are based on the default Hyperledger Fabric **access control list** (**ACL**), but the framework enables administrators to change those default values. To keep the discussion simple, we are focusing here on the default settings.

Organization level versus network level

If we were to define a policy that says: *All admins can update a channel definition*, how would we create a definition of what an "admin" is to suit every organization? Some small organizations might want everyone in the organization to be an admin, while a bank might have the absolute requirement for the segregation of duties.

Fortunately for us, Hyperledger Fabric caters for that situation via the use of two mechanisms:

- **Signature policy**: A signature policy indicates that a member of an organization must sign the transaction in order to fulfill the policy. However, it also needs to map to the correct member category of the organization. This can be controlled by the **membership service provider** (**MSP**) definition of each organization.

  Here's an example of a signature policy from a ConfigTX config file:

```
Policies:
    Readers:
        Type: Signature
        Rule: "OR('SampleOrg.member')"
```

In this example, any member of `SampleOrg` can act as a reader. The name `Reader` is the name of the policy. While you could use any name of your liking, the reality is that `configtx.yaml` predefines three policies:

- **Reader**: Associated with the ACL that allows read access
- **Writer**: Associated with the ACL that provides the ability to submit transactions and modify states
- **Admin**: Associated with the ACL that can modify the network configuration and policies

- **ImplicitMeta policy**: This type of policy acts at a higher level of abstraction to ensure that the identity that signs the transaction is recognized by its own organization as acting in the required role of the `ImplicitMeta` policy.

  Here's an example of an `ImplicitMeta` policy:

  ```
  Policies: &ApplicationDefaultPolicies
      Readers:
          Type: ImplicitMeta
          Rule: "ANY Readers"
  ```

Following on from the previous example, the `ImplicitMeta` policy would result in giving access to any member of the `SampleOrg` organization given that their members are automatically given the organization role of `Reader`.

Consortiums

At the consortium level, Hyperledger Fabric allows the declaration of organizations that can have visibility or manage the consortium. The primary capability a member of the consortium will have is to:

- View existing channels
- Create new channels
- Add and remove members of the consortium

It is important to note that an organization that would not be part of the consortium can still be invited to join a channel, but it will not have the ability to create new channels.

Channels

Channels follow a similar model to the consortium in the sense that members of the channel, given the access, can:

- Add new members to the channel
- Join peers to the channel
- Deploy smart contracts

Endorsements

This concept has been explored in previous chapters, so suffice it to say that an endorsement request is a form of policy that governs the process to submit transactions. By explicitly defining the participant that needs to vouch for a transaction, we are placing demands and constraints on organizations that will need to maintain peers and agree to support the execution of these transactions. Beyond the technical aspects, there is a certain level of liability that comes with the act of endorsing a transaction. As such, it should always be closely aligned to the business reality associated with the transaction.

There are many more controls that can be placed on a network. However, for the purposes of this chapter, we wanted to tie back the concepts of governance and explore how these concepts can be enforced by the blockchain foundation.

Summary

In a sense, governance is the human side of a business network. It is about how people come together and structure the decision-making process to ensure that all relevant parties are either consulted on or responsible for a decision. Governance needs to cover a broad spectrum of topics.

Technologists might be less enthused about the topic than others, but having a basic view of what it entails is useful to understand our working environments.

To sum things up, in this chapter, we explored how business models can have a profound impact on governance. Using these models, we looked at how to derive structures that meet business needs by addressing critical business processes. You have seen how organizations need to consider the approach of a centralized versus decentralized governance model. Finally, you learned that governance is required to support IT solutions; however, in turn, IT solutions also need to support governance processes.

A final point to keep in mind is that business models can be fluid. While an initiative might start as a founder-led network, it can evolve into a consortium or a community-based project. It is important to note that, although we looked at the models in isolation, the reality is that they are bound to evolve but need to remain aligned to the business value the networks provide.

Now that we have a good understanding of the effort and concepts surrounding the governance of a blockchain network, we will turn our attention to the key set of operational activities and events taking place on the network; from adding a new peer node to adding a new organization to a channel.

13
Life in a Blockchain Network

Your Fabric network should now be set up and running your application suite connecting different entities, managing a cross-organization trade through a set of smart contracts, and serving users through web interfaces. In addition, you should have instituted DevOps processes to help your developers and system administrators maintain code, push updates, and manage network configuration. You should also have mechanisms in place for testing and maintenance, and safeguards to minimize service interruptions.

Yet, the initial configuration and deployment do not represent a permanent state for your application. Change is a fact of life, as follows:

- Needs and expectations evolve, and this is especially true for a business network and workflow involving multiple collaborating entities, each of whom will have differing requirements at different points in time.

- In addition, it is expected that platform software itself will continually change and evolve even if the nature and function of an application are kept intact.

- Finally, any distributed service-oriented application (a description that can be applied to any Hyperledger Fabric application) must be prepared to handle changes in the numbers and identities of end users over time, necessitating software updates and hardware and software resource reallocation.

Over the lifetime of your blockchain network and distributed application, you will therefore see many changes that necessitate updates to code and configuration. The kinds of changes listed previously are not unique to Fabric networks, or even blockchains in general, but the mechanisms we will need to use and the considerations in selecting those mechanisms are quite specific to the platform. These, then, will be the main, though not the sole, focus of this chapter.

We will first examine the different ways in which your Fabric network structure and applications may need to be modified. Specific scenarios will be illustrated through sample code and configurations, and guidelines will be provided to help you make plans for system upgrades. We will then discuss application and network membership changes and the relevant considerations that apply to industry-scale blockchain applications. In the latter part of the chapter, we will delve into system maintenance: monitoring the health of your application and system resources and designing or upgrading your system to ensure high performance.

The following topics will be covered in this chapter:

- The Hyperledger Fabric blockchain and application life cycle with evolutions
- Adding or removing an organization's peer
- Adding a new organization to the network
- Channel configuration updates
- Upgrading smart contracts
- Framing new endorsement policies
- Upgrading the underlying platform
- System monitoring and performance
- Profiling containers and applications
- Measuring application performance

Modifying or upgrading a Hyperledger Fabric application

In the first part of this chapter, we will discuss how networks and applications evolve during their lifetimes and demonstrate how to perform common network operations and application modifications using code and Fabric tools.

Changing requirements and update modes

A distributed system built on blockchain technology, like any software system, is subject to change and needs to be continuously maintained to deliver proper functionality at the desired quality. Changes to a Fabric application require not just the usual software maintenance procedures of code and configuration changes, tests, and updates, but consensus-driven operations that are specific to blockchains. Let's examine the various ways in which the requirements of a Fabric network and its users change over time:

- **Software updates**: Changes and upgrades are an integral part of software maintenance. More frequently, modifications are required to fix bugs, performance inefficiencies, and security flaws (for example, think of the Windows Update Service). Less frequently, though almost equally inevitably, major design changes must be made to software to handle unanticipated challenges. Also, given that most applications depend on other (third-party) software, any upgrades in the latter trigger corresponding changes in the former. (Think of Windows service packs as an analogy.)

  In the Hyperledger Fabric world, you, as an application developer or system administrator, must support both application-level upgrades and platform-level upgrades. The former involves bug fixes and changes in application logic, and the latter involves changes to the underlying Fabric software.

  Software update processes for bug fixing and general maintenance are well known and can rely on the techniques discussed in *Chapter 10, Enterprise Design Patterns and Considerations*, for testing and reliable failover:

  - **Service applications**: If you recall the three-layer architecture of our canonical Fabric application, the layers above the smart contracts, which consist of web servers (exercising the Fabric SDK) and user interfaces, are typically under the control of a single organization, and they can therefore be updated through processes instituted within that organization.

  - **Smart contracts**: Updates are harder to make to smart contracts (or *chaincode*) though, as these are special pieces of software whose designs and APIs are collectively agreed upon by all the participating organizations. In Fabric 2, unlike in version 1, the organizations don't have to agree on an identical copy of the source code or binary for a given contract. It is enough for them to agree on a chaincode definition and record their approvals independently on the channel where that contract is to be deployed, as we saw in *Chapter 9, Network Operation and Distributed Application Building*.

Therefore, any update to a contract, which could be a mere change in definition or changes to the business logic, must also be consensus-driven. This is not as straightforward as pushing an update after going through a standard software modification and testing cycle. We will describe different contract upgrade processes in examples later in this section.

- **Platform software**: Finally, upgrades to the Fabric software have the potential to impact functionality and data and therefore must be done with care. We will describe the mechanisms and the pitfalls later in this section.

- **Changing resource requirements**: The resources you allocate to launch a network and deploy a distributed application are unlikely to satisfy changing user requirements over time. It is very likely that your application will receive increasing user traffic as time goes by, and no software improvement can make up for limits in hardware. Similarly, if we recall the requirements for reliability, availability, and serviceability, or RAS (see *Chapter 10, Enterprise Design Patterns and Considerations*), the proper functioning of a distributed application requires redundancy, failover, and load balancing across your system resources.

  In Fabric terms, what this translates to is that you may have to add nodes to your network for increased scale and fault tolerance. You may need more peers to serve transaction endorsement requests, and the network as a whole may need more orderer nodes to handle and balance the load of a currently bottlenecked ordering service (on the flipside, nodes can be removed to save on cost if traffic is too light). You may also need extra peer nodes in an organization for more reliable endorsement or extra orderer nodes for more reliable block creation through distributed consensus (though this may come at a performance cost). Regardless of the reason for the addition and removal of nodes in your network, you as a Fabric developer or administrator must support upgrades of this nature, and we will see how this can be done later in this section.

- **Changing user memberships**: Besides variations in user traffic, a business network must support changes in user memberships and system access levels over time. In Fabric terms, this implies adding or removing users or clients who are permitted to send requests to smart contracts and view ledger state. We have already discussed examples of member creations and authorizations in *Chapter 9, Network Operation and Distributed Application Building,* using the Fabric SDK, so this is not a topic we will discuss any further in this chapter.

Further down the stack, we may want to change channel- or organization-level policies to elevate or decrease privileges granted to existing organizations to make administrative changes. Though we will not discuss specific examples, we will demonstrate the channel configuration update mechanism that can be used to carry out such policy changes.

- **Changing application policies**: Transactions (contract invocations) in a Hyperledger Fabric application must satisfy endorsement policies, which are collectively decided on by the participants. It is possible, and even expected, that such policies will change over the course of an application's life cycle. An endorsement policy can be made less stringent for performance reasons (which we will discuss in the latter part of this chapter), as long as it assures a desired level of trust. For example, a policy requiring the signature of a member of every organization (like we configured for our trade contract in *Chapter 9, Network Operation and Distributed Application Building*) may be relaxed to a requirement for signatures from members of any two organizations. An endorsement policy can be made more stringent too if the current policy does not meet the level of trust desired by network participants. The mechanisms Fabric offers to modify endorsement policies will be discussed in examples later in this section.

- **Changing network and ledger configurations**: Finally, there will always be a need to modify the blockchain network itself to meet enhanced expectations. More organizations may want to participate in the network and the distributed application as time goes by, especially if the initial versions of the application have been validated through real-world operations. Existing organizations may want to leave too, for business or economic reasons. Even within a given organization, there may be a need to reallocate resources devoted to the application in question. Now, even though most distributed applications face these situations requiring enhancements and resource reconfigurations, blockchain applications face special challenges because of their unique nature. Recall that a blockchain is a shared ledger that must be validated and accepted by every participating network peer using commonly agreed-upon rules. This agreement extends to the structure and properties of the network itself, which is recorded on the ledger through consensus. We saw examples of this in *Chapter 9, Network Operation and Distributed Application Building*, where the channel joins and chaincode definition commitments resulted in the creation of transaction blocks.

In Hyperledger Fabric terms, an application is built on one or more channels (blockchain instances) whose rules and contents (that is, transaction data) are private to application participants and controlled collectively by them. Any changes to channel structure or policy require the new configuration to be recorded on the channel's ledger. Examples of changes requiring channel reconfigurations are the addition of a new organization with its own peer set; the removal of an organization; changes in peer or orderer addresses; the selection of different anchor peers within organizations; ordering service properties like block sizes and timeouts; channel access policies for reads, writes, and administration operations; hashing mechanisms; consensus mechanisms and clusters used for ordering. Although comprehensive coverage of channel configuration use cases is beyond the scope of this chapter, we will see how to make Fabric channel configuration updates in examples later in this section.

In the remainder of this section, we will cover the most common update procedures you will need to do on a live network. Some of these can be carried out using procedures we already know from the enterprise software world or have learned about in earlier chapters. But there are others that require special support from the blockchain platform, namely:

- **Channel configuration updates**: These are required to change network or channel properties. They cover the addition and removal of organizations, resource changes (the roles of peer and orderer nodes in their respective clusters), and changes in channel properties (policy and block creation rules, hashing, and consensus mechanisms).

- **Smart contract updates**: These are required to change contract properties, such as code and chaincode definitions (including endorsement policies).

To implement such upgrades in our trade network, we will need to augment the applications and tools demonstrated earlier in this book. Fortunately, the designers of the Fabric platform anticipated the kinds of network evolutions we have discussed in this chapter and have built capabilities for these that can be exercised using the CLI. The exercises we will go through in this chapter are of interest primarily to network operators rather than application developers. Only if a network modification or upgrade necessitates changes in application business logic will a developer need to be involved. Before we turn to implementation details, let's revisit the Fabric network life cycle illustrated in *Chapter 9, Network Operation and Distributed Application Building,* and modify it to incorporate system updates.

Fabric blockchain and application life cycle

Looking back at the process flow diagram in *Figure 9.1*, which was further expanded in Figures 9.4 and 9.5, we get a picture of how a network is launched and applications deployed on it are exercised at runtime. Missing from those diagrams are evolutions of the network and applications, of the form we have discussed in this chapter. *Figure 13.1* illustrates an expanded version of *Figure 9.1* with channel, contract, and platform updates called out explicitly. This diagram is not meant to be an exhaustive representation of all possible stages of a Fabric network or all possible changes, but it does show the ones you are most likely to encounter in practice and also covers the three modes listed in the preceding section.

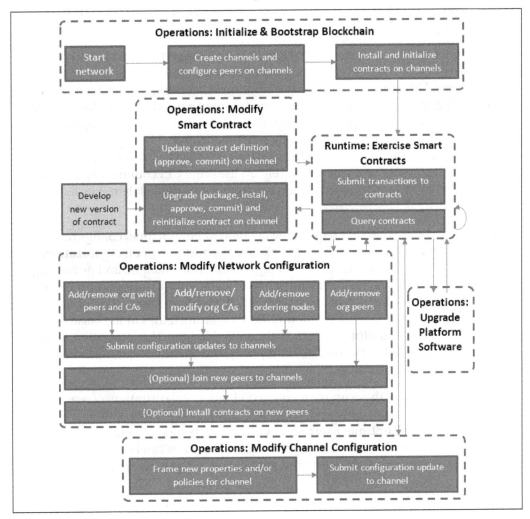

Figure 13.1: The evolutions in the life cycle of a blockchain network and application

The number of steps required may vary depending on the type of update we want to make, as you can see in the figure. Some, like peer additions and removals within an organization (see the **Operations: Modify Network Configuration** block in *Figure 13.1*) or upgrades of the platform software (see the **Operations: Upgrade Platform Software** block), require no changes to code nor the appending of blocks to the shared ledger. Any additions of peer nodes, either within existing organizations or in newly added ones, require the explicit joining of those peers to the channel through a similar procedure to the one we encountered in *Chapter 9, Network Operation and Distributed Application Building*. To assign endorsing roles to these new peers, the current version of a contract must be installed on those peers, again using a similar procedure to what we encountered earlier. The gossip protocol will then help these peers "catch up" with the rest of the network by eventually syncing the latest copy of the shared ledger.

Smart contract updates (see the **Operations: Modify Smart Contract** block) require a bit more work and result in commitments of blocks containing the new contract configurations. Updating the chaincode definitions, including endorsement policies, requires going through the approval and commitment procedures. Updating code, on the other hand, requires going through the full installation procedure, from packaging to commitment, and optionally a reinitialization. These processes are similar to those we ran in *Chapter 9, Network Operation and Distributed Application Building*, for the initial deployment and rely on the same CLI commands, though they allow the contract workflow to carry on from the current state rather than from a blank ledger.

Lastly, there are scenarios that require the creation of new channel configurations to represent deeper changes to the network, like the addition of an organization, changes in the ordering service cluster or algorithm, MSP changes, and governing policy modifications (see the **Operations: Modify Network Configuration** block again). Changing a channel configuration typically requires the creation of new channel or cryptographic artifacts, modifying specific attributes in the latest configuration, and committing a block to the shared ledger. This procedure requires some knowledge of network structure and policy and should be conducted with care by network administrators.

Before and after any of these updates are carried out, regular runtime operations consisting of sequences of contract transactions and queries may continue unimpeded (see the **Runtime: Exercise Smart Contracts** block). In the next few sections, we will describe how commonly required updates can be carried out, using our trade network and distributed application as the basis for demonstration.

Before we make code changes and run commands, let's understand what the blockchain looks like when the system undergoes different kinds of changes. *Figure 13.2* illustrates sections of a blockchain with different kinds of blocks representing different operations:

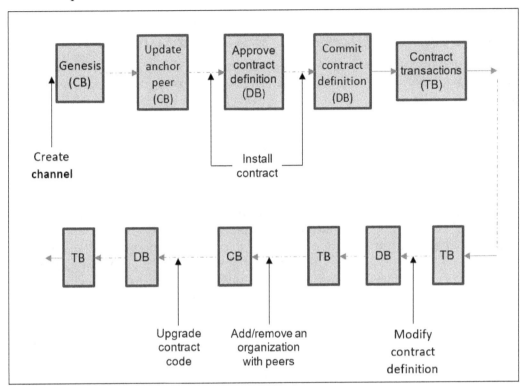

Figure 13.2: A section of a blockchain with configuration blocks, blocks containing contract deployment transactions, and regular contract transactions

Our blockchain (or in other words, the shared ledger transaction log) begins with a genesis block, which contains the initial configuration of the channel (as sketched out in the config.tx file). Subsequent anchor peer updates will append new **configuration blocks (CBs)**. An initial version of a contract can be deployed, resulting in a sequence of chaincode definition approval and commitment blocks, which we refer to as **deployment blocks (DBs)** (this is not a Fabric term). Subsequently, regular operation ensues, and transactions submitted to the contract are recorded in regular **transaction blocks (TBs)**, containing sets of transactions. A chaincode definition update at some stage will require approvals and commitments, resulting in more deployment blocks. If a new organization with peers is added, another configuration block will be appended, overriding the previous configuration block in the chain.

A new version of a contract requires the installation of the new code package, with the upgrade being recorded in new approval and commitment blocks. In between these configuration and deployment blocks, regular contract transactions will be submitted in blocks and appended to the chain.

Network organization resource updates

The first kind of update we will discuss is an extension of the existing trade network and does not involve any changes to channel properties or contracts. Consider a situation where an organization, say ImporterOrg, gets a lot of traffic resulting in its sole peer, peer0.importerorg.trade.com, being overloaded with requests. Or consider another situation where this peer occasionally fails or must be brought down for maintenance. For increased scale and fault tolerance, it is typically good practice (as we discussed in *Chapter 10, Enterprise Design Patterns and Considerations*) to keep redundant peers available and ready to share the load.

Hyperledger Fabric supports organizations having any number of peers for these purposes and, in addition, for redundant endorsements. For example, a contract could be defined with an endorsement policy that requires not one but two peers of ImporterOrg executing and signing transactions; this may be useful if the peer infrastructure is managed by untrusted third parties. All peers sync the latest ledger state using the gossip protocol and fetch blocks from the ordering service. (Note that one peer in each organization must be a designated anchor peer for these protocols to work.)

Adding a peer to an organization

Let's add a peer named peer1.importerorg.trade.com to ImporterOrg:

1. First, we need to create cryptographic artifacts using the cryptogen tool. We use the file bash/add_peer_importer/crypto-config.yaml to increment the configuration for ImporterOrg we used for our initial network (in bash/crypto-config.yaml):

```
PeerOrgs:
- Name: ImporterOrg
    Domain: importerorg.trade.com
    EnableNodeOUs: true
    Template:
      Count: 2
    Users:
      Count: 0
```

The `Template` count of 2 indicates that this organization should contain two peers, and the `Users` count of 0 indicates that it needs no extra users. We run `cryptogen` as follows (from the `bash` folder):

```
$ cryptogen extend --input=crypto-config --config=./add_peer_
importer/crypto-config.yaml
```

The tool interprets the configuration as an instruction to extend the existing cryptographic artifacts in the `bash/crypto-config/peerOrganizations/importerorg.trade.com/` folder as required. Since the folder already contains artifacts for one peer (`peer0`), the preceding command will create artifacts for another peer (`peer1`). The artifacts already created for users (one administrator and two regular users) are left undisturbed. You can run the preceding command through our `trade.sh` script as follows:

```
$ ./trade.sh createnewpeer
```

You will see the following folder getting created: `bash/crypto-config/peerOrganizations/importerorg.trade.com/peers/peer1.importerorg.trade.com/`. This contains certificates and keys for MSP-issued identities and for TLS communication, just like `peer0.importerorg.trade.com` does.

2. Using these newly created artifacts, we can now define the peer service configuration. Remember that a peer in ImporterOrg needs a CouchDB instance as a backing store for the ledger, as was configured in `bash/docker-compose-couchdb.yaml` for `peer0.importerorg.trade.com`. Therefore, we need to create containers for a new peer as well as a new CouchDB instance, which we do in `bash/docker-compose-another-importer-peer.yaml` as follows:

```
peer1.importerorg.trade.com:
  container_name: peer1.importerorg.trade.com
  extends:
    file: base/peer-base.yaml
    service: peer-base
  environment:
    - CORE_PEER_ID=peer1.importerorg.trade.com
    - CORE_PEER_ADDRESS=peer1.importerorg.trade.com:11051
    ......
    - CORE_PEER_LOCALMSPID=ImporterOrgMSP
    - CORE_LEDGER_STATE_STATEDATABASE=CouchDB
    - CORE_LEDGER_STATE_COUCHDBCONFIG_COUCHDBADDRESS=couchdb-
peer1.importerorg.trade.com:5984
  depends_on:
    - couchdb-peer1.importerorg.trade.com
  volumes:
```

```
       - /var/run/:/host/var/run/
       - ./crypto-config/peerOrganizations/importerorg.trade.com/
peers/peer1.importerorg.trade.com/msp:/etc/hyperledger/fabric/
msp
       - ./crypto-config/peerOrganizations/importerorg.trade.com/
peers/peer1.importerorg.trade.com/tls:/etc/hyperledger/fabric/
tls
       - peer1.importerorg.trade.com:/var/hyperledger/production
     ports:
       - 11051:11051
     networks:
       - trade
  couchdb-peer1.importerorg.trade.com:
     container_name: couchdb-peer1.importerorg.trade.com
     ......
     ports:
       - "8984:5984"
     networks:
       - trade
```

The peer, like all our other peers, is configured using base/peer-base.yaml as the base. It contains the usual environment variables for various service endpoints, with only the peer name (peer1.importerorg.trade.com) and the port (11051) modified. Any connection profile created for an application will use these names and ports for connectivity. A new CouchDB service named couchdb-peer1.importerorg.trade.com is created to listen on a unique port (8984), and the peer is configured to depend on this service using the CORE_LEDGER_STATE_COUCHDBCONFIG_COUCHDBADDRESS variable. Finally, as the peer's volumes section indicates, this peer uses the newly created MSP and TLS artifacts to join and participate in the trade network.

We can launch the peer and CouchDB services using the trade.sh script as follows (this uses docker-compose). Make sure you already have the initial network up using steps outlined in previous chapters before you run this:

```
$ ./trade.sh startnewpeer
```

You should see an additional peer and CouchDB instance when you run docker ps:

```
CONTAINER ID      IMAGE                              COMMAND                      CREATED
 STATUS           PORTS                                      NAMES
cd046b153a3c      hyperledger/fabric-peer:2.2.0      "peer node start"            1 second ago
 Created                                                     peer1.importerorg.trade.com
f8bf6ce72499      couchdb:2.3                        "tini -- /docker-ent..."     2 seconds ago
 Up 1 second      4369/tcp, 9100/tcp, 0.0.0.0:8984->5984/tcp   couchdb-peer1.importerorg.trade.c
om
```

Figure 13.3: A new peer and its backing CouchDB instance started for the importer organization

3. To join the peer to our two channels, run the following (As for our earlier peer joins, we rely on the `trade_cli` container for these operations. Make sure you have already created and bootstrapped the channels):

```
$ ./trade.sh joinnewpeer -c tradechannel
$ ./trade.sh joinnewpeer -c shippingchannel
```

The new peer is now connected to the network and will sync ledgers for both these channels from other peers using the gossip protocol! If you examine the code in `cli_scripts/channel.sh`, you will see that the join procedure involves fetching the oldest configuration block (or genesis block) for each channel and submitting a `peer channel join` CLI command using that block file.

The peer launch and join procedures were performed using code our reader is already familiar with from the discussions in earlier chapters. See `trade.sh` and `cli_scripts/channel.sh` for more details. You can also check the state of the blockchain using `trade.sh fetchconfig` to verify that no new blocks were created in the join operation.

Installing a smart contract on a new peer

We have created a validating and committing peer, which would be enough if fault tolerance was the purpose of expanding the network. But if we need the new peer to share traffic load and participate in endorsements, we must install contracts on it too. Though there is no shortcut command using `trade.sh` for this operation, we can do it quite simply on the `trade_cli` container using methods you are already familiar with.

Let's install the trade contract on `peer1.importerorg.trade.com`. As a prerequisite, we assume that this contract has already been installed on the peers of `ExporterOrg`, `ImporterOrg`, and `RegulatorOrg`, and its definition committed to `tradechannel`. So, you should see three separate containers running this contract on your machine. To install the contract on our new `ImporterOrg` peer, log in to the `trade_cli` container:

```
$ docker exec -it trade_cli bash
```

Set environment variables to assume the signing identity of the importer organization's administrator user (created for our initial network), the importer organization's MSP ID, the new peer's TLS credentials, and the new peer's service address and port:

```
$ export CORE_PEER_LOCALMSPID=ImporterOrgMSP
$ export CORE_PEER_MSPCONFIGPATH=/opt/gopath/src/github.com/
hyperledger/fabric/peer/crypto/peerOrganizations/importerorg.trade.com/
users/Admin\@importerorg.trade.com/msp
$ export CORE_PEER_ADDRESS=peer1.importerorg.trade.com:11051
$ export CORE_PEER_TLS_ROOTCERT_FILE=/opt/gopath/src/github.com/
hyperledger/fabric/peer/crypto/peerOrganizations/importerorg.trade.com/
peers/peer1.importerorg.trade.com/tls/ca.crt
$ export CORE_PEER_TLS_CERT_FILE=/opt/gopath/src/github.com/
hyperledger/fabric/peer/crypto/peerOrganizations/importerorg.trade.com/
peers/peer1.importerorg.trade.com/tls/server.crt
$ export CORE_PEER_TLS_KEY_FILE=/opt/gopath/src/github.com/hyperledger/
fabric/peer/crypto/peerOrganizations/importerorg.trade.com/peers/peer1.
importerorg.trade.com/tls/server.key
```

Package the `trade` contract as follows:

```
$ peer lifecycle chaincode package trade_v1.tar.gz --path ./contracts/
v1/trade/ --lang node --label trade
```

You should see a zipped archive named `trade_v1.tar.gz` created in the current folder. Now install the package on `peer1.importerorg.trade.com` as follows:

```
$ peer lifecycle chaincode install --connTimeout 300s trade_v1.tar.gz
```

Log out of the container and run `docker ps | grep dev- | grep trade-` to see the list of running trade chaincode containers. You should now see four containers running the `trade` contract, including the one we just installed, as follows:

```
86c378d42457        dev-peer1.importerorg.trade.com-trade-7548b931013419d78667b3faaf2fa16020b17c6ce
fc0e52c06b8dfed5f1d66aa-b0c8e00cce1111eb8cbf936efd67e1c41c8b3534e14ec77ff81cd9e3cb2dc6d6    "docker
-entrypoint.s…"    7 seconds ago        Up 5 seconds
       dev-peer1.importerorg.trade.com-trade-7548b931013419d78667b3faaf2fa16020b17c6cefc0e52c06b8dfed
5f1d66aa
fb2755d65069          dev-peer0.regulatororg.trade.com-trade-7548b931013419d78667b3faaf2fa16020b17c6c
efc0e52c06b8dfed5f1d66aa-02ce74f94cd69c8fca4c5559a50664825ddf2d6d4321419d1d357927bf562440    "docker
-entrypoint.s…"    2 minutes ago        Up About a minute
       dev-peer0.regulatororg.trade.com-trade-7548b931013419d78667b3faaf2fa16020b17c6cefc0e52c06b8dfe
d5f1d66aa
037213dfe72d          dev-peer0.importerorg.trade.com-trade-7548b931013419d78667b3faaf2fa16020b17c6ce
fc0e52c06b8dfed5f1d66aa-47825b1e7db0be27ddd41ece867b7c698b09731a1b84a64bef642c4de849e23e    "docker
-entrypoint.s…"    2 minutes ago        Up About a minute
       dev-peer0.importerorg.trade.com-trade-7548b931013419d78667b3faaf2fa16020b17c6cefc0e52c06b8dfed
5f1d66aa
78af2115b41b          dev-peer0.exporterorg.trade.com-trade-7548b931013419d78667b3faaf2fa16020b17c6ce
fc0e52c06b8dfed5f1d66aa-9c88ffd67f9c316565d651a1317d79038c799d4aac4970eee6852bd63220ac81    "docker
-entrypoint.s…"    2 minutes ago        Up About a minute
       dev-peer0.exporterorg.trade.com-trade-7548b931013419d78667b3faaf2fa16020b17c6cefc0e52c06b8dfed
5f1d66aa
```

Figure 13.4: Trade contract successfully installed on the new importer organization peer

The installation did not require any channel operations as we did not attempt to change the `trade` chaincode definition but rather just launch another instance of existing code.

You can install other contracts on this peer using a similar sequence of steps.

You can also update your `ImporterOrg` connection profile (used by the importer service application) to include a specification for `peer1.importerorg.trade.com` in addition to `peer1.importerorg.trade.com`. Using the augmented profile, the Fabric SDK will direct a contract query or transaction to either of these two peers, thereby spreading the load. Our project repository does not contain code to automatically augment the profile, but you can either modify the code or the profile directly using the methods demonstrated in *Chapter 9, Network Operation and Distributed Application Building*.

Removing a peer from an organization

The corollary of adding a peer for resourcing reasons is the removal of such a peer if its services are no longer needed. This is a very simple operation, requiring no more than bringing down the containers running the peer and its CouchDB instance, whose configurations are defined in `bash/docker-compose-another-importer-peer.yaml`. Use the `trade.sh` script to remove a peer as follows:

```
$ ./trade.sh stopnewpeer
```

This command runs `docker-compose` with appropriate parameters, as you can see if you examine the script code. If you run `docker ps`, you will see the peer and CouchDB containers now gone. If you had installed any contracts on this peer, they will be stopped as well. After you do this, you should update any connection profiles referencing the removed peer and make changes to applications targeting this peer so their operations are unaffected.

> Removing a peer is a very simple operation (and so is adding a new peer once its configuration has been generated) because organizations rather than peers are building blocks of Fabric channels and networks. Recall that the `configtx.yaml` file contains organization specifications with only an anchor peer specified (this is optional too) for a given organization. How many peers an organization chooses to employ in a network and channel is a decision that is left to that organization's administrators.

Channel configuration updates

As mentioned earlier in this chapter, there are many reasons why a channel configuration may have to be changed. As channel behavior is completely dictated by its configuration, and any update is recorded on the blockchain (hence overriding the previous configuration), this is a sensitive operation that must be restricted to privileged (admin) users, just like channel creation and joining and contract installations were. An exhaustive discussion and demonstration of channel configuration changes are beyond the scope of this book, but we will show the update mechanism using the CLI tools that Fabric provides. This mechanism can be applied to any configuration change; the only detail that will vary is the content of the proposed new configuration.

Adding a new organization to a live network

For demonstration, we will use a common situation any Fabric network operator will encounter in practice: adding a new organization and peers to the network and augmenting the distributed application to support this new organization. Consider our trade scenario where thus far, an exporter and its bank have shared an organization whose MSP (CA) and peer are maintained by the latter. The importer and its bank belong to a single organization as well, the logic being that banks have more incentive, as well as resources, to maintain peers and MSPs. But this logic may not hold forever. Let's say our exporter, who started out as a small-scale operator, gains higher profit and a higher reputation for honesty and quality over time. It is now a large-scale exporter of raw material with huge cash reserves and clout in the market. This creates an incentive for the exporter to "go it alone", that is, join the trade Fabric network as a peer organization rather than a dependent (or client) of a bank's organization. Another driver for independence is that the exporter may maintain accounts with banks other than our designated exporter's bank (represented by ExporterOrg in the network) and therefore would like to participate in multiple channels and multiple distributed applications (other than our trade application) running on a Fabric network.

Our goal is the following: allow the exporter to continue participating in the trade and shipping channels and the distributed application layered over it, but in its own organization, running its own MSP and its own network peer, independent of the bank. Also, no state or history must be lost in the process. *Figure 13.5* illustrates the network we would like to realize:

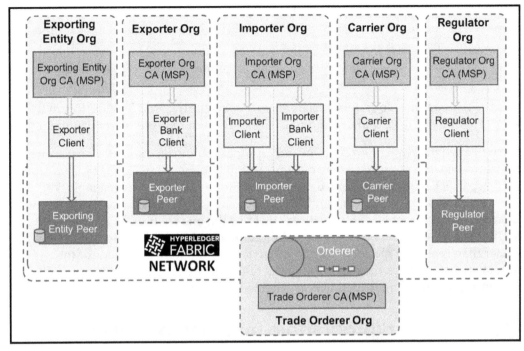

Figure 13.5: The augmented trade network with an organization, MSP, and peer for an exporter (or exporting entity)

We'll call the new organization `ExportingEntityOrg`, its MSP `ExportingEntityOrgMSP`, and the peer `exportingentity`. This is because new organizations and peers must have unique names, and the names `ExporterOrg`, `ExporterOrgMSP`, and `exporter` have already been taken in our network to represent the exporter's bank.

Prerequisites for adding a new organization to the network

We begin where we left off at the end of *Chapter 9, Network Operation and Distributed Application Building*. We assume that:

- You have a local copy of the `trade-network` repository
- You have the trade network up and running, with a Solo or Raft ordering service

- You have `tradechannel` and `shippingchannel` configured on the network with four contracts deployed: `trade`, `letterOfCredit`, `exportLicense`, and `shipment`, each at version v1

- You have four service-layer applications running: `exporter`, `importer`, `carrier`, and `regulator`

- You ran sample scripts in `apps/sample-cli-curl/` based on curl to run a workflow for a trade with the ID `trade-12` from request to final payment

We will need to create more channel and cryptographic artifacts for the components of `ExportingEntityOrg`, just as we did for our initial network in *Chapter 4, Setting the Stage with a Business Scenario*, using the `configtxgen` and `cryptogen` tools. We will need both a `configtx.yaml` and a `crypto-config.yaml` file for this purpose, but these can be incremental configurations, just like the one we used in the preceding section to add a peer to `ImporterOrg`. Maintaining incremental configuration files rather than replacing older ones also makes it easy for a network operator (or administrator) to track the evolution of the organization structure and resources. Our incremental configuration files are defined in the `bash/add_org/` folder.

Generating cryptographic material for the new organization

Our first step is to generate cryptographic material (certificates and keys for peers, users, and TLS communication) for a new peer and CA. The `crypto-config.yaml` file in `bash/add_org/` contains the `ExportingEntityOrg` specification:

```
PeerOrgs:
  - Name: ExportingEntityOrg
    Domain: exportingentityorg.trade.com EnableNodeOUs: true
    Template:
      Count: 1
    Users:
      Count: 1
```

As we can see, the specification is identical to the ones we defined for our initial four organizations, except that the MSP name and organization domain reflect the nature of the exporting entity organization. To generate the crypto material just for this organization, run the following command:

```
$ cryptogen extend --input=crypto-config --config=./add_org/crypto-config.yaml
```

The output is saved to `crypto-config/peerOrganizations`, where you will see a folder named `exportingentityorg.trade.com` in addition to the existing organizations' folders. This folder contains the keys and certificates for our new organization.

Generating channel artifacts for the new organization

Similarly, the `configtx.yaml` file in `bash/add_org/` contains only the specification of the exporting entity's organization in the `Organizations` section, as follows:

```
Organizations:
- &ExportingEntityOrg
  Name: ExportingEntityOrg
  ID: ExportingEntityOrgMSP
  MSPDir: crypto-config/peerOrganizations/exportingentityorg.trade.com/
    msp
  Policies:
    Readers:
      Type: Signature
      Rule: "OR(ExportingEntityOrgMSP.admin',
        ExportingEntityOrgMSP.peer', ExportingEntityOrgMSP.client')"
    Writers:
      Type: Signature
      Rule: "OR(ExportingEntityOrgMSP.admin',
        ExportingEntityOrgMSP.client')"
    Admins:
      Type: Signature
      Rule: "OR(ExportingEntityOrgMSP.admin')"
    Endorsement:
      Type: Signature
      Rule: "OR(ExportingEntityOrgMSP.peer')"
  AnchorPeers:
  - Host: peer0.exportingentityorg.trade.com
  - Port: 12051
```

This specification uses the same structure that every other (existing) organization and anchor peer uses; only the details are different: organization name, MSP ID, the path of the cryptographic material we just created, the service address, and the port.

To build the incremental configuration for `ExportingEntityOrg` on `tradechannel`, run the following command from the `bash` folder:

```
FABRIC_CFG_PATH=$PWD/add_org && configtxgen -printOrg
ExportingEntityOrgMSP -channelID tradechannel > ./channel-artifacts/
tradechannel/exportingEntityOrg.json
```

This is a different artifact from the ones we generated in *Chapter 4, Setting the Stage with a Business Scenario*. We don't need to build an orderer genesis block as the system channel is up and running. We don't need to generate a full channel configuration transaction nor a separate anchor peer configuration for the new organization. All we need is a JSON spec that contains information pertaining to the exporting entity's organization, namely, policies for reading, writing, and administration, and certificates for administrators, peers, root CAs, and TLS communication. This JSON will be used later to update the configuration of `tradechannel`.

 To ensure that `configtxgen` looks for the `configtx.yaml` file in the `add_org` directory, we must temporarily change the value of the `FABRIC_CFG_PATH` environment variable.

To build a similar incremental configuration for `ExportingEntityOrg` on `shippingchannel`, run:

```
FABRIC_CFG_PATH=$PWD/add_org && configtxgen -printOrg
ExportingEntityOrgMSP -channelID shippingchannel > ./channel-artifacts/
shippingchannel/exportingEntityOrg.json
```

In this case, the generated JSON `exportingEntityOrg.json` is identical in folders `channel-artifacts/tradechannel` and `channel-artifacts/shippingchannel` because we used the same `configtx.yaml` file, but we can envision situations where the same organization is configured differently (for example, the policies) for different channels.

Generating the cryptographic and channel artifacts in one operation

Instead of running `cryptogen` and `configtxgen` explicitly, you can use the `trade.sh` script. Just run the following command from `bash \`:

```
$ ./trade.sh createneworg -c tradechannel
$ ./trade.sh createneworg -c shippingchannel
```

These generate both cryptographic material in the crypto-config folder and the incremental channel configurations in the channel-artifacts folder.

Docker containers for the new organization

The incremental Docker network configuration for our new organization is specified in bash/docker-compose-exportingEntityOrg.yaml. Three container services are defined: a CA node serving as the organization's MSP peer, a peer node, and a CouchDB instance for the peer's ledger. Here is the CA node's configuration:

```
exportingentity-ca:
  image: hyperledger/fabric-ca:$CA_IMAGE_TAG
  environment:
    - FABRIC_CA_HOME=/etc/hyperledger/fabric-ca-server
    - FABRIC_CA_SERVER_CA_NAME=ca-exportingentityorg
    - FABRIC_CA_SERVER_TLS_ENABLED=true
    - FABRIC_CA_SERVER_TLS_CERTFILE=/etc/hyperledger/
    fabric-ca-server-config/ca.exportingentityorg.trade.com-cert.pem
    - FABRIC_CA_SERVER_TLS_KEYFILE=/etc/hyperledger/
    fabric-ca-server-config/priv_sk
  ports:
    - "12054:7054"
  command: sh -c 'fabric-ca-server start --ca.certfile /etc/
hyperledger/fabric-ca-server-config/ca.exportingentityorg.trade.com-
cert.pem --ca.keyfile /etc/hyperledger/fabric-ca-server-config/priv_sk
-b admin:adminpw -d'
  volumes:
    - ./crypto-config/peerOrganizations/exportingentityorg.trade.com/
    ca/:/etc/hyperledger/fabric-ca-server-config
    - ca.exportingentityorg.trade.com:/etc/hyperledger/fabric-ca-server
  container_name: ca.exportingentityorg.trade.com
  networks:
    - trade
```

You may notice that the configuration is similar to those defined for the four currently running CA nodes, as defined in bash/docker-compose-e2e.yaml. The differences lie in the container names, service address (ca.exportingentityorg. trade.com), the port mapped to the host (12054), paths to cryptographic material, and volumes, all of which are specific to the exporting entity's organization.

The configuration of the peer and its backing CouchDB instance will, likewise, be familiar to you, as the following snippets indicate:

```
peer0.exportingentityorg.trade.com:
  container_name: peer0.exportingentityorg.trade.com
  extends:
    file: base/peer-base.yaml
    service: peer-base
  environment:
    - CORE_PEER_ID=peer0.exportingentityorg.trade.com
    - CORE_PEER_ADDRESS=peer0.exportingentityorg.trade.com:12051
    ......
    - CORE_PEER_LOCALMSPID=ExportingEntityOrgMSP
    - CORE_LEDGER_STATE_STATEDATABASE=CouchDB
    - CORE_LEDGER_STATE_COUCHDBCONFIG_COUCHDBADDRESS=couchdb-peer0.
exportingentityorg.trade.com:5984
  depends_on:
    - couchdb-peer0.exportingentityorg.trade.com
  volumes:
    - /var/run/:/host/var/run/
    - ./crypto-config/peerOrganizations/exportingentityorg.trade.com/
peers/peer0.exportingentityorg.trade.com/msp:/etc/hyperledger/
fabric/msp
    - ./crypto-config/peerOrganizations/exportingentityorg.trade.com/
peers/peer0.exportingentityorg.trade.com/tls:/etc/hyperledger/
fabric/tls
    - peer0.exportingentityorg.trade.com:/var/hyperledger/production
  ports:
    - 12051:12051
  networks:
    - trade
couchdb-peer0.exportingentityorg.trade.com:
  container_name: couchdb-peer0.exportingentityorg.trade.com
  ......
  ports:
    - "9984:5984"
  networks:
    - trade
```

Note that the peer and CouchDB addresses and ports are unique to these nodes (to avoid conflicts with existing peers' and CouchDB instances' ports) and that they rely on MSP and TLS cryptographic material we generated earlier in this chapter. Also, all three containers are meant to be part of the trade Docker network, which is what we have been building channels and applications on.

Launching network components for the new organization

To start the peer, CouchDB instance, and MSP for our new organization, just run the following command (to run it as a background process and redirect output to a log file):

```
$ docker-compose -f docker-compose-exportingEntityOrg.yaml up > logs/
network-neworg.log 2>&1 &
```

Alternatively, you can use the `trade.sh` script as follows:

```
$ ./trade.sh startneworg
```

You can run this as a background process and redirect the standard output to a log file if you choose. Otherwise, you will see the various containers starting up and logs from each displayed on the console. From a different terminal window, if you run `docker ps -a`, you will see the following three additional containers:

```
CONTAINER ID         IMAGE                                                                          COMMAND
                     CREATED           STATUS          PORTS
       NAMES
97b88ba0f2e6         hyperledger/fabric-peer:2.2.0
                                                                                          "peer n
ode start"     9 seconds ago     Up 7 seconds    7051/tcp, 0.0.0.0:12051->12051/tcp
       peer0.exportingentityorg.trade.com
a2dfbe8bb0ad         couchdb:2.3
                                                                                          "tini -
- /docker-ent..."   11 seconds ago    Up 9 seconds    4369/tcp, 9100/tcp, 0.0.0.0:9984->5984/t
cp    couchdb-peer0.exportingentityorg.trade.com
525afae6d3f4         hyperledger/fabric-ca:1.4.8
                                                                                          "sh -c
'fabric-ca-se..."   11 seconds ago    Up 9 seconds    0.0.0.0:12054->7054/tcp
       ca.exportingentityorg.trade.com
```

Figure 13.6: Peer, backing CouchDB instance, and Fabric CA service containers for the new exporting entity organization

To stop the peer, CouchDB, and CA containers associated with the exporting entity's organization, you can run:

```
$ ./trade.sh stopneworg
```

Keep in mind that if you do this after the organization is joined to the channel and new applications have been launched, you may encounter failures as the new business logic (which we will discuss later) will rely partly on the new organization.

We are now ready to begin the process of reconfiguring the channel to accept the new organization. Note that we did not need to start the network components prior to the update, but we did so just to ensure that all network operations were completed before moving our focus to channel operations.

Updating the channel configuration

A channel's configuration is updated by creating a new configuration and submitting it to the channel, thereby creating a new configuration block that overrides the previous configuration block in the chain. As we demonstrated in *Chapter 9*, *Network Operation and Distributed Application Building*, and revisited in *Figure 13.2*, the channel creation step produced the initial configuration in the genesis block, and subsequent anchor peer updates (three for `tradechannel` and four for `shippingchannel`) appended new blocks and overrode previous configurations. The channel update we will perform is a four-step process:

1. Fetch the latest channel configuration from the blockchain
2. Parse and modify the configuration to produce a new one
3. Get enough signatures on the new configuration to fulfill channel policy
4. Submit a channel configuration update to record the new configuration

First, let's consider the tools required for this process.

Tools for channel configuration updates

Like we did for channel creations and joins, we will use the `trade_cli` container built on the `hyperledger/fabric-tools` Docker image to perform these steps. The logic resides in `cli_scripts/channel.sh` (just like the logic for channel creations and joins) and relies on the following tools that are already installed in the container:

- `peer`: This is the CLI tool used to run various channel and contract operations, as we demonstrated in *Chapter 9*, *Network Operation and Distributed Application Building*. It can be built from the Fabric source code.

- `configtxlator`: This is another CLI tool that can be built from the Fabric source code that allows users to create and manipulate channel configurations, and translate those configurations between **Protocol Buffers (protobuf)** and JSON formats. (For more details, see `https://hyperledger-fabric.readthedocs.io/en/latest/commands/configtxlator.html`.)

- `jq`: This is a command-line JSON processor for creating, parsing, and modifying JSON objects.

Fetching the latest channel configuration

Let's walk through the channel update steps as encoded in the function updateChannelConfiguration in cli_scripts/channel.sh. First, a folder named tmp_upgrade is created to save temporary files. The latest channel configuration block is downloaded to this folder using code we have already seen in *Chapter 9, Network Operation and Distributed Application Building*:

```
fetchChannelConfig ${CHANNEL_NAME}_config_block.pb
```

The CHANNEL_NAME variable will be set by the calling process and can assume the values tradechannel or shippingchannel. As you can see in the fetchChannelConfig function, the following peer CLI command fetches the block:

```
peer channel fetch config $BLOCKFILE -c $CHANNEL_NAME --connTimeout
120s >&log.txt
```

Parsing a channel configuration

Let's assume that CHANNEL_NAME is tradechannel for the subsequent steps. Returning to the updateChannelConfiguration function, the downloaded configuration block, which is in protobuf format (hence the extension .pb), must be converted to JSON for the configuration update to be applied. (We do this purely for convenience because it is easier to parse JSON and apply our intended configuration changes to it.) The configtxlator tool does this conversion as follows:

```
configtxlator proto_decode --input tradechannel_config_block.pb --type
common.Block | jq .data.data[0].payload.data.config > tradechannel_
config.json
```

The downloaded block is known to be of the protobuf type common.Block, a data structure that is shipped with Fabric. This block contains various pieces of information, but we are only interested in the channel configuration, which is extracted using jq from the field data.data[0].payload.data.config. (To get familiar with Hyperledger Fabric protobufs, you can visit https://github.com/hyperledger/fabric-protos.) The configuration is now recorded as JSON to tradechannel_config.json in the tmp_upgrade folder. If you view the contents of this file, you will see the underlying configuration structure of the channel and the various properties that can be updated. Currently, the properties of three organizations—ExporterOrg, ImporterOrg, and RegulatorOrg—are specified.

Modifying a channel configuration to include a new organization

Next, we will append the configuration we created for our new organization earlier in this chapter (`channel-artifacts/tradechannel/exportingEntityOrg.json`) to this JSON and create a modified configuration as follows:

```
jq -s '.[0] * {"channel_group":{"groups":{"Application":{"groups":
{"ExportingEntityOrg":.[1]}}}}}' tradechannel_config.json ../channel-
artifacts/tradechannel/exportingEntityOrg.json > tradechannel_modified_
config.json
```

If you view the contents of the modified configuration `tradechannel_modified_config.json`, you will see that it is very similar in structure to `tradechannel_config.json`. The difference is that it contains specifications for four organizations (including `ExportingEntityOrg`) where the latter contains only three.

We now convert both JSONs (the older configuration and the modified one) to protobuf formats. This step is required because we need to compute the delta (or difference) between the two, and `configtxlator` can only compute deltas between protobufs:

```
configtxlator proto_encode --input tradechannel_config.json --type
common.Config --output tradechannel_config.pb
configtxlator proto_encode --input tradechannel_modified_config.json
--type common.Config --output tradechannel_modified_config.pb
```

Computing a channel configuration update

Note that Fabric uses the protobuf schema `common.Config` to encode channel configurations. Now we can compute the delta or the incremental configuration that places `ExportingEntityOrg` in `tradechannel`:

```
configtxlator compute_update --channel_id tradechannel --original
tradechannel_config.pb --updated tradechannel_modified_config.pb
--output exportingEntityOrg_update.pb
```

The generated protobuf `exportingEntityOrg_update.pb` contains a full specification (policies and certificates) of `ExportingEntityOrg` and pointers to the existing three organizations (`ExporterOrg`, `ImporterOrg`, and `RegulatorOrg`). This is sufficient for a channel configuration update as the full specifications of the other organizations are already recorded on the `tradechannel` ledger in the latest configuration block.

We need to convert this protobuf, which is an instance of the protobuf schema `common.ConfigUpdate`, to JSON so we can create a **transaction envelope** (or wrapper):

```
configtxlator proto_decode --input exportingEntityOrg_update.pb --type
common.ConfigUpdate | jq . > exportingEntityOrg_update.json
```

Next, we need to create a transaction envelope using `jq`:

```
echo '{"payload":{"header":{"channel_header":{"channel_
id":"'tradechannel'", "type":2}},"data":{"config_update":'$(cat
exportingEntityOrg_update.json)'}}}' | jq . > exportingEntityOrg_
update_in_envelope.json
```

Finally, we need to use `configtxlator` again to convert this envelope to protobuf format so it can be submitted to the Fabric network:

```
configtxlator proto_encode --input exportingEntityOrg_update_in_
envelope.json --type common.Envelope --output exportingEntityOrg_
update_in_envelope.pb
```

Note that the transaction envelope is an instance of the protobuf schema `common.Envelope`.

Signing and submitting a channel configuration update

We now have an update in the form of a protobuf file `exportingEntityOrg_update_in_envelope.pb` in the `tmp_upgrade` folder. We just need to get it signed by a majority of administrators of the existing set of organizations that participate in `tradechannel`. As the channel currently has three organizations, two signatures will suffice, and as you can see in `cli_scripts/channel.sh`, we chose `exporterorg` and `regulatororg` for signing. (The majority policy was set by the rule `"MAJORITY Admins"` in the `Admins` attribute within the `Application` section in our `configtx.yaml` file.) Each administrator signs the configuration update using the following function call:

```
signConfigtxAsPeerOrg $org exportingEntityOrg_update_in_envelope.pb
```

This in turn runs the following `peer` CLI command (in effect) after setting the right environment variables for the given organization using the `setEnvironment` function:

```
peer channel signconfigtx -f exportingEntityOrg_update_in_envelope.pb
```

Signatures are accumulated in `exportingEntityOrg_update_in_envelope.pb`, which is now ready for submission to the ordering service. This is done using the following peer CLI command:

```
peer channel update -f exportingEntityOrg_update_in_envelope.pb -c
tradechannel -o orderer.trade.com:7050 --tls --cafile $ORDERER_CA
--connTimeout 120s >&log.txt
```

The value of `ORDERER_CA` should be set to the ordering service's TLS CA certificate path on the container's filesystem, whose default value is specified in `cli_scripts/channel.sh`.

Updating a channel configuration in one go

You can run all the above steps to update the configuration of `tradechannel` in a single command using `trade.sh`:

```
$ ./trade.sh updatechannel -c tradechannel -o 3
```

The `-o 3` switch tells the command to select two organizations (exporterorg and regulatororg) to sign the configuration update. If you monitor the output in `logs/network-cli.log`, you will see something like the following after a successful operation:

```
Updating the channel configuration to add ExportingEntityOrg...
Fetching the most recent configuration block for the channel
+ peer channel fetch config tradechannel_config_block.pb -c tradechannel --connTimeout 120s
+ res=0
+ set +x
2020-09-08 12:14:52.442 UTC [channelCmd] InitCmdFactory -> INFO 001 Endorser and orderer connection
s initialized

2020-09-08 12:14:52.444 UTC [cli.common] readBlock -> INFO 002 Received block: 13
2020-09-08 12:14:52.444 UTC [channelCmd] fetch -> INFO 003 Retrieving last config block: 3
2020-09-08 12:14:52.447 UTC [cli.common] readBlock -> INFO 004 Received block: 3
+ peer channel signconfigtx -f exportingEntityOrg_update_in_envelope.pb
+ res=0
+ set +x
2020-09-08 12:14:52.952 UTC [channelCmd] InitCmdFactory -> INFO 001 Endorser and orderer connection
s initialized
==================== peer0.exporterorg.trade.com signed update for channel 'tradechannel' ========
===============

+ peer channel signconfigtx -f exportingEntityOrg_update_in_envelope.pb
+ res=0
+ set +x
2020-09-08 12:14:53.035 UTC [channelCmd] InitCmdFactory -> INFO 001 Endorser and orderer connection
s initialized
==================== peer0.regulatororg.trade.com signed update for channel 'tradechannel' =======
===============

+ peer channel update -f exportingEntityOrg_update_in_envelope.pb -c tradechannel -o orderer.trade.
com:7050 --tls --cafile /opt/gopath/src/github.com/hyperledger/fabric/peer/crypto/ordererOrganizati
ons/trade.com/orderers/orderer.trade.com/msp/tlscacerts/tlsca.trade.com-cert.pem --connTimeout 120s
+ res=0
+ set +x
2020-09-08 12:14:53.122 UTC [channelCmd] InitCmdFactory -> INFO 001 Endorser and orderer connection
s initialized
2020-09-08 12:14:53.152 UTC [channelCmd] update -> INFO 002 Successfully submitted channel update
========= Channel update completed ===========
```

Figure 13.7: Successfully updated tradechannel configuration to add a new exporting entity organization

Similarly, you can add `ExportingEntityOrg` to `shippingchannel` using the following command:

```
$ ./trade.sh updatechannel -c shippingchannel -o 4
```

The `-o 4` switch tells the command to select three organizations (`exporterorg`, `importerorg`, and `carrierorg`), which is what is required in a four-organization channel to sign a configuration update.

Joining the new organization's peer to the channels

We have prepared both our channels to include the new organization. Earlier, we also started up a peer for this organization. Our next step is to join this peer to both the channels. This is a straightforward process that you ought to be very familiar with by now: we joined peers to channels in *Chapter 9, Network Operation and Distributed Application Building*, and also joined an additional `ImporterOrg` peer earlier in this chapter. Use the `trade.sh` script to join the exporting entity organization's peer to both channels as follows:

```
$ ./trade.sh joinneworg -c tradechannel
$ ./trade.sh joinneworg -c shippingchannel
```

The new peer is now connected to the network and will sync ledgers for both these channels from other peers using the gossip protocol! As with previous joins we performed, the process involves fetching the channel's genesis block and running a `peer channel join` CLI command using that block file. See `trade.sh` and `cli_scripts/channel.sh` for more implementation details. If you check for new blocks using `trade.sh fetchconfig`, you will find that no new blocks were created in these operations.

Setting the anchor peer for the new organization's peer on the channels

The sole peer in `ExportingEntityOrg` is now joined to both of our channels. We now need to set it as the anchor peer for the organization in each channel using configuration updates. The procedure to do this lies in the function `updateAnchorPeerForNewOrg` in `cli_scripts/channel.sh` and is similar in all but two respects to the procedure in `updateChannelConfiguration`, which we discussed earlier in this chapter. The first difference lies in the nature of the modified configuration; rather than appending a configuration for a new organization, we just need to modify an existing organization's configuration:

```
jq '.channel_group.groups.Application.groups.ExportingEntityOrg.
values += {"AnchorPeers":{"mod_policy": "Admins","value":{"anchor_
peers": [{"host": "peer0.exportingentityorg.trade.com","port":
12051}]},"version": "0"}}' ${CHANNEL_NAME}_config.json > ${CHANNEL_
NAME}_modified_config.json
```

As you can see, we set the anchor peer address to `peer0.exportingentityorg.trade.com` and the port to `12051`, corresponding to what was specified in the configuration file `add_org/configtx.yaml`.

The next difference lies in the signing logic: since a specific organization's configuration is being updated, we only need a signature from an administrator of that organization:

```
signConfigtxAsPeerOrg exportingentityorg exportingEntityOrg_anchor_
update_in_envelope.pb
```

Here `exportingEntityOrg_anchor_update_in_envelope.pb` is the channel update envelope (a protobuf of type `common.Envelope`) that is sent to the ordering service.

To update the anchor peer for the new organization in our two channels, run:

```
$ ./trade.sh updatenoworganchorpeer -c tradechannel
$ ./trade.sh updatenoworganchorpeer -c shippingchannel
```

If you examine the logs in any peer's container, you should see messages indicating how the peers are successfully discovering peers in other organizations and re-establishing gossip connections. For example, the logs on `peer0.regulatororg.trade.com` may indicate something like the following:

```
2020-09-08 12:22:57.169 UTC [gossip.gossip] JoinChan -> INFO 192 Joining gossip network of channel
tradechannel with 4 organizations
2020-09-08 12:22:57.169 UTC [gossip.gossip] learnAnchorPeers -> INFO 193 Learning about the configu
red anchor peers of RegulatorOrgMSP for channel tradechannel : [{peer0.regulatororg.trade.com 10051
}]
2020-09-08 12:22:57.170 UTC [gossip.gossip] learnAnchorPeers -> INFO 194 Anchor peer with same endp
oint, skipping connecting to myself
2020-09-08 12:22:57.170 UTC [gossip.gossip] learnAnchorPeers -> INFO 195 Learning about the configu
red anchor peers of ExporterOrgMSP for channel tradechannel : [{peer0.exporterorg.trade.com 7051}]
2020-09-08 12:22:57.170 UTC [gossip.gossip] learnAnchorPeers -> INFO 196 Learning about the configu
red anchor peers of ExportingEntityOrgMSP for channel tradechannel : [{peer0.exportingentityorg.tra
de.com 12051}]
2020-09-08 12:22:57.170 UTC [gossip.gossip] learnAnchorPeers -> INFO 197 Learning about the configu
red anchor peers of ImporterOrgMSP for channel tradechannel : [{peer0.importerorg.trade.com 8051}]
2020-09-08 12:22:57.196 UTC [committer.txvalidator] Validate -> INFO 198 [tradechannel] Validated b
lock [15] in 101ms
2020-09-08 12:22:57.196 UTC [gossip.privdata] prepareBlockPvtdata -> INFO 199 Successfully fetched
all eligible collection private write sets for block [15] channel=tradechannel
```

Figure 13.8: Regulator organization peer discovering other peers in the network and syncing configuration and data using the gossip protocol

This proves the success of our channel update operation to set an anchor peer for `ExportingEntityOrg` in `tradechannel`.

You can update both channels, start the new organization's components, join the new organization's peers to both channels, and set anchor peers on both channels, all in one go using the following command in the bash folder:

```
$ ./startAndJoinNewOrg.sh
```

Installing contracts on peers in the new organization

Our next logical step is to install one or more contracts involving the exporter entity's business workflow to the peer of our new organization so that this peer can play a role in endorsing transactions and serving contract queries to clients. For each contract we deployed in *Chapter 9, Network Operation and Distributed Application Building*, we will need to run the first three operations: packaging, installation, and recording an approval on the ledger. We do not need to repeat the commitment operation unless the chaincode definition itself changes.

We will perform these operations a little later, but purely as a prerequisite for contract upgrade. The contracts demonstrated earlier in this book using the version label v1 were developed with the four initial organizations in mind. The access control rules embedded in the v1 contract code are not cognizant of the new exporting entity organization. Hence the new organization's peer will be unable to meaningfully participate in transaction endorsements unless each contract's business logic is updated to take the members of ExportingEntityOrg into account.

Shortly, we will demonstrate the full incorporation of the new organization into the network (and channels) and the extension of the distributed application we have built over this network. We will do this through procedures that demonstrate how contracts and their definitions can be updated simultaneously.

Smart contract and policy updates

As we observed early in this chapter, a smart contract deployed on a channel is subject to change for a variety of reasons, including code bug fixes and maintenance, new business requirements, and the evolving needs of the participants. At other times, the chaincode definition, which includes the processing criteria for transactions submitted to a contract, may have to change while keeping the code intact. An example is a contract endorsement policy modification, which could be prompted by a change in the set of channel participants or even a change in the business relationship among existing participants.

Any of these types of updates can be performed using a small adaptation of the contract installation procedure we encountered in *Chapter 9, Network Operation and Distributed Application Building*. The bulk of the work lies in contract and service-layer application development, as we will see shortly.

Overview of contract update procedures

The steps we must carry out depend on whether we wish to just update the chaincode definition or update the code as well. To update the chaincode definition, we run the following steps in sequence:

1. **Approve a new chaincode definition**: Done by administrators of every organization that wish to install the contract on their peers and endorse transactions submitted to it

2. **Commit the new chaincode definition**: An administrator of any organization can do this after a majority of organization administrators (according to the Channel/Application/LifecycleEndorsement policy specified in configtx. yaml) have submitted approvals

To update the smart contract code, we need to carry out these two operations, but before that, we must package and install the code on the organizations' peers too. The full sequence of operations is as follows:

1. Package the new contract code

2. Install the new contract code on peers that are running the current version

3. Approve a new chaincode definition – done by organization administrators. The chaincode package version is part of the definition, and we must supply a new (and unique) version every time the code is modified

4. Commit the new chaincode definition

In the next section, we will demonstrate the latter procedure, involving both code and definition updates. To simply update a definition, you can adapt and apply a portion of that procedure.

Modification in contract business logic

Even a minor change in contract code will necessitate an upgrade. To keep things simple, we will not change the trade workflow at all, but rather remain faithful to the 12-step process sketched out at the beginning of *Chapter 4, Setting the Stage with a Business Scenario*. We will take the opportunity provided to us by the addition of an exporting entity organization to make certain necessary tweaks.

Overview of access control logic in the initial contract versions

Recall that our four smart contracts—trade, letterOfCredit, exportLicense, and shipment—were developed with four organizations in mind: ExporterOrg, ImporterOrg, RegulatorOrg, and CarrierOrg. Now we have added ExportingEntityOrg for exporters in our 12-step workflow who no longer must depend on ExporterOrg (run by a bank) as clients. But the contracts' access control logic assumes that an exporter is one that has an identity issued by ExporterOrgMSP and possesses a client attribute in its certificate. We can see this in the contract-wide access control rules as well as in trade instance-specific rules applied when a particular contract function is invoked.

Let's look at some examples. Start VS Code and load contracts in the workspace as follows:

1. Select **File** | **Add Folder to Workspace** from the top menu.

2. Navigate to your local copy of the trade-contracts repository. (You can also find this in the contracts folder within trade-networks if you have run all the exercises in this book.) Select the v1/trade folder, which contains the version of the contract code we installed and initialized in *Chapter 9, Network Operation and Distributed Application Building*.

3. Open the src/trade-contracts.ts file from the **Explorer** pane on the left of the window. The following screenshot shows the access control rules defined in the constructor of the trade contract. These cover banker and trader clients who possess credentials from ExporterOrgMSP and ImporterOrgMSP and regulators who possess credentials from RegulatorOrgMSP:

```
constructor() {
    super('TradeContract');
    this.aclRules[TradeContract.getAclSubject('ExporterOrgMSP', 'any')] = [ 'init' ];
    this.aclRules[TradeContract.getAclSubject('ImporterOrgMSP', 'any')] = [ 'init' ];
    this.aclRules[TradeContract.getAclSubject('RegulatorOrgMSP', 'any')] = [ 'init' ];
    this.aclRules[TradeContract.getAclSubject('ExporterOrgMSP', 'exporter')] =
                        [ 'acceptTrade', 'exists', 'getTrade', 'getTradeStatus', 'listTrade' ];
    this.aclRules[TradeContract.getAclSubject('ImporterOrgMSP', 'importer')] =
                        [ 'requestTrade', 'exists', 'getTrade', 'getTradeStatus', 'listTrade' ];
    this.aclRules[TradeContract.getAclSubject('ExporterOrgMSP', 'exporter_banker')] =
                                [ 'exists', 'getTrade', 'getTradeStatus', 'listTrade' ];
    this.aclRules[TradeContract.getAclSubject('ImporterOrgMSP', 'importer_banker')] =
                                [ 'exists', 'getTrade', 'getTradeStatus', 'listTrade' ];
    this.aclRules[TradeContract.getAclSubject('RegulatorOrgMSP', 'regulator')] =
        [ 'exists', 'getTrade', 'getTradeStatus', 'listTrade', 'getTradesByRange', 'getTradeHistory' ];
}
```

Figure 13.9: Access control rules set in the v1 version of the trade contract

4. Close the src/trade-contracts.ts file. Remove the trade contract from the workspace by right-clicking **Trade** in the **Explorer** pane and selecting **Remove Folder from Workspace** in the context menu.

5. Add the `v1/letterOfCredit` folder to the workspace.

6. Open the `src/main/java/org/trade/AccessControlUtils.java` file. The following screenshot shows, just as in the `trade` contract, access control rules framed for clients with credentials from two organization MSPs: `ExporterOrgMSP` and `ImporterOrgMSP`:

```java
public class AccessControlUtils {
    public final static String BUSINESS_ROLE_ATTR = "BUSINESS_ROLE";
    private final static Map<ACLSubject,String[]> aclRules = new HashMap<ACLSubject,String[]>();

    static {
        aclRules.put(new ACLSubject(Constants.importerOrgMsp, Constants.ANY_ROLE), new String[]{ "init" });
        aclRules.put(new ACLSubject(Constants.exporterOrgMsp, Constants.ANY_ROLE), new String[]{ "init" });
        aclRules.put(new ACLSubject(Constants.importerOrgMsp, Constants.IMPORTER_BANKER_ROLE),
                    new String[]{ "makePayment", "issueLC", "existsLC", "getLC", "getLCStatus" });
        aclRules.put(new ACLSubject(Constants.exporterOrgMsp, Constants.EXPORTER_BANKER_ROLE),
                    new String[]{ "requestPayment", "acceptLC", "existsLC", "getLC", "getLCStatus" });
        aclRules.put(new ACLSubject(Constants.importerOrgMsp, Constants.IMPORTER_ROLE),
                    new String[]{ "requestLC", "existsLC", "getLC", "getLCStatus", "getAccountBalance" });
        aclRules.put(new ACLSubject(Constants.exporterOrgMsp, Constants.EXPORTER_ROLE),
                    new String[]{ "existsLC", "getLC", "getLCStatus", "getAccountBalance" });
    }
```

Figure 13.10: Access control rules set in the v1 version of the letterOfCredit contract

New contract versions

To prepare our new five-organization network for full operation, we need new versions of the four contracts. These are available in the v2 folder in the `trade-contracts` repository (or the `contracts` folder within your local copy of `trade-network`). There are three kinds of changes you will observe:

- Updates to access control rules.
- Updates to contract API functions to ensure that trade instances are associated with `ExportingEntityOrgMSP` instead of `ExporterOrgMSP`.
- Initialization code that takes the current ledger state into account rather than beginning from a blank slate. (The initialization function must be updated so we don't inadvertently overwrite the current ledger state.)

We will discuss the changes made in two of our contracts, one written in TypeScript (`trade`) and another in Java (`letterOfCredit`). Similar changes were also made to the `exportLicense` and `shipment` contracts, which we will leave for you to examine.

Access control logic changes in the trade contract

Let's view changes to the `trade` contract in the v2 version.

Start VS Code and add the `v2/trade` folder to the workspace after removing any previously added folders. Then open the `src/trade-contracts.ts` file from the **Explorer** pane. Here is a screenshot illustrating changes in the access control rules:

```
constructor() {
    super('TradeContract');
    this.aclRules[TradeContract.getAclSubject('ExporterOrgMSP', 'any')] = [ 'init' ];
    this.aclRules[TradeContract.getAclSubject('ImporterOrgMSP', 'any')] = [ 'init' ];
    this.aclRules[TradeContract.getAclSubject('RegulatorOrgMSP', 'any')] = [ 'init' ];
    this.aclRules[TradeContract.getAclSubject('ExportingEntityOrgMSP', 'any')] = [ 'init' ];
    this.aclRules[TradeContract.getAclSubject('ExporterOrgMSP', 'exporter')] =
                    [ 'acceptTrade', 'exists', 'getTrade', 'getTradeStatus', 'listTrade' ];
    this.aclRules[TradeContract.getAclSubject('ExportingEntityOrgMSP', 'exporter')] =
                    [ 'acceptTrade', 'exists', 'getTrade', 'getTradeStatus', 'listTrade' ];
    this.aclRules[TradeContract.getAclSubject('ImporterOrgMSP', 'importer')] =
                    [ 'requestTrade', 'exists', 'getTrade', 'getTradeStatus', 'listTrade' ];
    this.aclRules[TradeContract.getAclSubject('ExporterOrgMSP', 'exporter_banker')] =
                    [ 'exists', 'getTrade', 'getTradeStatus', 'listTrade' ];
    this.aclRules[TradeContract.getAclSubject('ImporterOrgMSP', 'importer_banker')] =
                    [ 'exists', 'getTrade', 'getTradeStatus', 'listTrade' ];
    this.aclRules[TradeContract.getAclSubject('RegulatorOrgMSP', 'regulator')] =
        [ 'exists', 'getTrade', 'getTradeStatus', 'listTrade', 'getTradesByRange', 'getTradeHistory' ];
}
```

Figure 13.11: Access control rules set in the v2 version of the trade contract

Note that we have two additional rules permitting clients with credentials issued by `ExportingEntityOrgMSP`. One allows any member of the new organization to initialize the updated version of the contract. Another allows any client with an `exporter` certificate attribute issued by this MSP to perform the role of an exporter: it can submit an `acceptTrade` transaction and submit any of the queries supported by the trade contract API. The `acceptTrade` transaction is still permitted for a client carrying an `exporter` certificate attribute issued by `ExporterOrgMSP` because we want `ExporterOrg` to still support other trading entities as clients in exporter roles.

Further down in the file, you will see that the `init` function remains intact other than logging a different message. This is because this function is, in effect, a no-operation, and no key-value pairs need be recorded during the upgrade either:

```
/**
 * Perform any setup of the ledger that might be required.
 * @param {Context} ctx the transaction context
 */
@Transaction()
public async init(ctx: Context) {
    console.log('Upgrading the trade contract');
}
```

Figure 13.12: Updated initialization function in the v2 version of the trade contract

No other changes exist between the v1 and v2 versions of the trade contract.

Access control logic changes in the letterOfCredit contract

Now let's view changes in the `letterOfCredit` contract.

Remove the `trade` folder from the workspace and add the `v2/letterOfCredit` folder. Then open the `src/main/java/org/trade/AccessControlUtils.java` file. The following screenshot illustrates additions to the list of access control rules, permitting members of `ExportingEntityOrgMSP` to submit transactions and queries:

```java
public class AccessControlUtils {
    public final static String BUSINESS_ROLE_ATTR = "BUSINESS_ROLE";
    private final static Map<ACLSubject,String[]> aclRules = new HashMap<ACLSubject,String[]>();

    static {
        aclRules.put(new ACLSubject(Constants.importerOrgMsp, Constants.ANY_ROLE), new String[]{ "init" });
        aclRules.put(new ACLSubject(Constants.exporterOrgMsp, Constants.ANY_ROLE), new String[]{ "init" });
        aclRules.put(new ACLSubject(Constants.exportingEntityOrgMSP, Constants.ANY_ROLE), new String[]{ "init" });
        aclRules.put(new ACLSubject(Constants.importerOrgMsp, Constants.IMPORTER_BANKER_ROLE),
                     new String[]{ "makePayment", "issueLC", "existsLC", "getLC", "getLCStatus" });
        aclRules.put(new ACLSubject(Constants.exporterOrgMsp, Constants.EXPORTER_BANKER_ROLE),
                     new String[]{ "requestPayment", "acceptLC", "existsLC", "getLC", "getLCStatus" });
        aclRules.put(new ACLSubject(Constants.importerOrgMsp, Constants.IMPORTER_ROLE),
                     new String[]{ "requestLC", "existsLC", "getLC", "getLCStatus", "getAccountBalance" });
        aclRules.put(new ACLSubject(Constants.exporterOrgMsp, Constants.EXPORTER_ROLE),
                     new String[]{ "existsLC", "getLC", "getLCStatus", "getAccountBalance" });
        aclRules.put(new ACLSubject(Constants.exportingEntityOrgMSP, Constants.EXPORTER_ROLE),
                     new String[]{ "existsLC", "getLC", "getLCStatus", "getAccountBalance" });
    }
```

Figure 13.13: Access control rules set in the v2 version of the letterOfCredit contract

The "exporting entity" is allowed to initialize this contract and run all queries, like any other entity (banker or trader). Though the L/C contract allows the exporter's bank to submit transactions (`acceptLC` and `requestPayment`), it doesn't allow an exporter (formerly a member of `ExporterOrg` and now of `ExportingEntityOrg`) to submit any.

Query function logic changes in the letterOfCredit contract

Let's now examine changes that were required in query functions offered in the contract API, using `letterOfCredit` as an example.

Open the `src/main/java/org/trade/LetterOfCreditContract.java` file. Scrolling down, you will see changes in the `getLC` and `getLCStatus` functions compared to the v1 version. Here is a screenshot of the changes in `getLC`, with the new additions highlighted:

```
@Transaction()
public String getLC(Context ctx, String tradeId) {
    // Lookup L/C from given trade ID
    ChaincodeStub stub = ctx.getStub();
    String lcKey = getLCKey(stub, tradeId);
    byte[] lcBytes = stub.getState(lcKey);
    if (lcBytes == null || lcBytes.length == 0) {
        throw new ChaincodeException("No L/C recorded for trade '" + tradeId + "'");
    }

    LetterOfCredit lc = LetterOfCredit.fromJSONString(new String(lcBytes));
    String tradeExporterMSP = lc.getBeneficiary();
    // Exporter, represented by an exporter or exporting entity org MSP associated with this L/C,
    //      must match the caller's MSP
    // Allow the exporter bank to access this L/C too
    String callerMspId = AccessControlUtils.GetClientMspId(ctx);
    String callerRole = AccessControlUtils.GetClientRole(ctx);
    boolean isExportOrg = (callerMspId.equals(Constants.exporterOrgMsp) ||
                          callerMspId.equals(Constants.exportingEntityOrgMSP));
    boolean isExporterBank = (callerMspId.equals(Constants.exporterOrgMsp) &&
                          callerRole.equals(Constants.EXPORTER_BANKER_ROLE));
    if (isExportOrg && !isExporterBank && !tradeExporterMSP.equals(callerMspId)) {
        throw new ChaincodeException("'" + tradeId + "' does not belong to exporting entity MSP " +
                                    callerMspId);
    }

    String lcStr = new String(lcBytes);
    System.out.println("Retrieved L/C from ledger: " + lcStr);
    return lcStr;
}
```

Figure 13.14: The getLC function changes in the v2 version of the letterOfCredit contract

Recall that each trade instance in the workflow spanning our four contracts has an MSP ID representing the exporter. In the v1 contract, the ExporterOrgMSP keyword was used to represent the exporter in a trade. After the upgrade, we would like to create trades with exporters represented either by ExporterOrgMSP or ExportingEntityOrgMSP. An L/C associated with tradeid (the function argument) ought to be retrievable by a banker possessing credentials from ExporterOrgMSP (which is still the only organization MSP representing an exporter's bank). But it should only be retrievable by those clients (that is, exporters) that possess credentials from the right MSPs. Hence, we now look up the querying client's MSP ID and compare that with the exporter's MSP name recorded for tradeid on the ledger before returning a valid L/C, as you can see in the screenshot.

The getLCStatus function has identical additional logic, permitting the retrieval of L/C status by an exporter's bank or an exporter who is associated with the particular trade instance this L/C is associated with.

Initialization function logic changes in the letterOfCredit contract

Finally, let's examine changes in the initialization function offered in the letterOfCredit contract's API.

Now scroll back up the file to the init function. In the original version (v1) of the contract, the API required the transaction submitter to supply external channel and contract names for recording on the ledger. In v2, we allow the submitter to supply these names but don't mandate it. As the following screenshot indicates, if these names are supplied, the function overwrites the key values; otherwise, it just confirms the presence of the relevant keys on the ledger:

```java
@Transaction()
public void init(Context ctx, String ...params) {
    ChaincodeStub stub = ctx.getStub();
    if (params.length == 3) {
        byte[] tcBytes = stub.getState(Constants.tradeContractIdKey);
        if (tcBytes == null || tcBytes.length == 0) {
            throw new ChaincodeException("No trade contract id recorded on ledger");
        }
        byte[] schBytes = stub.getState(Constants.shippingChannelNameKey);
        if (schBytes == null || schBytes.length == 0) {
            throw new ChaincodeException("No shipping channel name recorded on ledger");
        }
        byte[] scBytes = stub.getState(Constants.shipmentContractIdKey);
        if (scBytes == null || scBytes.length == 0) {
            throw new ChaincodeException("No shipment contract id recorded on ledger");
        }
        System.out.println("No prameters provided. Reusing from ledger: Trade contract '" +
                        new String(tcBytes)+ "', shipping channel '" + new String(schBytes) +
                        "', and shipment contract '" + new String(scBytes) + "'");
    } else if (params.length == 6) {
        String tradeContractId = params[0];
        if (tradeContractId != null && tradeContractId.length() > 0) {
            stub.putState(Constants.tradeContractIdKey, tradeContractId.getBytes(UTF_8));
            System.out.println("L/C contract upgraded with Trade contract '" + tradeContractId + "'");
        }
        String shippingChannelName = params[1];
        if (shippingChannelName != null && shippingChannelName.length() > 0) {
            stub.putState(Constants.shippingChannelNameKey, shippingChannelName.getBytes(UTF_8));
            System.out.println("L/C contract upgraded with Shipping channel '" + shippingChannelName + "'");
        }
        String shipmentContractId = params[2];
        if (shipmentContractId != null && shipmentContractId.length() > 0) {
            stub.putState(Constants.shipmentContractIdKey, shipmentContractId.getBytes(UTF_8));
            System.out.println("L/C contract upgraded with Shipment contract '" + shipmentContractId + "'");
        }
    } else {
        throw new ChaincodeException("Expected 3 or 6 parameters, found " + params.length);
    }
}
```

Figure 13.15: Initialization function in the v2 version of the letterOfCredit contract supporting a different set of parameters than the v1 version

We must make another change to the init function. In the original version, a bank account was created for an exporter using its MSP ID (then `ExporterOrgMSP`) as the identifier. Now that the exporter entity has moved to a new organization, we need to create another account on the ledger using `ExportingEntityOrgMSP` as its identity. The following screenshot illustrates this account creation:

```
// Last 3 parameters are used to initialize a bank account for the exporting entity
String exportingEntityMSP = params[params.length - 3];
String exportingEntityBank = params[params.length - 2];
double exportingEntityAccountBalance = Double.parseDouble(params[params.length - 1]);
if (exportingEntityMSP != null && exportingEntityMSP.length() > 0 && exportingEntityBank != null &
        exportingEntityBank.length() > 0) {
    BankAccount exportingEntityAccount = new BankAccount(exportingEntityMSP, exportingEntityBank,
                                                exportingEntityAccountBalance);

    updateAccount(stub, exportingEntityAccount);
    System.out.println("Initialized exporting entity account: " + exportingEntityAccount.toJSONString());
}
```

Figure 13.16: Creating an account for the new exporting entity in the initialization function of the v2 version of the letterOfCredit contract

To verify that the `letterOfCredit` contract version v2 works, we have updated unit tests as well. We will leave it up to you to examine the changes. You can run the unit tests by opening the `src/test/java/org/trade/LetterOfCreditContractTest.java` file and clicking the `Run Test` link above the main class definition as follows:

```
Run Test | Debug Test
public final class LetterOfCreditContractTest {
```

Figure 13.17: Option to run unit tests for the v2 version of the letterOfCredit contract

After a successful test run, you should see a check mark to the right of `Debug Test` as follows:

```
Run Test | Debug Test | ✓
public final class LetterOfCreditContractTest {
```

Figure 13.18: Indication that all unit tests for the v2 version of the letterOfCredit contract passed

Endorsement policy updates

For the v1 version of our contracts, we had framed policies that required endorsements from every organization running a contract on one of its peers. For our demonstration, we will extend the policies to require an endorsement from an `ExportingEntityOrg` member for transactions on every contract installed on a peer of that organization. As it turns out, since all four of our contracts are installed on `ExporterOrg` peers, we must install them all on `ExportingEntityOrg` peers as well. Hence, we must use a new endorsement policy for each of the four contracts.

The following table illustrates the old and new policies for the contracts:

Contract	v1 Endorsement Policy	v2 Endorsement Policy
trade	AND('ExporterOrgMSP.member', 'ImporterOrgMSP.member', 'RegulatorOrgMSP.member')	AND('ExporterOrgMSP.member', 'ImporterOrgMSP.member', 'RegulatorOrgMSP.member', 'ExportingEntityOrgMSP.member')
letterOfCredit	AND('ExporterOrgMSP.member', 'ImporterOrgMSP.member')	AND('ExporterOrgMSP.member', 'ImporterOrgMSP.member', 'ExportingEntityOrgMSP.member')
exportLicense	AND('ExporterOrgMSP.member', 'RegulatorOrgMSP.member')	AND('ExporterOrgMSP.member', 'RegulatorOrgMSP.member', 'ExportingEntityOrgMSP.member')
shipment	AND('ExporterOrgMSP.member', 'ImporterOrgMSP.member', 'CarrierOrgMSP.member')	AND('ExporterOrgMSP.member', 'ImporterOrgMSP.member', 'CarrierOrgMSP.member', 'ExportingEntityOrgMSP.member')

Table 13.1: Contract endorsement policies

Upgrading contract code and endorsement policies on the channels

Now we are ready to carry out the upgrade process for each contract. For this exercise, we need to have the initial network up and running with two channels set up and four contracts installed. The ledger should have a full workflow recorded for a trade labeled trade-12. Further, the new organization's components should be running, and its peers joined to the two channels. (We assume that ImporterOrg only has one peer running, but you can modify the scripts yourself based on the instructions that follow to incorporate peer1.importerorg.trade.com into the upgrade process if you wish to.)

CLI code to upgrade a contract and its policy on a channel

We will upgrade the trade contract first, using the trade_cli container built on the hyperledger/fabric-tools image. The code for this lies in the upgradeContract function in bash/cli_scripts/chaincode.sh. The logic is straightforward, as you can see in the following:

```
upgradeContract() {

    ......

    installAndApproveContractOnNewOrg

    ......

    PEERORGLIST=$PEERORGLIST" exportingentityorg"
    CC_SEQUENCE_NUM=2
    packageChaincode
    installChaincode
    approveChaincodeDefinitions
    commitChaincodeDefinition
    initializeChaincode
)
```

As a prerequisite for an upgrade, we need to have four peers (peer0.exporterorg. trade.com, peer0.importerorg.trade.com, peer0.regulatororg.trade.com, and peer0.exportingentityorg.trade.com) running an instance each of the v1 version of the trade contract. The first step in the preceding code is a call to a function (installAndApproveContractOnNewOrg) that packages and installs this contract version on peer0.exportingentityorg.trade.com, and then approves the chaincode definition as an ExportingEntityOrg administrator.

Now we can run the five-step upgrade process — package, install, approve, commit, and initialize — as we have discussed earlier. We execute the same functions in chaincode.sh that were used to install and initialize the original versions of the contracts, as you can see in the preceding code. Only the sequence number in the chaincode definition is incremented to 2 (it was 1 earlier) and the exporting entity organization's peer is added to the list of peers on which the code should be upgraded. This function is executed in a container by the upgradeContract function in the trade.sh script as follows:

```
function upgradeContract () {

    ......

    if [ "$CONTRACT_NAME" == "trade" ]
    then
    CC_LANGUAGE=node
    PEERORGLIST="exporterorg importerorg regulatororg"

    ......

    docker exec -e CHANNEL_NAME=$CHANNEL_NAME -e NUM_ORGS_IN_CHANNEL=$NUM_
    ORGS_IN_CHANNEL -e PEERORGLIST="$PEERORGLIST" -e CC_LANGUAGE=$CC_
    LANGUAGE -e CC_LABEL=$CONTRACT_NAME -e CC_VERSION=v2 -e OLD_CC_
    VERSION=v1 -e CC_FUNC=$CONTRACT_FUNC -e CC_ARGS="$CONTRACT_ARGS"
    trade_cli scripts/chaincode.sh upgrade >>$LOG_FILE_CLI 2>&1

    ......
```

Various parameters are passed as environment variables to the `chaincode.sh` script:

- The channel name (`CHANNEL_NAME`) is `tradechannel` in this instance, which originally had three organizations (`NUM_ORGS_IN_CHANNEL`)
- The organizations for which the contract is to be upgraded (`PEERORGLIST`), which consist of the three original organization names, excluding the new organization (`exportingentityorg`), which is added in the `upgradeContract` function in `bash/cli_scripts/chaincode.sh`, as we saw in the earlier code snippet
- The contract name (`CC_LABEL`), the current version (`OLD_CC_VERSION`), and the new version (`CC_VERSION`) are also supplied, as are the name (`CC_FUNC`) and arguments (`CC_ARGS`) for the initialization function

Instructions to upgrade the trade contract on tradechannel

To upgrade the `trade` contract to version v2, just run the following (the parameters should be familiar to you by now):

```
$ ./trade.sh upgradecontract -c tradechannel -p trade -o 3 -t init
```

If the process is successful, you should see all the steps logged in `logs/network-cli.log`, ending in something like the following:

```
=================== Committed chaincode definition on channel 'tradechannel' ===================
=
+ peer chaincode invoke --connTimeout 120s -o orderer.trade.com:7050 --ordererTLSHostnameOverride o
rderer.trade.com -C tradechannel -n trade --isInit --tls true --waitForEvent --cafile /opt/gopath/s
rc/github.com/hyperledger/fabric/peer/crypto/ordererOrganizations/trade.com/orderers/orderer.trade.
com/msp/tlscacerts/tlsca.trade.com-cert.pem --peerAddresses peer0.exporterorg.trade.com:7051 --tlsR
ootCertFiles /opt/gopath/src/github.com/hyperledger/fabric/peer/crypto/peerOrganizations/exporteror
g.trade.com/peers/peer0.exporterorg.trade.com/tls/ca.crt --peerAddresses peer0.importerorg.trade.co
m:8051 --tlsRootCertFiles /opt/gopath/src/github.com/hyperledger/fabric/peer/crypto/peerOrganizatio
ns/importerorg.trade.com/peers/peer0.importerorg.trade.com/tls/ca.crt --peerAddresses peer0.regulat
ororg.trade.com:10051 --tlsRootCertFiles /opt/gopath/src/github.com/hyperledger/fabric/peer/crypto/
peerOrganizations/regulatororg.trade.com/peers/peer0.regulatororg.trade.com/tls/ca.crt --peerAddres
ses peer0.exportingentityorg.trade.com:12051 --tlsRootCertFiles /opt/gopath/src/github.com/hyperled
ger/fabric/peer/crypto/peerOrganizations/exportingentityorg.trade.com/peers/peer0.exportingentityor
g.trade.com/tls/ca.crt -c '{"function":"init","Args":[]}'

+ res=0
+ set +x
2020-09-08 13:24:39.000 UTC [chaincodeCmd] ClientWait -> INFO 001 txid [a9c79aa9966f9c0ee5867842d4c
5f4ceac54d61d5754bf6919904861aac57100] committed with status (VALID) at peer0.exportingentityorg.tr
ade.com:12051
2020-09-08 13:24:39.004 UTC [chaincodeCmd] ClientWait -> INFO 002 txid [a9c79aa9966f9c0ee5867842d4c
5f4ceac54d61d5754bf6919904861aac57100] committed with status (VALID) at peer0.regulatororg.trade.co
m:10051
2020-09-08 13:24:39.009 UTC [chaincodeCmd] ClientWait -> INFO 003 txid [a9c79aa9966f9c0ee5867842d4c
5f4ceac54d61d5754bf6919904861aac57100] committed with status (VALID) at peer0.exporterorg.trade.com
:7051
2020-09-08 13:24:39.022 UTC [chaincodeCmd] ClientWait -> INFO 004 txid [a9c79aa9966f9c0ee5867842d4c
5f4ceac54d61d5754bf6919904861aac57100] committed with status (VALID) at peer0.importerorg.trade.com
:8051
2020-09-08 13:24:39.022 UTC [chaincodeCmd] chaincodeInvokeOrQuery -> INFO 005 Chaincode invoke succ
essful. result: status:200
=================== Initialized chaincode on channel 'tradechannel' ===================
========= Chaincode upgraded ===========
```

Figure 13.19: Successful upgrade of trade contract to version v2 on tradechannel, ending with chaincode definition commitment and reinitialization

If you run docker `ps -a | grep dev- | grep trade-` to view the list of running trade chaincode containers, you will see four containers, each with the contract ID (trade) and a different peer service address appearing in the name as in the following screenshot (note the chaincode container corresponding to the new organization's peer):

```
f5e69c2ebe68          dev-peer0.importerorg.trade.com-trade-16acb4f4ebdc5c532c309ed4bd47154a3260c78d0
7278679e39bc7acc594b65e-2fa389c80c26d3db589012892f955e66f9d1ada4d9d5ad900d8f7da3a0066978
"docker-entrypoint.s…"   11 minutes ago     Up 11 minutes
          dev-peer0.importerorg.trade.com-trade-16acb4f4ebdc5c532c309ed4bd47154a3260c78d07278679e
39bc7acc594b65e
c71445e8ccbe          dev-peer0.regulatororg.trade.com-trade-16acb4f4ebdc5c532c309ed4bd47154a3260c78d
07278679e39bc7acc594b65e-753cd418bfee592b351cff07ec5832eac5eca96b44f9a50a00c339c0fd65f067
"docker-entrypoint.s…"   11 minutes ago     Up 11 minutes
          dev-peer0.regulatororg.trade.com-trade-16acb4f4ebdc5c532c309ed4bd47154a3260c78d07278679
e39bc7acc594b65e
0768cfe5e9f9          dev-peer0.exporterorg.trade.com-trade-16acb4f4ebdc5c532c309ed4bd47154a3260c78d0
7278679e39bc7acc594b65e-64f4a3e87054b7188b7ae279acd1ed46d9b129408d61d8a5966bc50ce4848d8c
"docker-entrypoint.s…"   11 minutes ago     Up 11 minutes
          dev-peer0.exporterorg.trade.com-trade-16acb4f4ebdc5c532c309ed4bd47154a3260c78d07278679e
39bc7acc594b65e
2eddeca976d0          dev-peer0.exportingentityorg.trade.com-trade-16acb4f4ebdc5c532c309ed4bd47154a32
60c78d07278679e39bc7acc594b65e-09ffe3bda3f1444be9d89d29ccea2b21cd6b2cf3c96bdad3f2417768452dcb32
"docker-entrypoint.s…"   11 minutes ago     Up 11 minutes
          dev-peer0.exportingentityorg.trade.com-trade-16acb4f4ebdc5c532c309ed4bd47154a3260c78d07
278679e39bc7acc594b65e
```

Figure 13.20: New trade chaincode containers corresponding to the three initial organizations and one new organization

If you select the container ID of any of these chaincode containers and view the logs using docker `logs <container-id>`, you will see something like the following (the highlighted statement is logged in the init function of the contract):

```
2020-09-08T13:24:36.478Z info [c-api:lib/handler.js]                    Successfully regi
stered with peer node. State transferred to "established"
2020-09-08T13:24:36.482Z info [c-api:lib/handler.js]                    Successfully esta
blished communication with peer node. State transferred to "ready"
Upgrading the trade contract
2020-09-08T13:24:36.515Z info [c-api:lib/handler.js]                    [tradechannel-a9c
79aa9] Calling chaincode Init() succeeded. Sending COMPLETED message back to peer
```

Figure 13.21: Messages indicating that the init function in the v2 version of the trade contract was executed

Instructions to upgrade the remaining contracts on their respective channels

Similarly, you can upgrade the other three contracts using the following commands:

```
$ ./trade.sh upgradecontract -c tradechannel -p letterOfCredit -o 3 -t
init -a '"[\"ExportingEntityOrgMSP\",\"LumberBank\",\"700000\"]"'
$ ./trade.sh upgradecontract -c shippingchannel -p exportLicense -o 4
-t init
$ ./trade.sh upgradecontract -c shippingchannel -p shipment -t init -o
4
```

Note that the `letterOfCredit` contract requires the arguments to be supplied as an array represented by a string. This is because the `init` function of this contract accepts a variable-length array of parameters (`String ...params`).

You should see an additional chaincode container for each contract launched by the exporting entity organization's peer. The upgrade of the smart contract layer of our distributed application is now complete!

Instructions to upgrade all contracts in one go

As an alternative to upgrading each contract individually, you can run all upgrades in one go using the following command in the `bash` folder:

```
$ ./sampleUpgradeChaincodeOperations.sh
```

Augmenting the distributed application

To complete the network upgrade picture, we need to create and deploy a service-layer application to serve the members of our new exporting entity's organization. Because our smart contract API has not changed, even though changes have been made internally in their functions, we don't need to modify our pre-existing applications: `exporter`, `importer`, `carrier`, and `regulator`. Following the same nomenclature, we will build and run a fifth application named `exportingentity`.

The code for this application lies in the trade-apps repository, like the other four applications. This application is developed using Java and Spring Boot, like the `importer` and `regulator` applications. If you load the application in VS Code, you will see that it resembles the other two in all respects other than the server port, REST API, and access control rules. We need to set a unique web server port to distinguish this application from the other four. If you open the `src/main/resources/application.properties` file, you can see that we use port number `8000` as follows:

```
server.port=8000
jwt.secret=fabrichacker
connectionProfilesBaseDir=/config/gateways/exportingentityorg
connectionProfileJson=connection.json
walletsBaseDir=/config/wallets/exportingentityorg
server.port=8000
```

Figure 13.22: The setting indicating that the exporting entity application's server will listen for incoming requests on port 8000

The source file `src/main/java/org/trade/exportingentity/`
`ExportingEntityController.java` contains the definitions and implementations of
the API routes, and access control rules governing those routes are specified in `src/`
`main/java/org/trade/exportingentity/ExportingEntityWebSecurityConfig.java` as
follows:

```
@Override
protected void configure(HttpSecurity httpSecurity) throws Exception {
    // We don't need CSRF for this example
    httpSecurity.csrf().disable()
        // dont authenticate this particular request
        .authorizeRequests().antMatchers("/register", "/login").permitAll()
        .antMatchers("/acceptTrade", "/requestEL", "/prepareShipment", "/getTrade", "/getTradeStatus",
                     "/getLC", "/getLCStatus", "/getEL", "/getELStatus", "/getShipmentLocation",
                     "/getBillOfLading", "/getAccountBalance", "/listTrades")
            .hasRole(SecurityUtils.clientRole)
        // all other requests need to be authenticated
        .anyRequest().authenticated().and()
        // make sure we use stateless session; session won't be used to store user's state.
        .exceptionHandling().authenticationEntryPoint(jwtAuthenticationEntryPoint).and().sessionManagement()
        .sessionCreationPolicy(SessionCreationPolicy.STATELESS);

    // Add a filter to validate the tokens with every request
    httpSecurity.addFilterBefore(jwtRequestFilter, UsernamePasswordAuthenticationFilter.class);
}
```

Figure 13.23: Access control rules governing the exporting entity application REST API

Like the other applications, this one exposes `register` and `login` functions to any
web client. The list of functions to invoke and query contracts is similar to that
offered by the exporter application for any user in a client role. This is the only user
role supported by the application and is mapped to a Fabric user with an exporter
certificate attribute.

The code for user registration and login, Fabric registration and enrollment, and
gateway-based invocation of contracts will be familiar to you by now, so we will
not go into the details here.

Preparing and running the application

Before launching the application, we must prepare it as follows:

1. In the `src/main/resources/application.properties` file, set the paths to
   the root wallet and gateway folders as appropriate, just as we did for the
   other applications in *Chapter 9*, *Network Operation and Distributed Application
   Building*.

2. Within the `wallets` folder, create a folder named `exportingentityorg` to
   store Fabric identities created by the `exportingentity` application.

3. Similarly, create an `exportingentityorg` folder in the `gateways` folder. We need to create a connection profile here with the name specified in the `connectionProfileJson` attribute in `application.properties`. By default, this is `connection.json`, though you can change the name if you wish.

4. As described in *Chapter 9, Network Operation and Distributed Application Building*, you can generate a connection profile in different ways:

   - Knowing the structure of the profile, you can create one manually.

   - For automated creation: You can first export a profile using the IBP extension in VS Code and modify it using the utility script `bash/utils/manage-connection-profile.js`.

   - Alternatively, you can use the same script to create a file named `connection.json` in `gateways/exportingentityorg/` as follows (run this from the `bash/utils/` folder):

```
$ node manage-connection-profile.js --generate
exportingentityorg ExportingEntityOrgMSP 12051 12054
--add-org
```

   Here, we supply the MSP ID (`ExportingEntityOrgMSP`), peer port (`12051`), and CA port (`12054`) corresponding to the new organization's configuration.

We are ready for launch. In VS Code, load the file `src/main/java/org/trade/exportingentity/ExportingEntityApplication.java` and click the **Run** link over the main function definition as follows:

```
@SpringBootApplication
public class ExportingEntityApplication {

    Run | Debug
    public static void main(String[] args) {
        SpringApplication.run(ExportingEntityApplication.class, args);
    }

}
```

Figure 13.24: Exporting the entity application main function with the option to launch highlighted

In the terminal window, you will see console output beginning with a Spring Boot logo and ending with messages indicating that a server has been started on Tomcat and is listening on port `8000`.

Exercising the augmented application

At this point, we assume that the five-organization trade network is running, with four contracts at version v2 and five applications corresponding to the different organizations running above the contract layer. An end-to-end trade workflow based on the identifier trade-12 is recorded on the ledgers through the contracts spanning tradechannel and shippingchannel and the four contracts. First, let's confirm that the records still exist after the contract upgrades. We will use our curl-based CLI scripts in the sample-cli-curl folder in trade-apps for this purpose and to exercise the exportingentity application:

1. Navigate to the sample-cli-curl folder in a terminal window. If you need to log existing users in again, if their JWT tokens have expired, run:

    ```
    $ . loginAll.sh
    ```

2. To get the list of trades currently recorded, run the following script, which assumes the importer's role (username importer):

    ```
    $ ./listTrades.sh
    ```

    You should see the following array consisting of exactly one trade identified by trade-12:

    ```
    {"result":true,"payload":"[{\"amount\":90000,\"descriptionOfGoo
    ds\":\"Wood\",\"exporterMSP\":\"ExporterOrgMSP\",\"importerMSP\
    ":\"ImporterOrgMSP\",\"status\":\"ACCEPTED\",\"tradeID\":\"tra
    de-12\"}]"}
    ```

3. Now register a user named exportingentity using the following command:

    ```
    $ ./registerNewOrg.sh
    ```

    You should see the following output:

    ```
    {"roles":["CLIENT"],"username":"exportingentity"}
    ```

    The wallet for the new organization (wallets/exportingentityorg/
    ExportingEntityOrgMSP/) will now contain two identity files: admin.id
    (registrar) and exportingentity.id (the Fabric client user representing an exporting entity member of ExportingEntityOrg).

4. Now log in the new user:

    ```
    $ . loginExportingEntity.sh
    ```

    An environment variable named JWT_EXPENT now contains the new user's JWT token.

5. Assume the role of importer and request a new trade identified by `trade-34` as follows:

```
$ ./requestNewTrade.sh
```

You should see the following output upon success:

```
{"result":true,"payload":""}
```

6. Assume the role of the exporting entity (`exportingentity`) for the subsequent commands. View the attributes of the requested trade using the following:

```
$ ./getNewTrade.sh
```

7. You should see the following output:

```
{"result":true,"payload":"{\"amount\":50000,\"descriptionOfGoods
\":\"Metal\",\"exporterMSP\":\"ExportingEntityOrgMSP\",\"importe
rMSP\":\"ImporterOrgMSP\",\"status\":\"REQUESTED\",\"tradeID\":\
"trade-34\"}"}
```

8. Running `./getNewTradeStatus.sh` will just return the status:

```
{"result":true,"payload":"{\"Status\":\"REQUESTED\"}"}
```

9. Now accept this trade as an exporting entity:

```
$ ./acceptNewTrade.sh
```

You should see the following output upon success:

```
{"result":true,"payload":""}
```

10. To verify the trade's acceptance, run:

```
$ ./getNewTradeStatus.sh
```

You should see the following:

```
{"result":true,"payload":"{\"Status\":\"ACCEPTED\"}"}
```

11. To view the list of trades the new user (`exportingentity`) is involved in, run:

```
$ ./listTradesNewOrg.sh
```

You should see an array with a single trade (`trade-34`) as follows:

```
{"result":true,"payload":"[{\"amount\":50000,\"descriptionOfGood
s\":\"Metal\",\"exporterMSP\":\"ExportingEntityOrgMSP\",\"import
erMSP\":\"ImporterOrgMSP\",\"status\":\"ACCEPTED\",\"tradeID\":\
"trade-34\"}]"}
```

12. Now switch back to the importer's role and view the list of trades the importer is involved in as follows:

```
$ ./listTrades.sh
```

You should see two trades in the returned array (`trade-12` and `trade-34`) as we have just one importer user in our distributed application who was involved in trades before and after the network upgrade:

```
{"result":true,"payload":"[{\"amount\":90000,\"descriptionOfGood
s\":\"Wood\",\"exporterMSP\":\"ExporterOrgMSP\",\"importerMSP\":
\"ImporterOrgMSP\",\"status\":\"ACCEPTED\",\"tradeID\":\"trade-
12\"},{\"amount\":50000,\"descriptionOfGoods\":\"Metal\",\"expor
terMSP\":\"ExportingEntityOrgMSP\",\"importerMSP\":\"ImporterOrg
MSP\",\"status\":\"ACCEPTED\",\"tradeID\":\"trade-34\"}]"}
```

13. To check the current account balance of `exportingentity`, run:

```
$ ./getExportingEntityBalance.sh
```

You should see the following output:

```
{"result":true,"payload":"{\"Balance\":700000.0}"}
```

You can continue the workflow for `trade-34` through the L/C, E/L, shipment, B/L, and payment operations to the end. Though we don't have curl-based CLI scripts in the `sample-cli-curl` folder for these operations, it is quite straightforward to create them as adaptations of the existing scripts. We will leave this as an exercise for you.

Platform upgrades

Your blockchain network must be prepared to run on new versions of the Hyperledger Fabric platform whenever a release is available. It is important that your application and network remain up to date with the platform, and new releases typically contain bug fixes and improved features that are likely to be important for enterprises. Currently, Fabric has an approximate release cycle of 3 months for minor releases (for example, `2.2` after `2.1`). Typically, each release is accompanied by a new source code branch (for example, `release-2.2`) and updated images in Docker Hub. Hyperledger Fabric CA follows a similar release process, though the frequencies may be different from that of Fabric.

A new release of Fabric implies new Docker images for the peer (`hyperledger/fabric-peer`) and orderer (`hyperledger/fabric-orderer`) nodes: you can either build these from source using docker or download them from Docker Hub (this will automatically occur when you are starting the network if the right image versions are not found on your system).

Similarly, a new Fabric CA release implies new Docker images for the CA (hyperledger/fabric-ca), which can be built from source or fetched from Docker Hub. You need to upgrade a live trade network's container images without disrupting the life cycle of the distributed application running over it. In this section, we will demonstrate how to do that.

For reference, you can view the current set of Docker images you have built or downloaded on your system using the following commands:

```
$ docker images | grep hyperledger/fabric-peer
$ docker images | grep hyperledger/fabric-orderer
$ docker images | grep hyperledger/fabric-ca
```

Given that the Fabric version we have been using for development (which was also the latest release at the time of publication) is 2.2, you should see something like the following for hyperledger/fabric-peer (you may see other image versions too if you built or fetched older images):

hyperledger/fabric-peer				2.2
	f8f2412f7ee8	2 months ago	54.9MB	
hyperledger/fabric-peer				2.2.0
	f8f2412f7ee8	2 months ago	54.9MB	
hyperledger/fabric-peer				amd64-2.2.0-
snapshot-0de7fc1	f8f2412f7ee8	2 months ago	54.9MB	
hyperledger/fabric-peer				latest
	f8f2412f7ee8	2 months ago	54.9MB	

Figure 13.25: List of fabric-peer Docker images on the local machine

We will perform an exercise where the trade network's orderer, peer, and CA nodes are upgraded. The steps to do this in a running application are as follows:

1. Download or build new versions of platform Docker images
2. Stop the components
3. (Optional) Make a backup of your components' states (channel ledgers for peers, system channel ledgers for orderers, and identities and credentials for CAs) for safety
4. Stop the running platform (orderers, peers, CAs) and chaincode containers
5. Delete the chaincode container images
6. Update the image versions in your configuration
7. Restart the components

You can also choose to stop, upgrade, and start each component in turn rather than all at once. You will need to stop all incoming requests (traffic) to the distributed application while this upgrade is going on, which you can do by stopping the application web servers.

Sample code to perform such an upgrade to our trade network lies in the upgradeNetwork function in our `trade.sh` script. First, we create a temporary folder to back up the ledgers and identities:

```
function upgradeNetwork () {
......
LEDGERS_BACKUP=./ledgers-backup
......
mkdir -p $LEDGERS_BACKUP
......
```

Next, we select the orderer nodes and `COMPOSE` file depending on whether our network is using a Solo or Raft orderer:

```
if [ "$ORDERER_MODE" = "prod" ]
then
  COMPOSE_FILES="-f $COMPOSE_FILE_RAFT"
  ORDERERS="orderer.trade.com orderer2.trade.com orderer3.trade.com
orderer4.trade.com orderer5.trade.com"
else
  COMPOSE_FILES="-f $COMPOSE_FILE"
  ORDERERS="orderer.trade.com"
fi
```

In the preceding code, `COMPOSE_FILE_RAFT` will map to `docker-compose-raft-orderer.yaml`. whereas `COMPOSE_FILE` will map to `docker-compose-e2e.yaml` (these variables are set in `trade.sh`).

We upgrade the orderer nodes as follows:

```
for ORDERER in $ORDERERS; do
  ......
  docker-compose $COMPOSE_FILES stop $ORDERER
  mkdir -p $LEDGERS_BACKUP/$ORDERER
  docker cp -a $ORDERER:/var/hyperledger/production/orderer $LEDGERS_
BACKUP/$ORDERER/
  docker-compose $COMPOSE_FILES up --no-deps $ORDERER >$LOG_FILE 2>&1 &
done
```

After an orderer container is stopped using docker-compose stop, its volume is still active, so we can copy the ledger contents to a folder on the host machine ($LEDGERS_BACKUP/$ORDERER) using docker cp. An orderer container built on the new version of hyperledger/fabric-orderer is then brought up using docker-compose up. (Before the last step, it is assumed that the Fabric version has been updated in the configuration; we will see how to do this shortly.)

Each peer node is upgraded using a similar procedure:

```
for PEER in peer0.exporterorg.trade.com peer0.importerorg.trade.com
peer0.carrierorg.trade.com peer0.regulatororg.trade.com; do
    ......
    docker-compose $COMPOSE_FILES stop $PEER
    mkdir -p $LEDGERS_BACKUP/$PEER
    docker cp -a $PEER:/var/hyperledger/production $LEDGERS_BACKUP/$PEER/
    ......
    CC_CONTAINERS=$(docker ps | grep dev-$PEER | awk '{print $1}')
    if [ -n "$CC_CONTAINERS" ] ; then
    docker rm -f $CC_CONTAINERS
    fi
    ......
    CC_IMAGES=$(docker images | grep dev-$PEER | awk '{print $1}')
    if [ -n "$CC_IMAGES" ] ; then
      docker rmi -f $CC_IMAGES
    fi
    docker-compose $COMPOSE_FILES up --no-deps $PEER >$LOG_FILE 2>&1 &
done
```

The only additional steps involve stopping chaincode containers associated with a given peer (using docker rm) and then deleting the Docker images those chaincode containers are built on (using docker rmi). (Note that we assume there are only four running peers in the preceding code. If you have additional peers running, like peer1.importerorg.trade.com or peer0.exportingentityorg.trade.com, you can modify trade.sh appropriately to upgrade them too.)

Finally, we upgrade the CA nodes using a similar procedure (stop, backup, restart):

```
for CA in exporter importer carrier regulator; do
    ......
    docker-compose $COMPOSE_FILES stop ${CA}-ca
    mkdir -p $LEDGERS_BACKUP/${CA}-ca
    docker cp -a ca.${CA}org.trade.com:/etc/hyperledger/fabric-ca-server
$LEDGERS_BACKUP/${CA}-ca/
    ......
```

```
    docker-compose $COMPOSE_FILES up --no-deps ${CA}-ca >$LOG_FILE 2>&1 &
 done
```

As with the orderers and peers, it is assumed that the Fabric CA version has been updated in the configuration before the last step (docker-compose up) is carried out. Also, the preceding code assumes that we have four active organizations; you can modify the code to add exportingentity in the for loop if that organization has been added to the network.

Upgrading a live four-organization trade network

To set new platform versions, you will need to edit two files:

- bash/.env: Modify the value of the IMAGE_TAG variable to set the new Hyperledger Fabric version. At the time of publication, this was set to 2.2.0 (corresponding to the latest release version). To set a new Hyperledger Fabric CA version, change the value of the CA_IMAGE_TAG variable, which was set to 1.4.8 at the time of publication. (You can modify one and not the other if a new release is not available for both.)

- bash/trade.sh: Modify the FABRIC_VERSION variable (set to 2.2 at the time of publication). You must update this if the first digit following the decimal in the new version (as set in .env above) is different. For example, if you change from version 2.2.0 to 2.2.5 in .env, no change is needed in trade.sh; but if the version changes from 2.2.0 to 2.3.1, you will need to set FABRIC_VERSION to 2.3. This change is needed to ensure that the hyperledger/fabric-tools image version matches that of hyperledger/fabric-peer and hyperledger/fabric-orderer. Such a check is done for every trade.sh operation done using the trade_cli container.

Let's say a new version of Fabric is released, labeled 2.3.1, and a new version of Fabric CA is released, labeled 1.4.9. All you need to do is make appropriate changes to these two files and run the following command from the bash folder:

```
$ ./trade.sh upgrade
```

Since we don't have a version 2.3.1 for Fabric or a version 1.4.9 for Fabric CA just yet, we can test this feature out by starting a network built on older Fabric images and then upgrading it to our default network that runs on Fabric 2.2.0 and Fabric CA 1.4.8 Docker images.

First, bring down the network if you are already running it:

```
$ ./trade.sh down
```

In .env, set IMAGE_TAG to 2.1.1 and CA_IMAGE_TAG to 1.4.7. In trade.sh, set FABRIC_
VERSION to 2.1. Bring the network up:

```
$ ./trade.sh up
```

You should see something like the following if you view the list of running
containers (using docker ps):

```
CONTAINER ID        IMAGE                              COMMAND               CREATED
  STATUS              PORTS                                 NAMES
6fde1bd34778        hyperledger/fabric-peer:2.1.1      "peer node start"        8 seconds ago
  Up 4 seconds        0.0.0.0:7051->7051/tcp                peer0.exporterorg.trade.com
0e636dc9a593        hyperledger/fabric-peer:2.1.1      "peer node start"       10 seconds ago
  Up 5 seconds        7051/tcp, 0.0.0.0:10051->10051/tcp    peer0.regulatororg.trade.com
d4572d4441de        hyperledger/fabric-peer:2.1.1      "peer node start"       11 seconds ago
  Up 6 seconds        7051/tcp, 0.0.0.0:8051->8051/tcp      peer0.importerorg.trade.com
62a45ca75833        couchdb:2.3                        "tini -- /docker-ent…"  15 seconds ago
  Up 7 seconds        4369/tcp, 9100/tcp, 0.0.0.0:5984->5984/tcp  couchdb-peer0.exporterorg.trade.c
om
89a4c8494142        hyperledger/fabric-peer:2.1.1      "peer node start"       15 seconds ago
  Up 6 seconds        7051/tcp, 0.0.0.0:9051->9051/tcp      peer0.carrierorg.trade.com
8677668de02b        hyperledger/fabric-ca:1.4.7        "sh -c 'fabric-ca-se…"  15 seconds ago
  Up 8 seconds        0.0.0.0:7054->7054/tcp                ca.exporterorg.trade.com
f618e79dcc02        hyperledger/fabric-ca:1.4.7        "sh -c 'fabric-ca-se…"  15 seconds ago
  Up 7 seconds        7054/tcp, 0.0.0.0:9054->9054/tcp      ca.carrierorg.trade.com
0f6ec5711b76        couchdb:2.3                        "tini -- /docker-ent…"  15 seconds ago
  Up 10 seconds       4369/tcp, 9100/tcp, 0.0.0.0:6984->5984/tcp  couchdb-peer0.importerorg.trade.c
om
d16ace1dbf86        hyperledger/fabric-orderer:2.1.1   "orderer"               15 seconds ago
  Up 7 seconds        0.0.0.0:7050->7050/tcp                orderer.trade.com
27570977de2b        hyperledger/fabric-ca:1.4.7        "sh -c 'fabric-ca-se…"  15 seconds ago
  Up 7 seconds        7054/tcp, 0.0.0.0:8054->8054/tcp      ca.importerorg.trade.com
69782f82a1c9        hyperledger/fabric-ca:1.4.7        "sh -c 'fabric-ca-se…"  15 seconds ago
  Up 11 seconds       7054/tcp, 0.0.0.0:10054->10054/tcp    ca.regulatororg.trade.com
3c613325bace        couchdb:2.3                        "tini -- /docker-ent…"  15 seconds ago
  Up 10 seconds       4369/tcp, 9100/tcp, 0.0.0.0:7984->5984/tcp  couchdb-peer0.regulatororg.trade.
com
```

Figure 13.26: List of trade network peer, CA, and orderer containers built on older image versions

Note that the (highlighted) peer, orderer, and CA images correspond to those set in
.env.

Now change IMAGE_TAG to 2.2.0 and CA_IMAGE_TAG to 1.4.8 in .env. In trade.sh,
change FABRIC_VERSION to 2.2. Trigger the network upgrade as follows:

```
$ ./trade.sh upgrade
```

Upon success, you should see something like the following if you view the list of
running containers (using docker ps):

```
CONTAINER ID        IMAGE                           COMMAND                    CREATED
   STATUS           PORTS                                    NAMES

5e4e58c3fb3b        hyperledger/fabric-ca:1.4.8     "sh -c 'fabric-ca-se…"   24 seconds ago
   Up 22 seconds      7054/tcp, 0.0.0.0:10054->10054/tcp        ca.regulatororg.trade.com
12ffa2ef9c5c        hyperledger/fabric-ca:1.4.8     "sh -c 'fabric-ca-se…"   37 seconds ago
   Up 33 seconds      7054/tcp, 0.0.0.0:9054->9054/tcp          ca.carrierorg.trade.com
4011b4a83b79        hyperledger/fabric-ca:1.4.8     "sh -c 'fabric-ca-se…"   52 seconds ago
   Up 48 seconds      7054/tcp, 0.0.0.0:8054->8054/tcp          ca.importerorg.trade.com
3d95a98e6278        hyperledger/fabric-ca:1.4.8     "sh -c 'fabric-ca-se…"   About a minute ago
   Up About a minute  0.0.0.0:7054->7054/tcp                    ca.exporterorg.trade.com
4b55c997d390        hyperledger/fabric-peer:2.2.0   "peer node start"         About a minute ago
   Up About a minute  7051/tcp, 0.0.0.0:10051->10051/tcp        peer0.regulatororg.trade.com
8c14e6420e8b        hyperledger/fabric-peer:2.2.0   "peer node start"         About a minute ago
   Up About a minute  7051/tcp, 0.0.0.0:9051->9051/tcp          peer0.carrierorg.trade.com
5fbb9a3caad2        hyperledger/fabric-peer:2.2.0   "peer node start"         About a minute ago
   Up About a minute  7051/tcp, 0.0.0.0:8051->8051/tcp          peer0.importerorg.trade.com
3ac9a1de2f44        hyperledger/fabric-peer:2.2.0   "peer node start"         About a minute ago
   Up About a minute  0.0.0.0:7051->7051/tcp                    peer0.exporterorg.trade.com
2ae5a7116b82        hyperledger/fabric-orderer:2.2.0 "orderer"                About a minute ago
   Up About a minute  0.0.0.0:7050->7050/tcp                    orderer.trade.com
62a45ca75833        couchdb:2.3                     "tini -- /docker-ent…"   7 minutes ago
   Up 7 minutes       4369/tcp, 9100/tcp, 0.0.0.0:5984->5984/tcp  couchdb-peer0.exporterorg.trade.
com
0f6ec5711b76        couchdb:2.3                     "tini -- /docker-ent…"   7 minutes ago
   Up 7 minutes       4369/tcp, 9100/tcp, 0.0.0.0:6984->5984/tcp  couchdb-peer0.importerorg.trade.
com
3c613325bace        couchdb:2.3                     "tini -- /docker-ent…"   7 minutes ago
   Up 7 minutes       4369/tcp, 9100/tcp, 0.0.0.0:7984->5984/tcp  couchdb-peer0.regulatororg.trade
.com
```

Figure 13.27: List of trade network peer, CA, and orderer containers built on new image versions after a platform upgrade

Note that the (highlighted) peer, orderer, and CA images correspond to those set in `.env`.

You can continue to run the distributed application without performing any special operations after the network upgrade. The channels set up before the upgrade will remain intact. Chaincode containers running the contracts will be recreated after the upgrade but will inherit the ledger state snapshot that existed just before the upgrade operation was carried out. The service-layer applications can continue to run without any stops and restarts.

 Platform changes may sometimes contain breaking changes in the contract and SDK API, which may necessitate an upgrade to the contract or service application code. Using our demonstration of contract upgrades in earlier sections of this chapter as a guide, you should now be well-equipped to simultaneously upgrade platform versions and contract code, should the need arise.

System monitoring and performance

You have now built your network and distributed application. You have also instituted various processes and mechanisms in anticipation of changes to the network structure and application logic over the course of its life. An additional, but no less essential, process that you must have in place and carry out from time to time is monitoring and performance measurement. Any production application you build for real-world users and institutions, especially in the enterprise world, must meet certain performance standards to be useful to end users and service providers. Therefore, knowing how well your distributed application performs, and striving to improve its performance, is a key maintenance task; any dereliction in this task may result in your network and application suite having short shelf lives.

The art (and science) of system performance measurement and analytics encompasses a broad and extensive set of topics, and it is not our intention to cover these topics deeply or exhaustively in this book. To get a deeper and broader understanding, you are encouraged to read other canonical texts on the topic (for example, `https://www.amazon.com/Systems-Performance-Enterprise-Brendan-Gregg/dp/0133390098`). We will instead offer some insight into the process of blockchain performance measurement and analytics and offer tooling suggestions to developers and system administrators.

Network operators in charge of system maintenance must periodically carry out the following sequence of tasks to ensure that the distributed application is performing at an acceptable level:

1. Observation and measurement
2. Evaluation (or analysis) and gaining insight (or understanding)
3. Restructuring, redesign, or reimplementation for improvement

In our discussion in this section, we will mainly focus on some aspects of the following:

- What it is important to measure in a Fabric application
- The mechanisms a Fabric application developer or administrator can use for measurement
- The performance-inhibiting aspects of Fabric any application developer or network operator should be aware of

Measurement and analytics

Before discussing Hyperledger Fabric in particular, let's understand what measurement and analytics for any distributed system entail. (A distributed blockchain application is one example of this class of systems.) The process of understanding how well a system performs begins with a comprehensive review of its architecture and listing the dependencies among the system's components. The next step is to institute mechanisms to monitor the different components and collect data attributes that have any bearing on performance, either continuously or at periodic intervals. The aggregate data must be periodically collected and analyzed to generate meaningful profiles of system performance; the expectation is that such profiles will provide insight into the working of the system and identify existing inefficiencies. System component monitors are also used to detect dips in performance that ought to be brought to the attention of administrators; this is especially important for user-facing systems. Periodic analysis of aggregated data can assure stakeholders that their system is consistently delivering a desired level of performance.

Such techniques and processes are well known in the world of distributed systems analytics and mobile analytics (a special case of the former.) Agents can be configured to observe or monitor a system component, either actively or passively. Active monitoring typically involves instrumentation (for example, by inserting a piece of code that periodically records data) to make them self-monitor their activities and gather information. Passive monitoring involves data collection using software that runs separately from the component being monitored. A pipeline is built to communicate recorded data periodically in a central repository, where it can be accumulated for later processing or processed and consumed immediately. The data may be modified before accumulation in the repository to make it easy to analyze. In data analytics parlance, such a pipeline is typically referred to as **extract-transform-load** (ETL). If the volume and frequency of data generation are very high, and if the number of data sources is very large, such analytics is also referred to as **big data analytics**.

In-depth coverage of ETL processes and big data analytics is beyond the scope of this chapter and book, but the takeaway for a blockchain developer or network administrator is that there are frameworks to measure and analyze distributed systems composed of servers and databases. A Fabric system is also composed of servers and databases at its core, with consensus mechanisms for transaction processing offering added twists. Examples of commercial analytics platforms include Splunk (`https://www.splunk.com/en_us/solutions/solution-areas/business-analytics.html`) and Apteligent (`http://www.apteligent.com/`) for general distributed systems, and Tealeaf (`https://www.ibm.com/in-en/marketplace/session-replay-and-interaction-analytics`) and Google Analytics (`https://developers.google.com/analytics/solutions/mobile`) for mobile applications. These frameworks can be used or adapted for blockchain networks and applications too.

Fabric system measurement considerations

An application built on Hyperledger Fabric, like our trade workflow, is, in effect, a **distributed transaction processing system**. So, what does a traditional transaction processing system look like? It typically consists of a database at the backend to store, process, and serve data. This database may be centralized or distributed, and in the latter case, maintain replicas or partitions. Between the database and end users lie one or more web servers or application servers to manage and run application logic. At the frontend lie one or more interfaces for users to interact with the servers.

Similarly, a distributed application built on Fabric (or any other blockchain technology) has a database in the form of a shared replicated ledger maintained collectively by peers. Smart contracts are analogous to stored procedures and views in a traditional database management system. Service-layer applications are traditional web or application servers. CLI applications and web interfaces for user interaction are exactly what you would use in a traditional transaction processing application. These upper-layer applications may independently submit transactions to a network, but in the backend, these transactions act on common shared ledgers. Transactions are validated, linked, and coordinated by contracts and consensus protocols to ensure that the integrity of ledger state snapshots is never violated.

Metrics for performance analysis

If a blockchain network and application is indeed a distributed transaction processing system, its performance ought to be affected by similar factors to those affecting a traditional DBMS-based transaction processing application. Hence, we can monitor and analyze the components of a Fabric network and application using techniques that could apply to any distributed system. Let's survey the factors that impact performance and their monitoring techniques.

The core of each application component is hardware that has common indicators of health and resource consumption, which we ought to monitor periodically. For every machine that is running a peer or orderer or CA, we need to track the following (this is not meant to be an exhaustive list, but it covers the needs of most systems):

- CPU usage
- Memory usage
- Disk I/O activity
- Available storage space
- Network bandwidth usage, latency, and jitter

These factors, especially CPU usage for processing-heavy systems, determine whether the network and application are operating at optimal performance levels. They are also crucial to understanding (or profiling) applications.

As we have seen in this book, a Fabric network can be configured in different ways. A peer or orderer process may run on a dedicated machine (physical or virtual), or multiple nodes in isolated Docker containers may share machines (like our trade network setup in this book). In a multi-container setup (using Docker Compose or Kubernetes), you will need to monitor the health indicators of not only the machines but also of each separate container. This consideration also applies to Fabric chaincode instances, which always run in dedicated Docker containers. We will look at some tools to measure container and application performance later in this section.

Moving up the stack from hardware to software, the performance of a Fabric application, like any other transaction processing system, has two characteristic metrics:

- **Throughput**: This is the number of transactions per unit time that your system can support. Fabric is a loosely coupled system, and every transaction goes through multiple stages in a pipeline consisting of independent components, namely, clients, peers, and orderers. The overall system throughput paints the most accurate picture of a distributed application's performance.

This is the measure of the entire pipeline's ability to process transactions: a transaction is one that begins when an application client submits it to a network gateway and ends when the client receives a response (using messages and events masked by an API) indicating whether the ledger has been updated. But we can also measure throughputs for stages in isolation, such as the ability of an endorsing peer to process endorsements or the ability of an ordering service to cut blocks. If we want to measure the orderer throughput, for example, we would need to collect statistics just for the portion of the pipeline where the ordering service receives an endorsed transaction and produces a block for dissemination to validating peers. Such isolated throughput measurements can be useful in capacity planning and bottleneck identification.

- **Latency**: Like all interactive applications, an important concern for a Fabric network or application designer is the typical time taken for a transaction submission to yield a response. This is **transaction latency**, and it is a distinct measure that is usually independent of processing capacity or volume. Like with throughput, we can measure the latencies of different pipeline stages in isolation—chaincode execution and endorsement, ordering and block creation, transaction validation and ledger commitment, and event notification. We can also measure inter-component communication latency to understand the limits of the network's communication infrastructure.

We can conceive of Fabric-specific performance metrics like replication efficiency, which could be defined as the time taken to synchronize ledger states across peers using the **gossip** protocol. But from a transaction processing perspective, throughput and latency are the metrics that will be at the forefront of system maintainers' concerns. Two primary goals must be kept in mind: maximizing throughput and minimizing latency. These goals apply not just to network operators and application developers, but also to blockchain platform engineers; applications typically will not be able to overcome the inherent limitations of platforms.

Fabric application performance measurement and data collection

Now that we are acquainted with the key performance metrics, let's look at some examples of hands-on measurement and data collection. We will use an Ubuntu Linux machine running our Docker container-based trade network for demonstrations, and let you apply similar methods (with the help of other measurement tools and texts) to different environments.

Measuring system health indicators

On any Linux machine, information about CPU, memory, and other activities can be found in the proc filesystem (typically mounted at /proc). In addition, an array of tools is publicly available to obtain specific pieces of information. The sysstat package contains many of them, for example, iostat to collect CPU and I/O statistics, pidstat to collect health statistics for each process, and sar and sadc to collect similar statistics as cron jobs. If sysstat is not already installed on your machine, you can install it using the following command (requiring elevated privileges): sudo apt install sysstat.

As an example, running iostat on a VM produces CPU usage and I/O statistics for drive partitions and logical volumes that look like the following:

```
Linux 4.4.0-173-generic (vagrant)        09/08/2020       _x86_64_        (2 CPU)

avg-cpu:  %user   %nice %system %iowait  %steal   %idle
           7.46    0.00    3.45    0.20    0.00   88.89

Device:            tps    kB_read/s    kB_wrtn/s    kB_read    kB_wrtn
loop0             0.00         0.00         0.00          8          0
sda               9.55        35.69       271.04     828766    6293864
dm-0             26.15        35.21       271.04     817577    6293840
dm-1              0.01         0.14         0.00       3264          0
```

Figure 13.28: Output of the iostat tool on a Linux machine

As another example, the vmstat tool presents a summary of the VM-wide information as follows:

```
procs -----------memory---------- ---swap-- -----io---- -system-- ------cpu-----
 r  b   swpd   free   buff  cache   si   so    bi    bo   in   cs us sy id wa st
 2  0      0 1220380 288504 1408748    0    0    18   140  843  196  7  3 89  0  0
```

Figure 13.29: Output of the vmstat tool on a Linux machine

For continuous per-process statistics, you can also use the well-known top command, or dstat (installed on an Ubuntu machine using sudo apt install dstat), which also generates output in CSV format for easy consumption. If you wish to connect your measurement mechanisms to an ETL analytics pipeline, nmon (http://nmon. sourceforge.net/pmwiki.php) is an easy-to-use tool for comprehensive performance data collection and reporting in well-known formats.

The following screenshot illustrates how nmon can be used to observe memory usage statistics:

```
-nmon—14g——————————Hostname=vagrant———Refresh= 2secs ——14:39.34———
 Memory Stats
                RAM     High     Low     Swap    Page Size=4 KB
 Total MB     5431.4    -0.0    -0.0    980.0
 Free  MB     1211.7    -0.0    -0.0    980.0
 Free Percent  22.3%  100.0%  100.0%  100.0%
               MB                MB                    MB
                        Cached= 1151.7    Active=  3377.5
 Buffers=      281.8 Swapcached=   0.0  Inactive =  513.1
 Dirty  =        0.0 Writeback =   0.0  Mapped   =  230.9
 Slab   =      224.3 Commit_AS = 10129.8 PageTables=  21.1
```

Figure 13.30: Memory usage statistics using nmon on a Linux machine

If you are running multiple components on a single machine, like we are with a Docker container-based trade network, you would like to observe per-component resource usage statistics. Here, the perf tool comes in handy as a performance counter and profiling tool for Linux. This tool is typically installed on an Ubuntu machine using the following command:

```
$ sudo apt install linux-tools-$(uname -r) linux-tools-generic
```

perf can collect profiles on a per thread, per process, and per CPU (or processor) basis. Data can be collected, and reports generated using the perf record command (with different switches); output data is stored in a file called perf.data in the folder the command was run in. This data can then be analyzed using the perf report command. Further, you can use bindfs (https://bindfs.org/) to map symbols in a perf report to processes running inside Docker containers. Lastly, perf stat can be used to collect system-wide statistics. The perf Wiki (https://perf.wiki.kernel.org/) gives more information about how to use this tool.

For Docker container-specific performance statistics, you should use Google's cAdvisor (Container Advisor) tool (https://github.com/google/cadvisor), which has native support for Docker containers. This runs as a daemon on your system and collects, aggregates, and processes information about running containers (in our scenario, these are the peer, orderer, and CA containers in the trade Fabric network). It keeps resource isolation parameters, historical resource usage, and network statistics for each container. Further, it exports this information through a web GUI for users to examine.

To launch cAdvisor within a Docker container on the machine on which you are running the trade network, run the following command (the version in the command was the latest at the time of publication):

```
$ sudo docker run \
   --volume=/:/rootfs:ro \
   --volume=/var/run/:/var/run:ro \
```

```
--volume=/sys:/sys:ro \
--volume=/var/lib/docker/:/var/lib/docker:ro \
--volume=/dev/disk/:/dev/disk:ro \
--publish=8080:8080 \
--detach=true \
--name=cadvisor \
--privileged \
--device=/dev/kmsg \
gcr.io/cadvisor/cadvisor:v0.36.0
```

If the image `gcr.io/cadvisor/cadvisor:v0.36.0` isn't already present on your system, it will be pulled from the repository. As a result of this command, cAdvisor will run in the background and expose a web server on `http://localhost:8080`. If you open this URL on your web browser, you will see an array of information, including statistics and graphs as you scroll down the page. A sample overview of the containers' resource consumption and a running graph of the total CPU usage of containers is illustrated in the following screenshot:

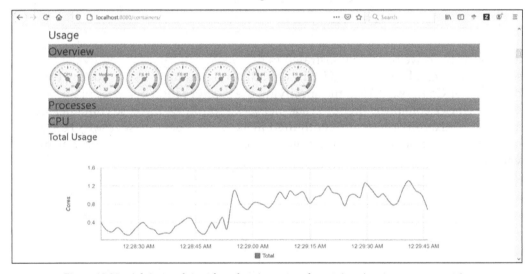

Figure 13.31: cAdvisor web interface showing network containers' resource usage metrics

If you are running your Fabric network components as containers on a Linux machine, you can use the tools demonstrated in this section to measure and compile statistics about the resource consumption of each component (Fabric network nodes as well as any service-layer applications you may be running).

Fabric support for component monitoring

Aside from using third-party tools like `sysstat` or cAdvisor, a network maintainer can also rely on *operations services* configured on peers and orderers to obtain health and behavioral information specific to each component. An operations service can be configured on a peer using its `core.yaml` file or on an orderer node using its `orderer.yaml` file, as demonstrated in `https://hyperledger-fabric.readthedocs.io/en/latest/operations_service.html`. The following snippet of code shows how an operations service in a peer is configured to listen on port 9443:

```
operations:
    listenAddress: 127.0.0.1:9443
```

> To view the current contents of these files, you can log in to the respective containers. For example, you can view the exporter organization's peer's configuration as follows:
>
> ```
> $ docker exec -it peer0.exporterorg.trade.com sh
> $ more /etc/hyperledger/fabric/core.yaml
> ```

Alternatively, as we have demonstrated in this book, you can make equivalent settings (or override the settings in the default configuration files) by editing the base Docker Compose YAML file specifying the configuration of a peer or an orderer service container. (In our `trade-network` repository, the base containers for a peer as well as an orderer are configured in `bash/base/peer-base.yaml`.) To start an operations service on port 9443, you can configure the following environment variable:

```
services:
    peer-base:
        image: hyperledger/fabric-peer:$IMAGE_TAG
        environment:
            ......
            - CORE_OPERATIONS_LISTENADDRESS=127.0.0.1:9443
            ......
```

To expose this service on the host machine, you should add a new entry in the `ports` section of each peer container's configuration in `bash/base/docker-compose-base.yaml` as follows (example of the exporter organization's peer service):

```
peer0.exporterorg.trade.com:
    ......
    ports:
```

```
......
- 9443:9443
......
```

You can configure ports for the other three peers (and the orderers in the appropriate Docker Compose file) similarly, but make sure you use unique values for each.

Once configured, an operations service exposes the following:

- Log information using a `/logspec` resource
- Component health using a `/healthz` resource
- Component metrics using either a `/metrics` resource or by pushing to a `statsd` daemon:
    - You can configure Prometheus (`https://prometheus.io/`) to expose metric values through /metrics (pull model) or run a StatsD statistics aggregation daemon (`https://github.com/statsd/statsd`) to collect metrics periodically sent by the component (push model).
    - An array of metrics is exposed, pertaining to chaincode and ledger activities, and the processing of transactions and blocks. (In the orderer's case, you will see metrics pertaining to Raft consensus). For a complete list, see `https://hyperledger-fabric.readthedocs.io/en/latest/metrics_reference.html`.

For more information on how to configure an operations service and access information exposed by it, you should refer to the official Fabric documentation: `https://hyperledger-fabric.readthedocs.io/en/latest/operations_service.html`. (A deeper examination of this feature is beyond the scope of this book, and we leave that as an exercise for you.)

Profiling containers and applications

Profiling network components, such as peers, orderers, and CAs running in Docker containers, can serve two purposes. First, health and resource usage numbers of the kinds we have seen tell us how well the application is performing. Second, if we can extract instruction-level information and program call stacks, we can not just track performance but also debug component flaws. As an example, tracking system calls made by a running Docker container allow us to build a profile of that container, and the `strace` tool can be used to do just that on Linux.

To get the process ID for one of our peer containers, first run:

```
$ docker inspect --format '{{ .State.Pid }}' peer0.exporterorg.trade.
com
```

The output will be a process ID; let's call it <pid>. Now run strace on that process:

```
$ sudo strace -T -tt -p <pid>
```

You should see a streaming output, which may look like the following screenshot:

```
strace: Process 7223 attached
14:55:45.434567 futex(0x2455b18, FUTEX_WAKE_PRIVATE, 1) = 1 <0.000028>
14:55:45.434693 futex(0x2455a18, FUTEX_WAKE_PRIVATE, 1) = 1 <0.000015>
14:55:45.434741 read(51, "\27\3\3\0/\f357\210\245\222\221b\37\200P\253\260]\2531\264\7\224\325\32f
\246KVI\202\\"..., 1746) = 52 <0.000012>
14:55:45.434841 futex(0xc000060848, FUTEX_WAKE_PRIVATE, 1) = 1 <0.000231>
14:55:45.435519 futex(0xc00044e148, FUTEX_WAKE_PRIVATE, 1) = 1 <0.000031>
14:55:45.435601 read(51, 0xc0031a2e00, 1746) = -1 EAGAIN (Resource temporarily unavailable) <0.0000
11>
14:55:45.435814 write(51, "\27\3\3\0\"\313+\355\211\3236\340\353Z\313\3\tOo\312\342<\356Yw\267\236\
231\303Q\326Z"..., 39) = 39 <0.000134>
14:55:45.436149 futex(0x24565c8, FUTEX_WAIT_PRIVATE, 0, NULL) = 0 <0.004018>
14:55:45.440427 futex(0x24565c8, FUTEX_WAIT_PRIVATE, 0, NULL) = 0 <0.003069>
14:55:45.443591 futex(0x24565c8, FUTEX_WAIT_PRIVATE, 0, NULL) = 0 <0.007346>
14:55:45.451038 futex(0xc00044e148, FUTEX_WAKE_PRIVATE, 1) = 1 <0.000024>
```

Figure 13.32: Output of strace on a peer process running within a Docker container on a Linux machine

To analyze the output, read the canonical strace documentation. Also, in your Docker Compose YAML file, you can configure a container to run strace internally. As an example, you can enable strace in peer0.exporterorg.trade.com by augmenting the container's configuration in bash/base/docker-compose-base.yaml as follows (the added configuration appears in bold):

```
peer0.exporterorg.trade.com:
  container_name: peer0.exporterorg.trade.com
  cap_add:
    - SYS_PTRACE
  security_opt:
    - seccomp:unconfined
```

Finally, to analyze your Fabric network units (peers, orderers, and CAs), all developed in Go, as well as contracts written in Go, you should use Go profiling. This will help you find out which parts of a program use more time and resources, and thereby help you improve its quality. Go has a built-in profiling tool called pprof (https://golang. org/pkg/net/http/pprof/). For a survey of the features this tool provides and to view examples, see https://blog.golang.org/profiling-go-programs. Before running the profiler, please ensure you have Go installed on the system (machine or container) in which the Go program being profiled is running.

To capture an application profile consisting of call graphs and run frequency (equivalent to CPU usage) of various functions in the graph, pprof requires a Go application to import certain libraries and run an HTTP server as follows (which typically listens on port 6060):

```
import "net/http"
import "net/http/pprof"
http.ListenAndServe("localhost:6060", nil)
```

Hyperledger Fabric provides built-in support for profiling Fabric peers; that is, it imports the preceding libraries and runs the profile server in the peer's source code (see https://github.com/hyperledger-archives/fabric/wiki/Profiling-the-Hyperledger-Fabric). In the base configuration of each of our peers (see bash/base/peer-base.yaml), profiling (or running the profile server on port 6060) is already enabled as follows (by setting the CORE_PEER_PROFILE_ENABLED environment variable to true):

```
services:
  peer-base:
    image: hyperledger/fabric-peer:$IMAGE_TAG
    environment:
      ......
      - CORE_PEER_PROFILE_ENABLED=true
      ......
```

What we have not done so far is to expose the pprof service to the host machine through container port mapping. We can do that now by adding a new entry in the ports section of each peer container's configuration in bash/base/docker-compose-base.yaml as follows:

```
peer0.exporterorg.trade.com:
  ......
  ports:
    ......
    - 6060:6060
    ......
```

You can add a similar port mapping entry in the other three peer containers' configurations too, though with different host port numbers for each: `peer0.importerorg.trade.com`, `peer0.carrierorg.trade.com`, and `peer0.regulatororg.trade.com`. Now you can run `pprof` on your host machine to capture and analyze the profiles of peers running within Docker containers. (Remember to restart your peer network after you make the preceding changes.) To test this out and capture a heap profile of `peer0.exporterorg.trade.com`, use `go tool` to hit the profile server and fetch the data as follows:

```
$ go tool pprof http://localhost:6060/debug/pprof/heap
```

In general, you can replace `localhost` with a different hostname or IP address in the preceding command. After saving a profile as a zipped archive in ~/pprof, the command will present you with a pprof shell to run analytics commands.

Instead of capturing an instantaneous profile snapshot, you can capture a 30-second CPU profile of the exporter organization's peer using the following command:

```
$ go tool pprof http://localhost:6060/debug/pprof/profile
```

After 30 seconds, this will generate a zipped archive in ~/pprof, and spew something like the following on your console:

```
Fetching profile over HTTP from http://localhost:6060/debug/pprof/profile
Saved profile in /home/vagrant/pprof/pprof.peer.samples.cpu.002.pb.gz
File: peer
Type: cpu
Time: Sep 8, 2020 at 3:02pm (UTC)
Duration: 30s, Total samples = 640ms ( 2.13%)
Entering interactive mode (type "help" for commands, "o" for options)
(pprof)
```

Figure 13.33: Collecting a 30-second CPU profile of the exporter organization's peer in the trade network using pprof

This command will also leave you with a pprof shell to run profiling commands and analyze the captured profile dump. For example, to get the top 20 most active functions or goroutines, run the command `top 20`. You will see something like the following:

```
(pprof) top 20
Showing nodes accounting for 500ms, 78.12% of 640ms total
Showing top 20 nodes out of 189
      flat  flat%   sum%        cum   cum%
     150ms 23.44% 23.44%      150ms 23.44%  runtime.futex
      90ms 14.06% 37.50%       90ms 14.06%  runtime.epollwait
      30ms  4.69% 42.19%       30ms  4.69%  runtime.usleep
      20ms  3.12% 45.31%       30ms  4.69%  crypto/elliptic.p256PointAddAsm
      20ms  3.12% 48.44%       30ms  4.69%  encoding/asn1.parseField
      20ms  3.12% 51.56%       20ms  3.12%  runtime.(*mcache).prepareForSweep
      20ms  3.12% 54.69%      210ms 32.81%  runtime.findrunnable
      20ms  3.12% 57.81%       20ms  3.12%  runtime.timeSleepUntil
      20ms  3.12% 60.94%       40ms  6.25%  syscall.Syscall
      10ms  1.56% 62.50%       10ms  1.56%  crypto/aes.(*gcmAsm).Overhead
      10ms  1.56% 64.06%       10ms  1.56%  crypto/elliptic.p256PointAddAffineAsm
      10ms  1.56% 65.62%       10ms  1.56%  crypto/elliptic.p256Sqr
      10ms  1.56% 67.19%       20ms  3.12%  crypto/x509.parsePublicKey
      10ms  1.56% 68.75%       10ms  1.56%  fmt.newPrinter
      10ms  1.56% 70.31%       10ms  1.56%  github.com/hyperledger/fabric/common/ledger/util/leveld
bhelper.(*DBHandle).GetIterator
      10ms  1.56% 71.88%       80ms 12.50%  github.com/hyperledger/fabric/common/policies.Signature
SetToValidIdentities
      10ms  1.56% 73.44%       10ms  1.56%  github.com/hyperledger/fabric/msp/mgmt.(*mspMgmtMgr).De
serializeIdentity
      10ms  1.56% 75.00%       10ms  1.56%  p256IsZero
      10ms  1.56% 76.56%       10ms  1.56%  p256SqrInternal
      10ms  1.56% 78.12%       10ms  1.56%  reflect.(*rtype).Kind
(pprof)
```

Figure 13.34: Profiling the top 20 most active functions or goroutines in the exporter organization's peer process using pprof

The tree command displays the entire call graph in textual form, a section of which will look something like the following:

```
(pprof) tree
Showing nodes accounting for 640ms, 100% of 640ms total
Showing top 80 nodes out of 189
----------------------------------------------------+-------------
      flat  flat%   sum%        cum   cum%  calls calls% + context
----------------------------------------------------+-------------
                                             50ms 33.33% |    runtime.findrunnable
                                             40ms 26.67% |    runtime.notetsleep_internal
                                             20ms 13.33% |    runtime.resetspinning
                                             20ms 13.33% |    syscall.Syscall
     150ms 23.44% 23.44%      150ms 23.44%               | runtime.futex
----------------------------------------------------+-------------
                                             90ms   100% |    runtime.findrunnable
      90ms 14.06% 37.50%       90ms 14.06%               | runtime.epollwait
----------------------------------------------------+-------------
      30ms  4.69% 42.19%       30ms  4.69%               | runtime.usleep
----------------------------------------------------+-------------
                                             30ms   100% |    crypto/elliptic.(*p256Point).p256Scal
arMult
      20ms  3.12% 45.31%       30ms  4.69%               | crypto/elliptic.p256PointAddAsm
                                             10ms 33.33% |    p256IsZero
----------------------------------------------------+-------------
                                             30ms   100% |    encoding/asn1.UnmarshalWithParams
                                             10ms 33.33% |    encoding/asn1.parseSequenceOf
      20ms  3.12% 48.44%       30ms  4.69%               | encoding/asn1.parseField
                                             10ms 33.33% |    encoding/asn1.parseSequenceOf
                                             10ms 33.33% |    reflect.(*rtype).Kind
----------------------------------------------------+-------------
```

Figure 13.35: A section of the exporter organization's peer process' call graph in textual form generated using pprof

You can also view the graph pictorially on a web page by running the web command in the pprof shell. (You will need to set the BROWSER environment variable appropriately for this.) Alternatively, you can generate an image file using the web command as follows:

```
(pprof) png
Generating report in profile002.png
(pprof)
```

Figure 13.36: Generating a pictorial representation of the exporter organization's peer process' call graph using pprof

In the preceding example, you will see a PNG image file containing the call graph generated in profile002.png in your current working directory. This will look something like the following:

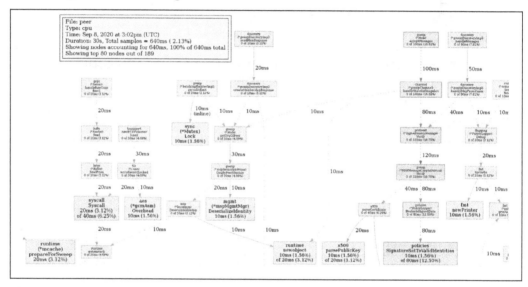

Figure 13.37: A section of the exporter organization's peer process' call graph in pictorial form generated using pprof

Figure 13.37 shows a section of the call graph image generated by the preceding command, with each box representing a function and the box's size indicating the frequency of that function (that is, the number of profile samples in which that function was running). Directed graph edges indicate calls made from one function to another, with the edges annotated by the time spent making such calls.

For more commands and analytical tools, you are encouraged to read the official pprof documentation and manuals.

Measuring application performance

Measuring the throughput and latency of your application requires conventional programming rather than exercising third-party tools of the kinds we have encountered in this chapter. It involves instrumenting your code to collect and record timing information. You will need to either (i) add logging or client-server communication (for remote reporting) instructions to record when an operation of interest is being performed, or (ii) add appropriate hooks that can enable or disable data collection as per your requirements.

Measuring latency is straightforward: you can record the time instants at which a transaction passes through different stages of the processing pipeline, from contract invocation through a gateway to receipt of a response indicating success or failure. To determine accurate latency figures for a particular type of transaction or for a particular pipeline stage, you should collect transaction data over a sufficiently long time period and analyze it using statistical tools.

To get throughput information, you will need to generate transaction loads of different volumes and different frequencies. Then you can increase the load on your application up to the point when the observed frequency of transaction commitment decreases below the transaction load generation frequency. To measure service-layer application performance in addition to contracts, peers, and orderers, you can tune transaction load by controlling the traffic that hits the web servers. Traffic generation tools are publicly available: for example, Apache JMeter™ (`https://jmeter.apache.org/`) is a Java-based tool to test web application performance by creating transaction load in a configurable manner. Just like in latency measurement, you will need to instrument your code to collect transaction volume figures. To experiment, you can vary machine characteristics (like available CPU and memory) and parameter values in the peer and orderer node configurations, such as block sizes and timeouts, (see *Chapter 4*, *Setting the Stage with a Business Scenario*). Observing throughput values for different configurations will enable you to determine ideal system characteristics for optimal performance.

Given all the information we can collect using the tools described in this section, an application or network designer can conduct advanced analytics to determine what parts of the system (for example, from a `pprof` call graph) are performing well, and what parts are bottlenecks. You can then try to remedy performance limitations by adding more resources to (that is, scaling up) "bottlenecked" components or re-engineer the system to make those components more efficient. Load balancing across redundant resources is another widely used technique to deliver high performance. Bottleneck detection and analysis is a very important topic in its own right, and you are encouraged to study texts and academic papers to gain a better understanding and extract lessons you can apply to your system.

Fabric engineering guidelines for performance

We will now move from the general to the specific. In this section, we will offer a commentary on Hyperledger Fabric performance, discuss salient characteristics of the platform that impact performance, and lay out guidelines for developers to extract the best performance from their applications.

Platform performance characteristics

The Fabric architecture and transaction pipeline should be very familiar to you by now. It is a complex distributed system and its performance depends on many factors, such as application (that is, contracts and services) characteristics, consensus algorithm, transaction size, block size, Fabric network size, and endorsement policies. The performance also depends on the capability of the underlying hardware and communication medium.

Several performance measurements of Fabric have been conducted, revealing that it can yield a throughput of several thousand transactions per second, though performance varies significantly depending on application characteristics, transaction types, network configurations, and system resources. Interested readers are directed to papers like *Hyperledger Fabric: A Distributed Operating System for Permissioned Blockchains* (https://arxiv.org/abs/1801.10228) and *Performance Benchmarking and Optimizing Hyperledger Fabric Blockchain Platform* (https://arxiv.org/abs/1805.11390) for more detailed information. You should note that these measurements were carried out using chaincode that performed very simple operations on network configurations that may not represent what a consortium of enterprises would use in production. Because Fabric is a general-purpose blockchain technology, performance is likely to vary considerably with application characteristics. Running a toy application on a small network will yield much higher performance numbers than a high-volume trading system spanning multiple real-world enterprises, for example. The hardware and deployment environment also make a difference: you will likely get higher performance for the same application on an **IBM Blockchain Platform** (**IBP**) instance than by running open source software on a public cloud, as IBP uses images that are optimized for performance. Yet, Fabric measurements, even with toy examples on simple network topologies, do establish baselines that tell enterprise customers what they can expect from the platform in commercial use. Good performance ultimately depends on your system having sufficient resources and the right configuration.

System bottlenecks

Inspection of the Fabric architecture and transaction pipeline reveals the likely bottleneck components. The ordering service is an obvious candidate. Every transaction *must* pass through this service and get included in a block to have a chance at ledger commitment. Therefore, the performance of the ordering service, in a way, sets the baseline for your distributed application's performance. Increasing orderer resources, either by adding more nodes or adding capacity to each individual node, may result in better performance, though up to a limit. Fabric is modular: you can replace the default ordering mechanism (Raft in version 2 of the platform) with one that meets your performance and fault tolerance needs. As the platform evolves and grows more popular, expect to see better and faster ordering algorithms becoming commercially available.

Transaction commitments to the ledger by validating peers may add more bottlenecks to your system: each transaction must be evaluated for satisfaction of the endorsement policy, the authenticity of endorsements, and the enforcement of database (ledger) integrity rules by handling read and write key conflicts. Cryptographic operations are heavy by nature, so the peers will be limited by resources available to them. Still, signature validations were made significantly more efficient in Fabric version 1, so the performance of this pipeline stage is significantly improved in Fabric version 2. As an enterprise application developer or network administrator, you can optimize performance by minimizing the possibility of transaction conflict within blocks (that is, transactions accessing and modifying the same version of a key) that eventually result in rejected transactions.

To reduce conflicts, you need to experiment with varying block sizes (remember that validation checks are made for conflicts among transactions within a block). Everything else being equal, larger blocks yield higher throughput, but the probability of conflicts increases too. You can design your contracts in ways that will minimize the possibility of conflicts among different invoke transactions. For an explanation of how Fabric detects and handles conflicts in blocks, see *Chapter 5, Designing Smart Contract Transactions and Ledger Data Structure*, in the *Multiversion concurrency control* section.

Configuration and tuning

In a Fabric network, you can configure various parameters to optimize your application's performance. Many of these parameter value settings, like network size, are driven by system requirements and are therefore hard to adjust for purely performance reasons.

But once a network topology is fixed, Fabric still allows operators an array of configuration parameters for the core components—peers, orderers, CAs, and databases. We saw several examples of these in *Chapter 4, Setting the Stage with a Business Scenario*. Parameter values can be set on a channel-wide basis in a configtx. yaml file. To configure a peer in isolation, you adjust core.yaml settings in the image or override them through environment variables in a Docker Compose YAML file.

One such adjustable parameter is the block size, as we discussed earlier in the context of minimizing transaction conflicts in a block. It is possible to determine the precise block size (both in bytes and in the number of transactions) that you should set for a network channel through experimentation (or the adjustment of the parameter until you achieve optimal throughput and latency). For example, measurements on a crypto-currency application called Fabcoin revealed an optimal block size of 2 MB (https://arxiv.org/abs/1801.10228). But even with a fixed upper bound, you must keep in mind that an increase in the number of transactions in a block will result in a higher rate of conflict and transaction rejections.

Your selection of transaction endorsement policy will also have a significant performance impact. The more peer endorsements a transaction needs, the more time it will take to validate the signatures at commitment time. Also, the more complex your policy (namely the more independent clauses, framed in Boolean or N-of syntax, it has), the longer the validation time will be. Now there is a trade-off to be made here. More endorsers and a more complex policy will usually provide higher assurance (reliability as well as trust for your channel ledgers), but it will also incur a performance cost (both throughput and latency). Therefore, a blockchain network operator must frame a suitable endorsement policy based on desired performance and trust levels.

There are various other factors that could affect the performance of a Fabric application: this includes overhead due to the *gossip* protocol among the peers to sync a channel's ledger contents, the number of channels a peer is joined to, and transaction arrival rates. At the hardware level, measurements reveal that CPU resources (that is, the number of cores and processing speed) have the highest impact on a component's (especially a peer's) performance. Generally, increasing the number of CPUs results in higher performance. If you are interested in more details, good papers to read on this topic are:

- *Performance Benchmarking and Optimizing Hyperledger Fabric Blockchain Platform, MASCOTS '18* (https://ieeexplore.ieee.org/document/8526892), also available at https://arxiv.org/pdf/1805.11390.pdf.

- *Hyperledger Fabric: A Distributed Operating System for Permissioned Blockchains, EuroSys '18* (https://dl.acm.org/citation.cfm?id=3190538), also available at https://arxiv.org/pdf/1801.10228.pdf.

Ledger data availability and caching

You can further improve the performance of your distributed Fabric application by extracting better performance from the ledger database (your network's backend) to minimize the stored data retrieval time (also called **data availability**). Several strategies have been devised for this in the database and distributed systems areas. We will outline two of them here.

Redundant committing peers

To increase data availability to client applications (that is, service-layer applications built on the Fabric SDK), additional committing peers may be deployed topologically closer to those applications accessing ledger data. A committing peer receives newly created blocks from the ordering service or from other peers in the network using the gossip protocol and maintains an up-to-date ledger by validating and committing the transactions in those blocks. It does not participate in the endorsement process and thus does not receive transaction proposal requests from clients. The peer process is fully dedicated to maintaining ledgers and responding to requests for data. An important consideration for network performance and system security configuration is the following: a committing peer ought to be located where it can gossip with other channel peers through low-latency network connections, and as a side effect, yield higher committing throughput.

Data caching

Data retrieved from a peer may be stored in an application cache so that future requests for that data can be served faster. To ensure that the cached data is up to date, the application must monitor changes in the underlying ledger and update the data periodically with a new ledger state. As you know by now, a peer emits event notifications whenever a new transaction is committed to the ledger. A client can subscribe to such notifications and determine whether the cache should be updated with new values after inspecting the content of transactions within the notifications.

Fabric performance measurement and benchmarking

We hope this section of the book has given you an understanding of why performance measurement and analysis are important, and some clues about how to make your Fabric networks and applications meet adequate performance standards. We will conclude by pointing you to tools that are maintained under the Hyperledger umbrella to measure performance (mainly throughput, latency, and resource utilization) using sample benchmark applications.

For an in-depth and comprehensive performance measurement tools suite specifically for Hyperledger Fabric, you should look at (`https://github.com/hyperledger/fabric-test`). In particular, PTE (`https://github.com/hyperledger/fabric-test/tree/master/tools/PTE`) is a flexible tool that can be used to create parameterized transaction loads for sample benchmark contracts. PTE can be used to generate throughput and latency numbers for any Fabric application you develop, though you will have to write additional configuration files with network and load characteristics.

Hyperledger Cello (`https://www.hyperledger.org/projects/cello`) is not a performance measurement tool but rather facilitates creating **Blockchain-as-a-Service** (**BaaS**). Cello is a blockchain provisioning and management system that enables the launching of networks on different platforms (VM, clouds, and container clusters). It provides an operational console for managing blockchains and can be used as an aid to launch, test, and measure sample networks before attempting a production deployment.

Hyperledger Caliper (`https://www.hyperledger.org/projects/caliper`) is a blockchain performance benchmarking framework that allows users to measure the performance of a specific blockchain solution with a set of predefined use cases. Caliper produces test results and reports containing various performance indicators, including throughput and latency. It currently supports the measurement of several Hyperledger solutions, namely Fabric, Sawtooth, Iroha, Burrow, and Besu. You should note that Fabric measurement support is comprehensive for version 1.x of the platform but currently limited for version 2.x; if you wish to benchmark a Fabric 2.x network (like our trade network), you may need to make appropriate adaptations to the Caliper source code.

Summary

A blockchain network operator's or developer's role does not end with the creation and bootstrapping of a network. They will be required to periodically maintain and augment such a network and any distributed application deployed on it for various business reasons other than administrative tasks like bug fixes. Operators and developers need to be skilled not just in design and implementation but also in monitoring, analytics, and assessing the impact of network modifications.

In this chapter, we have described various ways in which a Hyperledger Fabric network or a smart contract can change over its lifetime. We described in detail, using our trade application for demonstration, how organizations and peers can be added to a running network, how channel configurations can be augmented, how platforms can be upgraded, and how smart contracts and their associated definitions can be modified in a live network without adversely affecting the application state.

In the last portion of the chapter, we gave an overview of the tools a developer or system administrator can use to measure, analyze, and improve the performance of a Fabric blockchain application. We also provided guidelines for engineering a Fabric-based system for better performance.

With further research and development, the Hyperledger solution suite will no doubt be augmented with newer and better mechanisms to manage system upgrades and conduct performance assessments. This chapter should serve as a handy network maintenance guide for a Fabric network operator or developer.

In the next chapter, we will explore Hyperledger Fabric security.

14

Hyperledger Fabric Security

Hyperledger Fabric has a modular architecture. It has been designed to allow a known set of actors to participate and perform actions in a blockchain network (the so-called *permissioned blockchain*). Due to its modular nature, it can be deployed in many different configurations. The different deployment configurations of Hyperledger Fabric have varying security implications for the operator of the network, as well as its users.

At its core, Hyperledger Fabric is a **public key infrastructure** (**PKI**) system, and thus it inherits the security (and complexity) associated with such systems. At the time of writing this book, Hyperledger Fabric 2.1.1 has been released.

The security aspects of designing and implementing a blockchain network have been discussed in earlier application chapters; here, we intend to give a broader as well as a more in-depth view of security.

We will be covering the following topics in this chapter:

- Design goals impacting security
- Hyperledger Fabric architecture recap
- Network bootstrap and governance — the first step toward security
- Strong identities — the key to the security of the Hyperledger Fabric network
- Smart contract security
- Common security threats and how Hyperledger Fabric mitigates them
- Hyperledger Fabric and quantum computing
- GDPR considerations

Hyperledger Fabric design goals impacting security

To understand the security of Hyperledger Fabric, it is important to state the key design goals that impact security:

- **Existing members should determine how to add new members to the network**: The admission of new entities (members or organizations) to a Hyperledger Fabric-based network must be agreed upon by existing entities in the network. This principle is at the foundation of creating a permissioned blockchain. Instead of allowing any entity to download software and connect to a blockchain network without any verification, the current members in a Hyperledger Fabric-based blockchain network must agree upon a policy to admit new members (such as by majority vote). This policy is then enforced by the underlying mechanisms of Hyperledger Fabric. Upon the successful verification of such an admission policy, the digital credentials of a new member can be added to an existing network.

- **Existing members should determine how to update the network's configuration and work with smart contracts**: Similar to the first item, any change in the configuration of the network or deploying or instantiating a smart contract has to be agreed upon by the network members. Taken together, this and the preceding point give Hyperledger Fabric the ability to perform as a permissioned blockchain.

- **The ledger and its associated smart contracts (chaincode) may be scoped for relevant participating members to meet broader confidentiality and privacy requirements**: In public blockchain networks, all nodes have a copy of the blockchain ledger and execute smart contracts. While this property is intended to provide a globally transparent ledger, it leads to challenges in the privacy and confidentiality of participating organizations that must not only restrict the data to being exchanged solely among themselves, but also avoid disclosing the existence of a transaction for privacy and regulatory reasons. Thus, to maintain confidentiality and privacy, it is necessary to create a blockchain network in which information and the occurrence of transactions is only shared between relevant parties and not among every member in the network.

 Only members participating in a channel have to determine how to update the configuration of that channel.

- **Making their ledgers public is a decision of participating organizations**: The participating organizations in a Hyperledger Fabric-based network can keep their ledgers public (visible to the entire world) or private (visible to the relevant organizations). The decision to make ledgers publicly available is purely an administrative one and can be based on various factors, such as desired transparency among the participating organizations, as well as the public at large.

- **Smart contracts can be written in a general-purpose language**: One of the main design goals of Hyperledger Fabric is to allow smart contracts to be written in general-purpose languages such as Go and JavaScript. Obviously, allowing general-purpose languages for smart contract execution exposes the system to a variety of security issues if there aren't governance and processes in place to first verify and deploy smart contracts before execution and, second, monitor their behavior during execution. Even then, smart contracts written in a general-purpose language should be reasonably isolated to limit the harm they may inadvertently cause.

- **Transaction integrity must be ensured**: A transaction is an execution of a smart contract. The transactions must be created and stored in a way that will prevent them from being tampered with by other peers or will make it easy to detect any tampering. Typically, ensuring transaction integrity requires the use of cryptographic primitives.

- **Industry standards should be leveraged**: The system should leverage industry standards for asserting digital identities (for example, X.509 certificates), as well as for communication among peers (for example, TLS and gRPC).

- **Consensus processes should be separated from transaction execution and validation**: Existing blockchain networks combine transaction execution and validation with achieving consensus among nodes of a blockchain network. This tight coupling makes it difficult to achieve pluggability of the consensus algorithm as well as scaling the system.

- **Employ pluggability everywhere**: The system should have a modular design, and each module should be pluggable through standard interfaces. The ability to plug in modules specific to a network gives Hyperledger Fabric the flexibility to be used in a variety of settings. However, this pluggability also implies that two different instantiations of blockchain networks based on Hyperledger Fabric may possess different security properties.

To understand how these principles impact the security of Hyperledger Fabric, we will briefly explain the architecture of Hyperledger Fabric. Refer to earlier chapters for an in-depth explanation of the architecture.

Hyperledger Fabric architecture

The Hyperledger Fabric architecture for N participating organizations is illustrated in the following screenshot. An organization is a business entity that participates in a Hyperledger Fabric-based permissioned blockchain network and deploys the Hyperledger Fabric infrastructure such as peers, ordering nodes, smart contracts, and membership service providers.

In this section, we will describe this architecture in more detail from a security viewpoint:

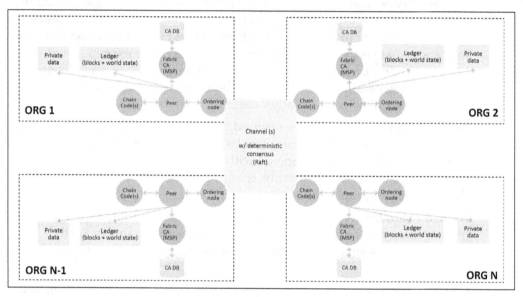

Figure 14.1: Hyperledger Fabric architecture

Fabric CA or membership service provider

The **membership service provider** (**MSP**) is responsible for creating digital identities for peers and users of a participating organization, validating identities, and is configured based on the root certificates and CRLs of one or more X.509 CAs. **Fabric Certificate Authority** (**Fabric CA**) is the recommended CA server for Fabric deployments, but it is possible to use other CA architectures, or even public CAs.

Fabric CA typically runs as a container, such as Docker or Kubernetes. Each Fabric CA server is configured with a backend database (the default being SQLite, with other options such as PostgreSQL or MySQL) that stores the registered identities, as well as their X.509 certificates. Fabric CA does not store the private keys of the users.

Peer

An organization participates in a Hyperledger Fabric-based network through a piece of software called a **peer**. The identity of the peer is issued by the MSP of the participating organization. A peer maintains the ledger, a cryptographically verifiable database of past transactions. The administrators of an organization interact with the peer to deploy and instantiate the smart contracts. Applications interact with the peers to update the ledger and share private data with other peers. Similar to Fabric CA, a peer also typically runs as a container, such as Docker or Kubernetes.

Smart contracts

A **smart contract**, or chaincode, is an application logic written in a high-level language, such as Go or JavaScript; when successfully executed, it reads and/or writes data that eventually gets committed to the ledger of the peers participating in a channel. A smart contract does not have direct access to the ledger. An organization can deploy zero or more smart contracts across one or more channels. An organization can also deploy multiple versions of a smart contract.

A successful update of a ledger based on an execution of smart contract requires an agreement on the existing state of the ledger being updated across applicable peers, and the new state.

Ledger

Each peer maintains a ledger for each channel, which records all of the transactions committed, as well as the corresponding world state generated by applying these transactions. The world state is a key/value store, and transactions update this key/value store by either creating new keys or modifying (or deleting) existing keys. Fabric supports basic range queries across keys in the world state when using LevelDB, as well as rich queries when using CouchDB.

 Note that a peer will only receive blocks to commit to its ledger from the channels that it participates in.

A peer can be part of zero or more channels.

Private data

With Hyperledger Fabric 1.1+, peers can choose to selectively share private data with a subset of peers in the channel through the private data feature. The blocks on the ledger only contain hashes of such data, while the private data is stored off the ledger in a private state database and can be directly shared with the relevant organizations. This feature is useful in a setting where it is more important to conceal the actual data, while the occurrence of transaction can still be visible to all participants in a channel.

Ordering node

The ordering node is responsible for receiving the transactions, ensuring that the transaction order (that is, which transactions will be written to the ledger first) is agreed upon by the peers, and it also performs basic access control on the channels. The ownership of ordering (whether by participants in the channel or other independent organizations) has always been a choice (since Fabric 1.0). Raft became available in Fabric 1.4.1 and allows multiple organizations to more easily share the responsibility for ordering, because jointly administering a Kafka cluster is generally challenging and not recommended.

Each ordering node participates in one or more or all channels in a Hyperledger Fabric-based network. The ordering nodes implement the Raft consensus protocol and perform the ordering operations (transaction order agreement) as discussed earlier. Depending on the volume of transaction traffic within a channel or any other operational needs, an organization can choose to have a separate ordering node per channel.

History of the ordering service in Hyperledger Fabric

In version 1.0 of Hyperledger Fabric, the peers would send a transaction (keys and associated values, along with the read/write set) to the ordering service. Thus, the ordering service had visibility of all data associated with transactions, which had implications from a confidentiality standpoint. In version 1.1 of Hyperledger Fabric, the client could send hashes of the transaction data (input and read/write set) to the ordering service while transferring the data associated with a transaction directly to the relevant peers.

In Hyperledger Fabric 1.0.0 to 1.4.0, the ordering service was implemented using Kafka. The Kafka-based ordering service has been deprecated in version 2. The Raft-based ordering service was introduced in version 1.4.1 and is now the recommended consensus type. Both Kafka-based and Raft-based ordering services are **crash fault tolerant (CFT)**, but not **Byzantine fault tolerant (BFT)**. However, the switch-over to Raft-based consensus provides for a decentralized consensus mechanism and is a stepping stone toward implementing BFT.

Although not shown in the diagram depicting Hyperledger Fabric architecture, peers, orderers, and Fabric CA use a pluggable cryptography service provider, which allows them to plug in new crypto algorithms, as well as **hardware security modules (HSMs)** (`https://en.wikipedia.org/wiki/Hardware_security_module`) for managing crypto keys.

Network bootstrap and data governance: the first step toward security

When organizations decide to form a permissioned private blockchain network using Hyperledger Fabric, they need to consider several governance aspects that will ultimately determine the overall security posture of the Hyperledger Fabric-based network. These governance aspects include, but are not limited to, the items discussed in this section.

Bootstrapping the network with known members

Bootstrapping the network is the first step in creating a Hyperledger Fabric-based blockchain network. The network typically represents the existing or new business relationships between the participating organizations. The organizations responsible for creating the network are typically known to each other through existing business relationships and have a lot of say in the purpose of the network, such as:

- Sharing data
- Defining the data schema to be shared among participants
- Establishing governance policies
- Determining if the participating organizations will keep their ledgers public
- Defining processes for admitting new members

We'll look into some of these responsibilities in more detail in the upcoming sections.

Defining the process for sharing data

Organizations participate in a Hyperledger Fabric-based network because they have a business need to share data to carry out their business operations. The processes for sharing business data and the data security need to be carefully defined, both within an organization and for other organizations with which the data will be shared. For example, does the other organization have equivalent security measures for safeguarding the shared data? What is the impact on the confidentiality and integrity of the shared data if the organization with which the data is shared is compromised?

Defining the data model of the shared data

Members must agree upon a common data model (data schema) that will be stored in the blockchain; the blockchain cannot be useful to its members otherwise. A common way to achieve this is to use a standard data schema—for example, **fast healthcare interoperability resources (FHIR – `https://www.hl7.org/fhir/overview.html`).** Because the data is stored for the duration of the network life cycle, the data schema should be carefully devised so that it does not run afoul of any compliance regulations, such as general data protection regulations (see the *GDPR considerations* section later in this chapter).

The data model is determined by the smart contract. The founding members of a network or a channel deploying a smart contract will determine the key/value pairs that get stored in a channel. Furthermore, the member will decide which data they will share with other members, and which data they will keep private to themselves or a subset of members. The data model should be devised so that it is useful for the business functions that members desire to accomplish, is reasonably future-proof, and does not inadvertently leak information. Recall that all participating peers in a channel store the committed transactions (and their key/value pairs).

 Establish a process for defining the data model that will be stored in a channel.

Mapping data sharing needs Hyperledger-based mechanisms for operational agility

An aspect that's often overlooked in the early stages of a Hyperledger Fabric-based network is determining the Hyperledger Fabric mechanisms that would be used to share data among the participating organizations. Often, that has to be determined at the business level. For example, are all participating organizations in a Hyperledger Fabric-based network going to share all information among themselves, or should the organizations share data directly among themselves? Do organizations need a proof of transaction to be visible to all participants even if the data is restricted from participants?

These business requirements, then, have to be mapped to the appropriate Hyperledger constructs, with an eye toward future expansion of the network and appropriate business needs. The principle of least privilege can help in determining the appropriate Hyperledger Fabric construct for sharing data. However, that approach can inadvertently lead to fine-grained data-sharing mechanisms (for example, Fabric channels comprising two participants, or multiple Fabric channels for specific functions among two participants) and create a management overhead.

Adding new members to the network (or channel)

Defining a policy for admitting new members in the network is paramount and is governed by the business needs of the network. There are several factors to be considered for such a policy. First, the new members joining a channel will have access to all ledger data stored within the channel. Without adequate analysis, information leakage can occur. Second, the admission of new members in a channel has the potential to impact the endorsement policies. This impact needs to be carefully considered. For example, if there were three participating organizations in a network and the endorsement required a majority vote, two out of three participating organizations are required to endorse a transaction. But if another member is added, three out of four members will be required to endorse the transaction. Without adequate planning, a transaction could be withheld from eventual commitment to the ledger, such as if the business processes at the newest members have not been fully defined, rendering them unable to endorse the transaction.

By default, the policy for admitting new members in a network (or a channel) is chosen by the majority (namely two out of two, two out of three, three out of four, and so on). The members may decide on any other policy for admitting new members in the network. Any change in the policy to admit new members will typically be decided through a business agreement. Once an agreement is reached, the channel configuration can be updated per the current policy to reflect the new policy for admitting new members.

> The creation of the genesis block, as well as subsequent transactions to update configurations or case of policies such as majorities/administrators, are privileged operations and must be approved by the peer administrator before being confirmed.

Deploying, instantiating, and upgrading smart contracts on peers in the network

Since smart contracts can update a ledger, it is important to define a process to prevent a malicious or buggy smart contract from being installed on one or more peers (see *Chapter 6, Developing Smart Contracts*).

Once members have decided to participate in a channel, they may choose to deploy and instantiate a smart contract. This defines how key/value pairs, which are scoped to a channel, will be updated or read from. A smart contract can define its endorsement policy — that is, it may require a digital signature from some or all peers in the network. Due to the permissioned nature of Hyperledger Fabric, a smart contract requiring a digital signature from a peer (endorsement) must be installed and instantiated on a peer. See *Chapter 6, Developing Smart Contracts*, and *Chapter 9, Network Operation and Distributed Application Building*, for more details on deploying smart contracts.

Prior to Hyperledger Fabric 2.0, the same exact smart contract (chaincode) package had to be installed on all peers wishing to execute a given smart contract. While this was convenient to ensure that all participants were running the same smart contract logic, it was challenging from a security perspective. Even if two organizations attempted to package the exact same smart contract sources, the two packages were still often different (because of differences in timestamps, archive order, and so on) and a "smart contract fingerprint mismatch" would occur. Similarly, all organizations had to roll out bugfixes in lockstep. If a bug was discovered, such as a nil pointer dereference, all members had to update their smart contracts at the same time to avoid the fingerprint mismatch problem; now, individual organizations may roll out fixes as soon as they are available, rather than requiring coordination with the rest of the network. When contract logic changes, it is still important to move to the new smart contract version in lockstep, but for many updates, this is not necessary.

Nevertheless, the participating organizations may still find it cumbersome to rewrite the smart contract with the same definition and may prefer to install one that has been developed by one of the participating organizations. Thus, it is important to define a formal governance process for smart contract development and verification in order for a peer to instantiate the smart contract.

 Establish a process for deploying smart contracts on your peer, including manual reviews and the verification of a digital signature of the smart contract author.

Strong identities: the key to the security of the Hyperledger Fabric network

Strong identities are at the heart of Hyperledger Fabric security. Creating, managing, and revoking these identities is critical to the operational security of Hyperledger Fabric-based deployment. The identities are issued and validated by an MSP. As shown in the previous Hyperledger Fabric architecture diagram, one logical MSP is typically associated with one peer. An MSP can validate any appropriate cryptographically signed identities. Hyperledger Fabric ships with a default MSP (Fabric CA), which issues X.509 certificates to the authenticated entities.

Bootstrapping Fabric CA

Fabric CA can be configured with an **Lightweight Directory Access Protocol (LDAP)** server or run in standalone mode. When running in standalone mode, it must be configured with a bootstrap identity that gets stored in its backend database. By default, a SQLite database is used, but for production usages, a PostgreSQL or MySQL database can be configured. Typically, the connection between the Fabric CA server and its database is over TLS if a standalone server is used.

For the rest of the chapter, we will refer to the bootstrap entity when running without the LDAP server as the **ca-admin**. The ca-admin and its password must be supplied on a bootstrap of the Fabric CA server, when running without an LDAP server.

In order for the ca-admin to interact with the server, it must submit a **certificate signing request (CSR)** to the Fabric CA server to obtain an X.509 certificate. This process is called **enrolling an identity,** or simply **enroll**, which we'll discuss in more detail shortly. With an X.509 certificate in possession, the ca-admin can then add other users, which we will explain next.

Keep the password of the admin user in a safe and secure place since this is the root user of your organization. Treat it as securely as you would treat the password of a root Linux user. Use it to create a new user with appropriate permissions, but never use this user for any other operation, except in the case of a security breach, where this user can be used to revoke the certificates of all enrolled entities.

Fabric CA provides two key operations in the system, namely register and enroll. We will explain these operations next.

Register

The **register** operation adds a new entity specified by an identifier to Fabric CA. The register operation does not create an X.509 certificate for the user; that happens in the enroll operation. It is up to the administrator of the Fabric CA server to define the policies and procedures for adding new users to the network.

There are some important points to consider while registering the users:

- If a policy is to register an email address then, upon subsequent enrollment, the user's email address will be encoded in the certificate. In Hyperledger Fabric, the certificate of the user issuing the transaction is stored in the ledger along with the committed transaction. Anyone can decode the certificate and determine the email address.

Carefully determine how new entities will be registered within a Fabric CA server, as their digital certificates will end up in the ledger when these entities issue transactions.

- Another important point to consider is how many enrollments are allowed for that user. Each enrollment results in a new certificate being issued to the user. In Hyperledger Fabric, a new user being registered can be enrolled a finite number of times, or can have unlimited enrollments. Typically, a new entity being enrolled should not be configured with an unlimited number of enrollments.

It is best to set the maximum number of enrollments to 1 for a new user. This setting ensures that there is 1-1 correspondence between an entity and its digital certificate, thus making the management of entity revocation easier.

- Since Hyperledger Fabric 1.1, it has been possible to define attributes for entities at the time of their registration. These attributes are then encoded in the X.509 certificate of an entity.

When used in standalone mode, upon successful registration, Fabric CA will create a unique password (if not supplied during registration). The ca-admin can then pass this password to the entity being registered, which will then use it to create a CSR and obtain a certificate through the enroll operation.

To register an entity in the Fabric CA server, an entity should have a set of roles. Fabric CA is configured with the following default roles:

```
hf.Registrar.Roles = client, user, peer, validator, auditor, ca
```

A Fabric CA server can register any entity that has one of these roles:

```
hf.Registrar.DelegateRoles = client, user, validator, auditor
```

A Fabric CA server can revoke a role:

```
hf.Revoker = true
```

A Fabric CA server can also register an intermediate CA:

```
hf.IntermediateCA
```

To register an identity in Fabric CA, an entity must have the `hf.Registrar` attribute. Roles are attributed with a comma-separated list of values, where one of the values equals the type of identity being registered.

Secondly, the affiliation of the invoker's identity must be equal to or a prefix of the affiliation of the identity being registered. For example, an invoker with an affiliation of `a.b` may register an identity with an affiliation of `a.b.c`, but may not register an identity with an affiliation of `a.c`.

Enroll

An entity in possession of an ID and secret can then enroll itself with Fabric CA. To do so, it generates a public/private key pair, creates a CSR, and sends that to Fabric CA along with the registered ID and secret in the `Authorization` header. Upon successful authentication, the server returns an X.509 certificate to the entity being enrolled. The entity sending the enroll request is responsible for managing the private key. These private keys should be stored in a secure fashion (such as in an HSM).

The CSR can be customized to generate X.509 certificates and keys that support the **Elliptic Curve Digital Signature Algorithm (ECDSA)**. The following key sizes and algorithms are supported:

Size	ASN1 OID	Signature Algorithm
256	prime256v1	ecdsa-with-SHA256
384	secp384r1	ecdsa-with-SHA384
521	secp521r1	ecdsa-with-SHA521

Revoking identities

Since Hyperledger Fabric is a PKI system, identities that must be removed from the system have to be explicitly revoked. This is done through standard **certificate revocation lists (CRLs)**. The CRLs need to be synchronized across all organizations to ensure that everyone detects the revoked certificate. The distribution of CRLs to other peers requires out-of-band mechanisms. If a root certificate or intermediate certificate must be revoked, the user can simply remove the certificate from the MSP configuration, and all its issued certificates will from that point on be considered invalid.

Practical considerations in managing users in Fabric CA

Typically, an organization has its own identity (LDAP) server for managing its employees. An organization may choose to participate in one or more Hyperledger Fabric networks, but only a subset of its employees may be onboarded to each network. The administrator of Fabric CA for each network may choose to register a subset of employees in each network. Since an employee must generate and manage a private key to successfully participate in a Hyperledger Fabric network, the responsibility of managing the private key and its corresponding digital certificate lies with the employee of an organization. Managing private keys and digital certificates is non-trivial, and this can place an undue burden on an employee and may lead to inadvertent key exposures. Since an employee needs to remember their organization-issued credentials (for example, username and password) to log on to the organization systems, an organization can choose to manage the private keys and certificates on behalf of its employees that participate in one or more Hyperledger Fabric networks. Depending on the industry, the private keys may be stored in HSMs, which will make it infeasible to tamper with the keys. The precise configuration of HSMs is beyond the scope of this chapter.

Smart contract security

In Hyperledger Fabric, as indicated previously, smart contracts (chaincodes) can be written in Go, Java, or JavaScript. The smart contract must be installed on a peer and then explicitly instantiated.

When instantiated using the `docker builder` command, each smart contract is built and then launched in its own Docker container. Starting with version 2.0, external builders can be utilized to build and run smart contracts without requiring a Docker daemon.

When running the smart contract inside a Docker container, it is important to understand what access this container may have to the network. If care is not taken in carefully reviewing the smart contract before it gets installed on the peer, and in isolating the network access for that smart contract, it could result in a malicious or misconfigured node probing or attacking the peer attached to the same virtual network.

How is a smart contract shared with other endorsing peers?

Starting in Fabric 2.0, it is encouraged that all users start with the same smart contract; it is not necessary for all organizations to install the same smart contract (chaincode) package across participating organizations. If users wish to share the same package to install, starting with the version 2.0 life cycle, smart contract packages are now plain `.tar.gz` archives, and users can easily open and inspect them.

In this scenario, the participating organizations establish a process for sharing the smart contract package with other organizations participating in a Hyperledger Fabric network. Since the smart contract must be installed on all endorsing peers, it is necessary to ensure the integrity of the smart contract through cryptographic mechanisms while sharing it with other peers. Please refer to *Chapter 11, Agility in a Blockchain Network*, for more details on the approach to share the smart contract.

Who can install smart contracts?

To install a smart contract on a peer, an entity's certificate must be installed on the node (stored in the local MSP) of the peer. Since installing smart contracts is a highly privileged operation, care should be taken that only entities with administrative capabilities have the ability to perform this operation. More specifically, the identity must have the Admin role for the peer's local MSP. In Fabric 2.0 the certificate does not need to be explicitly added if node **organizational units** (**OUs**) are enabled and an OU for the Admin role is set.

Smart contract encryption

An entity can choose to encrypt the key/value pairs by using an **Advanced Encryption Standard** (**AES**) encryption key at the time of smart contract execution. The encryption key is passed to the smart contract, which then encrypts the values before sending them in a proposal. The entities that need to decrypt the value (for example, to endorse a transaction) must be in possession of a key. It is expected that such encryption keys are then shared with other peers in an out-of-band manner.

Attribute-based access control

As you may remember from *Chapter 5, Designing Smart Contract Transactions and Ledger Data Structure*, one of the new features added with Hyperledger 1.1 was attribute-based access control. At the time of registering an entity, attributes can be specified for an entity, which then are added to the X.509 certificate upon enrollment. Examples of attributes include a role name such as an **auditor** that is agreed upon by the organizations participating in the network. When a smart contract is executed, it can check if an identity has certain attributes before the invoke or query operation. At a simple level, this allows application-level attributes to be passed down into the smart contract through an X.509 certificate.

Encoding attributes in certificates has its own set of pros and cons. On one hand, all the information associated with an identity is encoded in the certificate, thus decisions can be made based on attributes. On the other hand, if an attribute has to be updated, for example, when a user moves to a different department, the existing certificate must be revoked, and a new certificate has to be issued with a new set of attributes. While providing fine-grained security, a strict implementation of attribute-based control can create an operational and management overhead.

Common threats and how Hyperledger Fabric mitigates them

Hyperledger Fabric provides protection against some of the most common security threats and assumes that a participating organization (node operator) will manage the threats inherent in running such a system, while at the same time introducing new attack vectors inherent in data sharing and governance. In the following table, we will summarize the most common security threats, whether Hyperledger Fabric addresses them and how, or whether it is the responsibility of a node/network operator to address them:

Threat	Description	Hyperledger Fabric	Network/Node Operator
Spoofing	Use of a token or other credential to pretend to be an authorized user, or to compromise a user's private key.	Generates X.509 certificates for its members.	Manages certificate revocation list distribution among network participants to ensure that revoked members can no longer access the system.
Tampering	Modification of information (for example, an entry in the database).	Uses cryptographic measures (such as SHA256 or ECDSA) to make tampering infeasible.	Derived from Fabric.
Repudiation	An entity cannot deny who did what.	Tracks who did what using digital signatures.	Derived from Fabric.
Replay attacks	Replaying transactions to corrupt the ledger.	Uses read/write sets to validate the transaction. A replay of transactions will fail due to an invalid read set.	Derived from Fabric.

Information disclosure	Data exposed through intentional breach or accidental exposure.	Provides support for using TLS 1.2 for in-transit encryption. It does not encrypt ledger data at rest (the operator's responsibility).	It's the operator's responsibility to prevent information disclosure by following information security best practices for Fabric nodes as well as the applications interacting with the ledger. Further more, as part of data governance, the organizations must define the appropriate Fabric mechanisms for sharing data, especially when adding new members or new applications. If organizations decide to keep the ledgers private, then any leakage or compromise of one organization's ledger can impact the confidentiality and possibly integrity of other organization ledgers.
Denial of service	Making it difficult for legitimate users to access the system.	The operator's responsibility.	The operator's responsibility to prevent denial of service to the system.
Elevation of privileges	Gaining high-level access to the application.	Issued identities cannot upgrade their access (for example, create an identity) without manual review of access.	The responsibility of the network/node operator to audit a smart contract and to limit access and run smart contract containers with appropriate restrictions. (Fabric deployments typically run smart contracts in Docker containers.)

Ransomware	Using cryptographic or other means to prevent access to data on the filesystem.	Because it is a distributed system, generally speaking, the compromise of one peer should not impact the data integrity of other peers.	The operator's responsibility to ensure that ransomware cannot prevent access to a node's ledger.

Hyperledger Fabric and quantum computing

Hyperledger Fabric uses elliptic curve cryptography for digitally signing transactions. Elliptic curve cryptography relies on mathematical techniques that can be sped up using quantum computing (https://en.wikipedia.org/wiki/Post-quantum_cryptography). However, Hyperledger Fabric provides a pluggable cryptographic provider, which allows us to replace these algorithms for digital signatures with others. Moreover, according to the director of Information Technology Lab at NIST, the impact of quantum computing on the security of blockchain systems is at least 15 to 30 years from becoming a reality (https://www.coindesk.com/dc-blockchain-hearing-sees-call-for-congressional-commission/).

GDPR considerations

General data protection regulation (GDPR) (https://gdpr-info.eu/) is an EU law that defines how personal data is acquired, processed, and ultimately erased from a computing system. The definition of personal data in GDPR is quite broad — examples include names, email addresses, and IP addresses.

Blockchain, by design, creates an immutable, permanent, and replicated record of data. A blockchain network based on Hyperledger Fabric will obviously encompass these three properties. Thus, storing personal data on a blockchain network that cannot be deleted or modified can be challenging from the perspective of GDPR. Similarly, it is important to know with whom that personal data is shared.

The channel private data feature of Hyperledger Fabric provides a mechanism for determining the entities with which data is shared. In the case of channel private data, the data is never stored on a blockchain, but its cryptographic hashes are stored on the chain. Through a governance process, peers can determine the other peers to share this data with. The channel private data feature in Hyperledger Fabric can potentially provide a mechanism to store personal data off the chain, determining with whom this data is shared, while maintaining the integrity of this data through cryptographic hashes stored on the blockchain.

Hyperledger Fabric also stores the X.509 certificate of the entity creating the transaction in the digital ledger. These X.509 certificates can contain personal data. Hyperledger Fabric also provides a mechanism to prove the identity based on zero knowledge proofs, while hiding the actual value of the attribute. These zero knowledge proof-based credentials are then stored in the ledger in lieu of a traditional X.509 certificate and can potentially help toward GDPR compliance.

Summary

In this chapter, we first covered design goals of Hyperledger Fabric that are tied to security. We then described key concepts that impact the security of Hyperledger Fabric-based networks, such as network bootstrap, data governance, strong identities, and smart contract security. We then dove into the common Hyperledger security threats and how Fabric mitigates them.

We also briefly looked at the impact of quantum computing on Hyperledger Fabric.

We ended our discussion with GDPR considerations. In the final chapter, we will be looking at the next steps in Hyperledger and where it is heading in the future.

15

Blockchain's Future, Protocol Commercialization, and Challenges Ahead

We, the authors, certainly hope that this updated edition has been an interesting, informative, and educational journey. We have focused on bringing forth not only the **Hyperledger** centric landscape for blockchain technology projects, but also an overall business perspective that explains the challenges and adoption patterns that follow. This has been an interesting project for all of us, given the rapid pace of changes and the evolution in the blockchain technology landscape and Hyperledger frameworks and tools. We have attempted to ensure that the content not only provides a basis for a strong foundation, but also provides deeper insights into some of the core elements of blockchain business network solution design. As active members of the blockchain technical community and technology thought leaders, we all believe that we still have a long way to go in solving some complex issues such as a privacy, confidentiality, and scalability. We also have work to do in developing a network-centric approach to code and infrastructure management that leads to an economically viable solution with predictable transaction costs. This, in our opinion, is an important consideration as the business model that runs the business network depends on the cost predictability of network-processed transactions.

Looking ahead and beyond the scope and context of the topics covered in this book, it is vital to understand that the gap between today's centrally managed world and the complete decentralization of every aspect of business transaction is a spectrum, and the path to a complete decentralization that achieves the full promise of blockchain is not an easy one.

The transformational projects undertaken by industry leaders and industry consortiums are to be viewed as an effort to understand the technology, trust, and transaction risks prior to completely transitioning to the decentralized world most often professed by the industry challengers or startup entities. The spectrum itself is interesting, and innovation is incubating in both camps. It is vital to understand industry-specific innovation and adoption patterns, as they may indicate the readiness for production-grade blockchain-powered business networks.

Each chapter in this book has been carefully chosen to ensure that you are well equipped to consume the right content at the right depth. They also meaningfully address the broader-level conversation and implementation details you must have to address blockchain-based business and technology design for projects beyond **proof of concept (PoC)**. As practitioners, we have experienced first-hand the challenges of production readiness, and so we bring both the business understanding and technology acumen needed to devise a core blockchain network design that lays the foundation of a multiparty transaction network with built-in trust. The severe shortage of such acumen, a taxonomy, and common design patterns has been our primary motivation to expend our energies and time in devising the content of this book.

We would like to end this book with a summary that highlights some vital topics and ties together thematic elements of various chapters. We are doing this to ensure you have a cohesive understanding of the technology landscape, Hyperledger projects, and the divide between enterprise-driven blockchain technologies, which are primarily transformative, and the cryptoasset-driven world as a challenger and disruptor to every industry that aspires to employ blockchain to transform and reinvent itself. Regardless of the path, it is vital for us, as a community, to understand the motivations and technology advancements of both camps, as the innovation and resulting reinvention of business models will lead to new economic values aiming to change the world as we know it.

In this chapter, we'll look at the following:

- An overview of important Hyperledger projects
- Key issues between the disruptive side of blockchain and the more conventional side
- Interoperability
- Blockchain protocol commercialization
- Staying engaged with the technology and ecosystem

Summary of key Hyperledger projects

In this section, we'll summarize and review some key (at the time of writing) Hyperledger projects and the complementing values they provide to elements of blockchain technical design.

Hyperledger frameworks: business blockchain technology

As the blockchain industry evolves, so does the technology ecosystem that aims to support the evolution and aid in the industry adoption of various specialized technology frameworks. These specialized frameworks are constantly evolving to address various industry challenges such as interoperability, asset fungibility, and the trust divide, which we discussed in earlier chapters. While the business leaders focus on business models, governance, and risk model frameworks, the technologists of an enterprise are attempting to keep up with the technology advancements, evolution, and maturity that is so vital for industrial-grade deployment and for us to realize the true potential of blockchain technology. In this section, we'll summarize various Hyperledger projects, such as some of those illustrated in the following diagram, which represents its maturity and evolution:

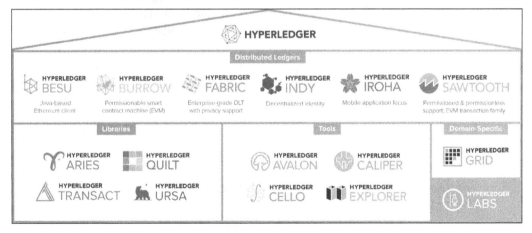

Figure 15.1: Hyperledger frameworks

(Source: Hyperledger.org, used under Creative Commons Attribution 3.0 Unported, https://creativecommons.org/licenses/by/3.0/)

Distributed ledger frameworks

Let's look at a few of the Hyperledger frameworks:

- **Hyperledger Besu**: The latest edition of the Hyperledger family of projects. This project is essentially an open source edition of the Ethereum client, which is written in Java. The goal of this project is to promote enterprise adoption of Ethereum as a public network, as well as to carve a path for the enterprise to leverage its investment in Java over the last two decades. One of the significant goals of this project is to enable the enterprise to explore and adopt Ethereum, either as a public network or a private-permissioned network.

- **Hyperledger Burrow**: A modular blockchain client with a permissioned smart contract interpreter built into the specification of the **Ethereum Virtual Machine (EVM)**. While adopting a different approach, Hyperledger Burrow, like Hyperledger Besu, aims to promote enterprise adoption of Ethereum as a public network.

- **Hyperledger Indy**: A distributed ledger, purpose-built for decentralized identity. Hyperledger Indy has received a lot of attention in the recent past due to a special emphasis on identity. The project aims to achieve the notion of a decentralized identity framework. It provides a set of tools and libraries for creating a model, as prescribed by the **privacy by design** approach, addressing shortcomings of the current notions of identity and its use in various industries.

- **Hyperledger Sawtooth**: Distributed ledger software that comes with a novel consensus algorithm, **Proof of Elapsed Time (PoET)**, that targets large distributed validator populations with minimal resource consumption. With the enterprise focused on the design thesis of making smart contracts safe and keeping ledgers distributed, Hyperledger Sawtooth supports both permissioned and permissionless models. By abstracting the trust systems and consensus from application development (that is, of system and smart contracts), Sawtooth negates the need for application developers to know the underlying design of the core system.

- **Hyperledger Iroha**: A business blockchain framework designed to be simple and easy to incorporate into infrastructural projects requiring distributed ledger technology.

- **Hyperledger Fabric**: A modular blockchain framework designed as a foundation for developing modular applications or solutions, including plug-and-play components like consensus and membership services.

The **Linux Foundation Hyperledger** Fabric has value-added enterprise-ready functionality, such as:

- Permissioned membership

- Performance, scalability, and levels of trust

- Data on a need-to-know basis

- Rich queries over an immutable distributed ledger

- Modular architecture supporting plug-in components for security and identity

- Protection of digital keys and sensitive data

This book has focused deeply on Hyperledger Fabric as a choice framework for enterprise blockchain technology.

Hyperledger libraries

The following is a list of Hyperledger libraries:

- **Hyperledger Quilt**: A library that offers interoperability between ledger systems by implementing **interledger protocol (ILP)**, which is primarily a payments protocol designed to transfer value across distributed ledgers and non-distributed ledgers.

- **Hyperledger Aries**: A set of libraries providing a toolkit for creating, transmitting, and storing verifiable digital credentials for individuals, assets, or interactions. These libraries include constructs like a shared cryptographic wallet as a client and communication protocols that enable interaction by addressing transmittal components between wallets. There is an assumption that the cryptographic support will be provided by another set of Hyperledger libraries—Hyperledger Ursa.

- **Hyperledger Ursa**: A set of libraries that provide cryptographic functions. This project is intended to provide the framework and tooling for decentralized key management and secure secrets management to other peer libraries and Hyperledger projects. This project represents a common components model to strengthen the security posturing of blockchain projects.

- **Hyperledger Transact**: A platform-agnostic library intended for handling the execution of smart contracts and transaction processing. The shared library handles all aspects of scheduling, state management, and dispatch. This project aims to achieve an extensible approach to managing smart contracts and their role in transaction processing. The goal of building a platform-agnostic model is to standardize smart contracts and transaction processing. This is achieved by providing an interpreter in a virtual machine called a *smart contract engine* and making it a black box for transaction processing.

Hyperledger tools

The following list includes several important Hyperledger tools:

- **Hyperledger Cello**: A tool that aims to bring the on-demand as-a-service deployment model to the blockchain ecosystem to reduce the effort required for creating, managing, and terminating blockchains.

- **Hyperledger Avalon**: A tool still in its incubation phase that provides a platform- and framework-agnostic model to improve performance, throughput, and latency, and a trust framework for the trusted execution of transactions while factoring in execution elements that may be off-chain.

- **Hyperledger Explorer**: A tool that allows exploration of various constructs of a blockchain network, such as transactions and their associated data, and network-related information such as block height, execution time, transactions, and other related information. This tool also permits navigating and traversing the network components that may be necessary for other business and monitoring functions. Hyperledger Explorer can view, invoke, deploy, or query blocks, transactions and associated data, network information, chaincodes, and transaction families, as well as any other relevant information stored in the ledger.

- **Hyperledger Caliper**: A blockchain benchmark tool that allows users to measure the performance of a specific blockchain implementation with a set of predefined use cases. It is an important tool in many use cases and industry applications. This tool produces reports around metrics such as **transactions per second** (**TPS**), latency, resource utilization, and so on. It is used for problem determination and solution inferences to solve technical problems that may hinder network **service-level agreements** (**SLAs**).

Hyperledger Composer

As of 29 August 2019, the Hyperledger Composer project is in deprecated status. None of the maintainers are actively developing new features.

Next, we'll discuss the future of blockchain.

Blockchain's future and the challenges ahead

Now that we've recapped our journey so far, we will present some of the key areas that we see as challenges and an opportunity for the future of blockchain solutions.

Addressing the divide: the enterprise blockchain and cryptoasset-driven ecosystem

There's been a significant divide between the world of cryptoassets—in the early days, **initial coin offerings (ICOs)**, and later, stablecoins and **security token offerings (STOs)**, on the one hand, and the world of regulated, conventional business on the other, the latter being led by the cooperative effort of financial institutions and banks to improve operational efficiency and so on. Both sides, however, have taken advantage of the benefits of blockchain to boost their market potential and further their goals.

The blockchain ecosystem—motivated by technological innovation, disruption, and newfangled models for doing business—has demonstrated what, at times, seems like juvenile behavior and occasional tantrums as it challenges the status quo. On both sides of the divide, this defiant behavior can be observed. On the former side, Bitcoin and other cryptoassets have dramatically shifted the traditional financial business model and introduced **decentralized finance**, or DeFi, challenging not only financial market infrastructure and business models, but also traditional regulatory frameworks for lending, payments, exchange, and fundraising.

Decentralized finance (DeFi) is the movement that leverages decentralized networks to transform old financial products into trustless and transparent protocols that run without intermediaries.

On the other hand, enterprises have introduced changes in the areas of settlement, interbank transfers, digital transparency, dissemination of information in a symmetrical fashion in supply chains, ways of generating trust between IoT devices, and so on. There are certainly differences on the two sides of the divide, but there's a common theme that blockchain isn't going anywhere and will continue to bring about transformation in various industries as it matures. Blockchain will uphold its promise to deliver greater efficiency and cost savings.

With the notion of permissionless blockchain, there's an outright rejection of convention. In the permissionless world, being able to accelerate innovation is a top priority — whether through new business design or technology. But, on the other side, there are conventional industries that are trying to adopt blockchain technology, either to keep up with the change they see around them or to transform their industry from within. Wherever an organization falls across this divide, the tenets of blockchain remain foundational, and an economic model for blockchain will help ensure its success.

With cryptoassets, digital assets, stablecoins, and STOs — the disruptive side of the blockchain divide — there's a strong inclination to invest in technology and talent, as well as leveraging synergies in the marketplace via incentive economics to facilitate the desired disruption and innovation. Tokenomics, for example, describes a system of cryptocurrency, a way of generating value in an IEO/STO network. The unit of value is in a co-created, self-governing network, and all participating parties can use it to their benefit.

Digital asset networks and STOs are largely funded by such cryptoassets. They defy traditional approaches to fundraising (through crowdfunding, for example). One of the more notable aspects of disruption brought by digital asset tokenization and STOs is an effort to distinguish a security from a utility coin. The model they are building emphasizes concepts like decentralization and open governance, transparency, innovation, and so on. Tokenized assets and STOs thus help pave the way to the future with cryptoassets, despite some initial ups and downs. They demonstrate the potential of value defined by a network that empowers innovation.

On the side of conventional industries and enterprises, the emphasis has been different. There's more focus on comprehending the new technology and how it might transform business through changing business ecosystems and networks, affecting regulation and compliance issues, and addressing privacy and confidentiality concerns. Enterprises are interested in quickly discovering use cases that will show results with the technology. Most businesses remain focused on an existing business models and growth plans, however, and as a result, many early projects haven't emphasized the blockchain tenets: that is, trade, trust, and ownership.

Moreover, enterprises are highly concerned with regulatory compliance and therefore less inclined toward disruptive models that could negatively impact current business operations.

In conventional industries, there's an appeal to aspects like symmetric dissemination of information, improving the efficiency of workflows and business processes, and controlling transactional data, which blockchain can facilitate. But there's a learning curve, and adoption is slower on this side of the divide. We've learned that enterprise blockchain design needs to take issues like confidentiality, privacy, scalability, and performance seriously. For enterprise blockchain networks, these issues can significantly impact cost and should therefore be central to network design. Ultimately, planning for blockchain implementations in conventional industries has helped inspire blockchain innovators to address these challenges. Organizations that see the promise of blockchain are bringing the best talent to bear on these issues. This is because it is all part of an agenda for progress.

The conventional, regulated enterprises we've been talking about are in permissioned networks, as opposed to permissionless ones. These permissioned networks will need to continue to uncover incentives to inspire other organizations to join them. Tokenomics, which works in the cryptoasset world, won't work for all conventional businesses for various reasons, so they'll have to find another business model to demonstrate value creation, distribution, and sharing within the network, while also facilitating innovation and modernization.

The last few years of blockchain, 2017-2019, were characterized by disruption and involved a lot of investment and education around the technology, as well as designing appropriate business models for implementing it. Now, in 2020, blockchain is starting to come into maturity, and industries should start to see the benefits it promises: a trust-based system that boosts efficiency. From the start, blockchain was intended to bring about greater efficiency in the marketplace through disintermediation, a shared network based on trust and transparency. Now is a great time to revisit the basics — those fundamentals of blockchain: trade, trust, and ownership. These fundamentals remain essential to optimizing blockchain engagements, and we've seen this repeatedly in our work with organizations all around the world. We have to remain alert to issues surrounding digital identity and assets, tokenization, settlement, ownership definitions and verification, governance, and so forth — the fundamentals outlined in this chapter. Staying aligned to these fundamentals is how we can safeguard robust blockchain networks that not only prevent fraud but also inspire confidence in financial systems in the digital era.

Interoperability: understanding business service integration

We have discussed that blockchain promises the value of multiparty networks and addresses the issues of time and trust. It does so by collapsing and flattening individual business processes into single processes with management enabled by constructs like smart contracts, transactional finality, channels, and ledgers, which are the records of transaction completion. We have also seen that, for various reasons, such as industry-driven regional networks and contextual networks, it may emerge that we will need to be connected not only to flatten the network-wide business process, but also to simply address the movement of value across the network. Furthermore, these networks may not necessarily be on a homogenous blockchain technology platform and may include other frameworks such as Ethereum, Corda, and so on. To add to this complexity, there are existing business systems that the enterprise manages for the sake of business analysis, reporting, regulatory and compliance systems, and so on. It would be cost-prohibitive for any enterprise to replace these (legacy) systems to adopt and join blockchain-powered networks. These emerging paradigms lead to two essential challenges:

- **Enterprise**: Ensuring seamless and meaningful integration with existing business systems
- **Business networks**: Keeping up with technology innovation and heterogeneity in the technology stack (and resulting trust systems)

These challenges must be addressed to ensure not only interoperability within the individual enterprise but also the business network being interoperable with other contextual networks. This is an area that all of us and the community, as a whole, need to focus on and address at a protocol level as it is an adoption imperative for blockchain network success.

Blockchain protocol commercialization: a "BizTech" agenda

As we dare to envision a world with decentralized control and governance based on distributed technology challenging every business model, as well as a governance structure built upon centralized business structures, we do have to ponder not just the shift but also the motivation, incentive, and monetization elements that will fuel and power the economic infrastructure to move things of value, thereby keeping up with changes to our perception (and subsequent realization) of value.

We can take a page from the internet phenomena, including its evolution and the monetization of its various layers, where each layer is more abstract than the lower ones, thus enabling a robust and modular system design. While there is a tight dependency between each layer, any one layer can be upgraded, patched, or completely replaced, with an impact on adjacent layers.

In this section, we will attempt to decompose blockchain into essentially four distinct layers to better understand and categorize the technology, security, scalability, service orientation, and collective economic contribution to the blockchain application design. While there are many layers and approaches proposed to simplify our understanding of complex blockchain technology spaces, the intent of our discussion here is to focus on the commercialization of blockchain protocols, as well as its collective impact on the overall costs of solution designs and the operational elements of the blockchain network. Many of the innovations in the foundational transaction protocol (layer 1), their enhancements around security and scale (layer 2), and the core services that utilize them (layer 3) manifest their economic model and strength with some kind of token, be it a cryptoasset or cryptocurrency governed by a crypto economic system in the blockchain network (mining, transaction processing, and so on). However, all of the collective constructs of the underlying layers and their respective token models feed into layer 4. This is the business application that creates a tapestry from services provisioned in layer 3, and extends the benefits of decentralized (or quasi-decentralized) blockchain networks in the form of speed, cost, transparency, and trust to network participants. Drawing an analogy from internet protocol layers, ideally, from a system design perspective, these layers should be abstract and modular and easily swappable, enabling business applications and underlying services to take advantage of innovations and their resulting (hopefully improved) cost structures at lower layers.

In discussing the governance structure of blockchain networks, we describe how the governance structure was fundamentally based on devised economic incentives driven by consensus in hopes of governing the network. This leads to defining governance—a body (centralized or decentralized) whose sole responsibility is to establish a set of laws or rules on which to base binding decisions in a given system.

While the genesis of blockchain, which was largely permissionless (for example, cryptoasset-based networks such as Bitcoin, Litecoin, and so forth), relied upon technology-based systemic governance comprising incentives and mechanisms of coordination, this systemic governance has its own set of challenges in the enterprise business networks attempting to exploit the tenets of blockchain technology.

In the enterprise world, which is largely regulated and relies upon (mostly) permissioned blockchain models, the system of checks and balances is complicated by transactions between competing entities, often with regulated data and a fiduciary responsibility, which can neither account for the tangible or systemically generated incentives (cryptoassets), nor have network-wide mechanisms of coordination due to privacy and confidentiality issues. So, tokens as digital assets or cryptoassets represent a vital part of the economic consideration at every layer, and most likely every layer either utilizes some form of token economy and establishes a monetization strategy in the form of utility as an incentive structure, or leverages a service-driven model that fuels the exchange of tokens as a fungible unit between the various participants in a network. While most token economic models thrive in truly decentralized structures, and many permissioned or quasi-decentralized models have seen the emergence of non-fungible tokens or a software as a service model to commercialize protocols, business networks and their business models that serve an ecosystem should determine the right model that fits the initiation and sustainable growth of the network, all while preserving the modularity of the solution design.

Most blockchain monetization strategies include (but are not limited to):

- **Token-based models:** Operation fees write to the blockchain-powered business network's distributed database
- **Tokens as a medium of exchange**: Lending or selling a token as a "step-through" currency
- **Asset-pair trading**: Monetizing margins
- **Commercialization of the protocol**: Technology services, including cloud and software labs and consulting services
- **The power of networks**: Extrapolating the power of networks and exponential power of co-creation models, leading to new business models and resulting economic value

The following diagram describes the various blockchain protocol layers and their commercialization model. This notion of protocol commercialization is essential to determine the commercial interest and monetization structure of the various entities involved, including technology providers, niche technology service providers, and entities that run their business on these blockchain-powered networks:

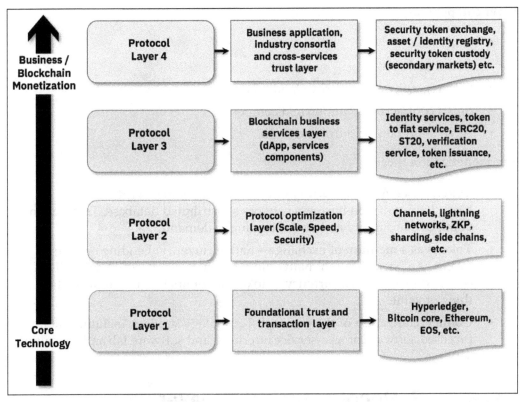

Figure 15.2: Blockchain protocol commercialization layers

Layer 1 – Foundational trust and transaction layer

This layer provides the foundational framework and the much-needed basic infrastructure to facilitate the network of trust and transactions technology. Similar to the basic networking layers (Ethernet/TCP/IP) that laid the foundation of information networks, a base trust layer, protocols, and standards are essential in order to move value, preserve the integrity of assets, and promote asset accountability for the network participants as they transact. And, just like the internet, these are global networks, implying that the burden of trust, availability, and resilience is immense, which makes the standardization of protocols vital.

Layer components:

- Consensus
- Data standards
- Cryptography and security standards
- Smart contracts — definition and composition
- Asset definition — control and audit

The monetization thesis:

- **Token-based model or utility tokens**: Operation fees written to the blockchain-powered business network's distributed database. Transaction volumes drive utility and usage, leading to demand.

- **Tokens as a medium of exchange — native currency**: Lending or selling tokens as a "step-through" native currency that acts as a utility, usually confined to a network currency or token denomination that represents a thing of value.

- **Commercialization of the protocol**: Technology services, including cloud (licensed software or as-a-service offerings) and software lab and consulting services.

Layer 2 – Protocol optimization layer

Drawing similarities from the internet, this layer provides useful protocols and standards that leverage the foundational network trust and transaction layer. While the focus of layer 1 is on infrastructure, a set of layer 2 protocols provides an avenue for modularity, as demanded by use cases, and addresses core issues that are either impossible to address at the base layer due to complexity and bloat, or simply are not the focus area of base layer protocols. Some examples include offline storage, privacy and confidentiality of users, assets, data, protocol optimization for performance and usability, and, most importantly, interoperability between various layer 1 protocols and standards.

Layer components:

- Scalability protocols
- Privacy and confidentiality
- Storage services — data and assets
- Interoperability — assets and chains

The monetization thesis:

- **Token as a medium of exchange**:Lending or selling tokens as a "step-through" or native currency that acts as a utility, usually confined to a network.

- **Asset-pair trading or bridged assets (tokens)**: Monetizing margins or simply using a bridged asset to provide interoperability between blockchain networks or different asset types. Transaction volumes drive utility and usage, leading to demand.

- **Commercialization of the protocol**: Technology services, including cloud (licensed software or as-a-service offerings) and software lab and consulting services.

Layer 3 – Blockchain business service layer

At this layer, we begin to see the emergence of business services and components that, again, build upon layer 1 and layer 2 and provide necessary components that are both interoperable and adhere to composable designs. The business application is able to leverage this to conduct business and drive transactions onto the network(s). These services provide singular units of a business service, such as identity, KYC, audit tokens, and so on. While today these services manifest in the form of dApps or smart contracts, these services should be abstracted from the underlying layers, making them agnostic to the underlying layer 1 and layer 2 and their respective token economies. It is also possible that the same services may exist in various layer 1-driven ecosystems to provide ubiquity, similar to mobile apps in various device-driven ecosystems.

Layer components:

- Asset tokenization
- Token interoperability and standards
- Asset transport and integrity
- Identity services
- Verification and validation services
- Asset exchange services: exchange and fungibility
- Audit and compliance services

The monetization thesis:

- **Tokens as a medium of exchange**: A native token-driven model. Operation fees write to the blockchain-powered business network's distributed database. Transaction volumes drive utility and usage, leading to demand.

- **Bridged tokens or utilizing native tokens**: Monetizing margins or simply using a bridged asset to provide interoperability between blockchain networks or different asset types. Transaction volumes drive utility and usage, leading to demand.

- **Commercialization of the protocol**: Technology services, including cloud (licensed software or as-a-service offerings) and software lab and business consulting services.

- **Business optimization services**: Provides consulting services around new business models and the co-creation elements of the platform.

Layer 4 – Industry/business application layer

Layer 4 is where blockchain tenets come alive and the true value and promise of blockchain technology is realized. For any industry to ramp up blockchain-powered applications, layer 3 business services are woven together to create a tapestry of industry-specific solutions, and they give birth to new business models and new industry participants and roles. This layer should ideally harness the innovation-led evolutionary business models and focus on business architectures that rely on the technology choice frameworks and modularity enabled by lower-layer protocols. Most token economic models thrive in truly decentralized structures, and many permissioned or quasi-decentralized models have seen the emergence of non-fungible tokens or software as a service models to commercialize protocols. However, business networks and their business models that serve an ecosystem should determine the right model that fits the initiation and sustainable growth of the network, all while preserving the modularity of the solution design.

Layer components:

- Industry-specific consortia
- Identity linkage services
- Asset exchange and fiat fungibility
- Asset custody-led services—ETFs and secondary markets

The monetization thesis:

- **Network effect**: Extrapolating the power of networks and the exponential power of co-creation models, leading to new business models and resulting economic value.

- **Transactional model**: Transaction volumes drive utility and usage, leading to demand and the creation of additional services.

- **Network growth**: Includes onboarding new participants and exploiting the resulting growth in business transactions and avenues for new business models.

- **Costs efficiencies and new business models**: Resulting from co-creation elements and platform approaches.

Adjunct business layer

Business link to any of the core four layers: there are many layers not linked with the preceding broadly defined four layers that may be essential to providing support services to some or all layers. This layer can be viewed as extensible services to the blockchain protocol commercialization landscape with blockchain specialization.

Layer components:

- Blockchain business model services
- Business structure and legal services
- Blockchain network operation services
- Audit and compliance services

The monetization thesis:

- **Network effect**: Extrapolating the power of networks and the exponential power of co-creation models, leading to new business models and resulting economic value.

- **Network services**: Specialized services to networks, consortia, and network participants.

- **Network operation services**: Providing neutrality to the network operational functions by managing technology services and business (continuity) services.

Next, we'll discuss modularity.

Devising modularity to avoid lock-in linkages

As the technology evolves, so does the business economics tied to it. It is therefore vital to devise a business architecture to be modular, enabling a key capability for the technology frameworks (mainly layers 1 and 2) to remain flexible and extensible. It is vital to understand the components that are grouped into these defined layers, which serve as a rubric to compare the various infrastructures, services, and frameworks in their respective layers and with their respective peers. This approach also aids in a componentized model for business network solution design, with varying degrees of **quality of service** (QoS) and trade-off options available to address the design specifications demanded by the use case and industry. The modularity and isolation of these layers provides a linked economic structure where the choice framework of every layer is tied to the cost structures and economic models of other dependent layers.

The intent behind blockchain protocol commercialization is to focus discerning levels of services and their economic impacts with their own monetization theses, as well as their collective impacts on the overall costs not only of solution designs but also of the operational elements of the blockchain network. And while many of the innovations are in foundational transaction protocols (*Layer 1*), their enhancements around security and scale (*Layer 2*) and the core services that utilize them (*Layer 3*) manifest their economic models and strengths in some kind of token, be it a cryptoasset or cryptocurrency governed by a crypto economic system in the blockchain network (mining, transaction processing, and so on). So, tokens as digital assets or cryptoassets represent a vital part of the economic consideration at every layer, and most likely every layer either utilizes some form of token economy and establishes a monetization strategy in the form of utility as an incentive structure, or leverages a service-driven model that fuels the exchange of tokens as a fungible unit between the various participants in a network. Most token economic models thrive in truly decentralized structures, and many permissioned or quasi-decentralized models have seen the emergence of non-fungible tokens or software as a service models to commercialize protocols. However, business networks and their business models that serve an ecosystem should determine the right model that fits the initiation and sustainable growth of the network, all while preserving the modularity of the solution design.

Scalability and economic viability of blockchain solutions

The focus on the scalability and economic viability of a blockchain solution is an important one as it addresses the longevity of the solution. We have already alluded to the fact that business design is reliant on the cost predictability of transaction processing.

This is because it is a cost component and a factor in the overall value of services provided on the network. Besides, for any system, let alone a transaction system to be ubiquitous and be adopted at global scale, speed and costs are two factors that simply cannot be ignored.

We needed to account for the inverse relationship between the compute costs due to security protocols (including encryption, cryptography, key management, and so on) and its impact on scalability (addressing speed and costs is an interesting paradox that presents an interesting challenge to us as practitioners). Therefore, we have employed various techniques, ranging from hardware-centric approaches (colocation, specialized ASIC processors, crypto accelerator cards, hardware security modules, and so forth) to software design-based decisions such as block data, channels, connection optimization, and so on. We have attempted to address some of these design principles and resulting choices; however, we also believe that every business network will have unique business requirements and integration challenges. These require professionals such as yourself to put on their thinking caps and apply what you have learned both from foundational and fundamental principles and also from the available options afforded by the platform, framework, and tools we have discussed in this book.

How can you help and stay engaged?

In this final section, we would like to invite you to get engaged in this blockchain journey and its evolution. There are many ways to get engaged, ranging from direct contributions to various open source and Hyperledger projects, to steering your enterprise projects in the right business direction and toward the right application of blockchain technology, with an acumen we hope the topics in this book help strengthen.

As practitioners, we have drawn a few observations from our engagements with clients and industry in general. These observations reflect on not only the trajectory of innovation and subsequent adoption, but also on challenges (and opportunities ahead). These observations are summarized in the following lists. While the summaries do not represent exhaustive lists, they certainly capture the essence of the state of blockchain's evolution at the time of writing this book.

Business-related observations are as follows:

- Despite currently lacking unanimous definitions and standards, blockchain technology is viewed as the next-generation technology that will disrupt the status quo in the existing market infrastructure and change the way financial institutions operate their day-to-day businesses.

- Blockchain continues to prosper first in markets (and ecosystems) that are less automated, less regulated, and less heavily traded, but with high clearing and settlements risks.

- The global regulatory apparatus has begun not only to take notice, but also to participate actively in providing guidance and regulatory frameworks for blockchain-based digital and cryptoassets.

- Systems built on top of a permissioned blockchain with a focus on logic optimization (enhancing workflows and business procedures) are more suitable candidates for markets and current ecosystem adoption.

- Clearing and settlement (the last mile for most value-based transactions) use cases are often identified as the most suitable for blockchain applications in markets and current ecosystems. We are cautiously optimistic about capital markets' adoption of blockchain technology and anticipate a steady increase in IT spending over the next 7 years.

- It is unlikely that blockchain technology will end up replacing entire markets and current ecosystems (especially capital markets).

- Despite the lack of successful implementation in markets and current ecosystems to date, all of the discussions about blockchain's potential benefits have resulted in at least one positive outcome: increased public discussions on how certain parts of capital markets and industry ecosystems are woefully inefficient and how technology, such as blockchain, and industry acknowledgement and consensus around existing shortfalls could help key market participants make tough choices that could create a solid foundation for future growth.

- Blockchain is creating opportunities for businesses to come together and create value in new ways by disintermediating participants in a business network, optimizing ecosystems, and reducing risk. Blockchain intrinsically supports a complete view of the provenance of transactions and assets being traded on a network. These benefits are addressing complex challenges across all industries, including supply chain management, health information exchange, financial services, and international trade.

Technology-related observations are as follows:

- With a distributed ledger, information can be shared between any participants on the network, eliminating the cost and complexity of involving intermediary layers to interconnect participants. When such a market-level approach can be achieved, we eliminate the need to implement bilateral transactions for each of the trading parties.

- Technology standards and protocols are still emerging, and entities like the Linux Foundation with Hyperledger (for technology standards), the **Enterprise Ethereum Alliance**, or **EEA**, (for industry standards), the Soverin Foundation (for identity standards), and several other foundations are paving the way for the community with diverse technology applications, ideas, and ideologies to come together to define a model and ensure that the evolution and subsequent adoption of blockchain is truly a community-driven process.

- There is a divide between the enterprise adoption patterns, which are largely permissioned, and the cryptoasset world, which is token- or crypto asset-based and often permissionless.

- The underlying technology application, however, is similar in both the permissioned and permissionless blockchain networks.

- Scalability, privacy, and confidentiality remain key challenges in all blockchain networks and technologies.

- Economic viability: Keeping transaction processing costs low and predictable is vital, and the race is on to reduce the computation overhead and cost with the advent of new and improved trust systems and consensus protocols.

- There's a severe shortage of blockchain technology skills and talent, thereby leading to further focus on the standardization and normalization of protocol adoption.

Discussing the business and technical observations leads to understanding systemic issues we need to work on together as a community, not only to promote the stability of technical design, but also to promote the business adoption of the technology to fulfill the promise of blockchain. At the outset, we discussed the importance of understanding the business domain and meaningfully applying technology to address complex systems that we are attempting to create. It is, therefore, vital to have the right balance of domain and technology skills as part of the solution development skills that are needed to effectively tackle the blockchain project challenges. In that spirit, we, as practitioners, have taken the liberty to introduce the focus areas in which we need to come together as a community to make blockchain real for business, and also realize the full potential of the technology. The focus areas we introduce by no means exhaustively cover everything domain-specific or everything that may need an additional technology-specific focus, but they do represent foundational elements we need to focus on to address the business facets of the digital transaction network we are attempting to redesign.

Our focus should be on developing the following blockchain domains:

- **Focus on digital identity constructs**: Digital identity is one side of the coin that addresses tenets like ownership, audit, KYC, and other business facets that are related to a transaction with respect to transaction initiations, contractual agreements, establishing ownership, culpability, and tracing for business and co-creation elements.

- **Focus on digital asset and digital fiat**: It is vital to address the duality of a transaction and ensure the linkage of digitized assets to either physical assets or dematerialized assets. Digital fiat or a collateral-backed digital asset is vital to address the last-mile issue of settlement. This is true for every transaction that involves a financial institution or financial instruments.

- **Technology design for digital asset tokenization**: Blockchain aims to build a trusted digital transaction network, and this network is envisioned to create a value network. Digital asset tokenization is a vital area to focus on in order to ensure that the digital manifestation reflects the real-world assets movement. This focus area will also reflect on the preceding focus area, *Focus on digital asset and digital fiat*. Technology design for digital asset tokenization represents an important technology design consideration as it encompasses various facets of trust, business models, incentive economics, and governance structure.

- **Security design of enterprise blockchain systems**: Security design becomes another vital technology design consideration. This is because we are building a digital transaction network with digital assets and digital identities (addressed in the previous three focus areas). Blockchain business network and network infrastructure security becomes an important consideration, along with trust systems comprised of crypto artifacts, consensus, transaction finality, and network communication. Cybersecurity concerns are heightened due to the severity and consequences of network breaches. This is not only to address business functions such as non-repudiation, privacy, and confidentiality, but also to address the foundational tenets of the trust network we aspire to build.

- **Devising appropriate blockchain business models**: Appropriate business models become a business design consideration. This focus area is vital for the economic viability, business growth, and longevity of the business network powered by blockchain. This focus area ensures the economics of investment, returns, membership, and derived benefits for an equitable participation by various ecosystem players to promote co-creation models and give birth to new business models and synergies that did not exist before.

- **Devising an appropriate governance structure**: Governance structure ensures the active and equitable participation of the blockchain ecosystem and network participants. This focus area is a business design consideration. The root of this focus area ranges from self-governing models (permissionless networks) to consortium-or joint venture business entity-defined defined quasi-autonomous governance structures. Governance structures are also instrumental in ensuring business attributes such as audit requirements, dispute resolutions, and reporting requirements.

Summary

We have, in crafting this book, focused on presenting well-balanced and relevant content to give a deeper understanding of the systemic issues we are trying to address with blockchain. The content is not only focused on a deep dive into the technology, but also on the technology's relationship with and relevance to the business network and ecosystem we are attempting to transform and disrupt. We hope you have benefitted from our collective experience. We have made a tremendous effort to craft the content based on our expertise, knowledge, experience, and, above all, personal commitment, and we also hope for a continued dialogue and your progressive involvement above and beyond the topics covered in this literature.

Another Book You May Enjoy

If you enjoyed this book, you may be interested in this another book by Packt:

Mastering Blockchain - Third Edition
Imran Bashir

ISBN: 978-1-83921-319-9

- Grasp the mechanisms behind Bitcoin, Ethereum, and alternative cryptocurrencies
- Understand cryptography and its usage in blockchain technology
- Understand the theoretical foundations of smart contracts
- Develop decentralized applications using Solidity, Remix, Truffle, Ganache, and Drizzle
- Identify and examine applications of blockchain beyond cryptocurrencies
- Understand the architecture and development of Ethereum 2.0
- Explore research topics and the future scope of blockchain technology

Leave a review - let other readers know what you think

Please share your thoughts on this book with others by leaving a review on the site that you bought it from. If you purchased the book from Amazon, please leave us an honest review on this book's Amazon page. This is vital so that other potential readers can see and use your unbiased opinion to make purchasing decisions, we can understand what our customers think about our products, and our authors can see your feedback on the title that they have worked with Packt to create. It will only take a few minutes of your time, but is valuable to other potential customers, our authors, and Packt. Thank you!

Index

Symbols

B

bakelite 99
balance payment
    making, as importer's bank 465
    requesting, as exporter's bank 465
basically available, soft state, eventual
        consistency (BASE) 66
before-image 229
benefit-cost ratio (BCR) 19
big data analytics 641
bill of lading (B/L) 112, 429
    issuing, as carrier 462
bindfs
    reference link 646
blockchain 3-5, 10, 30
    as governance tool 579
    benefits 99, 100, 554
    challenges 689
    divisions 10
    from enterprise perspective 20
    future 689
    infrastructure, integrating for whole
        enterprise 21
    interacting with 100, 101
    learning curve 12
    trust and accountability 13
    use cases, in enterprise 13
blockchain applications
    advantages, over current real-world
        processes 116
Blockchain-as-a-Service (BaaS) 660
blockchain, as governance tool
    network policies, managing 579
blockchain as governance tool,
      network policies
    channels 582
    consortiums 581
    endorsements 582
    organization level, versus network
        level 580, 581
    types 580
blockchain business network
    governance of 565-567
blockchain business service layer
    components 697
    monetization thesis 698

blockchain delivery
    economic model 11, 12
blockchain domain
    focus 704
blockchain framework
    selecting, business considerations 26, 27
    selecting, technology considerations 27
blockchain, in enterprise
    applications 14
    applications, selecting 14, 15
    use cases 13
blockchain monetization
    strategies 694
blockchain protocol
      commercialization 692-694
    modularity, devising to avoid lock-in
        linkages 700
blockchain protocol commercialization, layers
    adjunct business layer 699
    blockchain business service layer 697
    foundational trust and transaction layer 695
    industry/business application layer 698
    protocol optimization layer 696
blockchain roles
    business roles, mapping to 567-570
blockchain solutions
    building blocks 46
    capabilities 7, 8
    considerations 5
    core building blocks 6
    economic viability 700, 701
    scalability 700, 701
blockchain solutions capabilities
    auditing and logging 7
    enterprise authentication, authorization, and
        accounting requirements 8
    enterprise integration 7, 8
    monitoring 8
    reporting and regulatory requirements 8
blockchain technology 109
block creation
    verifying 388, 389
business
    observations 701, 702
Business API (BAPI) 477
business blockchain technology 685

identity, mapping 480, 481
message affinity 478-480
process alignment 477, 478
service discovery 480
integration design patterns 482
event-driven architecture 484
integrating, with operational data store for
blockchain analytics 483, 484
integrating, with system of record 482, 483
microservice 484
integration layer 490
CI perspective, considerations 493
considerations 493
interledger protocol (ILP) 687
internal rate of return (IRR) 19
interoperability 692
interprise synergy 21
Istanbul Byzantine fault tolerance (IBFT) 44

J

joint venture model 562
JSON querying syntax
reference link 207
JSON Web Tokens (JWTs)
reference link 430
JUnit
URL 194

K

know your customer (KYC) 28
Kubernetes
as platform, for Hyperledger Fabric 537-539

L

ledger 667
querying 269-272, 293, 294
querying, with EvaluateTransaction 295, 296
Ledger data availability 659
ledger notification
requesting 276-278
letter of credit (L/C) 108, 111, 429, 556, 557
accepting, as exporter bank 460
issuing, as importer's bank 460
requesting, as importer 460

processing, today 109
Linux Foundation Hyperledger 687
live four-organization trade network
upgrading 637-639
local memory 281
logging output 214
configuration 214, 215
standard error files, using 215, 216
standard output files, using 215, 216
logistics
terms 111

M

membership service
provider (MSP) 118, 175, 379, 666
Merkle tree 8
minting 84
Mocha
scenarios, mapping to 520, 521
Mocha framework
URL 519
modules 542
multi-network gateway 290-293
multi-party transactions 223, 226
identifier 227
invalid transactions 231, 232
proposal 227, 228
response 229-231
type 226, 227
valid transactions 231, 232
multiversion concurrency control
(MVCC) 67, 213, 214, 557

N

namespaces 294
net present value (NPV) 19
network
accessing 287, 288
bootstrapping, with known members 669
new members, adding to 671, 672
smart contracts, deploying
on peers in 672, 673
smart contracts, instantiating
on peers in 672, 673
smart contracts, upgrading
on peers in 672, 673

component monitoring 648, 649
containers, profiling 649-654
system health indicators, measuring 645-647
perf Wiki
reference link 646
permissioning 28
physical infrastructure
separating, from logical 269
platform upgrades, Hyperledger
        Fabric 633-636
playbook 542
pprof
reference link 650
principles, ICOs
decentralization 11
open governance (self-governance) 11
transparency 11
private data 330-332, 668
insert-style transaction 346, 347
recapping, on styles 339
private data collections 336-339
using 333
using, in smart contract 333-335
using, with transient data 335
private data consensus 338, 343-346
private data, insert-style transaction
insert-style smart contract 350-352
most important trade 347-349
private data, styles
application 341-343
organizations 341-343
verify-style transaction 339-341
production-grade ordering service
using 466-472
programming languages 255
modularity 256
selecting 256
type system, using 256
Prometheus
URL 649
promotion process
activities 491
aligning, to components 491
defining 490
life cycles 490
overview 494-497

promotion process, activities
continuous delivery (CD) 491
continuous integration (CI) 491
promotion process, life cycles
integration layer 490
smart contracts 490
proof of authority (PoA) 44
proof of concept (PoC) 684
Proof of Elapsed Time (PoET) 45, 686
proof of work (PoW) 3, 44
properties 80
Protocol Buffers (protobuf) 608
protocol optimization layer
components 696
monetization thesis 697
provenance 82
PTE
reference link 660
public key infrastructure (PKI) 663

Q

quality of services (QoS) 700
quantum computing
reference link 681
query
in complex topology 297, 299

R

radical openness 20
Raft
reference link 467
range queries 205, 206
ReadSet 211
reconciliation 100
redundant committing peers 659
reference architecture components, Hy-
        perledger Fabric
channel 53
client software developer kit (SDK) 54
consensus 54
contract services 53
events 54
ledger 54
membership services 53

V

W